JANE AUSTEN AND THE BLACK HOLE OF BRITISH HISTORY:
COLONIAL RAPACITY, HOLOCAUST DENIAL AND THE CRISIS IN BIOLOGICAL SUSTAINABILITY

KP

Korsgaard Publishing

www.korsgaardpublishing.com

"The quarrels of popes and kings, with wars or pestilences, in every page; the men all so good-for-nothing, and hardly any women at all - it is very tiresome; and yet I often think it odd that it should be so dull, for a great deal of it must be invention ... and invention is what delights me in other books" [Catherine Morland]

"Historians, you think," said Miss Tilney, "are not happy in their flights of fancy. They display imagination without raising interest. I am fond of history, and am very well contented to take the false with the true. In the principal facts they have sources of intelligence in former histories and records, which may be as much depended upon, I conclude, as anything that does not actually pass under one's own observation; and as for the little embellishments you speak of, they are embellishments, and I like them as such. If a speech be well drawn up, I read it with pleasure, by whomsoever it may be made..."

- Catherine Morland discussing History with Eleanor and Henry Tilney in Jane Austen (1818), Northanger Abbey [1]

"History is always written wrong, and so always needs to be rewritten."

- George Santayana (1953), The Life of Reason [2]

"The hidden parts of history, the covert sides, are more orderly and rational, but can be seen and understood only if you are told where to look. The holes in history are what make sense of the thing."

- Aarons and Loftus (1997) [3]

"The "control of nature" is a phrase conceived in arrogance, born of the Neanderthal age of biology and philosophy, when it was supposed that nature exists for the convenience of man."

- Rachel Carson (1964) [4]

"From the dawn of consciousness until the middle of our century man had to live with the prospect of his death as an individual; since Hiroshima, mankind as a whole has to live with the prospect of its extinction as a biological species."

- Arthur Koestler (1974) [5]

"We have come into this world to accept it, not merely to know it. We may become powerful by knowledge, but we attain fullness by sympathy."

- Rabindranath Tagore, quoted by Henry Miller (1992) [6]

To my dear late wife, Zareena née Lateef, who introduced me to the
works of Jane Austen

About the Author

The author, Dr. Gideon Maxwell Polya, is an Australian scientist, humanitarian writer, artist and activist. He was formerly a biochemistry researcher and academic, and taught university science students over 4 decades. He was the author of over 100 scientific publications, and is the author of the following huge books: "Biochemical Targets of Plant Bioactive Compounds. A pharmacological reference guide to sites of action and biological effects" (2003), "Jane Austen and the Black Hole of British History. Colonial rapacity, holocaust denial and the crisis in biological sustainability" (1998, 2008 and 2022 editions), "Body Count. Global avoidable mortality since 1950" (2007 and 2022 editions), "US-imposed post-9/11 Muslim Holocaust and Muslim Genocide" (2020), and "Climate Crisis, Climate Genocide & Solutions" (2021). He is a co-author of Søren Korsgaard et al., "The Most Dangerous Book Ever Published: Deadly Deception Exposed" (2020).

CONTENTS

18. 2022: neoliberal ignoring of reality now existentially threatens Humanity and the Biosphere [491].

Notes [532].

Bibliography [635].

DETAILED TABLE OF CONTENTS

3. The editing of the Austens and consequences of rustic amusement [42].

4. Jane Austen's siblings and their descendants [64].

7. The sensibility of Jane Austen's literary contemporaries [135].

18.4. War is the penultimate in racism, genocide the ultimate in racism –
revealing genocidally racist Churchill and Zionist quotes re brutally colonized
Palestine

18.5. A new and dangerous anti-science culture of blatant Trumpist lying

18.6. Anti-Arab anti-Semitism, anti-Jewish anti-Semitism, holocaust-
ignoring, nuclear terrorism, and colonial atrocities of US- and Zionist-
subverted IHRA countries

18.7. World hero Julian Assange imprisoned for revealing a huge body of
secret US documents

18.8. Nuclear weapons and climate change existentially threaten Humanity
and the Biosphere

18.9. Treaty on the Prohibition of Nuclear Weapons (TPNW)

18.10. A catastrophic plus 2 degrees Centigrade of heating is now effectively
unavoidable

18.11. Worsening Climate Genocide en route to only 1 billion people left by
2100

18.12. Catastrophic biodiversity loss in the Anthropocene Era

18.13. Negative carbon emissions back to 300 ppm CO_2 needed plus halving
population and halving economic activity

18.14. Deadly poverty, famine from war and climate change, entitlement, the
global South, and terracidal neoliberalism versus sustainable social humanism
(socialism)

18.15. Rich, neoliberal and racist Australia's ongoing commitment to US
wars, genocide, nuclear terrorism, and climate criminality
18.16. Polya's 3 Laws of Economics, user pays, carbon price, carbon tax, and
intergenerational equity

18.17. Covid-19-related avoidable deaths, Gerocide, holding rulers
responsible, and the 2020 pre-Covid-19 mortality baseline

18.18. All human rights for all including the sorely oppressed Palestinians

18.19. One-person-one-vote World Parliament for economics, human rights, entitlement and sustainability

18.20. Speak out!

Notes [532].

Bibliography [635].

PREFACE TO THE 2008 SECOND EDITION

I first became aware of the World War 2 Bengal Famine in about 1995 when I saw the movie "Distant Thunder" directed by the outstanding film-maker Satyajit Ray.[7] The film concluded with the statement that 5 million people had perished in the Bengal Famine. I was well aware of the Jewish Holocaust (6 million victims) – the more so because my father was a Jewish refugee from Nazism.[8] I went to my large personal library but found no record of the Bengal Famine except as a brief, several word entry in a German history encyclopaedia by B. Grun entitled The Timetables of History. A Chronology of World Events Based on Werner Stein's Kulturfahrplan.[9] I was appalled that such an immense, man-made catastrophe could occur at the same time as the Jewish Holocaust and with a similar death toll and yet be essentially erased from history and general public perception.

As an academic at a big university I had ready access to a big university library that had an excellent Indian collection. There I found a remarkable collection of Indian and European works dealing with the Bengal Famine. Because 1995 was the 50th anniversary of the end of World War 2, I wrote a succinct account of this atrocity and sent it to Mainstream media, politicians and leading academics around Australia. The response was almost comprehensive silence – the political, media and academic élite of Australia simply did not want to know about a man-made event as big as the Jewish Holocaust and "down to us".

There were several positive responses to my attempt to inform my fellow countrymen. An Indigenous Australian (Aboriginal) radio station interviewed me for the benefit of their remote Aboriginal listeners - to them the Bengal Famine was just a vastly bigger version of what had happened to Indigenous Australians in the 2 century Aboriginal Genocide. A very prominent Australian Vice Chancellor sent me the opinion he had commissioned from a top Australian academic "expert" on Indian history – unfortunately this academic historian was only concerned to lavish praise on British rule over India.

However, arising out of this "national informing process" a very detailed article by me entitled "The Forgotten Holocaust – the 1943 Bengal Famine" was published in a scholarly journal associated with the Macquarie University-based Centre for Holocaust and Genocide Studies in Sydney headed by outstanding genocide scholar Professor Colin Tatz. [10]

Senator Christobal Chamarette of the humanitarian and ethical Australian Greens tabled my concerns in a fine speech about the Bengal Famine in the Australian Senate in September 1995, an event about which Australia was informed by the Australian Broadcasting Corporation (ABC) reporting her speech – an astonishing and rare instance in which a Major Truth actually penetrated the Wall of Silence in Australia, the Land of Flies, Lies and Slies (spin-based untruths). [11] The rest was silence.

A very busy research scientist and academic teacher, I nevertheless considered it my moral obligation to inform people about the "forgotten holocaust", the man-made Bengal Famine in WW2 British-ruled India. With a background of 3 decades of scientific research and access to a fine Indian collection at the Dietrich Borchardt Library of Melbourne's La Trobe University, I proceeded to research the Bengali Holocaust in detail. However I quickly found that it was necessary to put this man-made event into a wider historical and cultural context. Thus the 1943-1945 Bengal Famine was the last of a succession of immense famines in British-ruled India that commenced with the man-made 1769-1770 Bengal Famine that killed 10 million Bengalis or one third of the whole population a mere dozen years after British conquest of Bengal at the Battle of Plassey (1757). However this catastrophe was also largely deleted from British History – this intellectual crime against Humanity being effected by successive generations of passively lying British academics, politicians and journalists.

At this point serendipity intervened. My dear wife Zareena is of Bengali and Bihari origin (her grandparents having all been "5-year slaves" of the British in Fiji towards the end of the brutal British indentured labor system, the so-called Fijian "Girmit" system). Educated under a colonial British system in Fiji and thence at high school and university in Australia, she was completely unaware of these immense catastrophes that had befallen her people. No members of her extremely numerous family I quizzed about this had ever heard of the Bengal famines. However Zareena being a well educated lady of the British Empire was well aware of Jane Austen and indeed introduced me to this wonderful writer through the novel "Northanger Abbey" - when I was about 50 years old, I must confess. This novel (only published after Jane Austen's death because of – you guessed it – "English censorship") contained an extraordinary speech by the heroine Catherine Moreland's "lover" Henry Tilney in which he reprimands her for imagining some family horror buried in the gothic Northanger Abbey:

"If I understand you rightly, you have formed a surmise of such horror as I have hardly words to -. Dear Miss Morland, consider the dreadful nature of the suspicions you have entertained. What have you been judging from? Remember the country and the age in which we live. Remember that we are English, that we are Christians. Consult your own understanding, your own sense of the probable, your own observation of what is passing around you. Does our education prepare us for such atrocities? Do our laws connive at them? Could they be perpetrated without being known, in a country like this, where social and literary intercourse is on such a footing, where every man is surrounded by a neighbourhood of voluntary spies, and where roads and newspapers lay everything open? Dearest Miss Morland, what ideas have you been admitting?"[12]

From the little I have told you above about British imperial lying by omission that continues today in Britain and its colonial progeny, the answers to Henry Tilney's questions about "connivance" and "perpetration" must in both cases be a resounding YES.

At this point my research widened into a more general inquiry into how such enormous crimes could be deleted from public perception in prosperous, literate, ostensibly free and democratic British –based societies. My eclectic book expanded to span literature, history and science, taking its cue from the admonition that history ignored yields history repeated. In introducing and leavening this sombre subject, my book initially deals with our heroine, Jane Austen, her life, connections, work and critics and describes the artistically legitimate, narrow social confinement of her novels. However such extraordinary selectivity has been illegitimately applied by a large body of "Austenizing" historians to whitewash colonial enormities and indeed Jane Austen and her Indian and other interesting connections have also been significantly "Austenized" as described in Chapter 5 of my book.

Specifically, "Jane Austen and the Black Hole of British History" deals with the Great Bengal Famine of 1769-1770 that killed 10 million people shortly after subjugation of Bengal by the rapacious British East India Company. This holocaust has been effectively deleted from history as have a further 2 centuries of such disasters in British India that culminated in the man-made Bengal Famine of 1943-1945 that killed as many as 4 million people in Bengal alone. The war-time Bengal Famine accounted for over 90% of total British Empire civilian plus military casualties of that conflict but has been effectively deleted from public perception.

The "forgotten holocaust" of Bengal occurred at the same time as the Jewish Holocaust and precise connections between these 2 horrendous events are explored in the book. However the people of Bengal - and indeed Third World people in general - are facing a major crisis in food availability in the 21st century occasioned by environmental degradation, industry-induced global warming, declining grain production, massive plant food diversion for biofuel and meat production and burgeoning populations. By honestly addressing the "forgotten holocausts" of the colonial past we can put resolution to the post-Holocaust crie de coeur "Never Again" and seriously address the crisis in biological sustainability that threatens the Third World and indeed the world as a whole.

The final chapters of my book dealt with the crisis in biological sustainability facing the world, the Australian response after 2 centuries of genocide, ethnocide and ecocide and how lessons from this resurrection of the "forgotten holocausts" of British history can guide us to humane solutions and prevent a catastrophe. My pessimistic view was that if a prosperous, educated, liberal democracy such as Australia would not respond to this moral message then why would less fortunate societies? That view has been justified by subsequent events as briefly outlined below.

I spent a lot of time and money trying to find a publisher for "Jane Austen and the Black Hole of British History" but my efforts failed in the aridity of remorseless and intrinsically racist Anglo-American holocaust-ignoring and holocaust denial. I accordingly published the book myself and sent copies to some major libraries, some major global figures and some decent writers and journalists. [13] The most amusing response I received was from the British Foreign Office on beautiful, thick, embossed paper: "The Prime Minister has instructed us to read your book. We have done so. Yours etc".

Nevertheless, publication of the book elicited useful responses from decent, anti-racist, humanitarian advocates from around the world. The nascent Sulekha organization (now the biggest Indian literary website in the world) commissioned me to write about this. [14] I gave lectures and interviews and published articles in magazines and books over the subsequent years. [15] I even made a nation-wide broadcast on the Australian ABC science program Ockham's Razor entitled "Bengali Famine" due to the intelligence and humanity of outstanding science journalist Robyn Williams who, in introducing my broadcast, said: "Can you turn science to history? To test it, I mean? You can't really do experiments on the past, so how could it be applied? Dr Gideon Polya insists that science does have a role in this regard, and he'll explain in a minute. But the point of such an exercise is important here, because the reason for Dr Polya's concern (and he's written a book about it) is one of the worst genocides on record, or not on record, unless you search long and hard." [16]

Well, I was not discouraged from my duty as a decent human being but was very disappointed by this extraordinary mainstream media, politician and academic refusal to acknowledge events of such enormity – behaviour that I have described as "politically correct racism" (PC racism) in which endlessly politically correct people and societies remorselessly ignore horrendous abuses at their hands of subject people of other races.

I continued with my extremely busy career as a teacher and researcher. In 2003, after some years of 7-days a week work, I published a huge pharmacological reference text "Biochemical Targets of Plant Bioactive Compounds. A pharmacological reference guide to sites of action and biological effects" (CRC Press/Taylor & Francis, New York & London, 2003). There was space in the 500 pages of detailed tables in this huge reference book for succinct, relevant, historical and cultural "snippets" and I made sure that the Awful Truth of the WW2 Bengal Famine was briefly mentioned in relevant places for the benefit of a generally scientific readership. [17]

I left full-time academic scientific work at this point and immediately devoted myself to researching a more general approach to this problem of Mainstream holocaust-ignoring that encompassed an even wider global perspective (in addition to part-time university and other tertiary institution science teaching, giving courses to the Australian University of the Third Age and a huge amount of humanitarian writing and advocacy published beyond the PC racist, Antipodean Land of Flies, Lies and Slies).

In short, my widened approach involved rational risk management (that, for example, makes aviation exceptionally safe). Rational risk management successively involves (a) getting accurate data about adverse events, (b) scientific analysis (this involving the critical testing of potentially falsifiable hypotheses) and (c) systemic change to minimize the risk of repetition of adverse events. [18] Unfortunately, as we are all too aware, this rational protocol is typically perverted by (a) lies, censorship and intimidation, (b) anti-science spin (involving the selective use of asserted facts to support a partisan proposition, and (c) blame and shame with no systemic change.

This perversion of rational risk management now threatens the Third World with climate change-driven decrease in agricultural productivity and huge global food price rises due to diversion of food for biofuel, climate change and globalization-based demand from the new Asian giants India and China [19]. Humanity as a whole is acutely endangered due to the threat to the Biosphere from anthropogenic global warming. [20]

Top American climate change scientist Dr James Hansen (head, NASA's Goddard Institute for Space Studies, New York City and adjunct Professor at Columbia University) has recently asserted that at 385 ppm (parts per million) atmospheric carbon dioxide (CO_2) concentration the world has already reached a tipping point at which all Arctic summer ice may be gone in several years rather than several decades, with immense implications for accelerating melting of the Greenland Ice Sheet, the West Antarctic Ice Sheet and the methane-rich American and Siberian tundra with consequent huge sea level rises. He advocates the need to rapidly reduce atmospheric CO_2 concentration to a safe and sustainable level of 300-350 ppm. Dr Hansen indicates that this will require cessation of fossil fuel burning and reduction of atmospheric CO_2 by re-afforestation, return of carbon to the soil as biomass-derived biochar and, if needed, generation of "global dimming" SO_2 aerosols. [21]

In a recent paper Dr Hansen and colleagues have provided a daunting prospect: "Paleoclimate data show that climate sensitivity is ~3 deg-C for doubled CO_2 [carbon dioxide; atmospheric CO_2 280 ppm pre-industrial], including only fast feedback processes. Equilibrium sensitivity, including slower surface albedo feedbacks, is ~6 deg-C for doubled CO_2 for the range of climate states between glacial conditions and ice-free Antarctica. Decreasing CO_2 was the main cause of a cooling trend that began 50 million years ago, large scale glaciation occurring when CO_2 fell to 450 +/- 100 ppm [parts per million], a level that will be exceeded within decades, barring prompt policy changes. If humanity wishes to preserve a planet similar to that on which civilization developed and to which life on Earth is adapted, paleoclimate evidence and ongoing climate change suggest that CO_2 will need to be reduced from its current 385 ppm to at most 350 ppm". [22]

Top UK climate scientist Dr James Lovelock FRS has dire projections in "The Revenge of Gaia" (2006): "I describe a simple model where the sensitive part of the Earth system is the ocean; as it warms, so the area of the sea that can support the growth of algae grows smaller as it is driven ever closer to the poles, until algal growth ceases. The discontinuity comes because algae in the ocean both pump down carbon dioxide [by photosynthesis] and produce clouds [through cloud-seeding dimethyl sulphide production]. Algae floating in the ocean actively remove carbon dioxide from the air and use it for growth; we call the process "pumping down" to distinguish it from the passive and reversible removal of carbon dioxide as it dissolves in rain or sea water. The threshold for the failure of the algae is about 500 parts per million (ppm) of carbon dioxide, about the same as it is for Greenland's unstoppable melting". More recently (2007) Dr Lovelock has said that over 6 billion people will perish this century if climate change is not urgently and requisitely addressed. [23]

However a combination of biofuel-, climate change- and globalization-driven food price hikes (wheat price has doubled in 12 months, rice price has doubled in 3 months) means that the world is now facing a disaster possibly 100 times greater than the man-made, food-price-driven Bengal Famine that killed 6-7 million in Bengal and adjoining provinces when the price of rice ultimately quadrupled. The United States (US) is currently using about 9% of its wheat, 25% of its corn and about 15% of its grain in general to produce biofuel. The United Kingdom (UK) has committed to large increases in the use of biofuels over coming decades, has recently announced subsidies for biofuel and supports the European Union (EU) target requiring 10 per cent of petrol station fuel to be plant-derived biofuel within 12 years. However the huge and intrinsically genocidal US diversion of 15% of its grain crop to biofuel production has had a huge impact already on soaring global food prices – the world is already facing a global food crisis with alarm being expressed by UN, FAO and other scientific experts. [24] Thus the UK Chief Scientific Adviser, Professor John Beddington CMG, FRS (Professor of Applied Population Biology at Imperial College, London.) has described the devastating potential of food shortages as an "elephant in the room" problem commensurate with that from climate change and warns that biofuel diversion (e.g. for canola oil- or palm oil-derived biodiesel and grain- or sugar-derived ethanol) is threatening world food production and the lives of "billions": "It's very hard to imagine how we can see the world growing enough crops to produce renewable energy and at the same time meet the enormous demand for food. The supply of food really isn't keeping up." [25]

We are running out of oil and the price of crude oil has now exceeded US$100 per barrel. However the proposition that crop-based biofuels represent a "green" solution to fossil fuel burning and the "peak oil" phenomenon has been shown to be incorrect. Recent US research by Fargione and co-workers and published in the prestigious scientific journal Science has shown that diversion of land to growing biofuel crops can produce an enormous "CO_2 debt" from use of machinery, fertilizers, release of carbon from the soil and loss of CO_2 sequestration by trees and other plants:

"Increasing energy use, climate change, and carbon dioxide (CO_2) emissions from fossil fuels make switching to low-carbon fuels a high priority. Biofuels are a potential low-carbon energy source, but whether biofuels offer carbon savings depends on how they are produced. Converting rainforests, peatlands, savannas, or grasslands to produce food crop–based biofuels in Brazil, Southeast Asia, and the United States creates a "biofuel carbon debt" by releasing 17 to 420 times more CO_2 than the annual greenhouse gas (GHG) reductions that these biofuels would provide by displacing fossil fuels. In contrast, biofuels made from waste biomass or from biomass grown on degraded and abandoned agricultural lands planted with perennials incur little or no carbon debt and can offer immediate and sustained GHG advantages." [26]

In the first edition of "Jane Austen and the Black Hole of British History" I referred to the diaries of General Wavell and observed (p141): "On October 15 1943 in Cairo on his way out to India, Wavell inspected Indian troops and spoke to Casey about food. Casey said Australia had had a bad wheat harvest, Canada could just supply U.S. and British deficiencics and that the Argentinians had burnt their surplus of 2 million tons as fuel on the railways in the absence of coal, of which there was a world shortage." [27] Now in 2008 Americans and Europeans are burning biofuel in their cars while 4 billion fellow human beings on Spaceship Earth are malnourished and facing starvation.

In assessing adverse outcomes the bottom line is excess death (avoidable death, avoidable mortality, excess mortality, deaths that should not have happened). Excess deaths for a country can be calculated from the difference between deaths actually occurring and deaths expected for a peaceful country with the same demographics. Thus the over 6 billion excess deaths predicted by Professor Lovelock from climate change will overwhelmingly be non-violent excess deaths (although Western military might ensures that the victims will not escape the "passive killing fields").

In 2007 I published an analysis of global excess death entitled "Body Count. Global avoidable mortality since 1950". Based on UN Population Division demographic data, it calculated excess death and under-5 infant mortality for every country in the world since 1950. The results are horrendous: 1950-2005 excess deaths totalled 1.3 billion (for the world), 1.2 billion (for the non-European world) and 0.6 billion (for the Muslim world). These horrendous estimates are consonant with independently determined estimates for 1950-2005 under-5 infant deaths of 0.88 billion (the World), 0.85 billion (the non-European world) and 0.4 billion (the Muslim world). [28]

As you might well imagine, such information is unacceptable to racist, lying Mainstream media and politicians and unacceptable to the same Anglo-American publishing culture that has kept most people ignorant of the World War 2 Bengali Holocaust. Ever the optimist about human nature, I wasted much time and money looking for a Mainstream publisher and ultimately published myself. I have sent over one hundred copies of "Body Count" to libraries and humanitarians around the world to assist their humanitarian advocacy – and to contribute intelligently to the first key step of global risk management, namely provision of fundamental adverse outcome data.

Unfortunately we live in an obscene world of massive lying by omission in which the politically correct racist (PC racist) corporate, media, politician and academic Establishments of the Western Murdochracies simply do not want to know about the consequences of their actions. At this point one has to turn to one of the world's most important bioethicists for guidance. Professor Peter Singer (De Camp Professor of bioethics at Princeton University, a professor at the University of Melbourne and held by some to be the world's most influential living philosopher because of his work on animal rights) has stated: "we are responsible for what we do and for what we fail to do." [29]

Professor Singer has controversially argued for the humane "active euthanasia" of severely disabled infants. At present many experienced hospital doctors will administer pain relief but not sustenance to such infants by way of "passive euthanasia". According to Singer: "Doctors who deliberately leave a baby to die when they have the awareness, the ability, and the opportunity to save the baby's life, are just as morally responsible for the death as they would be if they had brought it about by a deliberate, positive action." [30]

These ethical injunctions are acutely relevant to Spaceship Earth on which 4 billion hover near starvation with an over-fed First World in charge of the flight deck. Indeed they become more acutely relevant when there is mass avoidable mortality in countries under violent First World occupation such as Occupied Haiti, Occupied Somalia, Occupied Palestine, Occupied Syria, Occupied Iraq and Occupied Afghanistan. We must note that it is extremely rare for Asian, African or Latin American countries to invade and occupy other countries – the only such countries involved in such obscenities at the moment are US-backed Ethiopia (in Occupied Somalia), US-backed Turkey (in Northern Cyprus) and US-backed Apartheid Israel (in Occupied Syria and Occupied Palestine).

Thus "Year 2005 under-5 infant deaths" / "year 2005 population" is 370,000 / 29.9 million (Occupied Afghanistan); 122,000 / 28.8 million (Occupied Iraq); 82,000 / 8.2 million (Occupied Somalia); 31,000 / 8.5 million (Occupied Haiti); and 3,000 / 3.7 million (Occupied Palestinian Territory) – as compared to 1,500 / 20.2 million (Occupi-er Australia) and 800 / 6.4 million (Occupi-er Israel).

"Year 2005 annual under-5 infant death rate" (i.e. as a percentage: deaths for every 100 under-5 year old infants in 2005 in a particular country) was 6.7% (Occupied Afghanistan); 2.8% (Occupied Iraq); 5.5% (Occupied Somalia); 2.7% (Occupied Haiti); and 0.47% (Occupied Palestinian Territory) – as compared to 0.12% (Occupi-er Australia) and 0.12% (Occupi-er Israel). [31]

My book "Body Count" gave details of excess mortality for every country in the world since 1950, laboriously estimated using conservative assumptions (it took over a year to do these calculations, country by country in 5 year steps (or pentades). However, an empowering method for estimating "excess deaths" arose from the completed analysis. Thus for impoverished Third World countries the under-5 infant deaths are about 0.7 (70%) of the excess deaths for all age groups. Accordingly, if you know the under-5 infant deaths for such countries (e.g. from UNICEF or UN Population Division data) you can quickly estimate the excess deaths by dividing this number by 0.7. [32]

A major contributor to the carnage in Occupied Palestine, Occupied Iraq and Occupied Afghanistan is the war criminal failure of the Occupiers to supply life-sustaining requisites as demanded unequivocally by the Geneva Convention Relative to the Protection of Civilian Persons in Time of War. Thus, according the World Health Organization (WHO), the "annual total per capita medical expenditure" permitted in Occupied Iraq by the US Coalition is $135 (2004) as compared to $19 (Occupied Afghanistan), $2,560 (UK), $3,123 (Australia) and $6,096 (the US). [33]

It is useful here to present the relevant articles of the Geneva Convention Relative to the Protection of Civilian Persons in Time of War [34]:

Article 55

To the fullest extent of the means available to it the Occupying Power has the duty of ensuring the food and medical supplies of the population; it should, in particular, bring in the necessary foodstuffs, medical stores and other articles if the resources of the occupied territory are inadequate.

The Occupying Power may not requisition foodstuffs, articles or medical supplies available in the occupied territory, except for use by the occupation forces and administration personnel, and then only if the requirements of the civilian population have been taken into account. Subject to the provisions of other international Conventions, the Occupying Power shall make arrangements to ensure that fair value is paid for any requisitioned goods.

The Protecting Power shall, at any time, be at liberty to verify the state of the food and medical supplies in occupied territories, except where temporary restrictions are made necessary by imperative military requirements.

Article 56
To the fullest extent of the means available to it, the Occupying Power has the duty of ensuring and maintaining, with the cooperation of national and local authorities, the medical and hospital establishments and services, public health and hygiene in the occupied territory, with particular reference to the adoption and application of the prophylactic and preventive measures necessary to combat the spread of contagious diseases and epidemics. Medical personnel of all categories shall be allowed to carry out their duties.
If new hospitals are set up in occupied territory and if the competent organs of the occupied State are not operating there, the occupying authorities shall, if necessary, grant them the recognition provided for in Article 18. In similar circumstances, the occupying authorities shall also grant recognition to hospital personnel and transport vehicles under the provisions of Articles 20 and 21.
In adopting measures of health and hygiene and in their implementation, the Occupying Power shall take into consideration the moral and ethical susceptibilities of the population of the occupied territory.

The infant deaths, the excess deaths and the legal obligations of Occupiers in these Occupied Countries are clear – but lying, racist, holocaust-ignoring mainstream media, politicians and mendicant academics simply look the other way – just as they have looked the other way in relation to the Bengal Famine and indeed the whole 2 century horror of British rule over India. It can be estimated that excess deaths in British India totalled 1.5 billion – a number that would astonish Anglo-Celts (and indeed many of their Subjects) brought up on the myth of Pax Britannica and the nobility of British civilization.

The perversion of rational risk management through successive (a) lying, (b) spin and (c) blame and shame (with war being the ultimate obscenity) is horribly illustrated by the remorseless post-1950 US Asian wars that have so far been associated with 25 million Indigenous Asian excess deaths (mostly non-violent and mostly women and children). Each war was associated with false and shabby "justifications" – the only real basis was US geo-political strategy.

The Korean War was associated with about 1 million excess deaths. Only 3 years after the end of the Indo-China War (excess deaths totalling 13 million) the US embarked on backing a fundamentalist Muslim war against the pro-woman, socialist régime in Afghanistan, this eventually precipitating a Soviet invasion in 1979 and a war that was associated with excess deaths totalling 2.9 million for the period 1979-1989. The subsequent civil war was associated with 3.3 million excess deaths in the period 1989-1999.

After 9/11 the Bush Administration told the appropriate stories. While no Afghans or Iraqis had been involved in the attacks according to the official Bush story, both Afghanistan and Iraq were bombed, invaded and occupied with horrendous loss of life. Two US think tanks have recently reported that the Bush Administration told a total of 935 lies about Iraq alone in the post-9/11 pre-invasion period (e.g. false assertions of Iraqi-Al Qaeda links, uranium oxide supplies and Weapons of Mass Destruction being the most notorious lies). [35]

Indeed there is widespread expert, intelligence and scholarly scepticism about many aspects of the "official 9/11 story". A substantial proportion of Americans believe that their government was at least passively complicit in the atrocity. Even former Vice President Al Gore, while dismissing complicity assertions, has lambasted the Bush Administration for criminal negligence prior to 9/11. [36]

In November 2007 the former 7-year president of Italy, law professor, senator-for-life and Western intelligence intimate, Franceso Cossiga, told a top Italian newspaper that the US CIA and Israeli Mossad were responsible for 9/11, had done this to enhance US and Zionist interests and that Western intelligence agencies were aware of this. [37]

The consequences of this horrendous violence, lying, spin and blame-and-shame perversion of rational risk management has been terror hysteria, anti-Arab anti-Semitism and Islamophobia, huge violations of civil rights domestically and of human rights abroad and Western involvement in horrendous war crimes in Muslim lands. Post-invasion excess deaths in the Occupied Palestinian, Iraqi and Afghan Territories (as of March 2008) total 0.3 million, 1.7-2.2 million and 3.3-6.6 million, respectively, and there are 7 million, 4.5 million and 4 million refugees, respectively. [38]

The Western world is variously complicit in UK state terrorism, US state terrorism, US-backed Israeli state terrorism and Palestinian Genocide, Iraqi Genocide and Afghan Genocide, noting that "genocide" is here defined according to Article 2 of the UN Genocide Convention: "In the present Convention, genocide means any of the following acts committed with intent to destroy, in whole or in part, a national, ethnic, racial or religious group, as such: a) Killing members of the group; b) Causing serious bodily or mental harm to members of the group; c) Deliberately inflicting on the group conditions of life calculated to bring about its physical destruction in whole or in part; d) Imposing measures intended to prevent births within the group; e) Forcibly transferring children of the group to another group". [39]

What can decent people do? Peace is the only way but silence kills and silence is complicity. Decent people are obliged to bear witness, to get through the Mainstream media Wall of Silence and to inform others about these atrocities. Informing others is the first step in the rational risk management process that successively involves (a) data, (b) science and (c) systemic change. Since publishing the first edition of "Jane Austen and the Black Hole of British History", "informing others" is what I have been doing, with "Body Count. Global avoidable mortality since 1950" a major vehicle of this pro-Peace, pro-Truth, humanitarian enterprise.

I have been lecturing, broadcasting and writing thousands of articles and letters to media around the world. I have also made formal complaints to the International Criminal Court (ICC), most recently submitting a detailed complaint against Australia for on-going Australian complicity in Indigenous Genocide (Aboriginal Genocide, 90,000 excess Indigenous Australian deaths 1996-2007; Iraqi Genocide, 1.5-2 million Indigenous Occupied Iraqi excess deaths in 2003-2007; Afghan Genocide, 3-6 million Indigenous Occupied Afghanistan excess deaths in 2001-2007) and Climate Genocide (complete loss of some Island Nations; 16 million avoidable deaths globally each year and increasingly climate change-impacted; and over 6 billion deaths predicted by the end of the century due to greenhouse gas pollution profligacy; and with Australia being the World's worst developed country for annual per capita CO_2 pollution). [40]

This Second Edition has essentially only involved minor clarification of the Jane Austen family tree and typographical and other minor corrections to the 1998 First Edition text. Accordingly, in reading the main text please remember that it was written 10 years ago and referenced by a literature available then. However in addition to this Preface, detailed, documented Postscript comments at the end of each chapter bring the text up to date and thus provide a cogent record of Anglo-American Alliance holocaust commission, holocaust denial, genocide commission, genocide denial and "History ignored yielding History repeated" in the decade since the publication of the First Edition.

Dr Gideon Polya

Melbourne, Australia

September, 2008

PREFACE TO THE 2022 THIRD EDITION

The fundamental message of the 1998 First Edition of "Jane Austen and the Black Hole of British History" [41] is that that history ignored yields history repeated. The most fundamental human right is the right to life, and decent folk who respect human rights are obliged to bear witness to deadly atrocities imposed by war and deprivation.

Continuing horrendous mass mortality through violence and war-imposed deprivation has marred the 21st century, with much of this carnage associated with US imperialism as described in my 2020 book "US-imposed Post-9/11 Muslim Holocaust and Muslim Genocide" [42]. However the First World-dominated world order meant that as estimated in 2004 about 16 million people died avoidably annually from imposed deprivation in the Developing World. This ongoing Global Avoidable Mortality Holocaust was described in country-by-country detail in my huge 2007 book "Body Count. Global Avoidable Mortality Since 1950" [43]. These continuing mass mortality disasters made a 2008 Second Edition necessary involving 2008 updating Postscripts at the end of most chapters, as described above in the Preface to the 2008 Second Edition of "Jane Austen and the Black Hole of British History" [44].

In 2021 I published an extensively revised and updated Second Edition of "Body Count. Global Avoidable Mortality Since 1950" [45]. The good news was that global avoidable mortality (and the related parameter of under-5 infant mortality) had halved in the 16 years from 2004 to 2020. However the bad news was that in 2020 annual global avoidable mortality totaled 7.4 million and global under-5 infant mortality totaled 5.3 million. [45] Further, worsening man-made global warming that impelled production of the First and Second Editions has now reached a dangerous level as described in the new and final Chapter 18 of the present 2022 Third Edition of "Jane Austen and the Black Hole of British History".

The present Third Edition of "Jane Austen and the Black Hole of British History" is essentially the Second Edition plus a detailed final Chapter 18 entitled "2022: neoliberal ignoring of reality now existentially threatens Humanity and the Biosphere". To aid the reader of this huge book and to obviate the need for an impossibly huge Index for this encyclopaedic work, the sections of each chapter have all been numbered (e.g. 1.1, 1.2 etc for Chapter 1) and the titles of each of these numbered sections are provided in a Detailed Table of Contents.

The 1998 First Edition of "Jane Austen and the Black Hole of British History" [41] warned that in the absence of requisite action Bengal and other low lying nations face catastrophe from global warming with mortality that will dwarf that in massive famines under British colonial rule. A quarter century on that dire threat is presently being realized, with our Anthropocene World experiencing mass species extinction and extraordinary forest fires, droughts, tropical storms and floods. Key "tipping points" are presently being approached or exceeded. Indeed in my huge 2020 book "Climate Crisis, Climate Genocide & Solutions" [46] I conclude that a catastrophic plus 2 degrees Centigrade temprature rise is now effectively unavoidable, but we are obliged to do everything we can to make the future "less bad" for our children and future generations.

In the absence of requisite action the World faces a worsening Climate Genocide in which 10 billion people will die en route to a sustainable human population in 2100 of only about 1 billion people. [46] Humanity and the Biosphere are existentially threatened by nuclear weapons and climate change. One of Humanity's greatest minds, theoretical physicist Stephen Hawking, has stated succinctly that "We see great peril if governments and societies do not take action NOW [my emphasis] to render nuclear weapons obsolete and to prevent further climate change". [47]

This worsening threat is now disastrously compounded by neoliberal greed coupled with anti-science denialism and a widely supported culture of blatant Trumpist and populist lies and falsehood. [48] While outstanding world hero, Australian journalist Julian Assange, has been already incarcerated for 10 years and faces death in a US prison for truth-telling reportage, decent people must follow his example and bear witness to deadly, dangerous and evil realities such as those described in this book.

Finally, I must express my profound thanks to humanitarian worker, activist and publisher Søren Korsgaard for his enthusiasm, dedication and technical proficiency in this humanitarian truth-telling project. Peace is the only way but silence kills and silence is complicity. History ignored yields history repeated.

Dr Gideon Polya

Melbourne, Australia

May, 2022

Chapter 1

Introduction - truth, reason, science and history

"...I am rather inclined to suppose him a very respectable Man;...but it also has been declared that he did not kill his two Nephews, which I am inclined to believe true; & if this is the case, it may also be that he did not kill his wife..."

- Jane Austen on Richard III in The History of England (1791) [1]

1.1. History ignored yields history repeated, and the ruler is responsible for the ruled.

Ultimately this book is impelled by the oft-quoted assertion "Those who cannot learn from the past are condemned to repeat it." [2] It addresses excesses of the past that have almost completely disappeared from general history books and from general perception and which are set to recur in the next century for similar reasons of greed and moral torpidity. My argument is about historiography, science and humanity and is specifically concerned with the people of Bengal and their immediate future that threatens to outdo their tragic past in terms of human suffering and loss of life imposed by greedy and morally unresponsive foreigners.

Two centuries of British rule in India were repeatedly accompanied by horrendous human disasters due to callous exploitation by those responsible for their enslaved subjects, the human toll from these events amounting to scores of millions of people. [3] The two principal disasters suffered by Bengal were the Great Bengal Famine of 1769-1770 that consumed about 10 million people [4] and the Bengal Famine of 1943-1944 that ultimately swept away as many as 5 million people through starvation and attendant disease in the latter half of World War 2. [5] In between these 2 appalling events Bengal, and indeed India, suffered 2 centuries of famine and merciless exploitation that killed scores of millions and reduced hundreds of millions of people to wretched lives on the edge of the abyss.

Leaving to one side the precise mechanisms involved, the administering authority bears the responsibility for such events. The metropolitan community that would thus rule others has a continuing responsibility to ensure that at the very least such crimes against humanity are recorded, remembered and learned from by all. This has clearly not happened pursuant to the above disasters and this dereliction is indeed the subject of the present work. Holocaust denial of this kind and a continuing global commitment to blind economic expansion have created a crisis in biological sustainability that will resolve itself over the next century.

While the world has ostensibly departed from the era of explicit imperial colonialism, the present "neo-colonial" world order means that the poor and weak are subject to the rich and powerful by other means. An ostensibly free Bengali ryot (peasant farmer) couple and their children today are no less subject to the men of the City of London (now linked with the men of New York, Chicago, Washington and Zurich) than were their counterparts of 230 or indeed of 60 years ago. However the economic power of these latter day First World versions of the East India Company men is not accompanied by any formal or publicly acknowledged responsibility for their subjects. Global warming attendant upon the irresponsibility and greed of the industrial world is likely in the next century to visit upon the people of Bengal a disaster that will dwarf the horrors of their colonial past.[6]

We live in a global village and the "first world", "northern", "developed" societies are relatively well informed in principle about the present and likely future situation of the debt-ridden, impoverished people of the subject "third world".[7] However such wretched people are in reality of minimal concern to us and their transient invasion of our lives (principally via television) can be dispelled by a flick of a switch. Like the servants and other common folk in the neighbourhoods of an exquisite Jane Austen novel, these people are largely anonymous, ignored and unlamented in the rich tapestry of our elevated, hygienic lives.

Nevertheless barriers to humane sensibility are substantially dispelled by social or familial intimacy. While the West Indies represented a major source of contemporary wealth, its indigenous or slave inhabitants do not intrude into the world of Jane Austen's literary art except for the elegant "half mulatto, chilly and tender" Miss Lambe, made "the most important and precious" of her young ladies' party and indubitably acceptable by her wealth and consequent social position in the unfinished novel Sanditon. [8]

The growth of the British Empire in the 19th century was inevitably accompanied by increasing racism reflecting ruler-subject power relations and Miss Lambe would not have had the same social acceptability in 1850 - nor indeed in 1950 - as in 1800. Nevertheless post-war migration from former colonial countries, consequent social intercourse and intermarriage and the politically correct ideals of the modern global village have today generally restored normal interpersonal decencies if not a practical sense of collective social responsibility towards vulnerable Third World countries that will be critical in the coming catastrophe.

1.2. The present author's connections

It is useful for the reader to know from what patch of the social and intellectual woods the writer is coming from. To convince the reader that the underlying social responsibility argument of this book does not stem from a "holier than thou" position borne of superior moral and intellectual sensibilities of the writer, I should admit at the outset to having been married to a woman of ultimately Bihari and Bengali origin for over 30 years and we have 3 lively children. Her grandparents were among indentured labourers to the Pacific islands of Fiji from Bihar, Bengal and other parts of India early this century, [9] her paternal grandparents leaving India and crossing the kala pani (the Black Water) on the Ganges in 1913. In the rapid advance characteristic of such colonial societies, my wife's mother, Habiban (daughter of Tez Ali), became a school teacher (and indeed was known in her community of Nausori and Suva as "Teacher"); my wife's father, Abdul Lateef MBE (son of Kassim and Bedami), became a lawyer, distinguished himself in public life and was a member of a parliamentary delegation that negotiated independence for Fiji from Britain in 1970.[10] Of their unusually small family of only 6 children, the 3 sons are lawyers and the 3 daughters are, respectively, a science graduate/teacher-librarian, a secretary and a highly-positioned anthropology PhD working for a major international bank.

Any one of the millions of Bengali victims of past British imperial or mercantile policy is not simply another nameless statistic of the Third World suffering to which we have become innured through the "compassion overload" induced by the daily news. To a significant extent any such victim can be perceived as connected with any Bengali extended family, not so much for the commonplace crime involving the victim's suffering and death at foreign hands so many years ago, but for the present-day, continuing crime of racially- and culturally-selective forgetting.

The continuing white-washing of history is an offence as well as a danger to present-day people of the same ilk and indeed to all of us. In Germany and in France today it is an offence to deny the Jewish Holocaust, the Judeocide of World War 2, there being a penalty of up to 5 years imprisonment for this offence in Germany.[11] The Bengali Holocaust (first described in these terms by Jog (1944)[12] and indeed also by the Manchester Guardian in 1944)[13] has been completely forgotten in many standard general histories. One supposes that the deletion from public perception has been sustained by some general acceptance of the notion that somehow Bengalis don't matter. My personal interest in this "holocaust ignoring" derives from a familial involvement in both tragedies.

On my father's side I am descended from a prosperous, substantially "assimilated" Austro-Hungarian Jewish family that had progressively entered the mainstream of Hungarian society in the latter half of the 19th century. [14] My great grandfather Jakab Pollak (Polya) (1844-1897) was a lawyer-economist and utterly dedicated scholar who, incidentally, translated into Hungarian Adam Smith's An Inquiry into the Wealth of Nations (1776) (a work that draws upon the Great Bengal Famine of 1769-1770 as an example of the failure of economic managers). [15] It appears that access to Jakab Polya's translation of this "capitalist" classic was restricted to professional economists in communist Hungary. This family made substantial contributions to industry, culture, scholarship and science. Thus my grandfather Jeno (Eugene) Polya (1875-1944/45) was a great surgeon (of Polya/Billroth gastrectomy fame) who performed some 50,000 surgical interventions and published some 500 scientific works.[16] His brother, George (Gyorgy) Polya (1887-1985), was a very famous mathematician (most generally known for his classic book How to Solve It), with an immensely productive career spanning 7 decades in Budapest, Zurich and Stanford University, Palo Alto, California.[17] A third brother, Laszlo Polya (1891-1915/16), is presumed to have died as a soldier in the Austro-Hungarian Army on the Eastern Front during the First World War and one can only guess at the contributions he would have made if he had survived. This family was effectively wiped from the face of Europe in World War 2, the survivors (including those who had wisely left before the Holocaust) scattering principally to England, America and Australia.[18] My father, John (Janos) Bela Polya, fled to Australia and thence to Tasmania (as far away from the lunacy of Europe as one could go) and distinguished himself as an organic chemist and staunch defender of academic and intellectual decencies.[19] My grandmother's cousin, Dr. Edith Bone (née Hajos), went to England but was arrested in Budapest on returning to Hungary in 1949 as a journalist for the Daily Worker. She escaped during the Hungarian Revolution of 1956. Her remarkable mind-over-matter survival in solitary confinement in prison is described in Seven Years' Solitary

(1957), a work that, with other such accounts, is a testament to courageous self-possession at the edge of the abyss. [20]

The destruction of the Hungarian Jews (and the failure of the world to save this last major surviving body of Jews in German-occupied Europe) [21] is not unconnected with the contemporaneous "Forgotten Holocaust" in Bengal. As we will see, Winston Churchill, as a major wartime leader of Britain and the British Empire, was critically connected in different capacities with both events, a reality not apparent from his famous histories. [22]

1.3. History is written by the victors

The victor writes history, or more generally stated, the non-vanquished writes history. The Egyptian Pharoah Ramses II (1301-1234 BC) was well held by the Hittites at the Battle of Kadesh on the River Orontes in Syria (1296 BC) and was lucky not to have been comprehensively demolished. Ramses II commissioned his servants to render this near-disaster as a great victory for posterity. In his account of the discovery of the Hittite Empire, Narrow Pass, Black Mountain, C.W.Ceram (1955) describes this licence thus:

"Today it is known that these reports inspired by Ramses were shameless falsifications of history. They are the first examples of we have of such rewriting of history." [23]

Tudor recorders of history - no doubt concordant with the wishes of victorious Henry VII and his son Henry VIII - would have it that Richard III had eliminated most of his own important relatives including the 2 young Princes kept in the Tower of London. This was transmuted by Shakespeare into his famous play The Tragedy of King Richard the Third [24] but has been the subject of sensible scepticism as cogently and entertainingly described in The Daughter of Time by Josephine Tey (1951) and The Trial of Richard III by Drewett and Redhead (1984). [25] Nevertheless Hicks (1992), while accepting the reality of Tudor "demonization" of Richard III, also accepts his responsibility for the disappearance of the Princes. [26] As the quotation at the beginning of this Chapter indicates, young Jane Austen had a healthy scepticism about Richard's supposed guilt at the age of 16. Nevertheless basic, essential data concerning Kadesh and Richard III has survived - the Battle of Kadesh was fought, but the outcome is arguable; the "little bastards" were murdered in the Tower, but we can debate the culprit.

The bottom line for both scientific and historical scholarship is respect for the basic data. An extraordinary aspect of the history of the famines of Bengal is the elimination of the actuality of these immense tragedies from general and even specific histories and their consequent absence from general current perception. This book explores this Black Hole of British history that has consumed even the most horrendous realities. We are using the term Black Hole in several senses in this book. We are familiar with the astronomical Black Holes that have such a massive concentration of mass that even light (illumination in a physical and metaphorical sense), cannot escape. This nomenclature in turn surely derives from the "historical" Black Hole of Calcutta. This was a tiny room in which 146 British prisoners were supposedly incarcerated overnight on 20-21 June 1756 and from which emerged only 23 survivors. This event has gone into our language and is routinely used daily to represent any situation involving unproductive and irreversible consumption of valuable resources. However, as we will see, the Black Hole and attendant events and people are intimately linked to Jane Austen and her family. Further, this major element of demonizing British Imperial iconography may not even have happened or, if it did, has been immensely exaggerated. [27] The Black Hole in this disquisition represents a number of things: the historical "event", a very destructive, racially-loaded imperial myth, a metaphor for the extraordinary "ignoring" or "disappearing" of major historical realities by society and its academic elders and the human and biosphere catastrophe if the current crisis in biological sustainability is not resolved satisfactorily in the next few decades.

1.4. Jane Austen and historiography

Jane Austen was born in 1775 - 5 years after the apocalyptic semi-depopulation of Bengal, the richest province of the Indian sub-continent, under the remorseless fist of the East India Company. She was born into a family with manifold connections with British imperial expansion and specifically with Bengal. [28] Her life was spent in a fashion not dissimilar to that of the leisure life of civilized, educated people today - a modestly comfortable life of gentle family pleasures, of books, music, art, sociability, tamed nature and conversation. Her exquisite novels, written at the time of the Napoleonic Wars, are like a pool of tranquillity, a moral oasis in a period of horrendous violence and awfulness. [29]

One maximal human lifespan of about 125 years from Jane Austen's untimely death in 1817 brings us back in time to the accession of William III and Mary (1689), the beginning of the end of Catholic Highland Scotland and the commencement of a military struggle with France that would conclude with the Battle of Waterloo (1815). 1692 saw the Massacre at Glencoe of Jacobite Highlanders and the major English naval victory over the French at Cap de la Hogue in a conflict that would evolve into one of the first major wars of modern times, the War of the Spanish Succession (1702-1713). This war was qualitatively different from others in that it involved "modern", large-scale offensive carnage and generated immense wealth from attendant domestic and foreign activities for its chief administrators, notably Sir Winston Churchill's ancestor John Churchill, the Duke of Marlborough, and his Paymaster, Jane Austen's relative James Brydges, the first Duke of Chandos and the great-uncle of Jane Austen's mother. [30] The same span of years forward in time brings us to the commencement of World War 2, the ultimate war to beat all preceding wars in human history in terms of human carnage and commercial profit.

If we go back about 250 years (or 2 maximal human life spans) from the year of Jane Austen's death, we come to the accession of Queen Elizabeth I of England (1558), the entrenchment of a Protestant establishment and the commencement of an aggressive expansion of England into the greater world of the Americas, Africa and the East Indies. Advance 250 years from 1817 and we come to the late 21st century at which point the global environmental and economic consequences of moral and intellectual unresponsiveness and of thoughtless and aggressive expansion will be all too apparent.

One cannot criticize Jane Austen, the Artist, for the confinement of her art to the gentle and comfortable domesticity of the English Upper Class of circa 1800. Her novels deal with English Home Counties gentlefolk with annual incomes in the range of about 200 to 10,000 pounds and are delicious exercises in conversation and manners concerned with the matching of young men and women consonant with love and future material practicalities. It is not for us to cavill at the fact that the violent ugliness of the real world does not intrude into her world. There is no more room for the wretched, starving masses (British or Bengali) in the art of Jane Austen (1775-1817) than in the Arcadian landscapes of John Constable (1776-1837). [31] One notes, however, that the common folk of England had an assured place in the overwhelmingly powerful landscapes of Joseph Turner (1775-1831), a contemporary of Jane Austen and John Constable. [32]

Nevertheless Jane Austen was there and her family and connections were intimately involved in the process of preserving and extending the national and international hegemony of her class. The very displacement of her art from the attendant violent realities has provided a paradigm for what can charitably be seen as the remarkable, continuing English capacity for highly informed self-delusion about the world and their place in it. [I hasten to add that my maternal ancestry derives from early settlers to South Australia, Tasmania and Victoria from Cornwall, Devon and Middlesex as well from Gaelic Scotland. Thus a maternal great-great-great grandfather was a game

keeper (in Ilesworth near Twickenham, London) whose son went out to
Van Dieman's Land (Tasmania) and there married a woman from
Argylleshire in the Scottish Highlands. Other forebears were
Devonshire free settlers in Willunga, South Australia. I can thus surely
be credited with a licence to be suitably critical of my own lot.]

Self-delusion is not confined to the English - indeed it is
asserted that the essential difference between man and beast is not the
ability to make tools, use language or to deceive one's fellow creatures
but the capacity of man to deceive himself. We all do it, whether we
are a Tory academic historian like G.M.Trevelyan erasing Irish or
Indian famines from history, [33] a Jewish intellectual facing death in a
concentration camp [34] or a starving Bengali woman returning to
prostitution with the war-time British Military Labour Corps to
preserve the life of herself and her child. [35]

Jane Austen herself has posed a germane series of questions
that are directly relevant to this problem. In Northanger Abbey the
heroine, Miss Catherine Morland, affected by the somewhat Gothic
atmosphere of the Tilney family home and the romantic horrors of Mrs
Radcliffe's novels, conceives the fantasy that General Tilney (the father
of her beloved, Henry Tilney) has done away with the late Mrs Tilney.
(Let us remind ourselves that the late Mrs. Tilney is merely one soul as
compared to the millions of Bengal, Bihar and Oudh despatched
through the rapacity of the East India Company in the eighteenth
century alone). Henry reproves Catherine as follows:

"If I understand you rightly, you have formed a surmise of such horror
as I have hardly words to -. Dear Miss Morland, consider the dreadful
nature of the suspicions you have entertained. What have you been
judging from? Remember the country and the age in which we live.
Remember that we are English, that we are Christians. Consult your
own understanding, your own sense of the probable, your own
observation of what is passing around you. Does our education prepare
us for such atrocities? Do our laws connive at them? Could they be

perpetrated without being known, in a country like this, where social and literary intercourse is on such a footing, where every man is surrounded by a neighbourhood of voluntary spies, and where roads and newspapers lay everything open? Dearest Miss Morland, what ideas have you been admitting?" [36]

Catherine at this point rushes off to her room "with tears of shame".

This present book sets out from the beautiful, decent, articulate and morally sensitive microcosm of Jane Austen's life and art to explore her family and connections, her world and the appalling, continuing holocaust that was British imperialism in India. We will inspect the historical realities and the soldiers, administrators and scholars that contributed to our dim perception of the man-made tragedies of Bengal. In doing so we will nibble at a large literature and discover that not only have the Bengal holocausts and similar events been essentially deleted from generally-perceived history but even the more interesting and entertaining aspects of the lives of Jane Austen and her connections have been similarly rendered fit for polite society.

1.5. Science and the Austenizing of history

This "Austenizing" of history deserves to be addressed seriously. It is quite acceptable and legitimate for an artist such as Jane Austen to choose her medium and message just as it is perfectly reasonable for old-fashioned epicureans to delete "religion, sex and politics" from dining table conversation. However in academic scholarship, and ultimately in the areas of perception and policy in the parts and the whole of society, it is important that the basic facts are known. It is only then that we can begin to construct models, hypotheses and theories and to make predictions about matters pertaining to the future of our world. The ugly facts of Imperial Britain in circa 1800 were not relevant to Jane Austen's literary masterpieces but they are relevant to our understanding of history, human responsiveness and the likelihood of future catastrophes.

An experimental scientist has an advantage over the historian in that he can assess the data, generate an hypothesis and then set out to test the hypothesis experimentally. Indeed Karl Popper defined the scientific process as involving the construction and testing of potentially falsifiable hypotheses - an hypothesis was "scientific" in his perception if it could be experimentally tested. [37] This procedure leads to progressive refinement of scientific models when they are on the right track and points up major problems when there are major missing elements in the collective scientific perception of the systems under study. Such problems can be addressed by the formulation and testing of new hypotheses and are often successfully dealt with through technological advances.

While this sort of scientific advance can be seen to be evolutionary and incremental it is also clear that occasionally "revolutions" occur in our collective perception of reality. [38] Thus one of the classic examples of this sort of change in perception is provided by the Copernican revolution. It is indubitable that the sun rises in the morning, passes across the sky and then sets, to rise in roughly the same position again the following day. Our simple perception of this daily passage may lead us to infer (as did the Egyptian astronomer Ptolemy) that the Sun may orbit the Earth. However the revolutionary perception of Copernicus (and thence Galileo and Kepler) was that a simple model to explain this and a huge body of additional astronomical data involves the Earth revolving on an axis and actually orbiting around the Sun. [39]

This example provides a salutory lesson that "self-evident" and "general" perception and inference do not necessarily equate with reality, a proposition that applies not only to experimental science but also to historiography and the "social sciences" such as economics. It is notable that George Soros, the Hungarian Jewish investor, philanthropist and former undergraduate student of Karl Popper at the London School of Economics, has applied a critical "Popperian" approach to dealing with the gap between perception and reality in the marketplace - with evident sustained empirical success that has earned him billions as well as the accolade of being "the world's greatest investor" and "the world's greatest philanthropist". However Soros has also applied such analysis of perception/reality gaps to societies in disequilibrium and in particular to the old Soviet Union that have changed rapidly and catastrophically when the divergence between policy and reality became unsustainable. [40] The same sort of analysis is relevant to the looming conflicts involving expanding human populations, the impact of environmental change on agricultural productivity and sustainability, the dramatic decline in biodiversity and indeed the survival of major elements of the biosphere and of billions of human beings.

Historians have a difficulty in that the data they have is simply the collected flotsam of past eras and past events. Occasionally new technology provides a radical new way of accessing this information store (as seen in modern archaeology). However the historian, unlike the experimental scientist, cannot in general perform experiments to test "Popperian" hypotheses. An historian cannot re-run the Battle of Waterloo in the flesh after the fashion of the fictional re-run by historian Miss Hazlestone in Tom Sharpe's hilarious Riotous Assembly, in this instance a re-run of the Battle of Isandhlwana involving Zulu and white psychiatric inmates as protagonists. [41] However modern computers provide conceivable avenues for "re-running" historical models of such events with the attendant perturbation of particular variables (such as the Prussian General Blucher arriving at Waterloo earlier or later).

Cosmologists and evolutionary biologists have a problem akin to that of historians in that critical events they are concerned with are believed to have taken place literally billions of years ago. It has been possible to perform laboratory experiments demonstrating the formation of amino acids and other key "monomeric" components of living systems from electric discharges through an inferred "pre-biotic" atmosphere of methane (CH_4), nitrogen (N_2), carbon dioxide (CO_2) and water (H_2O). [42] However no in vitro construction of even the simplest "self-replicating" chemical system has been achieved. Man-made "evolution" through processes akin to Darwinian "natural selection" are readily demonstrable as in plant and animal breeding (through selection of desirable traits) and in molecular biological selection processes in the laboratory. The changes in the distribution of dark and pale moths in Industrial England (the so-called "industrial melanism") is readily explained in terms of the camouflaging of darker moths in a grimy, sooty environment and their differential selection within a moth population. Nevertheless, while Darwinian evolution in its crude essence is accepted by virtually all biologists, major problems exist with establishing the molecular details of how self-repairing and self-replicating systems (i.e. living organisms) arose and how evolution actually happened. [43]

Scientists have an ethical commitment to the "data"- they cannot pick and choose to suit their hypothesis. However scientists can typically get more data, repeat experiments, quantitate reproducibility and apply statistical arguments to their data. Historians have a peculiar responsibility towards the "facts of history" because these "facts" are essentially all the data they have. Of course it may well be that some "facts" are considered to be more important than others but the legitimacy of the licence offered by such value judgements has worn very thin when major catastrophes are ignored by major historians. The basic data should be given and then we can dispute the relevance of the victims to the "big picture" of human experience. Thus the historian G.M. Trevelyan in his History of England (1952) totally ignores the Bengal Famines - and indeed any famine in India - and, while effusive about the marvellous benefits of the imposition of the British Imperial Way, has nothing to say about the "native" recipients of this largesse or the supplanted and perverted cultures. [44]

Finally we should return to the predictive value of history either as typically purveyed by our parochial historians or properly dealt with in an ethical and scientific sense. At this point in time there is a fine balance between global population and available food. There are serious predictions of a substantial decline in staple food production in tropical countries next century due to global warming [45] and even optimistic projections predict a doubled global population by the mid-21st century. [46] The populous tropical "Third World" is under dire threat of famine next century. A human disaster of an unthinkable magnitude and awfulness is looming if there is to be a continuation of the view in "First World" countries that such people are irrelevant to the grand sweep of human progress or are otherwise undeserving of human compassion. The biosphere is facing a man-made crisis involving catastrophic decline in biological diversity and an immense threat to biological sustainability as we have known it. [47] And yet it is by and large "business as usual" for the world, the "Asian Tigers" have been progressing in leaps and bounds and there is manifestly insufficient global action now to steer us away from disaster. The lotus eaters prefer to remain unruffled and unmoved:

"O let us shut the future out,

Lest thoughts should poison with the shaft of doubt

The happy now!" [48]

This book sets out to describe some of the most horrendous crimes against humanity and how they have been almost completely deleted from general perception by the media, academics and "elders" of my own "British" culture. It presents the further contention that the world has to come to terms with these past realities in order to vigorously address collapsing biological sustainability. Of course nobody likes doom and gloom and "shame" is one of the most distorting feelings. I am reminded of a cartoon by George Booth (1974): a clergyman is being chased out of a New England church by his enraged flock and the reason is apparent when we see the church noticeboard announcing the title of the sermon: "Are we all prostitutes?" A gem that is also germane to our disquisition is a further cartoon by Booth (1977) showing a tribe of people on a flat plain and one individual asserts "It is so!". His tribe respond with a plethora of negatives: "No! Hell no!Absolutely not!" until a huge hirsute figure appears clutching the edge of the horizon and declares "It is so!", whereupon the whole tribe reverts to "Yes! Verily. Without doubt it is so! You damn betcha it is so if he says it is so!" [49]

In writing about the horrendous genocide and abuse of humanity in our past, the continuing "holocaust denial" of our culture and the crisis in biological sustainability that threatens our humanity, I am conscious that a modicum of leavening may be required. We all like to read a trenchant literary or other "cultural" critique in the press, our pleasure influenced no doubt by the principle that "there but for the grace of God go I". I have no criticism to offer of Jane Austen's literary vehicle per se, this being a matter of choice for the Artist. However, while conceding that some of the most effective historiography is suffused with the Art of Poetry, I nevertheless demand that historians, like scientists, respect the basic data. Thus, among other things, this book is a catalogue of some of the most surprising examples of historical deletion or oversight that I have called "Austenizing". At the more innocuous end of the historiographical spectrum, we have the Austenizing of the more interesting and indeed scandalous aspects of the lives of Jane Austen's connections that would appeal to the mischievous and voyeuristic in all of us. At the heavy end of the spectrum, we have what could be described as sustained, widespread "holocaust ignoring" that effectively amounts to massive "holocaust denial" in our culture. We are all familiar with the horrors of the Jewish Holocaust, yet the contemporaneous man-made Bengal Famine has been effectively deleted from general perception - this substantially Muslim Holocaust has become a Forgotten Holocaust.

This "holocaust denial" in our culture has blunted our responsiveness to inhumanity and is part of a more general failure to face up to the present reality that threatens biological sustainability and the lives of billions. However some hope remains if those with power and resources can tunnel through the wall of several centuries of dishonest and racially- and culturally-biased historiography, see the awful carnage that has been so well hidden and give resolution to the post-Holocaust plea: "Never again".

1.6. 2008 Postscript

As outlined in the Preface, major scientific bodies such as the American Association for the Advancement of Science (AAAS) [50], the US National Academy of Science [51], the UK Royal Society [52], other national and global scientific bodies, [53] and the Inter-governmental Panel on Climate Change (IPCC) [54] are warning of the dire threats to humanity from unaddressed greenhouse gas pollution, global warming and climate change. Indeed top US climate scientist Dr James Hansen (NASA) says that at the current 385 ppm atmospheric CO_2 we have already passed a tipping point and must urgently return to a safe and sustainable 300-350 ppm CO_2 to avoid catastrophe for humanity and mass species extinctions. [55] Professor James Lovelock predicts over 6 billion will perish this century due to climate change. [56] Biofuel-, climate change- and globalization-driven food price changes already threaten "billions" according to the UK Chief Scientist Professor John Beddington. [57] Yet climate sceptic Bush America still refuses to sign the Kyoto Protocol and it is "business as usual" as the major climate criminal countries, the US, Canada and Australia, continue to pollute and ignore the Climate Emergency and Sustainability Emergency facing Spaceship Earth. [58]

Chapter 2

The editing of Jane Austen's maternal connections - the Leighs and Brydges

"It is a truth universally acknowledged that a single man in possession of a good fortune, must be in want of a wife".

- Jane Austen in Pride and Prejudice (1813) [1]

"My idea of good company, Mr Elliot, is the company of clever, well-informed people, who have a great deal of conversation; that is what I call good company." [Anne Elliot] "You are mistaken," said he gently, "that is not good company, that is the best. Good company requires only birth, education and manners, and with regard to education, it is not very nice. Birth and good manners are essential; but a little learning is by no means a dangerous thing in good company, on the contrary, it will do very well. My cousin, Anne shakes her head. She is not satisfied. She is fastidious." [Mr. Elliot]

- Anne and Mr. Elliot in Persuasion (1818a) [2]

"I wish him happy with all my heart, & hope his choice may turn out according to his own expectations, & beyond those of his Family - and I dare say it will. Marriage is a great improver - & in a similar situation Harriet may be as amiable as Eleanor. - As to Money, that will come You may be sure, because they cannot do without it."

- Jane Austen letter to Cassandra (1808) concerning the coming marriage of Edward Bridges with Harriet Foote (her sister Eleanor having also married a Bridges) [3]

2.1. The "Austenizing" of Jane Austen's life

Jane Austen's art in each of her novels is concerned with the rarefied social interactions of a limited set of people essentially belonging to a single social class, the key young participants being potentially marriageable subject to age, inclination and financial constraints. The essential beauty of each creation lies in the sum of the delicious descriptions of people, their interactions and their elegant conversations. These highly moralistic "games" require no paraphernalia of additional social complexity or the drama of physical violence. There was no need for the awfulness of the real world to intrude into Jane Austen's novels for these realities would have simply detracted from the medium, the ménage and the message.

The artist can be highly selective in choosing the elements of creation without compromising truth or beauty. However the historian, like the scientist, is bound by the data - to operate otherwise is not merely "unethical", it is utterly pointless and counterproductive. Nevertheless "bias" inevitably intrudes into both historical analysis and science. When the "bias" in the latter leads to cavalier disregard of the data, the process has become fraudulent fantasy. The boundary between illegitimate and legitimate selectivity is more hazy in the area of historical analysis because of differential, culturally-biased weightings given to the data and to the historical models accomodating them. Nevertheless in some instances, to be detailed later in this book, the neglected historical reality is of such quantitative and qualitative importance that the illegitimacy should be palpably evident.

While the world of Jane Austen's novels was a highly selective, tranquil and comfortable slice of the society in which she lived, the treatment of her own life and connections by her numerous biographers is remarkably uneven in content. While the former can be seen as stylishly focussed art, the latter is a good example of the way in which historical realities are deleted, softened and prettified to satisfy a racial and cultural mythology of social "naiceness". This "Austenizing" or deleting and sweetening of the lives of the Austens can be seen as vastly less serious than the extraordinary sanitizing of British colonial enormities by historians, but it is nevertheless qualitatively of the same nature.

The Jane Austen novels have spawned a substantial Jane Austen-based academic industry that provides a rich body of data on the sensitivities of those engaged in historical reportage and analysis relating to Jane Austen. In detailing the forebears, life and connections of Jane Austen we will keep a quantitative tally of the deficiencies of such reportage. Of the large number of books dealing with the life of Jane Austen, [4] easily the most comprehensive and sensible is P. Honan's Jane Austen. Her Life (1987)[5] and for much of what is asserted in the following few chapters about Jane Austen and her connections the reader can regard this excellent work as a "default" reference.

Jane Austen (1775-1817) was born in her parents' home, the rectory of the village of Steventon in Hampshire, England on 16th December 1775. She was the 7th of 8 children born to her mother Cassandra (1739-1827) and her father the Reverend George Austen (1731-1805), the rector of Steventon from 1761 and who had married Cassandra (née Leigh) in 1764. The other siblings were, in order of birth, (the later Reverend) James (1765-1819), George (1766-1838) (a disabled person, put out to evidently excellent care), Edward (1767-1852) (who changed his surname to Knight in 1812), the (later Reverend) Henry Thomas (1771-1850), Cassandra Elizabeth (1773-1845) (Jane Austen's dear sister), the (later Admiral Sir) Francis William (1774-1865) and (the later Admiral) Charles John (1779-1852).

At the outset of this disquisition we will see that even this simple historical reality of immediate family members and relationships is subject to "Austenizing" (in this instance by Austen descendants themselves) arising from English manners and sensibilities. Thus James Edward Austen-Leigh (1798-1874), the son of the Reverend James Austen, completely deletes disabled George from Jane Austen's family in his biography of his Aunt Jane, A Memoir of Jane Austen (1870).[6] Similarly, Mary Augusta Austen-Leigh (1838-1922), in her Personal Aspects of Jane Austen (1920), also deletes poor George [7] and other works on Jane Austen perpetuate the absence. Of a selection of 30 works dealing with Jane Austen's life (albeit with markedly different degrees of detail and emphasis), a total of 7 do not mention brother George, namely Austen-Leigh (1870), Austen-Leigh (1920), Johnson (1926), Johnson (1927), Lascelles (1939), Nicolson (1991) and Smith (1890).[8]

Maybe, like starving Indians, Irish, Scots or even starving Englishmen, the disabled were not "naice" subjects for the polite society addressed by some of these authors. Perhaps the "family" authors did not want an "unfortunate" aspect of their lovely family to be exposed to the public, or, for all we know, they were themselves the victims of prior "Austenizing" by their senior relatives.

It gets worse. Before considering Jane's own life and work, it is useful and entertaining to look at her forbears, the ancestors of her father George Austen and her mother Cassandra Leigh. We are indebted to the scholarship of Halperin (1984), Hodge (1972), Honan (1987), Lane (1984, 1986, 1996), Smithers (1981) and Tucker (1983) in particular [9] and others [10] for a wealth of information relating to Jane Austen's connections. Ladies first...

2.2. The family of Jane Austen's mother, Cassandra Leigh

An early distinguished ancestor of the Leighs was Sir Thomas Leigh (1504?-1571), a Lord Mayor of London and Jane Austens's great great great great grandfather. His union with Alice Barker (the niece of Sir Rowland Hill) produced via Sir Thomas Leigh (Baronet, died 1626) a line of Leighs of Stoneleigh (of which more later) and via Rowland Leigh the Leighs of Adelstrop. The latter, with inputs from the Brydges and Perrot families, finally led to Jane Austen's mother Cassandra Leigh. The family lineages involved are simply presented below in quasi-Biblical fashion with spaces between generations and asterisks (*) marking siblings (JA refers to Jane Austen).

2.3. The Leighs of Adelstrop:

Rowland Leigh (JA great great great grandfather) married the daughter of the Earl of Berkeley & begat

Sir William Leigh (died 1632; JA great great grandfather) who married Elizabeth Whorwood & begat

Theophilus Leigh of Adelstrop (died 1724; JA great grandfather) who, in marrying again, married Mary Brydges (sister of James Brydges, 1st Duke of Chandos, of which much more later) & begat

*William Leigh (died 1757; JA great uncle) &

*Theophilus Leigh (died 1785; Master of Balliol, 1724-1785; JA great uncle) &

*Thomas Leigh (Rector of Harpsden, died 1763; JA grandfather).

William Leigh (died 1757; JA great uncle) married Mary Lord & begat

* Rev. Thomas Leigh who married Mary &

*James Leigh (1724-1784) who married Lady Caroline Brydges (daughter of Henry Brydges (1708-1781), the 2nd Duke of Chandos, and who thus shared a common great-grandfather with her husband in James Brydges, 8th Baron Chandos) & begat

James Henry Leigh (1765-1823) who married the Hon. Julia Twistleton (daughter of 13th Baron Lord Saye and Sele and sister of Mary Cassandra Twistleton, who was observed by Jane Austen at Bath and was regarded as an "adultress") & begat

Chandos Leigh (1791-1850) (1st Baron Leigh of Stoneleigh).

Theophilus Leigh (died 1785; JA great uncle) begat

Cassandra Leigh (1744-1826) (youngest daughter of the Master of Balliol, friend of the novelist Fanny Burney and cousin of Cassandra Austen née Leigh) who thence married Reverend Samuel Cooke (1741-1820) (of Cotsford, Oxfordshire and Vicar of Great Bookham, Surrey) & begat

*Reverend Theophilus Leigh Cooke (1776-1846) &

*Reverend George Leigh Cooke (1780-1853) &

*Mary Cooke

<u>Thomas Leigh</u> (died 1763; JA grandfather) married Jane Walker (of the Perrot line) & begat

* Thomas Leigh (disabled; JA uncle) &

*James Leigh (later Leigh-Perrot, JA uncle) &

*Jane Leigh (JA aunt) &

*Cassandra Leigh, Jane Austen's mother

2.4. The Chandos line:

James Brydges (d. 1714) (8th Baron Chandos; JA great great uncle) begat

*Katherine, Anne, Emma, Elizabeth, Henry &

*Mary Brydges (q.v., who subsequently married Theophilus Leigh) &

*James Brydges (1673-1744) (1st Duke of Chandos) who married twice, latterly (1713) without issue to his beautiful cousin Cassandra Willoughby (daughter of Francis Willoughby & Emma Barnard, sister of 1st Baron Middleton and step-daughter of Sir Josiah Child, a

governor of the East India Company) but firstly to Mary Lake (d.1712) who begat

*9 children of which only 2 survived, namely the elder

*John (1705-1727) (Lord Caernarvon, who had daughters Catherine & Jane) & the younger

*Henry Brydges (1708-1781) (2nd Duke of Chandos) who begat

*Lady Caroline Brydges (q.v., who married her relation James Leigh) &

*James Brydges (1731-1789) (3rd Duke of Chandos)

Two further members of this line were the siblings

*Sir Edgerton Brydges (1762-1837) (a writer unappreciated by Jane Austen and who unsuccessfully claimed the Chandos barony which thence ceased; he fled England in debt and died abroad) &

*Anne Brydges (born 1749) (a good friend and confidant of Jane Austen) who married the Reverend Isaac George Lefroy (Rector of Ashe; his elder brother Anthony Lefroy, commander of the 9th Light Dragoons, had a son Tom Lefroy who touched Jane Austen's heart) & begat

*3 children &

*Ben Lefroy (1791) who married Anna Austen (1793-1872) (daughter of James Austen) & begat

*6 children &

*Fanny C. Lefroy (1820-1885) who wrote The Family History.

2.5. The Perrot line:

James Perrot (d.1724) (of Northleigh, Oxfordshire; JA great great grandfather) married Anne Dawtrey & begat

Jane Perrot (JA great grandmother) who married Dr John Walker (JA great grandfather) and thence begat

Jane Walker (1704-1768, Cassandra Leigh's mother, JA grandmother).

2.6. The Leighs of Stoneleigh:

Sir Thomas Leigh (Baron of Stoneleigh) (d.1626; JA great great great great uncle) begat

Thomas, 1st Lord Leigh (1643) who begat

Thomas Leigh (1652-1710) (2nd Lord Leigh of Stoneleigh) who married Eleanor Watson (daughter of the 2nd Baron Rockingham) and then Lady Anne Wentworth (daughter of the 1st Earl of Strafford, Charles I's minister beheaded in 1641) & begat

Edward Leigh (1684-1738) (3rd Lord Leigh) who begat

Thomas Leigh (1713-1749) (4th Lord Leigh) who married Maria Rebecca Craven (sister of the 5th Lord Craven) & begat

*Edward Leigh (1742-1786) (5th Lord Leigh, died unmarried 1786) &

*Mary Leigh (successor to Stoneleigh who died unmarried 1806 & thence

the property and title fell to Chandos Leigh (q.v.), 1st Baron Leigh of Stoneleigh).

2.7. The Cravens and Lloyds

The Cravens and Lloyds come into the picture in that they were connected with a 16th Century Lord Mayor of London, had high Tory Royalist connections and ultimately connected themselves through friendship and marriage to the Austen family and the Leigh family of Stoneleigh. We can begin this lineage with 2 brothers Sir William Craven and Henry Craven.

Sir William Craven (1548?-1618) (Lord Mayor of London) begat

William Craven (1606-1697) (1st Earl of Craven; Royalist leader linked as lover and even husband to Elizabeth Stuart, Queen of Bohemia, daughter of James I and grandmother of George I).

Henry Craven (1543-1603) (brother to Sir William Craven) gave rise to

*William Craven (1668-1711) (2nd Lord Craven) &

*Charles Craven (1682-1754) (Governor of South Carolina) &

*John Craven.

William Craven begat

William Craven (1700-1739) (3rd Lord Craven) who married Anne Tylney

Charles Craven begat

Martha Craven (died 1825) who married Reverend N. Lloyd and begat

*Mary Lloyd (1771-1843) (who married James Austen as his 2nd wife in 1797) &

*Martha Lloyd (1765-1843) (who married Francis Austen as his 2nd wife in 1828)

<u>John Craven</u> begat

*William Craven (1705-1769) &

*Maria Rebecca (q.v.) (who married Thomas Leigh, 4th Lord Leigh) &

*John who begat

William Craven (1738-1791) (5th Lord Craven) who married Lady Elizabeth Berkeley (1750-1828) (later Margravine of Brandenburg-Ansbach; playwright) & begat

William Craven (1770-1825) who married Louisa Brunton (1785?-1820) (famous actress).

2.8. The Leigh-Perrots - Cassandra's siblings and their connections:

The Leigh/Brydges line represented by Rev.Thomas Leigh (Jane Austen's maternal grandfather) now joins with the Perrot/Walker line represented by Jane Walker (granddaughter of James Perrot and Jane Austen's maternal grandmother) to yield Jane Austen's mother Cassandra Leigh.

<u>Rev. Thomas Leigh</u> (JA grandfather) married Jane Walker (JA grandmother) & begat

*Cassandra Leigh (1739-1827; JA mother) who married George Austen (1731-1805; JA father) &

*Thomas Leigh Junior (died 1821; disabled; JA uncle; in care, possibly with George Austen) &

*James Leigh (later Leigh-Perrot; JA uncle) (died 1817) who married
Jane Cholmeley (1744 -1836) (JA aunt; the niece of Sir Montague
Cholmeley of Lincolnshire; she was accused of theft entailing possible
capital punishment or transportation) &

*Jane Leigh (JA aunt) who married Reverend Dr Edward Cooper
(1728-1792) and begat

*Reverend Edward Cooper (1770-1835; JA cousin) (curate of
Harpsden; rector of Hamstall-Ridware, Staffordshire; married Caroline
Isabella Lybbe Powys who died in 1838) &

*Jane Cooper (later Lady Jane; JA cousin) (who was a great friend of
Jane Austen and died tragically from a carriage accident in 1798; she
married Thomas Williams, RN, who was knighted in 1796, became an
admiral and was Charles Austen's captain in several ships)

2.9. A brief overview of Cassandra Leigh's connections

Inspection of Cassandra's relatives and connections makes it
clear that the Austens were not a simple clerical family of modest
means cast adrift from the powerful establishment in an isolated rustic
oasis. Cassandra's "mob" (to use a rather fluid Australian term)
included Lord Mayors of London, a Minister of Charles I, a
notoriously wealthy Paymaster to Marlborough's forces, earls, barons,
dukes and their grand ladies, a Governor of South Carolina, an admiral,
a military commander, a famous Master of Balliol College at Oxford, a
celebrated woman writer and a famous actress as well as a number of
humble clergymen. We will see later that the Reverend George
Austen's "mob" was similarly blessed with English establishment
notables. These connections traversed the spectrum of acceptable
society from modest clergymen to grand people having direct dealings
with royalty. Thus Sir Thomas Leigh entertained Charles I at
Stoneleigh Abbey and the king's sister, Elizabeth Stuart (later Queen of
Bohemia, grandmother of George I and reputed lover of Willliam, 1st
Earl of Craven) was brought up at nearby Coombe Abbey.

Since not too many could share in the post-Reformation cake and be accomodated in the clerically comfortable to the ducally opulent layers of the Establishment, it is not surprising that multiple family re-connections should occur. Thus the Cravens are linked to the Stoneleigh Leighs (and hence the Austens) by the union of Maria Craven with Thomas, 4th Lord Leigh and we see that the Craven descendants Mary Lloyd and Martha Lloyd became the second wives of widowed James Austen and Francis Austen, respectively. The death in 1806 of Mary Leigh, life tenant of Stoneleigh Abbey, meant that Chandos Leigh (like Jane Austen a great grandchild of Theophilus Leigh of Adelstrop, and whose other early ancestor Sir Thomas Leigh, Lord Mayor of London, was also a shared ancestor with the Stoneleigh Leighs and his "cousins" Cassandra Leigh and her daughter Jane Austen) ultimately became the legal owner of this grand establishment (cf. Mansfield Park).

Consanguinity was certainly the "go" among the Chandos mob and indeed among the English ruling class in general. Cassandra Leigh's cousin James Leigh was the great-nephew of James Brydges (1st Duke of Chandos) and married Lady Caroline Brydges, the daughter of Henry Brydges (the 2nd Duke of Chandos) and hence the granddaughter of James Brydges - this couple thus shared a common great-grandfather. At a more intimate level, after the death of his first wife Mary, James Brydges (1st Duke of Chandos and corrupt Paymaster to the Forces) married his beautiful cousin Cassandra Willoughby in 1713, but they had no children. A further such marriage in the family was opposed and thereby prevented: Martha Bourchier (daughter of James Brydges' sister Katherine) fell in love with Alexander Jacobs (son of James Brydges' sister Elizabeth). Alexander went overseas with his regiment and Martha was entered into an unsatisfactory marriage with Henry Perrot, an intimate of Brydges (cf. Brandon in Sense and Sensibility). [11]

It should be noted that while first cousin marriage is prohibited in some religious and legal systems, it is possible in others. Thus in traditional Chinese custom such a union might be possible but a non-consanguinous union involving partners having the same family name would be prohibited. In hindsight this prohibition can be justified in terms of minimizing the deleterious effects of inbreeding. [12] The Australian aboriginal "skin name" system of tribal sub-group identification and constraints on in-law connections was able to minimize in-breeding in the context of relatively small tribal groups. [13] However one presumes that such regulations may actually have stemmed from innate or societal incest taboos. In some American states first cousin marriage was prohibited and in some others it was permitted provided there was no issue. Thus Albert Einstein's allegedly "lost son" in Czechoslovakia may have ended up there due to the kindly fostering out of the product of his second marriage to the widowed daughter of his father's cousin. [14] The Reformation in England led to a slightly more liberal interpretation of religious injunctions but the taboos specified in Leviticus Chapters 18 and 20 basically remained in place and some non-consanguinous unions between people related only through marriage were prohibited. In Jane Austen's times first cousins were permitted to marry, although there was some social discouragement. [15] As we will see later, such consanguinous unions recur in the Austen family and in Jane Austen's novels.

All families will have "skeletons in the cupboard" and the Cassandra "mob" are no exception. Of interest to me in this disquisition is how some of the more interesting members of this tribe are treated by the numerous biographers of Jane Austen or by historians in general where this is appropriate. We have already seen how poor George Austen Junior has been erased from history by some of his sister's more delicate biographers. Accordingly, for various reasons, we will examine a limited set of such people encountered so far who have been treated unevenly by historians, namely James Brydges, Edgerton Brydges, James Leigh-Perrot, Jane Leigh-Perrot and Mary Cassandra Twistleton.

2.10. James Brydges, Paymaster to the Forces and First Duke of Chandos

James Brydges (1674-1744), the great-uncle of Cassandra Leigh (Jane Austen's mother) and great-great-uncle of Jane Austen, was born into the prosperous Chandos family which had estates in Herefordshire, Worcestershire and Gloucestershire. Having secured presentations to King William III and to the Prince of Denmark, he was nevertheless unsuccessful in attempts to gain a potentially lucrative post in the Excise Department. He was subsequently elected to Parliament in 1698 (not without some opposition from Sir Thomas Southwell), noting that the electoral process was notoriously corrupt and particularly so in Herefordshire. His assiduous lobbying paid off with his appointment as a commissioner of the Admiralty in 1703. With the commencement of the War of the Spanish Succession against the Spanish and French (1701-1713), Brydges saw further opportunities and, through his friendship with the Duke of Marlborough, took up the position of Paymaster to the Queen's Forces Abroad. His subsequent generous gift of a valuable ring to the Duchess had to be declined. While not in a position to determine policy, Brydges was able to make a large fortune. He had excellent connections: his aunt Beata Danvers was a lady-in-waiting to Queen Anne (who had assumed the Crown in 1702) and Brydges was friendly with the treasurer Godolphin and the great general Marlborough.

James Brydges made not a small fortune - he made a gigantic fortune. Handling over 15 million pounds of funds in his period as Paymaster he was able to exploit his position by borrowing from such funds and investing them for short-term profit (deriving from interest on such capital and from differential exchange rates for foreign currencies) until the funds actually had to be paid. Through his connection with Marlborough (who did quite nicely himself out of war and its attendant profitable possibilities) and with Marlborough's aide Lord Cadogan, Brydges was well placed for insider-trading based on knowledge of future alarms, battles or peace initiatives crucial for investment outcomes. Nevertheless Brydges was careful to avoid explicit criminality and the closest he came to this (depending upon your judgement) was through supplying inferior equipment to his poor countrymen who were later defeated on the Spanish Peninsular.

It has been estimated that Brydges was worth several hundred pounds a year when he commenced as Paymaster in 1705 but when he retired from the position in 1713 his fortune was worth 600,000-700,000 pounds. With increasing unpopularity of the war (especially its attendant taxation burden) and increasing Tory power in Parliament and in the Court, the gravy train was set to come to a close.

When the Tories led by Harley and St John mounted the Peculation Charges in Parliament against the Whig administration involving lost funds asserted to amount to 35 million pounds, Brydges encountered a rather tricky phase of his life. He corresponded with Harley (a distant relative) and secured special treatment involving his separation from Marlborough and the others. This in turn enabled him to stay in office and brave the storm (his resignation could well have implied guilt). While the Duchess of Marlborough's influence at Court was supplanted by that of Mrs Abigail Masham (also a distant relative of Harley), Brydges curried favour with Mrs Masham (giving her a lavish gift of plate) and his cause was no doubt assisted by his aunt Beata Danvers.

In the event he survived while not discarding his obligation to the disgraced Marlborough. However with coming of peace in 1713 (the year of the Treaty of Utrecht), Brydges felt able to resign as Paymaster. With Anne seriously ill, the Tory leaders Oxford and Bolingbroke favoured a Stuart succession involving the return of James (Anne's half brother) while the Whigs favoured Sophia of Hanover or her son George. Brydges with continuing excellent judgement distanced himself from the Tories and plumped for the Hanoverian camp. On George's accession to the throne in 1715 and the re-instatement of Marlborough as Captain General of the Army, Brydges made generous gifts of jewellery or money to the King's mistresses Melusina von Schulenberg (later the Duchess of Kendal) and Sophia Kielmansegge (later the Countess of Darlington) and to the King's close advisers Baron von Bernstorff and Baron von Bothmer. He subsequently secured some modest bureacratic sinecures and set about alternative business ventures.

Capital-rich Brydges was in a splendid position to invest in the great entrepreneurial adventures of his day. Brydges was connected with the Turkey Company through his grandfather Sir Henry Barnard and his brother-in-law Alexander Jacob. Sir Josiah Child (1630-1699), a Director and subsequently Governor of the East India Company, was the step-father of Brydges' second wife Cassandra Willoughby (Brydges' beautiful cousin whom he married in 1713 after the death of his first wife Mary). Child conducted his business affairs with great vigour and ruthlessness (to the extent of securing all of the revenues of the Willoughby estate after marrying Cassandra's mother and only surrendering them to the legitimate heirs after extensive legal action). Brydges was associated with the slave trade through the Royal African Company and, through Sir Hans Sloane FRS, had an interest in African medicinal plants. Unsuccessful ventures for Brydges included the Mississippi Company of John Law (which eventually collapsed) and the notorious South Sea Company. When the South Sea Bubble burst, Brydges lost 50,000 pounds, Cassandra lost 11,000 pounds and her mother also lost substantially.

The immense wealth of James Brydges is reflected in fine buildings designed and built at his behest by architect-surveyor John Wood in Bath (a key location in Jane Austen's life and literary work). His Edgeware palace Canons was remarkable at the time for its magnificence and appointments. An indication of the lavishness of his lifestyle is given by his maintenance of a 27-member orchestra at an annual charge of 1,000 pounds (about 100,000 pounds in today's money). George Frederick Handel wrote 12 anthems as well as other choral works and overtures for James Brydges. While not having any children by Brydges, Cassandra was kept very busy helping to run this great establishment and helping her step-children and ultimately their children.

Of particular interest to us here is the manner of wealth generation involved, the impact of the Brydges on the Leighs and hence the Austens, the continuing connections between these families and the surprising total or near total deletion of this immensely wealthy operator from a substantial number of standard, and indeed specialist, historical texts, including Jane Austen biographies. Thus, while a number of detailed accounts of James Brydges and his connections have been published,[16] Brydges receives minimal or no mention in a number of English histories dealing with his period. [17] Of our selection of 30 works dealing with Jane Austen's life [8] only 11 mention James Brydges and of these only 4 allude to his pecuniary adventures, namely Honan (1987), Lane (1984), Tucker (1983) and Watkins (1990).

2.11. Sir Edgerton Brydges

Sir Edgerton Brydges is a minor player in this story. He was connected to Jane Austen through the Brydges line. His sister Anne Lefroy was a good "older" friend to Jane Austen and her nephew Tom Lefroy was perhaps Jane's first love. Edgerton Brydges was a novelist but Jane Austen did not approve of his literary style. Jane Austen commented thus on one of his works:

"We have got "Fitz-Albini"; my father bought it against my private wishes, for it does not quite satisfy my feelings that we should purchase the only one of Edgerton's works of which his family are ashamed. That these scruples, however, do not at all interfere with my reading it, you will easily believe. We have neither of us finished the first volume. My father is disappointed - I am not, for I expected nothing better. Never did any book carry more internal evidence of its author. Every sentiment is completely Edgerton's. There is very little story, and what there is is told in a strange, unconnected way. There

are many characters introduced, apparently merely to be delineated.
We have not been able to recognize any of them hitherto, except Dr
and Mrs Hey and Mr Oxenden, who is not very tenderly treated." [18]

Conversely, Sir Edgerton Brydges never suspected that she was
an author. [19] Edgerton Brydges (1762-1837) pursued an unsuccessful
claim for the restoration of the Chandos aristocratic position which had
finally lapsed. The last direct descendant to inherit what was left of the
massive estates was Lady Anna Eliza Brydges (1780-1836). Her father,
James Brydges the Third Duke of Chandos (1731-1789), had died
prematurely (after his wife had pulled away a chair on which he was
about to sit) and her mother had gone mad. The Lady Anna Eliza
Brydges / Richard ("Temple") Grenville match had been arranged in
principle in 1786 in Bath when the girl was merely 6 but was later
opposed by Lady Caroline Brydges (her aunt and also a guardian),
giving rise to all kinds of romantic subterfuge between the pair.
However the union eventually took place in 1796 but later soured
because of the profligacy and habitual adultery of Richard Grenville,
Duke of Buckingham, who adopted the title of Duke of Chandos and
Buckingham. Their eldest son, the Marquess of Chandos, was also a
spendthrift. The Grenville family eventually disposed of most of the
Chandos and Buckingham fortune during the 19th Century. [20] Sir
Edgerton Brydges scores 13 mentions out of 30 possible [8] in our "quiz"
but only 2 works, namely Honan (1987) and Halperin (1984), refer to
his quixotic bid for aristocratic restoration. The "De Bourgh" of Jane
Austen's unpleasant aristocratic dowager Lady Catherine De Bourgh in
Pride and Prejudice is evidently a joke at Sir Edgerton Brydge's
expense, this having been an alternative name for his tribe in the dim
past.

2.12. James and Jane Leigh-Perrot

James and Jane Leigh-Perrot were much humbler people than
the Brydges but were comfortably well off gentry nevertheless and of
course had a lot to do with Jane. James Leigh, Jane's maternal uncle,

adopted the name Perrot after his maternal great-aunt persuaded her brother to will estates at Northleigh to his great-nephew. He duly received this property in 1751 and as a condition of the settlement changed his name to Leigh-Perrot. James sold the estates to the Duke of Marlborough and thence lived at his home Scarlets at Hare Hatch (near Reading) and at Bath. His wife Jane (or Jenny) Cholmeley was born in Barbados, her father having married into the Willoughby family (q.v.). Jane's "Aunt Perrot" was very proud of the ancient and noble lineage of the Perrots (pre-conquest, over with the Conqueror and one supposedly the natural-born son of Henry VIII as well as family connections that variously founded Trinity College and St. John's College).

Wills can have a somewhat corrosive effect on happy families. After his death in March 1817, James' will was not happily received and had long-reaching effects. James had no children and essentially left everything to his wife with a conditional generous future provision for his nephew James Austen and 1,000 pounds to each of the Austen children who survived their Aunt Perrot. Jane Austen's terminal illness was exacerbated by knowledge of the will, for she was very conscious of the financial problems and constraints of her siblings. Indeed Jane Austen died about 4 months later. Her reaction to the will was rather severe:

"A few days ago my complaint appeared removed, but I am ashamed to say that the shock of my Uncle's Will brought on a relapse, & I was so ill on friday & thought myself so likely to be worse that I could not but press for Cassandra's returning with Frank after the funeral last night, which she of course did, & either her return, or my having seen Mr Curtis, or my Disorder's chusing to go away, have made me better this morning." [24]

Jane Leigh-Perrot lived on to a ripe old age of 92. Shortly after her husband's death she settled a generous income on her great-nephew James Edward Austen who later assumed the name Austen-

Leigh (after the fashion of his benefactor Great-Uncle James Leigh-Perrot and indeed of his Uncle Edward Knight née Austen). James Edward Austen-Leigh inherited Scarlets and indeed most of the Leigh-Perrot wealth and is the author of the particularly gentle and circumspect A Memoir of Jane Austen (1870). The Will from which he benefited so greatly, but which had such a negative impact on his family and on the last months of Jane Austen's life, was deleted (together with so much else) from his biography [25] and indeed from 13 out of our sample of 30 Jane Austen biographies.

Jane Leigh-Perrot was fortunate to have lived so long or to have lived so long in England. In 1799, about 6 months after a visit of Jane Austen to her relations in Bath, her Aunt Jane was involved in a serious charge. Jane Leigh-Perrot had purchased a card of black lace for about 1 pound at the millinery shop of Miss Elizabeth Gregory. However she was subsequently accosted by Miss Gregory in the street and a card of white lace was found, together with the black lace, in the parcel that had been wrapped up in the shop. James Leigh-Perrot gave their address to the milliner's shop assistant, Charles Filby, on his request. Some days later an anonymous letter concerning lace stolen from a shop was received by the unfortunate couple. Subsequently she had to appear before the Mayor and Magistrate of Bath who remanded her in prison for trial.

She was in remand in Ilchester for 7 months facing a possible death sentence (since the alleged shoplifting involved goods worth more than 5 shillings) or transportation to Botany Bay in New South Wales (since the allegedly stolen goods were worth more than 12 pence). Her own counsel Joseph Jeckyll apparently considered her a kleptomaniac. A trip to London in the company of her gaoler Edward Scadding failed to secure bail and she returned to gaol in Ilchester. At her trial at Taunton she read a statement in her own defence, her position being strengthened by her social position, excellent references from men of substance and evidence that Charles Filby had been bankrupted and had made a similar wrapping-up error in the past. Jane

Leigh-Perrot was acquitted by the jury but the matter inevitably gave rise to speculations: had the acquittal been purchased or had she been subject to a process of blackmail?

An interesting East Indies connection makes its appearance in this affair of Jane Leigh-Perrot. One of the men of substance who acted as a rather crucial character witness for her was George Vansittart, MP for Reading in Berkshire. His brother was Henry Vansittart, former Governor of the Presidency of Fort William (Calcutta) from 1760-1764 during a period of some of the worst mercantile excesses of the Company men in Bengal. He was very helpful to the cause of Mohammed Reza Khan, the chief minister of the "native" government of Bengal during the period of the so-called "Dual Government" instituted by Robert Clive after the Battle of Plassey in 1757 and the person responsible for collecting taxes for the Company at the time of the Great Bengal Famine. Henry Vansittart retired to England a wealthy man and indeed used his wealth to become an MP after the fashion of many Company men. He was recalled to duty when news of the Bengal disasters reached London and was sent out to Calcutta with 2 other newly appointed Commissioners in 1770 on the Aurora. The Aurora was lost at sea with all aboard. [26]

George Vansittart was a Company man in Bengal at the time and indeed during the Great Bengal Famine was a Supervisor involved in overseeing tax-collection. He was a very good friend of Warren Hastings (first Governor-General of Bengal and an important friend of Jane Austen's parents). After his service for the Company he retired to England and took over his late brother's seat in Parliament. He would have known the Leigh-Perrots since the Leigh-Perrot estate Scarlets was in Berkshire. It is not unlikely that he would have been aware of Jane Leigh-Perrot's relationship to George Austen given that the latter and George Vansittart had a common friend in Warren Hastings. It is also likely that Hastings was friendly with the Leigh family in Gloucestershire. [27]

James Austen was very solicitous to his Aunt and Uncle during the Trial. Mrs Austen suggested that Jane and Cassandra should keep Aunt Jane Leigh-Perrot company during her remand (an offer that was not taken up). James Austen's son James Edward Austen-Leigh deleted these unpleasant happenings from his A Memoir of Jane Austen (1870) as have other Austenizing biographers. Thus with respect to our selection of 30 Jane Austen histories, [8] James Leigh-Perrot scores 27/30 for being mentioned but only 17/30 describe The Will. Jane Leigh-Perrot scores 25/30 for being mentioned and 20/30 for reportage of her close shave with the noose or Botany Bay, Australia.

2.13. Mary Cassandra Twistleton

Our last example of the sanitizing of this part of Jane Austen's life relates to Lord and Lady Saye and Sele and their daughters, Julia Twistleton, who married James Henry Leigh of the Adelstrop Leigh family, and Mary Cassandra Twistleton. Lord Saye and Sele was unbalanced and disposed of himself in a desperate and bizarre fashion using a razor and a sword. Jane observed Mary Cassandra, who appeared "quietly and contentedly silly", and her lively friends at Bath. She wrote of this in correspondence with her sister Cassandra and commented on the supposed married lover, a middle-aged Mr Evelyn whom she had met, travelled out with and found pleasant and harmless:

"I then got Mr Evelyn to talk to, & Miss Twistleton to look at; and I am proud to say that I have a very good eye at an Adultress, for tho' repeatedly assured that another in the same party was the She, I fixed upon the right one from the first. - A resemblance to Mrs Leigh was my guide. She is not so pretty as I expected; her face has the same defect of blandness as her sister's, & her features not so handsome; - she was highly rouged, & looked rather quietly and contentedly silly than anything else. - Mrs Badcock & two young Women were of the same party, except when Mrs Badcock thought herself obliged to leave them, to run round the room after her drunken Husband. His avoidance, & her pursuit, with the probable intoxication of both, was an amusing scene. - The Evelyns returned our visit on Saturday; - we were very happy to meet, & all that; they are going tomorrow into Gloucestershire, to the Dolphins for ten days." [28]

" Mrs Evelyn called very civilly on Sunday, to tell us that Mr Evelyn had seen the Mr Philips the proprietor of No 12 G.P.B. and that Mr Philips was very willing to raise the kitchen floor; ...I assure you inspite of what I might chuse to insinuate in a former letter, that I have seen very little of Mr Evelyn since coming here; I met him this morning for only the 4th time, & as to my anecdote about Sidney Gardens, I made the most of my Story because it came in to advantage, but in fact he only asked me whether I were to be at Sidney Gardens in the evening or not. - There is now something like an engagement between us & the Phaeton, which to confess my frailty I have a great desire to go out in; - whether it will come to anything must remain with him. - I really beleive [sic] he is very harmless; people do not seem to be afraid of him here, and he gets Groundsel for his birds & all that." [29]

This sort of slippage from virtue appears in Jane Austen's Mansfield Park in which Maria Rushworth née Bertram runs away from her boring rich husband with interesting Henry Crawford. However what was good enough for a hygienic Jane Austen novel was possibly not sufficiently "naice" for a number of her biographers. Thus Mary Cassandra Twistleton scores only 5/30 for being named and for speculation about her allegedly adulterous conduct.

The reader will now have begun to get a feel for the range of Jane Austen's connections and the surprising variations in the historiography applied to them. These connections on her mother's side ranged from high nobility to humble clergymen and already we see the importance of wealth generation in India for some of these people (Sir Josiah Child, Cassandra Brydges née Willoughby, James Brydges, George and Henry Vansittart and Warren Hastings). Those who had returned wealthy from India (Bombay, Madras or Bengal) were referred to as nabobs (derived from nawab, the name for a Mughal prince). [30] They excited some envy at home as well as moralistic concern over the nature of their wealth acquisition. The rapacity of these colonial overlords was to seriously exacerbate the first and most appalling of 2 centuries of famines in British India, the Great Bengal Famine of 1769-1770. [31]

2.14. 2008 Postscript

Some further books on Jane Austen became available. [32] Mary Cassandra Twistleton was indeed an "adulteress". [33] Jane Austen visited Stoneleigh Abbey in 1806 (cf Mansfield Park). [34]

Chapter 3

The editing of the Austens and consequences of rustic amusement

"My father is glad to hear so good an account of Edward's pigs, and desires he may be told, as encouragement to his taste for them, that Lord Bolton is particularly curious in <u>his</u> pigs, has had pigstyes of a most elegant construction built for them, and visits them every morning as soon as he rises."

- Jane Austen, letter to Cassandra (1798)[1]

"Nothing can be said in his vindication, but that his abolishing Religious Houses and leaving them to the ruinous depredations of time has been of infinite use to the landscape of England in general."

- Jane Austen on Henry VIII and the countryside in The History of England (1791)[2]

"She returned just in time to join the others as they quitted the house, on an excursion through its more immediate premises; and the rest of the morning was easily whiled away, in lounging round the kitchen garden, examining the bloom upon its walls, and listening to the gardener's lamentations upon blights, - in dawdling through the green-house, where the loss of her favorite plants, unwarily exposed, and nipped by the lingering frost, raised the laughter of Charlotte, - and in visiting her poultry-yard, where in the disappointed hopes of her dairymaid, by hens forsaking their nests, or being stolen by a fox, or in the rapid decrease of a promising young brood, she found fresh sources of merriment."

- Marianne at Cleveland in Sense and Sensibility (1811)[3]

3.1. The Austen paternal half of Jane Austen's forebears

The paternal half of Jane Austen's forebears are no less interesting than the Leighs, Cravens, Brydges and Perrots, although they lack the lordly connections of the latter. The Austens were a prosperous Kentish lot involved in agriculture, wool manufacture and other practical occupations. The Jane Austen scholars have provided a wealth of information about the Austen side of Jane Austen's inheritance.[4] The Austens and their close connections descended from John Austen of Horsmonden as outlined below and there are a number of particularly useful accounts of these connections. [5]

3.2. John Austen I of Horsmonden and his immediate descendants:

John Austen I (1560-1620, JA great great great great grandfather) of Horsmonden begat

*John Austen II (1585-1650) &

*Francis Austen I (1600-1688, JA great great great grandfather) of Grovehurst who begat

John Austen III (1629-1705, JA great great grandfather) who begat

*Jane Austen (the original; JA great great aunt) who married Stephen Stringer (JA great great uncle)

*John Austen IV (died 1704, JA great grandfather) of Broadford (who begat John Austen V) &

*Anne who married John Holman.

3.3. The original Jane Austen's line:

Jane Austen (original; JA great great aunt) married Stephen Stringer (JA great great uncle) & begat

*Mary Stringer (who married her cousin John Austen V) &

*Hannah Stringer who married William Monke & begat

Jane Monke who married Thomas Brodnax (later Knight) of Godmersham who begat

Thomas Knight II (died 1794) of Godmersham and Chawton who married Catherine Knatchbull (died 1812) but had no issue (these were the adoptive parents of Jane Austen's brother Edward Knight née Austen who had the same great great grandfather, John Austen III, as Thomas Knight II).

Our Jane Austen's brother Edward Austen was adopted by this couple and in 1797 Catherine assigned the estates to Edward who took the name Knight on the death of his foster mother. The Knatchbull family will resurface later.

3.4. John Austen IV of Broadford's descendants:

<u>John Austen IV</u> (JA great grandfather) married Elizabeth Weller (died 1721) and begat

*Elizabeth Austen (1695-),

*John Austen V (1696-1728, JA great uncle),

*Francis Austen II (1698-1791) (a solicitor of the Red House, Sevenoaks),

*Thomas Austen (1699-1772) (an apothecary),

*William Austen (1701-1737) (a surgeon and George Austen's father),

*Robert Austen (1702-1728) &

*Stephen Austen (1704-1751) (a stationer selling medical books and bibles).

John Austen V (JA great uncle) married his cousin Mary Stringer & begat

John Austen VI (1716-1807, JA great uncle) who married Joanna Weeks (died 1811).

Francis Austen II (JA great uncle) married Anne Motley and thence Jane Lennard.

Thomas Austen (JA great uncle) begat

Henry Austen (a clergyman at West Wickham until he lost faith and resigned).

William Austen (Jane Austen's paternal grandfather) married Rebecca Walter (née Hampson; JA grandmother) (died 1733) & begat

*Philadelphia Austen (1730-1792, JA aunt),

*George Austen (1731-1805) (Jane Austen's father; rector of Steventon from 1761),

*Leonora Austen (no issue. JA aunt) &

*Hampson (no issue, JA uncle).

Rebecca's son by a Mr Walter, William Hampson Walter, married Susanna Weaver & begat Philadelphia Walter (died 1834) (a cousin of Jane Austen) who married George Whitaker.

3.5. Philadelphia Austen went out to India and there married Tysoe Saul Hancock (a surgeon and business associate of Warren Hastings, he died in 1775 in India) & (almost certainly through adultery with Warren Hastings) begat

3.6. Elizabeth (Eliza) Hancock (1761-1813) (Jane Austen's lively cousin) who married Jean Capote, Comte de Feuillade (guillotined in 1794) & begat

Hastings Capote, Comte de Feuillade (1786-1801) (sickly and subject to fits) & thence married Henry Thomas Austen (her cousin; Jane Austen's brother) (no issue).

3.7. George Austen married Cassandra Leigh and begat

*James Austen (1765-1819) (clergyman),

*George Austen (1766-1838) (possibly deaf, suffered fits and was put out to care),

*Edward Austen (Edward Knight from 1812) (q.v.) (1767-1852) (of Godmersham and Chawton),

*Henry Thomas Austen (1771-1850) (clergyman and failed banker),

*Cassandra Elizabeth Austen (1773-1845),

*Francis Austen (1774-1863) (later Admiral Sir Francis),

*<u>Jane Austen (1775-1817)</u> &

*Charles Austen (1779-1852) (later an Admiral).

3.8. A brief overview of the Austens

An interesting feature of this sequence of relatives and connections is the recurring consanguinity that we also saw with Cassandra's "mob". Thus John Austen V (1696-1728) married his cousin Mary Stringer, the daughter of Jane Stringer (née Austen) and Stephen Stringer. A further instance is that of Henry Austen (1771-1850) who married his cousin Elizabeth (Eliza) Hancock (1761-1813), the ostensible daughter of Philadelphia Hancock (née Austen) (George Austen's sister) and Tysoe Saul Hancock (but almost certainly fathered by Warren Hastings). Henry was the lucky man in this in the sense that his brother James also had an interest in cousin Eliza. Eliza, like Mary Crawford the anti-heroine in Jane Austen's Mansfield Park, was not very keen on a clerical partner. Mary Lloyd eventually married the widowed James Austen and disapproved of Eliza (somewhat like goody-goody Fanny in Mansfield Park who disapproved of lively Mary Crawford and her interest in clerical Edmond, who indeed ends up marrying Fanny, his very sisterly cousin).

Another recurring theme of the Austen and the Leigh tribes is the rejoining of distant familial connections. Thus Edward Austen lived with his distant relatives Thomas Knight and his wife Catherine (née Knatchbull). Thomas Knight shared a great-great grandfather with Edward's father George Austen, namely John Austen III (1629-1705). After the death of his foster father Edward received the Godmersham and Chawton estates and eventually took on the name Knight after the death of his foster mother (Edward's uncle James Leigh-Perrot and his nephew James Edward Austen-Leigh did likewise). Edward's daughter Fanny Knight (Jane Austen's favourite "neice") married Sir Edward Knatchbull and hence rejoined these strands. However Fanny's brother Edward married Mary Dorothea Knatchbull (Sir Edward's daughter by a previous marriage). This non-consanguinous union (subsequently blessed by 7 children) had the embarrassing consequences that Fanny Knatchbull (née Knight/Austen) became simultaneously the sister-in-law and aunt as well as stepmother of Mary Dorothea Knatchbull.

The George Austen family connections are less grand than the up-side of the Leighs and Perrots but have a similar bottom line of clergymen living off the clerical dispensations of their wealthy relatives who had been effective at wealth generation. Mary Crawford (the anti-heroine in Mansfield Park with some barely muted contempt for the social passivity of clergymen) would surely have appreciated the caustic line about academics in the play The Department by the amusing, incisive and deadly accurate Australian playwright David Williamson: "those who can do, and those who can't teach".[6] The clergymen included Henry Austen (son of George Austen's uncle Thomas Austen), George Austen and George's sons James Austen and Henry Thomas Austen. Whereas Henry Thomas Austen (Jane Austen's brother) turned to being a clergyman after bankruptcy, his earlier namesake forsook the cloth after losing faith in the Holy Trinity.

The more practically useful members of the George Austen "mob" include farmers, wool processors and merchants, an apothecary, a book seller, a solicitor and a surgeon. However it must be appreciated that George Austen supplemented his income by farming nearby acres courtesy of a rich relation and tutored several live-in sons of the wealthy (including George Hastings (1757-1764), the son of Warren and Mary Hastings).

3.9. Warren Hastings and the Austens

There is a substantial literature dealing with the life and times of Warren Hastings and a number of detailed biographies have been written.[7] Hastings (1732-1818) came from an old landed family dating back to William the Conqueror. His mother died giving birth to him at Churchill and his father disappeared after leaving Warren and his sister Anne in care of a village foster-mother Mary Ellis. The father Penyston Hastings, a clergyman, remarried two further times, firstly to the daughter of a tradesman and then to a lady in Barbados, where he died. The grandfather, Penyston Hastings, was the rector of Daylesford. The family home Daylesford had been sold by Warren's great-grandfather in 1715 and it was subsequently demolished. His childhood was spent in his grandfather's home in the care of his aunt Elizabeth Hastings and he was aware of the Daylesford lands that he dreamed in his youth might one day return to him. He was sent to his uncle Howard

Hastings' house at Westminster and attended the Westminster School with Elijah Impey (later to be encountered as Chief Justice in Bengal) and the poet William Cowper (of whom more later also).

In 1749 Hastings' uncle died and his guardian Joseph Creswicke, a distant relative, took him away from Westminster, to the chagrin of the headmaster who appreciated Hastings' intelligence. Hastings finished a course in merchants' accounts in 1749 and his guardian (later to be an East India Company Director) enabled him to become a "writer" in the Company. In 1750 he sailed for India, disembarking at Fort William on the Hooghli in Bengal. In 1752 Hastings was sent to Kasimbazaar, an important trading post. When the young Nawab of Bengal Siraj-ud-dauhlah moved against the British in 1756 Hastings was captured in the countryside and taken to the Nawab's capital, Murshidabad. Vernet, the head of the Dutch factory was very kind to him (and in later years Hastings was to pay his widow a pension of 300 pounds a year). Hastings heard of the Black Hole of Calcutta (in which 146 British prisoners from the capture of Fort William were supposedly locked up overnight in a tiny cell and from which only 23 emerged alive the next morning). Hastings was able to visit the survivors, including their leader Holwell. When the survivors were sent to the Dutch station at Fulta, Hastings stayed on at Murshidabad.

As life under Siraj-ud-dauhlah became more problematical, Hastings escaped to the Dutch station at Chinsura and then to Fulta. At Fulta he married Mary Buchanan née Elliott, the widow of Captain Buchanan who had died in the Black Hole incident.or otherwise in defence of Fort William - according to Davies (1935), Feiling (1966), Moon (1947), Stephen & Lee (1964) and Turnbull (1975). It is intriguing to see that some biographers.of this immensely important man - namely Gleig (1841), Lawson (1905), Lyall (1907), Malleson (1894) and Trotter (1890) - have identified his first wife as the widow of a Captain Campbell from Madras who had succumbed to disease. According to the Black Hole version, Mary Buchanan had escaped to

Fulta from Fort William with her 2 infant daughters. Hastings was involved in the recapture of Fort William and may have also been with Clive at the Battle of Plassey in 1757. Hastings' first child George was born in 1757 and a daughter Elizabeth was born in 1758, but she survived only several weeks. His wife Mary died of an illness in 1759. His affection for Mary is reflected in the subsequent sustained payment of a pension to her Goanese maid Peggy.

In 1760 Tysoe Hancock, a friend of Robert Clive, came up from Madras to take up the position of surgeon at Kasimbazaar (Hastings had differed with Clive over the appointment and preferred the doctor who had cared for Mary). Tysoe Hancock had met and married Philadelphia Hancock née Austen, George Austen's sister, in Madras in 1753. Philadelphia had no doubt suggested sending George Hastings to stay with George and Cassandra Austen at Steventon in 1760. Bengal was an extremely unhealthy place for Europeans [8] and Hastings had already lost his wife Mary and his daughter Elizabeth. Mary's 2 daughters had already been sent back to their grandmother in Ireland. Hastings supported them financially and also attempted to recover their late father's estate for them. Hancock and Hastings became friends and indeed business partners at a time of unchecked entrepreneurial profligacy in Bengal.

We will return to Hastings in later chapters but at this instance we wish to consider the intimate connection that was formed between Hastings and the Austens. George Hastings was unfortunately to die in 1764 of fever at Steventon after being assiduously nursed by George and Cassandra Austen. Mrs Austen felt the loss as if it were of her of her own child.

Philadelphia Hancock fell pregnant in 1761 and gave birth to Eliza, Jane Austen's lively cousin, in December of that year. She was named after Hastings' dead daughter by Mary. The Hancocks returned to England in 1765 but Tysoe Hancock returned to India and was never to see his family again, dying in 1775. Hastings provided an extraordinarily generous trust fund of 10,000 pounds for his god-daughter (and, almost certainly, real daughter) Eliza Hancock. The trust generated an income of about 400 pounds per annum. Philadelphia and Eliza lived in the West End of London, visited the Walters and the Austens and also travelled to Germany, Flanders and France. George Austen acted as the trustee for Eliza's trust fund and his uncle Francis Austen acted as Tysoe Hancock's attorney. It is likely that Philadelphia drew excessively from both sources. Eliza and her mother did not lack for money and after Eliza married the Comte de Feuillade she evidently contributed to a prosperous lifestyle. Both mother and daughter were lively, good-humoured and sociable women.

Hastings' paternity of Eliza is very likely for a variety of reasons:

- the absence of pregnancy for 8 years until the Hancocks' coming to Kasimbazaar and the lack of subsequent pregnancy;

- the circumstances of the recently widowed Hastings and the comfort he received from Philadelphia who was probably a friend of Mary's from before the time of their departure for India in 1751 as poor, unmarried young women;

- the common orphaned background of both Hastings and Philadelphia that ultimately sent both to India for fortune and marriage, respectively;

- the close attachments of Hastings to other married women, namely the widowed Mary Buchanan / Campbell and the Baroness "Marian" Imhoff, both of whom he married;

- the extraordinarily generous trust fund for Eliza worth about 250,000 pounds in today's money;

- the opinion of Clive, a person close to both Hastings and Hancock;

- the continuing close connection of Hastings, Philadelphia and Eliza over many years.

In 1780 Philadelphia wrote to Hastings:

"Knowing your heart as I do and being convinced in spite of appearances it is not changed for your friends, I cannot refuse you the satisfaction of knowing my daughter, the only thing I take comfort in, is in perfect health". [9]

Lord Clive wrote to his wife in 1765 warning her of Philadelphia, who was returning to England with Hancock and "Betsy" (Eliza):

"In no circumstances whatever keep company with Mrs. Hancock for it is beyond a doubt that she has abandoned her self to Mr. Hastings, indeed, I would rather you had no acquaintance with the ladies who have been in India, they stand in such little esteem in England that their company cannot be of credit to Lady Clive." [10]

Hancock, who had returned alone to India in 1769, opposed the return of Philadelphia and "Betsy" to Bengal on account of the bad moral climate of the place. He attributed the coolness of Lady Clive in England to the machinations of Lady Jenny Strachey (née Kelsall), the wife of Clive's secretary Sir Henry Strachey. Tysoe Saul Hancock died in Calcutta in 1775. Philadelphia died in England in 1792.

From the mouth of babes we may discern something of the truth. Young Jane Austen in her unfinished novel Catherine or The Bower (written in 1792) describes an unsuitable marriage in India borne of straightened circumstances. This is likely to have resembled that of Hancock and Philadelphia at Cuddalore near Fort St David in 1753, shortly after Philadelphia's arrival:

"The eldest daughter [Cecilia] had been obliged to accept the offer of one of her cousins to equip her for the East Indies, and tho' infinitely against her inclinations had been necessitated to embrace the only possibility that was offered to her, of a Maintenance; Yet it was one, so opposite to all her ideas of Propriety, so contrary to her Wishes, so repugnant to her feelings, that she would have preferred Servitude to it, had Choice been allowed her -. Her personal Attractions had gained her a husband as soon as she had arrived at Bengal, and she had been married nearly a twelvemonth. Splendidly, yet unhappily married. United to a Man of double her own age, whose disposition was not amiable, and whose Manners were unpleasing, though his Character was respectable. Kitty [Catherine] had heard twice from her friend since her marriage, but her Letters were always unsatisfactory, and though she did not openly avow her feelings, yet every line proved her to be Unhappy. She spoke with pleasure of nothing, but of those Amusements which they had shared together and which could return no more, and seemed to have no happiness in view but that of returning to England again. Her sister had been taken by another relation the Dowager Lady Halifax as a companion to her Daughters, and had accompanied her family into Scotland about the same time of Cecilia's leaving England. From Mary therefore Kitty had the power of hearing more frequently, but her Letters were scarcely more comfortable -... The Summer passed away unmarked by any incident worth narrating, or any pleasure to Catharine save one, which arose from the receipt of a letter from her friend Cecilia, now Mrs Lascelles, announcing the speedy return of herself & Husband to England." [11]

After the death of Eliza in 1813, the widowed Henry Austen visited Warren Hastings at Daylesford and afterwards gave Jane Austen the report that the great man had really liked Pride and Prejudice. In a letter to her sister Cassandra, Jane Austen reports in turn:

"Mr. Hastings never <u>hinted</u> at Eliza in the smallest degree." [12]

A final assessment we have of what Jane Austen thought of this matter is surely in Sense and Sensibility, the most "Indian" of her novels and a work that, as described in detail in Chapter 6, appears to provide a barely disguised version of the Hastings-Hancock affair. There is a large literature dealing specifically with the life of Warren Hastings and his activities in India. However as far as I am aware, discussion of Hastings' fathering of Eliza Hancock is essentially confined to a small body of excellent specialist analyses of the life of Jane Austen. [13]

3.10. Sheep, fox-hunting, Tasmania and scientific advice

We have seen that George Austen's "mob" have a different flavour to that of his wife Cassandra née Leigh. His forbears and connections outlined above included a solid basis of Kentish rural gentry involved in agriculture and in particular in wool production and processing. It is tempting to suppose that the Thomas Austin (sometimes spelled Austen) from near Geelong in Victoria, who introduced the wild rabbit into Australia to support his sporting predilections, might also be connected to the George Austen Austens. [14] [I have a familial connection with the Australian Austen sheep family but as far as I am aware the evidence is wanting of any direct connection with this "mob" and the Austens of our present concern.] One member of Jane Austen's family who did come uncomfortably close to coming to Australia was Jane Leigh-Perrot who faced the possibility of transportation to Botany Bay until her acquittal of the theft charge at the Taunton Assizes (Chapter 2).

Nevertheless there are some interesting connections to be made between the Kentish sheep farmers and their generic (if not necessarily genetic) sheep-raising ilk in Australia. This is most dramatically seen in Tasmania (formerly Van Dieman's Land) where the aboriginal inhabitants (about 6000 at the time of first settlement in 1804) were almost completely destroyed. by the settlers. Some of the aboriginal tribes had a custom of seasonal migration from the Midlands plains up to the Highlands. The slow-moving sheep were much easier to kill than the agile and nocturnal pademelons, Eastern Grey kangaroos and

Bennet's wallabies but spearing sheep produced a violent reaction from the European settlers. [15]

Like the Tasmanian aborigines, the Tasmanian tiger is popularly supposed to have been totally eliminated by the European settlers and for similar reasons. The Tasmanian tiger, thus named because of a striped back and tail, is a remarkable case of "convergent evolution", being a marsupial that resembles a short-haired dog. The Tasmanian tiger or thylacine (Thylacinus cynocephalus) was a rather fastidious carnivore in its choice of edible parts and was accordingly a somewhat wasteful diner. The thylacine, like the aborigines, found sheep attractively less agile and more susceptible than other big herbivores. The thylacine and the aborigines were accordingly both hunted down by the settlers "that sheep may safely graze". The last Tasmanian tiger in captivity died in the Hobart zoo in 1933. However there is a set of accounts of sightings by sensible and competent people over the years up to the present that suggest that a very small population of these animals still survives in remote forested parts of Tasmania. [16]

One such possible "tiger" area is the Tarkine Wilderness that is adjacent to the lands of the Van Dieman's Land Company in northwest Tasmania and which is being currently staunchly defended by Tasmanian "Greens" against the unholy destructive alliance of government and business bent on its "development". Maybe when the last of the remaining forests of Tasmania have been wood-chipped for conversion into Japanese toilet paper the controversy about the existence or extinction of the elusive Tasmanian tiger will be finally be resolved.

The settlement of Tasmania was achieved in the early days with the assistance of the slave labour of convicts transported initially to the notorious convict prisons at Port Arthur on the Tasman peninsular east of Hobart and at Macquarie Harbour on the inhospitable west coast. Convicts were treated with great brutality and escaped convicts who became "bushrangers" behaved in kind. Convicts were subject to ferocious lashing, were used in lieu of plough horses and were readily hung. The sufferings of these wretched people is described in Marcus Clarke's novel For the Term of His Natural Life and the convicts and the convict heritage of Tasmania is dealt with in a number of other works. [17]

The legacy of the convict stonemasons is seen in the re-creation of fine aspects of the England of Jane Austen's day, especially in the rich Midlands, in the form of Georgian mansions, churches, other public buildings and elegant bridges. [18] The anglicising of the Tasmanian environment has not ceased since settlement. The political establishment is still locked into a "development" model that has seen the wilful destruction of great forests (including remarkable temperate rain forests and stands of fabulous but endangered trees such as Huon pine), the flooding of lakes such as the exquisite Lake Pedder and of river valleys (that have not even been assessed in a sensible scientific fashion) and the destruction or near-extinction of remarkable wild-life. What has happened in Tasmania is a crime against the world and the process is still continuing. There is a continuing notion of transforming all but a nominal skerrick of nature into an ordered and highly productive state. In the Midlands this can amount to a simulacrum of the Home Counties known to Jane Austen, involving modest Georgian mansions set in parks with ordered pastures dotted with sheep, cattle, copses of introduced trees and dams and lakes stocked with trout. This continuing devastation amounts to sustained and remorseless blasphemy. The extraordinary beauty of what is still being destroyed can be best appreciated on the ground in the shrinking wilderness but is also recorded in the paintings, poetry, photography and impassioned writing of sensitive Tasmanians. [19] Small wonder that the insensitive political establishment of Tasmania should have legislated that the punishment for private, adult, consensual expression of homosexual love should be 25 years in prison. [20] (This has fortunately been recently reversed).

The free settlers that started coming to Tasmania at the beginning of the 19th century, in the latter half of Jane Austen's life, did in effect to Tasmania what their ilk did to the Scottish Highlands - clearing the land of people and trees and replacing the people with sheep. Those Scottish Highlanders that did not starve to death had the chance of escaping with their lives and some of their culture to America or to Australia, a course also followed by many impoverished common folk of England. [21] [One line of my rather cosmopolitan family derives from a woman from the Western Highlands of Argyll who married the son of a Middlesex gamekeeper. Both may have been servants of the famous Tasmanian colonial diarist, water colourist and landowner Louisa Meredith in the mid-19th century.] The Tasmanian aborigine had nowhere to go and their culture is essentially gone, although there are several thousands of mixed-race descendants of Tasmanian or Mainland aboriginal women and their European partners still living in Tasmania and proud of their heritage. In an awful testament to the perpetuation of racism in Australia, a major Australian corporate leader with intellectual pretensions recently declared that the aboriginal women would have been happy to have been raped by Europeans because their own menfolk were so ugly. [22]

3.11. Sport, rabbits, ecocide and science

Domestic rabbits came on the First Fleet to Botany Bay in 1788 but did not spread appreciably. Sporting shooting and fox hunting were the sport of the gentry of the time (including some of Jane Austen's brothers back in the Home Counties). "Wild" rabbits were originally introduced into Tasmania and "took off" in numbers. Thomas Austin of Barwon Park (near Geelong) introduced 24 wild rabbits for "sport" in 1859 and within 6 years 20,000 were killed on his property alone. By 1887 10 million were killed in the first 8 months of the year alone. The rabbit subsequently spread in plague proportions across the sub-tropical and temperate parts of the continent and has contributed to the extinction of numerous small marsupial species. The rabbit and other introduced and now feral creatures (notably cats, dogs, foxes, pigs.

goats, horses, camels and water buffalo to name the larger animals) have caused immense damage to ecosystems throughout Australia as have the hard-hoofed sheep and cattle that range over a substantial part of the country that is not utter desert. Energetic attempts have been made to control the rabbit, the feral import which has caused the most damage. Poisoning, shooting, ripping up of warrens and even a transcontinental "rabbit-proof" fence are still employed. [23]

A major advance involved introduction of the Myxoma virus from South America. This virus is essentially specific for the rabbit and closely related creatures (although suckling mice are also susceptible), the infectious disease being called myxomatosis. After an initial experimental trial in the Murray River valley in 1950, the virus "took off" in an extraordinary fashion and within several weeks had spread throughout south-eastern Australia with tremendous effect. However the spread of myxomatosis by mosquitoes coincided with an increased incidence of Murray Valley encephalitis in humans (this disease being caused by a completely different virus). To allay public fears, in 1951 three leading Australian scientists were inoculated with the Myxoma virus, namely Sir MacFarlane Burnet (later a Nobel Prize winner for immunological discoveries), Sir Ian Clunies Ross (Chairman of the Commonwealth Scientific and Industrial Research Organization, CSIRO) and Professor F. Fenner (from the John Curtin School of Medical Research, Canberra where Peter Doherty did immunological research in the 1970s that would earn him the Nobel Prize in 1996). The public announcement was made in Federal Parliament by the Minister in Charge of CSIRO, Mr. R.G. (later Lord) Casey (who we will encounter later in relation to his role in the Bengal Famine of 1943-44).

The postwar introduction of the myxomatosis virus had a tremendous initial effect but ultimately increased rabbit resistance and a decreased viral virulence has progressively reduced the effectiveness of the virus. [24] However 2 major new strategies deserve some consideration here in a disquisition that links the continuing values and conduct of Jane Austen's people to global catastrophe. One major approach involves molecular engineering of a viral vector that will introduce the gene (DNA) coding for particular proteins found on the surface of rabbit ova or sperm (the female and male sex cells, respectively, involved in the process of fertilization). As infected rabbits will start producing these proteins, these in turn will be targeted by antibodies produced by the immune systems and the consequence will be infertility. [25] The "safety" of this procedure with respect to us (or indeed to other animals with an immune system) depends upon the "host range specificity" of the engineered virus (or of its descendants that will evolve in the "natural world" after its release). As long as the virus is specific for the rabbit alone (and as long as this remains so in the long term out in the wild), this remains a "safe" procedure. However a significant worry to some observers of this multi-million dollar research program and future application of its results is the possibility that the "host range specificity" may change. Clearly such specificity changes do occur in the long term on an evolutionary time-scale but relatively short term changes in viral host specificity are clearly possible as evidenced by the spread of influenza virus from birds to man and the likely extension of HIV from certain monkeys to man. In the event that the "experts" are wrong one can conceive a scenario of a whole continent in quarantine (insofar as that is possible with the movements of traditional Indonesian fishermen, drug smugglers and migratory birds and other migratory species) in order to protect the rest of the world.

This leads us to the further control measure that is already operating as a result of the "experts" getting their quarantine arrangements wrong - the accidental release in Australia of the "rabbit specific" calicivirus that causes Rabbit Haemorrhagic Disease. This virus is supposedly "rabbit specific" and was trialled in the wild on an ostensibly "safely" quarantined island off the South Australian coast. The "experts" evidently failed to consider the possibility of birds, insects or other organisms transmitting the virus to the mainland. In the event, such transmission occurred before necessarily limited "host range specificity" studies had been completed and the virus has spread extensively since 1995 throughout the Continent. [26]

One would like to be sanguine about the outcome although such lay confidence is not helped by the admitted mistakes of the "experts" to date and the opinion of a calicivirus "expert" from a calicivirus research centre in the US who considers that the virus concerned and related viruses may have actual "host range specificities" that are much broader than hitherto recognized (not to mention the possibilities arising from mutation and natural selection). A modest possibility remains that some interesting indigenous Australian animal that has evaded the experimental purview of the "experts" may bite the dust for eternity. At the other end of the speculatory spectrum, we can imagine any number of scary scenarios ranging from minor human skin excrescences (found already with a closely related calicivirus) to the doom of humanity. On balance, scientists plump for the calicivirus solution as a sensible means of stopping the rabbit plague that represents a continuing environmental catastrophe on a continental scale (there are about 300 million rabbits in Australia). However the reservations offered thus far concerning host range specificity and the stringency of testing are quite sensible. [27]

Nevertheless we must bear in mind the potential dangers of irreversible human actions effected for the best of reasons but with possible dangerous consequences e.g. animal-human transplants (xenografts), invasion of tropical rain forests and animal cell viral vaccine culture (novel human viral pathogens) and genetic engineering for large-scale crop monocultures (loss of "wild" or "primitive" crop plant genetic resources). [28] (However it seems that other concerns in relation to transgenic plants, notably the spread of particular genes to other plants in the field or the wild, are fears that have not been sustained with hard evidence.) [29] To this list of perturbations we can add climatological and biological consequences of environmental pollution. [30] This has been explored at great length by the sanatorium inmates of Thomas Mann's The Magic Mountain [31] but is surely most simply expressed in the Greek myths of Pandora's Box and of the Fate of Prometheus. [32]

All of which seems a long way from fox-hunting by the Home Counties gentry of the late 18th century but the causal connection should be sufficiently clear to be not laboured further. The moral and philosophical connections between Jane Austen's world, its successors and ours are also fairly apparent. The indubitable rightness of the well-washed and well-educated to alter the world and the essential irrelevance of the views and concerns of mere mortals such as common folk or other subject people was widely accepted then and is perhaps even more strongly accepted today in a sociologically modified sense. The "indubitably right" are no longer the gentry of Jane Austen's novels (our upper middle class) but the "experts" of government and big business, mendicant academics and the "wisely and properly" instructed representatives of the people and their duly charged agents. Those who would gainsay such people are bold indeed. [33] We will see later in Chapter 15 how anonymous "expert" advice rendered to government could ultimately kill millions of Bengalis in the mid-20th century as surely as the individual and collective entrepreneurial activities of people of Jane Austen's class in the 18th century.

3.12. The reporting of the Austen connections

The point can be repeated that Jane Austen, the artist, used a very limited social palate for her creations for perfectly legitimate reasons of style, taste, modus operandi and compatibility. However the same licence cannot be accorded historians including biographers of Jane Austen. The most comprehensive and simultaneously most socially-responsive biography of Jane Austen of which I am aware is Jane Austen. Her Life by Park Honan (1987) that can be used as a default reference for matters relating to Jane Austen in the present work. Honan (1987) details the likelihood of the Hastings-Hancock affair. However of a sample of 30 works dealing with Jane Austen's life and connections [34] only 5 allude to Hastings' likely paternity of

Eliza, namely Lane (1984), Lane (1986), Lane (1996), Honan (1987) and Tucker (1983). In addition, an inexplicit perception of this kind is articulated by Jane Hodge (1972) in The Double Life of Jane Austen in detailing the 10,000 pounds provided by Hastings for Eliza and her mother ("It makes one wonder, just a little"). Further, in a book of literary criticism, Ruoff (1992) speculates that Hastings may have been the father as well as the godfather of Eliza Hancock. [35]

In relation to this sparse reporting of a major connection in Jane Austen's life, it is interesting to apply the same analysis to reportage of other connections of the Austen line. If we consider the same 30 biographies we can score reportage of Eliza Hancock, her husband Jean Capotte the Comte de Feuillade and their son, Philadelphia Hancock, Tysoe Hancock and Warren Hastings and his son George Hastings. We find that 27 report Eliza, 24 Philadelphia Hancock, 20 Tysoe Saul Hancock and 22 report Warren Hastings. However only 5/30 report Eliza's origin, Philadelphia's adultery, Dr. Hancock's cuckolding or Warren Hastings' paternity of Eliza. While 25/30 refer to Eliza's husband, 20 to her son and 17 to Hastings' son George, the untimely deaths of these people score 24, 12 and 16, respectively, out of 30.

As we have seen in the previous chapter, many Jane Austen biographers have failed to include a variety of interesting aspects of Jane Austen's connections in their works. The present example represents one of the more interesting connections pertaining to Jane Austen's life. Eliza was one of her more important relations, intimates and influences and this lively woman quite clearly appears as Lady Susan in Lady Susan, Mary Crawford in Mansfield Park and Eliza in Sense and Sensibility. Nevertheless, despite a huge literature on Jane Austen, this affair is completely absent from nearly all the biographies of Jane Austen's life.

In the context of an English historical and literary tradition that has by and large buried the unimaginable holocaust that was 2 centuries of British India, what is the importance of the likely generation of one new life by an unsatisfied, passionate woman and a widowed, passionate man in the hot, dangerous world of Kasimbazaar in 1760? Hastings had a major impact on his world that continues to this day and still affects the lives of hundreds of millions of people. His daughter/god-daughter Eliza, borne of a lively mother, has clearly lived on in major novels that today still have immediacy, universality and a moral message. But whether the persons are great or small, the biologically critical minimum human social compound is that of man, woman and child. The bald statistic of ten million swept away by famine in Bengal in 1770 barely begins to grapple with the pungent tragedies of so many compounds of man, woman and child at that time and in subsequent centuries. The gross, collective statistics of human disasters allow for scientific analysis and prediction and leave the sensitive with a practical resolution that this should never recur. However the numbers are not readily comprehensible in an emotional sense. It is the individual realities that directly impinge on our human sensibilities and are comprehended in a devastating, tangible way. All the data are important, the individual elements and the immense collective edifice.

3.13. 2008 Postscript

Further books deal with the Hastings Eliza scandal [36] and Tasmanian history [37].

Chapter 4

Jane Austen's siblings and their descendants

"I believe I never told you that Mrs Coulthard and Anne, late of Manydown, are both dead and both died in childbed. We have not regaled Mary with this news." ... "I have just received a note from James to say that Mary was brought to bed last night, at eleven o'clock, of a fine little boy, and that everything is going on very well."

- Jane Austen letter to Cassandra on Saturday November 17 and thence on Sunday November 18 (1798)[1]

"What must I tell you of Edward? Truth or falsehood? I will try the former, and you may choose for yourself another time. He was better yesterday than he had been for two or three days before - about as well as while he was at Steventon. He drinks at the Hetling Pump, is to bathe tomorrow, and try electricity on Tuesday. He proposed the latter himself to Dr. Fellowes, who made no objection to it, but I fancy we are all unanimous in expecting no advantage from it."

- Jane Austen letter to Cassandra (1799)[2]

"She [Catherine] was heartily ashamed of her ignorance - a misplaced shame. Where people wish to attach, they should always be ignorant. To come with a well-informed mind is to come with an inability of administering to the vanity of others, which a sensible person would always wish to avoid. A woman, especially, if she have the misfortune of knowing anything, should conceal it as well as she can."

- Jane Austen, Northanger Abbey (1817)[3]

4.1. Jane Austen's siblings and their descendants

From the above extracts we can see the perceived importance to Jane Austen of contentment and peace of mind and the happiness of others. Her world revolved about her immediate family and other dear connections. The editing out of social reality in her novels can be seen as her artistic prerogative. However for conduct in "real life" she evidently also espouses a pragmatic avoidance of discomforting truth in the interests of general happiness. In this she can be seen to be so very English and in good company with British historiographers. With this in mind we can proceed to inspect the lives of her siblings and their descendants. We will see later how these lives have been "Austenized" in the interests of "naiceness". The key "default" references for this chapter are Halperin (1984), Hodge (1972), Honan (1987) and Lane (1984, 1986, 1996), and of these the most comprehensive is Honan (1987). [4]

James Austen firstly married Anne Matthew (died 1795) in 1792 & begat

Anna Austen (1793-1872) who married Benjamin Lefroy (q.v.; of the Brydges line) in 1814 & begat

7 children including Fanny C. Lefroy (1820-1885) (q.v.; author of Family History).

James Austen thence married Mary Lloyd (1771-1843) (q.v.; of the Craven line, sister of Martha Lloyd, friend of Cassandra and Jane and who would later marry the widowed Francis Austen) in 1797 & begat

*Caroline Austen (1850-1880; unmarried, no issue; author of My Aunt Jane Austen) &

*James Edward Austen (later Austen-Leigh) (q.v.; author of A Memoir of Jane Austen, 1870) who married Emma Smith in 1828 & begat 10 children including

*Cholmeley Austen-Leigh (1829-1899) (named thus in deference to Jane Leigh-Perrot; one of his children Kathleen married Edward Impey (a descendant of the Impeys from near Basingstoke, Wiltshire that

included the notorious Elijah Impey); another child Richard Arthur Austen-Leigh (1872-1941) co-authored the 1913 Life of Jane Austen)

*William Austen-Leigh (1843-1921) (who died unmarried; co-authored Life of Jane Austen with his nephew Richard) &

* Arthur Henry Austen Leigh (1836-1917) (who married Violet Hall-Say & begat 7 children).

George Austen had no issue.

Edward Austen (Knight after 1812) married Elizabeth Bridges (1773-1808) & begat

11 children (Elizabeth dying in 1808, 2 days after the birth of the last) including:

*Fanny Knight (1793-1882) (Jane Austen's favourite niece) who married Sir Edward Knatchbull (1820) & begat 9 children including Edward Hugessen Knatchbull (1829-1893) (1st Baron Brabourne1880; edited 1884 Letters of Jane Austen). Fanny became simultaneously the sister-in-law and aunt as well as stepmother to her step-daughter Mary Dorothea Knatchbull when Mary Dorothea married Fanny's brother Edward (see below).

*Edward Knight (1794-1879) who married his step-niece Mary Dorothea Knatchbull in 1825 & begat 7 children and thence married Adela Portal in 1840 & begat a further 9 children.

*George Knight (1795-1867) who married Hilare, Countess Nelson in 1837 (no issue).

*Henry Knight (1797-1843) who married firstly Sophia Cage and thence Charlotte Northey & begat children from both marriages.

*William Knight (1798-1873) who married firstly Caroline Portal and thence Mary Northey & begat children from both unions.

*Elizabeth Knight (1800-1884) who married Edward Royd Rice in 1818 & begat 15 children.

*Marianne Knight (1801-1896) who died unmarried.

*Charles Knight (1803-1867) who died unmarried.

*Louisa Knight (1804-1889) who married Lord George Hill in 1847 (after the death of her sister Cassandra Jane) & begat 1 child.

*Cassandra Jane (1806-1842) who married Lord George Hill in 1834 & begat 4 children.

*Brook John (1808-1878) who married Margaret Pearson (no issue).

Henry Thomas Austen (1771-1850) firstly married Eliza de Feuillade (1761-1813) (his cousin) in 1797 (no issue) and thence married Eleanor Jackson in 1820 (no issue).

Cassandra Elizabeth Austen (1773-1843) died unmarried.

Francis William Austen (1774-1865) married Mary Gibson (died 1823) & begat

* Mary Jane Austen (1807-1836),

*Francis William Austen (1809-1858),

*Henry Austen (1811-1854),

*George Austen (1812-1903) &

*Catherine Anne Austen (1818-1877) (a novelist) who married John Hubback in 1842 & begat

John Henry Hubback (1844-1939) (co-author with his daughter Edith of Jane Austen's Sailor Brothers) who married Mary Ingram & begat

7 children including John Austen Hubback (1878-1969) (Governor of Orissa) and Edith Charlotte Hubback (1876-1947) (co-author of Jane Austen's Sailor Brothers).

In 1828 Francis Austen married Martha Lloyd (1765-1843) (q.v.; of the Craven line; sister of Mary Lloyd, James Austen's second wife).

Jane Austen (1775-1817) died unmarried.

Charles John Austen (1779-1852) (later Admiral) married firstly Frances Palmer (daughter of John Palmer, Attorney General of Bermuda and a resolute persecutor of Methodists; she died in childbirth in 1814) & begat

*Cassandra Esten Austen (1808-1897) (died unmarried),

*Harriet Jane Austen (1810-1865) (died unmarried),

*Frances Palmer Austen (1812-1882) (who married her cousin Francis William Austen (1809-1858) (q.v.; son of Francis Austen) & begat 6 children) &

*Elizabeth (died 1814).

In 1820 Charles Austen married Harriet Palmer (the sister of his first wife Frances) & begat

*Charles John Austen (1821-1867) who married Sophia de Blois in 1848 (with issue).

*George Austen (baby died 1824),

*Jane Austen (baby died 1825) &

*Henry Austen (1826-1851) who died unmarried.

4.2 Austen family writings and first cousin unions

An interesting feature of this tree is the recurring consanguinity in the Austens that we saw with Cassandra's "mob". Thus John Austen V (1696-1728) married his cousin Mary Stringer, the daughter of Jane Stringer (née Austen) and Stephen Stringer. A further instance is that of Henry Austen (1771-1850) who married his cousin Elizabeth (Eliza) Hancock (1761-1813) the ostensible daughter of Philadelphia Hancock (née Austen) (George Austen's sister) and Tysoe Saul Hancock, but who was almost certainly fathered by Warren Hastings. Henry was the lucky man in this in the sense that his brother James also had an interest in Eliza but was rejected because of his clerical commitment.

Another recurring theme of the Austen and the Leigh tribes is the rejoining of distant familial connections. Thus Edward Austen lived with his distant relatives Thomas Knight and his wife Catherine (née Knatchbull). After the death of his foster father Edward received the Godmersham and Chawton estates and eventually took on the name Knight (Edward's uncle James Leigh-Perrot and his nephew James Edward Austen-Leigh did likewise). Edward's daughter Fanny Knight (Jane Austen's favourite "neice") married Sir Edward Knatchbull and hence rejoined these strands. However Fanny's brother Edward married Mary Dorothea Knatchbull (Sir Edward's daughter by a previous marriage). This union (blessed by 7 children) was non-consanguinous but had the embarrassing consequence that Fanny became simultaneously the sister-in-law and aunt as well as stepmother of Mary Dorothea.

A further feature of the Austen family was the compulsion to put pen to paper that transcended the simple necessity of writing letters to loved ones in those days. James started a periodical The Loiterer at Oxford in 1789 that ran for 60 issues until 1790, with James contributing 27 articles and Henry 10. In addition to her novels and the so-called Juvenilia of her "teenage" years, Jane Austen conducted a lifetime of correspondence with her close relatives, notably with her sister Cassandra. Members of the following generations followed this example. While Catherine Anne Austen, daughter of Francis Austen, was a novelist, the others with a literary bent confined themselves to recording the family. Thus Jane's nephew James Edward Austen-Leigh (son of the Reverend James Austen) wrote his A Memoir of Jane Austen and his sister Caroline wrote My Aunt Jane Austen. James Austen-Leigh's son William Austen-Leigh and William's nephew Richard Arthur Austen-Leigh co-authored Jane Austen: Her Life and Letters. A Family Record (1913). The Reverend James Austen's granddaughter Fanny Lefroy (1820-1885) wrote a Family History (unpublished manuscript), the grandson of Edward Knight, Edward Hugessen Knatchbull (1st Baron Brabourne) edited Letters of Jane Austen in 1884 and Admiral Francis Austen's grandson John Henry Hubback co-authored Jane Austen's Sailor Brothers with his daughter Edith Charlotte Hubback. This literary effusion continued with Mary Augusta Austen-Leigh (1920) Jane Austen: Her Life and Letters, Hugesson (1960) Kentish Family and Joan Austen-Leigh (1983). [5]

Jane Austen's siblings were not as conventional and bland as some biographers would have us believe (and, for all I know, as they believed them to be). The ultimate in blandness was A Memoir of Jane Austen of James Edward Austen-Leigh (who even edits out disabled brother George from the account). The best biography I have encountered in a relatively brief journey is Honan's Jane Austen. A Life. We can give a rather arbitrary numerical score reflecting relative biographical excellence (as comprehensiveness) as outlined below.

We give a simple numerical score of 1 to each biography for actually naming each sibling. We then give an additional score of 1 for naming in some way for each sibling the primary juicy story that would definitely interest the News of the World. We could then consider a set of n biographical accounts of Jane Austen's life available in an excellent antipodean university library and give each sibling a reportage score out of n (for being named) and a juicy attribute score (maximum value also n). We can also give each biography a score expressed (conveniently if somewhat improperly) as a percentage of the maximum score of 14 (7 siblings; 2 points maximum per sibling; 2 x 7 = 14).

Since James Edward Austen-Leigh is dead and Honan (1987) gets full marks we can safely apply this game to these two biographers. The siblings (juicy attribute in parentheses) are as follows: James (father-in-law General Matthew's unfair requirement to repay a huge amount of unauthorised West Indies salary plus interest); George (not normal due to episodic fits, possibly deaf and dumb and put out to care); Edward (litigation against him over his inheritance of the Knight estates); Henry (goes bankrupt and costs some of his relatives a pretty penny too in the process); Cassandra (committed the crime of burning a whole lot of Jane's letters); Francis (discreet transfer of East India Company bullion from China to England and incidentally involving Directors' concern over the death of a Chinese) and Charles (court martial over the loss of a ship off Turkey).

Since James Austen-Leigh only mentions 6 siblings (George is deleted) and mentions none of their "attributes" he scores 43%; Honan scores 100%. Of course this "game" is somewhat arbitrary since the various "Jane Austen" works being considered differ considerably in basic objectives and scope. Further, "attributes" other than those listed above could have been chosen. Nevertheless, from the 2 examples given the reader can get a feel for the sort of variation in comprehensiveness encountered in our target set of Jane Austen histories. We can now proceed to briefly survey the lives of Jane's siblings, conscious of issues of subsequent reportage and of the social realities of the time that did not become part of the artist's social palette in the creation of the novels. We can then "score" these siblings for "reportage".

4.3. The lives of Jane Austen's sister and six brothers

James Austen (1765-1819) was educated at home and then at
St. John's College, Oxford from 1788 as "Founders kin" with a fee
remission. He founded The Loiterer periodical that ran to 60 issues in
1789-1790 to which he, Henry and others contributed and which
teenage Jane read. Curate at Deane for his father, he married Anne
Matthew (daughter of General Edward Matthew) in 1792. The same
year her father was billed for a mistakenly non-authorised salary as
Governor of Grenada. With interest the bill became 24,000 pounds
when it had to be paid after his death in 1805. Anne had one child
(Anna, born 1793) and died in 1795. He was in love with Eliza and
may have proposed (circa 1796). He re-married, to Mary Lloyd in
1797, and became Rector at Steventon in 1801 when George Austen
retired to Bath. He was particularly solicitous to Aunt Jane Leigh-
Perrot during her remand and trial and was left funds by his Uncle
James Leigh-Perrot on his death in 1817 in the will that upset Jane and
her other siblings. Scholarly and literary, he influenced the literary
beginnings of Jane and no doubt also of his children by Mary, James
Edward (born 1798) and Caroline (born 1805), who both published
accounts of Jane Austen.

George Austen (1766-1838) was evidently disabled. He had
episodes of fits and could possibly have been deaf and dumb (as
inferred from Jane Austen referring to her being able to communicate
by hands to a deaf man). George was put out to care with a local
woman. His uncle Thomas Leigh had a similar problem and Eliza's son
Hastings had fits. Of our set of 30 biographical works on Jane Austen,
7 delete George from history and 10 fail to mention his disability.

Edward Austen (Edward Knight from 1812) (1767-1852)
was "adopted" by a wealthy distant relative Thomas Knight and his
wife who were childless. He married Elizabeth Bridges (daughter of
Sir Brook Bridges of Goodnestone, Kent) in 1791 and they had 11
children, Elizabeth dying some days after the last birth in 1808.

Thomas Knight died in 1794 and in 1797 Mrs Knight gave over the estates at Godmersham (where they primarily lived), Chawton (where Edward and his family often stayed especially after Mrs Austen, her daughters and Martha Lloyd moved to Chawton Cottage on the estate) and Steventon (where George Austen was permitted to farm several hundred acres to supplement his Rector's livings). When Mrs Knight died in 1812 Edward assumed the name Knight under the terms of his foster-father's will. However he was subsequently served with a writ of ejectment from the Chawton estate (mansion, cottage and lands) by a presumed heiress in 1814 and had to settle the matter eventually with a large payout. A kind, affectionate and avuncular man, he did not go to university but spent a long, prosperous and pleasant life in charge of his estates and took assiduous care of his sisters, his mother and his family. Apart from trips and the terminal months at Winchester, Jane Austen spent the last highly productive years of her life (1809-1817) at Chawton Cottage on Edward's estate in Hampshire.

Henry Austen (1771-1850), like his brother James, was first educated at home by his father and then sent to Oxford on a "Founder's kin" Fellowship at St. John's College. Like James he also was in love with the lively Eliza. He was more adventurous than James (a consideration that would have swayed Eliza who is reputed to have rejected James on account of his purely clerical ambitions). Henry joined the Oxford Militia in 1793 and, after the death of Eliza's husband the Comte de Feuillide by the guillotine in 1794, resumed his suit to Eliza. Eliza commented on his rejection of a clerical career to her cousin Philadephia (Philly) Walter: "I believe he has now given up all thoughts of the Church, & he is right for he is certainly not so fit for a parson as a soldier". Eliza informed Warren Hastings of the impending match "I have consented to an Union with my Cousin, Captain Austen, who has the honour of being known to you." Henry and Eliza travelled to France in 1802 to recover the late Comte's estates but were lucky to escape back to England in 1803 due to Eliza's French and liveliness. Henry went into partnership in a London bank in 1807 and they opened a branch at Alton (near Chawton). He became

Receiver-General for Oxfordshire in 1813 and in that year Eliza died, Jane travelling to London to comfort Henry. Unfortunately he was bankrupted in 1816 and his brother Edward Knight and his Uncle James Leigh-Perrot lost substantial sums in the process (Jane lost most of her meagre royalties). Henry took orders in 1816, served as Chaplain to the British Embassy in Berlin in 1817 and then took over the living at Steventon. He married Eleanor Jackson in 1820 but had no children from either of his marriages. Handsome, intelligent, articulate, lively and energetic he was Jane's favourite brother and he assisted her in publication dealings.

Cassandra Austen (1773-1845) was Jane's lifetime companion and shared a period of childhood schooling away from home with Jane. Cassandra was good-humoured but more self-possessed and calm than Jane. The great tragedy of her life was her engagement to the Reverend Thomas Fowle who was a cousin of their intimates Mary and Martha Lloyd (who were to become the second wives of James and Francis Austen, respectively). Thomas Fowle went out to the West Indies as a Chaplain to the regiment of his relation Lord Craven but tragically died of yellow fever at San Domingo in Hispaniola in 1797. He left a small bequest to Cassandra. Cassandra and Jane were loving sisters and corresponded at length when apart. However on Jane's death a substantial amount of correspondence, notably for the period 1797-1801 which was emotionally tumultuous for both women, was destroyed by Cassandra. Cassandra nursed Jane and was with her dear sister right to the end.

Francis Austen (1774-1865) had a distinguished naval curriculum vitae: entered the Royal Navy Academy, Portsmouth (1786); midshipman on the frigate Perseverance to India (1792); commissioned (1792); lieutenant on the armed brig Minerva (1792); on the sloop Lark that helped convoy Princess Caroline to England for marriage to the Prince of Wales (1795) [a marriage that subsequently involved scandalous un-Austenly behaviour on the part of both the Prince and his rudely rejected wife]; on the London that blockaded a

Spanish fleet in Cadiz (1797); involved in some dubious way with the East India Company on the Perseverance requiring him to leave the ship at Madras and later petition for expenses home - it appears that his father's representations to Hastings on his behalf connected him to Company business (1798); Commander on the sloop Peterel in a fleet with Nelson (1799), this ship sinking 2 French ships and capturing the 42-gun La Ligurienne (1800); Flag Captain on the 98-gun Neptune (this appointment being due to Admiral Gambier, a relative of his sister-in-law Anne Matthew) (1801); stationed at Ramsgate on coastal defence (1803); on the Leopard with Rear-Admiral Louis blockading Boulogne (1804); captain of the 80-gun Canopus (formerly Le Franklin and captured by Nelson at the Battle of the Nile) and assisted Nelson in a trans-Atlantic chase after Villeneuve to the West Indies and back (1805); sent to get supplies at Gibraltar, Francis missed out on the Battle of Trafalfgar (1805); on Canopus at the Battle of St Domingo in which all the French participants were captured or destroyed (1806); married Mary Gibson and lived at Southampton with Jane, Cassandra, Mrs Austen and Martha Lloyd (1806); captained the St Albans that convoyed transports carrying soldiers to the Peninsular War (1808); removed survivors from the Peninsular campaign (1809); commanded a navy fleet protecting East Indiamen sailing to China and back via Madras, returning from this trip with 13 ships worth 2 million pounds including silver bullion worth 470,000 pounds delivered discreetly to the Company agents at Deal, this trip occasioning a payment of 1000 guineas and Directors' concerns over the death of a Chinese associated with a dispute and a 6-week delay to trading in China (1810); Commander of the Elephant in the North Sea and Baltic (1811-1813); on half-pay variously at Portsmouth, Chawton and Alton, he was made CB (1815); Mary died leaving 11 children (1823); he married Martha Lloyd (1828); he received a number of honours and important positions subsequently including KCB (1837), Rear-Admiral (1830), Vice-Admiral (1838), Commander-in-Chief, West Indies (1844), Admiral (1848), GCB (1860) and Admiral of the Fleet (1863). A dignified and notably religiously observant man, he died in 1865 after a lifetime of distinguished service. His second wife was a dear friend of Jane and who came to live with the Austen women after the death of George Austen in 1805.

Charles Austen (1779-1852) followed his brother Francis into the Royal Navy Academy at Portsmouth (1791). His subsequent career was as follows: midshipman on the 32-gun Daedalus under Captain Thomas Williams who was married to Charles' cousin Jane née Cooper on his mother's side (1792); he was on the Unicorn when it captured the 44-gun frigate La Tribune (1796); commissioned and sailed with the 16-gun Scorpion (1797); while his father unsuccessfully applied to Admiral Gambier for Charles' transfer to a frigate (a good prospect for gaining commercial prizes), Charles' representation direct to Lord Spencer saw him transferred as second lieutenant to the frigate Tamar (1798); he was subsequently posted to the Endymion under the now Sir Thomas Williams (1798); on the Endymion under Captain Charles Paget when it captured 3 men-of-war and 2 privateers, he was promoted to 1st lieutenant (1803); made Commander of the 18-gun sloop Indian (1804); he served in North America and married Frances Palmer (the daughter of John Palmer, the Attorney-General of Bermuda who vigorously enforced laws against Methodists) (1807); he was transferred to the flag-ship Swiftsure (1810) and to the frigate Cleopatra (1810) before returning home (1811); he was Flag-Captain on the Namur at the Nore where he had major responsibilities for Thames and eastern ports navy recruits (1811-1814); Frances died giving birth to her 4th child Elizabeth who also died subsequently (1814); Captain of the 32-gun Phoenix in the Mediterranean; court martialled on the Boyne in the Mediterranean for the loss of the Phoenix in a storm off Turkey - he was acquitted (1816), the fault lying with the Greek pilots; he married Frances' sister Harriet in 1820 (they subsequently had 4 children); Captain of the frigate Aurora (1826); commanded the Bellerophon and was awarded the CB for the bombardment of St Jean d'Acre (1840); Rear-Admiral of the Blue (1846); commanded the East Indies and China station on the Hastings; he died of cholera on a steam sloop on the Irrawaddy during war in Burma (1852). Handsome, courageous, affectionate, fond of children,

Charles Austen was a model for Jane Austen's portrayal of noble, decent Navy men.

4.4. The score - the Austenizing of Jane Austen's siblings

Of a sample of 30 books dealing with Jane Austen's life [6] all but 7 mention all of her siblings, these 7 deficient histories failing to mention her disabled brother George for reasons about which we can only speculate. Indeed of 23 histories mentioning George, only 20 mention that he was deaf or dumb. This reservation is shown by his family and their descendants. Thus Jenkins (1973) observes:

"Of Mrs Austen's first four children, the third, George, was subject to fits and was never able to live with the family, and the temperament of the Austens is nowhere better shown than by the fact that, affectionate and forthright as they were, beyond the statement of his death in 1827, not a single word in reference to him is discoverable in any of their printed memoirs or correspondence." [7]

While all of the 30 histories actually mention the rest of Jane Austen's siblings, there are big differences in how singular attributes of these siblings are dealt with. Thus only 15 mention Cassandra's destruction of a swag of Jane Austen's letters (the ultimate in Austenizing is an Austen Austenizing an Austen), 5 the East Indies adventures of Francis Austen, 20 the bankruptcy of Henry Austen, 9 the litigation over the inheritance of Edward (Austen) Knight, 6 the naval court martial of Charles Austen and only 14 mention James Austen as a potential beneficiary of the will of Uncle James Leigh-Perrot. The Austenizing goes even further and thus while 9 histories mention James Austen's first father-in-law General Matthew, only 1 mentions his financial embarrassment over having to repay a huge sum deemed to have been "non-approved" salary for service in Grenada. [8]

Of course this analysis could be taken further in all kinds of interesting ways. I will leave it up to a future American successor to Morris J. Zapp, Professor of English at the State University of

Euphoria USA,[9] to provide a detailed analysis of everything in this regard based upon a state-of-the-art, computer-based analysis of the relevant holdings of the Library of Congress or the Cornell University Library. Suffice it to say that the present sample shows that, for a variety of reasons, the more interesting aspects of the lives Jane Austen's siblings have been generally reported in a less than comprehensive fashion.

4.5. 2008 Postscript

Further relevant books on Jane Austen became available. [10]

Chapter 5

The editing of Jane Austen's life

"There were very few beauties, and such as there were were not very handsome. Miss Iremonger did not look well, and Miss Blount was the only one much admired. She appeared exactly as she did in September, with the same broad face, diamond bandeau, white shoes, pink husband, and fat neck. The two Miss Coxes were there: I traced in one the remains of the vulgar, broad-featured girl who danced at Enham eight years ago; the other is refined into a nice, composed-looking girl, like Catherine Bigg. I looked at Sir Thomas Champneys and thought of poor Rosalie; I looked at his daughter, and thought her a queer animal with a white neck. Mrs Warren, I was constrained to think a very fine young woman, which I much regret. She danced away with great activity. Her husband is ugly enough, uglier even than his cousin John, but he does not look so very old. The Miss Maitlands are both prettyish, very like Anne, with brown skins, large dark eyes, and a good deal of nose. The General has got the gout, and Mrs Maitland the jaundice. Miss Debary, Susan, and Sally, all in black, but without any statues, made their appearance, and I was as civil to them as circumstances would allow me."

- Letter from Jane Austen to Cassandra (1800)[1]

"For what do we live, but to make sport for our neighbours, and laugh at them in our turn?"

- Mr. Bennet in Pride and Prejudice (1813)[2]

5.1. Jane Austen's life, times and writing

This book is not meant to be a detailed analysis of Jane Austen's life. Literature aside, Jane Austen's life was very "ordinary" and I am not a Jane Austen scholar with the patience and resolution to devote an academic life to the mundane minutiae of another person's existence. I am concerned with social consequences of her writing and of the world vision and moral responsiveness of her class, a class that ended up conquering half the world and imposing their might and manners on their subjects. Her class still rules the roost, whether it is domiciled in London, New York, Bonn or Paris. These civilized, highly-educated, hygienic people of noble personal aspirations will nevertheless visit destruction on swathes of humble people in the world in the cause of their life-styles, investment portfolios and superannuation schemes just as their predecessors did in Jane Austen's day.

It is a rather strange aspect of Jane Austen's writing that while the annual income of her comfortably off to filthy rich characters is a crucial element in every plot, the actual basis for this wealth is not detailed in most cases. Rare, anonymous or near-anonymous characters appear as servants, teachers, governesses, sailors, soldiers, farmers, solicitors or apothecaries. Jane Austen presumably did not have to spell out for the perceptive or informed reader that the rural estates were food-producing operations and not simply extensive rural parks for the hunting, fishing, aesthetic appreciation and variously-motivated strolling of the gentry. In some cases the "pay" or "prizes" of naval captains is referred to, as is the importance of West Indian estates. The East Indies, so intimately connected with her family, is actually explicitly referred to in Sense and Sensibility, albeit briefly, in this the most patently "Indian" of her novels.

With these concerns in mind, let us now consider Jane Austen's life and how her biographers have done to her life what (for what I choose to regard as perfectly legitimate artistic reasons) she did to the life of her wider society. The reader may care to read Chapter 6 (dealing with her novels) before reading the present Chapter 5 (which deals with her life) or vice versa. The former course would allow the reader the unprejudiced, speculative amusement of linking the realities, and especially the characters, of Jane's familial world to the world of her creation. For much of what follows the reader is referred to

Halperin (1984), Hodge (1972), Honan (1987) and Lane (1984, 1986, 1996) in particular. [3] Some particularly attractive books provide (in addition to historical and social detail), charming pictorial presentations of the houses, gardens and houses of Jane Austen's life and her novels. [4]

5.2. Jane Austen's parents

George Austen (1735-1805) was educated at the Tonbridge School (thanks to the help of his uncle Francis Austen) and gained a scholarship that took him to Oxford. After a succession of employments and advances, namely as an assistant master at Tonbridge School, a deacon in 1754, taking priest's orders in 1755 and a proctor at Oxford, he formally became the Rector of Steventon in Hampshire from 1761 (thanks to his distant relation Thomas Knight). He finally took up this latter position in a practical sense after marrying Cassandra Leigh (1739-1827) in 1764. Cassandra (named after her beautiful great-aunt Cassandra Brydges, Duchess of Chandos, who was both cousin and second wife of James Brydges, First Duke of Chandos) was the daughter of the Reverend Thomas Leigh who was Rector of Harpsden in Oxfordshire, Fellow of All Soul's College and a brother of Theophilus Leigh, Master of Balliol College, Oxford.

In addition to the "living" of Steventon in Hampshire, George Austen later gained the "living" of the nearby Deane parish in 1773 (thanks to his uncle Francis Austen). He supplemented his income by farming adjacent lands courtesy of Thomas Knight and tutored a number of boys (including George Hastings) who actually came to live with his family in the rectory. His finances were not great and his income amounted to about 600 pounds per year, payment of the expenses of a growing family being assisted on occasion by loans or gifts from kind relatives.

At the beginning of their life at Steventon the Austens cared for George Hastings, the son of Warren Hastings and his first wife Mary (who died 1759 in Kasimbazaar, Bengal). Mary was formerly Mary Elliott and had applied in 1751 for permission to go to Fort St. David at about the same time as Philadelphia (they were both young, unmarried and poor and may indeed have been friends). Mary married Captain Buchanan who died in the Black Hole of Calcutta in 1756 and she subsequently married Warren Hastings. (We have previously noted in Chapter 3 the pre-World War I versus post-World War I assignations of Hastings' wife as the widow of Captain Campbell or of Captain Buchanan, respectively). George Hastings was sent to England in the care of Francis Sykes in 1760, a year after the death of his mother and presumably through the suggestion and good offices of Philadelphia Hancock (née Austen). We have already seen that George Austen's sister Philadelphia was an intimate friend of Warren Hastings. George Hastings was cared for in the Austen home but tragically died from diphtheria in the Steventon rectory in 1764.

5.3. Jane Austen at Steventon 1775-1801

Jane Austen was born at Steventon on 16th December 1775. Her godmothers were her paternal great-aunt Jane Austen (wife of Francis Austen) and Mrs Musgrave, the wife of the Reverend James Musgrave (a relative on the Perrot side). Her godfather was the Reverend Samuel Cooke, husband of Cassandra Leigh, Mrs Cassandra Austen's cousin, the daughter of Theophilus Leigh, and who was to publish an historical novel Battleridge in 1799. Jane Austen was kept swathed in a swaddling cloth and initially given to the care and subsequent weaning with an experienced woman in nearby Deane.

Her only sister Cassandra was 2 years older and thus began a close lifelong friendship. Indeed it is useful to remind ourselves at this point of the ages that her various siblings other than the youngest Charles (1779-1852) attained in the year of Jane's birth: James (1765-1819), 10 years; George (1766-1838), 9; Edward (1767-1852), 8; Henry (1771-1850), 4; Cassandra (1773-1845), 2; Francis (1774-1865), 1.

In 1782 Jane and Cassandra were sent away for board and schooling in reading, writing and arithmetic with Mrs Ann Cawley (née Cooper) at Oxford. Mrs Cawley was the widow of a Principal of Brasenose and was the sister of Jane's uncle the Reverend Edward Cooper whose daughter Jane Cooper was also with them at Oxford. At Southampton with Mrs Cawley in 1783 all 3 girls came down with "putrid throat" or typhus. Responding to a letter from Jane Cooper, Mrs Jane Cooper and her sister Mrs Cassandra Austen came down immediately to recover their children. The tragic aftermath of this affair was the subsequent death of Mrs Cooper from the infection.

Jane and Cassandra as well as Jane Cooper were subsequently sent to the Abbey School for girls, a sister school to an adjacent and well-regarded boys' school in Reading. At this establishment they had lessons in French, Italian, needlework, English and history. Jane finally left this school at the end of 1786, at the age of 11. Her subsequent education at home derived from a large library and her family and encompassed piano, drawing, dancing, sewing, embroidery, history and literature. Jane Austen read poetry, enjoyed Richardson's Sir Charles Grandison (which she later converted to a play) and other novels. Her brother James had founded a literary journal The Loiterer, for which Henry also wrote, and Charles and Cassandra also had a literary bent. Jane and her family performed plays in the barn behind the rectory including The Rivals by Richard Sheridan.

On her own part Jane Austen's first literary efforts included letter-based novels, plays, histories and poems, the collective body being now referred to as the Juvenilia. Her novels-in-letters included Love and Freindship (sic) (written in 1790 and dedicated to her cousin Eliza), Lesley Castle (written in 1791 and dedicated to Henry Austen, her favourite brother) and finally the mature and delicious Lady Susan (written in 1794 and having a delightfully naughty anti-heroine evidently based on Eliza Austen née Hancock). Other Juvenilia include the unfinished work Catherine or The Bower, The History of England (written in 1792) and numerous letters. [5]

In addition to her immediate family, Jane had close friends in the vicinity of Steventon. Mrs Anne Lefroy (née Brydges) was the wife of the Rector of Ashe, the Reverend Isaac Peter Lefroy, and the sister of Sir Edgerton Brydges who wrote novels, published and was unsuccessful in his claims to the revival of the Chandos aristocratic position. Her brother-in-law Anthony Lefroy, who commanded the 9th Light Dragoons, was the father of Tom Lefroy, who was linked romantically in a fashion to Jane. Mrs Lefroy was a lively friend to Jane and one of her children Benjamin married Jane's niece Anna, the daughter of James Austen, in 1814 (thereby re-linking the Austens and the Brydges).

Mary Lloyd (1771-1843) and her elder sister Martha Lloyd (1765-1843) lived with their parents the Reverend Nowys Lloyd and Mrs Lloyd at the Rectory of Deane. After the death of Reverend Lloyd, the family moved to nearby Ibthorp when Reverend James Austen moved into the Deane rectory with his new wife Anne (née Matthew). Mary and Martha were good friends of Jane and her family and later were to marry (in both cases as second wives) James (1797) and Francis (1828), respectively. Cassandra was engaged to the Reverend Thomas Fowle (brother of Mrs Lloyd's brother-in-law and a former pupil of George Austen) but on tour of duty as a chaplain with Lord Craven's regiment, he sadly died of yellow fever in Hispaniola in 1797.

Elizabeth (Eliza) Hancock (1761-1813) stayed with her cousins at Steventon on a variety of occasions. She was a very pretty, lively woman who played the harp.[6] She was flirtatious and interested in the Steventon amateur dramatics. Both Henry and James succumbed to Eliza's charms and Henry married Eliza in 1797. Eliza can be seen as a model for some of the less insipid and less constrained women in Jane Austen's novels such as Lady Susan in Lady Susan, Isabella in Northanger Abbey, Mary Crawford in Mansfield Park and Eliza, the daughter of Eliza in Sense and Sensibility.[7]

Other friends of Jane Austen included her cousin Jane Cooper who married Thomas Willliams (later Sir Thomas) under whom Charles had served in several ships. Lady Jane died tragically in a carriage accident in 1798. A friend and relation of both Eliza Hancock and Jane Austen was their cousin Philadelphia (Phylly) Walter (they all shared a common grandmother in Rebecca Austen). Jane and Cassandra attended local balls at the homes of the local gentry, of which the Bigg Withers at Manydown and the Bridges at Goodneston are particularly notable, and accordingly met many young men and women of the surrounding area. It is from this period that Mary Russell Mitford quotes her mother Mrs Mitford as saying of Jane that she was the "prettiest, silliest, most affected, husband-hunting butterfly". The validity of this notorious quotation has been questioned since Mrs. Mitford had moved away from Steventon when Jane was too young to have been observed in this respect. However she did not move away that far, indeed only about 15 miles away, and presumably would have maintained her connections. Miss Mitford's gossip about the young Jane and description of the 40-year old Jane was made in 1815 and stands as interesting, necessarily anecdotal data:

"I have discovered that our great favourite Miss Austen is my countrywoman; that Mama knew all her family very intimately; and that she herself is an old maid (I beg her pardon - I mean young lady) with whom Mama before her marriage was acquainted. Mama says that she was then the prettiest, silliest, most affected husband-hunting butterfly she ever remembers and a friend of mine who visits her now says that she has stiffened into the most perpendicular, precise, taciturn piece of "single blessedness" that ever existed, and that till Pride and Prejudice showed what a precious gem was hidden in that unbending case, she was no more regarded in society than a poker or a fire screen or any other thin, upright piece of wood or iron that fills its corner with peace and quiet. The case is very different now; she is now a poker but a poker of whom everyone is afraid." [8]

As a young woman, Jane Austen evidently interacted with young men of whom 4 are of particular note, namely Tom Lefroy, Edward Bridges, Harris Bigg-Wither and an unknown young man at the seaside. We will briefly consider the first 2 of these these particular interactions at this point. Tom Lefroy was the nephew of Jane's neighbour and good friend Anne Lefroy. In Jane's own words in a letter to Cassandra:

"You scold me so much in the nice long letter which I have this moment received from you, that I am almost afraid to tell you how my Irish friend and I behaved. Imagine to yourself everything most profligate and shocking in the way of dancing and sitting down together. I <u>can</u> expose myself, however, only <u>once more</u>, because he leaves the country soon after next Friday, on which day we are to dance at Ashe after all. He is a very gentlemanlike, good-looking, pleasant young man, I assure you. But as to our having ever met, except at the three last balls, I cannot say much; for he is so excessively laughed at about me at Ashe, that he is ashamed of coming to Steventon, and ran away when we called on Mrs Lefroy a few days ago." [9]

However Tom Lefroy was sent away to Ireland and quite possibly for the obvious financial, professional and class reasons that recur in Jane Austen novels. Tom Lefroy was young and from a highly-placed family and set to study law (indeed many years later he became Lord Chief Justice of Ireland). Jane's family was very respectable and no doubt she was a gifted, articulate, out-going and agreeable young woman but any financial contribution her father could have made to a marriage would have been very meagre. Jane writes sadly:

"At length the day is come on which I am to flirt my last with Tom Lefroy and when you receive this it will be over. My tears flow as I write of the melancholy idea." [10]

In old age Tom Lefroy confessed to a boyish love for Jane and one therefore could assume a warm mutual attraction. Some years later Jane reveals an evidently hurt and proud diffidence in relation to news of Tom Lefroy from her friend Mrs Lefroy:

"Mrs Lefroy did come last Wednesday ... I was enough alone to hear all that was interesting, which you will easily credit when I tell you that of her nephew she said nothing at all, and of her freind very little. She did not once mention the name of the former to <u>me</u>, and I was too proud to make any enquiries; but on my father's afterwards asking where he was, I learnt that he was gone back to London on his way to Ireland, where he is called to the Bar and means to practise." [11]

Edward Bridges was the brother of Elizabeth Bridges who married Edward Austen (Knight) in about 1792. Edward was the fifth son of Sir Brook Bridges and Lady Bridges of Goodneston and had a dozen siblings. He was interested in Jane and indeed asked her, as guest of honour, to commence a ball at Goodneston as his partner. Edward may have made his interest clear to the point of actual proposition.

During this period Jane Austen visited the homes of various connections and in particular the Lefroys at Ashe, the Bridges at Goodnestone, the Bigg-Withers at Manydown, her brother Edward Austen and his wife Elizabeth (née Bridges) at Godmersham Park in Kent, the Lloyds at Ibthorpe, her brother James and his wife Mary (née Lloyd) at Deane and her Uncle James and Aunt Jane Leigh-Perrot in Bath. The arrest and remand of Mrs Leigh-Perrot occurred in August 1799, about 6 weeks after a visit by Jane Austen. In 1800 the Reverend George Austen - possibly for reasons connected with his age, his health, his son the Reverend James (who took over Steventon), the Leigh-Perrots and the prospects of more society for his daughters - abruptly decided to remove his family to Bath. Jane, returning from Ibthorpe with Martha Lloyd, supposedly fainted at the shock announcement.

In this period Jane Austen wrote Lady Susan, a novel in letter form that was not published in her life-time (1794/1795), Elinor and Marianne (the early version of Sense and Sensibility) (1795), First Impressions (the first version of Pride and Prejudice) (1796/1797), Sense and Sensibility (based on its predecessor) (1797) and Susan, that was to become Northanger Abbey (1798/1799). [11]

5.3. Jane Austen at Bath 1800-1806

The relocation to Bath was not without significant loss to Jane. 500 books from their library and Jane's pianoforte that could not be taken were ultimately sold. Jane no doubt keenly felt the loss of her beloved countryside. Jane and her mother went first to stay with the Leigh-Perrots in the Paragon and to look for a suitable place. They eventually settled on a house at Sydney Place that overlooked countryside. The beautiful city of Bath, famous for its mineral springs from Roman times, was not without a familial connection in addition to the Leigh Perrots. Some of the grand buildings owed their erection to Cassandra's great-uncle James Brydges, the first Duke of Chandos.

Jane Austen attended parties and functions at the Upper Rooms at Bath (immortalized in Northanger Abbey and Persuasion) and there observed her relative Mary Cassandra Twistleton and met her alleged married lover Mr. Evelyn. [13] While Jane did not evidently like Bath, the society and circumstances certainly well served her muse.

While on holiday at Teignmouth (the seat of Sir John Shore, who we will encounter as an observer of the horrendous Great Bengal Famine of 1769-1770), Jane Austen evidently met and fell in love with a young clergyman who was visiting his brother, a local doctor. The affection was returned and the young man was to rejoin them on their holiday. However the young man died and thus Jane in this sense suffered the same misfortune as her sister Cassandra. The happy ending allotted to every one of her heroines was not to be Jane's.

In the middle to late 1802 Jane successively visited James and Mary at Steventon, Edward and Elizabeth at Godmersham Park and then the Bigg-Withers at Manydown Park near Basingstoke. This was an ancient family that included the famous 18th century lawyer Sir William Blackstone and George Wither, the 17th century poet. Harris Bigg-Wither (he preferred Wither), his widowed sister Elizabeth and two further sisters Catherine and Alethea Bigg were in residence at the time of Jane's visit. Harris proposed to Jane (6 years his senior) and she accepted. However overnight Jane had second thoughts and by the morning her personal feelings (or lack thereof) had overcome the very considerable personal, social and financial advantages of the match. She withdrew her consent and her brother James took her back to Bath. Jane had done what perhaps Maria Bertram should have done in relation to the rich but not particularly attractive Mr Rushworth in Mansfield Park.

In 1803 Jane visited Ramsgate, where her brother Francis was quartered on account of his responsibility for defences in that part of the coast against a possible French landing. Frank had met his future wife Mary Gibson in Ramsgate. Jane was aware of the attractions of the seaside for the infirm and wrote rather sneeringly of the nervous indisposition of Edward Bridges' wife Harriet (née Foote) who had visited Ramsgate. The health-giving aspects of the seaside resort reappears in the unfinished Sanditon and the south coast military presence is a key ingredient in the plot of Pride and Prejudice. [14] Jane and her family visited the picturesque south coast town of Lyme Regis. Jane took walks along the Lyme Regis Cobb (or sea wall), made famous in Persuasion through the accidental fall from it of Louisa Musgrove in which she misses the arms of her erstwhile "lover" Captain Wentworth and is seriously hurt. At about this time (1803/1804) Jane Austen commenced writing The Watsons which she was not to finish given the upset of this period. Susan was offered for publication and sold to Crosby & Co. for 10 pounds. The conclusion of her first work, Lady Susan, was probably written in 1805. [15]

The Austens moved to Green Park Buildings, a location closer to waters of the Pump Room for the ailing Reverend George Austen who eventually died in 1805. One supposes that the fragility of George Austen is reflected in the accounts of filial solicitude in Emma and the unfinished The Watsons. [16] Jane Austen wrote thus of her father to her brother Francis:

"...Your affectionate heart will be greatly wounded, & I wish the shock could have been lessen'd by a better preparation; - but the Event has been sudden, & so must be the information of it. We have lost an Excellent Father ... His tenderness as a Father, who can do justice to?...The Serenity of the Corpse is most delightful! - It preserves the sweet, benevolent smile which always distinguished him." [17]

George Austen's death left Mrs Austen in a difficult financial position with an annual income of 210 pounds that was regularized by various contributions from Henry (50 pounds pa), James (50 pounds pa), interest on the late Tom Fowle's legacy of 1,000 pounds to Cassandra, 100 pounds pa from Edward and 50 pounds pa from Francis (this being the half accepted of what Francis had actually offered to the family in a secret deal released by Henry). The family moved again, in this instance to 25 Gay Street, and reduced their staff to only one maid by dismissing a man and another maid. When Mrs Lloyd died, her daughter Martha came from Ibthorpe to live with the Austens (she was to marry Francis as his second wife in 1828). In 1808 the family moved to Trim Street and then left Bath for good.

The Austens (and Martha) visited Clifton and then Adelstrop in Gloucester to visit Mrs Austen's cousin the Reverend Thomas Leigh whose nephew had inherited the magnificent and historic Stoneleigh Abbey on the death of his distant relative Mary Leigh in 1806, and the Austens accompanied him to this new estate. From this splendid environment, Thomas Leigh and Lady Saye and Sele, the Austens went to Hamstall-Ridware in Staffordshire to stay with the Reverend Edward Cooper, Jane Austen's cousin on her mother's side. Finally, after a visit to James and Mary at Steventon, the Austen family and Martha ended up in Southampton with Francis and his wife Mary.

5.4. Southampton (1806-1809)

Mrs Austen, Cassandra, Jane, Martha, Francis and his wife Mary shared lodgings until they found a suitable house to rent in Castle Square. The Austen women and Martha lived with Frank and his wife in Southampton for about 2 and a half years. Southampton was conveniently close to Portsmouth where Francis expected to resume a new naval command. Indeed only a few weeks after establishing themselves at Castle Square Francis took command of HMS St Albans and was thence abroad on active service, escorting East India Company ships to the Far East and participating in the war against France off Spain and Portugal. Francis was away when his first child Mary Jane was born in 1807.

The Castle Square house had a garden for their pleasure and entertainment through theatre, balls and parties. Jane and Cassandra made visits to Edward and his wife Elizabeth (née Bridges) at Godmersham and Henry and his wife Eliza in Brompton on the outskirts of London. Jane visited Edward's "foster mother" and generous benefactor Mrs Catherine Knight at her home White Friars at Canterbury and met George Moore, son of the Archbishop of Canterbury, who had married Elizabeth's sister Harriet (Harriot) Bridges. Jane Austen's opinion of George Moore is exquisitely put:

" & another five minutes brought Mr Moore himself, just returned from his morn'g ride. Well! - & what do I think of Mr Moore? - I will not pretend in one meeting to <u>dislike</u> him, whatever Mary may say; but I can honestly assure her that I saw nothing in him to admire. - His manners, as you have always said, are gentlemanlike - but by no means winning." [18]

Two of the Bigg sisters, Alethea and Catherine, visited Jane and Cassandra at Southampton in 1808. Catherine was shortly to marry a much older man, the Reverend Herbert Hill, 2 dozen years her senior and the uncle of the poet Robert Southey. The "older man" as an acceptable husband for a heroine appears as Mr Knightley in Emma and as Colonel Brandon in Sense and Sensibility. [19]

Tragedy struck the family in late 1808: Elizabeth Austen died some days after giving birth to her 11th child (Brook John). Cassandra, Edward and all but 2 of his children were at Godmersham Park at the time. The 2 eldest boys Edward and George were at Winchester School and returned home via Steventon and a short stay with Jane at Southampton. Subsequently Edward suggested Chawton Cottage, adjacent to Chawton Manor, in Hampshire as a suitable place for the Austen women. Chawton Cottage, a substantial 2-storey dwelling in Chawton village near Alton, was located near the junction of a road from Basingstoke with the road from Southampton to London via Winchester. Henry had a banking branch at nearby Alton, Edward was able to stay periodically at Chawton House (although it had been let to the Middletons until 1812) and Chawton was relatively close to James and his family at Steventon.

Shortly before the Austens finally left Southampton for Chawton in 1809, Jane Austen wrote to Crosby & Co. under the pseudonym Mrs. Ashton Dennis inquiring after her still unpublished novel Susan and offering another copy of the manuscript if needed. They replied that they held the publishing rights but she could re-purchase her manuscript at the original price of 10 pounds.

5.5. Chawton 1809-1817

The Chawton Cottage had 6 bedrooms and thus had plenty of room for visitors. Jane and her family interacted with the Rector of Chawton, Reverend Papillon, his niece Eleanor Papillon and with the Middletons who leased Chawton House until 1812. John Charles Middleton, a widower, had 6 children and a sister-in-law Maria Beckford assisted with their care. A niece of the latter, Charlotte-Maria

Beckford provided, in old age, a description of Jane at this time at variance with the rather full-cheeked and somewhat combative person of the surviving sketch by Cassandra: tall, thin, spare, with high cheek bones, good colour and joyous, intelligent, sparkling eyes; good-humoured, great fun with children but perhaps rather reserved with strangers. [20]

Jane Austen's nieces and nephews would variously stay at Chawton cottage or at Chawton House. Edward took possession of Chawton House in 1813 and his family returned to be there for the warmer months from 1813 onwards. Through such interactions and through correspondence, Jane took a keen interest in her nieces and nephews and had a particular critical and affectionate interest in the literary aspirations of James' daughter Anna and Edward's daughter Fanny. Henry's wife, his cousin Eliza, died in 1813 and Jane visited Henry at his place at Covent Garden, London and attended the theatre. Jane also visited Edward's family at Godmersham Park.

With four women to run the household, Jane Austen was able to devote a lot of time to her writing in this period. Jane would write in the company of her mother and of Cassandra and Martha, using ordinary sheets of paper that could be put away as social circumstances demanded and eventually collated, folded and combined. Sense and Sensibility was revised and prepared for publication (1809-1811) and finally published (1811). This was followed by Pride and Prejudice (finished 1812; published 1813), Mansfield Park (written 1811-1813; published 1814) and Emma (written 1814-1815; published 1816) and the writing of Persuasion (1815-1816). Susan was finally published posthumously as Northanger Abbey in 1817/1818 as was Persuasion but now, for the first time, under the name of the author in both cases. [21]

In 1815 Henry was negotiating with a new publisher, John Murray, for his sister in relation to the newly-completed Emma, but fell ill. Jane came to care for him at Hans Place in London. Henry's physician Mr Hayden charmed Jane. One of his colleagues, who was a physician to the Prince Regent, passed on the intelligence that the Prince enjoyed her novels and kept a set in each of his residences. The Librarian of Carlton House, the Reverend James Clarke, invited her to a tour of the Prince's magnificent palace and she felt obliged to respond by dedicating Emma to the Prince in the most gracious of language. [22]

In 1816 Henry Austen's bank collapsed and he and his partners were declared bankrupt. The collapse cost Edward 2,000 pounds, James Leigh-Perrot 10,000 pounds and Jane Austen lost her banked literary earnings. Henry took Holy Orders and became a curate assisting the Reverend Papillon at Chawton. Brother Charles had difficulties at this time in addition to relatively modest losses in the banking collapse. His ship Phoenix was lost in a storm off Turkey and he was up for court martial. He was ultimately acquitted. This bad year also saw the worsening of Jane Austen's health. The transformation of the gay young thing of the 1790s to the apparently "most perpendicular, precise, taciturn" woman of 40 described anecdotally by Miss Mitford [23] may relate to the progress of her disease, surmised to be the adrenal cortical insufficiency of Addison's Disease. Outward appearances can be very deceptive and a good-humoured personality can address the behavioural impact of corticosteroid insufficiency and indisposition [as I know from all too real personal experience]. Reproduced below is a lovely example of the delightful enthusiasm, warmth, love and witty good-humour of Jane Austen at the age of 41 writing to her niece Fanny Knight (daughter of Edward) (20 February 1817):

"My dearest Fanny,

You are inimitable, irresistable. You are the delight of my Life. Such Letters, such entertaining Letters as you have lately sent! - Such a description of your queer little heart! - Such a lovely display of what Imagination does. - You are worth your weight in Gold, or even in the new Silver Coinage. - I cannot express to you what I have felt in reading your history of yourself, how full of Pity & Concern & Admiration & Amusement I have been. You are the paragon of all that is Silly & Sensible, common-place and eccentric, Sad & Lively, Provoking and Interesting. - Who can keep pace with the fluctuations of your Fancy, the Capprizios of your Taste, the Contradictions of your Feelings? - You are so odd! - It is very, very gratifying to me to know you so intimately. You can hardly think what a pleasure it is to me, to have such thorough pictures of your Heart. - Oh! what a loss it will be when you are married. You are too agreeable in your single state, too agreeable as a Neice. I shall hate you when your delicious play of Mind is all settled down into conjugal & maternal affections." [24]

Jane Austen's health worsened in 1816 and one presumes that her condition was not improved by the surfeit of bad family news. She suffered back pains and Cassandra took her to Cheltenham for the spa waters in April. She visited Kintbury where, according to Mary Jane Fowle's account to Caroline Austen, she recalled old places with a particularity that had the prescience of mortality. She returned to Chawton via Steventon.

5.6. The final year - 1817

At the beginning of 1817 Jane Austen had begun her final, albeit unfinished, work Sanditon. She was only able to complete 12 chapters. She suffered backache, nausea and weakness that could prevent her from walking out. Cassandra and Edward took her out riding on a donkey, her siblings walking beside her. Her condition fluctuated and she was optimistic and cheerful to her loving family. The death of her uncle James Leigh-Perrot at the end of March and the revelation of his will brought on a relapse. In Jane's own account:

" but I am ashamed to say that the shock of my Uncle's Will brought on a relapse". [25]

The will left 1,000 pounds to each of Mrs Austen's children who survived Mrs Leigh-Perrot. He left the property at Bath and Scarlets in

Berkshire to his wife and left funds, subject to her disposition, for James Austen who had been so solicitous during their troubles. (James Austen was not to actually directly benefit but his son, James Austen - later Austen-Leigh - did inherit.)

Jane was finally confined to bed or to the sofa, suffering weakness, abdominal pains, nausea, vomiting and skin depigmentation. It has been suggested that she was suffering from the terminal stages of Addison's disease deriving from autoimmunity- , tuberculosis- or cancer-induced destruction of the adrenal glands. She made out a will, leaving the little she had to her dear sister Cassandra subject to 50 pounds to Henry and 50 pounds to his housekeeper Madame Bijion. She subsequently also left a gold chain to her niece and god-daughter Louisa Knight and a lock of hair for Fanny Knight. It was felt that she would be better off in nearby Winchester where expert medical care would be available. She was lodged at 8 College Street, the lodging having been arranged by Elizabeth Heathcote (née Bigg), one of Lovelace Bigg's daughters at Manydown now resident in Winchester. Dr Giles Lyford was in attendance and diagnosed a wasting disease but was unable to affect its course. Jane, good-humoured as ever, wrote to Edward:

"Mr. Lyford says he will cure me, & if he fails I shall draw up a Memorial and lay it before the Dean & Chapter, & have no doubt of redress from that Pious, Learned and Disinterested Body". [26]

Elizabeth Heathcote and her sister Alethea visited Jane daily. On occasion she was taken out in a wheelchair. Her last day was one of pain and to inquiry as to her needs she replied: "Nothing but death". Her last words: "God grant me patience. Pray for me, oh pray for me!" [27] Dr. Lyford relieved her pain, probably by laudanum from Bengal, and she lapsed unconscious, dying early in the morning of 18th July 1817.

5.7. The editing of Jane Austen's life

We have already seen how the more interesting aspects of the
lives of many of Jane Austen's family and connections have been
variously found less than interesting by her biographers. The same
treatment has been meted out to Jane Austen's own life, despite the
really exemplary nature of her life in a personal, social, moral and
creative sense. Of course one must appreciate that some of the books
dealing with Jane Austen's life are not primarily biographies and, as
discussed in Chapter 1, people will apply different value judgements
about the importance of particular historical events. However, given
Jane Austen's modest domestic life and her literary genre that was
concerned with commonplace, everyday social interactions, any details
of her social behaviour and in particular of any potentially "romantic"
encounters with men can be seen to be very important. However
analysis of a large number of books concerned with the life and work
of Jane Austen reveals wide variation in the treatment given to such
matters.

This is illustrated by the treatment by Jane Austen's biographers
of her significant "suitors" or subjects of her serious affection. At one
end of the spectrum we have the definitive Jane Austen. Her Life by
Park Honan (1987) that deals with Tom Lefroy, Edward Bridges,
Harris Bigg-Wither and the unknown young clergyman at the seaside
as men linked romantically to Jane Austen. On the other hand we have
A Memoir of Jane Austen by James Edward Austen-Leigh (1870) who
discreetly refers only to the latter affair as a possible attachment. In
between we have various combinations of reportage. [28]

A further example is the rather Jane Austen-like comment
about Jane Austen by Mrs Mitford reported by her daughter Mary
Russell Mitford, namely that she was "the prettiest, silliest, most
affected, husband-hunting butterfly". [29] Probably because this
description represents a rare insight into Jane Austen's character from
a contemporary, this is quoted in 18 out of our sample of 30

biographies of Jane Austen surveyed, although various writers are concerned about the accuracy of the remarks. [30]

We can extend the intrinsically rather arbitrary "quantitative" analysis we applied in Chapter 4 to Jane Austen's siblings to consider a wider range of her connections. I have set up a set of 30 connections (including her siblings) and 30 corresponding newsworthy attributes associated with these people of the kind that one might find reported in a popular newspaper such as the News of the World. For each book in our set of 30 published accounts of Jane Austen's life we determine whether the connection is named and whether the attribute is mentioned, while noting that some of these books are not primarily biographical. We can then sum the data for each connection and each corresponding attribute as shown in the following table:

Connection	Attribute	Person named	Attribute mentioned
Austen, Cassandra	destruction of letters	30	15
Austen, Charles	court martial	30	6
Austen, Francis	East Indies adventures	30	5
Austen, George	disabled & fits	23	20
Austen, Henry	bankruptcy	30	20
Austen, James	Leigh-Perrot inheritance	30	14
Bigg-Wither, Harris	rejected marriage proposal	21	21
Bridges, Edward	romantic interest	8	6
Brydges, Sir Edgerton	unsuccessful Chandos claim	13	2
Brydges, James	gigantic peculation	11	4
De Feuillade (Capote), Hastings	sickly, fits, early death	20	12
De Feuillade (Capote), Jean	guillotined, alleged conspiracy	25	24
Hancock, Elizabeth	fathered by Hastings	27	5
Hancock, Philadelphia	productive adultery with Hastings	24	5
Hancock, Tysoe Saul	cuckolded by friend Hastings	20	5
Hastings, Warren	real father of Eliza	22	5
Hastings, George	Hasting's son, died in the Austens' care	17	16
Knatchbull, Dorothea	married step-uncle Edward Knight Jr	2	2
Knight, Edward Jr	married step-niece Dorothea Knatchbull	8	2
Knight (Austen), Edward	litigation over Knight inheritance	30	9
Knight, Fanny	step-daughter's sister-in-law & aunt	27	2
Lefroy, Thomas	Jane's first romance	24	24
Leigh, Thomas	retarded brother of Cassandra & James Leigh	4	4
Leigh-Perrot, James	upsetting will with restricted benefits	27	17
Leigh-Perrot, Jane	capital trial for alleged theft of cloth	25	20
Matthew, General	forced repayment of unauthorised pay	9	1
Mitford, Mrs	Jane "butterfly" gossip	18	18
Russell Mitford,	Jane "butterfly" gossip	22	16

Mary			
Twistleton, Mary Cassandra	supposed Bath adulteress	5	5
Unknown clergyman	Jane's romantic friend who died	19	19

The above simply provides an overall summary of the surprising absences in Jane Austen historiography that have been dealt with in the last few chapters. The Austenizing of Jane Austen simply shows that even something as relatively simple and straightforward as the life of a modest English country spinster is not immune from selective reportage. The above data is the more surprising because of the sustained, huge interest in this delightful writer and the consequently very large literature that exists concerning her life and work. We will now turn to a brief description of Jane Austen's finished and unfinished novels and document the extent to which the "real" world was permitted to intrude into the world of her Art.

5.8. 2008 Postscript

Further relevant books on Jane Austen became available. [31]

Chapter 6

The rare intrusion of humble social reality into Jane Austen's novels

"I would rather work for my bread than marry him."

- Miss Frederica Vernon in Lady Susan (1794)[1]

"I would rather be a teacher in a school (and I can think of nothing worse) than marry a man I did not like."

- Emma in The Watsons (1804)[2]

"There are certainly not so many men of of large fortune in the world, as there are pretty women to deserve them."

- in Mansfield Park (1814)[3]

"A large income is the best recipe for happiness that I ever heard of. It certainly may secure all the myrtle and turkey part of it."

- in Mansfield Park (1814)[4]

"Single women have a dreadful propensity for being poor, which is one very strong argument in favour of matrimony, but I need not dwell on such arguments with _you_, pretty dear."

- Letter from Jane Austen to her niece Fanny Knight (Austen) (1817) [5]

6.1. Jane Austen's novels in the social context of her times

It is useful to very briefly summarize the essential plots and dramatis personae of Jane Austen's novels before making a necessarily very brief catalogue of instances in which the "real" world of radically socially stratified war-time England of circa 1800 actually intrudes into the lordly mansion, manor house, gentleman's cottage or rectory of her literary constructions. Such intrusions in her novels are about as frequent as references to famine or genocide in standard British history texts or indeed in British historical texts in general that are not devoted specifically to such unpleasant subjects.

The world in which Jane Austen lived was the comfortable lot of the gentry that represented one percent of the population. The bulk of the population lived in dire poverty, rural families were being dispossessed, urbanized and disempowered by the Enclosures,[6] and a significant proportion of the male population was involved in the carnage of the Napoleonic Wars.[7] It was a time at which women were in a subordinate position, childbirth was dangerous and a caesarean typically resulted in death from infection within days.[8] Men were flogged to death in the Navy.[9] Thousands of petty criminals were confined on hulks and thence transported to the gross brutalities of penal servitude in America and (after American Independence) to New South Wales and Van Dieman's Land.[10] Convicts would be sentenced to hundreds of lashes for minor misdemeanors in circumstances in which as few as 30 lashes could be fatal.[11] Petty theft could attract a death sentence, a prospect with which Jane Austen's Aunt Jane Leigh-Perrot was all too familiar.[12] If life was tough for the ordinary people of Merrie England, then spare a thought for the victims of expanding British imperialism from the Scottish Highlands to the South Pacific.[13] Slavery was in its heyday in Africa and the Americas,[14] the rapacious taxation of indigenous farmers or tenant farmers was the "go" from Ireland to India[15] and the extermination of Australian and Tasmanian aborigines had just commenced.[16] However the horror to surpass all others was the famine in Bengal that had destroyed about 10 million people in 1769-1770 and from which it would take Bengal about 40 years to recover. Indeed that dreadful period of Bengali economic and demographic recovery would largely coincide with the period of Jane Austen's life.[17]

We will now briefly examine Jane Austen's novels and assess the minimal extent to which social realities intruded upon the "naice" world they describe. We will deal with the novels in order of their completion in the hope of espying a trend of increasing maturity, social consciousness or indeed of increasingly "common" values or sensibilities acquired in a slowly democratizing society.

6.2. Lady Susan (completed 1794) [18]

The events unfold in a series of letters principally between Lady Susan Vernon and her confidante Mrs Alicia Johnson of Edwards Street and between Lady de Courcy of Parklands and her daughter Mrs Catherine Vernon, wife of Lady Susan's brother Charles Vernon of Churchill (cf John Churchill, associate of JA great great uncle James Brydges). The calculating and flirtatious Lady Susan, recently widowed and with a 16 year-old daughter Frederica, detaches Sir James Martin from ordinary Miss Manwaring, the daughter of jealous, rich Mrs Manwaring and poor but very attractive Mr Manwaring of Langford with whom she flirts. This was reported to the de Courcy ladies via gossipy Charles Smith, a friend of Reginald de Courcy, the son of Lady and Sir Reginald de Courcy. Lady Susan leaves Langford (unwanted by Mrs Manwaring) and repairs to Churchill (where she is unwanted by Mrs Vernon), leaving Frederica in the care of Miss Summers of Wigmore Street.

Lady Susan's sensible plan is to marry dull Reginald de Courcy (cf Brydges-related de Bourgh in P & P) in the expectation of his father's demise and for Frederica to marry silly, rich Sir James Martin. Frederica dislikes Sir James, escapes from Wigmore Street, is recaptured 2 streets away and is brought to Churchill by her uncle Charles Vernon. Sir James Martin imposes himself briefly at Churchill and Frederica, forbidden from complaining to the Vernons, entreats an increasingly indignant Reginald de Courcy of her distress at the plan. Lady Susan smooths the affair with her lover Reginald but visits town to see Mr. Manwaring who has seen Mrs Johnson who acts as a go-between. Lady Susan cannot visit Mrs Johnson's house (this having been forbidden by Mr. Johnson) and entertains Mr. Manwaring daily at her lodgings. Unfortunately Mr Johnson (somehow apprised of Lady Susan's presence in town, possibly as a result of the de Courcy ladies' correspondence with each other) delays his gout-impelled trip to Bath. Reginald de Courcy and the jealous Mrs Manwaring arrive at Edwards Street in town simultaneously and all is revealed after the latter cross-examines her husband's servant about his conduct.

In the wash-up, Reginald de Courcy returns to Parklands and his connection with Lady Susan is over. Mrs Johnson is forced by her husband to bid adieu to her dear friend and end all intercourse. The Manwarings part and Miss Manwaring comes to town, dresses well and resumes her pitch for Sir James Martin. However Lady Susan cheerfully survives: an influenza scare sends Frederica back to Churchill from her mother and the eventual marriage of the daughter to Reginald de Courcy is foreshadowed when the pain of his former attachment to the mother has faded. Lady Susan marries rich Sir James Martin, her happiness only being conceivably qualified by "her husband, and her conscience". Concludes naughty, ironic Jane: "For myself, I confess that I can pity only Miss Manwaring, who coming to town and putting herself to an expense of clothes, which impoverished her for two years, on purpose to secure him, was defrauded of her due by a woman ten years older than herself."

Analysis of Lady Susan: This delicious tale with intriguing under-currents actually fleetingly adverts to humble "reality" on several occasions: a servant, Wilson, brings word of Reginald's intended departure from Churchill and conveys Lady Susan's desire to talk with him, thus enabling the subsequent rapprochement; Mrs Manwaring extracts intelligence of her husband's misbehaviour from his servant; disease surfaces as an influenza scare. While the more rarefied financial realities of the plot are quite clear, the social bottom line is perhaps inadvertently put into the words of poor Frederica when she complains to Reginald de Courcy about the proposed match to Sir James Martin: "I would rather work for my bread than marry him."

6.3. **Northanger Abbey** (originally submitted as Susan in 1803) [19]

Oh so nice Catherine Morland leaves her parents' country home to visit Bath with her childless neighbors the friendly Allens. She briefly encounters a pleasant young clergyman Henry Tilney. They subsequently meet Mrs Allen's now-widowed friend Mrs Thorpe and thence the Thorpe children Isabella and John (a friend of James Morland at Oxford). Catherine and Isabella take to each other. When Henry re-appears at a ball, Catherine has to decline him because of her engagement to John for the evening. John behaves in a rather high-handed manner in not stopping the carriage on Catherine's demand and unilaterally cancelling an engagement of Catherine to walk with Henry and his sister Eleanor. Catherine rushes to the Tilneys to explain to them and their father, General Tilney. Catherine, Henry and Eleanor subsequently walk to the Beechen Cliff of Bath and discuss art and novels (including Mrs Radcliffe's gothic Mysteries of Udolpho). Isabella becomes engaged to James Morland but the financial contribution to the couple by Mr Morland senior is necessarily (and accordingly disappointingly) modest. Isabella subsequently publicly flirts with Henry's brother, the dashing Captain Tilney (cf Anne Tylney Craven link and Manydown Park of the Bigg family).

Catherine is invited to the Tilneys' Northanger Abbey (cf Stoneleigh Abbey) and in transit Henry induces a spooky atmosphere that is reinforced by the Abbey itself when they arrive. Catherine has a disturbing evening occasioned by finding in a secret cabinet a document that turns out to be a laundry list in the morning. Catherine fantasizes about the reserved General Tilney - has he murdered his late wife or secreted her in the Abbey? Henry disabuses Catherine of this fantasy: "this is England, we are Christians, how can you think such a thing?" They visit Henry's parsonage nearby and Catherine is charmed. Henry and the General have to leave on business and Catherine and

Eleanor entertain each other. Catherine receives a letter from Isabella indicating the end of her engagement to James and the role of Captain Tilney in this.

Catherine is suddenly told to leave on orders of the General and is precipitately returned to her parents unescorted. Henry later appears and explains the General's incorrect intelligence from the vindictive John Thorpe that she is penniless, this totally counteracting Thorpe's earlier assertion that she came from a very well-off family. The Morlands will not consent to her marrying Henry unless the General agrees. He does so when Eleanor's beau (he of the laundry list) becomes a viscount and marries Eleanor. Henry and Catherine Tilney live happily ever after.

Analysis of Northanger Abbey: The "real" world intrudes minimally into this moral construction only to the extent that there are nameless servants; General and Captain Tilney are soldiers in England at the time of the Napoleonic wars; of Mrs Thorpe's' sons, John is at Oxford, Edward is at Merchant-Taylors' (the school in London that Robert Clive of India attended before he was sent off to India as a "writer" in the East India Company) and William is at sea (in the Navy or on an East Indiaman or another merchant vessel). Of course a major interest of this novel for us in this disquisition is Henry's passionate defence of the nobility and unimpeachable decency of English civilization that could not possibly admit of the possibility of Catherine's fantasy about the General murdering or otherwise sequestering his wife:

"Remember the country and the age in which we live. Remember that we are English and we are Christians. Consult your own understanding, your own sense of the probable, your own observation of what is passing around you. Does our education prepare us for such atrocities? Do our laws connive at them? Could they be perpetrated without being known, in a country like this, where social and literary intercourse is on such a footing, where everyman is surrounded by a neighbourhood of voluntary spies, and where roads and newspapers lay everything open?" [20]

6.4. The Watsons (left unfinished 1804) [21]

The heroine Emma Watson returns to her sickly and widowed father in Surrey after 14 years in the care of her aunt Mrs Turner. Mr Turner has died and his widow has accompanied her new husband Captain O'Brien to Ireland. Her elder sister Elizabeth Watson lost her love Mr Purvis to another thanks to her sister Penelope's setting Purvis against her. Elizabeth has been disappointed with lady-killer Mr Tom Musgrave (900 pounds per annum) whom she now detests. Penelope Watson frets over Musgrave who slighted her over a further sister Margaret. Penelope is interested in an old Dr. Harding in Chichester and is now to spend time with her solicitor brother Robert Watson and his sharp wife Jane at Croydon. A further brother Sam Watson is a surgeon. He loves Mary Edwards, the only daughter of wealthy and sociable Mr and Mrs Edwards but faces stiff competition from Captain Hunter. Mary will have 10,000 pounds on marriage.

Emma attends a ball at the Edwards' and sees Mary Edwards surrounded by Red-coats (notably Captain Hunter). The Osborne Castle mob arrive: widowed Lady Osborne, her son Lord Osborne, his former tutor the Reverend Howard, Mrs Blake (the Reverend Howard's widowed sister) and Mrs Blake's 10 year-old boy Charles. Emma gallantly dances with little Charles (who has been forsaken by Miss Osborne, engaged by Captain Beresford) and gains the approbation of the Reverend Howard and Mrs Blake. Elizabeth stays overnight and the next day avoids Musgrave's invitation to drive her home.

The Watsons are visited by Tom Musgrave and by Lord Osborne who has also noted Emma's beauty and invites her to observe their hunting with hounds. Days later Robert Watson and his wife Jane (an only daughter worth 6,000 pounds when she married) arrive from Croydon with Margaret Watson (they have left their little daughter behind). This couple make pointed judgements about Mrs Turner and her financial dispositions and Emma is tearful in recalling the death of her uncle. Tom Musgrave, whom Margaret loves, drops by.

Jane Austen did not finish The Watsons, perhaps because of the coincidence of the plot and its composition with the infirmity and death of her beloved father in 1805. According to Cassandra, Mr. Watson was to die, Emma is forced to depend upon Robert and Jane but declines Lord Osborne's offer of marriage. Despite Lady Osborne's love for the Reverend Howard, he finally marries Emma.

Analysis of The Watsons: The unfinished account has a much more bourgeois complement than her other novels: we encounter a banker and his sons, another wealthy urban family in the Edwards, a surgeon, the inevitable clergyman, a solicitor and a plethora of Red-coat officers as well as the noble Osbornes. Servants, including an old Watson family retainer called Nanny, appear in the novel. Social attitudes quickly reveal themselves: Mr. Edwards dislikes his daughter's being about the military officers (see P & P) and as for Emma's brother, "Sam is only a surgeon". Emma opines: "I would rather be a teacher at a school (and I can think of nothing worse) than marry a man I did not like" and Elizabeth goes further: "I would rather do anything than be a teacher at a school". [22]

6.5. Sense and Sensibility (1811) [23]

Mr Henry Dashwood dies leaving his Sussex estate, including Norland Park, to his son by a previous marriage, John Dashwood. Mrs Dashwood and her daughters, sensible Elinor, emotional Marianne and very young Margaret, move to Barton Cottage on the Devonshire estate of a generous relative, hearty, sociable Sir John Middleton of Barton Park. Elinor quietly bears her removal from Edward Ferrars, the brother of John Dashwood's wife the sharpish Fanny: an attachment had developed between them since Edward had spent a lot of time at Norland Park. The Dashwood women are frequently entertained at

Barton Park by hearty Sir John, reserved, children-absorbed Lady Middleton and her mother, the cheerful, gossipy Mrs Jennings.

Colonel Brandon, a reserved older man, loves Marianne. She loves the charming Mr Willoughby whom she has encountered when slipping on an outing with her sister. Willoughby somewhat improperly shows her over Allenham which he expects to inherit from his relative Mrs Smith. A social engagement is interrupted by the Colonel's urgent, unexplained removal to London. Marianne is bereft when Willoughby abruptly departs. Edward Ferrars appears but is strangely confused and despondent; he has been visiting a former tutor. Mrs Jennings' pregnant daughter Charlotte and her discourteous husband come and go to be replaced at Barton Park by the two Miss Steeles. Lucy Steele confides to Elinor, with the latter's sworn secrecy, that Edward is engaged to her - the tutor he has been visiting is her uncle. Elinor bears her loss quietly while Marianne is increasingly distraught over hers.

Mrs Jennings is going to London to be with Charlotte and takes Elinor and Marianne with her. Marianne cannot get any communication from Willoughby but finally encounters him at a ball, is snubbed and subsequently receives a cruel terminating letter from him. Colonel Brandon tells Elinor about Willoughby's unworthiness. Brandon was raised with an orphaned relative Eliza whom he loved. Rich Eliza is to be unhappily married to Brandon's brother at her guardian uncle's insistence but her planned elopement with Brandon is betrayed by a maid and Brandon is sent away. Returning from his regiment in India some years later he traces Eliza: she has divorced, had a life of sin and has borne a child "from her first guilty connection", also Eliza, whom she bestows upon Brandon on her deathbed. Eliza was sent to a school but was equally as lively as her mother and was productively impregnated by Willoughby. Colonel Brandon perforce had a duel with Willoughby in which neither was wounded; Eliza and her baby were rescued and removed to the countryside by Colonel Brandon. This intelligence does not enliven the inconsolable Marianne: "She felt the loss of Willoughby's character yet more heavily than she had felt the loss of his heart."

Edward's engagement to Lucy is opposed by his sharpish sister Fanny and his plain nasty mother Mrs Ferrars who wants him to marry a rich Miss Morton. Despite Mrs Ferrars' determination to cut him off from his fortune as the elder son if he marries Lucy, he persists with his engagement out of honour if not of love. He is cut off and his brother Robert is elevated as heir and favoured son. Colonel Brandon respects Edward's decency and offers him via Elinor the "living" of Delaford, his country location. Charlotte Palmer having given birth, the Palmers, the Dashwood girls and Mrs Jennings all go to Cleveland, the Palmers' place in Somersetshire, 80 miles from Barton and 30 miles from Willoughby at Combe Magna. Marianne falls seriously ill. The futile doctor Mr Harris attends and as the illness worsens, Colonel Brandon is sent off to fetch Mrs Dashwood from Barton. Summoned by the noise of a carriage from her sister's bedside, Elinor rushes downstairs to encounter Willoughby. He explains his conduct to Elinor. Mrs Smith of Allenham had heard of Willoughby's impregnation of Eliza II but her offer to restore him in her favour if he married her was declined. He therefore decamped to London and became engaged to the rich Miss Sophia Grey. Miss Grey discovered the Marianne attachment through her letter and dictated Willoughby's cruel letter of termination. On learning of Marianne's illness he had rushed over to Cleveland. He still loves Marianne but she is lost for ever.

On their return to Barton Cottage, Marianne recovers her health and spirits and becomes more resolved, dignified and occupied. A servant Thomas brings the intelligence that he has seen Mr. Ferrars and his new bride in the locality on their way to Mr Pratt (Miss Lucy's uncle) at Plymouth and that the handsome Miss Lucy, now Mrs Ferrars, has spoken to him at length (and in our hindsight most deceptively). Elinor maintains her forbearance and Marianne has hysterics. When Edward appears Elinor inquires after "Mrs Ferrars" -

no, not his mother but "Mrs Edward Ferrars" - and then Edward reveals that it is Robert who has married Lucy. Elinor can control herself no longer - she almost rushes from the room and bursts into tears of joy. Elinor marries Edward and they remove to Delaford parsonage, Mrs Ferrars having re-admitted him as a son and given him 10,000 pounds. Robert remains her favourite on 1,000 pounds a year. Marianne through her frequent visits to Delaford eventually marries Colonel Brandon.

Analysis of Sense and Sensibility: Sense and Sensibility goes further than any other Jane Austen novel in actually giving a voice to the common folk. While natural-born Henrietta of Emma does talk after a fashion, for most of the novel we are assured that she is a daughter of a gentleman and is certainly schooled and treated as such. Only at the end of the novel do we discover that she has been an unwitting social contaminant. While her "common" suitor Mr Martin, a farmer, pens a letter that "would not have disgraced a gentleman", we find later that Mr. Knightley has composed it for his tenant farmer. In Sense and Sensibility, Thomas, the mere man-servant of Mrs Dashwood at Barton Cottage is not only named but is permitted an extensive verbatim account of his encounter and conversation with Mrs Ferrars (née Steele) at Exeter that runs to 3 pages.

Other servants and maids have an anonymous existence in the novel but some of these "common folk" have a more critical role in the story than that of Thomas, who is simply the vehicle for transmitting a farcical misapprehension engendered by the mischievous deceit of Lucy, the new Mrs Robert Ferrars. Thus when Elinor wants to find out where Marianne has been with Willoughby "she had actually made her own woman inquire of Mr. Willoughby's groom, and that she had by that method been informed that they had gone to Allenham". In Colonel Brandon's tale of Willoughby's infamy, a servant intervenes critically to destroy his life with Eliza: "We were within a few hours of eloping together for Scotland. The treachery, or the folly, of my cousin's maid betrayed us". Many years later, in searching for a servant he discovers his cousin Eliza: "Regard for a former servant of my own, who had since fallen into misfortune, carried me to visit him in a spunging house, where he was confined for debt; and there, in the same house, under a similar confinement, was my unfortunate sister." [Note again the unabashed consanguinariousness!]

Some estimate of the value of servants is indicated by the fact that Mrs Dashwood has an income of only 500 pounds a year and yet "Her wisdom, too, limited the number of their servants to three - two maids and a man, with whom they were speedily provided from amongst those who had formed their establishment at Norland". When Willoughby offers Marianne a horse for riding, the need for a groom is readily accepted:

"As to an additional servant, the expense would be a trifle".

While Sense and Sensibility is less Naval and Military than some of the other novels (e.g. Northanger Abbey, Mansfield Park, Pride and Prejudice, Persuasion and The Watsons) it is certainly the Austen novel most explicitly and intrinsically linked to the affairs of the East India Company and Warren Hastings in India. Colonel Brandon has served in a regiment in the East Indies and this experience is amplified in the following exchange between Marianne and Willoughby in which they are discussing the "neither lively nor young" Colonel Brandon:

"Willoughby asserts that "he has always answered my inquiries with the readiness of good-breeding and good nature." "That is to say," cried Marianne contemptuously,"he has told you that in the East Indies the climate is hot, and the mosquitoes are troublesome." "He would have told me so, I doubt not, had I made any such inquiries; but they happened to be points on which I had been previously informed". "Perhaps," said Willoughby," his observations have extended to the existence of nabobs, gold mohrs, and palanquins." [24] [A "gold mohr" is like a gold sovereign - indeed my Indian wife wears a "mor-hurr" impressed with George V on a gold chain around her neck.]

The connections between Warren Hastings and India in this novel extend to the names, conduct and locations of some of the characters. While "Middleton" is the name of the Austens' neighbour at Chawton who rented Chawton House from Edward Knight (née Austen), it is also the name of Warren Hastings' associates in Bengal, the brothers Samuel and Nathaniel Middleton. Nathaniel Middleton was involved in the outrages against the famous Begums (Muslim princesses) of Oudh, their eunuchs, the ladies of their zenana and their treasury that were the most celebrated of Hastings' infamies paraded at the impeachment proceedings (at which Nathaniel Middleton testified). [25] John Middleton was the second-in-command to James Lancaster on the first East India Company expedition and Henry Middleton commanded the second such expedition. [26] Willoughby was the family name of Cassandra Brydges (née Willoughby), wife of James Brydges (the first Duke of Chandos and Jane Austen's great-great uncle ancestor). Cassandra Willoughby's stepfather was Sir Josiah Child, a Governor of the East India Company. [27] A long bow can be drawn about the name of Colonel Brandon himself: he is a "nabob" or a wealthy returned East India man. [28] Jane was fond of charades and word games (see Emma in particular) and the reverse of Brandon, nodnarb, and its anagrams, nardnob, narbnod, nnarbod, narbodn, nnardob and nardobn come close to nabob. Colonel Brandon has set himself up nicely in Somerset at Delaford House and the great dream of Warren Hastings was to re-acquire and restore the family home at Daylesford in Worcestershire - a dream he realized on his return to England despite the huge expenses incurred by his impeachment. The close friendship of Middleton and Colonel Brandon is mirrored in the loyal association of Nathaniel Middleton and Warren Hastings. [29]

The Colonel Brandon-Warren Hastings connection gains greater solidity when one considers the tragic tale of the 2 Elizas. We have already seen that Hastings is very likely to have had an affair with

Jane's aunt Mrs Philadelphia Hancock (née Austen) and fathered Eliza. Brandon has an affair with a to-be-married woman, namely his brother's wife-to-be Eliza I. The second Eliza, Eliza II, comes from "the first guilty connection" of Eliza I which one supposes could indeed be Brandon prior to their sprung elopement. Philadelphia / Eliza I and Eliza / Eliza II are rather lively women. Both Philadelphia and Eliza I die prematurely (cancer and consumption, respectively) and both Eliza and Eliza II are left with an infant without a father (through the guillotine and desertion, respectively). [30] The duel between Brandon and Willoughby may indeed be a reflection of the famous duel between Hastings and his intractable enemy Philip Francis in Calcutta (1780) in which the latter was wounded but survived to resume his active animosity against Hastings in Bengal and in England. [31]

A final intriguing connection: Hastings had an affair with Baroness Imhoff, the wife of the painter Baron Imhoff. If connecting oneself with the romance of a noble, globe-travelling painter is sensibility, then subsequently marrying one of the most celebrated and wealthy men of the world shows sense. The Baron and the Baroness were divorced amicably, allowing the Baroness to marry Hastings (although it appears that Hastings used his influence to have the cuckolded husband removed from the East Indies). Just as Colonel Brandon finally takes his Marianne to Delaford, so Warren Hastings took Mrs Anna Maria Chapuset "Marian" Hastings home to Daylesford. [32]

Jane Austen provides an intriguing insight in a letter to Cassandra (15 September 1815): "And Mr. Hastings! I am quite delighted with what such a man writes about it [Pride and Prejudice]. Henry sent him the books after his return from Daylesford, but you will hear the letter too... I heard Edward last night pressing Henry to come to Gm [Godmersham], & I think Henry engaged to go there after his November collection. Nothing has been done as to S & S. The books came to hand too late for him to have time for it, before he went. Mr.

Hastings never <u>hinted</u> at Eliza in the smallest degree ... I long to have you hear Mr. H.'s opinion of P & P. His admiring my Elizabeth is particularly welcome to me." [33]

6.6. Pride and Prejudice (1812) [34]

Kind but paternally indulgent Mr Bennet and his silly, talkative wife Mrs Bennet have 2 sensible older daughters, articulate Elizabeth (Lizzie) and demure Jane, as well as 2 younger, silly, flirtatious daughters, Lydia and Kitty, and a serious youngest daughter, Mary. Mr Bingley rents nearby Netherfield Park and arrives with his 2 nasty sisters (one of them married) and extremely wealthy but reserved Mr Darcy of Pemberley. At a local ball Bingley dances with Jane, but Darcy offends the Bennet connections by dancing only with the Bingley sisters and Lizzie overhears him declining Bingley's suggestion to dance with her. They meet subsequently at the Lucas ball with the Bingley-Jane connection strengthening but with Lizzie responding proudly to Darcy. Jane is invited to dine at Netherfield but cannot go by carriage, rides there, catches cold and has to stay there abed. Lizzie walks over, muddying her petticoats and provoking the Bingley sisters' scorn. Lizzy stays to care for Jane and verbally fences with the sisters and Darcy.

Simultaneously pompous and sycophantic cleric Mr Collins is heir to the Bennet estate, which is entailed, and proposes to marry Jane to resolve this family difficulty. Alerted by Mrs Bennet to the Bingley-Jane affection, he shifts his attention to Lizzie. Lydia and Kitty are excited by the arrival of a regiment at nearby Meryton where Lizzie meets an officer, Wickham, and observes the coldness of Darcy towards him. Wickham indicates that Darcy has refused to fulfil the obligations toward him made by Darcy's late father. Bingley gives a ball at Netherfield at which Wickham is not present. Jane dances with Bingley, Lizzie spars with Darcy and Mrs Bennet and her younger daughters are variously embarrassing. The next day Collins proposes to Lizzie who says no to the consternation of Mrs Bennet and the pleasure of Mr Bennet. Collins then successfully proposes to Lizzie's plain friend Charlotte Lucas.

The Bingleys depart for London to be followed by Jane who stays with her aunt and uncle, the friendly and perceptive Gardiners. Miss Bingley pays one frosty visit in London, alluding to a possible Bingley connection with Darcy's sister Georgiana, but there is no visit from Bingley. Mrs Gardiner warns Lizzie against Wickham who has made some kind of attachment to a plain girl who has inherited 10,000 pounds. Lizzie is invited by Collins and Charlotte to the Hunsford Parsonage on the Rosings estate of Collins' patron, the arrogant and nasty Lady Catherine de Bourgh, to and about whom Collins is revoltingly sycophantic. Lady Catherine has a delicate young daughter. Mr Darcy and his cousin Colonel Fitzwilliam stay at Rosings and there is much traffic between Rosings and the Parsonage. Fitzwilliam tells Lizzie that Darcy has been able to scotch some unfortunate alliance involving his friend Bingley. Mortified and angry, Lizzie pleads indisposition to excuse herself from the latest Rosings occasion and stays back at the Parsonage, only to receive a visit from an exquisitely uncomfortable Darcy. His ardently meant but clumsily expressed proposal is comprehensively rejected and Lizzie tasks him about his treatment of Jane and Wickham and for his ungentlemanly behaviour (the worst cut of all). The next day Darcy gives her a letter that admits and accounts for his scotching of a Bingley-Jane marriage (citing the gross behaviour of her family and Jane's demureness having been interpreted as lack of enthusiasm). The letter also describes Wickham's dishonesty, profligacy and attempted seduction of Georgiana. Lizzie is partly convinced.

Lizzie and Jane return home. The regiment has left for Brighton and Lizzie and Jane decide to keep Wickham's misdeeds unreported since he is now gone. Lydia is invited to stay with an officer's wife at Brighton and is permitted to do so by Mr Bennet against Lizzie's advice. Lizzie goes on a tour of Derbyshire with the Gardiners. They take in Darcy's magnificent palace Pemberley, Darcy is praised by the housekeeper and to their surprise Darcy returns unexpectedly early. He is solicitous to the Gardiners, Mr Gardiner is invited to fish on the estate and all are invited to tea where Lizzie meets Georgiana and fends off the nasty Bingley sisters. A further invitation is cancelled in a tearful meeting with Darcy when a note from Jane describes Wickham's elopement with Lydia. Lizzie returns home and the Gardiners repair to London.

A letter from Mr Gardiner brings good news to the Bennets: the couple have been found, they have married, Wickham has been transferred to a northern regiment, Wickham's debts have been paid and a financial settlement arrived at for the marriage. The couple visit and Lydia lets slip that Darcy was at the wedding. Mrs Gardiner confirms that Darcy was responsible for everything. Bingley returns to Netherfield and the Bingley-Jane affair is on again. Lady Catherine visits for an intemperate hectoring of Lizzie about Darcy having been promised to Miss de Bourgh. Lizzie refuses to undertake not to marry Darcy. Darcy hears of this from Lady Catherine and returns. Lizzie's thanks to Darcy for his interventions preface a course to wedded bliss.

Analysis of Pride and Prejudice: Common social reality intrudes minimally into this delicious novel. We have the reminder of the on-going war with France in the arrival of the regiment and its subsequent re-location to Brighton. Jane cannot take a carriage and rides a horse over to Netherfield (and thence gets drenched and takes ill) because the farm labourers are taking in the harvest and cannot be disturbed in the process. The power and irresistable charm of this novel lies in the dignity, self-possession and wit of the deliciously articulate Lizzie living in a world in which women are at an enormous disadvantage. It is also a determinedly honest novel: thus for all her proud intelligence, Lizzie concedes the very real temptation of the wonderful world of Pemberley. Of immediate relevance to the moral thrust of the present disquisition is the lesson deriving from the failure of Lizzie and Jane to reveal Wickham's misdeeds - history ignored yields history repeated.

6.7. Mansfield Park (1813)[35]

Sir Thomas Bertram is the master of Mansfield Park and has an elder son, fun-loving Tom, a younger son, dignified, responsible Edmond, and 2 daughters Maria and Julia. One of Lady Bertram's sisters marries Reverend Norris and the other marries well below her station to a Marine, Mr Price of Portsmouth, and has a horde of children including our heroine Fanny. When Reverend Norris dies, a penny-conscious, self-interested Mrs Norris lives on nearby but has much to do with Mansfield Park. She encourages Sir Thomas to foster Fanny but in the event declines to participate in her care. Fanny arrives and leads a subdued life, missing her brother William and being subordinate to everybody. Edmond is very kind to her and Fanny becomes the companion of Lady Bertram. Sir Thomas goes off to Antigua to fix up his estate problems. Henry Crawford and his sister Mary come to stay with their half-sister Mrs Grant, the wife of the gluttonous Reverend Grant, the local vicar.

Maria is engaged to dull, rich Mr Rushworth of Sotherton Court, Julia is interested in Henry, Henry in Maria and Mary in Tom until he leaves and thence in Edmond. On a trip to Sotherton Court Fanny sees Maria go off in the gardens with Henry and Rushworth and Julia are jealous. Mary is frankly contemptuous of Edmond's plans for being a cleric. Tom returns with his friend Yates and a theatrical performance is planned to which Mrs Norris assents. Moralistic Fanny and Edmond disapprove but Edmund is persuaded to play opposite Mary and they practise before Fanny. A carpenter decorates Sir Thomas' office and in the middle of a rehearsal Sir Thomas returns and puts a stop to it all. Maria marries Rushworth for his money and they leave for Brighton with Julia.

Mary oscillates with Edmond and Henry sets on Fanny. Fanny's brother William was formerly started in the Navy with the help of Sir Thomas and comes to stay. A ball is given for Fanny and William at which Fanny wears William's present of a cross on a chain provided by Edmond rather than the one impressed on her by Mary, a gift from Henry and which does not accomodate the cross. Henry goes to London with William and on return explains that he has introduced William to his uncle the Admiral and thereby secured his promotion to lieutenant. Fanny is conscious of Henry's fickleness and looseness and rejects his proposals, despite the earnest intervention of kindly Sir Thomas and of Mary. The Crawfords return to London and Fanny is sent to Portsmouth to stay with her own family so that she can see the real world and appreciate the consequences of her indulgence in rejecting Henry.

At Portsmouth Fanny sees her "awful" mother and father, siblings, slatternly servant and dirty, crowded abode. In addition to William (who is at sea), a further salvageable sibling is Susan. A letter from Mary mentions a Yates-Julia affair, Henry visits and Edmond writes but is still concerned by Mary's unsoundness. Lady Bertram writes and advises of Tom's illness borne of his gay life. Events now move quickly: Mary writes and outrageously implies that Tom's demise would solve her problem with Edmond as a cleric for he would then be master of Mansfield Park rather than the Rector at nearby Thornton Lacy. Mary writes again urging Fanny to reject a dreadful rumour. However the rumour turns out to be true: Henry has run away with Maria and Julia has eloped with Yates. In the wash-up Edmond spurns Mary who takes Henry's crime too lightly; Henry leaves Maria who is divorced by Rushworth and goes to live in disgrace with Mrs Norris; Julia marries Yates; Tom recovers. Edmond and Fanny finally declare their love and marry and Susan takes her place as Lady Bertram's companion.

Analysis of Mansfield Park: The most sexual and titillating of the novels, Mansfield Park allows a glimpse of the real world of people as biological entities e.g. Maria's liaison in the gardens at Sotherton, the play-part pairings, Maria's attraction for Henry and subsequent flagrant flight and adultery and the elopement of Julia. However the most powerful passion in all of this is the extraordinary flowering of essentially consanguinous love between Fanny and Edmund, the two most constrained, upright and "sound" of the characters. Jane Austen is surprisingly quite comfortable with what amounts to a translation of brother-sister love to realisable first cousin marriage. Such realised or considered connections between first cousins occurred in Jane's immediate family as with Eliza Hancock-James Austen and Eliza Hancock-Henry Austen and among her forbears as with John Austen-Mary Stringer and James Brydges-Cassandra Willoughby. It is worth reiterating that the suit of James Austen for Eliza Hancock was not realised because of her contempt for his clerical plans that is reflected precisely in the attitudes of Mary Crawford. The subsequent non-consanguinous marriage of Jane's nephew Edward Knight to her niece Fanny Knight's step-daughter Mary Dorothea Knatchbull had this quality as indeed in a more remote sense did Francis Austen's second marriage to Martha Lloyd who had lived with Jane, Cassandra and Mrs. Austen for so long (including several years with Francis and Mary and the Austen women at Southampton).

In addition to the inevitable shadowy servants and the carpenter, we now actually get to see the awfulness of people and their dingy lives at the bottom of the servant-retaining barrel, the world of Fanny's real family at Portsmouth. Implicit in the novel are greater realities as well: the Antigua estates, no doubt worked by slaves from Africa, and the naval realities of Portsmouth, Mr Price, William and the Admiral. George Austen acted as an agent for Antiguan estates and variously made representations to his family connections Warren Hastings and Admiral Gambier on behalf of his naval sons Francis and Charles. [36] This novel certainly has the most "social realism" of all of Jane Austen's works with the intrusions of advanced London attitudes, the Navy, Antiguan estates, the opportunity for prolonged physical intimacy in the Sotherton gardens, the awful lives of the lower gentry, the indulgence of young men, adultery, elopement and brotherly-sisterly love leading to consanguinous physical passion. However even a rude 20th century Antipodean fellow such as myself is taken aback by Mary Crawford's assertion about her familiarity with Admirals:

"Certainly, my home at my uncle's brought me acquainted with a circle of admirals. Of Rears, and Vices, I saw enough. Now, do not be suspecting me of a pun, I entreat." [37]

6.8. Emma (1815)[38]

Emma Woodhouse (about 20) lives with her widowed, ageing father at Hartfield. Her sister Isabella has married Mr John Knightley and her former governess, Miss Taylor, has married Mr Weston. Mr John Knightley's brother, Mr George Knightley (mid-30s), is a friend of Emma and her father. Mr Knightley disapproves of Emma's claims to have "matched" Miss Taylor with Mr. Weston and is angry when Emma is involved in the rejection of the proposal of farmer Robert Martin by her young friend Harriet. Harriet has stayed at the Martins' farm with Mrs Martin, her son Robert and his sisters. Knightley is particularly annoyed since he helped to compose the letter of Martin, who is his tenant at Abbey-Mill Farm. Harriet is the "natural born" daughter of a presumed gentleman and is being schooled by Mrs Goddard in her establishment in the nearby village of Highbury. Emma plans a match between Reverend Elton and Harriet. After a dinner at the Westons, Emma occupies a carriage home with Elton who makes a passionate proposal which she rejects. Elton subsequently marries a snooty lady from Bath.

Emma has as local acquaintances old Mrs Bates, her exceptionally talkative daughter Miss Bates and Mrs Bates' orphaned grand-daughter Jane Fairfax. Jane has been brought up by Colonel Campbell. However the Colonel is visiting relatives in Ireland and his daughter has married Mr Dixon. Jane Fairfax, who has come to stay with her grandmother, is accomplished but reserved. Mr Weston has a son, Frank Churchill, by his now-deceased former wife and who has been adopted by her parents. Everybody is in anticipation of his first ever visit to his father and all are charmed when he arrives. He visits Jane, having met her previously, but excites comment when he goes to London to get his hair cut. At a party given by the lesser gentry the

Coles, Knightley brings Miss Bates and Jane. Mrs Weston and Emma speculate about a possible Knightley-Jane match - Emma disapproves because this would threaten the inheritance of the Isabella-John Knightley offspring. Jane Fairfax receives a piano from an unknown benefactor - Emma fantasizes to Frank Churchill that it may be a token of illicit love from Mr Dixon, newly married to Miss Campbell. A ball is held at the local inn at which Elton snubs Harriet but Knightley is promptly gallant. The following day Harriett is rescued from importuning gypsies by Frank. Harriet subsequently disposes of some mementos of Mr Elton and Emma starts contemplating a Frank-Harriet connection. However a Frank-Emma possibility emerges for the prescient reader.

A day-time affair is held at Knightley's Donwell Abbey (cf Stoneleigh Abbey) at which the guests eat fresh strawberries from the field. Jane Fairfax is pestered by remorselessly nosey Mrs Elton about taking up a governess position and eventually walks home. Frank turns up late and an outing is fixed for the morrow on Box Hill. On that occasion Frank is very friendly with Emma who is very rude to the dreadfully loquacious Miss Bates. Tasked by Knightley, Emma drops by at the Bates' next day to make amends for her rudeness. However there is fuss and delay before she is admitted: Jane Fairfax is ill and cannot be disturbed. However Miss Bates adverts to Jane's intended departure as a governess.

Frank has returned home because of the illness of Mrs. Churchill which soon translates to her demise. Emma speculates further on a Frank-Harriet connection. Her further attentions to the sick Jane Fairfax are declined. Finally the dénouement: Mrs. Weston explains to Emma that Frank has been secretly engaged to Jane Fairfax and that the death of his possessive foster-mother has permitted marriage to poor but beautiful Jane. The odd behaviour of Jane and Frank at Donwell and afterwards arose from a lover's tiff. Emma dispels the Westons' concerns that she has been attached to Frank. Emma tells Harriet and discovers that Harriet is not attached to Frank either but evidently likes Knightley for his gallantry. Emma speaks to Knightley of the Frank-Jane affair and of her lack of attachment to Frank. Knightley declares his love for Emma. Emma writes to Harriet to break the news but her concerns are misplaced. Harriet, who has gone to London, has now accepted farmer Martin and it transpires that her father is a tradesman. Mr Woodhouse is unhappy about losing his daughter but a spate of robberies in the area convinces him of the benefits of having a son-in-law at Hartfield.

Analysis of Emma: Emma is an honest but offending book that portrays the unwise fantasies, patronising match-making and social snobbery of the heroine. In Jane Austen's own words:

"I am going to take a heroine whom no one but myself will much like." [39]

Indeed Jane herself played these games in the sense of parlour speculation. Thus she writes in a letter to Cassandra (1 October 1808) :

"Our party at Mrs. Duer's produced the novelties of two old Mrs. Pollens & Mrs. Heywood, with whom my Mother made a Quadrille Table; & of Mrs. Maitland & Caroline, & Mr. Booth without his sisters at Commerce. - I have got a Husband for each of the Miss Maitlands; - Coln Powlett & his Brother have taken Argyle's inner House, & the consequence is so natural that I have no ingenuity in planning it. If the Brother shd luckily be a little sillier than the Colonel, what a treasure for Eliza." [40]

Of all Jane Austen's novels, Emma strays closest to the downside boundary of the gentry. Old Mrs. Bates, Miss Bates and Jane are gentry with little money, Jane is facing the dreadful prospect of becoming a governess (jokingly comparing the "governess-trade" with the "slave-trade" in Volume 2, Chapter 17) and Mrs Elton sprays her snobbish venom (notably at the nouveau riche Tupmans from industrial Birmingham in Volume 2, Chapter 18). Harriet is assumed to be a gentleman's natural born (out of wedlock) daughter because her education at Mrs Goddard's establishment has been generously secured. Emma disingenuously distances herself from Harriet's decision on Martin's proposal but makes it clear that an affirmative would have ended their friendship:

"While you were in the smallest degree wavering I said nothing about it because I would not influence; but it would have been the loss of a friend to me. I could not have visited Mrs. Robert Martin of Abbey-Hill Farm. Now I am secure in you for ever ... Dear affectionate creature! - You banished to Abbey-Mill Farm! - You confined to the society of the illiterate and vulgar all your life! I wonder how the young man could have the assurance to ask it. He must have a pretty good opinion of himself." [41]

When the Harriet match is finalised, the joy is enhanced by the discovery that Harriet's father is a well-off tradesman and not a gentleman after all:

"The event, however, was the most joyful, and every day was giving her fresh reason for thinking so. - Harriet's parentage became known. She proved to be the daughter of a tradesman, rich enough to afford her the comfortable maintenance which had ever been her's, and decent enough to have always wished for concealment. - Such was the blood of gentility that Emma had been so ready to vouch for! - it was likely to be as untainted, perhaps, as the blood of many a gentleman: but what a connexion had she been preparing for Mr. Knightley - or for the Churchills - or even for Mr. Elton! - The stain of illegitimacy, unbleached by nobility or wealth, would have been a stain indeed... Harriet, necessarily drawn away by her engagements with the Martins, was less and less at Hartfield: which was not to be regretted. - The intimacy between her and Emma must sink; their friendship must change into a calmer goodwill; and, fortunately, what ought to be, and must be, seemed already beginning, and in the most gradual, natural manner." [42]

Life on the downside of the social divide intrudes further with the inevitable unnamed servants, townsfolk and even a named employee, William Larkins, the manager of Mr Knightley's estate. However Jane Austen goes further: Emma actually visits the poor of the parish and we see Harriet beset by a small group of begging "gypsies" who no doubt are going to be rudely treated by the law for their impertinence. It is not clear whether these are Romany gypsies (of medieval Indian origin) or simply some of the Enclosure-generated, homeless, wretched poor of England in those times. A final surprise is encountered in Emma for the Jane Austen reader - the heroine actually attends church on no less than 2 occasions, firstly at Harriet's wedding and secondly at her own. Thus:

"Before the end of September, Emma attended Harriet to church, and saw her hand bestowed on Robert Martin with so complete a satisfaction, as no remembrances, even connected with Mr. Elton as he stood before them, could impair. - Perhaps, indeed, at that time she scarcely saw Mr. Elton but as the clergyman whose blessing at the altar might next fall on herself. - Robert Martin and Harriet Smith, the latest couple engaged of the three, were the first to be married." [43]

The novel ends with Emma's own wedding with satin and lace:

"The wedding was very much like other weddings, where the parties have no taste for finery or parade; and Mrs. Elton, from the particulars detailed by her husband, thought it all extremely shabby, and very inferior to her own. - "Very little white satin, very few lace veils; a most pitiful business! - Selina would stare when she heard of it." - But in spite of these deficiencies, the wishes, the hopes, the confidence, the predictions of the small band of true friends who witnessed the ceremony, were fully answered in the perfect happiness of the union."
[44]

These are the only occasions in Jane Austen's novels in which we are taken inside a church, this being the more surprising coming from the daughter of a clergyman and the sister to 2 others. Attendance at church, one supposes, would have represented one of the most obvious acceptable means of "boy meets girl' and certainly of "boy sees girl' and vice versa. Perhaps respect for her father, the clergy and the Church constrained Jane Austen from such a profane employment in her novels.

6.9. Persuasion (1816) [45]

Sir Walter Elliot of Kellynch Hall is widowed with 3 daughters, namely Elizabeth (29) and Anne (27) who are unmarried and a younger daughter Mary who has married Charles Musgrove. Sir Walter's expenses force him to retire to Bath and rent out Kellynch Hall to Admiral and Mrs Croft née Wentworth. Anne was once attached to Mrs Croft's brother Captain Wentworth but Lady Russell, a good friend of hers and of her father, dissuaded her from the match because of his modest finances. Lady Russell and Anne disapprove of the friendship between Elizabeth and Mrs Clay, the widowed daughter of Sir Walter's business adviser Mr Shepherd. In the event Sir Walter, Elizabeth and Mrs Clay go off to Bath.

Anne stays with Charles and Mary Musgrove at Uppercross, just down from the Great House. Anne had rejected the suit of Charles and he then turned to Mary. Mr and Mrs Musgrove have 2 daughters, Henrietta and Louisa, who live with them at the Great House. The Crofts move in to Kellynch Hall and Captain Wentworth comes to stay. He has made a modest fortune through naval victory and is now set to marry. He is interested in both Louisa and Henrietta, the latter being the object of the affection of her cousin Charles Hayter. Anne is looking after one of Mary's boys (who has had a fall) when Captain Wentworth is brought round to visit. They meet further at the Crofts' and on a long walk in the countryside with the Musgrove siblings that takes them as far as the Hayter estate. On this occasion Anne gets a lift back with the Crofts.

Captain Wentworth, Anne, Charles, Mary, Henrietta and Louisa go to Lyme Regis by the seaside where they meet Captain Harville, his wife and Captain Benwick, who was engaged to Harville's dead sister. Benwick and Anne find common ground in poetry. Anne and a handsome stranger exchange interested looks at the inn. The next day they all stroll by the sea. Louisa jumps from the stone stairs on the side of the Cobb (sea-wall) and is caught by Wentworth. However when she insists on repeating the jump, Wentworth is unprepared and Louisa falls and loses consciousness. Anne is prepared to stay to nurse Louisa but Mary insists on staying. Anne returns to stay with Lady Russell and learns of Louisa's slow recovery before she and Lady Russell go to Bath.

At Bath Anne meets her cousin Mr Elliot, who turns out to be the handsome stranger at Lyme Regis. Mr Elliot is set to inherit Kellynch Hall but has been estranged from Sir Walter. Lady Russell encourages an Anne-Elliot connection. Sir Walter and Elizabeth meet up with the wealthy Carterets. Anne visits an old friend, the now-widowed, poor and ill Mrs. Smith. Surprising news comes that Louisa is now recovered and engaged to Captain Benwick. Anne is secretly pleased that Wentworth is free. Wentworth comes to Bath and his successive meetings with Anne make her feel that it is "on" again. On their meeting at a concert with the Carterets, Anne is disappointed that Elliot's presence has kept her from Wentworth.

Mrs. Smith has heard of an Elliot-Anne connection from her nurse but when disabused of this by Anne reveals that Elliot is a cad who has helped to ruin her husband and is preventing her from recovering a modest inheritance. He has designs on Anne and is now of a mind that inheriting the title and Kellynch Hall is worth it and he is in Bath to scotch any Mrs Clay-Sir Walter connection. Charles and Mary Musgrove and the Harvilles all come to Bath and at a big gathering Anne espies Elliot, who is supposed to have gone to London, talking in the street with Mrs Clay. The following day Anne attends the Musgroves and Harvilles. With Wentworth composing a note to her in the background, Anne talks to Harville of the faith of women who keep up their love. When everyone leaves, Wentworth gives his note to Anne declaring his earnestness. Anne is much overcome and Charles Musgrove sees her home, only to be overtaken by Wentworth who takes over this charge. Mutual love is revealed and all is set for bliss. Elliot goes back to London with Mrs Clay and they may deserve each other. Anne-Wentworth, Louisa-Benwick and Hayter-Henrietta are the happy outcomes.

Analysis of Persuasion: "Reality" intrudes minimally in this novel, principally in the "Naval" sense with the Crofts, Wentworth, Harville, Benwick and the dead Musgrove lad who sailed with Wentworth. Again we have proposed or realised first cousin consanguinity as with Henrietta-Hayter, Elizabeth-Elliot and Anne-Elliot. However this is a very personal novel dealing with 2 principal characters, the former lovers Anne and Wentworth. The story is of sustained affection with shades of Jane Austen's "first love", Tom Lefroy, and the disapproval of the match by Jane's friend Mrs Lefroy. The romantic tension of the tale lies in the conduct of Anne and Wentworth with other supporting elements introduced, as in a symphony, that contribute to the sense of loss that can nevertheless be ultimately repaired.

6.10. Sanditon (unfinished; 1817) [46]

Mr and Mrs Parkers' carriage overturns and Mr Parker suffers a sprain when they travel to the "wrong" Willingden on the Sussex coast looking for a surgeon for their seaside resort Sanditon ("One mile nearer to London than Eastbourne"). They depart from the kind care of Mr and Mrs Heywood after some days and bring Charlotte Heywood with them to their resort development surrounding their Trafalgar House near the village of Sanditon. Rather mean, mercenary and extremely rich, Lady Denham (formerly a Miss Brereton) has had 2 husbands: Mr Hollis, who bequeathed her Sanditon House and a big estate and Sir Henry Denham, who left her the title. Denham's son Sir Edward, Baronet of Denham Park, and his sister, Miss Denham, are relatively poor and Lady Denham is well aware of their interest in her wealth. Edward would like to cement this interest through his courting of Lady Denham's relative and companion Miss Clara Brereton.

Mr Parker's lively and good-looking young brother Sidney and his somewhat hypochondriac further siblings Arthur, Susan and the rather pointlessly busy Diane turn up at Sanditon. Diane believes she has through a gossipy process secured two sets of visitors for the resort. In the event there is actually one party rather than two: Mrs Griffiths, who runs a finishing school at Camberwell, arrives with 3 charges, the wealthy West Indian Miss Lambe, "half mulatto, chilly and tender", and the two Miss Beauforts. Charlotte discusses poetry and literature with the rather flowery Sir Edward and observes his careful attendance on Clara Brereton. Charlotte eventually gets to see Sanditon House.

Analysis of Sanditon: All was set for another interesting social and conversational collage but Jane Austen's illness intervened. As with The Watsons, a "finished" version of Sanditon has been devised and published. The unfinished Sanditon has a rather modern, "real estate and resort development" feel about it and the existence of a lot of ordinary human beings is adverted: servants, harvesters (men, women and children), fishermen, shopkeepers, farmers, cottage renters, teachers, physicians, a surgeon, a vegetable gardener and even a librarian, Mrs Whitby. Jane Austen's worsening, unameliorated illness at the time of the writing of Sanditon provides empirical justification for Lady Denham's indignant speech on doctors:

"Lord! my dear sir," she cried, "how could you think of such a thing? I am very sorry you met with your accident, but upon my word you deserved it. - Going after a doctor! - Why, what should we do with a doctor here? It would only be encouraging our servants and the poor to fancy themselves ill, if there was a doctor at hand. - Oh! pray, let us have none of the tribe at Sanditon. We go on very well as we are. There is the sea and the downs and my milch-asses - and I have told

Mrs Whitby that if anybody enquires for a chamber-horse, they may be supplied at a fair rate - (poor Mr. Hollis's chamber-horse, as good as new) - and what can people want for more? - Here I have lived seventy good years in the world and never took a physic above twice - and never saw the face of a doctor in all my life, on my own account. - And I verily believe if my poor dear Sir Harry had never seen one neither, he would have been alive now. - Ten fees, one after the other, did the man take who sent him out of the world. - I beseech you Mr. Parker, no doctors here." [47]

Some particular medical protocols were clearly effective (e.g. Jane Austen's friend Mrs Anne Lefroy inoculated about a thousand of the poor with Dr. Jenner's vaccine). [48] However medical intervention only became really effective as a whole from about the mid-20th century onwards with the discovery of antibiotics. [49] Cartwright (1977) has provided statistics on the growth of the population of England plus Wales from the Middle Ages that can be summarized as follows: 1300 (4 million); 1377 (2.1 million, the fall being due to the Black Death of the bubonic plague); 1700 (5 million, it having taken several hundred years to recover from the effects of the Black Death); 1851 (18 million); 1876 (23 million); 1900 (32 million). In seeking an explanation for the extraordinary increase in population in the 18th and 19th centuries (a matter which also concerned Malthus), [50] Cartwright (1977) finds that this cannot be explained in terms of the modest decreases in infant mortality due to better medical practice: "We cannot therefore accept Professor Trevelyan's opinion that population growth "was due mainly to improved medical service" and must look for some other explanation". His explanation relates to agricultural progress and in particular the growing of crops for winter feed for livestock (that would previously have been slaughtered, dressed and salted down). He concludes: "Some fresh meat, larger supply of vegetables, and more milk in winter may have reduced the childhood rather than the infant mortality". [51]

Of course the greatly increased urbanization of Britain in the 18th and 19th century associated with the Enclosures and the Industrial Revolution meant that survival for the vast body of urban poor involved purchase of requisite food. The engine of the Industrial Revolution, and hence a key financial support for the urban populace, was the cotton-based textile industry. Before British conquest in the mid-18th century, Bengal was a rich, sophisticated and populous country with agriculture based heavily on rice production and an urban industry that led the world in cotton-based textile manufacture. We will see in Chapter 13 how this prosperous land was rapaciously exploited and great swathes reduced to wasteland through appalling, exploitation-linked famine. The textile industry was destroyed and Bengal effectively became an agararian economy devoted to production of cotton, jute, indigo and opium in addition to rice. The former leading textile manufacturer of the world became a raw cotton producer for Britain and the bare-subsistence Bengalis became a captive market for British cloth. [52]

We have seen that the ugly realities of wider society did not intrude into Jane Austen's novels. Nevertheless colonial operations do intrude significantly (if inexplicitly) as a background of necessary activity for the fortune of society. Thus Sir Thomas Bertram is compelled to leave the pleasures of Mansfield Park to address the problems of his West Indies estates, the custom of a wealthy West Indian is important for Sanditon and many of Jane Austen's characters are involved in the defence of overseas interests against the French. Colonel Brandon is a nabob who has made his fortune in the East Indies and it is that wealth which has created Delaford (Daylesford) and enables a happy and prosperous conclusion in Sense and Sensibility, Jane Austen's "Indian" novel.

6.11. Some conclusions concerning Jane Austen's art

Jane Austen's novels dealt with a very limited aspect (courtship and marriage suitability) of the lives of a very small minority of the

English population, the prosperous gentlefolk. However just as a single painting or a piece of music can be profound while being necessarily confined in material substance, so each of her novels has both emotional and technical depth. In construction, economy of word and flashes of elegance her novels can be seen to be related to great painting and music, in which there is also an orderly underlying scaffolding, technical competence and transfixing, exquisite elements. The charm, universality and popularity of Jane Austen's work lies in the apparent domestic simplicity of her stories and the self-possession of her heroines that capture the hearts of her readers. The genius of her work lies in the literary construction and the elegant use of language.

If I were to find a popular cultural equivalent to Jane Austen's novels in our complicated, sophisticated modern world I could suggest top-class women's tennis - a game circumscribed by a restricted locus, well-defined rules and the authority of the umpire and linesmen, but providing an absorbing experience for the audience through the genius of the players. Pushed well into the background there is also a lot of money involved. A metaphorical and indeed artistic element is provided by the differences in style, focus and personality of the players: the cheerful, good-humoured self-possession of teenage Swiss Martina Hingis (readily relatable to the best of Jane Austen's heroines), the determined self-control of South African Amanda Coetzer, the Gallic intensity of Mary Pierce, the brilliant resolve of German Steffi Graf or the furious vigour of Spanish Aranxe Sanchez Vicario. The absorption lies in the fluctuating fortunes, the battle of wills and temperament, the skill and the flashes of sheer brilliance.

If I were to find an equivalent in painting I could suggest the work of Vermeer (1632-1675), his beautifully constructed scenes of civilized, gentle domesticity, charm and placid warmth being rendered unforgettable by the powerful and faithful use of light. Of immediate relevance to the substance of Jane Austen's life and work are Vermeer's domestic paintings of young women, and in particular those works in which women are reading letters or writing. [53] A musical equivalent might well be the work of Mozart in which there is again powerful scaffolding, technical genius and flashes of exceptional beauty that grip the listener. Indeed the construction of Jane Austen's novels has been previously related to that of works by Mozart. [54] In all three - Austen, Vermeer and Mozart - there is also a confident simplicity and lack of pomposity or pretension that make for universal appreciation.

It would be a mistake to dismiss Jane Austen's work as socially irrelevant or a-political. Her self-possessed heroines are all in vulnerable social positions and in the background there are obvious economic realities that will constrain their actions. Nevertheless her articulate heroines survive through dignity, intelligence and the powerful use of language. In this sense Jane Austen's work is feminist but all of humanity can benefit from the moral lessons of her art. No matter what our place in the world, we are all empowered by the dignified, intelligent and articulate use of words.

6.12. 2008 Postscript

An even more careful analysis of quantitative times (months and years) repeatedly referred to in Sense and Sensibility in relation to the Eliza I and Eliza II story reveals remarkable consistency with the hypothesis of Brandon as the father of Eliza II, this in turn clearly suggesting that Jane Austen was actually very cleverly saying that Hastings was indeed the actual father of her cousin Eliza Hancock. Thus, for example, in Chapter 31 Brandon says that Eliza II was "about three years old" after he returns to England "nearly three years after this unhappy period" (of discovered elopement, Brandon's "banishment" to a "distant relation" and hence "the East Indies" and Eliza's marriage to Brandon's brother when his "father's point was gained") and a further "six months" after this return and actually discovering Eliza I and Eliza II – all consistent with Brandon as father and a gestation period of 9 months. In Chapter 8 we are told that Brandon is 35 and in Chapter 31 that Eliza II is 18; Chapter 31 further tells us that Brandon and Eliza were "nearly the same" age and Eliza I was 17 when she was forced into marriage with his brother – further consistency with Brandon as the father of Eliza II. Indeed Brandon states thus of his "guardianship" of Eliza II: "I called her a distant relation; but I am well aware that I have in general been suspected of a much nearer connection with her". In Catherine or The Bower, (see p22, Chapter 3), Jane Austen's first attempt at telling the Warren Hastings/Aunt Philadelphia story, the name Cecilia (patron saint of music) is used rather than Philadelphia (lover of the Delphic i.e. lover of music and poetry) and Mrs Philadelphia Hancock (Hancock meaning "having cock" i.e. having game) becomes Mrs Cecilia Lascelles (Lascelles being the name of the Earl of Harewood, with "harewood" also implying part of an estate "having game"). I subsequently published other accounts of Sense and Sensibility as a thinly disguised account of the Hastings paternity of Jane Austen's cousin Eliza. [55] The last paragraph of this chapter is acutely relevant in 2008 as the mainstream media, politicians and academics of the Western Murdochracies continue to ignore the horrendous human cost of the ongoing Iraqi Genocide and Afghan Genocide (as of 2008, post-invasion excess deaths total 2 million and 3-7 million, respectively; post-invasion under-5 infant deaths total 0.6 million and 2.3 million, respectively; and refugees total 4.5 million and 4 million, respectively). Yet apart from myself, as far as I know the only writers on Earth (population 6.6 billion) actually referring to the Iraqi Holocaust and/or the Iraqi Genocide are Dr Mark Weissbrot (Just Foreign Policy), Dr Paul Craig Roberts (Father of Reaganomics), John Pilger (outstanding Australian-UK writer) and Tariq Ali (outstanding Pakistani-UK writer) and, apart from myself, the only scholar referring to the Afghan Genocide is top US law academic Professor Ali Khan. [56]

Chapter 7

The sensibility of Jane Austen's literary contemporaries

"Nay, mama, if he is not to be animated by Cowper! - but we must allow for differences of taste. Elinor has not my feelings, and therefore she may overlook it, and be happy with him. But it would have broke my heart had I loved him, to hear him read with so little sensibility."

- Marianne Dashwood on Edward Ferrars' being unmoved by Cowper in Sense and Sensibility (1811)[1]

"Well, Marianne," said Elinor, as soon as he had left them, "for one morning I think you have done pretty well. You have already ascertained Mr. Willoughby's opinion in almost every matter of importance. You know what he thinks of Cowper and Scott; you are certain of his estimating their beauties as he ought, and you have received every assurance of his admiring Pope no more than is proper."

- Elinor Dashwood gently mocking her sister Mariannne in Sense and Scnsibility (1811)[2]

"It is not seemly nor of good report

That thieves at home must hang, but he that puts

Into his overgorged and bloated purse

The wealth of Indian provinces, escapes."

- William Cowper in The Task (1785) [3]

7.1. The social responsiveness of Jane Austen's literary contemporaries

We have seen how Jane Austen has by and large totally ignored the great events of her time, both at home and abroad, as well as the existence of the common folk and the servants that appear to be to her world what electronic devices are to ours - unobtrusive servomechanisms for our comfort to be addressed when needed. How did Jane Austen's contemporaries respond to inhumanity applied either at home or abroad at that time? In particular, what were the responses of Jane Austen's favourite writers or other writers that she read? Living most of her life in the country, Jane Austen would have been aware of the lot of the common folk. Like her siblings she was left for some time as a baby with a local woman. It is likely that her brother George was cared for (together with his uncle Thomas Leigh) in a lowly home. She made charitable visits to the poor and must have been aware of the extraordinary wretchedness of so many ordinary people as described by George Crabbe and other contemporary poets.

7.2. George Crabbe (1754-1832) was a favourite poet of Jane Austen. Indeed Jane Austen's letter to Cassandra from Henry Austen's place at Henrietta Street, Covent Garden, London (1813) suggests that she is more than simply an enthusiastic fan (but one strongly suspects that her enthusiastic comments about Crabbe are simply a romantic joke that a young woman of today might make about a sports hero, singing idol or movie star):

"I must get a softer pen. - This one is harder. I am in agonies. - I have not yet seen Mr. Crabbe ... We had very good places in the Box next to the Stage box - front and 2d row; the three old ones behind of course. - I was particularly disappointed at seeing nothing of Mr. Crabbe. I felt sure of him when I saw that the boxes were fitted up with Crimson velvet". [4]

In letters to Cassandra from Godmersham Park (1813) she writes in the same vein:

"No; I have never seen the death of Mrs Crabbe. I have only just been making out from one of his prefaces that he probably was married. It is almost ridiculous. Poor woman! I will comfort him as well as I can, but I do not undertake to be good to her children. She had better not leave any." [5] and

"Miss Lee I found very conversable; she admires Crabbe as she ought. - She is at an age of reason, ten years older than myself at least. She was at the famous Ball at Chilham Castle, so of course you remember her. - By the bye, as I must leave off being young, I find many Douceurs in being a sort of Chaperon for I am put on the Sofa near the Fire & can drink as much wine as I like."[6]

Nevertheless, unlike his admirer Jane Austen, Crabbe was prepared to "tell it like it is" and indeed in The Borough, Letter XX he quite specifically addresses the failure of writers to describe the realities of life:

"I've often marvel'd, when by night, by day,
I've mark'd the manners moving in my way,
And heard the language and beheld the lives
Of lass and lover, goddesses and wives,
That books, which promise much of life to give,
Should show so little how we truly live."[7]

In The Village Crabbe makes the same point:
"--- paint the Cot, As Truth will paint it, and as Bards will not:"[8]

In The Borough, Letter XXII, The Poor of the Borough: Peter Grimes, Crabbe writes of a fisherman who has impoverished boys on relief in the work-house bound over to him as virtual slaves to be beaten and starved:

"Peter had heard there were in London then -
Still have they being! - workhouse-clearing men,
Who, undisturbed by feeling just or kind,
Would parish boys to needy tradesmen bind;
They in their want a trifling sum would take,
And toiling slaves of piteous orphans make.
Such Peter sought, and when a lad was found,
The sum was dealt him, and the slave was bound ...
Pinned, beaten, cold, pinched, threatened , and abused -
His efforts punished and his food refused -
Awake tormented - soon aroused from sleep -
Struck if he wept, and yet compelled to weep,
The trembling boy dropped down and strove to pray,
Received a blow, and trembling turned away,
Or sobbed and hid his piteous face; while he,
The savage master grinned in horrid glee;
He now the power he ever loved to show
A feeling being subject to his blow.
Thus lived the lad, to hunger, peril, pain,
His tears despised, his applications vain;
Compelled by fear to lie, by need to steal,
His bed uneasy and unblessed his meal,
For three sad years the boy his tortures bore,
And then his pains and trials were no more." [9]

The enclosures of formerly common land proceeded apace through her
lifetime and Jane Austen no doubt encountered the sorry consequences
of this for her humble neighbours. Poor farmers were pushed off their
land and, unable to produce food for themselves and their families, had
to work for wages that could prove insufficient when war-time
economic conditions and urban demand pushed up the price of grain.
This human tragedy was repeated again and again in the British
Empire, from the Home Counties to Scotland, from Ireland to India

and culminated in the worst of such social disasters, the man-made
Bengal Famine of 1943-44. The rural displacement of the enclosures
would have been familiar to Jane Austen. Several thousand Enclosure
Acts were enforced during her lifetime and the following anonymous
poem conveys the essential injustice:

"They hang the man and flog the woman
That steals a goose from off the common
But leave the greater criminal loose
That steals the common from the goose."[10]

7.3. Oliver Goldsmith (1730-1774) was read in the Austen home and
no doubt Jane Austen was familiar with The Deserted Village:

"Sweet Auburn! loveliest village of the plain,
Where health and plenty cheered the laboring swain,
Where smiling spring its earliest visit paid,
And parting summer's lingering blooms delayed ...
Yes! let the rich deride, the proud disdain,
These simple blessings of the lowly train,
To me more dear, congenial to my heart,
One native charm, than all the gloss of art ...
Ye friends to truth, ye statesmen, who survey
The rich man's joys increase, the poor's decay,
'Tis yours to judge how wide the limits stand
Between a splendid and a happy land ...
Even now the devastation is begun,
And half the business of destruction done;
Even now, methinks, as pondering here I stand,
I see the rural virtues leave the land ..."
and concluding with Dr. Johnson's additions:
"That Trades's proud empire hastes to swift decay,
An ocean sweeps the labored mole away;
While self-dependent power can time defy,
As rocks resist the billows and the sky."[11]

7.4. William Cowper (1731-1800), born in a rectory, was evidently a great favourite of Jane Austen and the Austen household and is mentioned in a number of her works. William Cowper was a very dear friend of Lady Anne Austen, the widow of Sir Robert Austen, Baronet [12]. The latter and the Steventon Austens had a common ancestor in John Austen of Horsmonden (1560-1620). [13] Cowper's schoolfellows at Westminster included Warren Hastings (intimately connected with the Steventon Austens) and Hastings' close friend and partner in infamy in the East Indies, Elijah Impey. Cowper recalls this in a poem written in 1792, 3 years before Hastings' acquittal of the impeachment charges, published in 1803 and dedicated "To Warren Hastings, Esq. by an old school-fellow of his at Westminster" :

"HASTINGS! I knew thee young, and of a mind,

While young, humane, conversable, and kind,

Nor can I well believe thee, gentle THEN,

Now grown a villain, and the WORST of men.

But rather some suspect, who have oppress'd

And worried thee, as not themselves the BEST." [14]

Cowper suffered fluctuations of mood that one presumes may have added to the power of his poetry but which could make life difficult for his dear friends such as Lady Austen and his patron Mrs Unwin. The Austens cannot but have been moved by his earnest humanity. Cowper was aware of the sufferings of enslaved Africans and Indians and the obloquy attaching to England as a consequence. Thus in Expostulation (composed in 1781; published 1782) he writes passionately about the exploitation of the Indians:

"Why weeps the muse for England? What appears
In England's case to move the muse to tears?
From side to side of her delightful isle,

Is she not cloth'd with a perpetual smile? ...
Hast thou, though suckled at fair freedom's breast,
Exported slav'ry to the conquered East,
Pull'd down the tyrants India served with dread,
And rais'd thyself, a greater in their stead?
Gone thither arm'd and hungry return'd full,
Fed from the richest veins of the Mogul,
A despot big with pow'r obtain'd by wealth,
And that obtain'd by rapine and by stealth?
With Asiatic vices stor'd thy mind,
But left their virtues and thine own behind;
And, having truck'd thy soul, brought home the fee,
To tempt the poor to sell himself to thee! ...
Say not (and, if the thought of such defence
Should spring within thy bosom, drive it thence)
What nation amongst all my foes is free
From crimes so base as any charg'd on me?
Their measure fill'd, they too shall pay the debt
Which God, though long forborn, will not forget.
But know that wrath divine, when most severe,
Makes justice still the guide of his career,
And will not punish, in one mingled crowd,
Them without light, and thee without a cloud.
Muse, hang this harp upon yon aged beech,
Still murm'ring with the solemn truths I teach;
And, while at intervals, a cold blast sings
As through the dry leaves, and pants upon the strings,
My soul shall sigh in secret, and lament
A nation scourg'd yet tardy to repent.
I know the warning song is sung in vain,
That few will hear, and fewer heed the strain:
But, if a sweeter voice, and one design'd
A blessing to my country and mankind,
Reclaim the wand'ring thousands, and bring home
A flock so scatter'd and so want to roam,

Then place it once again between my knees;
The sound of truth will then be sure to please :
And truth alone, where'er my life be cast,
In scenes of plenty or the pining waste,
Shall be my chosen theme, my glory to the last."[15]

In Charity (composed in 1781) Cowper pleads for the decent treatment
of the simple natives being encountered by European adventurers and
explorers, citing the exemplary conduct of the martyred South Seas
explorer James Cook (1728-1779) [16] in this regard:

"Fairest and foremost of the train, that wait
On man's most dignified and happiest state,
Whether we name thee Charity or love,
Chief grace below, and all in all above,
Prosper (I press thee with a pow'rful plea)
A task I venture on, impell'd by thee...
When Cook - lamented, and with ears as just
As ever mingled with heroic dust -
Steer'd Britain's oak into a world unknown,
And in his country's glory sought his own,
Wherever he found man, to nature true,
The rights of man were sacred in his view.
He sooth'd with gift, and greeted with a smile,
He spurn'd the wretch that slighted or withstood
The tender argument of kindred blood,
Nor would endure that any should controul
His free-born brethren of the southern pole.
But, though some nobler minds a law respect,
That none shall with impunity neglect.
In baser souls unnumber'd evils meet,
To thwart its influence, and its end defeat.
While Cook is lov'd for savage lives he sav'd,
See Cortez odious for a world enslav'd!
Where wast thou then, sweet Charity? where then,

Thou tutelary friend of helpless men?"[17]

Sadly, Cowper's exhortation fell on deaf ears as the British Empire spread toward the southern pole. Van Dieman's Land (later, Tasmania) was first settled in 1804 and within a century of this poem's publication virtually all of the Tasmanian Aborigines were dead. The brave woman Truganini, the last "full-blood" Aborigine, died in 1876. White Tasmanian mythology regards her as the last Tasmanian Aborigine, a position belied by the establishment of the Cape Barren Island Aboriginal reserve in 1881 and the existence of several thousand Tasmanian Aborigines today, the descendants of Tasmanian and "Mainland" Australian Aboriginal women and European men. [18] In Book II of The Task (published in 1785 and familiar to Jane Austen), Cowper rails against slavery in The Time-piece:

"I would not have a slave to till my ground,
To carry me, to fan me while I sleep,
And tremble when I wake, for all the wealth
That sinews bought and sold have ever earn'd.
No: dear as freedom is, and in my heart's
Just estimation priz'd above all price,
I much rather be myself the slave,
And wear the bonds, than fasten them on him.
We have no slaves at home. - Then why abroad?
And they themselves, once ferried o'er the wave
That parts us, are emancipate and loos'd.
Slaves cannot breathe in England; if their lungs
Receive our air, that moment they are free;
They touch this country, and their shackles fall.
That's noble, and bespeaks a nation proud
And jealous of the blessing. Spread it then,
And let it circulate through ev'ry vein
Of all your empire; that wherever Britain's pow'r
Is felt, mankind may feel her mercy too." [19]

Cowper assumes the slave's part in his poem The Negro's Complaint (written in 1788; published in 1793):

"Forc'd from home, and all its pleasures,
To Afric's coast I left forlorn;
To increase a stranger's treasures,
O'er the raging billows borne.
Men from England bought and sold me,
Paid my price in paltry gold;
But, though theirs they have enrolled me,
Minds are never to be sold ...
Deem our nation brutes no longer
Till some reason ye shall find
Worthier of regard and stronger
Than the colour of our kind.
Slaves of gold, whose sordid dealings
Tarnish all your boasted pow'rs,
Prove that you have human feelings'
Ere you proudly question ours." [20]

Cowper reiterates the message in The Morning Dream (1788) in which Britannia makes "Freemen of Slaves" [21] and in Sweet Meat Has Sour Sauce or, The Slave-Trader in the Dumps (written 1788, published in 1836) in which the slave-trader bemoans the end of his trade. [22] However the message gets rather close to home in the Home Counties drawing rooms in the poem Pity the Poor African (written 1788; published 1800):

"I own I am shock'd at the purchase of slaves,
And fear that those who buy them and sell them are knaves;
What I hear of their hardships, their tortures, and groans,
Is almost enough to draw pity from stones.
I pity them greatly, but I must be mum,
For how could we do without sugar and rum?
Especially sugar, so needful we see?

What? give up our desserts, our coffee and tea?" [23]

While Jane Austen refers to estates and fortunes in the West Indies in Mansfield Park and Sanditon, she is "mum" about the enslavement realities involved. While Jane Austen makes only fleeting reference to the wealth acquired by nabobs in the East Indies in Sense and Sensibility, she would have read Cowper's passionate condemnations of those involved.

7.5. Robert Burns (1759-1796) was certainly read by Jane Austen although one supposes that she had not encountered any of the large and very entertaining body of his bawdy poetry, of which the following is a good example:

"I hae three ousen in my plough,
Three better ne'er plough'd ground, jo.
The foremost ox is lang and sma',
The twa are plump and round, jo ...
I hae ploughed east, I hae plough'd west,
In weather foul and fair, jo;
But the sairest ploughing e'er I plough'd,
Was ploughing amang hair, jo." [24]
While being chiefly concerned with matters Scottish, Burns was aware of the sorry lot of the half-starved Indians as is made clear by his poetical petition to the Scottish representatives of the House of Commons in relations to excise impositions on whisky:

"Ye Irish lords, ye knights an' squires,
Wha represent our brughs an' shires,
An' doucely manage our affairs
In parliament,
To you a simple poet's prayers
Are humbly sent.
Alas! my roupit muse is hearse;
Your Honors' hearts wi' grief 'twad pierce

To see her sitten on her arse
Low i' the dust,
An' screechin, out prosaic verse,
An' like to brust!
Tell them wha has the chief direction,
Scotland an' me's in great affliction,
E'er sin' they laid that cursed restriction
On aqua vitae;
An' rouse them up to a strong conviction,
An' move their pity ....
Let half-starv'd slaves in warmer skies
See future wines rich-clust'ring rise ;
Their lot auld Scotland ne'er envies,
But, blythe an' frisky,
She eyes her free-born martial boys
Tak aff their whisky.
What tho' their Phoebus kinder warms,
While fragrance blooms an' beauty charms,
When wretches range in famish'd swarms
The scented groves,
Or, hounded forth, dishonour arms
In hungry droves.
Their gun's a burden on their shouther;
They downa bide the stink o' powther;
Their bauldest thought's a hank'ring swither
To stan' or rin,
Till skelp! a shot - they're aff, a' throu'ther,
To save their skin.
But bring a Scotsman frae his hill,
Clap in his cheek a Highland gill,
Say "Such is royal George's will,
An' there's the foe!"
He has nae thought but how to kill
Twa at a blow....
Scotland, my auld respected Mither!

Tho' whyles ye moistify your leather,
Till where you sit, on craps o' heather,
Ye tine your dam -
Freedom and Whisky gang tegither!
Tak aff your dram!" [25]

"For a' that", Burns was employed by the Commissioner of Excise and was instructed to act and not to think. [26] The resultant Creed of Poverty pins down the general problem of social circumstances and free expression:

"In politics if thou would'st mix,
And mean thy fortunes be;
Bear this mind - be deaf and blind;
Let great folks hear and see."[27]

The vicious hounding of the Highland Scots, that began with the Glorious Revolution and the Massacre of Glencoe and accelerated appallingly after the defeat of the 1745 rebellion at the Battle of Culloden, continued in various forms throughout the 18th and 19th centuries. [28] Robert Burns' father, William Burness, may have been "out" in the forty-five (i.e. part of the rebellion) and while he escaped arbitary death at the hands of the English he could only gain employment (and hence live) when his loyalty was formally certified by his parish. Burns was constrained by a régime that oppresses his land to this day. In the words of his biographer Allan Cunningham:

"His steps were watched and his words weighed; when he talked with a friend in the street, he was supposed to utter sedition; and when the ladies retired from the table and wine circulated with closed doors, he was suspected of treason rather than of toasting..." [29]

Burns could nevertheless passionately declare for justice and liberty in a generalized fashion as in his dedication to the 2nd edition of his works:

"Dedication to the noblemen and gentlemen of the Caledonian hunt. My Lords and gentlemen: A scottish bard, proud of the name, and whose highest ambition is to sing in his country's service, where shall he properly look for patronage as to the illustrious name of his native land: those who bear the honours and inherit the virtues of their ancestors? ... May corruption shrink at your kindling glance; and may tyranny in the ruler, and licentiousness in the people equally find you an inexorable foe! I have the honour to be, With sincerest gratitude and highest respect, My Lords and Gentlemen, Your most devoted humble servant, Robert Burns (Edinburgh, April 4, 1787)." [30]

Burns rails against slavery and despotism in the following poetical prayer:

"Grant me, indulgent Heav'n, that I may live
To see the miscreants feel the pains they give,
Deal Freedom's sacred treasures free as air,
Till slave and despot be but things which were." [31]

While constrained from comment in relation to the fate of the Scottish Highlanders, Burns was able to write of the cruelty of slavery in America in The Slave's Lament:

" It was in sweet Senegal that my foes did me enthral,
For the lands of Virginia O;
Torn from that lovely shore, I must never see it more,
And alas I am weary, weary O!
All on that charming coast is no bitter snow or frost,
Like the lands of Virginia O;
There streams for ever flow, and there flowers for ever blow,
And alas I am weary, weary O!
The burden I must bear, while the cruel scourge I fear,
In the lands of Virginia O;
And I think on friends most dear, with the bitter, bitter tear,
And alas I am weary, weary O!" [32]

7.6. John Shore (later Sir John Shore, Lord Teignmouth, 1st Baron Teignmouth) (1751-1834) was a distinguished British administrator in India and was an eye-witness to the Great Bengal Famine of 1769-1770. The awful, unimaginable, physical consequences of despotism and slavery in the East Indies - the wretched mass starvation of the conquered and rapaciously over-taxed Bengalis in 1769-1770 - was recorded by Shore in a poem:

"Still fresh in memory's eye the scene I view,
The shrivelled limbs, sunk eyes, and lifeless hue;
Still hear the mother's shrieks and infant's moans,
Cries of despair and agonizing moans,
In wild confusion dead and dying lie; -
Hark to the jackal's yell and vulture's cry,
The dog's fell howl, as midst the glare of day
They riot unmolested on their prey!
Dire scenes of horror, which no pen can trace,
Nor rolling years from memory's page efface." [33]

7.7. Samuel Johnson (1709-1784) was evidently a significant influence on Jane Austen's writing and was in communication with the Austen family intimate Warren Hastings. At the time that the famous Hindu Bengali official Nandakumar was hung (having been sentenced to death by Hastings' friend and judicial collaborator Judge Elijah Impey), thousands in Calcutta were moved by this dreadful event. Within a day or so of the execution Warren Hastings penned a letter on Persian poetry to Dr.Johnson. [34] Dr. Johnson was accordingly apprised somewhat of conditions in Bengal. He is offered the observation:

"It is remarkable that the most unhealthy countries where there are the most destructive diseases, such as Egypt and Bengal, are the most populous." Dr. Johnson replies "Countries which are the most populous have the most destructive diseases. That is the true state of the proposition." [35]

Dr. Johnson did not apparently have a very high opinion of Bengalis and is reported as calling the East Indians "barbarians". [36] Boswell talks with Dr Johnson "of accusations against a gentleman for supposed delinquencies in India". Dr. Johnson's response (presumably in defence of his correspondent Warren Hastings, then facing attacks and eventual impeachment in Parliament) is an elegant argument: "What foundation there is for accusation I know not, but they will not get at him. Where bad actions are committed at so great a distance, a delinquent can obscure the evidence till the scent becomes cold; there is a cloud between, which cannot be penetrated: therefore all distant government is bad. I am clear that the best plan for the government of India is a despotick governour; for if he be a good man, it is evidently the best government; and supposing him to be a bad man, it is better to have one plunderer than many. A governour, whose power is checked, lets others plunder, that he himself may be allowed to plunder; but if despotick, he sees that the more he lets others plunder, the less there will be for himself, so he restrains them and though he himself plunders, the country is a gainer, compared with being plundered by numbers." [37]

7.8. Richard Brinsley Sheridan (1751-1816) the famous parliamentary orator, theatrical entrepreneur and playwright, was the most celebrated literary defender of the rights of the oppressed Indians of Oudh and Bengal. [38] Jane Austen was obviously well aware of his theatrical works, as made apparent in the theatrical discussions in Mansfield Park. In addition the Austen family would have closely followed the impeachment and trial of their intimate Warren Hastings before Parliament and known of the 2 most extraordinary speeches by Sheridan during those proceedings (see Chapter 12). [39] The first of these (delivered on 7th February 1787) was concerned with whether Hastings should be impeached on account of his crimes against the Begums of Oudh (and as we will see, inspired the indignation of the poet Lord Byron). Sheridan's passion for the down-trodden Indian subjects of the East India Company was translated into the play Pizarro, his very popular adaptation of The Spaniards in Peru (or The

Death of Rolla) by the German Augustus von Kotzebue (1761-1819) that deals with the conquest of the Peruvian Incas by the Spaniards. The German play was a sequel to his play The Virgin of the Sun, both plays being dramatizations of The Incas, a novel by Jean-Francois Marmontel (1723-1799). Pizarro (originally played by Mr Barrymore) questions the Peruvian Orozembo who is then mortally wounded by Pizarro's lieutenant Darvilla for his bold contempt of the invader. Against the entreaties of his mistress Elvira (played by Mrs Siddons) and his clerical mentor Las-Casas, Pizarro proceeds against the Incas led by Atalibo, King of Quito, and his commanders the Inca Rolla and the Spaniard Alonzo. Prior to the battle, Rolla makes a great speech to the Incas (of which more below) and Alonzo secures Rolla's promise to care for his wife Cora and his child if he falls in battle. Alonzo is captured and, despite Elvira's entreaties, Pizarro is resolved to torture him to death as a traitor. Rolla, scorned by Cora on revealing his promise, replaces Alonzo in captivity by subterfuge but refuses to slay the sleeping Pizarro at the behest of disaffected Elvira. Discovered by the waking Pizarro, Elvira faces death by torture but the chivalrous Rolla is released. Cora runs to the escaped Alonzo only to see her child kidnapped by lurking Spaniards. Rolla is recaptured but released at the order of Pizarro. However Rolla spies the kidnapped child in the camp and escapes, mortally wounded, with the infant. Rolla restores the child to Alonzo and Cora and then dies. The Peruvians seek revenge and attack the Spanish camp. Pizarro fights with Alonzo but is slain, having been distracted by the re-appearance of Elvira who has been freed by Pizarro's secretary, Valverde, who loves her. Pizarro's deputy Almagro submits and the Spaniards leave Peru. Elvira has the last substantive speech:

"Cherish humanity - avoid the foul examples thou hast viewed - Spaniards returning to your native home, assure your rulers, they mistake the road to glory or to power. - Tell them, that the pursuits of avarice, conquest, and ambition, never yet made a people happy, nor a nation great".

These words reiterate elements of the great speech of Rolla to the Incas prior to the battle, which in turn directly derives from the great parliamentary speeches of Sheridan against the invasion, exploitation and despoiling of the East Indians. Rolla declaims:

"... Your generous spirit has compared as mine has, the motives, which, in a war like this, can animate their minds and ours. - They, by a strange frenzy driven, fight for power, plunder, and extended rule - we, for our country, our altars, and our homes. - They follow an Adventurer, whom they fear - and obey a power which they hate - we serve a monarch whom we love - a God whom we adore. - Whene'er they move in anger, desolation tracks their progress! - Where'er they pause in amity, affliction mourns their friendship! - They boast, they come but to improve our state, enlarge our thoughts, and free us from the yoke of error! - Yes - they will give enlightened freedom to our minds, who are themselves the slaves of passion, avarice, and pride. - They offer us their protection - Yes, such protection as vultures give to lambs - covering and devouring them! - They call on us to barter all of good we have inherited and proved, for the desperate chance of something better which they promise. - Be our plain answer this: The throne we honour is the people's choice - the laws we reverence are our brave Fathers' legacy - the faith we follow teaches us to live in bonds of charity with all mankind, and die with hope of bliss beyond the grave. Tell your invaders this, and tell them too, we seek no change; and, least of all, such change as they would bring us." [40]

Those speaking for the desolated Indian provinces of Bihar, Bengal, Oudh and Rohilkund could not have put their case more cogently.

7.9. Lord Byron (George Byron, 6th Baron Byron) (1788-1824) [41] immortalized Sheridan's passionate defence of the down-trodden Indians in the following poem:

"When the loud cry of trampled Hindostan
Arose to Heaven in her appeal to man,
His was the thunder, his the avenging rod,
The wrath - the delegated voice of God!
Which shook the nations through his lips, and blazed,
Till vanquished senates trembled as they praised." [42]

Lord Byron's passion for the rights of such imperial subjects translated into his active support for the Greeks in their fight for independence against the Ottoman Empire. In 1824 Lord Byron died of a fever in that struggle for freedom and self-determination and has become a national hero of the Greek people. [43]

7.10. Jane Austen confined her moralistic narratives to the lives of the rich

We have now seen the life, connections and works of Jane Austen and glimpsed the surprisingly different degrees of comprehensiveness with which her historians have dealt with these various matters. We have scanned the social conscience of her literary contemporaries and found that a variety of the greatest poets and writers of the time (including some of her favourite writers) were moved to passion by the gross injustices perpetrated by British imperialism on down-trodden colonial subjects throughout the world. To be scrupulously fair to Jane Austen, the precious little of the "real world" that does intrude into her novels (albeit minimally and then only implicitly) does include some major social phenomena of the time: the sophisticated, cultured lives of the landed or sinecured rich (all of her novels); nabob wealth from the military occupation of the East Indies (Sense and Sensibility); wealth from slave plantations in the Americas (Emma, Mansfield Park and Sanditon); war against the French (all of her novels except for Lady Susan, Sanditon and Emma); trade, tradesmen, professions and commerce (throughout her novels); the extraordinary social divide between the 1% rich or comfortable and the 99% down-trodden, impoverished non-persons of Britain (all of her novels); the displaced, homeless rural poor (the Gypsies in Emma); improved agriculture (Emma). A notable omission is reference to massive expansion of English urbanisation and manufacturing industry at the time [44], apart from references to manufactured goods, notably textiles, and a brief pejorative comment by Mrs Elton in Emma about Birmingham:

"People of the name of Tupman, very lately settled there, and encumbered with many low connections, but giving themselves immense airs, and expecting to be on a footing with the old established families. A year and a half is the utmost that they can have lived at West Hall; and how they got their fortune nobody knows. They came from Birmingham, which is not a place to promise much, you know, Mr. Weston. One has not great hopes from Birmingham. I always say there is something direful in the sound: but nothing more is positively known of the Tupmans, though a good many things are suspected; and yet by their manners they evidently think themselves the equal even to my brother, Mr. Suckling, who happens to be one of their nearest neighbours. It is infinitely too bad." [45]

Jane Austen's essentially rural perspective is summed up in the following snippet from a rare letter from Jane Austen (Chawton, 1811) that actually refers to Birmingham and the major contemporary English enterprise of manufacturing:

"I like your new Bonnets exceedingly, yours is a shape which always looks well, & I think Fanny's particularly becoming to her. - On Monday I had the pleasure of receiving, unpacking & approving our Wedgewood ware. It all came very safely, & upon the whole is a good match, tho' I think they might have allowed us rather larger leaves, especially in such a Year of fine foliage as this. One is apt to suppose that the Woods about Birmingham must be blighted. - There was no Bill with the Goods - but that shall not screen them from being paid. I mean to ask Martha [Lloyd] to settle the account. It will be quite in her way, for she is just now sending my Mother a Breakfast set, from the

same place. I hope it will come by the Waggon tomorrow; it is
certainly what we want, & I long to know what it is like, & as I am
sure Martha has great pleasure in making the present, I will not have
any regret. We have considerable dealing with the Waggons at present;
a Hamper of Port & Brandy from Southampton, is now in the
Kitchen." [46]

While Jane Austen steered clear of politics it is clear where her
sympathies lie - with the landed Tory gentlemen and the aristocracy.
While she loved Crabbe and Cowper she did not follow their example
and defend human social decencies at home or abroad. The following
exchange between poor but beautiful Jane Fairfax and thoroughly
unpleasant and self-opinionated Mrs Elton in Emma is as close as we
get to social commentary (and indeed Jane Austen makes a joke about
it in comparing the "slave trade" and the "governess-trade"):

"When I am quite determined as to the time, I am not at all afraid of
being long unemployed. There are places in town, offices, where
inquiry would soon produce something. - Offices for the sale - not
quite of human flesh - but of human intellect." [Jane Fairfax] "Oh! my
dear, of human flesh! You quite shock me; if you mean a fling at the
slave-trade, I assure you Mr. Suckling was always rather a friend to the
abolition." [Mrs. Elton] "I did not mean, I was not thinking of the slave
trade," replied Jane; "governess-trade, I assure you was all that I had in
view; widely different as to the guilt of those who carry it on; but as to
the greater misery of the victims, I do not know where it lies." [Jane
Fairfax] [47]

For all that her literary references to the "big world" are
fleeting and inexplicit, Jane Austen's novels, being prosaic, domestic
and business-like, cannot totally avoid these glimpses of reality. Indeed
later and vastly more passionate, romantic, physical and sensational
works such as Wuthering Heights by Emily Brontë (1818-1848) and
Jane Eyre by Charlotte Brontë (1816-1855), are actually even more
divorced from "global realities". [48] It is because Jane Austen's novels

deal with pecuniary practicalities and everyday social discourse in such a sensible, dispassionate way that one becomes aware of the absence of wider social description and social commentary. This absence is the more obvious given the manifold "imperial" connections of her family and the interconnected "imperial" as well as "landed" sources of their prosperity. However Jane Austen was a fine artist and as for her choice of medium one can ultimately only say "chaçun a son gout". Before proceeding to a detailed consideration of the British Imperial realities underlying the prosperity of Jane Austen's connections and class, we will now briefly sample the judgements that other writers have applied to her Art.

Chapter 8

The judgement of Jane Austen's peers and successors

"Mrs Hall, of Sherborne, was brought to bed yesterday of a dead child, some weeks before she expected, oweing to a fright. - I suppose she happened unawares to look at her husband."

- Letter of Jane Austen to Cassandra (1798)[1]

"Miss Blachford is agreeable enough; I do not want People to be very agreeable, as it saves me the trouble of liking them a great deal."

-Letter of Jane Austen to Casssandra (1798)[2]

"& at the bottom of Kingsdown hill we met a Gemtleman in a Buggy, who on minute examination turned out to be Dr Hall - & Dr Hall in such very deep mourning that either his Mother, his Wife or himself must be dead."

- Letter of Jane Austen to Cassandra (1799)[3]

"Only think of Mrs Holden's being dead! - Poor woman, she has done the only thing in the World she could possibly do, to make one cease to abuse her."

- Letter of Jane Austen to Cassandra (1813)[4]

"What should I do with your strong. manly, spirited Sketches, full of Variety & Glow? - How could I possibly join them on to the little bit (two Inches wide) of Ivory on which I work with so fine a Brush, as produces little effect after much labour?"

-Letter of Jane Austen to her nephew James Edward Austen (1816)[5]

8.1. Literary critics of the moral quietude of Jane Austen's writing

As the above quotations illustrate, Jane Austen could bring a hard, critical eye to bear on others and indeed upon her own work. At this point in our disquisition it is useful to take stock and consider the judgements on Jane Austen delivered by her peers and by her successors. It is appropriate to do this now before we consider the progress of the juggernaut of British imperialism and corporate greed up to the present day and the accompanying failure of social criticism and restraint. Jane Austen's work represents a pool of highly moral quietude that resolutely ignores the dreadful times in which it is set. We have already seen the passion that the times evoked in kindred literary spirits and indeed in poets who numbered among Jane Austen's favorites. What did her countrymen - particularly writers and politicians - think of her work and did any perceive and attempt to resolve the apparent paradox of highly moral writing that makes no reference to the horrendous immorality of the times?

8.2. Jane Austen's contemporaries

Jane Austen's novels were not published under her name in her lifetime and those of her novels that were published appeared towards the end of her all too short life. Accordingly general criticism, positive and negative, was limited. James Austen-Leigh points out in his A Memoir of Jane Austen (1870) that Jane Austen was not directly involved with the literary scene of the day. Thus James Austen-Leigh writes:

"Jane Austen lived in entire seclusion from the literary world: neither by correspondence nor by personal intercourse was she known to any contemporary authors." [6]

The critical feedback she obtained came from family, friends, family connections and occasionally through second-hand reports from others. Thus we know from her letters the pleasure that approbation brought her and she refers in her letters to a variety of people who have made nice comments about her work. As we have already seen, she was particularly chuffed by the approbation of Warren Hastings:

"Lady Robert is delighted with P. & P - and really <u>was</u> so as I understand before she knew who wrote it - for, of course, she knows now. - He [Henry] told her with as much satisfaction as if it were my wish. He did not tell <u>me</u> this, but told Fanny. And Mr Hastings - I am quite delighted with what such a Man writes about it. - Henry sent him the Books after his return from Daylesford - but you will hear the Letter too ... I long to have you hear Mr. H.'s opinion of P & P. His admiring my Elizabeth so much is particularly welcome to me." [7]

Through Henry's physician she was taken on a tour of Carlton House in 1815 and received the warming intelligence from the Prince Regent's Librarian, the Reverend James Stainier Clarke, that the Prince liked her work so much that he kept a set of her novels in each of his palaces. She dedicated Emma to the Prince in appropriately lavish language.[8] From her correspondence with the Reverend Clarke (who had suggested a novel about the Royal Family) we obtain refreshing opinions of Jane Austen about her own work written in a typically matter-of-fact and precise fashion. [This correspondence is reproduced in Heath (1961)]. Thus in relation to Emma she writes:

"I am strongly haunted by the idea that to those readers who have preferred Pride and Prejudice it will appear inferior in wit, and to those who have preferred Mansfield Park inferior in good sense." [9]

In relation to the suggestion of writing an historical novel Jane Austen is precise and to the point:

"You are very kind in your hints as to the sort of composition which might recommend me at present, and I am fully sensible that an historical romance, founded on the House of Saxe Cobourg, might be much to the purpose of profit or popularity than such pictures of domestic life in country villages as I deal in. But I could do no more write a romance than an epic poem. I could not sit seriously down to write a serious romance under any other motive than to save my life; and if it were indispensable for me to keep it up and never relax into laughing at myself or at other people, I am sure I should be hung before I had finished the first chapter. No, I must keep to my own style and go on in my own way; and though I may never succeed again in that, I am convinced that I should totally fail in any other." [10]

A review of her work in 1818 pins down her succint description of the world known to her and the embarrassing precision of her descriptions of our social foibles:

"In imagination, of all kinds, she appears to have been extremely deficient; not only her stories are utterly and entirely devoid of invention, but her characters, her incidents, her sentiments, are obviously all drawn exclusively from experience .... Her merit consists altogether in her remarkable talent for observation; no ridiculous phrase, no affected sentiment, no foolish pretension seems to escape her notice. It is scarcely possible to read her novels, without meeting with some of one's own absurdities reflected back upon one's conscience; and this, just in the light in which they ought to appear." [11]

While "cut off from contemporary authors" Jane Austen must have been known to many of them. Thus Sir Walter Scott says in his diary:

"That young lady has a talent for describing the involvement of feelings and characters of ordinary life which is to me the most wonderful I have ever met with. The big bow-wow strain I can do myself, like any now going; but the exquisite touch which renders ordinary commonplace things and characters interesting from the truth of the description and the sentiment is denied to me." [12]

Scott appreciated the precision of her Art, its merits and faults:

"The author's knowledge of the world, and the peculiar tact with which she presents characters that the reader cannot fail to recognize, reminds us something of the merits of the Flemish school of painting. The subjects are often not elegant, and certainly never grand; but they are finished up to nature, and with a precision which delights the reader. This is a merit which it is very difficult to illustrate by extracts, because it pervades the whole work, and is not to be comprehended from a single passage....[the merit] consists much in the force of a narrative conducted with much neatness and point, and a quiet yet comic dialogue in which the characters of the speakers evolve themselves with dramatic effect. The faults, on the contrary, arise from the minute detail which the author's plan comprehends. Characters of folly or simplicity, such as those of old Woodhouse [Emma's father] and Miss Bates [Emma's endlessly loquacious acquaintance] are ridiculous when first presented, but if too often brought forward or too long dwelt upon, their prosing is apt to become as tiresome in fiction as in real society" [13] and "There is a truth of painting in her writings which always delights me. They do not, it is true, get above the middle classes of society, but there she is inimitable." [14]

Other 19th century writers were to give Jane Austen mixed reviews and the reader is referred in particular to Halperin (1975), Heath (1961) and Southam (1976a,b) for detailed accounts of such criticism. [15] In a detailed review, T.B. Macaulay (as we will see elsewhere, a thoroughly decent and morally responsive man) was a great fan of Jane Austen and comments on her importance and upon her avoidance of high-blown emotions or the obsessive passions that he calls "humours". By way of example he refers to "the insane desire of Sir Edgerton Brydges [brother of Jane Austen's friend Anne Lefroy] for a barony to which he had no more right than to the crown of Spain." Macaulay gives great praise indeed:

"Shakespeare has had neither equal nor second. But among the writers who, in the point which we have noticed, approached nearest to the manner of the great master, we have no hesitation in placing Jane Austen, a woman of whom England is justly proud... A line must be drawn, we conceive, between artists of this class, and those poets and novelists whose skill lies in the exhibition of what Ben Jonson calls humours... Seeing that such humours exist, we cannot deny that they are proper subjects for the imitations of art. But we conceive that the imitation of such humours, however skilful and amusing, is not an achievement of the highest order; and, as such humours are rare in real life, they ought, we conceive, to be sparingly introduced into works which profess to be pictures of real life. Nevertheless, a writer may show so much genius in the exhibition of these humours, as to be fairly entitled to a distinguished and permanent rank among the classics. The chief seats of all, however, the places on the dais and under the canopy, are reserved for the few who have excelled in the difficult art of portraying characters in which no single feature is extravagantly overcharged." [16]

It is a shame that Jane Austen was cut off from literary intercourse, the more so since she was a keen and critical reader of contemporary literature as we have seen in the previous chapter. We can sense this loss in her girlish desire to see her favourite poet Crabbe in the flesh at the theatre in London as revealed in her letter to Cassandra from Henrietta Street: "I was particularly disappointed at seeing nothing of Mr. Crabbe." [17] One of her contemporaries, her nephew James Austen-Leigh, does allude to the societal absences in her novels in a generalized way:

"She was always careful not to meddle with matters with which she did not thoroughly understand. She never touched on politics, law, or medicine [sic], subjects which some novel writers have ventured on rather too boldly, and have treated, perhaps, with more brilliancy than accuracy. But with ships and sailors she felt herself at home, or at least could always trust to a brotherly critic to keep her right. I believe that no flaw has ever been found in her seamanship either in "Mansfield Park" or in "Persuasion"." [18]

James Austen-Leigh in a further commentary on the novels praises "the fidelity with which they represent the opinions and manners of a class of society in which the author lived" and provides a succint summary of the philosophical position in her novels:

"They were certainly not written to support any theory or inculcate any particular moral, except indeed the great moral, which is to be generally gathered from an observation of the course of actual life - namely, the superiority of high over low principles and of greatness over littleness of mind." [19]

This reflects the position of Richard Whately who appreciated Jane Austen's low-key moral approach and the fidelity of her approach to reality - indeed an Aristotelian coupling of precise observation and reason:

"Miss Austin has the merit (in our judgement most essential) of being evidently a Christian writer: a merit which is much enhanced, both on the score of good taste, and of practical utility, by her religion being not at all obtrusive.... The moral lessons of this lady's novels, though clearly and impressively conveyed, are not offensively put forward, but spring incidentally from the circumstances of the story; they are not forced upon the reader, but he is left to collect them (though without any dificulty) for himself: her's is that unpretending kind of instruction which is furnished by real life; and certainly no author has ever conformed more closely to real life, as well as in the incidents, as in the characters and descriptions. Her fables appear to us to be, in their own way, nearly faultless.... We know not whether Miss Austin ever had access to the precepts of Aristotle; but there are few, if any, writers of fiction who have illustrated them more successfully... Her minuteness of detail has also been found fault with; but even where it produces, at the time, a degree of tediousness, we know not whether that can be justly reckoned a blemish, which is absolutely essential to a very high excellence." [20]

G.H. Lewes writing in 1852 agrees with Macaulay:

"First and foremost, let Jane Austen be named, the greatest artist that has ever written, using the term to signify the most perfect mastery over the means to her end. There are heights and depths in human nature Miss Austen has never scaled nor fathomed, there are worlds of passionate existence into which she has never set foot; but although this is obvious to every reader, it is equally obvious that she has risked no failures by attempting to delineate that which she had not seen. Her circle may be restricted, but it is complete. Her world is a perfect orb, and vital. Life, as it presents itself to an English gentlewoman peacefully yet actively engaged in her quiet village, is mirrored in her works with a purity and a fidelity that must endow them with interest for all time. To read one of her books is like an actual experience of life: you know the people as if you had lived with them. The marvellous reality and subtle distinctive traits noticeable in her portraits has led Macaulay to call her a prose Shakespeare....There is nothing of the doctinaire in Jane Austen; not a trace of woman's mission; but as truthful, charming, humorous, pure-minded, quick-witted, and unexaggerated of writers, female literature has reason to be proud of her." [21]

The exquisite prose of Jane Austen failed to impress Charlotte Brontë. In a letter to G.H.Lewes in 1848 she criticises Jane Austen for the lack of precise description of the material reality of the limited world she dealt with:

"What did I find? An accurate daguerrotyped portrait of a commonplace face; a carefully fenced, highly cultivated garden, with neat borders and delicate flowers; but no glance of a bright vivid physiognomy, no open country, no fresh air, no blue hill, no bonny beck. I should hardly like to live with her ladies and gentlemen, in their elegant but confining houses." [22]

Charlotte Brontë in a further letter to Lewes (1848) rails passionately against his proposition (as recorded by Brontë) that while "Miss Austen is not a poetess, has no "sentiment"....no eloquence, none of the ravishing enthusiasm of poetry" should nevertheless be acknowledged as "one of the greatest artists, of the greatest painters of human character, and one of the writers with the nicest sense of means to an end that ever lived":

"Can there be a great artist without poetry? What I will call - what I will bend to, as a great artist - cannot be destitute of the divine gift. But by poetry, I am sure, you understand something different to what I do, as you do by "sentiment". It is poetry, as I comprehend the word, which elevates that masculine George Sand, and makes out of something coarse something godlike." [23]

In a letter to W.S. Williams in 1850, Charlotte Brontë again passionately adverts to the lack of passion in Jane Austen:

"I have likewise read one of Miss Austen's works, Emma - read it with interest and with just the degree of admiration which Miss Austen herself would have thought sensible and suitable - anything like warmth or enthusiasm, anything energetic, poignant, heartfelt, is utterly out of place in commending these works: all such demonstration the authoress would have met with a well-bred sneer, would have calmly scorned as outré and extravagant. She does her business of delineating the surface of the lives of genteel English people curiously well; there is a Chinese fidelity, a miniature delicacy in the painting: she ruffles her reader by nothing vehement, disturbs him by nothing profound: the Passions are unknown to her... what the blood rushes through, what is the unseen seat of Life and the sentient target of death - this Miss Austen ignores; she no more, with her mind's eye, beholds the heart of her race than each man, with bodily vision sees the heart in his heaving breast. Jane Austen was a complete and most sensible lady, but a very incomplete and rather insensible (not senseless) woman...." [24]

G.H.Lewes is still highly laudatory in an 1859 essay but admits concern with the limited pallette of Jane Austen's work:

"Miss Austen's two-inch bit of ivory is worth a gallery of canvas by eminent R.A.s, but it is only a bit of ivory after all." [25]

Julia Kavanagh (1862) addressed the limited social, emotional and descriptive range in Jane Austen's work but, unlike Charlotte Brontë, regarded these limitations as positive merits:

"The grand, the heroic, the generous, the devoted, escaped her, or, at least, were beyond her power; but the simply good, the dull, the lively, the mean, the coarse, the selfish, the frivolous, she saw and painted with a touch so fine that we often do not perceive its severity. Yet inexorable it is, for it is true. To this rare power Miss Austen added another equally rare - she knew where to stop. Two qualities are required to write a good book: to know what to say and what to withhold. She had the latter gift, one which is rarely appreciated: it seems so natural not to say more than is needed! In this respect she must have exercised great judgement, or possessed great tact, since her very qualities are those that lead to minuteness." [26]

Richard Simpson in about 1870 was concerned with the lack of concern for social issues and the lack of connection with the ordinary person in Jane Austen's work:

"She had no interest for the great social and political problems which were being debated with so much blood in her day. The social combinations which taxed the calculating powers of Adam Smith or Jeremy Bentham were above her powers. She had no knowledge how to keep up the semblance of personality in the representation of a society reckoned by averages and no method of impersonating the people or any section of the people in the average man." [27]

Simpson (1870) further perceived an emotional constraint, a regulation of feelings by reason:

"Miss Austen seems to be saturated with the Platonic idea that the giving and receiving of knowledge, the active formation of another's character, or the more passive growth under another's guidance, is the truest and strongest foundation of love. Pride and Prejudice, Emma and Persuasion all end with the heroes and heroines making comparisons of the intellectual and moral improvement which they have imparted to each other. The author has no fear of the old adage, "Wise lovers are the most absurd." " [28]

Goldwin Smith in 1890 approaches critical analysis of Jane Austen's work in the same vein as James Austen-Leigh and it is well to note his straightforward, philosophically minimalist views before we consider the mountain of profound, intestinal, deconstructionist, statistical and psychoanalytical assertions generated by her 20th century critics (and which surely would have amused Jane Austen immensely):

"Criticism is becoming an art of saying fine things and there are really no fine things to be said about Jane Austen. There is no hidden meaning in her; no philosophy beneath the surface for profound scrutiny to bring to light; nothing calling in any way for elaborate interpretation... Jane Austen's characters typify nothing, for their doings and sayings are familiar and commonplace. Her genius is shown in making the familiar and commonplace intensely interesting and amusing. Perfect in her finish and full of delicate strokes of art, her works require to be read with attention, not skimmed as one skims many a novel, that they may be fully enjoyed. But whoever reads them attentively will fully enjoy them without the help of a commentator." [29]

8.3. Non-English opinions of Jane Austen

At this point it useful to gather some non-English opinions in order to distance ourselves from any parochial sentimentality. The reader is referred to Southam (1987) for a detailed compilation of criticism over the period 1870-1940, including the opinions of American writers. [30] Joseph Conrad, not an Englishman, was the author of passionate, powerful stories set in the heat, danger and colour of the tropical East. We cannot be surprised in the least with his comment in a letter to H.G. Wells in 1913:

"What is all this about Jane Austen? What is there in her?" [31]

A similar cultural gulf appears in the opinions of Samuel Clemens (1835-1910), better known as Mark Twain, whose democratic sensibilities were evidently profoundly offended by her writing, as revealed by the following snippets:

"Jane Austen's books, too, are absent from this library [on a ship]. Just that one omission alone would make a fairly good library out of a library that hadn't a book in it" (1896). [32]

"I often want to criticize Jane Austen, but her books madden me so that I can't conceal my frenzy from the reader; and therefore I have to stop before I begin" (1898). [33]

"It seems to me a great pity that they allowed her to die a natural death." (1909). [34]

"When I take up one of Jane Austen's books such as Pride and Prejudice, I feel like a bar-keeper entering the kingdom of heaven. I know what his sensations would be and his private comments. He would not find the place to his taste and he would say so" (anecdotal account of a conversation in 1909). [35]

Henry James was also dismissive, Jane Austen having left him unsatisfied:

"Jane Austen, with her light felicity, leaves us hardly more curious of her process, or of the experience in her that fed it, than the brown thrush who tells his story from the garden bough; and this I freely confess, in spite of her being one of those shelved and safe, for all time..." (1906). [36]

"Who could pretend that Jane Austen didn't leave much more untold than told about the aspects and manners even of the confined circle in which her muse revolved? Why shouldn't it be argued against her that where her testimony complacently ends the pressure of appetite within us presumes exactly to begin?" (1914). [37]

The judgement of the eminent American writer Edmund Wilson (1945) is authoritative:

"There have been several revolutions of taste during the last century and a quarter of English literature, and through them all perhaps only two reputations have never been affected by the shifts of fashion: Shakespeare's and Jane Austen's." [38]

The French woman Léonie Villard appreciated the female aspect of Jane Austen's work at the level of the socially-conditioned heroine and commences her Jane Austen: Sa Vie et Son Oevre (1924) with a vulnerable image:

"Smiling and very much alive, sometimes half-concealing her grace beneath a veil of shyness, or cloud of melancholy, a young girl is invariably the heroine of a novel by Jane Austen." [39]

However Villard quickly gets to the heart of the matter: unlike "romantic" novelists such as Fanny Burney (author of Evelina and Cecilia and a friend of Cassandra Austen's cousin Cassandra Leigh, daughter of Theophilus Leigh, Master of Balliol), Jane Austen recognizes in her writing the biological and social realities that qualify or condition the "love" of sensible women:

"Having fallen in love at the first sight with a handsome stranger, Evelina ... is simply in love with love...The truth which Jane Austen is the first to bring forward is that the majority of women regard love in quite another fashion. Studying woman's soul from within, she does not hesitate to paint it as it generally is. Ruthlessly she despoils it of the imaginary qualities in which man has decked it when he formulates conclusions which cannot be either disinterested or due to direct observation...The genius of Shakespeare alone, up to this point, had divined the fact that even the greatest, noblest, tenderest love in a woman does not necessarily exclude all practical considerations, all links with everyday reality." [40]

On Jane Austen's Art, Villard quotes Jane Austen herself, writing to her nephew James Edward Austen: "What should I do with your strong, manly, vigorous sketches, full of variety and glow? How could I possibly join them on to the little bit of ivory (two inches square) on which I work with so fine a brush as produces little effect after much labour." [41] Villard concludes that Jane Austen's work "is that of a miniaturist or illuminator" and provides the following judgement:

"If the artist's chief triumph lies in concealing the effort of creative activity so well that his work seems absolutely spontaneous, Jane Austen must be ranked among the greatest literary artists, the greatest "artificers" of letters ... The next qualities to admire are the exact symmetry always given to the story itself, the perfection with which the means employed are adapted in order to arrive at a particular effect ... In this symphony of family life, with its slender joys and cares as light as thistledown, every component part belongs to the whole, and brings its quota to the effect of all ..." [42]

However in her final words Villard (1924) comes to the heart of our present disquisition - the gulf between the serene lives of the people of Jane Austen's novels and the real world:

"They are happy and fortunate, and take their good fortune as their due, and accept without demur, without "useless repining", the fact of the necessitous lives around them. Their serenity, their infinite contentment with themselves and their lives, separates them, by a great distance, from ourselves who have learned that which their common-sense outlook had not even then even suspected - for we have learned the need for social justice and the brotherhood of mankind." [43]

8.4. 20th century English writers

There is a very large literature of criticism of Jane Austen's work [44] and for excellent compilations of such criticism the reader is referred to a number of works, notably those of Watt (1963), Halperin (1975) and Southam (1987). [45] It is useful at this point to glimpse some of the opinions of 20th century writers who had substantially discarded the sentimentality and prejudice of the prior imperialist era.

Virginia Woolf was conscious of the deceptive ordinariness of Jane Austen's characters, the fierce dedication of her "fans" and the loss to literature occasioned by her early death:

"Anybody who has had the temerity to write about Jane Austen is aware of two facts: first, that of all the great writers she is the most difficult to catch in the act of greatness; second, that there are twenty-five elderly gentlemen living in the neighbourhood of London who resent any slight upon her genius as if it were an insult to the chastity of their Aunts" (1923). [46]

"The balance of her gifts was singularly perfect. Among her finished novels there are no failures, and among her many chapters few that sink markedly below the level of others... Vivacious, irrepressible, gifted with an invention of great vitality, there can be no doubt that she would have written more, had she lived, and it is tempting to consider whether she would have not written differently" (1924). [47]

A loyal band of "Janeites" continued to grow in the 20th Century, warmed no doubt by the straight-forward judgements of writers such as R. Brimley Johnson (1924):

"She wrote books because she loved books, and for no other reason. She did not study human nature, but loved men and women; and her realism sprang from loyalty to her friends." [48]

Johnson (1924) gives credit to Samuel Richardson (1689-1761), novelist, printer and bookseller, as an author with similar motives to those of his reader and successor Jane Austen, a love of books and a desire to write more accurately about real people of his experience. He ascribes a "passion for truth" to Jane Austen:

"Her passion for truth, in fact, appears in individual character-drawing, is inspired by individual circumstances, when the author feels in her bones that her people are really alive. It is not the realism or passion of the reformer - of life or of art. Her ideal in man came to be the ardour and confidence of Captain Wentworth that "seemed to foresee and to command his prosperous path"; just as his ideal in woman was "a strong mind, with sweetness of manner"." [49]

In 1927 the witty Arnold Bennett (1867-1931) attacked the Janeites, the growing band of Jane Austen "fanatics" and has a reasonable judgement about Jane Austen's achievement:

"Jane Austen? I feel that I am approaching dangerous ground. The reputation of Jane Austen is surrounded by cohorts of defenders who are ready to do murder for their sacred cause. They are nearly all fanatics. They will not listen. If anyone "went for" Jane, anything might happen to him. He would assuredly be called on to resign from his clubs... I do not even agree that Jane was a great novelist. She was a great little novelist. She is marvellous, intoxicating: she has unique wit, vast quantities of common sense, a most agreeable sense of proportion, much narrative skill. And she is always readable. But her world is a tiny world, and even of that tiny world she ignores, consciously or unconsciously, the fundamental factors. She did not know enough of the world to be a great novelist. She had not the ambition to be a great novelist. She knew her place; her present "fans" do not know her place, and their antics would without doubt have excited Jane's lethal irony."[50]

J. Bailey (1931) gives voice to the sentimentality of Jane Austen's fans in the following:

"The extraordinary spread of the cult of Jane Austen would have surprised nobody more than herself. What it has been can be crystallized in a single word. Fifty years ago she was Miss Austen. To-day she is always Jane."[51]

R. Brimley Johnson (1924) similarly brims with affection for the unaffectedness of Jane Austen's writing and concurs with the views of Villard (1924):

"Can we doubt that the genius of Jane Austen had its birth in the love and the criticism of books; that it matured through her love of man? ... Hers is not "Art for the sake of Beauty" or even "Art for Truth's sake"; but is "above all Art for the pleasure she took in certain aspects of life." She has no desire whatever to "edify" or "instruct"."[52]

However R. Brimley Johnson (1927) is quite well aware of the unruffled normality and lack of violent drama in Jane Austen's work:

"It is a remarkable fact, characteristic of Jane Austen's lack of sensational emotion, that no death occurs, of characters actually present, in any of these novels. The influence of death, indeed, is strongly felt by Frank Churchill [in Emma]; but this is the only occasion in which death occurs during this story."[53]

In a 1937 poem the poet H.W.Auden (1907-1973) addresses the commonsense in matters matrimonial of many of Jane Austen's female characters:

"You could not shock her more than she shocks me;
Beside her Joyce seems innocent as grass.
It makes me most uncomfortable to see

An English spinster of the middle class
Describe the amorous effects of "brass",
Reveal so frankly and with such sobriety
The economic basis of society."[54]

Auden is clearly much more perceptive than H.G.Wells who rudely declared (1938):

"The English Jane Austen is quite typical. Quintessential I should call her. A certain ineluctable faded charm. Like some of the loveliest butterflies - with no guts at all." [55]

We will return to H.G.Wells later to deal with his equally careless treatment of History.

Kingsley Amis (1957) was sensibly contemptuous of the "cringing self-abasement" of Fanny in Mansfield Park and asserted of Jane Austen "that her judgement and her moral sense were corrupted" in this her best work in his judgement. He declares that "Edmond and Fanny are both morally detestable" and that their endorsement by the author "makes Mansfield Park an immoral book". [Fanny's feelings] "are made odious by a self-regard utterly unredeemed by any humour" and "the character of Fanny lacks self-knowledge, generosity, and humility ... it is a monster of complacency and pride who, under a cloak of cringing self-abasement, dominates and gives meaning to the novel." [56] C.S. Lewis (1954) adjudges her as exhibiting "cheerful moderation, She could almost have said with Dr. Johnson, "Nothing is too little for so little a creature as man." If she envisages few great sacrifices, she also envisages no grandiose schemes of joy. She is the daughter of Dr. Johnson: she inherits his commonsense, his morality, even much of his style." [57] B.C. Southam (1977) sums up her literary position thus: "it is with Jane Austen that the novel takes on its distinctively modern character in the realistic treatment of unremarkable people in the unremarkable situations of everyday life." [58]

8.5. Jane Austen and the feminist perspective

Women in 1800 had a very subordinate place in a society that was very tough for the underclass. [59] Fay Weldon (1984) in Letters to Alice on First Reading Jane Austen provides a grim picture of England at that time and particularly of the lot of women: the heavy physical demands of survival and the dangers of childbirth, abortion and disease, including sexually-transmitted disease in cities such as London where 1 in 7 women was a prostitute. [60] Women of Jane Austen's class had gentler lives but childbirth was a common danger as instanced by the untimely deaths of Frances Austen (Charles' first wife) and Elizabeth Austen (Edward's wife).

Economic considerations imposed the central consideration for the young women in Jane Austen novels: find a suitably prosperous husband and preferably one that you can love. A young gentlewoman without means or a dowry could become a governess or, like Philadelphia Austen and Mary Buchanan (later Hastings) (née Elliot), go out to India or elsewhere to find a husband. Current attitudes to women can be gauged from the following 1794 advice for young ladies:

"You must first lay it down for a foundation in general, that there is inequality in the sexes; and that for the better oeconomy of the world, the men, who were to be the lawgivers, had the larger share of reason bestowed upon them." [61]
The following poem by Alexander Pope (a poet evidently admired by Jane Austen) conveys the same "sexist" flavour:

"Nothing is so true as what you once let fall,
"Most women have no Characters at all."
Matter too soft a lasting mark to bear,
And best distinguish'd by black, brown or fair." [62]

As pointed out by Villard and others, Jane Austen's heroines generally maintained a dignified, intellectual position in a male-dominated world. At one extreme we have Elizabeth Bennet of Pride and Prejudice who maintains a dignified position through wit and irony but even she admits to being tempted by the glories of Pemberley. At the other end of the spectrum we have Fanny Price in Mansfield Park who maintains her position in a resolutely moral but subordinate and self-effacing fashion. [63] A powerful message in Jane Austen's novel is the triumph of self-possession and intelligence over the arbitrariness of fortune, authority and prejudice. In Jane Austen's microcosms this courageous intelligence is the staff of her heroines but the message is empowering for everyone. This view has been cogently expressed by Sulloway (1989):

"Because Austen wrote as though hostile relationships between adults and children, rich and poor, socially established or obscure - that is between the empowered and the disempowered - are paradigms for the female predicament, to say nothing of the human predicament, as indeed they are, she has now become the woman for all seasons." [64]

8.6. The Jane Austen industry

The foregoing gives an outline of the reactions of highly accomplished men and women of letters to Jane Austen's work. However a substantial industry of Jane Austen scholarship (that has greatly expanded in the postwar years) ranges over history [65], literary criticism [66], word usage [67], sociology (including religion) [68], music [69], Juvenilia, letters and completion of unfinished works [70], feminism [71] and lifestyle and urban/rural landscape [72] (these being in many cases overlapping categories). Brief inspection of some of the more eclectic of these works gives something of the flavour of the industry. Hudson (1992), Sibling Love and Incest in Jane Austen's Fiction, picks up on the consanguinity (most notoriously Edmond and Fanny in Mansfield Park) and non-consanguinous familial "closeness" (e.g. Elinor Dashwood and Edward Ferrars in Sense and Sensibility) and then runs with the ball. [73] Wallace (1983), Jane Austen and Mozart. Classical Equilibrium in Fiction and Music, deals with elements of literary and musical expression, namely equilibrium, balance, proportion, symmetry, restraint, passion, sobriety, bacchanalia, happiness, sadness, morbidity, wit and lyricism. By way of example, among other comparisons he compares Pride and Prejudice with Mozart's Piano Concerto No. 9 (K 271). [74] One of the more unusual of such works is Burrows (1987), Computation into Criticism, which involves quantitative analysis of word usage by Jane Austen. One of the findings of Burrows (1987) is that of 2,342 words uttered by the regal Lady Catherine De Bourgh (in Pride and Prejudice), 5 are "we, us or our" whereas of 2,034 words uttered by Admiral Croft (he and his wife being an inseparably affectionate couple in Persuasion) 50 are first person plural pronouns. [75] Suggested further areas for profitable trans-Atlantic Jane Austen scholarship (especially at the Science/Literary Deconstruction interface) could be "Jane Austen and the psychological consequences of early weaning", "Jane Austen, celibacy and literary constraint", "Mood, perception and hormonal cycling revealed in Jane Austen's letters" ...

8.7. Jane Austen and 19th century sensibilities

Jane Austen cannot surely be blamed for the social insensitivity of her later readers. But that disclaimer cannot deny the likelihood that the civilized and moral world of her novels helped to establish a paradigm for perception of British society and its ruling class as noble, highly moralistic and exquisitely decent in social interactions. She has surely made a very substantial posthumous contribution to the glorious mythology of the British Empire and the English Way that is still deeply rooted in world culture. A limited number of 19th century examples will suffice.

Disraeli had apparently read Pride and Prejudice 17 times and we could reasonably conclude that he was "sold" on Jane Austen and her world. This was the man who in his support for the Corn Laws had

a direct involvement in the Irish Famine (of which more later). [76] From
a 20th century post-Holocaust perspective there is something
transcendently awful in a Jew being involved in genocide. Thus
sensitive Jews would have a particularly profound horror of the
massacre of the 200 Arab villagers of Deir Yassin in 1948 by the Irgun
Zwei Leumi to which the later Israeli Prime Minister Menachem Begin
belonged at the time. [77] The Irish famine, assisted by the callousness
and greed of Benjamin Disraeli and his colleagues, swept away as
many as 1 million people and sent 1.5 million more overseas from
"Erin's Island". [78]

No doubt Winston Churchill, very much a 19th Century man
for all his 20th Century exploits and distantly connected to the Austen
tribe, would have been introduced to Jane Austen's novels in his youth.
Churchill must remain our hero for his resolute warnings about the
Nazi threat and his participation in its extirpation. However we must
encounter Churchill later in relation to Gallipoli and the consequent
Armenian Genocide, the survival of the British Empire, hatred for
Indians, the bombing of Pearl Harbor, the fall of Singapore, the man-
made Bengal Famine of 1943-1944 and the laundering of British
history (Chapter 15). Churchill comments:

"I decided to read a novel. I had long ago read Jane Austen's Sense and
Sensibility, and now I thought that I would have Pride and Prejudice...
What calm lives they had, those people! No worries about the French
Revolution, or the crashing struggle of the Napoleonic Wars. Only
manners controlling natural passion so far as they could, together with
cultured explanations of any mischances." [79]

I reiterate that Jane Austen's chosen, highly-circumscribed Art
form has certainly not set out to hide or deceive - indeed the opposite is
quite clearly true. Yet the tranquillity and unruffled decency of her
highly moral world as perceived and relished by Imperial participants
from Disraeli, through Kipling to Churchill has contributed to the
noble self-image of those involved at the top end of what was in reality

an immensely destructive and imposing colonial Empire. This in turn
has contributed to the extraordinary "Austenizing" of British Imperial
history that is the subject of the following chapters.

8.8. 2008 Postscript

The fundamental messages of the WW2 Jewish Holocaust (6 million
dead) and of the WW2 Holocaust in general (30 million Slav, Jewish
and Roma dead) are "zero tolerance for racism" and "never again to
anyone". Yet 160 years on from Benjamin Disraeli and the Irish
Famine, racist Zionists running Apartheid Israel support the invasion,
occupation, dispossession, disempowerment, mass imprisonment and
ethnic cleansing of the ongoing Palestinian Genocide; deny the
Armenian Genocide (1.5 million killed); and support the Bush-ite US
Iraqi Genocide (4 million excess deaths, 1990-2008) and Afghan
Genocide (3-7 million excess deaths, 2001-2008). [80] Also see shocking
revelations of Jewish Israeli anti-Arab anti-Semitic sentiment [81]. For
many more opinions on Jane Austen's writing see "Jane Austen
Antipodean Views". [82]

Chapter 9

The East India Company, the Black Hole and the conquest of Bengal

"Mr. Children's two Sons are both going to be married, John & George - They are to have one wife between them; a Miss Holwell, who belongs to the Black Hole at Calcutta."

- Jane Austen in a letter to Cassandra (1796). [1]

"Gentoos in general are as degenerate, crafty, superstitious and wicked a people as any race in the known world, if not eminently more so, especially the common run of Brahmins."

- John Zephania Holwell (survivor and chronicler of the Black Hole of Calcutta and grandfather of the above Miss Holwell). [2]

"By God, Mr Chairman, at this moment I stand astonished at my own moderation!"

- Lord Robert Clive responding to Parliamentary cross-examination in 1773 over his immense personal pecuniary advancement in Bengal. [3]

9.1. The consequences of passive and active Austenizing

We have seen how Jane Austen, the artist, quite legitimately confined her moral exercises to a rarefied, genteel slice of English society. Our concern is that historians have illegitimately applied the same social editing in their portrayal of British society and the Empire. We have already seen how this Austenizing has been applied (albeit relatively innocently) to Jane Austen's life and connections. It is useful to now briefly sketch the origins of the East India Company and the conquest of Bengal that contributed immensely to the prosperity of the privileged part of society to which Jane Austen belonged. In doing so we will draw upon a large historical literature that deals with this saga of the 17th and 18th centuries with varying degrees of comprehensiveness and humanity. [4]

Austenizing involves both passive and active distortion of reality. The passive process involves ignoring unpleasant realities of which the most glaringly obvious in our disquisition is the avoidable death by starvation and attendant disease of tens of millions of remorselessly exploited colonial subjects in Bengal and elsewhere in the Indian Empire. [5] The active process involves the construction of heroes and anti-heroes, racial stereotyping and romantic mythologising. Such constructions can be very powerful and can mobilize whole nations. The dreadful story of the Black Hole of Calcutta is an example of such powerful "Empire-building" iconography. There is a standard "Black Hole story" that is recounted in essence in a large number of British histories with different degrees of detail and commentary (indeed on occasion with the qualification that the reader is surely aware of the matter). [6] Nevertheless some declare that the "Black Hole" incident did not actually happen [7] and others believe the event was grossly exaggerated if it did. [8]

The present chapter traces the foundation of the East India Company and the ultimate British invasion of Golden Bengal in the 18th century. At that time Bengal was one of the richest countries in the world in an agricultural, industrial and cultural sense. [9] The "Black Hole" incident in 1756 arose out of the last successful Bengali defence of their country against a merciless invader. The subsequent treacherous defeat of the last completely independent Bengali ruler, the Nawab Siraj-ud-daulah, by the British under Robert Clive at the Battle of Plassey in 1757 delivered control of Bengal to the East India Company. [10] The final defeat of the last Bengali resistance under the "puppet" Nawab Mir Kasim and his allies by the British under Major Hector Munro, at the Battle of Buxar in 1764, delivered the people of Bengal, and indeed of the whole Gangetic plain, into the hands of merciless foreign exploiters. [11] Within half a dozen years of the Battle of Buxar, 10 million people - one third of the remorselessly impoverished population of Bengal - would perish in the Great Bengal Famine, one of the most horrendous events in all of human history. The most extraordinary Austenizing ensured that the British ruling class, Jane Austen's people, escaped censure and accordingly continued a "business as usual" process of murderous exploitation over nearly 2 centuries in India. That process involved the deaths of scores of millions through famine, culminating in the "forgotten holocaust" of Bengal in the latter half of World War 2. [12] The same moral blindness, supported by resolute Austenizing on the part of academics, media and politicians, is set to turn the tropical parts of the planet into a global Bergen-Belsen by the middle of the 21st century. [13]

9.2. Foundation and expulsion from the Spice Islands

The exciting story of the foundation and expansion of the East India Company is described in a variety of enthralling texts. [14] The East India Company was formally established by the signature of Queen Elizabeth I of England on New Year's Eve 1600. England was at war with Spain and Portugal (who had divided the world, and in particular the New World, between themselves). The Portuguese had established themselves in India and the East Indies and the Dutch were also trading from the islands of the East Indies. The overland passage to the East was blocked by the Ottoman Empire, whose navy patrolled the Mediterranean. Francis Drake had circumnavigated the world in 1572-1580 and Albion was set to bestride the world.

In January 1601 the first East India Company fleet set sail to the Spice Islands of the East Indies under the command of Captain Lancaster. By the time the Cape of Good Hope was reached, scurvy (due to vitamin C deficiency) had decimated the crew and the Guest was abandoned. In 1602, after a voyage of 18 months, the fleet reached Achin in northern Sumatra. Lancaster presented gifts and presents from Queen Elizabeth to the King of Achin who granted the Englishmen freedom to trade, entertained them and inquired after Queen Elizabeth. It should be noted that in the culture of that part of the world, women can have a prominent position in relation to government, inheritance and property rights. Lancaster captured a Portuguese galleon and used the coin of the prize to purchase spices (notably pepper, the dried berries of Piper nigrum (Piperaceae), a tropical climbing vine). Sending one ship back to England, Lancaster traded with the Dutch at Bantam in Java, where his deputy commander John Middleton died. After further adventures, including peaceful trade with French and Dutch vessels at St Helena and a huge storm, the fleet returned to London in 1603 but of 460 men who had ventured out only 278 returned. Lancaster was knighted by the new monarch James I, became a proprietor of the Company and thence wisely stayed home.

Over the next decades the enterprise continued and expanded. Henry Middleton commanded the next fleet that completed the return voyage to Bantam, Java and to the Molucca Islands with the loss of 1 ship. A third expedition under Captain Keeling (immortalized in the Cocos-Keeling Island group in the Indian Ocean) returned with an extraordinarily profitable cargo of cloves (the dried flower buds of Syzygium aromaticum = Eugenia caryophyllata (Myrtaceae), a tropical evergreen tree). The increasing activity led to ship-building at Deptford and timber yards at Reading but eventually the Company commenced leasing ships. After 2 decades the Company employed 2,500 seamen and was distributing substantial dividends to its shareholders.

The growing trade led to increasing conflict with the Dutch in the East, even though England and Holland were ostensibly at peace in Europe. The Dutch, Portuguese and subsequently the English built forts to protect key bases and conflict erupted between these competing interests in various places. John Jourdain, president of the Company's Java factory at Bantam, was killed in a naval engagement with the Dutch in 1620. The conflict with the Dutch East India Company led to the Amboina massacre in the Moluccas in which the Dutch arrested 18 Englishmen for spying on the Dutch fort, the Dutch having elicited this intelligence from torturing a Japanese mercenary of the English. The English were tortured and all but 2 beheaded. The Amboina massacre did not endear the Dutch to the English and no doubt contributed to the anti-Dutch Navigation Act of 1651 (confining importation of goods into England to English shipping) and the genesis of the Anglo-Dutch Wars of 1652-1654 and 1665-1667. In the wash-up of the latter conflict, the English gave up their Java factory in 1667 and swapped Surinam for New Amsterdam (later New York) with the Dutch in the Americas. The Portuguese lost their fort at Hormuz (at the entrance to the Persian Gulf) to the English and lost Ceylon to the Dutch.

The commercial stakes were very high in these conflicts in terms of the trade to Europe of spices such as pepper, cloves, nutmeg (the seeds of Myristica fragrens (Myristicaceae), an evergreen tree native to the Moluccas) and cinnamon (the seeds of Cinnamomum zeylanicum (Lauraceae), a bushy, evergreen tree of Ceylon, South India, Sumatra and Burma). Other plant products of great value were tea (the dried leaf tips of Camellia sinensis = Thea sinensis (Dipterocarpaceae), an East Asian evergreen bush), coffee (seeds of Coffea arabica (Rubiaceae), an Arabian bush) and the narcotic laudanum or opium (the latex of the immature fruits of Papaver somniferum (Papaveraceae), the opium poppy of Asia). The blue dye from the indigo plant (Indigofera species (Leguminosae) indigenous to Bengal and Java), Chinese silk and porcelain and Bengali silk and muslin were also valuable goods traded to Europe.. The Europeans also traded in slaves for work on plantations or for purposes of sexual abuse. The Dutch seized slaves for their plantations in the East Indies. The Portuguese had a vile reputation for slaving in coastal regions of Bengal, slaves being secured by thin canes passed through holes made in the palms of their hands. Shah Jehan ordered the extirpation of Portuguese slavers from Bengal. The English were also involved in slavery in the East. Female slaves as young as 12 were bought and hired for prostitution.

Adam Smith has described the conduct of the Dutch in the Spice Islands in relation to maximizing their profits from spices and maintaining their monopoly. In order to keep the price high in Europe they would burn excess spices from the harvest and to keep others from engaging in the trade they would also destroy spice-producing trees. However another option was also exercised by the Dutch to maintain their monopoly and to keep prices high:

" If the produce even of their own islands was much greater than what suited their market, the natives, they suspect, might find some means to convey some part of it to other nations; and the best way, they imagine, to secure their own monopoly, is to take care that no more shall grow than what they themselves carry to market. By different arts of oppression they have reduced the population of several of the Moluccas to nearly the number which is sufficient to supply with fresh provisions and other necessaries of life of their own insignificant garrisons, and such of their ships as occasionally come there for a cargo of spices. Under the government of even the Portuguese, however, these islands are said to have been tolerably well inhabited. The English company have not yet had time to establish in Bengal so destructive a system. The plan of their government, however, has had exactly the same tendency. It has not been uncommon, I am well assured, for the chief, that is, the first clerk of a factory, to order a peasant to plough up a rich field of poppies, and sow it with rice or some other grain. The pretence was, to prevent a scarcity of provisions; but the real reason, to give the chief an opportunity of selling at a better price a large quantity of opium, which he happened then to have on hand. Upon other occasions the order has been reversed..." [15]

After discussing monopolistic usurpation of foreign and inland trade in particular goods in Bengal and similar restraints on production to maximize profit, Adam Smith (1776) concludes prophetically:

"In the course of a century or two, the policy of the English company would in this manner have probably proved as completely destructive as that of the Dutch". [16]

9.3. The first footholds in India

The first direct Company contact with the Mughal Emperor of India was by their representative William Hawkins. His ship arrived at Surat in 1608 and following difficulties with the hostile Portuguese and after making suitable presents to the local authorities and Mughal representatives, he set off for the Imperial Court at Agra. The Emperor Jahangir took to Hawkins, who could speak Turkish, gave him a position and a Christian Armenian bride. Hawkins ultimately left but died in transit to Bantam. His widow subsequently married a Company man in London.

The English established a factory at Surat and 2 English ships secured a victory against 4 Portuguese galleons in 1612. When Jahangir initiated hostilities against the Portuguese, a small English fleet of 4 vessels under Nicolas Downton successfully repulsed a much larger Portuguese fleet of 6 galleons, 2 further ships and a large number of smaller vessels. Sir Thomas Roe was sent to Agra with a message from James I seeking peaceful trade. At his audience with Jahangir he declined to touch the ground with his head. He gained recognition of a circumscribed, non-military, Company presence at Surat and Agra that was subject to the laws of the land. His advice to the Company on his return home was for civilized trade: "it is an error to affect garrisons and land wars in India". [17]

Fort St George was founded by Francis Day in 1640 on the south eastern coast of India on land granted by the local ruler. It was made a Company "presidency" in 1653 and in 1658 was put in charge of Company affairs in Bengal and on the Coromandel coast. With a small English population of several hundred and ten times as many Portuguese, it was a lively place. Factional conflict in 1665 required the despatch of Company forces to restore order. This station was to become the city of Madras (now Chennai). In 1661 Charles II received the island of Mumbai (Bombay) on marrying the Infanta of Portugal. The Company obtained the island for a nominal rental and for providing a substantial loan. Thus was the beginning of the mega-city of Bombay (now Mumbai again).

The first probings of Bengal began in 1633. A factory was established at Hooghly, on the river of the same name, and trade commenced in a difficult physical and political environment. Notwithstanding the earlier advice of Sir Thomas Roe, in 1686 Job Charnock led a Company army of 300 men plus Portuguese mercenaries and Rajput sepoys (Indian soldiers) against a Mughal army of 12,000 men. In the event the English were forced to withdraw from Hooghly and the Mughals took Surat on the west coast. The Emperor Aurangzib (son of Shah Jahan and Mumtaz Mahal [remembered by the Taj Mahal], grandson of Jahangir and the Rajput Manmati and great-grandson of Akbar), was concerned with English naval dominance of the Arabian Sea and the security of pilgrims taking the haj to Mecca. Accordingly he made peace with the English and his subordinate, the Nawab of Dacca, was ordered to permit an English return to Bengal. Charnock established Fort William at Kalikata on the River Hooghly. Charnock married a Brahmin widow he had saved from the suttee funeral pyre. Charnock died in 1693 and in 1699 this settlement was made a third Indian presidency of the Company. This settlement was eventually to become the great city of Calcutta.

In 1685 Sir John Child became Captain-General and Admiral of India, based at Bombay. The Company became responsible for English interests in India. The first tea from China was sold in London in 1657 and towards the end of the century the Company began a trade involving opium from India to China to obtain the coinage required to purchase Chinese tea. With the Revolution in England and the establishment of William and Mary, a rival English East India Company was established. Amalgamation into the United Company of Merchants of England Trading in the East Indies, the "East India Company", occurred in 1709. The Company had a statutory monopoly of trade with the East Indies and "interlopers" were acted against. Thomas Pitt (1653-1726), "Diamond Pitt" (the grandfather of William

Pitt the Elder, 1st Earl of Chatham), was a celebrated 'interloper" who nevertheless became a Company man as Governor of Fort St George in 1697. An outstanding example of an Englishman surviving and making good in the service of the Company, he returned home with great wealth, including the famous Pitt diamond. His descendants William Pitt the Elder and William Pitt the Younger led England against the French in the Seven Years' War and the Napoleonic Wars, respectively. [We have already seen the connection of the "Austen" Leighs to the East India Company via Cassandra Willoughby, second wife of James Brydges and step-daughter of Sir Josiah Child, a Director and thence a Governor of the Company. [18] Our artistic heroine Jane Austen and William Pitt (the 1st Earl of Chatham) shared a common ancestor in Sir Thomas Leigh, Lord Mayor of London. [19]]

The "Glorious Revolution" that finally secured the Protestant establishment of England ushered in an ethos of imperialism and global commercial expansion that wreaked havoc upon the world, is still a dominant global driving force and which is currently set to destroy the world. For all of the grandeur and high culture of the 18th century, the lives of the ordinary English people and of their subjects, from the Scottish Highlands to the colonies, were vile. G.M. Trevelyan, the master of Austenizing history, has a mellifluous view:

"The Revolution gave to England an ordered and legal freedom, and through it gave her power. She often abused her power, as in the matters of Ireland and of the Slave Trade, till she reversed the engines; but on the whole mankind would have breathed a harsher air if England had not grown strong. For her power was based not only on her free Constitution but on the maritime and commercial enterprise of her sons, a kind of power naturally akin to freedom, as the power of great armies in its nature is not." [20]

9.4. Dupleix and the French ascendancy in India

The English under William III were at war with the French from 1689-1697 (concluded by the Treaty of Ryswick). Under Queen Anne and generaled by Marlborough, the English were subsequently engaged in the bloody War of the Spanish Succession (1701-1714) (the Anglo-French conflict being concluded by the Treaty of Utrecht in 1713). However these Anglo-French conflicts had not spread to India. Joseph Francois Dupleix came to India in 1722 and by 1731 had become the Governor of the French Company station of Chandernagore, upriver from Calcutta. Dupleix made a great success of this operation and was made Governor of Pondicherry in 1742. Pondicherry, lying between the British establishments of Fort St George (Madras) in the north and Fort St David in the south, had been the key French base on the Coromandel coast since 1683. This was a time of great uncertainty in the south of India: the English and French were poised in competition and the Hindu Marathas had conquered most of the Carnatic and captured the capital Arcot, about 100 miles inland from Madras and from Pondicherry.

Admiral La Bourdonnais, the Governor of the island of Mauritius in the Indian Ocean, had made naval preparations for the coming conflict with the English in India. In 1744 came the formal declaration of war between England and France. Louis XV was unwilling to commit forces to India. Accordingly, Dupleix proposed a truce east of the Cape of Good Hope but this was rejected by the English. An English fleet captured 4 French ships and in 1746 the French under Dupleix and La Bourdonnais made alliance with the Nawab of the Carnatic and moved against Madras. While Madras was now a substantial city of 250,000 inhabitants, it was poorly defended by only 200 English troops and a contingent of sepoys. After a short bombardment, Madras surrendered to La Bourdonnais. [Back home the last battles to be fought on English and indeed on British soil were associated with the second Jacobite Rebellion. The defeat of the young pretender Charles at Culloden in Scotland on April 16th 1746 lead to

the Clearances of the Scottish Highlands]. An English fleet under
Admiral Edward Boscawen arrived carrying Royal English troops -
these were the first British Army troops to serve in India. With the
Company forces of Major Stringer Lawrence and the Royal troops
under his command, Boscawen besieged Pondicherry but the French
resisted successfully. The French were now in a very strong position in
the Carnatic.

Under the terms of the Treaty of Aix-la-Chapelle Madras had to
be handed back to the English. However Dupleix proceeded apace to
secure a formidable position in the Carnatic (not without the assistance
of his vigorous wife and her brother M. d'Auteuil). Dupleix set up their
favourite as Nizam of Hyderabad and another favourite as the Nawab
of the Carnatic. The British set up a rival claimant in Mohammed Ali
but, yielding to French power, he was under siege in the fortress city of
Trichinopoly by 1750. Given the formal peace between England and
France, the English and French made a qualified deal to minimize
European casualties. A French army under the Marquis de Bussy
defended Hyderabad and the Nizam ceded the province of the Northern
Circars to pay for the maintenance of this army. Dupleix realised the
extraordinary value of the revenues that could be made from millions
of subject Indians and indeed acquired immense wealth before his
recall to France.

9.5. Clive, Stringer, the Marathas and British ascendancy in the Carnatic

The first substantial territorial acquisition of the East India
Company dates from this period, namely a coastal strip of land at
Devicotah. Stringer Lawrence had organized the Company forces
sensibly after the fashion of the British Army and is regarded as the
founder of the British Army in India. The situation in southern India
was critically poised: the Mughal authority was non-existent and the
English and French had come to appreciate the relative ineffectiveness
of indigenous Indian forces as compared to well-armed, well-trained

and well-led European troops or sepoys trained and led by European officers.

A plan was devised (possibly by Clive or by others) to attack Arcot, the capital of the Carnatic, and hence relieve Mohammed Ali at Trichinopoly. Thomas Saunders, the Governor at Fort St David, permitted Clive to lead the venture. The 1,100-strong garrison defending Arcot withdrew in the face of only 200 English soldiers, 300 sepoys and 8 officers. Clive sensibly acceded to advice to concentrate on defending Arcot. A second success by Clive was a night attack on enemy forces encamped nearby but his small army was to face a mounting siege by accumulating forces involving the original defenders, 4,000 men sent north from investing Trichinopoly and 150 French soldiers from Pondicherry. With food, water and ammunition running low, the diseased and malnourished defenders were in a desperate position after a siege of 50 days. At this point a Maratha army of 6,000 men intervened and set themselves for Arcot. The Nawab's son attempted negotiation and indeed bribery and then launched an attack with his army of 10,000 men. However panicking elephants stampeded back into the attacking army, the Nawab's son withdrew (to be later executed by the Marathas), 600 French sepoys changed sides and Mysore allied itself to the British. Stringer defeated the French and their allies at Trichinopoly in 1752, Clive defeated D'Auteuil and Mohammed Ali became de facto Nawab of the Carnatic.

The French were not yet done. With De Bussy established firmly in Hyderabad, Dupleix resorted to a combination of diplomatic and military moves to restore the French position elsewhere. He was able to remove the support of Mysore and the Marathas for the British, captured 200 Swiss mercenaries travelling by ship from Madras to Fort St David and invested the latter fort. However Lawrence defeated the French forces at Fort St David and held them elsewhere. At this critical junction Dupleix was recalled to France, his replacement arriving in 1754 (noting the substantial time-lag involved in the round trip to France and metropolitan decision-making). The French East India

Company was seriously concerned with the conduct of costly wars at the expense of trade and failed to accept Dupleix's assertion of the immense wealth to be made through taxation of millions of Indian farmers. Dupleix returned to France a very rich man. His successor made peace with the English (and returned the captured Swiss mercenaries). In hindsight, the French East India Company had effectively at this point thrown away the chance of creating what would surely have been (from a cultural point of view) an extraordinary French empire in India.

9.6. Bengal administration before Plassey - Murshid Quli, Shuja-ud-din, Alivardi and Siraj-ud-daulah

Before it was raped by the British, Bengal was one of the most prosperous places on the face of the earth. The immense fertility of the silt-derived soil, ample water and sunlight ensured high and consistent agricultural production. The manufacture of indigo and textiles as well as a plethora of other needs made for a very solid manufacturing as well as agrarian base for this society. The flow of money in the government revenue system was organized thus: ryot (peasant) to zamindar (local ruler responsible for law, relief, protection, river embankments, loans to ryots) to amil (revenue collector) to nawab (ruler of Bengal, who was also Diwan, or revenue raiser for the Emperor, and Nazim, or Supreme Magistrate) and finally to the Mughal Emperor (with appropriate diminutions at each stage). Revenue also entered this stream from appropriate taxation of merchants and manufacturers. This sophisticated society required banking, the Jagan Seth banking family being of major commercial and political importance. The reader is referred to an excellent account of this period by Sinha (1967). [21] This rich, well-organized society was described as one in which "the peasant was easy, the artisan encouraged, the merchant enriched and the prince satisfied" by Harry Verelst, the East India Company Governor of Bengal in 1767-1769, immediately prior to the famine that was to desolate the country and destroy one third of the population.

Murshid Quli Khan ruled a prosperous Bengal for the first few decades of the 18th century, imposing a good civil admistration while being unable to control the Afghan and other Muslim military adventurers at his court. After Shuja-ud-din, Alivardi came to power in 1740 through violent usurpation after killing the legitimate heir Sarfaraz at Giria. Alivardi had to deal with an increasingly pushy European presence as well as threats from the Marathas. He appointed his grand-nephew Siraj-ud-daulah as his successor in 1751 and in 1756 Siraj-ud-daulah (1737-1757) became the last Nawab of a Bengal free of British domination. For what was to follow you can choose between versions that align themselves more with the invaded [22] or with the glorious British invaders [23].

The British quickly resolved to dispose of Siraj-ud-daulah. The Nawab had, like his predecessor Alivardi, objected to the continuing British evasion of trading duties. The Company justification for this was a 1717 firman (or official pronouncement) from Emperor Farrukh Siyar granting the Company an exemption from such duties in exchange for a small annual fee. The Nawab insisted on some payments from the English, Dutch and French by way of affirming his right to tax such commercial activity. Nevertheless it was clear that the Company and those involved in private trade were abusing this dastak (trading permit) system and Siraj-ud-daulah was prepared to stand his ground on this quite legitimate matter. However the Nawab faced an extraordinarily difficult situation since the Afghan Ahmad Shah Abdali had invaded India in 1756, seizing Lahore in 1756 and Delhi in 1757. The Anglo-French conflict in South India and consequent conspiracies of Shah Nawaz and Nizam Ali at Hyderabad added to the strategic knife-edge. The Marathas represented a continuing threat as well and Siraj-ud-daulah, while dealing with the French, was clearly unwilling to alienate the British in such a dangerous environment. Nevertheless the British mounted plots against him in his own court that would eventually lead to his military defeat and death. The principal "traitors" were Mir Jafar, Roy Durlabh and Yar Latif with the assistance of the Jagan Seths and the merchant Omichand.

In 1755 war erupted between the French and the English in North America and in 1756 the Seven Years' War (1756-1763) commenced. With the imminence of war and the experience of the Carnatic, the Europeans looked to their defences in Bengal. However Siraj-ud-daulah demanded that such military preparations should cease. While the French acceded acceptably, the British declined to do so. Siraj-ud-daulah invested Fort William with an army of 50,000 men. The British Governor Roger Drake and the garrison commander, Captain George Minchin, attempted to hold a perimeter around the fort but the Bengali forces were simply too great against a British garrison of only 520. Evacuation of women and children to ships on the Hooghly was effected at night of the 18th and the morning of the 19th of June. While Mary Carey, the part-European wife of one of the British soldiers was not allowed to embark on the Dodaldy (despite the protestations of some European wives), 2 officers who were partners in the ship insisted on remaining on board in safety.

On the 19th of June the situation worsened: there were about 2,000 Indian women and children as well as soldiers and traders in the fort, food was short, some soldiers were mutinous and casualties were mounting. The one surgeon was engaged amputating all day. Panic over the rumor that gunpowder had run out precipitated a stampede that trampled 2 sentries. People left in a flotilla of craft. As the last boats left for the Dodaldy, Captain Minchin and other officers also fled to be joined by Governor Drake. The Dodaldy sailed downstream when Drake boarded. The chief magistrate John Zephania Holwell, while not the most senior person, took command, distributed food, treasure, liquor and gunpowder and organised resistance to enable final evacuation. In response to a message from Holwell, a Company vessel the Prince George sailed upriver but ran aground on a sandbar. Captain Young of the Dodaldy would not endanger his overloaded vessel and could not assist. The Prince George was eventually set ablaze by Bengali fire arrows.

On the 20th of June the end came in sight of the Company fleet that declined to assist with their gunnery. A truce was arranged with the Nawab but this was evidently violated by the defenders firing on the Bengalis with cannons and muskets and the attack resumed. However when some defending soldiers opened the gates in the afternoon the battle was lost. The victorious Nawab entered the fort. While there was the possibility of a settlement, discharge of a gun by a drunken European soldier in a brawl decided the Nawab to order the imprisonment of the British.

9.7. Holwell's version of the Black Hole

According to the accounts given by Holwell (which are very likely to be grossly exaggerated but are nevertheless generally accepted by the vast majority of histories), at 8 p.m. 145 men plus Mary Carey were imprisoned in the cell known as the Black Hole that was 18 feet long and 14 feet 10 inches wide. The Black Hole rapidly became a hell of squashed bodies, excrement, urine, vomit, sweat, airlessness and thirst. People were trampled, drank their own urine out of thirst and pleaded with the guards for relief. Clothing was removed and hats waved to ameliorate the conditions but the expedient of men rising and falling on their haunches to allow air led to the trampling and suffocation of the exhausted. Holwell was in a position near a window but surrendered his position to the press. After a further spell at the window for air, drinking his own urine and sucking moisture from his shirt, Holwell returned to the interior, lay down beside Mary Carey and her dead husband and lost consciousness. The guards offered some water but nobody was prepared to rouse the sleeping Nawab. At 6 a.m. in the morning, after the unconscious Holwell was propped up for the guards to see, the 23 survivors were released. Among the dead was Captain Buchanan whose widow would later marry Warren Hastings. The survivors, including Holwell and Mary Carey, were taken to Murshidabad. Holwell gave several versions of these events and in 1758 published his final "146 in and 23 out" version. [24]

The Dutch and French commanders in Bengal sensibly paid off the Nawab. The British survivors were released but the widowed Mary Carey (a 15-16 year old part-Portuguese woman) was retained in the zenana for the pleasure of the Nawab. She later fell into the hands of Siraj-ud-daulah's successor, Mir Jafar, but eventually escaped or was otherwise released 6 years later at the behest of Governor Henry Vansittart. [25]

9.8. The Black Hole as a Big Lie of British History

The Black Hole made a powerful contribution to the iconography and psychopathy of British imperialism. It no doubt contributed to negative attitudes towards Indians held by the British in subsequent centuries and to the contempt for Indians of particular powerful people such as Winston Churchill. The hatred of the latter for Indians was to contribute to one of the most appalling crimes of the 20th Century and indeed of human history - the death of about 4 million Bengalis in the man-made famine of 1943-1946. [26]

Over the years scepticism grew in relation to the Holwell story: Holwell's probity was highly arguable; there were only several hundred Europeans in the settlement anyway; the dimensions of the Black Hole were inconsistent with the number of people claimed to have been incarcerated. In addition, contemporary historians, including people considered to be pro-British, evidently did not think the matter of any substance. J.H. Little in Bengal Past and Present (1915-1916) perceived inconsistencies and "blew the whistle" on the tale. [27] Einbinder (1972) also considered the evidence and concluded that the story had no substance in reality. Einbinder (1972) succintly summarized the evidence provided by Little (1916) concerning the veracity of the Black Hole story: the tale was essentially based on the words of J.Z. Holwell (a liar and a rogue), was not mentioned in a key Indian history of the time that nevertheless records other Indian atrocities against the British, was not substantiated by Clive and his colleagues and contains extraordinary inconsistencies (notably details of fellow prisoners that surely could not have been apparent in the virtually pitch-black conditions). [28]

Gopal (1963b) has summarized much of this evidence and concludes that something happened but that Holwell's account was greatly exaggerated. Gopal concludes: "One is therefore driven to the conclusion that the Black Hole was not as ghastly a tragedy as it has been made to appear". Gopal cites better documented atrocities performed by the British on Indians during the Indian Mutiny (the Indian War of Independence) in 1857 (execution by being tied to the muzzle of cannon and being "blown away", the public hanging of hundreds, burning of villagers, massacres of Indian civilians, bayoneting and burning alive of victims). Gopal (1963b) cites an incident on 1 August 1857 in the Amritsar district in which hundreds of sepoys were confined to a round tower. After several hundred had been taken out and shot, the survivors refused to come out. However in the morning nearly all of those remaining were found to have died from exhaustion and partial suffocation, some 45 in all. Gopal cites 49 prisoners "blown away" from guns after a revolt in Malerkotla in 1872 and a further "Black Hole" occurred as recently as 1921 when 66 out of about 70 prisoners died when confined to a scorching railway goods wagon. [29]

Iris Macfarlane (1975) has made a very convincing case that the investment of Fort William by Siraj-ud-daulah was probably part of a plan to dispose of him. In essence she proposes that the sort of plot that had a dramatically successful military and financial outcome for Clive and his associates at the Battle of Plassey (1757) was set in place by Holwell and the same set of Bengali collaborators in 1756. Indeed of the 2 plots the 1756 plan would surely have been the more likely to have succeeded. That it did not can be ascribed to the confusion of the siege. The actuality of the Black Hole according to Holwell and the consequent demonizing of Siraj-ud-daulah can be very plausibly disputed, the most compelling evidence coming from the implausibility of Holwell's changing account and the reactions of people at the time.

Clive's subsequent description of Siraj-ud-daulah as "a man of courage and humanity" is astonishingly inconsistent with the Holwell account. However it must be stated that Siraj-ud-daulah's behaviour was manifestly noble and humane no matter the version that is accepted, for the noble Prince was asleep during the night and disposed of the survivors generously. Macfarlane (1975) concludes that there could have been no more than 64 Europeans in the Black Hole anyway, that the total number is likely to have been about 9-20 and that maybe only 2 previously wounded men died. [30]

The Black Hole makes a "ripping yarn" and the highly coloured version of Barber (1966), The Black Hole of Calcutta, a Reconstruction, is entertaining reading redolent of the imperialist adventures of the Chums Own Annuals that I read as a child in Tasmania, that all-white, southern-most outpost of the British Empire. Barber's book includes, among many such bloodthirsty descriptions, the graphic account of how Juggernath Singh, chief footman of the detained merchant Omichand, unaccountably murders 13 women and 3 children in Omichand's compound. The victims approach in a line, the first woman tears her dress from her breasts, is stabbed in the heart and falls soundlessly to the ground. She is followed in the same fashion by the remaining 15 victims. [31] However the ugly story of 2 centuries of British Imperial global slaughter tells us that the Black Hole is more than simply a ripping yarn and may well have been for entrenched British racism what the Little Hugh of Lincoln story or the Protocols of the Elders of Zion have been for British or European anti-Semitism, respectively. The canard of Little Hugh of Lincoln being murdered by Jews for his blood arose 60 years after the death of the wonderful St Hugh, Bishop of Lincoln, who had courageously defended Jews from mobs in an era of violent anti-Semitism that resulted in pogroms and the ultimate exclusion of Jews from England. The power of such racially-specific lies has been dealt with by a number of writers, a relatively recent example being the account by Koestler (1971) of transient, anti-Semitic mass hysteria in Orleans in 1969 occasioned by the fictitious disappearance of as many as 26 women via Jewish fashion boutiques. [32]

Notwithstanding the immense amount of recapitulation of the "received version" of the Back Hole, the critics are on strong ground. In the monumental work The History and Culture of the Indian People. The Maratha Supremacy, edited by Majumdar and Dighe (1977), Datta concludes: "But Holwell's story of the "Black Hole" has been proved by modern researchers to be untrue" . [33] Even the name itself - so evocative of irresistable awfulness - is misleading since it was the name used then for a "local lock-up or temporary gaol". [34] According to Edwardes (1977) (a qualified believer, estimating no more than 64 incarcerated): "It was an emotive name, but only the usual one given officially by the English to any garrison lock-up normally used for confining drunken soldiers, and not abandoned by the army until 1868 ... It grew, however, into one of the great imperial myths - a justification for the Victorian empire." [35] The Victorian chronicler E.H. Nolan indeed expressed the British view of the time very well: "The whole transaction admits of no defense: it was an exemplification of Mohammedan insolence, intolerance, and cruelty ... if ever a nation had cause of war, Great Britain then had. That people would have been unworthy of an empire which did not rise to punish the author of such a crime." [36] [In current times the anti-Islamic fervour in the West culminating in the horrors of the Gulf War has had the same flavour. "Patriotism is the last refuge of a scoundrel" [37] and the fantastic Allied successes in the Gulf War have masked the immense military-industrial complex profits from the affair. A heart-wrenching piece of propaganda used by the Allies was the canard of the Kuwaiti babies thrown out of humidicribs thence destined for Baghdad. Just as the Black Hole helped to obscure 2 centuries of oppression and massive human rights abuse, so Allied propaganda (some true, some false) about the undoubted, genocidal inhumanity of Saddam Hussein has helped to obscure the awful realities: the deaths of hundreds of thousands of Iraqi conscripts and the dreadful impact of war and sanctions on that half of the Iraqi population who are simply children.

[38] We will later encounter passionate anti-Islamic sentiment in the writings of H.G. Wells, who managed not to notice either the 1770 or the 1943 Bengal holocausts in his Outline of History. [39]]

Holwell could hardly have admitted to the truth of a "1756" plot given the substantial European casualties and financial cost, no more than Winston Churchill could admit to his likely fore-knowledge (not communicated to his Allies) of the indefensibility of Singapore in 1941/42 and the nature and time of the attack on Pearl Harbor by the Japanese in December 1941. [40] Nor could Churchill admit to the actuality of the appalling Bengal Famine of 1943/44 in his History of the Second World War [41] while admitting as much (if not his culpability) in secret communication to Roosevelt. [42]

A monument was erected in memory of the Black Hole by J.Z. Holwell after he became Governor of Fort William but by 1821 it had fallen into disrepair and was removed (the very removal of the monument suggesting an absence of substance to the tale). [43] By the middle 1880s the site was noted in carefully dimensioned paving at the entrance to a lane adjacent to the Calcutta General Post Office. [44] Viceroy Lord Curzon restored the monument in 1902 with much imperial rhetoric[45], notwithstanding the horrendous famine that had afflicted India at the time and the supposed shortage of money for famine relief. [46] Rabindranath Tagore subsequently made the following comment on the second Calcutta monument to the victims of the Black Hole: "A big thumb of stone, raised in the midst of a public thoroughfare, to proclaim to the heavens that exaggeration is not a monopoly of any particular race or nation". [47] The second Black Hole monument was finally destroyed by the Bengal Provincial Government under Premier Fazl-ul-Haq in 1940. [48] However 3 years later the malignant effect of the Black Hole myth solidified into horrible reality with the conscious, sustained decisions of the war-time British authorities that permitted the Bengal Famine of 1943-44. [49]

9.9. Clive and the conquest of Bengal

The final disposal of Siraj-ud-daulah was now only a matter of time despite his conciliatory attitude to the British. The situation in the west with Ahmad Shah Abdali occupying Delhi forced him to send forces to Patna in Bihar under Ramnarayan. The situation in Hyderabad, the French-British conflict and British concern about Siraj-ud-daulah's approaches to the French led to a conspiracy involving collaboration of members of his court with the British that ultimately sealed his fate as well as that of Bengal and millions of Bengalis.

Robert Clive had been appointed Governor of Fort St David and was made a Lieutenant-Colonel in the army, this enabling him to command both British Army and Company soldiers. The recapture of Calcutta was an imperative and Clive was made the Commander-in-Chief. A force of 1,000 European soldiers, about 1,000 sepoys, 5 navy men-of-war and 7 other armed vessels left for Calcutta in 1757. The naval fleet was under the command of Vice-Admiral Watson. Clive led his army in a dawn attack on the Nawab's army of 12,000 foot soldiers, 18,000 cavalry and 40 guns. The British rapidly broke through the Indian line, recaptured Fort William and accepted the Nawab's request for peace talks. The British subsequently captured Chandernagore from the French with the naval bombardment from Watson's fleet and his control of the river being a crucial aspect. Clive had entered into negotiations with Siraj-ud-daulah's uncle Mir Jafar who was one of the Nawab's key commanders and who aspired to the throne. However a Hindu merchant Omichand, who acted as an intermediary, got greedy and threatened betrayal unless he was exorbitantly recompensed. Clive drew up 2 agreements, one on white paper and countersigned by Watson that gave Omichand nothing and another on red paper that agreed to Omichand's demands. The honorable Watson refused to sign the latter but his signature was forged on the document by Henry Lushington (who was to subsequently die in the Patna Massacre in 1783). Clive set out with 2,000 European troops, 1,000 sepoys and 12 guns to meet the Nawab's army of 50,000 that included a French company as well as French gunnery officers.

The Nawab's forces formed a semi-circle about the British who had their backs to the river at the village of Plassey. The battle commenced with an artillery barrage but with the onset of rain at midday the disciplined and experienced British kept their ammunition dry whereas the Bengalis were unable to continue firing. The subsequent Bengali cavalry charge was met with artillery from the British and stampeding Indian elephants disrupted the attack. The British infantry under Eyre Coote launched a successful counter attack that became a rout when the treachery of Mir Jafar, Roy Durlabh and Yar Latif led to the critical witholding of forces. Siraj-ud-daulah fled to Murshidabad before the advancing British. Clive took Murshidabad and installed Mir Jafar as Nawab. Mary Carey was apparently retained in the zenana of the newly-installed Nawab Mir Jafar for his pleasure - she either escaped or was released some years later at the instance of the then Governor Henry Vansittart and lived to old age, dying in 1801. [50] Clive and the Company were generously rewarded by the new Nawab under the terms of the "deal". Clive himself was paid 234,000 pounds.

Siraj-ud-daulah fled for safety to Bihar with one of his wives but was captured and cut to pieces on the orders of Mir Jafar's unpleasant son Miran. Siraj-ud-daulah was only 24 years old at the time of his death. He was the last independent ruler of Bengal until independence from Britain in 1947, nearly 2 centuries later. Despite the awfulness of the "Black Hole" story and the attendant disapprobation attaching to the Nawab, Siraj-ud-daulah is generally exonerated for culpability by historians going along with the Holwell story - the Nawab was asleep, his men dared not wakc him and he treated the survivors humanely when apprised of the situation. [51] Nevertheless some unpleasant stories are told of Siraj-ud-daulah e.g. his allegedly having had pregnant women opened up to satisfy his curiosity and having his soldiers overturn boat-loads of people on the River. [52]

9.10. The final defeat of the French

In 1758 the French embarked on what was to be a final push to secure an Indian empire. A force under the command of an Irish Frenchman Tom O'Lally (known as the Comte de Lally) landed in South India and captured Fort St David. With the collaboration of Bussy's forces from Hyderabad, Lally attacked Madras but was frustrated by the naval superiority of the British. Clive sent an army to occupy the Northern Circars in the absence of Bussy, defeating the French at Masulipatam. Bussy's removal to the south and the loss of the Northern Circars prompted the Nizam of Hyderabad to change sides. In 1760 Sir Eyre Coote of Plassey fame marched against Lally who was besieging Wanderwash. Coote's forces comprising 1,700 Europeans, 3,500 sepoys, 1,500 cavalry and 15 artillery pieces defeated a much larger French force of 2,500 French Army and French Company soldiers, 10,000 sepoys, 3,000 Marathas and 20 guns. In the following year Pondicherry fell to a siege, Lally again being defeated by Coote. Lally was returned to England having been taken prisoner at Pondicherry. Against advice he returned to France, was tried for alleged treason at Pondicherry and beheaded. Bussy returned to France an extremely wealthy man. The Treaty of Paris of 1763 which concluded the Seven Years' War allowed the return of Pondicherry to the French but French power was finally broken in India.

9.11. The defeat of the Marathas at Panipat by the Afghans

During the period of the Seven Years' War the British in Bengal had to contend with the Dutch and with aggression from adjoining Oudh. In 1758 the Vizier of Oudh invaded Bengal but his army was defeated at Patna. The defeat of the Dutch at Chinsura in 1759 left Bengal to the British and finally removed the Dutch from India. While the Marathas played a key role in the fluctuating fortunes of Britain and France in southern India during this period, events involving the Marathas were being played out in the Gangetic plain to the west that did not directly involve the Company but which would have some impact on subsequent Company operations in India. In the west a massive confrontation occurred between the Hindu Marathas and the Muslim forces of the Afghan invader Ahmed Shah Abdali who had conquered northern India, including Delhi. Ahmed Shah made the emperor appoint Nujib-ud-daulah prime minister and also appointed a viceroy at Lahore to rule the Punjab. Ahmed Shah retired victorious to Afghanistan but the Hindu Marathas took advantage of his absence to invade northern India. While Balaji Baji Rao, the Maratha Confederacy Peshwa (prime minister), advanced through Central India, his brother Rughanath Rao invaded the north. Rughanath Rao conquered Delhi, Lahore and finally, the Punjab. However this aggression into the previously Muslim dominated north led to an immediate reaction. Nujib-ud-daulah organized a Muslim confederacy and Ahmed Shah returned in force in the winter of 1759-1760. Ahmed Shah recaptured the Punjab, Lahore and Delhi. The Maratha Confederacy responded in kind, the Peshwa sending a huge force from Poona under his son Wiswas Deo to confront the Muslim forces. Wiswas Deo was joined by the armies of other Maratha generals and the stage was set near Delhi at Panipat for a massive battle.

The Maratha army comprised 75,000 cavalry, 15,000 infantry and 200 guns. In addition 15,000 Pindaris (freebooters) as well as banditti elements were associated with the Maratha army. Opposed to them were 28,000 Afghan cavalry as well as over 50,000 infantry and cavalry from Ahmed Shah's allies. The huge Maratha horde had initial great success against the right wing of the Muslim army and their artillery and rockets drove back the centre commanded by Ahmed Shah's Vizier. The Vizier successfully rallied his forces with reinforcements from Ahmed Shah who killed or halted fleeing soldiers and committed all his reserves to a counterattack. The counterattack was withstood for a short time by the huge Maratha army but Afghan advances and the death of the Maratha leader precipitated a collapse and a rout. The fleeing Marathas were butchered by the pursuing Afghan cavalry and indeed by the peasantry over the countryside. The Peshwa wisely deferred further engagement, his confederates having suffered such an enormous loss. Remarkably, Ahmed Shah did not capitalize on this immense victory that was the outcome of one of the greatest battles ever between Hindu and Muslim forces in India: he simply returned home to Afghanistan with his booty, leaving a Muslim-ruled region that would be eventually brought under British domination and thence subjection in the succeeding decades.

9.12. Mir Jafar, puppet Nawab of the British

In Bengal Clive appointed the young Warren Hastings as the Company representative at Mir Jafar's court at Murshidabad. The new régime faced problems with threats of Shah Allam to Bihar and rebellions in Midnapore and Patna involving connections of the late Siraj-ud-daulah. Mir Jafar objected to Ramnarayan, ruler of Bihar, but Clive thought it politic to keep friendly with the latter. In 1760 Clive returned home an extremely wealthy man. He was reputed to be the richest man in England. The British position was very strong with the French finally excluded from Bengal and the Bengalis incapable of mounting a serious threat against the British again. Back in Bengal Holwell took over as Acting Governor of Calcutta, to be succeeded in turn by Henry Vansittart. Holwell's view was that the Company should take over Diwani or imperial revenue collection. Although Clive had rejected an offer of this from Shah Allam before he left, this became a reality by 1765. Conversely, Clive had made suggestions to London that with 2,000 European soldiers he could conquer India but such conquest was not to be completed for some decades yet. With the example of Clive before them, the other men of the Company cashed in on the circumstances. They were law unto themselves and were not subject to the taxation or jurisdiction of the Nawab or his officers, from whom they exacted substantial contributions. They could compete unfairly with Bengali traders and merchants who were subject to both indigenous and British authority. The outstanding "debt" of the Nawab to the Company had to be paid off.

Mir Jafar was essentially a British puppet but had the trappings of power that was an irritant to the British. His son Miran had definite dislikes including Roy Durlab who was eventually removed with reluctant British assent. A young son of Siraj-ud-daulah disappeared, others from the previous regime were imprisoned and 2 Begums were thrown into the river with weights attached to their legs, their hands beaten as they clawed at the gunwhale. Miran was disliked and distrusted by the British (which is possibly why he has got such a poor press) and one suspects that he reciprocated the sentiment and dreamed of freedom from the British. He was involved in all kinds of sorties with the British General Caillaud involving strategic positioning against the Dutch, the French, Oudh and the residual Mughal Empire. Miran was supposedly (and most implausibly) struck by lightning while in his tent, an event that has given rise to considerable speculation since that he was murdered by Caillaud or other Englishmen. [53] With Miran dead and the army restless for payment, Governor Henry Vansittart was finally moved to persuade Mir Jafar to step down and go to Calcutta. He was replaced by his son-in-law Mir Kasim.

9.13. Mir Kasim's revolt and the Patna Massacre

The impetus for the changeover to Mir Kasim appears to have been mercenary, the responsible Company officers gaining financially from Mir Kasim in the same way that Clive had benefited from Mir Jafar. The "deal" in this case involved huge payments to the Company for the revolution, including transfer of particular districts to the Company, and, most significantly, the transfer of Bengali land to the Company to pay for the upkeep of Company forces. However Mir Kasim was a relatively responsible leader and attempted some reforms to assist indigenous commerce. The British had a monopoly of external trade with Europe and also profited immensely from an exemption from taxes on internal trade in Bengal. The dealings of the British through their gomastahs (agents) could be exploitataive and violent. These exclusive trading rights were of course very damaging for Bengali merchants and manufacturers. Mir Kasim abolished taxes on trade in order to restore indigenous competitiveness with respect to the Europeans. Governor Henry Vansittart and his friend Warren Hastings had some sympathy for Mir Kasim but the overwhelming greed of the majority of Company men overcame their sensible scruples.

Armed conflict arose out of these pressures. Ellis, the chief of the Patna factory, took violent action to avert the intervention of the soldiers of Mir Kasim bent on enforcing the Nawab's residual authority. Ellis and his men were captured by the Nawab's soldiers as they were looting Patna, but the Bengalis in turn were overcome by a Company force. Mir Kasim massacred their Bengali prisoners including Ramnarayan and the Seths. After threatening that further British advance would precipitate massacre of his British prisoners, Mir Kasim carried out his threat with the infamous Patna massacre of Ellis, Lushington and about 50 other British captives as well as many other prisoners. The outrageous Patna massacre of several hundred prisoners (supervised by a ruthless European mercenary, an Alsatian Walter Reinhard known as Samroo) [54] did not achieve the notoriety of the "Black Hole" event in the absence of a good publicist. Adams, who recaptured Patna, would have been well-advised to have backed off and secured the release of his fellow Englishmen. [55] [By a strange conjunction of events, my wife's paternal grandfather (dada) Kasim came from within several kilometers of the Black Hole of Calcutta and her paternal grandmother (dadi) Bedami was from a village near Patna. Kasim, a Muslim, and Bedami, a Hindu, both left Calcutta on the Ganges in 1913 for temporary slavery in the sugar cane plantations of Fiji.]

Mir Kasim was pushed out of his position by the Council in 1763 and Mir Jafar was restored to his nominal position as Nawab for a second term from 1763-1765. Mir Kasim fled to neighbouring Oudh and was succoured by the Nawab of Oudh to whom the Mughal Emperor Shah Allam had also fled from Delhi after its capture by the Marathas. The Nawab of Oudh, Shuja-ud-daulah, and the deposed Nawab of Bengal, Mir Kasim, invaded Bengal in 1764 but were met by a numerically inferior but better equipped and trained British force under Major Hector Munro at Buxar on the Ganges. Major Munro disposed of a sepoy mutiny by "blowing away" mutineers from cannons [56] and then proceeded to dispose of the enemy "without". A component of the Mughal army was sacrificed to the pursuing Company forces to allow for the destruction of a bridge of boats that allowed the major part of the army and the 2 Nawabs to escape. Major Munro was angered by this eventuality because he had lost the opportunity to seize the jewels of the Nawabs. This victory firmly established the authority of the British over Bengal, giving them effective control over neighbouring Oudh, Bihar and Orissa as well as substantially intruding into the affairs of the Mughal Emperor.

Mir Kasim assumed the existence of a refugee who represented a formal but actually insubstantial threat to the British in Bengal. He died in Shahjahanabad in 1777, the last Nawab of Bengal to have led an army against the British invaders. Mir Kasim's puppet Nawab successors included the restored Mir Jafar (1763-1765 in addition to his 1757-1760 period), Najm-ud-daulah (1765-1766), Saif-ud-daulah (1766-1770) and Mubarak-ud-daulah (1770-1793).

9.14. Clive and the Bengal Settlement of 1765

Clive returned to India in 1765 as the Governor of the Calcutta Presidency and set about straightening things out with characteristic energy. A treaty with Oudh allowed the Nawab a form of independence although a small part of his territory was hived off and given to the Mughal Emperor. The Treaty of Allahabad with the Mughal Emperor restored his nominal authority over the areas controlled by the Company. In return the Emperor gave the company the power of Dewani (the authority to collect revenue) in Bengal. The

Nawab was theoretically in charge of the civil administration of Bengal but the Company was charged with collecting taxes. A proportion of such taxes would go to the Emperor, a further sum to the Nawab and the rest was to be retained by the Company. In the event Clive allowed the "native" government to collect taxes. This "native" administration was headed by Mohammed Reza Khan, the chief minister of the very young Nawab Najm-ud-daulah appointed by the Company after the victory at Buxar. Mohammed Reza Khan was a very effective administrator and tried to meet the financial obligations placed upon him by the Company.

The period from 1760-1765 has been described by Sir Alfred Lyell as "the only period of Anglo-Indian history which throws grave and unpardonable discredit on the English name". [57] More discreditable times were yet to come and Clive's reforms did not eat too severely into the profitability of his subordinates although they certainly were not popular. The junior Company men felt some indignation`that Company servants were excluded from private trading except for senior employees who were permitted to trade in salt. A mutiny among the military officers who had suffered a loss of some commercial outlets was snuffed out.

Clive returned home in 1767 to face a lot of inquiry into his wealth from his enemies and the envious. While the House of Commons formally asserted in a motion that Clive had made 250,000 pounds in Bengal during his first stint as Governor, it also passed a motion stating that "Robert, Lord Clive, did at the same time render great and meritorious service to his country". Clive died in 1774 at his own hand, probably from stabbing himself with a penknife in a water-closet after having used it to sharpen the quill of a lady. [58] However he was suffering from depression and pain from illness and an alternative story (possibly deriving from friends or family) was that he died of a laudanum (opium) overdose. [59]

Between Clive's departure in 1767 and the arrival of Warren Hastings in 1772, Bengal was formally governed by Verelst and then by Cartier. As we will document in Chapter 10, it is a period that is remarkably skirted in most British histories and indeed completely ignored by some [60] - and for good reason. A time of exceptionally cruel taxation of the Bengalis by the British, it was also a period that includes the disastrous famine that swept away 10 million people, one third of the total population, perhaps the most horrendous single decimation in the history of mankind. It has nevertheless been treated minimally by most historians [61] although a small set of historians have been moved by the enormity of the disaster. [62] We will deal with this period in some detail because, while supposedly having little impact on formally recognized British "history" as displayed by British historiography, it certainly had an immense impact on Bengal for the next half century as detailed by Hunter (1871). It also had a significant impact on Adam Smith, the "father" of modern economics, who deals with this Bengal famine and its causes in his seminal book An Inquiry into the Wealth of Nations. [63] The immense wealth extracted from Bengal provided capital for the British Industrial Revolution. This in turn would drive further British conquest and incidentally decimate the Bengal textile industry that had helped to fuel the expansion of the Company in the 18th century. [64]

The "Black Hole", something that may have been no more than an exaggerated concoction, has been of vastly greater concern to British historians than the British-exacerbated famine that killed 10 million Bengalis in 1769-1770 and crippled a populous and sophisticated society. The Black Hole is typically treated with precise and indignant detail but the Great Bengal Famine, when rarely alluded to, is dismissed in a dozen words. Dodwell (1963b) castigates J.H. Little (1916) for his disposal of the "Black Hole" with a confident, patronising academic pomposity: "Altogether the controversy seems to have arisen from the perplexities of a student unaccustomed to the conflicts of evidence which the historian has perpetually to encounter." [65] Honi soit qui mal y pense. In Dodwell (1963a), The Cambridge

History of India, the relevant chapter by Dodwell manages to completely ignore the Great Bengal Famine of 1769-1770. [66]

Chapter 10

The Great Bengal Famine of 1769-1770

"Let other pens dwell on guilt and misery".

- Jane Austen in Mansfield Park (1814) [1]

"Remember that we are English, that we are Christians. Consult your own understanding, your own sense of the probable, your own observation of what is passing around you. Does our education prepare us for such atrocities?"

- Henry Tilney in Northanger Abbey (1818) [2]

"Between 1769 and 1770 a third of the population of Bengal died of famine."

- Winston Churchill (1965) [3]

"Nonsense, isn't it! Millions starving, then and now, I hear you protesting. And Jane Austen! What are you going on about? All I can answer is, plaintively, man, and especially woman, does not live by bread alone: he has to have books."

- Fay Weldon in Letters to Alice on First Reading Jane Austen (1984) [4]

10.1. Bengal immediately after Clive's departure

There is a copious literature dealing with the period of British conquest and consolidation in Bengal that culminated in the disastrous Bengal Famine of 1769-1770 and we will draw upon the more detailed histories that deal with this catastrophe. [5] However, as we have already seen in Chapter 9, there are substantial differences in how one of the greatest disasters of humanity has been treated by historians.

With the departure of Robert Clive from Bengal in 1767, the Governorship of Bengal fell to Harry Verelst. Mohammed Reza Khan had to deal with Francis Sykes who was the Company's resident at Murshidabad.. Sykes was of course insistent on maximizing tax receipts and was involved in all kinds of trading. Sykes was replaced by Richard Becher. While Becher would send his gumashtahs (agents) into the country to conduct private trade, he was not obsessed with the ruthless wealth generation imperative of Sykes and other such Company men. Mohammed Reza Khan found a more sympathetic person in Becher and could more readily put a case to the Governor and Council in Calcutta in relation to limitations on how much could be squeezed out of a suffering land. The impositions on the Bengalis included the massive and often violently secured overtaxing of farmers and other abuse of the people, whether weavers, merchants, ryots or zamindars, through trade restrictions, monopolies, enforced acquisition of goods at the purchaser's price and the brutality of gumashtahs (the agents of the Company men).

The British Government, impressed with the potential for wealth to be made from Bengal, demanded 400,000 pounds per annum for the British Treasury. This in turn provided greater pressure for revenue raising in Bengal. In 1769 Hyder Ali of Mysore invaded the Carnatic and the defense of the region by British forces represented another major drain on Company resources. The Council in Calcutta wanted to introduce a system of Supervisors involving Europeans in directly overseeing revenue collections and reporting on conditions. This system began early in 1770 as famine was beginning to take a grip on Bengal.

Verelst left Bengal at the end of 1769 and was replaced as Governor by John Cartier. The puppet Nawab Saif-ud-daulah died early in 1770 and was replaced by Mir Jafar's fifth son Mubarak-ud-daulah. The latter's mother was Babbu Begum but the mother of the preceding two Nawabs, Munni (little) Begum, had originally been a slave girl of Babbu Begum's mother and from this had risen to a position of great power at court. She disliked Mohammed Reza Khan, despite his best endeavors, and a delicate problem of Begum precedence arose on the accession of Mubarak-ud-daulah. Mohammed Reza Khan's solution was that the new Nawab's mother should have real authority at court but as a matter of etiquette should regard Munni Begum as her superior. Munni Begum felt her loss keenly and translated her animosity into action when Warren Hastings arrived in 1772.

10.2. Basic biological survival realities in Bengal

Before considering the disastrous consequences of the British invasion and irresponsible exploitation of Bengal, it is useful to consider the agrarian bottom-line underlying the "nabobs, mohrs and palanquins" perceived by Jane Austen and her contemporaries. [6] Rice is the basic food staple of the Bengalis and there are three significant rice harvests per year in the highly productive, silt-enriched paddy fields of Lower Bengal, namely the spring paddy (boro), summer paddy (aus) and the winter paddy (aman) harvests with typical relative total yields of about 1, 7 and 21, respectively. The actual yields per acre of these crops are actually rather similar but the differences in aggregate amount derive from the different types of locations in which they are grown, for there are agriculturally important differences in terrain even in this real-life "Flatland".

The spring rice (boro) is harvested in February to May. The seed is broadcast in November to January into low lying wetlands that retain moisture such as drying river beds and swamps. It can grow and survive without additional rain and inundation but obviously additional water will assist the yield. The summer rice (aus) is harvested in late July to September. It is planted in late March and April on relatively high land at the same sort of level as housing or protective levees and benefits from the longer hours of summer sunshine and is crucially dependent on rain. The winter paddy (aman) is the most important rice crop and is harvested from late October to February. It can be planted by either simply broadcasting seed or by transplanting from nurseries, in both cases into prepared fields that will be flooded as a result of monsoonal rain . The rice plants grow well in such flooded conditions and the rice stalks can be extremely long. The rice roots can survive low oxygen concentrations and even if roots are detached from the substratum, adventitious roots can supply nutrient. [7]

The consumption of rice by Bengalis is typically very substantial. Thus average annual rice consumption by Bengalis in the straightened circumstances of the early 1940s was about 90 kilograms per person for a bare-subsistence family. This basic staple is nutritionally expanded with pulses (used to make a legume porridge or dahl), vegetables such as spinach (palungshagh) or eggplant (baygun) and fruit. In hindsight, from a biochemical perspective, the pulses provide a better complement of amino acids and green vegetables provide essential minerals and vitamins. This diet is further complemented (as can be afforded) with varying amounts of salt, sugar, spices, fruit, milk and milk products such as clarified butter (ghee), meat, shrimps (chinlri march) and fish. [8] From this we can see the modest requirements for human survival in Bengal in 1770.

Since rice represents the major component of this diet we can attempt to put a price on human survival at that time and hence the "value" put on the lives of each of the 10 million who were to perish. Later in this disquisition we can attempt similar estimates of the "values" of the lives of some victims of genocide in World War 2: a starving Hindu Bengali pandit, a Muslim Bengali mother driven to sexual submission or a Hungarian Jewish professional man sent to Auschwitz. While the Great Famine of Bengal in 1769-1770 derived from drought and hence a major food deficit, it must be appreciated that the administration that ferociously taxed the Bengali peasant (or ryot), ruled the waves and exported Bengali opium to China and Bengali muslin, silk, saltpetre and indigo to Britain would have had the resources to address its obligations to its starving subjects. [9]

The price of rice in Calcutta in 1770 was Rs 0.77 per maund. [10] Taking a 1770 exchange rate of about 0.11 pound per Rupee, [11] 1 maund = 37.4 kilogram and 90 kilograms as the annual average per capita rice consumption, [12] we can use such assumptions to estimate the Calcutta market cost of feeding one Bengali at the time for 1 year at about 0.2 pounds. If we adopt the bottom-line estimate of annual per capita famine relief to actual recipients in Bengal in 1944 at 30 kilogram of grain [13] we can divide the above estimate by three to get a rock-bottom estimate of the per annum cost of a Bergen-Belsen type of survival at 0.07 pounds, or about one shilling and sixpence per person. The total annual cost of bare subsistence for those 10 million who perished would thus on this account have been 700,000 pounds, similar in magnitude to the additional 400,000 pounds demanded of the Company by the British Government in 1769. [14]

Considerations such as this make one realise that it would indeed have been very cheap for Marianne's mother to have hired an additional servant to care for Willoughby's gift of a horse. The above figures are revealing in comparison with the annual incomes of other good people of Sense and Sensibility (admittedly several decades later) such as Mrs. Dashwood (500 pounds), Colonel Brandon (2,000 pounds) and Edward Ferrars (1,000 pounds if he marries Miss Morton). [15] In comparison, in the early 1770s (one third of the rural population having died), Fort William coolies were paid Rs.4 per month (i.e. about 5 pounds per annum). [16] With these estimates in mind, let us now examine the genesis and course of the Great Bengal Famine.

10.3. The beginning of the famine

The most detailed account of the genesis, course and consequences of the Great Bengal Famine is that of Hunter (1871) [17] but a number of additional corroborative accounts have also been given. [18] In 1768 there had been a partial failure of the rice crop but this had not affected the rent-wracking returns to the administration of the "Dual Government" of Mohammed Reza Khan and the Company. This however led to increased prices in early 1769 (the price rose by about 10% in Calcutta). Although tax receipts continued as usual, rain was deficient in northern Bengal and some local officers expressed some concern at this stage. In September 1769 the summer aus harvest was sufficiently good initially to enable the promise of substantial exports to Madras. However the September rains ceased unexpectedly and large crop losses ensued with fields of rice reduced to paddocks of dried straw. Despite mounting concerns from local officials, Governor Verelst gave no warning to his superiors, although such advice (signed by his successor John Cartier before his accession) was sent to London. Verelst left office at the end of the year and was replaced by John Cartier.

By February 1770 it was clear to Cartier that famine was abroad and he informed the Court of Directors, assuring them that revenue was unaffected although temporary remissions could be entertained in particular cases of difficulty. The spring boro crop also failed its previous promise but the Council actually increased the land-tax for the next year by 10%, acting on the advice of Mohammed Reza Khan. The sanguinity of the Council in Calcutta is surprising, especially since the "native" tax collectors had every incentive, humanity aside, to maximize any difficulties encountered in meeting the merciless demands of the Company. By the middle of the year famine was an obvious and established reality throughout Bengal, Bihar and Orissa.

10.4. The awfulness of the catastrophe

In the absence of any significant prior attempts at mitigation, a catastrophe consumed Bengal - city, town, village and countryside alike. In the absence of grain for food the ryot could progressively sell off his cattle and implements in order to buy food. Seed grain was consumed and ultimately all that was left were the leaves of trees and grass. Children were sold into bondage. The nightmare led to the living feeding on the dead. Fields were strewn with the dead and dying. No doubt other horrors recorded 60 years ago in Bengal [19] also obtained in Bengal in 1770, such as vultures, jackals and dogs eating those so weakened with hunger that they could not move or resist.

Refugees flooded into the cities and disease complicated the tragedy. Dogs, jackals, birds of prey and even tigers would cleanse Bengali communities of dead bodies in those days. However the death toll was so great that bodies accumulated in the streets with consequent disease. A smallpox epidemic had commenced at the beginning of 1770 in Murshidabad and even the great were not safe: the young Nawab Saif-ud-daulah died of the disease in March 1770. The awfulness of the carnage was such that words were inadequate: the observers were evidently in the same sort of dulled perceptional state as the first soldiers and journalists to enter concentration camps towards the end of World War 2. [20] A letter from the Calcutta Council to the Court of Directors of the Company in London on 12th December 1770 states: "It is scarcely possible that any description could be an exaggeration". [21] To repeat the words of eye-witness John Shore (later Lord Teignmouth):

"Still fresh in memory's eye the scene I view,
The shrivelled limbs, sunk eyes, and lifeless hue;
Still hear the mother's shrieks and infants moans,
Cries of despair and agonizing moans." [22]

Charles Grant was also an eye-witness and graphically described the "lingering multitudes" feeding off the leaves and bark of trees; fields, streets and passages strewn with bodies; people constantly removing bodies and floating them downriver on rafts; the impossibility of avoiding the frantic cries; the offensive smell of rotting bodies; the violation of eating taboos and even children eating their dead mothers and mothers feeding on their dead children. [23] In all of this remember that in such cataclysms the children represent the largest group of victims. The rains came in mid-1770 and a good summer aus harvest was obtained. However it came too late for huge numbers of people. No doubt many died of starvation or disease in sight of the ripening abundant harvest. The rains also brought disease to a population weakened by starvation.

10.5. Counting the cost

It was estimated by Warren Hastings after his return to India that the famine had swept away at least one third of the population. [24] In mid-1770 it was estimated that 3 eighths of the population had perished and that a half of the farmers and their families would perish. Grant provides a very conservative estimate of 3 million deaths but Hunter estimates 10 million. The country took literally 4 decades to recover from the disaster. In the immediate aftermath there were insufficient people to farm the land and large tracts of land were left uncultivated. The famine had a disastrous impact upon industrial activity, notably upon the major weaving trade. [25]

10.6. The observations of a relation visiting Jane Austen's uncle in Bengal

A chillingly brief eye-witness account of this depopulation is given by Philip Dormer Stanhope in his Genuine Memoirs of Asiaticus. This Stanhope is not the same as the Philip Dormer Stanhope, the 4th Earl of Chesterfield, who died in 1773. Stanhope arrived in Calcutta in 1774 and was presented to Warren Hastings by Jane Austen's uncle, Tysoe Hancock, with whom Stanhope was staying because of prior acquaintance and because Stanhope was related to Philadelphia Hancock (née Austen). In Stanhope's own words, "You know I went out particularly recommended to Mr. Hancock, whom I previously knew in England, and whose lady is my near relation." Stanhope was received well by Hastings, a very good friend and business partner of Hancock, and learned from the latter that Hastings would try to obtain a position for him with the "Nabob of Oude". In the event Stanhope was advised to return to Madras where he had hopes of gaining a post on the recommendation of Hastings. However he was shipwrecked off the Bengal coast at the beginning of 1775 but made it to shore. A village of Indians was persuaded by a lascar (seaman) to take them to Calcutta, which they reached after various adventures. Thus various members of their party disappeared and the chief mate (notorious for his violence and for the murder of lascars) was seized and carried off by a tiger (noting that the tigers of that part of Bengal could be as big as small cows). In the middle of this account he describes the desolation of Bengal (now, and indeed before the Great Famine, the most densely populated part of the planet), five years after the holocaust:

"We proceeded, by easy marches, through a country beautiful, by nature, but utterly destitute of cultivation;" [26]

Stanhope returned to the hospitable Hancock in Calcutta. He ultimately saw service with Mohammed Ali, the Nawab of Arcot, and returned to England in 1778. [27]

10.7. The desolate country

Stanhope's chilling observation is confirmed by the observations of the remorseless British tax-collectors over the next few years: one third of the country had reverted to waste land. Even 19 years after the famine, Lord Cornwallis (Governor-General 1786-1793) concluded that one third of Bengal was jungle. For one and a half decades after the famine the population continued to decrease because of the differential mortality of children during the famine. Renewed population growth awaited the growth to sexual maturity of children born after the famine. The population 20 years after the famine was estimated to be about 27 million, about what it had been in 1769. [28] We will see later that there was a similar huge demographic "deficit" after the 1943/44 famine of about 11 million people about 7 years after the end of the famine. [29]

A major consequence of the famine was a dramatic change in the social strata. Two thirds of the zamindars, the landowners, were ruined because the British remorselessly insisted upon the payment of the land taxes despite the fact that the human basis for wealth generation had been so severely damaged. The demands were extracted with violence where necessary, as indeed had happened in pre-famine times. Zamindars unable to meet their "debts" to the British blood-suckers had to surrender their property and in some cases their liberty as well. In the district of Beerbohm the local prison was filled with "revenue prisoners" nearly 2 decades after the disaster. It should be appreciated that the British insisted in general on payment of the taxes regardless of the famine and indeed the demand proposed for 1770/71 (1,524,567 pounds) was 10% higher than in the previous year. Arrears had to be paid and were remorselessly exacted. Remissions were rare: thus of 1,380,269 pounds demanded in 1769/70, only 65,355 pounds was mercifully remitted. In comparison, the receipts in the "good" period of 1768/69 were only slightly higher at 1,525,485 pounds.

A major rural reality after the famine was an excess of land and a shortage of people to till it. This had a number of consequences for landowners and for the peasants (ryots). The ryot was in demand by zamindars and this then generated 2 classes of farmer: those who continued on their traditional patch and those that came from elsewhere. The Company, concerned by the potential losses of revenue, encouraged migration of peasants from neighbouring Oudh. Zamindars competed with each other for ryots, offering lower rents and protection. [30]

The destitution and reversion of so much countryside to wilderness created further problems for the peasants. Tigers represented a great menace - they could be extremely large. There is a horrible account of firewood collectors being attacked by a tiger and scattering in haste with one of their number being seized and eaten. The survivors then return, confident that the tiger's appetite has been satisfied. Another account describes a person escaping to the water only to be seized when the tiger swims out. [31] Elephants also posed a major threat and the diminished community resources decreased the ability of the peasants to defend themselves against elephants.

Bandits (banditti) represented a major threat to the depleted and impoverished peasantry, spreading rape, murder and pillage across the countryside. Such bands of violent men could be former soldiers, people from the hill country, displaced peasants and religious sanyasis or faquirs who could couple religious devotion with violent robbery. Huge bands of thousands of displaced and impoverished peasants afflicted the countryside. In addition there were "traditional" robbers belonging to the robber castes, namely the dacoits and thugs. The traditional ryot and zamindar relationship obliged the latter to provide some measure of protection in return for the rent, but the British imposition and the famine disrupted this social compact. This violence spread to the cities and was most dramatically associated with incendiarism. Thus a huge fire in Calcutta in 1780 destroyed 15,000 homes and killed several hundred people. [32]

10.8. Responsibility for the famine

Responsibility for disasters of this kind must lie heavily with the administering power. Those who would rule others are responsible for their welfare. "No governance without responsibility" applies as much to those ruling the starving millions of colonial Bengal in 1770 as to successive Australian governments and the disastrous, "Third World" health problems of "outback" tribal Aborigines in "post-colonial" Australia approaching the year 2000. The British did not respond effectively to the growing reports of famine, first in the north and then throughout the whole of Bengal and adjoining regions. Bengal was a huge, lucrative place in which the peasants were being "farmed" for revenue and one senses that (within certain constraints) famine would have been regarded as a natural phenomenon affecting Bengalis in much the same way that drought might affect livestock numbers in outback Australia. The same callousness was to repeat itself over the subsequent centuries in Australia, other parts of India, Ireland and repeatedly in Bengal. [33]

Relief was offered in Calcutta and Murshidabad but was woefully inadequate. Hunter (1871) gives an estimate of 9,000 pounds provided for relief by the Company for a starving population of 30 million (as compared to the taxation receipts of over 1.3 million pounds for 1769/70). This relief amounted to 0.07 of a penny for each Bengali and was about a thousand times lower than the cost of rice for a normal Bengali diet. [34]

The issue of hoarding and constraint on trade is complicated. As Adam Smith (1776) has argued in relation to famines in general and to the Great Bengal Famine in particular, it is important for food prices to be de-regulated to allow food to reach its most urgent destination naturally, to allow the market to inform people unambiguously of impending shortages and to impose timely economies on the consumers. Bengal was a tightly regulated milch-cow for the Company and its employees, with considerable profits to be made from grain in an economy regulated for the benefit of a miniscule number of Europeans. Hunter (1871) has argued cogently that in the Bengal famine of 1865-1866 deregulation of private trade had a very positive effect and that such a deregulated rice market would have helped in the Great Bengal Famine. However there was widespread belief that European traders exploited the elevated price of rice for their benefit in this disastrous situation. Further, Europeans were in a position to force starving peasants to grow crops for products other than food and controlled grain shipments. The outrageous financial exactions on the peasantry (demands actually increased in this period) was an effective sentence of death for millions. According to Ballhatchet (1965):

"But in spite of the Bengal famine of 1770, which was thought to have carried off one-third of the population, the revenue was, in the government's words "violently kept up to its former standard"." According to Roberts (1909b):

"While its servants accumulated vast fortunes, the finances of the Company were far from prosperous, and Bengal itself, already plundered by corrupt native officials, was scourged by a terrible famine in 1769-70. A sinister commentary upon the administration of this time is afforded by the fact that though a third of the inhabitants of Bengal are said to have perished, the revenue collections of 1771 exceeded those of 1768, the year preceding the famine."

The shortage of cash to buy food was compounded by the rises in the price of rice. Thus Bose (1993) comments that there was actually a shortage of labour prior to the famine (and hence the disaster was not "Malthusian") and that lack of bullion and artificially elevated prices was the problem: "The "violent upswing" in prices was much greater than the shortfall in production would have "nominally justified"." [35]

Bengal is in general a waterway-rich country and this would have provided an avenue for grain importation that was not realised in reality. Hunter compares the situation in Bengal in 1770 with that in Orissa in 1866 in which a rice-exporting province was struck by famine at a time of low food stocks, limited landward access and harbors unusable in the monsoon season. These factors combined to devastate Orissa while the remainder of the region with adequate access to external food escaped a catastrophe. Hunter has argued that the Great Bengal Famine derived from want of effective transportation as well as from deterrence of private trade and lack of money to buy grain if available. [36]

Ultimately in any famine the real determinant of life or death is access to food and money to purchase food. Amartya Sen has used the notion of "entitlement" to describe a type of social share that if too small results in famine and death. [37] Food deficit situations that are emotionally and superficially perceived as due to drought can in many cases be seen to simply derive from an inability to purchase. In Bengal in 1770 the British exercised tight control over a "human farm", declined significant amelioration and had sucked the society dry of the resources needed to purchase grain from elsewhere. There was indeed a dearth of cash in a society milked to support Madras and for remittances to England. This deficiency is expressed simply by Gardner (1971):

"The country had been swept by one of the most terrible famines it had ever known. There was a shortage of currency owing to the export of gold and silver to China to purchase tea." [38]

10.9. The historical record

A variety of eye-witness accounts of the famine exist, including letters from people intimately involved such as Company men, notably Supervisors, and from Indian dignitaries such as Mohammed Reza Khan. Officials such Charles Grant and John Shore recalled and recorded these dreadful times. We have seen that even chance travellers such as Stanhope were touched by these events several years after their occurrence. [39] A detailed account of Bengal (and Company finances) is given by Warren Hastings and his colleagues in a letter to the Court of Directors in London in 1772 in which they estimate the loss of one third of the whole population. [40] Other details are provided by the communications from the Company men to the Directors but we have already noted that there was no advice about the famine actually signed by Governor Verelst who departed at the end of 1769. [41]

Some variously detailed accounts of the famine have been written. [42] The most detailed and sympathetic account of the famine is given by Sir William Hunter (1871) in The Annals of Rural Bengal. This humane history records eye-witness accounts and details the genesis, actuality, consequences and causes of the famine and of related events in India. [43] Perhaps the best known writer who commented in various ways on the famine was Adam Smith (1776) in his An Inquiry into the Wealth of Nations. It is a sad testament to the unresponsiveness of the world that one of the earliest and most widely read works on economics that dealt with these matters in an incisive and deeply humane way should have over several centuries still failed to move the world to rational action. [44] [It is of interest to note that my lawyer-economist great-grandfather Jakab Polya translated Adam Smith's classic into Hungarian but public access to this translation of a "capitalist" work was apparently restricted in post-war Communist Hungary.] From these texts we go to a large number of excellent texts (mostly dealing specifically with Indian history) that, while not going into elaborate detail, nevertheless deal concisely with the actual occurrence and dimensions of the tragedy. [45] From these we then descend to works that dismiss this extraordinary event in a few words and, in particular, those in which the paucity of treatment is stark contrast to the depth of treatment given to vastly less significant matters in an "Indian" or other "colonial" context. [46]

Kaye (1853) in detailing changes to revenue collection in 1772 admits that: "The country was at this time in an impoverished condition, for there had been a mighty famine in the land..." [20 words for 10 million victims.] [47]

Sir Alfred Lyall P.C., K.C.B., D.C.L. came close to the mark in condemning British abuses in Bengal in the most trenchant terms but evidently did not get quite close enough: "By investing themselves with political attributes without discarding their commercial character, they produced an almost unprecedented conjunction which engendered intolerable abuses and confusion in Bengal. This is the only period of Anglo-Indian history which throws grave and unpardonable discredit on the English name. During the six years from 1760 to 1765, Clive's absence from the country left the Company's affairs in the hands of incapable and inexperienced chiefs, just at the moment when vigorous and statesmanlike management was needed." After his history re-enters a time zone of creditable English behaviour, Lyall (1916) devotes 9 words to a famine that consumed 10 million: "The Madras Presidency drifted into that ruinous war with Hyder Ali that has already been described; and in 1770 a terrible famine had desolated Bengal." [48] Lyall

(1907) was similarly economical in his biography Warren Hastings:
"and in 1771 a wasting famine had visited Bengal". [49]

Wilbur (1945) takes this diminution even further. Chapter 18 (Clive,
Pondicherry , and Plassey) concludes with the suicide of Clive : "In
February, 1767, he left the shores of India for the last time ... Ill and
discouraged over the attitude of the public, the hostility and treachery
of men in high places, on November 22, 1774, he took his life at his
home in Berkeley Square." (pp 272-273). Verelst, Cartier and the Great
Bengal Famine are erased from history and Chapter 19 commences:
"In 1772 there was appointed to the governorship of Bengal ... Warren
Hastings." Wilbur (1945) nevertheless actually alludes to some kind of
difficulty on p278: "Widespread famine, sickness, and poverty among
Bengal workers impaired the returns from the farms." [14 words]. [50]

Winston Churchill's A History of the English-Speaking Peoples
provides a zenith for this coyness about the period 1765-1772.
Churchill deals with this period in a similar fashion and with similar
verbal economy. Thus on pp 225-226: "A few years later he [Clive]
died by his own hand. * * * Clive was soon followed in India by ...
Warren Hastings... The Mahrattas seized Delhi and menaced Oudh.
Madras was threatened, and even Bombay, hitherto so peaceful, was
involved in the civil wars. Between 1769 and 1770 a third of the
population of Bengal died of famine. Throughout these ordeals Warren
Hastings held fast to an austere way of life." [51]

Edwardes (1967) discusses famine in India and while mentioning that
"Before 1858, there had been frequent famines in India" fails to deal
with the 1770 famine, presumably because his book is confined to the
period 1772-1947. However Edwardes (1961) in his history of India
yields ten words for 10 million: "Oppression and exploitation were
aggravated, in 1770, by a disastrous famine." [52]

Gardner (1971) continues this historiographical tradition with an
almost famine-free Clive Chapter 5 and Hastings Chapter 6 interfacing.

However in writing about Hasting's accession in 1772 he does admit that: "The country had been swept by one of the most terrible famines it had ever known." [53]

Carey (1882) is similarly inexplicit: "One [famine] which extended over 1770 and 1771 was the most terrible in its consequences, but others of shorter duration occasioned unspeakable suffering." [54]

Dunbar (1951) alludes to oppression of the peasantry at this time that incidentally affects revenue: "Unfortunately it was soon obvious that the collection of revenue was being accompanied by widespread extortion and injustice, evasion by the victimised peasantry, and, incidentally, considerable loss to the government. This cried out for reform, and the first act of Warren Hastings, when he became governor at Fort William in 1772, was to set up an English board of revenue under himself." [55]

Feiling (1966) briefly refers to the "great famine": "As he went on tour this summer, he [Warren Hastings] tells Aldersey "it is an exhausted country and has been much oppressed." For everywhere he saw marks of the great famine, when dogs and vultures had fed on the million dead, and whole villages had gone back to jungle." [56]

Hunter, while the author of the most detailed and impassioned description of the famine, namely Hunter (1871), Annals of Rural Bengal, [57] is less fullsome 20 years later in Hunter (1890): "Lord Clive quitted India for the third and last time in 1767. Between that date and the governorship of Warren Hastings in 1772, little of importance occurred in Bengal beyond the terrible famine of 1770, which is officially reported to have swept away one third of the inhabitants. The dual system of government, established in 1765 by Clive, had proved a failure." [58]

Gleig (1841) in his monumental 3 volume work on Warren Hastings has a few words to spare for the 10 million: "while, as if to sum up the measure of evil, first war and then famine came like a scourge upon the provinces. It was in Bengal that the famine raged with such a fury as to cut off in the course of one year full one third of the inhabitants." [59]

Finally we should recognize that there is a large body of books dealing with British history, including British colonial history, that do not specifically refer at all to the Great Bengal Famine of 1769-1770, one of the most devastating events in human history prior to the 20th century. [60] Thus Porter (1983), The Lions's Share. A Short History of British Imperialism 1850-1983, is even less explicit. The problem of famine in India is mentioned in general and indeed specifically: "British India was in quite a lot of trouble in 1877-1878. As well as the Afghan War, a famine which killed 5 million, and what The Times called "an ominous restlessness" among the natives ..." There is no mention of the (pre-1850) Great Bengal Famine nor of the (pre-1983) Bengal Famine of 1943-1944. [61]

The remarkable near-total deletion of the Great Bengal Famine from Dodwell (1963a) The Cambridge History of India Volumes 1-6 is alleviated by several very brief non-quantitative references to the 1770 event in the contributions of Lovett (1963a,b) in the 19th century section of the opus. In contrast, the one volume Oxford History of India by Spear (1975) deals with both events. Fortunately for Cambridge, various volumes of The New Cambridge History of India, specifically those written by Bayly (1988), Bose (1993) and Marshall (1987), resurrect the 1770 Famine. Roberts and Ballhatchet (both of Oxford) also rescue Cambridge by briefly mentioning the 1770 famine in their contributions, namely Roberts (1909b) and Bullhatchet (1965) in The Cambridge Modern History and The New Cambridge Modern History, respectively. However we will see in Chapters 14 and 15 that Cambridge also appears to suffer from a strange forgetfulness in relation to the Bengal Famine of 1943-44. [62]

In terms of human death toll and destruction wreaked on a sophisticated human society, the Great Bengal Famine must rank with "well-known" pre-20th century events as catastrophic as the medieval

European Black Death and the Mongolian conquests under Genghis Khan, [63] the decimation of the population of Mexico [64] and the carnage of the African slave trade [65] while being smaller in magnitude than the total carnage associated with the Tai Ping rebellion in 19th century China. Nevertheless this massive disaster is scrupulously avoided by a large number of histories. Several of these Austenizing works bear specific mention because they are "classic" historical texts, namely H.G.Wells' The Outline of History [66] and the History of England by G.M. Trevelyan, O.M., Master of Trinity College 1940-1951 and formerly Regius Professor of Modern History in the University of Cambridge. [67] Wells (1956) and Trevelyan (1952) manage to delete all mention of famine in British India from their works. G.M. Treveleyan was the grandson of Charles Trevelyan who performed a similar bureaucratic job in relation to starving Ireland and starving India of Imperial Britain of the 19th century as Albert Speer did for the Nazi German empire in Europe during World War 2. [68]

We have already seen that the Black Hole of Calcutta has a highly arguable reality and that, if it occurred at all, [69] the outrage ranges from the "standard version" of 23 survivors out of 146 imprisoned [70] to perhaps as few as 9-20 imprisoned of whom 2 died. [71] It is remarkable that of a list of 27 works not mentioning the Great Bengal Famine but expected to do so (listed in footnote 60), 11 nevertheless mention the Black Hole "outrage". [72] One is reminded of the aphorism from that monster of the 20th century, Joseph Stalin, that "A single death is a tragedy, a million deaths is a statistic." [73] and more recently, that of Ben Elton (1996) through his Police Chief Cornell in Popcorn: "There's two results to every event, what actually happened and what people think happened. That's a fact, pal, and if you believe you can ignore it, then you don't have no election to face come the spring." [74] The conclusion of Iris Macfarlane (1975) is germane to our disquisition at this stage:

"So there it was, the Black Hole of Calcutta, a nothingness...The legend grew and grew as the sweaty agonies of those men and women were required to set against oversights of humanity of the white man now in charge: the famine of 1770 for instance, when ten million Bengalis died while the revenue continued to be collected." [75]

10.10. Postscript - merciless, remorseless rapacity

The following considered and "expert" observations of this disaster provide a chilling sequence and conveys the remorselessness of the "farming" of Bengali peasants and workers that was to continue for nearly 2 centuries. It is also provided for the benefit of the English readers who, at one end of a likely spectrum of disapprobation, may consider me "unsound" and at the other, "an Aussie slagging off the Poms".

"When the Bengal famine of 1770 occurred, believed to have swept away one-third of the population, little attempt at relief was made, though this, with Bengal's network of waterways was practicable. The cruel severity with which the revenue continued to be collected at this time delayed recovery for many years."

- Encyclopaedia Britannica (1977, 1979). [76]

"In 1770, some months after the introduction of the new [Supervisor] system, there was a dreadful famine which killed one-third of the population of Bengal, but the famine, instead of melting the hearts of the Englishmen concerned, whetted their hunger for money... the ryots were compelled to sell their rice to the monopolizing Europeans...to sell even the seed requisite for the next harvest."

- Gopal (1963a). [77]

"In 1770 Nature added to the ruin done by man. A famine carried off some millions, perhaps one third, of the inhabitants. The survivors lived on roots or leaves, and sold their children; the dead lay heaped in the streets of Calcutta, and epidemic followed famine. Both

Englishmen and Indian ministers were accused of profiting by the shortage of food."

- Feiling (1966). [78]

"In 1770 there was a terrible famine in Bengal. One-third of the population died. Yet it was reported in England that the Company's servants were making fortunes out of the sufferings of the starving population by speculating in foodstuffs. And, while the Company's servants gained wealth, the Company itself, despite all its conquests, was on the verge of bankruptcy. In 1769 the adventurer Hyder Ali, of Mysore, invaded the Carnatic, devastating and plundering; and the cost of sending armies from Bengal to resist completed the Company's undoing. Instead of paying 400,000 pounds to the British Treasury, they had to borrow money from Government."

- Muir (1929). [79]

"It has been registered as truth in the pages of history, has been the public subject of religious lamentations, has been examined in verse, and still remains such a foul stain upon British character as the annals of any people can hardly parallel."

- Grant (1792), while disputing the validity of the accusation of British entrepreneurs profiting from the food shortage. [80]

"it is enough that various estimates put the losses at between one-third and one-fifth of all the people of Bengal, and that this famine was over long before Leadenhall Street were made aware of it by falling off in revenue."

- Woodruff (1965). [81]

"The Great Famine of Bengal kills 10 million Indians wiping out one-third of the population in the worst famine thus far in world history.

Britain's East India Company increases its demands on Bengal's remaining 20 million people to insure a "reasonable profit"."

- Trager (1979).[82]

"It was to be the first famine-experience of the English, and they had made no provision for it. The misery was terrible... In summing up, 2 years later, the effects of the famine on the population, the Governor-General in Council declared that in some places one-half, and, on the whole, one-third of the inhabitants had been destroyed. It need scarcely be added that this terrible calamity affected the proprietors of East India in a manner to them the most vital: - it destroyed their prospect of large dividends."

- Malleson (1985). [83]

"The ravages caused by the famine of 1770, it is true, contributed a great deal to their failure to secure the promotion of agriculture and improvement in the state of administration. But until 1772, that failure proceeded most from the fundamental defect of policy which had kept power divorced from responsibility."

- Misra (1959). [84]

"Even among those that were not altogether abandoned many square miles of the richest country lay untilled, and one set of revenue agents after another failed to wring the land-tax out of the people. In 1772, the old farmers having thrown up their task in despair were superseded and dragged down to the debtors' prison in Calcutta for arrears... When the British undertook the direct management of the district, nearly twenty years after the famine, they found the jail filled with revenue prisoners, not one of whom had any prospect of regaining his liberty... while the country every year became a more total waste, the English Government constantly demanded an increased land-tax."

- Hunter (1871). [85]

"A terrible famine in Bengal in 1770 created such havoc and desolation that even in 1789 Cornwallis wrote: "I have no hesitation in declaring that one-third of the territories in Bengal under the Company's administration is now reduced to a jungle inhabited by beasts." Yet the total amount of revenue fixed by Cornwallis as the basis of the Permanent Settlement was much higher than the annual revenue realised during the preceding 28 years."

- Majumbar (1976).[86]

"What is called trade between one country and another to the mutual advantage of both, was, in the case of India, its exploitation by Britain ... The world had not known a trade of this kind: it had to be kept going even in the years of famines when millions died of starvation; the economy had been so manouvered that the income the British made in India was not affected by economic distress in the country."

- Gopal (1963a). [87]

"We have outdone the Spaniards in Peru. They were at least butchers on a religious principle, however diabolical their zeal. We have murdered, deposed, plundered, usurped - nay, what think you of the famine in Bengal in which three millions perished being caused by a monopoly of the servants of the East India Company?"

- Horace Walpole. [88]

"Bengal on which the Company had become accustomed to draw for meeting deficits elsewhere, was afflicted in 1770 by an appalling famine in the course of which, so the Governor and Council later informed the Director, one-third of the population is believed to have died."

- Moon (1989). [89]

"Such gross expropriation of the country's wealth and the total neglect of its economy led to chronic want. Eventually it burst forth in a virulent famine in 1770 with a seasonal failure of rain and the manipulation of grain stocks by the profit-hunting English officials and the Indian agents."

- Mukherjee (1958). [90]

"the jobbery and peculation that played havoc both with the trade and revenue of Bengal ... In 1770, the year when Cartier succeeded Verelst, broke out the terrible famine which slew more than a third of the people in Bengal, and turned large tracts of the country into tiger-haunted jungle."

- Trotter (1890). [91]

"At last the dreadful famine of 1770-71 desolated and depopulated the whole country. Terrible reports reached England that the Company's servants had leagued with the native officials to buy up all the grain and sell it at famine prices."

- Wheeler (1860). [92]

"While the servants of the Company were thus wrangling over fine points of jurisdiction, one of the worst tragedies of human history befell Bengal. This was the Bengal famine of 1770 in which nearly a third of the population is said to have been swept away. The absence of a government, properly speaking, and the action of self-seeking men in cornering grains, intensified the severity of the famine."

- Majumdar & Dighe (1977). [93]

The Great Bengal Famine of 1769-1770 and its genesis and aftermath clearly involved the family and connections of Jane Austen. The famine occurred just prior to her birth and it would take about 40 years - the span of Jane Austen's life - to recover from the disaster..

We have no record in Jane Austen's writing about the matter. We should finally recall the words of the great Thomas Babington Macaulay, describing the Great Bengal Famine in his essay on Lord Clive:

"Every servant of a British factor was armed with all the powers of his master; and his master was armed with all the power of the Company. Enormous fortunes were thus rapidly accumulated at Calcutta, while thirty millions of human beings were reduced to the extremity of wretchedness ... In the meantime, the impulse which Clive had given to the administration of Bengal was constantly becoming fainter and fainter. His policy was to a great extent abandoned; the abuses which he had suppressed began to revive; and at length the evils which a bad government had engendered were aggravated by one of those fearful visitations which the best government cannot avert. In the summer of 1770, the rains failed; the earth was parched up; the tanks were empty; the rivers shrank within their beds; and a famine, such as is known only in countries where every household depends for support on its own little patch of cultivation, filled the whole valley of the Ganges with misery and death. Tender and delicate women, whose veils had never been lifted before the public gaze, came forth from the inner chambers in which Eastern jealousy had kept watch over their beauty, threw themselves upon the earth before the passers-by, and, with loud wailings, implored a handful of rice for their children. The Hooghly every day rolled down thousands of corpses close to the porticos and gardens of the English conquerors. The very streets of Calcutta were blocked up by the dying and the dead. The lean and feeble survivors had not energy enough to bear the bodies of their kindred to the funeral pile or to the holy river, or even to scare away the jackals and vultures, who fed on human remains in the face of day. The extent of mortality was never ascertained; but it was popularly reckoned by millions ... and indignation soon began to mingle itself with pity. For it was rumoured that the Company's servants had created the famine by engrossing all the rice of the country; that they had sold the grain for eight, ten, twelve times the price at which they had bought it; that one

English functionary who, the year before, was not worth a hundred guineas, had, during that season of misery, remitted sixty thousand pounds to London. These charges we believe to be unfounded." [94]

This "coloured" but nevertheless powerful prose of Macaulay would certainly have been known to his grandson, G.M. Trevelyan, who would exclude any mention of Indian famine, whether of 1770 or 1943, from his History of England (1952). [95] Winston Churchill certainly read Macaulay, would have read this account of the Great Bengal Famine and indeed made slight reference to this disaster in his A History of the English-Speaking Peoples (1965). [96] Bengal would suffer nearly 2 more centuries of rapacious exploitation but before this 2 century Holocaust ended, the same ruthless inhumanity would visit another famine of gigantic proportions upon the people of the most prolific food producing area of the planet. Sir Winston Churchill, evidently unmoved by the passion of the great Macaulay over the Great Bengal Famine of 1769-1779, would preside over the latter day Bengal Famine of 1943-45 which would consume as many as 5 million people. [97]

10.11. 2008 Postscript

The Great Bengal Famine of 1769-1770 is described in Schama's A History of Britain (2002) but unaccountably the 1943-1945 Bengal Famine (6-7 million victims in Bengal, Bihar, Orissa and Assam) is missing from this otherwise excellent 3-volume history. [98] In contrast, in my huge pharmacological text Biochemical Targets of Plant Bioactive Compounds. A Pharmacological Guide to Sites of Action and Biological Effects (2003) I had occasion to mention the 1769-1770 Bengal Famine in the contexts of Table entries pertaining to morphine (from opium) and rice α-amylase inhibitor protein. [99] This extraordinary holocaust-ignoring in relation to the Great Bengal Famine of 1769-1770 is to be found in some further recent histories.

As discussed in the Preface to the Second Edition and elsewhere in this book, this extraordinary holocaust-ignoring is de rigeur in the Western Murdochracies. Thus I recently published an article entitled "Palestinian, Iraqi, Afghan, Biofuel and Climate Genocide – silence kills and silence is complicity" in the Maine, US magazine Liberalati but the average citizen, while aware of the Jewish Holocaust (6 million victims), would be unaware of what I was talking about since none of these other holocausts and genocides are even mentioned by the Western Mainstream media, even though they are current and continuing. [101]

Chapter 11

Warren Hastings and the conquest of India

"That is to say," cried Marianne contemptuously, "he has told you that in the East Indies the climate is hot, and the mosquitoes are troublesome."

"He would have told me so, I doubt not, had I made any such inquiries; but they happened to be points on which I had previously been informed."

"Perhaps," said Willoughby, "his observations may have extended to the existence of nabobs, mohrs, and palanquins."

- Marianne Dashwood and Mr. Willoughby discussing Colonel Brandon, returned home from India, in Sense and Sensibility (1811). [1]

"The Lands had suffer'd unheard of Depopulation by the Famine and Mortality of 1769. The Collections violently kept up to their former Standard, had added to the distress of the Country, and threatened a general Decay of the Revenue, unless immediate Remedies were applied to prevent it. The farming System for a course of Years subjected to proper checks and regulations, seem'd the most likely to afford relief to the Country, and both to ascertain and produce the real value of the Lands without violence to the Ryots."

- Warren Hastings, letter to the Secret Committee of the East India Company (1772). [2]

"The civil offices of this government might be reduced to a very scanty number, were their exigency alone to determine the list of your covenanted servants, which at this time consists of no less a number than two hundred and fifty-two, and many of them the sons of the first families in the Kingdom of Great Britain, and everyone aspiring to the rapid acquisition of lakhs (1,00,000 rupees) [sic; = 100,000 rupees] and to return to pass the prime of their life at home."

- Warren Hastings, letter to the Court of Directors of the East India Company (1781). [3]

"Shall you expect to hear from me on Wednesday or not? - I think you will, or I should not write, as the three days & half which have passed since my last letter was sent, have not produced many materials towards filling another sheet of paper. - But like Mrs Hastings , "I do not despair -" & you perhaps like the faithful Maria may feel still more certain of the happy Event."

- Jane Austen letter to Cassandra (1800) [their father's cousin Miss Maria Payne was essentially Mrs Marian Hasting's companion at Daylesford in Worcestershire]. [4]

"Nobody ever feels or acts, suffers or enjoys, as one expects! - I do not at all regard Martha's disappointments on the Island; she will like it better in the end. - I cannot help thinking and re-thinking of your going to the Island so heroically. It puts me in mind of Mrs Hastings' voyage down the Ganges, and if we had but room to retire into to eat our fruit, we wd have a picture of it hung there."

- Jane Austen letter to Cassandra (1808) [Cassandra's trip to the Isle of Wight with Martha Lloyd is related to the William Hodges painting at Daylesford of Mrs Hastings' heroic Ganges trip in aid of her sick husband.] [5]

11.1. Warren Hastings returns to India

After the dreadful events of the Great Famine one might have supposed that a chastened Company would have changed its tune significantly and proceeded with somewhat greater sensitivity in its treatment of its Indian subjects. This was not to be despite the fact that the East India Company was now operating in the context of a far better informed and increasingly indignant metropolitan population. After 14 years in Bengal under Robert Clive and Henry Vansittart, Warren Hastings had returned home in 1764 frustrated by the Calcutta Council. However he was to return to India and to glory as recounted in a copious literature dealing specifically with his life [6] or with this period of Indian history. [7] He was recalled to India and given a post as deputy in charge of Madras. In 1772 he was appointed Governor of Fort William to replace John Cartier. Hastings immediately commenced dealing with the aftermath of the Great Bengal Famine and cleaning the stables.[8]

The dual system of government was finally disposed of: the Nawab and his advisers had no more say in the affairs of Bengal. The Nawab Saif-ud-daulah had died in 1770 and Hastings ensured that the young new Nawab, Mubarak-ud-daulah, was given a greatly reduced allowance. Collectors were appointed to actually raise revenue in the countryside with the help of native assistants. The Collectors also had a judicial function, being in charge of civil law administration in the districts. The Collectors were also in position to advise the Council in Calcutta. While criminal law remained in "native" hands, courts of appeal for civil and criminal law, respectively, were established in Calcutta. Mohammed Reza Khan at Murshidabad and Shaitab Ali in Bihar were removed from office and imprisoned. They were prosecuted for financial irregularities but were eventually acquitted - they had merely done their masters' bidding. A Board of Revenue was established and a 5-year plan for revenue collection put in place.

11.2. The Rohilla War

The Marathas gradually recovered from their enormous defeat at Panipat in 1761 and by 1769 were again invading northern India, raiding Rajputana and Rohilkhand and eventually seizing Delhi. The Maratha leader Sindhia returned the Moghal Emperor Shah Alam to Delhi in return for his handing over Allahabad and Kora, cities that the Emperor had received from Clive in 1765 in the settlement following the defeat of Oudh at the Battle of Buxhar in 1764. Hastings responded by formally cutting off the Moghal's tribute (worth about 260,000 pounds per annum), which actually had not been paid anyway since 1769/70. Hastings further concluded the Treaty of Benares in 1773 with the Nawab Wazir of Oudh that specified the return of Allahabad and Kora to Oudh in exchange for 500,000 rupees and a continuing contribution for the support of Company forces. However at this meeting Hastings agreed to assist the Nawab Wazir of Oudh in a campaign against Rohilkhand, thus initiating British involvement in the controversial Rohilla War.

Rohillkhand is a region of 12,000 square miles north of the Gangetic plain. It had a population at that time of about 6 million that was predominantly Hindu. The dominant, ruling tribe were Rohillas and Pathans who had come from Afghanistan. In 1772 the Nawab of Oudh and the head chief of the Rohillas, Hafiz Ramat Khan, concluded a treaty of defence against the increasingly threatening Marathas by which it was agreed that the Rohillas would pay Oudh 400,000 rupees for successful succour in the event of a Maratha invasion. The treaty was witnessed by Sir Robert Barker. In 1773 the Marathas did invade and an army from Oudh, assisted by the British, forced their retreat. However Rohilla refused payment, Oudh requested British assistance to enforce the obligation and Hastings obliged. An army from Oudh and a British force under Colonel Champion invaded Rohilkhand in 1774 and at the Battle of Miranpur Katra the Rohillas were defeated and Hafiz Rahmat Khan slain in battle. Rohilkhand was seized by Oudh and 20,000 Rohillas expelled.

The destructive British involvement against people in a region remote from them and not otherwise in conflict with them was regarded with great disapprobation back in England. Colonel Champion commented at the time on indescribable violence, oppression and cruelty on the part of the Oudh soldiery but he was to soften this in giving evidence at the Parliamentary Hastings Impeachment proceedings a dozen years later back in England.

11.3. Parliament intervenes

The growing public perception of the wealth of the returning Company men or "nabobs" and recognition by shareholders in the Company that their due was being intercepted by their employees led to pressure for greater government control over the Company and its affairs in India. This had initially led to the requirement for 400,000 pounds per annum to be paid into the Exchequer by the Company during the period 1769-1772. A compensatory measure was the relief from duty of Company tea being sent to Ireland and to America. Tea thus exported by the Company to America could therefore compete more effectively with smuggled tea. It was East India Company tea that was thrown into Boston Harbor by the "no taxation without representation" American activists in 1773.

The Company had sent out a commission composed of former Governor of Bengal, Henry Vansittart, as well as Colonel Forde and Scrafton in 1769 to investigate Bengal abuses but their ship of passage, the Aurora, was lost with all aboard in the Indian Ocean. Losses of revenue associated with the Bengal famine and the cost of military operations in southern India made a dent in Company profits and in 1773 the Directors successfully obtained a loan of 1 million pounds from the Government to enable the troubled Company to stay afloat. However the quid pro quo of this support was Parliamentary intervention into affairs in India, and the Act of Parliament specifying this loan also regulated dividends and required reporting to the Treasury.

A second Act of Parliament, Lord North's so-called Regulating Act, provided a new constitution for the Company. A board of Directors was to be elected for 4 years, and a quarter were to retire each year and remain unelectable for 1 year. In India the head of the organization would be a Governor-General based in Calcutta and he would preside over a Council composed of 4 other members, the Governor-General having the casting vote. The Council would govern all three Presidencies in India and would report to the Directors in London who would in turn report to the Treasury about finances and to the Secretary of State about other matters. In addition a Supreme Court was set up with a Chief Justice and 3 puisne judges.

The first Governor-General was Warren Hastings, the first Councillors Lieutenant-General Clavering, Monson, Barwell and Philip Francis. The first Chief Justice was Elijah Impey, who had attended the Westminster School with both imperialist Hastings and the sensitive, humanist poet William Cowper. Just as Hastings was intimately connected with the Austen family in the 18th and 19th centuries, so the Impey family became connected by marriage with the Austens in the 19th century.[9] The annual salaries are instructive: the Governor-General received 25,000 pounds, each Councillor 10,000 pounds and the Chief Justice 8,000 pounds. However these salaries evidently did not suffice and were generously supplemented in various ways.

Things started badly on the arrival in Calcutta in 1774 of 3 of the Councillors, namely Francis, Monson and Clavering. They objected to an insufficiency of guns in the welcoming salute and quickly made it clear that they were set to constrain Hastings. While condemning the Rohilla War, the Council demanded that Colonel Champion get 400,000 rupees from the Nawab of Oudh in return for the earlier defeat of the Marathas and also ordered Captain Nathaniel Middleton, Resident at Lucknow, to hand over confidential correspondence with Hastings. When the Nawab Wazir of Oudh, Shuja-ud-daulah, died in 1775, the Council upped the payments to the Company by his successor for maintenance of the British forces and also insisted that Benares become Company territory.

11.4. The judicial murder of Nandkumar

Hastings was under attack from the Council but, in a process not unconnected with this hostility, was subject to formal complaint to the Council by the leading Hindu dignitary Nandkumar in 1775. It was alleged that Hastings had received a bribe from the widow of Mir Jafar, the indomitable Munni Begum. The allegation was supported by testaments from the Indian community and had some substance in the sense that he had actually received 150,000 rupees from her on a trip to Murshidabad. Hastings fought back: he refused to be arraigned in front of the Council by Nandkumar and dissolved the Council meeting. He refused to pay the money into the Company treasury and brought a charge of conspiracy against Nandkumar. Very conveniently a charge of forgery was now brought against Nandkumar by a Calcutta merchant.

Nandkumar was tried before Chief Justice Elijah Impey and 3 other judges, was found guilty and hanged. The Council did not show mercy towards a man who had helped their purposes and the judicial murder of such a prominent Indian citizen (5 years after the death of 10 million Bengalis in the famine) would have had a salutory effect on the Indian citizenry by demonstrating the consequences of having the temerity to accuse an important person such as Hastings. In addition to having been at school with Hastings, Impey had also benefited from his friend through a generous additional judicial appointment that effectively doubled his salary. It has been argued that if this was a corrupt decision then the other judges would have had to be persuaded as well. This actually seems likely, since isolated men of a common cultural, professional and racial ilk would be expected to stick up for their own in such circumstances. The prolonged duress of widowed, part-European Mary Carey says a lot about such attitudes. [10]

The execution of Nandkumar shocked the Calcutta community and was one of the grounds for the later impeachment of Warren Hastings. In addition to his deadly faux pas in accusing Hastings, Nandkumar had also informed the Company in London via an intermediary, Robert Gregory, of the gross abuses during the period of the Great Bengal Famine. [11] Nandkumar had collaborated with Mir Jafar and his son Miran, had tried to keep revenue details from the

English, insisted upon formal ratification of arrangements with the Mughal Emperor on the accession of Nawab Najm-ud-daulah, opposed Mohammed Reza Khan and was detested by Warren Hastings from the very first. [12] For all that Nandkumar was a wealthy Bengali, he can be legitimately viewed as a patriot. [13] (One is reminded in this of the hanging in 1916 of Irish patriot Roger Casement, the great man who blew the whistle on ghastly Belgian colonial abuses in the Congo). [14] According to T.B. Macaulay "It is a remarkable circumstance that one of the letters of Hastings to Dr. Johnson has been dated a very few hours after the death of Nuncomar" [15] (actually, it appears, 2 days after the hanging). [16]

Starvation, trauma and utter impoverishment had crushed physical resistance from the Bengalis. The most potent result of the judicial murder of Nandkumar was the stifling of dissent and complaint. In the words of T.B. Macaulay (1840): "The voices of a thousand informers were silenced in an instant. From that time, what difficulties Hastings might have had to encounter, he was never molested by accusations from natives of India." [17]

11.5. Conflict with Mysore, Hyderabad and the Marathas

It is useful at this point to consider the build up of military tensions in the south of India over the preceding decade. The key players were Hyder Ali (who had deposed the previous ruler of Mysore), the Maratha Confederacy (that dominated Central India as well as threatening Bombay, northern India and southern India), the Nizam of Hyderabad and the British. In terms of dangerousness we could rank the British over the Marathas and Mysore, with Hyderabad being the least effective. In 1765 the Company allied itself with Hyderabad against Mysore and the Marathas but the Nizam of Hyderabad had betrayed them. Nevertheless the British under Colonel Smith were able to defeat a combined "native" force at the Pass of Changana and at Trincomali in 1767. However at the subsequent Treaty of Masulipatam in 1768 the Madras Presidency made peace with the Nizam of Hyderabad in terms that were hostile to Mysore. The fighting continued with Mysore (but with Hyderabad standing aside) and eventually Mysore forced the British to a peace in which all conquests were restored and the British agreed to assist Mysore against the Marathas. However when indeed the Marathas invaded Mysore in 1771 the British reneged on their commitment to Mysore and thereby further enhanced the enmity of Hyder Ali.

As we have already seen, these adventures put considerable strains on the finances of the Company at a very difficult time. When Hastings took over as Governor-General in Calcutta his difficulties with his 3 opponents on the Council constrained his ability to deal effectively with the other Presidencies and he was lumbered with consequences of their continuing to indulge in plots and wars with Indian native states.

In 1775 the Bombay Presidency very unwisely signed the Treaty of Surat that supported the claim of Raghunath Rao (Raghoba) to the position of Peshwar of the Marathas in return for the ceding of Bassein and the island of Salsette. Hastings and the Council opposed this unilateral action but major hostilities having broken out, they sent Colonel Upton to Poona to make peace with the Peshwar of the Marathas. Under the Treaty of Purandhar (1776) the British surrendered their gains (except for Salsette) and gave up support for Raghunath Rao. However (with the accompanying delay of transmission), the Directors disapproved and permitted Hastings to renew support for Raghunath Rao, which he did on his casting vote on the Council and against the position of his enemy Francis. This was an expensive and unfortunate decision borne of anti-French paranoia in relation to the presence in Poona of a Frenchman who, it transpired, was not in fact an agent of the French Government.

The Bombay forces were not successful against the Marathas and Bombay concluded an unauthorized Treaty of Wargaon (1779) that surrendered all gains. The Council forces rejected this treaty, resumed hostilities and had some success. In 1780 Goddard marched across India from the Jumna and captured Ahmadabad and Bassein. Popham captured the "impregnable" fortess of Gwalior (1780). However Goddard was unsuccessful in an advance on the Maratha capital Poona and Hastings was forced to an accomodation with the Marathas. Hastings made peace with the Maratha chief Sindhia, who regained territory west of the Jumna at the Treaty of Salbai (1782), Raghunath Rao's claims to be the Peshwar were dissolved and Bombay retained Salsette. After 4 years of war all parties were essentially back to where they had started.

In the south the Madras Presidency supported Mohammed Ali, the Nawab of the Carnatic, in defeating and imprisoning the Raja of Tanjore in 1773. This period was associated with corruption involving the native court and Company men (notably the scandal of the "Nawab of Arcot's debts") and required repeated intervention by the Directors and the Council in Bengal. The confusion of Madras and the misplaced alliance of Bombay with Raghunath Rao, allowed Haidar Ali to collect a confederacy involving Mysore, the Marathas and Hyderabad and to invade the Carnatic in 1780. A British force under Baillie was surrounded and destroyed, Munro had to flee to Madras, leaving behind his guns, and Arcot was captured by Haider Ali. While the French possessions of Pondicherry and Chandernagore had been captured (France having declared war on Britain in 1778), there was the danger of a forthcoming French naval expedition.

Hastings responded effectively to the emergency. Pearse led an army from Bengal to the south, the Raja of Berar was detached from the enemy and the Treaty of Salbai with Sindhia removed the Marathas from the conflict. Eyre Coote defeated Haidar Ali at Porto Novo on the Coromandel coast south of Fort St David in 1781. In this battle a British force of 8,500 lost only 300 men having been opposed by Haidar Ali's force of 65,000. The discipline of the British infantry "squares" together with the help of gunfire from a warship offshore combined to defeat a much larger force of cavalry in a battle that ranks with Buxhar and Plassey as a military tour de force. Eyre Coote, together with Pearse, fought Tipu, Haidar Ali's son at Pollilore. Eyre Coote subsequently defeated Haidar Ali at Solingar. Negapatam and Trincomali were captured. This flow of good fortune was followed by the defeat of Braithwaite by Tipu at Tanjore and the landing of 2,000 Frenchmen by Admiral De Suffrein after an engagement with Admiral Sir Edward Hughes off Pulicat. Haidar Ali and the French captured Cuddalore from the British in 1782. The famous Bussy returned too late to India to team up with Tipu who had gone off to battle on the Malabar coast. Hughes was able to hold De Suffrein in great sea battles but De Suffrein recaptured the crucial port of Trincomali. Nevertheless the French naval forces had to run the gauntlet of the British navy on their way to India and the arrival of a further British fleet under Admiral Sir R. Bickerton tipped the balance for the British.

In 1783 Tipu captured Bednore and put Mangalore under siege. However Fullarton invaded Mysore, capturing Palghat and Coimbatore and threatening the capital Seringapatam before being recalled by Governor Lord Macartney who was sueing for peace. Tipu delayed agreement until Mangalore had fallen and then accepted the Treaty of Mangalore that temporarily restored peace to south India. The conflict against the Marathas and against Tipu would be resumed with great vigour after Hastings left India.

11.6. The bullying of Chait Singh of Benares

Because of the expenses incurrred by the adventures in the south and west of India and with the ostensible excuse of the declaration of war by the French, in 1778 Hastings demanded an additional 50,000 pounds for "war expenses" from Chait Singh, the Raja of Benares, in addition to the normal levy of 225,000 pounds. The Raja asked that the levy be confined to 1 year but Hastings insisted on immediate payment. When the Raja asked for a delay of 6 months, Hastings demanded full payment in 5 days and declared that a delay would be treated as outright refusal. In 1779 the demand was repeated and when Company troops moved against him the Raja paid the 50,000 pounds plus a fine of 2,000 pounds for the attendant military expenses.

In 1780 a further demand for 50,000 pounds was made. Chait Singh offered a "present" to Hastings of 20,000 pounds, which Hastings accepted. This was used for the war against the Marathas and the Company Treasurer in Calcutta and Director Sullivan were informed, as were the Directors in London at a later date. Nevertheless the 50,000 pounds was also exacted and Hastings then made further demands. Asked for 2,000 cavalry, the Raja argued this down to 1,000 but did not deliver exactly what was demanded. Accordingly Hastings now demanded a fine of 500,000 pounds from the Raja.

Hastings traveled to Oudh and the Raja met him at Buxhar, but Hastings deferred any reply to his pleas until he arrived at Benares. At Benares Hastings refused a personal interview, reiterated his demands in writing and rejected the Raja's written response. The culmination of this extraordinary bullying was Hastings' arrest of the Raja. At this point the Raja's troops rebelled against the British, slaughtering sepoys and some British officers. Hastings fled to Chanar and the Raja, innocent of the rebellion, also fled. The revolt was put down and the Raja, dispossessed of his domain, fled to the Marathas of Gwalior. He was replaced by his nephew who was compelled to pay an enormously increased annual tribute of 400,000 pounds to the Company.

The consequences of exorbitant demands, bullying and consequent rebellion, war and grievous taxation was the devastation and impoverishment of a formerly prosperous province. This appalling episode was also raised as an item of the Hastings impeachment. As with other actions of Hastings, the treatment of Chait Singh has been justified for various reasons by British Establishment historians. One supposes that gentlemen brought up with the bastardizing and brutality of the English public school fag system would have had a relatively relaxed attitude to this socially destructive episode of remorseless bullying. However for the people of the Gangetic plain, the disruptions of war and the impositions of taxation meant severe exacerbation of the dreadful famine of 1782.

11.7. The robbing of the Begums of Oudh

After the death of the old Nawab Wazir of Oudh, Shuja-ud-daulah, his son and successor Asaf-ud-daulah fell into arrears with the Company. In 1775 the widow of Shuja-ud-daulah agreed to the representations of the British Resident to pay her son a further 300,000 pounds on top of 260,000 pounds he had already received, it being agreed that no more payments would be made. The Council agreed to this arrangement. However in 1781, under pressure of his arrears, the Nawab asked for the treaty to be set aside, to which Hastings readily agreed on the dubious excuse that the Begums had supported Chait Singh of Benares. The Nawab had second thoughts about ripping off his mother and grandmother but Hastings insisted and despatched forces to Fyzabad to assist the Nawab's soldiers to effect the robbery of the Begum's treasure and jagirs (estates). Captain Nathaniel Middleton's forces invaded the women's quarters, seized the eunuchs and subjected them to imprisonment and starvation for about a year to extract the whereabouts of the treasure.

The matter of the Begums of Oudh excited further indignation back home in England, not the least because of the unseemliness of Englishmen bullying and robbing noble women of their money, jewels and jagirs and violating the perceived sanctity of their quarters (the zenana). This was further grist to the Impeachment mill several years later. Hastings was to spend much of 1784 organizing the affairs of Benares and Oudh to his satisfaction, his earlier interventions having brought great distress from famine to the province. If people are unable to produce food (because of drought and military activity) and cannot buy food (because of grievous taxation), they simply starve.

11.8. The duel with Francis

The domination of the Council by his opponents was a big burden for Hastings that was relieved when Monson died in 1776 and Hastings could use his casting vote to have his way. However his position was seriously jeopardized when his agent in London mistakenly tendered Hastings' resignation as Governor-General. The Directors appointed General Clavering as his successor but Hastings when apprised of the matter resisted and his school chum Chief Justice Impey supported him (but not to the extent of forcing Clavering out as a Councillor and as Commander-in-Chief as Hastings demanded). Clavering died in 1777 and was replaced by the famous Eyre Coote on the Council. When Barwell decided that he wanted to return home to enjoy his profits, a deal was done with Francis so that Hastings would not be disadvantaged in the voting on the Council and the arrangement was set down on paper by the Advocate-General. In the event Francis continued his opposition which Hastings now could consider as "dishonour" and a duel ensued in 1780.

Hastings' second was the heroic Colonel Pearse and Francis' was Colonel Watson. Hastings, on his own account, allowed Francis to fire first but the pistol missed fire. Still resolved to go second, Hastings observed Francis take aim twice and then withdraw. Accordingly he then took aim and fired, Francis' pistol going off at the same time. Francis collapsed wounded but recovered and left Bengal. [We have already seen the connections between Sense and Sensibility and the life of Warren Hastings in Chapter 6. The duel between the cad Willoughby and Colonel Brandon in Sense and Sensibility very likely reflects the celebrated duel between Philip Francis and Warren Hastings.]

That was not to be the end of Philip Francis in Hastings' life. Francis was widely believed to be the author of the caustic "Letters of Junius" published in various journals before his arrival in Bengal and which satirised men of position. He had maintained a position of opposition to Hastings' policies right from the start, although it should be appreciated that Francis' position was more in accord with the formal position of the British Government and his opposition to the Bombay Maratha adventures was sensible. On his return to England he made sure to apprise others of what had been going on in India and this appreciation ultimately led to Hastings' Impeachment.

11.9. Impey, Fox, Pitt the Younger and further Parliamentary intervention

In addition to his judicial murder of Nandkumar, the Chief Justice Elijah Impey earned an unpleasant reputation for himself in other matters of adjudication. The Council was in conflict not only with Hastings but with his friend Impey. When the Council overrode their authority and told zamindars to ignore the judges, Impey and his colleagues declared the Council in contempt. Hastings softened the impasse by making Impey the President of the Company's Court of Appeal (worth an additional 6,500 pounds per annum). This was not regarded favourably back home since it appeared to compromise the independence of the Supreme Court (surely compromised rather seriously anyway). In 1781 Parliament passed an Act removing the Governor-General from the authority of the Supreme Court and Impey was brought home. An attempt to impeach Impey on the basis of his bad reputation was unsuccessful.

Parliamentary interest in India began to hot up at this point (fuelled no doubt by whistle-blowing Philip Francis). In 1781 a new Act extended the Company's Charter for 10 years but determined that three quarters of post-dividend surplus was to go into the Treasury and that the Government should have access to Company communications sent to as well as received from India. A select committee and then a secret committee of inquiry into Indian judicial matters were set up that led to the resolution of Parliament in 1782 that Hastings and the President of Bombay should be recalled. Hastings escaped this through the fall of Rockingham's Government but his troubles were just beginning.

In 1783 the Coalition Government of Fox and North proposed major changes by which the Company would be under much greater Government control with Directors being nominated by Parliament. Pitt (the grandson of a famous Company man) vigorously opposed the Bill and although it was passed in the Commons it was defeated in the Lords. When Pitt returned triumphant to Parliament after subsequent elections, his Tory Government brought down the India Act of 1784 that dramatically changed the administration of India. A Board of Control composed of the Chancellor of the Exchequer, a Secretary of State and 4 Privy Councillors was headed by a Privy Councillor acting as President of the Board and who was to have great executive power. The Board's orders were to go forth to India through a secret committee of the Directors and the shareholders could not countermand decisions of the Board of Control. In India the Governor-General and a Council of 3 would have unambiguous authority over all Presidencies.

Hastings was unhappy with Pitt's India Act, resigned and returned to England in 1785. However the metropolitan concerns about India that had led to parliamentary interventions culminating in Pitt's India Act had built up to an extent resulting in moves for Hastings' impeachment. The Impeachment of Hastings was as close as we have ever come to holding a major War Crimes Trial over the appalling abuses of British imperialism.

11.10. 2008 Postscript

The present day crucifixion of Occupied Iraq provides a parallel with the British post-Famine exploitation of Bengal. Professor Noam Chomsky has spelled out what ordinary Western citizens had already worked out for themselves before the US, UK and Australian invasion of Iraq – that it was about oil. Thus Professor Chomsky states: "the huge energy resources of the region were recognized by Washington sixty years ago as a "stupendous source of strategic power," the "strategically most important area of the world," and "one of the greatest material prizes in world history." Control over this stupendous prize has been a primary goal of U.S. policy ever since, and threats to it have naturally aroused enormous concern". [18] Post-invasion violent plus non-violent excess deaths in Occupied Iraq totalled 1.7 - 2.2 million as of March 2008. In addition one can estimate 1.7 million Sanctions excess deaths (1990-2003), 1.2 million under-5 infant deaths under Sanctions, 0.2 million Iraqi Gulf War deaths, 0.6 million post-invasion infant deaths (UNICEF) and 4.5 million Iraqi refugees (UNHCR). [19] The Sanctions, Gulf War and Invasion and Occupation of Iraq have come at a huge human cost and amount to an Iraqi Holocaust and an Iraqi Genocide as defined by the UN Genocide Convention. [20]

Chapter 12

The impeachment of Warren Hastings and the judgement of history

"Lady Robert is delighted with P. & P - and really <u>was</u> so as I understand before she knew who wrote it - for, of course, she knows now. - He told her with as much satisfaction as if it were my wish. He did not tell <u>me</u> this, but he told Fanny. And Mr. Hastings - I am quite delighted with what such a Man writes about it. - Henry sent him the Books after his return from Daylesford - but you will hear the Letter too ... Nothing has been done as to S & S. The Books came to hand too late for him to have time for it, before he went. Mr Hastings never <u>hinted</u> at Eliza in the smallest degree ... I long to have you hear of Mr H's opinion of P & P. His admiring my Elizabeth so much is particularly welcome to me. "

- Letter of Jane Austen to Cassandra (1813) [re Henry Austen's trip to Warren Hastings at Daylesford and Hastings' admiration of Pride and Prejudice. Unfortunately Henry was not able to transmit a copy of Sense and Sensibility and we do not know what Hastings thought of a novel evidently based on his own life.] [1]

" - he shortly found himself arrived at politics; and from politics, it was an easy step to silence."

- Henry Tilney with his sister Eleanor and Catherine Morland on top of Beechen Cliff overlooking Bath in Northanger Abbey (1818) [2]

"This rich and flourishing kingdom may be totally subdued by so small a force as two thousand Europeans, and the possession thereof maintain'd and confirmed by the Great Mogul upon paying the Sum of 50 Lakhs per annum paid by former soldiers."

- Robert Clive (1758) [3]

"(the East India Company government) is one of the most corrupt and obstructive tyrranies, that probably ever existed in the world."

- Edmund Burke (circa 1790) [4]

"When you cried for peace, and your cries were heard by those who were the object of it, I resisted this and every other species of counteraction by rising in my demands, and accomplished a peace, and I hope everlasting, with one great state [the Marathas]; and I at least afforded the efficient means by which a peace, if not so durable, more reasonable at least, was accomplished with another [Tipu]. I gave you all, and you have rewarded me with confiscation, disgrace, and a life of impeachment."

- Warren Hastings speech to Parliament [5]

12.1. Accountability

It is worthwhile to consider the impeachment of Warren Hastings in some detail because it is one of the rare occasions when a perpetrator of imperial enormities has actually had to answer to his own people. It can be seen as a very imperfect attempt to address appalling injustice and inhumanity but which has been largely dismissed in hindsight by British Establishment historians as the vicious persecution of a great man.

12.2. Moves against Hastings

Much has been written about this remarkable event and the reader is referred to biographies of Warren Hastings, [6] the account by Thomas Babington Macaulay in particular, [7] other germane works dealing with the times [8] and more general historical texts that deal briefly with the matter. [9] A major figure in the Parliamentary process was Richard Brinsley Sheridan, the famous orator and playwright, [10] and the reader is referred in particular to transcriptions of his extraordinary Parliamentary speeches on Hastings' conduct in the East Indies. [11] Warren Hastings returned to England with his new wife "Marian", the former Baroness Maria Chapuset Imhoff. An elegant and sophisticated woman, she was much admired in society. Hastings took steps toward his later recovery of Daylesford (a lifetime ambition) but storm clouds were gathering. Edmund Burke had foreshadowed charges against Hastings in Parliament.

Things came to a head in Parliament when on 24th January 1786, the first day of the session, Major Scott, a friend of Hastings, raised the matter of unseen charges against Hastings that Burke had forshadowed in the previous session and reminded the House that Hastings had been back in England for some months. He rather unwisely suggested that the House should fix the earliest day possible for discussing these charges. Burke replied with an allusion to a challenge by Henry IV of France to the Duke of Parma to immediately bring his forces to battle, the Duke replying "that he knew very well what he had to do, and was not to be directed by an enemy." Burke eventually brought the matter before the House and successfully moved for copies of correspondence between Hastings and the Company directors to be put before the House. Burke subsequently called for other documents relating to Hastings' administration in India but with limited success.

After some debate in Parliament Burke called for the impeachment of Hastings on the basis of 22 charges, of which the principal ones are briefly listed below:

1. Hiring British forces out for the extirpation of the innocent Rohillas.

2. Witholding from the Moghul Emperor Shah Alam his 260,000 rupee share of the Diwani receipts from Bengal, Bihar and Orissa.

3. Extortion, dispossession and expulsion inflicted upon Rajah Chait Singh of Benares.

4. Impositions on the rulers of Oudh.

5. Ruination of the previously prosperous province of Faruckabad (the environs of Benares).

6. Impoverishing and depopulating the whole of the previously prosperous province of Oudh.

7. With abuse of power overturning ancient Indian establishments and imposing extravagant contracts and inordinate salaries.

8. Improper, unauthorised receipts of money used for improper and unauthorised purposes.

9. Having resigned in proxy and then denying and reversing it.

10. Treachery to Muzuffer [Muzaffar] Jung who had been placed in his care.

11. Extravagance and bribery to enrich his friends and dependants.

All of these charges were undoubtedly correct in hindsight but Hastings had the support of Pitt and the Tories in Parliament. Hastings was permitted to address the House in a short speech and was given permission to read his defence over 3 days, this being subsequently tabled. While the Rohilla charge was rejected (67 for, 119 against), Parliament responded to Fox's account of the mistreatment of the Rajah Chait Singh by accepting it as a grounds for impeachment (119 for, 79 against). The support of the Chancellor of the Exchequer for the motion was regarded as treachery by the Hastings camp.

At the beginning of 1787 these preliminary hearings continued with Nathaniel Middleton and Sir Elijah Impey giving evidence before the House. On February 7th 1787 Sheridan was called upon to address the matter of the resumption of the jaghirs and the confiscation of the treasure of the princesses of Oudh. Sheridan rose to give one of the most remarkable speeches in parliamentary history that was to be matched by a similar performance in the following year.

12.3. Sheridan's speech on the Begums of Oudh

According to the chronicler of this speech, Sheridan pointed out that numerous past deliberations of Parliament and its committees had:

"incontrovertibly established this plain broad fact, that parliament directly acknowledged that the British name and character had been dishonoured, and rendered detested throughout India, by the malversation and crimes of the principal servant of the East India Company...Was parliament mis-spending its time, by inquiring into the oppressions practised on millions of unfortunate persons in India, and endeavouring to bring the daring delinquent, who had been guilty of the most flagrant acts of enormous tyranny and rapacious peculation, to exemplary and condign punishment?... Their conduct in this respect, during the course of the preceding year, had done them immortal honour, and proved to the world, that however degenerate an example of Englishman some of the British subjects had exhibited in India, the people of England collectively, speaking and acting as their representatives, felt, as men should feel on such an occasion, that they were anxious to do justice, by redressing injuries, and punishing offenders, however high their rank, however elevated their station."

Sheridan addressed the sorts of arguments which in reality would be the line taken by a succession of apologists for Hastings, namely: "that the guilt of Mr. Hastings was to be balanced by his successes; that fortunate events were a full and complete set-off against a system of oppression, corruption, breach of faith, peculation and treachery."

He asserted that the fact that Parliament, including Pitt, accepted the treatment of Chait Singh as a grounds for impeachment proved that Burke was not motivated by malice or other unworthy motives (a position rejected by the Hastings apologists). Sheridan took great flights of indignation that, depending upon your point of view, were either hyperbole or well-justified assertions (married to an Indian for over 40 years, I admit to the latter prejudice). Sheridan asserted that he believed:

"the conduct of Mr.Hastings in regard to the Nabob of Oude and the Begums, comprehended every species of human offence. He had proved himself guilty of rapacity at once violent and insatiable - of treachery, cool and premeditated - of oppression, useless and unprovoked - of breach of faith, unwarrantable and base - of cruelty, unmanly and unmerciful. These were the crimes of which, in his soul and conscience, he arraigned Warren Hastings; and of which he had the confidence to say he should convict him."

Sheridan addressed the Hastings argument that somehow the Begums' wealth belonged to the young Nawab with the sarcastic descriptive "as if he meant to insinuate that there was something in Mahomedanism which rendered it impious in a son not to plunder his mother" and read a pathetic plea from young Nawab's mother for Hastings' help to relocate them safely if indeed they were to be impoverished.

A critical defence of Hastings was that the Begums (the princesses of Oudh), had been involved in the Benares rebellion, a proposition for which there was no evidence. However Sheridan, in adverting to this, brought up the matter of Chief Justice Impey's helpful "legal" opinion given to the Governor-General on this matter and had great scorn for Impey, summoned by his friend to assist in the crime:

"Mr. Hastings with so much art, proposed a question of opinion, involving an unsubstantiated fact, in order to obtain even a surreptitious approbation of the measure he had predetermined to adopt. "The Begums being in actual rebellion, might not the nabob confiscate their property?" "Most undoubtedly," was the ready answer of the friendly judge. Not a syllable of inquiry intervened as to the existence of the imputed rebellion; nor a moment's pause as to the ill-purposes to which the decision of a chief justice might be perverted ... Sir Elijah pursued his progress; and passing through a wide region of distress and misery, explored a country that presented a speaking picture of hunger and nakedness ... Thus, whilst the executive power in India was perverted to the most disgraceful inhumanities, the judicial authority also became its close and confidential associate - at the same moment that the sword of government was turned to an assassin's dagger, the pure ermine of justice was stained and foiled with the basest and meanest contamination."

Australian readers may hark back to the events of 2 centuries later, in 1975, in which an Australian Chief Justice Garfield Barwick offered advice to Governor-General Kerr that encouraged him to dismiss the democratically elected Whitlam government in circumstances of parliamentary constraints on public money supply and (so it is widely believed) a notion in Washington that the Australian Government was less than totally loyal to the American Government. [12]

Sheridan dealt with the affidavits of the Resident Nathaniel Middleton, Colonel Hannay, Colonel Gordon, Major McDonald, Major Williams and others with great scorn for what he perceived to be loose, hear-say testimonies affected by time and consideration for Hastings. Sheridan concluded with great passion that he:

"heard of factions and parties in that house, and knew they existed ... But when inhumanity presented itself to their observations, it found no division among them: they attacked it as their common enemy... They could not behold the workings of the heart, the quivering lips, the trickling tears, the loud and yet tremulous joys of the millions whom their vote of this night would for ever save from the cruelty of corrupted power. But though they could not directly see the effect, was not the true enjoyment of their benevolence increased by the blessing being conferred unseen? Would not the omnipotence of Britain be demonstrated to the wonder of nations, by stretching its mighty arm across the deep, and saving by its fiat distant millions from destruction? And would not the blessings of the people thus saved, dissipate in empty air? No! if I may dare use the figure, - we shall constitute Heaven itself our proxy, to receive for us the blessings of their pious gratitude, and the prayers of their thanksgiving. - It is with confidence, therefore, Sir, that I move you on this charge, "that Warren Hastings be impeached"."

12.4. Pitt's defection

Sheridan's speech kept his audience spell-bound, confirmed his allies and converted his opponents. Fox declared that everything he had ever read or heard dwindled into nothing in comparison. Hastings' supporter Pitt, in the words of the chronicler, acknowledged "that it surpassed all the eloquence of ancient or modern times, and possessed every thing that genius or art could furnish, to agitate and controul the human mind". The debate was indeed adjourned after arguments that the speech had been so compelling that time was needed to allow people to cool before voting. The debate was resumed the next day with Philip Francis supporting impeachment and Hastings being supported by various people including Major Scott and George Vansittart (who would several years later defend Jane Austen's aunt with a character reference to help save her from Botany Bay or the gallows).

Pitt thought that the treatment of the princesses appeared cruel and criminal, treaty obligations contraindicated the resumption of the jaghirs, the seizure of the treasures had to be condemned, these offences were aggravated by making the young Nabob the instrument of robbing his mother and that Hastings had erred in stifling orders from the Directors against the Begum proceedings. The motion for impeachment on the grounds of the extortion of the Begums was carried overwhelmingly (175 for, 68 against) on 8 February 1787.

The apologists for Hastings have striven to excuse or explain this turn-around by Pitt but the simplest explanation lies in the words of the central players on Hastings' side. Pitt, while rejecting most of Burke's charges as justifying impeachment, was convinced by the charges relating to the extortion of the Rajah Chait Singh and of the Begums of Oudh. Similarly Pitt's colleague Dundas (President of the Board of Control of the East India Company), in a letter to Hastings' successor in India, Lord Cornwallis, declared that the impeachment was not pleasing to them "but the truth is, when we examined the various articles of the evidence against him with his defences, they were so strong, and the defences so perfectly unsupported, it was impossible not to concur." This position of Dundas reflected the current flow of political machinations in the East India Company. [13]

12.5. The trial and Sheridan's second Begum speech

The trial of Warren Hastings commenced on 13 February 1788 in Westminster Hall and involved numerous charges that mostly involved Oudh. The stars for the prosecution were Edmund Burke, Fox and Sheridan. While Sheridan's orations outdid those of his companions, Burke was also a master of oratory:

"I impeach him in the name of the people of India, whose rights he has trodden under foot, and whose country he has turned into a desert. Lastly, in the name of human nature itself, in the name of both sexes, in the name of every age, in the name of every rank, I impeach the common enemy and oppressor of all." [14]

Burke pulled few punches in his denunciations, ranging from the "low" and "vulgar" upbringing of Hastings, through the "providential flash of lightning" (that supposedly killed Mir Jafar's son Miran and permitted the installation of Mir Kasim as a temporarily pliant Nawab of Bengal), to extravagant assertions about the life-style and morality of the famous Munni Begum. [15]

The second speech by Sheridan on the Begum charge was delivered on 3 June 1788 and was extraordinarily well attended on account of the first. The approaches were crowded by 8 o'clock in the morning but the peers did not arrive until noon. The chronicler narrates Sheridan's earnest declaration of disquiet about the state of India:

"To convince their lordships that the British government - which ought to have been a blessing to the powers in India connected with it - had been a scourge to the natives, and the cause of desolation to the most flourishing provinces in Hindostan, he had only to read a letter that had been received not long since from Lord Cornwallis, the present governor-general of Bengal. In that letter the noble lord stated he had been received by the Nabob Visier with every mark of friendship and respect; but the honours he received at the court of Lucknow had not prevented him from seeing the desolation that overspread the face of the country, the sight of which had shocked his very soul. He spoke to the nabob on the subject, and earnestly recommended it to him to adopt some system of government that might restore the prosperity of his kingdom, and make his people happy. The nabob's answer was strikingly remarkable. That degraded prince said to his lordship, that as long as the demands of the English government upon the revenue of Oude should remain unlimited, he (the nabob) could have no interest in establishing any system of economy; and whilst the English should continue to interfere in the internal government of his country, it would be in vain for him to attempt any salutary reform; for his subjects knew that he was only a cypher in his own dominions, and therefore laughed at and despised his authority and that of his ministers."

Sheridan dealt with criteria for acceptable evidence, especially in relation to the affidavits of Hastings' witnesses Middleton, Impey, Goring, Gilpin, Scott, Shore and Holt, and then proceeded to the dramatic exposition on the violation of the zenana (the women's rooms) that no doubt would have distressed the ladies present (such as the companions of the Prince Regent). He declared that Hastings' witnesses had established the nobility of the Begums and the sanctity of the zenana. Sheridan declaimed:

"The confinement of Turkish ladies was in a great measure to be ascribed to the jealousy of their husbands; in Hindostan the ladies were confined, because they thought it contrary to decorum that persons of their sex should be seen abroad: they were not the victims of jealousy in the men; on the contrary, their sequestration from the world was voluntary; they liked retirement, because they thought it best suited to the dignity of their sex and situation: they were shut up from liberty, it was true; but liberty, so far from having any charms for them, was derogatory to their feelings; they were enshrined rather than innured; they professed a greater purity of pious prejudice than the Mahomedan ladies of Europe and of other countries; and more zealously and religiously practised a more holy system of superstition. Such was their sense of delicacy, that to them the sight of man was pollution; and the piety of the nation rendered their residence a sanctuary. What, then, would their lordships think of the tyranny of the man who could act in open defiance of those prejudices, which were so interwoven with the very existence of the ladies of that country, that they could not be removed but by death? What, he asked, would their lordships think of the man who could threaten to profane and violate the sanctuary of the highest description of the ladies in Oude, by saying that he would storm it with his troops, and remove the inhabitants from it by force?"

Sheridan detailed the friendship of Hastings and the late Nawab, the surrender of 550,000 pounds to the young Nawab by the Begums, the approval of these arrangements by the Council in 1775 and Hastings' receipt of a temporarily rather well-hidden 100,000 pounds from the young Nawab at Chunar in 1781. The origins of this money was described as follows:

"It was not given by the nabob from the superflux of his wealth nor in the abundance of his esteem for the man to whom it was given. It was, on the contrary, a prodigal bounty, drawn from a country depopulated -

no matter whether by natural causes, or by the grinding of oppression. It was raised by an exaction which took what calamity had spared and rapine overlooked; - and pursued those angry dispensations of Providence, when a prophetic chastisement had been inflicted upon a fated realm. The secrecy which had marked this transaction was not the smallest proof of its criminality."

Sheridan's speech had to be spread over several days in which he detailed the events involved in the extortion of Chait Singh, the rebellion at Benares and the subsequent extortion of the Begums. He argued passionately for the downtrodden ryots and the rights of man. On June 13 Sheridan concluded his oration thus:

"This is the call on all to administer to truth and equity, as they would satisfy the laws and satisfy themselves, with the most exalted bliss possible, or conceivable for our nature, - the self-approving consciousness of virtue, when the condemnation that we look for will be one of the most ample mercies accomplished for mankind since the creation of the world! My lords I have done."

He sank exhausted into the arms of a fellow parliamentarian.

12.6. The outcome

Hastings spent a huge amount of money in his defence over the period of the trial. The total expenditure has been estimated at 100,000 pounds and the costs involved a substantial amount spent on pamphleteering. [16] One is reminded again of Henry Tilney's assertion in Northanger Abbey: "Does our education prepare us for such atrocities? ... Could they be perpetrated in a country like this, where social and literary intercourse is on such a footing... where roads and newspapers lay everything open?" [17] In the event the outcome was acquittal for Warren Hastings in 1795 but his reputation and finances had been severely tried in the lengthy 7 year process. Time heals, and even Sheridan approached him in 1804, explaining that he had argued simply as a matter of high principle and that no personal animosity was involved in his great Parliamentary speeches. [18]

Warren Hastings retired to Daylesford with Marian (as the nabob Colonel Brandon had retired to Delaford with Marianne) and devoted himself to the pleasures of rural life and society. His rehabilitation came with the successes of the Napoleonic Wars. Thus in 1813 he was awarded an honorary doctorate in civil law at the University of Oxford to the cheers of the students and in 1814 the East India Company extended his annuity for the rest of his life. Hastings was drawn into banquets where he met dignitaries, including foreign rulers such as the Czar of Russia and the King of Prussia. [19] All the members of the House of Commons stood in respect as Warren Hastings left the chamber after testifying on Indian matters in 1813. [20]

12.7. The verdict of history

British historians are torn between great respect for Hastings as a great "Empire builder" and the fact that he had been subject to such a sustained process of public criticism following a period in which immense social disruption in India was associated with highly suspect administration and immense European enrichment. Bearing in mind the immensity of the human cost of the Great Bengal Famine of 1769-1770 and the subsequent famine and devastation of the Gangetic plain in 1782, it is useful to see the judgements of British historians on a major player in the conquest of India.

T.B. Macaulay was highly critical of aspects of Hastings' rule in India but nevertheless concluded that: "His internal administration, with all its blemishes, gives him a title to be considered one of the most remarkable men in our history." [21]

Malleson (1894) concludes that " {Great Britain's] sons will not fail to recognize, in the face of the scurrilities of Burke, the distortions of Macaulay, and the calumnies and inaccuracies of Mill, that no nobler son ever devoted to his country's interests a life more pure, a prescience more profound, talents more commanding, than did the second founder of British India, the Right Honourable Warren Hastings." [22]

Kaye (1853) praised the administrative changes that Hastings brought to India and claims that his successor in 1786, Lord Cornwallis, found administrators "with little resemblance to the old denizens of the Augean stables which, twenty years before, Clive had so courageously ventured to cleanse." [Scores of millions were yet to perish in war, famine and disease before India was to be free of such noble integrity.] [24]

Lyall (1916) concludes that "All preceding Governors had been servants of the East India Company; and Hastings, the first of the Company's Governors-General, had been the scape-goat of an awkward and unmanageable governing apparatus, hampered by divided authority, and distracted by party feuds in Calcutta and London." [25]

Reid (1947) declares of the Impeachment proceedings,: "No acquittal has ever been more justly earned ... It is almost as nauseating an example of England's ingratitude as the indictment of Clive: and one wonders, reading the lives of these great founders of the Indian Empire, what magic spell England wields that, with such examples before their eyes, men were still ready to devote their lives to her service, knowing that the greater the success of their efforts, the less would be their reward." [26]

More recent historians have sustained this complimentary message.

Gardner (1971) refers to Dundas, President of the Board of Control of the East India Company, as having "played a sinister part in the long and distasteful story of Warren Hastings's impeachment." [27]
Woodruffe (1965) concludes thus of Hastings: "And though he was wrong about the administration of Bengal, he worked patiently and

indomitably for the right things. He worked always to instil into the Company's servants habits of industry and a sense of responsibility for the people of India." [28]

Wilbur (1945) referred to Hastings as the "Savior of Bengal" and applies an astonishing "Emperor's clothes" argument to account for the Impeachment: "One of the strangest aspects of the life of the East India Company's servants in India, plainly disclosed in the impeachment of Hastings, was the preponderance of personal jealousies, petty rivalry, and sheer vindictiveness of spirit shown in the letters written by the vast majority of the Company's servants, from the lowest clerk to those of the highest rank in India, to friends and relatives in England." [29]

"Holocaust ignorer" H.G. Wells (1959) perceived the "romanticism" of the English transformation of Clive and Hastings into national heroes: "The country which had once put Clive and Hastings on trial for their unrighteous treatment of Indians was now persuaded to regard them as entirely chivalrous and devoted figures. They were "empire builders"." [30]

Muir (1929) recognized a useful side to the matter: "The fact of his impeachment was a proof that Britain had now awakened to the magnitude of the Indian problem and was determined to secure good government. But this was a cruel reward for noble service. The impeachment lasted for seven years. But the cost of the trial used up nearly all his savings, and he was left a poor man. He was still young, but Britain had no further use for one of the greatest of her sons." [31]

The Encyclopaedia Britannica (1977) endorses this position thus; "Most historians, while recognizing Burke's absolute sincerity, now feel that Burke was attempting to pin the evils of a situation on one individual and that he had chosen the wrong one ... It is difficult not to regard this long-drawn-out ordeal as a serious injustice. At the most it made some contribution to the process by which standards were being laid down for the future conduct of British rule in India." [32]

Bearing in mind the reality of 2 centuries of famine culminating in the Bengal Famine of the Second World War, several post-war conclusions are intensely pertinent to our disquisition.

<u>G.M. Trevelyan</u> (1952) defends Hastings: "He saved British rule in India in spite of all [inadequate means, Philip Francis], but was not without making the kind of mistakes a strong man is likely to make in difficult emergencies. For these acts, much exaggerated and misconstrued by the malignity of Francis and the imagination of Burke, Fox and Sheridan, he was impeached in Westminster Hall. Those famous proceedings, substantially unjust to Hastings, even though they resulted in his acquittal, had the advantage of bringing Indian problems and responsibilities to the notice of British statesmen and the British public. Burke preached the right ideal of our obligations to the Indians, but misunderstood the relation of Hastings' governorship to the problem." [33]

<u>Carter and Mears</u> (1960) endorse this noble view, borne of Austenizing, with a similar rosy position: "False as were most of the accusations against him, his trial did good in one way. Burke's eloquent appeal on behalf of the suffering millions of India, whom he supposed Hastings to have misruled, awoke a sense of responsibility in Britain towards peoples under our rule." [34]

Nevertheless, after the Indian Mutiny of 1757 there was a sensible appreciation that there may surely have been some substance to Indian grievance. In a Parliamentary debate at the time, Sir George Cornewall Lewis provided what we could take as an unbiased and disinterested judgement on Hastings' period in India:

"I do most confidently maintain that no civilised Government ever existed on the face of this earth which was more corrupt, more perfidious and more rapacious than the Government of the East India Company from 1765 to 1784." [35]

We will now see to what extent the "sense of responsibility" of the British rulers for their Indian and other colonial subjects was "awoken" as we briefly scan the next 2 centuries of war, exploitation, famine and genocide that was the reality of the British Empire. However before doing so it is well to present the germ of an idea that will slowly assume greater proportions as we proceed through our catalogue of inhumanity. The British represented a numerically insignificant minority in India but they imposed their will through sophisticated weaponry, highly disciplined soldiery, divide-and-rule policies and the use of well-fed sepoys and other indigenous collaborators. Nevertheless, despite these "equalizers", there was still an enormous disparity in numbers and their vulnerability was revealed in the Indian Mutiny of 1857 when "well fed" Indian sepoys were finally forced to rise against their British masters.

Disease and war aside, the British had a lovely life in the East. [36] Thus in the 18th century in Bengal, a gentleman's day could begin with the escort from his bedchamber of his Bengali woman, followed successively by ablutions, breakfast, eventual commercial duties and evening social entertainments. His long day would end in the arms of his latest dusky maiden [37] However even more exciting sport was provided by the wild animals that were much more plentiful then than they are now. In Bengal in the 18th century, according to accounts in Nair (1984), tigers, dogs and jackals could perform a sanitary function in disposing of rubbish and indeed human corpses (from the streets or left below the high tide mark on riversides). Tigers could be very aggressive and attack even large groups of people to seize their victim. [38] [Henry Fane (1817-1868) wrote a fascinating account of his 5 years in India as aide-de-camp of the Commander-in-Chief of the Indian Army (1835-1840) and tells a story of a wolf seizing the child of one of the seyces, or grooms. "It was asleep between its mother and father, the former having her arms around it; and in spite of this and the immediate pursuit, the animal managed to clear off with its prize." [39] One is reminded of the prolonged Chamberlain affair arising from scepticism in the judicial process that a dingo had taken their baby at

Ayer's Rock (Uluru) in Central Australia.] Of sporting shooting in India none was more dangerous than hunting the tiger, a beast that could be as big as a small cow in size. [40] In the "classic" tiger hunts, the pukka sahib, armed to the teeth, would venture out on a howdah mounted on top of an elephant and accompanied by a small army of armed servants and beaters - all this for one admittedly dangerous foe. [41] However one should seriously consider: what is the most dangerous creature of all? Surely Man. For all the armaments, skill, courage and discipline of the British soldiers, in the 18th century there were literally only several thousand of them to guard an Indian empire encompassing 100 million subjects.

It is likely that the reduction of the vast bulk of the population of India to life on the edge of bare survival was a matter of deliberate strategic policy of the British over 2 centuries of occupation. While individual acts of British barbarity, such as "blowing away" mutinous sepoys from cannons, were decisions by military men on the spot at the time, the empirical reality of hundreds of millions living at the edge of the abyss for 2 centuries instructs us that the British rulers found this acceptable in practice over the whole period of their occupation of India. This policy not only maximized income but would have dramatically decreased the ability of the Indians to rise against their cruel persecutors.

We will see that during World War 2, the "frontier"' provinces of Bengal and Assam were arenas for armed unrest and "terrorism" and were of major strategic concern to the Indian authorities and to the Home Government. [42] It is likely that a similar policy of "starvation into submission" was applied (either consciously or by moral default) to war-time Bengal half a century ago as it was to India over the preceding 2 centuries. Dropping an atomic bomb on Hiroshima to destroy a city and kill 100,000 people was the result of a specific decision taken at the time, as was the subsequent destruction of Nagasaki. However to permit famine and attendant disease to inflict immense suffering and cause as many as 5 million deaths in war-time

Bengal over several years amounts to deliberate policy. While the crimes of the British in the early decades of occupation of India went unpunished and have been largely deleted from public perception, the same can be said of what was done repeatedly to India in the following 2 centuries.

12.8. 2008 Postscript

One is left almost speechless when one considers the immensity of the crimes being committed today by the Anglo-American Alliance against what Sheridan back in 1788 called "Mahomedan ladies" in his indignant speech and the extraordinary Silence of contemporary Mainstream media, politicians and academics. The Anglo-American Alliance is party to: what is a Palestinian Genocide (post-1967 excess deaths 0.3 million, post-invasion under-5 infant deaths 0.2 million, 7 million refugees, 4 million Occupied Palestinians – half of them children, three quarters women and children - imprisoned in an increasingly abusive Prison); Iraqi Genocide (1990-2003 excess deaths 1.7 million, 1.2 million under-5 infant deaths, 0.2 million Gulf War deaths; 2003-2008 post-invasion excess deaths 1.7-2.2 million, post-invasion excess under-5 infant deaths 0.6 million, 4.5 million refugees); Afghan Genocide (post-invasion excess deaths 3.3-6.6 million, post-invasion under-5 infant deaths 2.3 million, 4 million refugees); Biofuel Genocide (16 million people die avoidably every year due to deprivation and deprivation-exacerbated disease in the post-colonial neo-colonial world and the new colonial world of the American Empire; this is increasingly impacted by huge food price rises driven in part by legislatively-mandated diversion of food for biofuel in the UK, US and EU; UK Chief Scientist Professor John Beddington FRS says that "billions" are threatened by the biofuel diversion); and Climate Genocide (Professor James Lovelock FRS says that over 6 billion will perish this century due to unaddressed anthropogenic greenhouse gas pollution and consequent global warming). This immense set of current crimes is stringently non-reported by mainstream media, politicians and academics in the

Western Murdochracies (ostensible democracies in which major media conglomerates such as the Murdoch Empire have a hugely disproportionate say in election outcomes and public policy). I and others have attempted to report this carnage via Alternative Media e.g. see my article "Palestinian, Iraqi, Afghan, Biofuel and Climate Genocide – silence kills and silence is complicity" in the Maine, US magazine Liberalati and other articles. [43] 2005 Nobel Laureate Harold Pinter in his Nobel Prize Acceptance Speech called for arraignment of Bush and Blair before the International Criminal Court over their horrendous crimes in Iraq, stating (informed by grossly under-estimating media reports) : "How many people do you have to kill before you qualify to be described as a mass murderer and a war criminal? One hundred thousand? More than enough, I would have thought. Therefore it is just that Bush and Blair be arraigned before the International Criminal Court of Justice." [44] Some other great writers have also expressed outrage. [45] My response (see above Iraq statistics): "4 million? More than enough I would have thought". I have made formal complaints over Anglo-American and Australian war crimes to the International Criminal Court. [46]

Chapter 13

Colonial famine, genocide and ethnocide

"The Hindoo appears a being nearly limited to mere animal functions and even in them indifferent. Their proficiency and skill in the several lines of occupation to which they are restricted, are little more than the dexterity of which any animal with a similar conformation but with no higher intellect than a dog, an elephant, or a monkey, might be supposed to be capable of attaining. It is enough to see this in order to have full conviction that such a people can at no period have been more advanced in civil policy."

- Lord Hastings (Lord Moira, Marquess of Hastings and Governor-General of India, 1813-1823) (1813) [1]

"The trifling quantity of piece goods which Bengal still exported is for the most part made from English twist."

- C.E. Trevelyan (1835), reporting on the effective destruction of the centuries-old Bengal textile industry. [2]

"The population of the town of Dacca [a key textile centre] has fallen from 150,000 to 30,000 or 40,000, and the jungle and malaria are fast encroaching on the town."

- C.E. Trevelyan (1840), reporting to a Parliamentary Committee on the destruction of the Dacca textile industry. [3]

"This being altogether beyond the power of man, the cure had been applied by the direct stroke of an all-wise Providence in a manner as unexpected and unthought of as it is likely to be effectual."

- C.E. Trevelyan (1846) (the responsible Undersecretary for the Treasury, commenting on the Irish famine as a "cure" for overpopulation). [4]

"the great object of saving life and giving protection from extreme suffering may not only be as well secured, but in fact will be far better secured, if proper care be taken to prevent the abuse and demoralisation which all experience shows to be the consequence of ill-directed and excessive distribution of charitable relief."

- Report of the Indian Famine Commission 1880 [5]

"In my judgement any government which imperilled the financial position of India in the interests of a prodigal philanthropy would be open to serious criticism. But any government which, by indiscriminate alms-giving, weakened the fibre and demoralised the self-reliance of the population would be guilty of a public crime."

- Lord Curzon, Viceroy of India on the 1900 Indian Famine (January 1900) [6]

"I have the honour to state that there are no Aborigines in my district."

- Reverend James Walker (1846), reporting on the total elimination of indigenous people from the North Parramatta district of New South Wales, Australia.. [7]

13.1. Famines in India 1770-1943

The above considered assertion by Lord Hastings in 1813 was about the people that created one of the earliest major human civilizations, [8] an extraordinary culture most evident in literature, music, art and architecture (such as the Taj Mahal or the great Hindu temples) [9] and one of the world's most technically and philosophically sophisticated societies by the time of British invasion in the mid-eighteenth century. [10] Famine is not simply a deficiency of food production in a particular area. It derives from the inability of people in a particular area to either harvest or purchase food. [11] Before the British invaded and enslaved Bengal, this part of the world had a highly productive agricultural and manufacturing economy. Not content with the enslavement and rapacious taxation of the farmers, the British shifted crop production from food crops to indigo, opium, cotton and jute. From a situation in which Bengal was initially a major exporter of textiles to Britain, the textile industry was remorselessly destroyed by differential duties and Bengal was reduced to a cotton-producing captive market for British textiles. Desperate poverty was thus imposed upon formerly prosperous Bengal and, with variations, upon India as a whole by a remorseless invader. A Governor-General of the East India Company described this succinctly in 1835: "The misery hardly finds a parallel in the history of commerce. The bones of the cotton-weavers are bleaching the plains of India." [12]

After the great famine in Bengal in 1769-1770 one would have supposed that a morally responsive conquering nation would have taken stock and taken steps to ensure that such awful events would not recur. This was not the case. We have seen that the British under their hero Hastings extended their hegemony in various capacities to Rohilkund, Delhi, Benares and Oudh in the north and finally disposed of French imperial dreams in the south of India. However this process inevitably produced great distress in concert with the vagaries of climate. Combinations of taxation, war, the burning of crops and drought brought famine to Madras in 1781 and more generally to the Carnatic, Mysore and the Bombay region in 1781-1783. Drought affected the west of India (Thar, Pakar and Sind) in 1782-1784 and in 1782-1784 drought, war and crop burning brought famine to Madras, Bengal, Bombay and Upper India. [13]

We have seen in the previous chapter that generalized concerns in relation to the distress of Indian subjects were raised during the impeachment proceedings but to no avail. The proceedings evidently became more concerned with the rights of Indian princes and princesses and Hastings was ultimately acquitted. India was to suffer nearly 2 centuries of recurrent famine under British rule. It should be stated clearly at this point that after the independence of India and Pakistan in 1947, while scarcities and localized famine distress occurred on occasion, there was by and large no recurrence of the massive, catastrophic famines of the kind suffered under British rule. (The biggest South Asia post-war famine events were those in Bihar in 1966-1967 and in Bengal in 1974). [14] That this dramatic post-independence amelioration occurred despite massive population increases can be primarily attributed to the application of modern technology and the replacement of callous British rulers by indigenous governments that, for all their faults, evidently had a vastly greater humanitarian concern for their subjects. [15]

Prior to conquest by the British, India had experienced immense famines that were basically caused by drought and in some cases severely exacerbated by war or excessive revenue-raising. Thus about 80 famines - nearly all occasioned by drought but in some cases greatly affected by war or excessive taxation - occurred in various parts of India from the prolonged 293-282 BC famine in Bihar up to the famine in 1759 in the Bombay area that was caused by wars of the Marathas. The invasion of northern India by Timur caused famine in 1399 and the wars of Aurangzeb caused famine in the 17th Century. However the indigenous rulers, and indeed also the Moghal rulers, variously perceived an obligation to ameliorate the suffering due to drought-induced famine through the purchase of food, the opening up of food stores, the construction of irrigation works and the employment of famine victims on these and other public works. [16]

As we will see, the British were not totally unmoved. Improvements to roads, the installation of railway lines, the construction of irrigation works (especially in the Punjab) and a succession of Famine Commissions resulting in the refining of "Famine Codes" towards the end of the 19th Century all helped to mitigate the effects of drought. However the real killers were the utter impoverishment of the Indian people to satisfy British greed and the not unconnected administrative apathy borne of entrenched racism. In the simple but profound words of Kachhawaha (1985): "The administration failed to realise that it had an obligation to save every human life. The relief measures were not undertaken promptly and were generally half-hearted and inadequate to meet the situation. " [17]

The Indian sub-continent covers a vast area and contains a multiplicity of cultures. For geographical and other reasons some regions were more susceptible to famine than others. Greenough (1982) has compiled a list of recorded famines in India from about 290 BC to 1944 AD and has categorised various regions of India in terms of famine propensity as reflected in the number of historical famines. Thus (in order of risk) "high" propensity areas were the upper Gangetic valley and the northern Deccan, "middle high" areas included Punjab-Kashmir, southern Deccan, Peninsular west coast, Rajasthan-Sind, middle Gangetic valley and Peninsular east coast and "middle low" areas included Gujarat, West Bengal-Bihar and Central India. The well-watered and highly productive regions of Orissa and East Bengal had the lowest famine propensity and it is accordingly of particular note that these regions suffered horrendously from famine during the British administration of India. [18]

The nature and occurrence of famines in India has been reported extensively. About 4 dozen famines occurred in India since the Battle of Plassey (1757) and it is beyond the scope of this book to describe in detail this immense carnage that swept away tens of millions of people in ghastly circumstances. Nevertheless I feel obliged to offer at least the following chronology of imperial mass murder interspersed (in square brackets) with some relevant events elsewhere in the Empire. The major sources for this catalogue are Cook & Stevenson (1991), Ghosh (1944), Greenough (1982), Kachhawaha (1992), Langer (1952), Maloo (1987), Roberts (1958), Sen (1981) and Spear (1965). [19]

[Battle of Plassey 1757];

Bombay (1759); Bengal, Bihar (1769-1770); Madras (1781); Carnatic, Mysore, Bombay (1781-1783); Thar, Pakar, Sind (1782-1784);

Madras, Bombay, Bengal, Oudh, northern India (1782-1784); northern Deccan, Bengal (1787);

[invasion of Australia (1788)];

Bombay, Gujarat, Deccan, Hyderabad, Kutch, Orissa, Marwar, Madras (1790-1793); Rajasthan (1796);

[inadvertent and "forgotten" second settlement on the East Coast of Australia on Preservation Island in Bass Strait by substantially Bengali shipwrecked sailors bound for Sydney from Calcutta (1797)];

north-west provinces, Kutch, Bombay, central India, Rajasthan, Hyderabad, Deccan (1799-1804); Bombay (1806-1807); Carnatic (1806-1807); Bombay, Sind, Gujarat, Agra, Rajasthan, north-western provinces (1812-1813); Madras (1812-1814); north-west provinces, Rajasthan, Deccan, Sind (1819-1822); Deccan, Bombay, Madras, Gujarat (1823-1825); Sirohi (1824); famine due to over-taxation and disorder in Mewar (1828); Punjab (1827-1828);

[abolition of slavery in the British Empire (1833)];

Deccan, Madras (1831-1833); Ajmer, Cawnpore, Bundelkhand, Gujarat, Deccan, Rajasthan, Punjab (1832-1834); Madras, Deccan, Punjab, Gujarat (1833-1835); north-west provinces, Rajasthan, Punjab (1837-1838); Gujarat (1838-1839); Deccan (1845);

[the first Maori War (1843-1848); the Irish Famine (1845-1850, 1 million dead, 1.5 million emigrated); the potato famine in Scotland (1848-1849)];

Rajasthan (1847-1849);

[the Taiping rebellion and associated famine in China took 20-100 million lives (1850-1864)];

Madras, Deccan, Rajasthan, Bombay (1853-1855); Orissa, Bihar, Gunjam, Hyderabad, Mysore (1856-1857);

[Indian Mutiny (1857-1858); end of rule in India by the East India Company (1858); first Indian indentured labourers - 3-year slaves - to South Africa (1860)];

north-west provinces, Punjab, Rajasthan, Gujarat (1860-1862); Deccan (1862);

[abolition of slavery in the U.S.A. (1865)];

east coast, Orissa, Bihar, west Bengal, Madras, Deccan, Bombay (1866); north-west provinces, Rajasthan, Deccan, central provinces, Punjab, Gujarat (1868-1870); north-west provinces, Bihar, Oudh, Bengal, Bundelkhand (1873-1874);

[cession of Fiji (1874); death of Truganini, the last "full-blood" Tasmanian (1876)];

Madras, Bombay, Mysore, Hyderabad (1876-1878); north-west provinces, Kashmir, Punjab, Uttar Pradesh, Rajasthan (1877-1878); north-west provinces, Deccan (1879-1880);

[commencement of indentured Indian labour - 5-year slavery - to Fiji (1879)];

west Bengal, Bihar (1884-1885); central provinces (1886-1887); Orissa, Ganjam (1888-1889); Garhwal, Bengal, Bihar, Madras, Rajasthan (1890-1892); central provinces (1894); north-west provinces, Bengal, Madras, central provinces, Bombay, Punjab, Bihar, Hyderabad, Rajasthan, Bundelkhand (1896-1897); Punjab, Rajasthan, central provinces, Bombay, Hyderabad (1899-1900); Gujarat (1900-1902);

[the Boer War (1899-1902); death of Queen Victoria (1901); genocide of the Hereros and Namas of South West Africa by the Germans (1904-1907)];

Bombay, Deccan, Rajasthan (1905-1906); Bihar, Bengal (1906-1907); Uttar Pradesh, central provinces (1907-1908);

[the First World War (1914-1918); the Armenian Genocide (1915-1923); influenza epidemic killed 27 million world-wide, 17 million in India (1918-1919); East Africa Famine (1919-1920), end of the indentured labour or girmit system of Indians to Fiji (1920); the Russian Famine (1921); last major massacre of Australian aborigines, northwest Australia (1926); famine in China (1920-1921, 1928-1930); the Ukraine Famine (1928-1933); Japanese invasion of China (1937); Niger famine (1942); Hunan famine, WW2 China; the Second World War and the Jewish Holocaust (1939-1945)];

Rajasthan (1939-1940); Bengal, Bihar, Assam, Orissa (1943-1946).

In briefly considering this disastrous catalogue we should indicate the more serious of the pre-20th Century famines, namely those in Bengal, Bihar and Orissa (1769-1770), Rajasthan, Oudh and elsewhere in northern India (1782-84), Rajasthan, Bombay, Gujarat and north-western provinces (1812-1815), north-western provinces, Punjab and Rajasthan (1837-1838), Madras, Deccan, Bihar, Bengal and particularly Orissa (1866), Rajasthan and northern India (1868-1870), and throughout much of India from Hyderabad to Rajasthan and the Punjab (1899-1900). The 1769-1770 and 1899-1900 famines were the worst and the 1943-1944 Bengal Famine was in the same league of massive catastrophe.

While the consistent primary cause of these famines was drought, the ultimate cause of death was lack of resources to purchase food in these times of scarcity - in the parlance of Amartya Sen, a deficiency of "entitlement". [20] The administering power had imposed a system of remorseless revenue collection without realistically accepting responsibility for its millions of starving subjects. This situation was exacerbated by the immense damage done to Indian industry and hence earning capacity by restrictive trading practices of the British, notably through imposition of prohibitive tariffs excluding Indian goods from Britain. This is well illustrated by a dramatic set of statistics relating to Indian textile exports to and imports from Britain in the 19th Century: the value in rupees of cotton goods exported/imported in 1815/16 was 13,151,427/263,800 but by 1832/33 this proportion has shrunk to 822,891/4,264,707. [21] A further major impact was war, both in the sense of paying for this senseless pursuit and the actual damage and disruption caused by war. Thus war conducted by the British or their foes clearly contributed to famines in the period of conquest 1759-1807, the Indian Mutiny period of 1856-1857 and the Second World War period of 1939-1945. In order to get a better feel for these events we will specifically focus on 2 radically different areas, namely relatively dry to desert Rajasthan and lush, well-watered Bengal, to illustrate the courses of famine in British India.

13.2. Famine in Rajasthan

Detailed accounts of famine in Rajasthan have been written by Maloo (1987) and Kachhawaha (1992). [22] Rajasthan (the land of Rajputs) is divided into two distinct areas by the Aravali range running southwest to northeast. The west-northwestern 60% of the territory is comprised of the very dry states of Jaisalmer, Bikaner and Marwar. The east-northeast states of Jaipur, Ajmer, Merwara, Kishengarh and Alwar variously have the benefit of wells and irrigation and to the south Sirohi, Mewar, Dungarpur and Banswara are hillier and have better rainfall. The eastern fringe of Rajasthan includes Bharatpur, Dholpur and Karauli in the north and Kotah, Bundi, Jhalawar and Tonk in the south.

Before the British arrived there had been drought-induced famines in various parts of Rajasthan: Marwar in the reign of Rao

Rajal who opened his granaries to the people (1309-1313); Ajmer and elsewhere in which people were driven to cannibalism and the Moghal Emperor Akbar instituted public works relief at Nagaur (1570); Mewar and elsewhere in which a large lake was constructed near Udaipur as part of famine relief (1660-1661); Marwar (1698-1770); Jaipur (1711-1716); Sojat, Raipur and Jetaran in Marwar (1742); Rajasthan generally (1747); Marwar (1756).

After the firm establishment of the British in large swathes of northern, eastern, southern and western India, famine became endemic to this region. The immense famine that afflicted northern India in 1782-84 during the "reign" of Warren Hastings had a particularly bad effect on the northern-most state of Bikaner. A further huge famine afflicted Rajasthan in 1812-1813 that caused massive losses of cattle and crops and depopulated large swathes of the country. This was followed by famines or severe scarcities affecting parts of Rajasthan (1819-1822), Mewar and Sirohi (1833), Alwar, Bharatpur, Dholpur, Karauli and Jaipur (1838-1840), Ajmer and Marwar (1848) and various parts of Rajasthan (1853-1855) and northwestern Rajasthan and Alwar (1860-1862).

The last 4 decades of the 19th century saw massive famines in Rajasthan. In 1868-1869 famine particularly affected Marwar, Bikaner, Ajmer and Merwara and killed one third of the population of Marwar, Bikaner and Ajmer. About 480,000 people died in Marwar alone and a further 1,000,000 emigrated, leaving the state largely depopulated. It has been estimated that 1,250,000 people perished in Rajasthan as a whole.

In 1877-1878 major scarcity of food in Rajasthan forced substantial emigration, Alwar losing 10% of its population in this way, and a similar period of scarcity occurred in 1891-1892 occasioning implementation of the Famine Code for Native States for the first time. Failure of the monsoon in 1896 caused famine that particularly affected Bharatpur, Bikaner, Dholpur, Jaisalmer and Marwar in the northern half of Rajasthan and precipitated relief measures.

In 1899-1900 one of the worst famines to occur in British India severely affected many parts of India including Rajasthan. The worst affected area was the western two thirds of Rajasthan including Jaisalmer, Bikaner, Marwar (20,000 deaths), Mewar (223,000 deaths) and Tonk. Cholera and malarial epidemics inevitably accompanied starvation. 1,000,000 million people starved to death in a Rajasthan reduced to the semblance of Bergen-Belsen. About 750,000 people emigrated out of the province to escape the famine.

The appalling sequence of events in Rajasthan and elsewhere in India in the course of the 19th Century led to Famine Commissions and the promulgation of Famine Codes for dealing with such emergencies (of which more later). However the disasters kept occurring into the 20th Century. Thus there was a major period of scarcity throughout most of Rajasthan in 1901-1902 and explicit famine in 1905-1906 that affected Ajmer, Merwara, Alwar, Bharatpur, Dholpur, Jaipur, Marwar and Mewar. Various parts of Rajasthan suffered scarcities over the next 40 years with Ajmer, Merwara, Bharatpur, Bikaner, Banswara, Bundi, Marwar and Mewar being particularly affected in 1915-1916. India made a major contribution in men and material to the British war effort but any British gratitude did not extend to the people of Rajasthan, a contemptible passivity that was to recur during the Second World War. In 1939-1940 most of Rajasthan suffered explicit famine that was nevertheless to be dwarfed by the Bengal Famine of 1943-1945.

13.3. Famines in Bengal between the 1769/70 and 1943/45 holocausts

In 1782-1784 northern India suffered a grievous famine that has been alluded to above. This famine was complicated by war and attendant rapacious taxation of the kind brought up in the Hastings Impeachment. The Company administration was aware of the problem and even set up a Committee but with results that are not apparent. Well-watered Bengal escaped the worst of this famine which devastated Madras and Bombay as well as Oudh and other parts of northern India.

In 1865 failure of expected rains led to fears about the winter harvest that were cruelly realised. 1866 saw widespread famine in Bengal, Bihar, Orissa and other parts of India including the Carnatic, Madras and Bombay. In the middle of 1866 the authorities refused to accept that there was a serious problem and only commenced importation of food in June when it became apparent that soldiers and prisoners could not be fed. The occurrence of rain in August and attendant disease compounded the problems of those weakened by starvation. The famine had the greatest impact in West Bengal (Midnapore, Bankura, Nadia, Murshidabad and Hughli) and Orissa. Orissa, like Bengal, was a major rice producer and exporter but storms prevented the necessary importation of food by sea. The total loss of life was in excess of 1 million people with 750,000 dying in Orissa alone. The devastation was seen to be so enormous that the Board of Revenue was criticized by the subsequent Famine Commission in 1867 and the Board subsequently professed regret for their tardiness in appreciating the extent of the impending disaster, remitting land taxes, importing food and taking other relief measures. [23]

In 1873-1874 famine again struck Bengal, Bihar and nearby provinces, the winter rice crop in Bengal being only three eighths of normal. However in this instance the humanity and intelligence of one man, Sir George Campbell, the Lieutenant Governor of Bengal, saved millions from disaster and this despite the contemptible unresponsiveness of the Home Government and the Central Government of India. 70 years later General Wavell (Viceroy of India) and the Australian R.G. Casey (Governor of Bengal) were to energetically address the horrendous wartime Bengal Famine in the face of Home Government unresponsiveness and after disastrously ineffectual responses from their predecessors, Linlithgow in Delhi and

Herbert in Calcutta, respectively. Sir George Campbell responded quickly to the crisis through importation of food, introduction of relief works and systematic provision of relief food throughout Bengal. Nevertheless the Viceroy, Lord Northbrooke, declined to prohibit the continuing export of rice to Ceylon, the West Indies, Mauritius, England and elsewhere in the Empire, a position supported by the Home Government - free trade must go on. [24]

In 1875-1876 food was still scarce in Bengal but famine was averted. Similarly shortages in 1884-1885 and 1892 did not cause catastrophic famine in Bengal. However in 1896-1897 severe famine affected all of northern India including Bengal. Fortunately the dreadful famine of 1899-1900 that swept away several million people in a huge area of India - Punjab, Rajasthan, Central Provinces, Bombay and Hyderabad - had much less impact on Bengal. Ghosh (1944) writes with bitterness and contempt about the grandeur of the Delhi Durbar of 1902 held at immense expense shortly after one of India's worst famines. Famine recurred in Bengal and Bihar in 1906-1907 but, scarcity aside, Bengal was then free of famine for nearly 40 years. [25]

13.4. Responses to Indian famines by the British

The British had a major responsibility for famine in India in a clear and fundamental way - they had imposed themselves gratuitously and violently upon a complex sub-continent and became the rulers. The unspoken contract between the rulers and the ruled in civilised human societies is that the ruled pay their taxes and get something back in return from the rulers - whether this be bread and circuses, leadership in war or relief at times of natural disaster such as periods of food scarcity and famine. The conduct of the British in India - for all the immense propaganda to the contrary in relation to dams, railways, law and Pax Britannica - reveal them to be merely thieves and slave-masters with a callous disregard for their subjects right up to the time they finally got the message and left. Indeed it is the thesis of this book that the process of exploitation and imposition has not yet finished and that Gadarene European mercantilism will impose an even more dreadful exaction from the Indians (and others) in the next century as a price for their sharing the biosphere with the "master culture".

Specifically, the British were responsible for famine in India in many ways: through wars, rapacious land taxes, export of food, conversion of land use to growth of non-food cash crops and destruction of indigenous manufacturing industry through discriminatory taxes and violence. We have seen, for example, the dramatic decline of the Indian cotton industry brought about through highly discriminatory tariffs blocking Indian exports to Britain. In times of food scarcity people in India survived through the help of their rulers and other people who had a sense of social obligation imbued by the steady evolution of their society over thousands of years. However ultimately, in the absence of food in their immediate environment, hungry people had to buy it from elsewhere. Colonial policies led to significant conversion of food crops to industrial cash crops (e.g. cotton, jute, opium, tea and indigo) and damage to ancient Indian industries (in favour of metropolitan industry and its sales to a captive market). These pressures diminished food supply and the ability of Indians to buy food. Yet the British right to the end maintained the economic fiction that the famines of India were "acts of God" rather than the clear and appalling reality that they were due to the actions of the colonial overlords.

There is a horrible story that I have been told by a number of Indian scholars and which relates to the Bengali muslin weavers of Dacca. It was said that muslin from Dacca was so fine that a sari made from this material could be drawn through a wedding ring. The manufacture of Dacca muslin was disposed of by the British through the expedient of chopping off the thumbs of the weavers - or so the story goes. The only published versions of this story that I have seen are of 2 kinds - one more or less as above and the other involving self-

mutilation by brutally oppressed weavers. The latter story tells of
Bengali raw silk winders cutting off their own thumbs to prevent their
being forced to wind silk by the brutal Company agents. [26] Of course
the absence of a satisfactorily documented "written" account does not
necessarily invalidate the tale (as we can see from the oral traditions of
aboriginal people in Australia or ragas in India). If indeed it is merely
a story, then it nevertheless serves as a powerful metaphor for the
social, agricultural and industrial disruption due to the British in India
that visited Bergen-Belsen conditions to swathes of the sub-continent
in virtually every decade of British rule for 2 centuries of
unprecedented holocaust. Karl Marx (1853) described precisely how a
combination of British imperialism and technology impoverished
Bengal and the rest of India:

"It was the British intruder who broke up the Indian hand-loom and
destroyed the spinning wheel. England began with driving the Indian
cottons from the European market; it then introduced twist into
Hindustan and, in the end, inundated the very country of cotton with
cotton. From 1818 to 1836 the export of twist from Great Britain to
India rose in the proportion of 1 to 5,200. In 1824 the export of British
muslins hardly amounted to 1,000,000 yards while in 1837 it surpassed
64,000,000 of yards. But at the same time the population of Dacca
decreased from 150,000 inhabitants to 20,000. This decline of Indian
towns celebrated for their fabrics was by no means the worst
consequence. British steam and science uprooted, over the whole
surface of Hindustan, the union between agricultural and
manufacturing industry." [27]

The British did inquire into the famines as they occurred. A
commission of 3 experienced men was sent out to Bengal in 1772 to
inquire into the conduct of affairs but unfortunately the commissioners
did not arrive, the ship taking them to India, the Aurora, having been
lost at sea with all hands. Nevertheless official inquiry into the 1769-
1770 famine was made and evidence adduced of speculation in food
by Company men. Other analyses and reports of famine in India were

published. [28] The great Adam Smith commented on the Bengal famine of 1769-1770 in relation to his proposition that scarcity should never translate into famine provided there is no constraint on normal free trade. In his view inappropriate regulations and restraints by the British administrators simply compounded the problem at the time of this famine in Bengal. [29] Imposition of differential duties by the British through simple regulation abolished both the foreign and domestic market for Bengali and Indian textiles and brought horrendous suffering to millions. [30] We will see later that ultimately British "regulations" killed a million people in the Irish famine. [31] In the Bengal famine of 1943-1945, British regulations (significantly enacted a week before the Japanese attack on Pearl Harbor) gave individual provinces the power to control their own food trade. This has been described as a "tragic step" and a "fatal mistake" that helped to seal the fate of millions of Bengali famine victims. [32]

As famine recurred throughout the nineteenth century, the British would earnestly analyse the data and this inevitably led to palliative measures. Thus the improvements to ports and roads and the building of railways increased the capacity to bring food into famine areas. Storms that prevented the supply of Orissa by sea in 1866 were responsible for an immense loss of life in that famine. Major irrigation works in the Punjab provided greater security against the effects of climatic oscillations. Famine Commissions were conducted and ultimately revised versions of Famine Codes were promulgated. Improved irrigation was seen as a major beneficial move to prevent famine with improved transport and relief work programs as effective responses to famine. However the continuing reality was that Indians lived on the edge. For those who worked for money to buy food (or had been forced into this situation through drought), a downward shift in their income coupled with an upward shift in the price of food would lead to disaster. The Famine Codes indicated a growing moral sensibility on the part of the British. [33] However the very existence of these regulations could impair effective response. Thus the acting Governor of Bengal in 1943, Sir T. Rutherford, informed the Viceroy of India that he had not actually declared a famine because this would have obliged him to implement the measures laid down in the Famine Codes. [34]

13.5. The context of global genocide

It is useful at this point to put the British crimes against humanity in India into the context of what they had been up to elsewhere and what other European powers were doing. In considering European colonial excesses we will be largely concerned with the span of 2 maximal human lifetimes (2 times 125 years) on either side of the year of Jane Austen's death (1817). This takes us roughly from the accession of Queen Elizabeth I in England (1558) to a point just after the middle of the 21st century, by which time global warming changes would already have wreaked disastrous "entitlement" changes for the people of the tropical third world (see Chapter 16). We will be largely concerned with the activities of the British (both at home and abroad) but will intersperse our account with the more revolting "colonial" activities of some other powers.

13.6. Africa

The slave trade in Africa began with the Portuguese obtaining slaves from indigenous slave traders on the coast of Mauretania in the 15th century. The trade was initially Africa-based (e.g. the Portuguese trading slaves to Africans in return for Angolan gold and running slave-based plantations on Sao Tomé off the African coast). The conquest of the New World and the setting up of plantations in South and North America and in the West Indies dramatically increased the slave trade and brought the Dutch, French and British into the act. In the 17th century the Dutch moved into the trade in Angola to service their plantations in South America but were eventually pushed out by the Portuguese.

The major years of the trade were 1750-1850, nicely bracketing the life of Jane Austen. A total of about 11-20 million slaves were sent to the Americas but this estimate can be increased by about 25-50% to include those that died in the appalling imprisonment, shipping and physical punishment impositions of the process. The regions of activity stretched down the coast from West Africa to Angola. The Arabs were heavily involved on the East coast of Africa. The economic impact on England and other slaving countries was enormous. Slavery and attendant economic activity helped to fund the capital accumulation needed for the Industrial Revolution and associated expansion elsewhere. The general procedure involved coastal acquisition of slaves captured and brought in from the interior followed by trans-Atlantic shipment and re-sale. The overall process involved enormous violence, social disruption and substantial losses during transportation. While African population growth compensated for these depredations, the trade as such distorted African societies in substantial contact with Europeans and imposed parasitic and exploitative indigenous "slaving" classes upon African societies.

Through the lobbying of decent people of the likes of the Quakers and poets such as William Cowper (see Chapter 7), pressure mounted against the slave trade. However the abolition of the slave trade was not simply due to the altruism and goodness of a noble people (we recall Henry Tilney declaring to Catherine Morland: "Remember the country and the age in which we live. Remember that we are English, that we are Christian".) Contrary to the "goodness" myth and ostensible public assertion, it is likely that slavery was abolished by Britain because it became expensive and uneconomic. It is a much better proposition to employ "free" workers who are subject to State authority and have no choice but to work for you or to starve. Britain was the leading slave trading country and lead the way in abolishing the slave trade in Britain and its dominions in 1807. Slavery in British colonies was abolished in 1833 and this example was followed successively by the French, the Danes, the South American republics, the USA (1865), Spanish Cuba (1888) and Portuguese Brazil (1888). [35] However we will see later (p129) that British and

Australian slavery would occur later in the Pacific as so-called "blackbirding" for Melanesian sugar plantation labour.

The abolition of the slave trade on the part of Europeans brought expansion of "legitimate" commercial activity to Africa involving palm oil in West Africa and farming by the Dutch Afrikaners, Portuguese, Germans and the British in Southern Africa. This simply involved the violent seizure of African lands and the expansion of "efficient" scientific European agriculture. The British expansion in this respect led to the agricultural settlement of Rhodesia and eventually of the high country of Kenya, which was ideal for coffee production. The Great Trek of the Afrikaners from the Cape colony into the Transvaal led them into conflict with African tribes, substantial but incomplete seizure of African lands and use of indigenous labour. The British expansion into Natal led to conflict with the Zulus and the celebrated Zulu wars. The Natal and Kenya expansions resulted in the need for labour and the introduction of Indian and Chinese labour. The Portuguese extended agricultural activity in Mozambique and Angola and the Germans (of whom more later) seized African lands for cattle farms in South West Africa. [36] The nineteenth century saw the division of Africa between the European powers namely Britain, France, Spain, Portugal, Belgium, Germany and Italy. This acquisition phase produced some conflicts of exceptional violence and horror that we will now briefly deal with in rough chronological order.

The Zulus were ruled by Shaka from 1818 to 1828, when this monster was assassinated. This was a time of pressures deriving from the northward movement of the Europeans from the Cape of Good Hope and the Zulus made space for themselves through frightful expansion and genocide. Shaka organized his soldiers into a merciless military machine that in battle would approach the enemy as a crescent, the horns of which would close up to encircle the foe. Everyone thus trapped would be systematically slaughtered. The women, children and elderly of his opponents would be all murdered.

Some young women might be occasionally spared for sexual purposes but Shaka saved young men for his own army. Shaka created zones of death around his kingdom in which nobody was left alive and maintained the security of his domain by keeping his neighbours in a state of utter terror. Shaka was a prototype of Hitler, Stalin and Pol Pot - they all ruled their territories by force of arms complemented by the sheer terror of remorseless mass-murder. [37]

The British and the Afrikaners moved north into regions depopulated by the Zulus under Shaka and defeated the Zulus and other African tribes in a succession of encounters during the nineteenth century. Major events included the massacre of Piet Retief and his followers by the Zulus under Dingaan and the subsequent defeat of the Zulus at the Battle of Blood River by the Afrikaners (1838); war between the British and the Kaffirs resulting in the defeat of the Kaffirs in the War of the Axe (1847-1848); the mass-starvation of the Kaffirs (1856); the final Kaffir War (1877-1878); and the Zulu War of 1879 which saw initial Zulu victory over the British but eventually the inevitable Zulu defeat. As we will see later it was not just the indigenous people of Southern Africa who gave the European imperialists a run for their money in the 19th century, despite the impossible odds of spears against guns. [38] [As a child I used to borrow "ripping" British Imperial adventure books from the personal library of a kindly, elderly Mrs Walker who lived up the hill on Mount Stuart Road on Mount Stuart in Hobart, Tasmania (our road and hill being named after Mount Stuart Elphinstone, the great British India administrator, and indeed diverging from Elphinstone Road further down Mount Stuart). One of my favourites was Sanders of the River, who would go out to Africa armed with his "equalizers" and, with the help of "friendly natives", would wreak havoc on dissident Africans. In hindsight, these tales had very much an Old Testament flavour about them, with the hapless African "savages" as Canaanites, the "friendly natives" as Israelites and Sanders being someone like Joshua, an agent of the Lord's Will and who has the advantage of transcendental destructive powers. Well might they have said "God is an Englishman"].

The ancient land of Egypt was invested by the British, exciting events in a Boy's Own Annual sense being the bombardment of Alexandria and the occupation of Cairo by the British (1882), the capture of Khartoum in the Sudan - with the attendant massacre of General Gordon and his garrison by the followers of the Mahdi (1885) - and the reconquest of the Sudan by General Lord Kitchener at the Battle of Obdurman in which Churchill participated (1896). Bad treatment of the vanquished by the British under Kitchener included the maltreatment and murder of the wounded. Pelling (1974), in recounting this episode, quotes Churchill's comment about Kitchener: "He may be a general - but never a gentleman." [39]

The Anglo-Boer War (1899-1902) followed the successful fight for independence of the Transvaal Afrikaners against the British (1880-1881) and the British desire to reassert authority after the discovery of gold on the Witswatersrand in 1896. This conflict involved 300,000 British Empire soldiers pitted against the Boer farmers. The British herded captured Boer women and children into concentration camps where there were massive casualties. About 10% of the Afrikaaners perished and there was a particularly high death rate among children. As a result of this war Britain gained the South African goldfields but also earned great disapprobation in Europe for treating white folks so badly. However other European powers had also dirtied their reputations in Africa as the following examples show. [40]

The Congo region became the venue for rapacious rubber collection and appalling cruelties by the Belgians. King Leopold of the Belgians had attempted to get interest in forming a Belgian equivalent of the East India Company that would do to China what that Company had done to India. Fortunately for the Chinese there were no takers and Leopold turned to the Congo. The International Association for the

Exploration and Civilization of Central Africa was set up (ostensibly to suppress the slave trade) in 1876. H.M. Stanley (of "Dr Livingstone, I presume" fame) was recruited after his famous trans-Africa trip to act as an agent of the Belgian part of the committee. He returned to Africa and set up Belgian stations in the Congo. The International Association of the Congo was set up and received international recognition. This period of Central African history was attended by all kinds of exciting diplomatic to-ing and fro-ing between the Belgians, British, Portuguese, Germans and the French and also saw European defeat of Arab slave traders. Risings by the Batetalas on the Upper Congo were suppressed by the Belgians (1896) and the Portuguese suppressed a revolt in Angola (1902).

The Belgians extracted rubber from the indigenous inhabitants of the Congo with unbelievable cruelty - women and children were captured and violated, Africans were mutilated or just simply murdered out of hand on a huge scale. The chopping off of hands was a favourite device to punish Africans for insufficient collections. Smoked ears and hands were tendered by the agents as evidence of their enthusiasm. Evidence from a variety of witnesses described appalling atrocities and the widespread and near-total destruction of African communities. The graphic account by E.D. Morel entitled Red Rubber, the Story of the Rubber Slave Trade Flourishing on the Congo in the Year of Grace 1907 raised great public indignation in Britain, the US and Germany, as did the reports of the British consul Roger Casement. [41] Sir Roger Casement, the decent and good man who had so earnestly pleaded the cause of the horribly afflicted inhabitants of the Congo, was hung by the British in 1916 for his support for Irish self-determination. [42]

South West Africa was seized by the Germans in the 19th century and they proceeded to dispossess the native inhabitants of their land, territory lying between the coastal sandy Namid desert and the Kalahari desert on the east. This arid country was sparsely populated by the Ovambo (125,000) in the north, the Hereros (80,000) in the central region of Hereroland and the Namas (20,000) in the southern Namaland. The Hereros were nomadic herdsmen and the Germans, after the fashion of their British cousins in similarly arid Australia, simply seized native lands as well as maltreating the Hereros by rape, imprisonment, flogging and murder. The Hereros were ultimately forced into revolt through the expansion of the German railways and hence of German pastoralists and their herds. These encroachments were set to destroy their very ability to survive in this relatively harsh environment.

The Hereros revolted in 1904 under the leadership of Samuel Maharero and had major initial successes. They conducted themselves very honourably in relation to non-combatants, including non-Germans. The Germans came back with great ferocity and effected the first of a number of 20th century genocides on their slate. The Hereros had no answer to artillery and machine guns and the Germans instituted a deliberate policy of total extermination. Ultimately the survivng Herero women and children were driven into the desert to die. The proto-Nazi General von Trotha who was responsible for these enormities wrote: "This uprising is and remains the beginning of a racial struggle, which I foresaw for East Africa as early as 1897 in my reports to the Imperial Chancellor". About 50% of Hereros and Namas taken prisoner died in captivity i.e. were murdered. Overall these proto-Nazi colonial Germans wiped out 80% of the Hereros and 50% of the Namas in South West Africa. [43]

The struggle of Africans for their lands and liberty was fought out over several centuries in all parts of Africa, the bloodiest struggle being the Algerian war of independence against the French that cost over a million lives. The most notable successes in a British colonial context were the successful campaigns of the Mau Mau of the Kikuyu in Kenya (leading to independence), the Zimbabweans (independence) and the African National Congress (democracy achieved 1995). However of relevance to these processes and our concern with India was the system that brought indentured labour from India to South

Africa and East Africa. These workers were essentially "3 year slaves", becoming free again on the expiry of their contract. These people and their "free" immigrant compatriots made a good "go" of it in Africa and certainly contributed to political development in an increasingly racist environment. Gandhi had lived, worked and organized for public and political decency in South Africa. Indians contributed to the failure of Kenya to become a white-dominated minority-ruled country after the fashion of South Africa or Southern Rhodesia and were actively involved in the ultimate destruction of Apartheid in South Africa. [Just as my father-in-law Abdul Lateef MBE believed in the equality of man and to that end was actively involved in the creation of institutional access - to secondary education, golf, the Club, the law, parliament - for everyone in colonial Fiji (and ultimately to global institutions through independence), so an Osman Latief insisted on his right to travel by train in colonial South Africa]. [44]

Nevertheless it is abundantly clear that the myth of British Imperial decency, sustained by the Austenizing of history, contributed to a view among those who matter in Britain, the US and Europe that the quintessentially (and in many cases actually) Nazi South African Nationalists, their supporters and their English "running dogs" were somehow respectable and honourable in a way that the Africans, "Coloureds" and Indians were not. This was certainly the attitude among conservative Australians up to a few years ago (and for all I know still is behind club doors). This had a sustained public expression over several decades after the Sharpeville Massacre (1960) in relation to economic and sporting boycotts of South Africa. On a very celebrated occasion in 1987, the Anglican Archbishop of Cape Town, Archbishop Desmond Tutu, a good-humoured, passionate and good man, who was visiting Australia at the time, was vehemently condemned as a "witch doctor ... breathing hatred" by an outspoken Returned Soldiers' League official. [45] The sanitized view of British Imperial history contributed to the pragmatic and far too tolerant attitudes to white minority regimes in Southern Rhodesia and South

Africa and hence the longevity of these obscenities. The Nationalist imposition on South Africa for half a century has been an immense human and social disaster.

13.7. America

The invasion of the Americas commenced with the voyage of Christopher Columbus in 1492. Santo Domingo on the island of Hispaniola became the initial capital of Spanish colonial rule in the New World. Disease and violent enslavement decimated the indigenous population. African slavery was introduced there in 1500. By 1535 the first of many genocides in the New World had eliminated the indigenous Arawak Indian population (variously estimated to be up to several million in number in 1492). For maltreatment of the Arawaks, Columbus was arrested and taken back to Spain in 1500 on orders of King Ferdinand and Queen Isabella, these being the monarchs responsible for the expulsion of Jews and Moors from Spain but who paradoxically favoured the conversion of the Indians. Columbus was forbidden entry to Hispaniola again.

The defeat of the Aztecs at Otumba by the Spanish under Cortes in 1500 and the subsequent conquest of the Aztec empire was followed by defeat of the Maya Indians. The Spanish brought disease that decimated the Indian populations. In Peru Pizarro (see Chapter 7) seized the Inca Atahualpa, ransomed him for a gigantic fortune, murdered him in 1533 and then defeated the demoralised Incas and seized their capital Cuzco. Throughout Spanish and Portuguese American possessions disease, maltreatment, taxation and brutal enslavement took an enormous toll of the indigenous Indian population. Even the altruistic missionary process contributed to the epidemics through mass gatherings and consequent transmission of disease. The 19th century saw the deliberate genocide of Indians in Argentina, Paraguay and Uruguay to permit cattle ranching and horrendous crimes against Peruvian and Brazilian Amazonian Indians associated with settlement and rubber collection.

The French colonial expansion in North America brought inadvertent and deliberate destruction upon the Indians. The French alliance with the Huron Indians against the Iroquois and other European interests along the St. Lawrence resulted in the destruction of the Hurons by the Iroquois, only one Huron tribe surviving by the middle of the 17th century. French expansion up the Mississippi River in the early 18th century finally met with resistance from the Natchez Indians. In 1731 a combination of the Choctaw Indians and the French defeated the Natchez who were then sold into slavery in the West Indies plantations and disappeared from history. [46]

The English first became actively involved in American affairs through the slave trading of John Hawkins in the mid-16th century and the attacks on Spanish ships and establishments by Drake and Cavendish. These adventures and the explorations of these and other sailors such as Frobisher, Gilbert and Davis ultimately led to the first unsuccessful attempts to establish a colony in Virginia in the late 16th century under the auspices of Sir Walter Raleigh. The Jamestown settlement led by Captain John Smith was established in Virginia by the London Company in 1607, which went into tobacco and was also involved in Bermuda. [If one wishes to be comprehensive in this catalogue of colonial mayhem it is worth noting that in the First World every year about 1 in every 1000 people dies of smoking-related disease. With a global population now of about 6 billion and with smoking an epidemic in some major countries such as China, it is estimated that smoking kills about 5 million people a year - a death toll greater than that from that scourge of humanity, malaria]. The Pilgrim Fathers arrived at Cape Cod in the Mayflower in 1620 and set up a colony outside the jurisdiction of the London Company. Catholic settlement in Maryland took place in 1633 and Lord Saye and Sele (whose tribe was later connected with the Leighs and the Austens) was involved in settlement in Massachusetts in 1635. The Dutch West India Company purchased Manhattan Island from the Indians for 24 dollars in 1626. The Dutch pushed out the Swedes from New Sweden on the Delaware in 1655 and were in turn turfed out of North America in 1664 with the surrender of New Amsterdam to the English, who renamed the colony New York. [47]

When the first European settlements were made in Virginia and New England epidemics of disease contracted from previous contact with European fishermen and adventurers had already swept through the Indian populations. The plague epidemic in 1614-1616 and the smallpox epidemic of 1633-1634 had a big impact. However loss of land, winter food stores and livelihood together with European violence compounded the problems for the Indians. The notion of vacuum domicilium, or unoccupied land, was accepted by the Europeans, this convenient notion being encouraged by the depopulation due to disease. (We will see later that the same notion of terra nullius, or empty land, justified the wholesale removal of traditional lands from Australian aboriginals). Roger Williams had his opinions burnt and was banished from Salem for arguing for Indian land rights. While most Indian tribes were too disadvantaged to resist the Europeans effectively, the Pequots of southern Massachusetts resisted, only to be defeated by the English in alliance with the Narragansett Indians. The Pequots were exterminated, many of those not directly killed being burnt to death in their wigwams. Prisoners were taken to sea and thrown overboard. The Pequots disappeared from the world in 1637-1638. The Naragansett Indians were forced to fight back and achieved success in 1675 against the English, but inevitably they too followed the path of the Pequots into oblivion. [48]

As the English colonies expanded and prospered, the surviving Indian communities in "settled" areas, ravaged by war, violence and disease and deprived of lands and traditional livelihood, shrank into political irrelevance. However resistance continued on the frontier. There is evidence that the Europeans deliberately used smallpox infection of Indians to wipe out their opponents. British military authorities at Fort Pitt (later Pittsburgh) gave blankets from the smallpox hospital to Indians in order to cripple a revolt in the mid-18th century. The British commander-in-chief in America, Sir Jeffrey

Amherst, had directly advocated this procedure and the Delawares, Mingo and Shawnee were consequently swept with a smallpox epidemic. It is interesting to observe that while Jane Austen's friend Mrs Lefroy helped in the cowpox vaccination of local villagers against smallpox following the discovery of this procedure by Edward Jenner in 1796, [49] English settlers in America had already applied this device for the protection of their slaves. It appears that deliberate biological warfare was applied in North America as an instrument of genocide.

The "Indian question" re-appeared politically in relation to westward expansion of European settlement. The revolt of the colonies against the British was impelled by considerations such as "no taxation without representation" and the rights of local entrepreneurs to operate without metropolitan, Parliamentary restrictions and impositions. The Boston Tea Party was a demonstration against the monopoly of the East India Company and its relief from duties on tea imports from the East in England that were nevertheless to be paid in the American colonies. The British Government had imposed a restriction on westward expansion of the colonies in 1763, concerned by the cost of providing military protection. George Washington was strongly opposed to this constraint on the dispossession of Indians on the frontier and beyond and it became a significant issue in the rebellion of the colonies in 1775. The final defeat and concession of the British in 1783 gave the Americans their independence and freedom of economic and territorial expansion that was to dispossess the remaining aboriginal inhabitants in the west. [50]

By 1800 the American European population was about 5 million and the Indian population had shrunk to about 600,000. The 19th century saw Americans move west taking with them the remorseless logic of the American mercantile tradition, of "free trade" garnished with moralistic, religious and nationalistic rhetoric and instinctively pragmatic "democracy" coupled with profoundly entrenched racism. The Indians in their path were inevitably subdued, dispossessed, swept aside or moved on. The "divide and rule" policy of using particular tribes to help suppress others was very effective for the Americans but ultimately the collaborators shared the fate of their earlier victims. Thus the Cherokee accommodated and collaborated in the suppression of the Shawnee and the Creek Indians. However they were finally evicted from their lands in Georgia and forcibly removed to west of the Mississippi in a process associated with massive loss of life (25% of the population dying in the Cherokee Removal). Chickasaw, Choctaws and Creeks were also deported from their lands.

With the discovery of gold in California the indigenous Indians came in for the routine of mass murder, enslavement, rape, disease and dispossession. Thus the Yuki Indians of Northern California suffered a population decline of from 3,500 in 1848 to merely 400 in 1880 as a result of these vile processes. Associated with massive population decline and dissolution of formal Indian social organization came the process of ethnocide associated with assimilation of surviving Indians into mainstream society and decline of cultural integrity, a process to be seen elsewhere in the English-speaking world with the indigenous people of Australia, New Zealand, Canada, South Africa and indeed of the Celtic people of Ireland, Wales, Scotland and Cornwall. [It is amusing to note an anecdote from an academic Ulsterman in this connection. He asserts that because of substantial migration of Gaelic-speaking people from northern Ireland to America in the 18th century, the revolutionary Americans seriously considered Gaelic as an option for a national language for America, English just winning over Gaelic which in turn did vastly better than the biblically-inspired Hebrew option].

As the Americans spread over the Great Plains to the Rocky Mountains and beyond, the Indians in these parts found their economy disrupted through disease, violence, mass murder, dispossession and the slaughter of wildlife necessary for their survival. In the early 1860 the Americans mobilized cavalry regiments to meet a perceived threat from horse-riding Indian tribes such as the Sioux, Cheyenne, Arapaho, Apache, Comanche and Kiowa. The Sioux were defeated by General

Sibley at Wood Lake in Minnesota in 1862 but other Indian tribes continued resistance. The Cheyenne under Chief Black Kettle were prepared for peace against overwhelming odds but in 1864 were massacred - men, women and children - by the Americans under Chivington at Sand Creek in Colorado. The American government provided "reservations" for the Cheyenne and Arapahos in 1865, a policy that was extended to other Plains Indians such as the Apache, Comanche, Kiowa and Sioux. However the authorities were ever ready to remove lands from such reservations to meet the needs of the immense European population streaming west over the Plains.

Wildlife destruction and removal of lands cut at the basis of biological survival for the Plains Indians and starvation compounded the problems of disease. The bison (Bison bison) numbered an estimated 60 million in the mid-19th century but were virtually pushed to the very edge of total extinction. The American passenger pigeon (Ectopistes migratorius) was numbered in billions and yet became totally extinct by 1814. The advance of the railways, the slaughter of buffalo and the continuing flood of settlers (stimulated further by the discovery of gold in the Black Hills of Dakota) pushed the Sioux into revolt. Custer and his men were massacred by the Sioux under Chief Sitting Bull at Little Big Horn in 1876, for which the Americans exacted salutory revenge upon the Sioux. The Nez Perce Indians under Chief Joseph were defeated in 1877 and the Apache in Arizona and New Mexico under Chiefs Victorio and Geronimo were finally forced to concede to the might of the U.S. Army in 1886. Geronimo's Apache tribe (together with the Apache scouts who had tracked them down and persuaded a final surrender), were carted off to Florida in cattle trucks to imprisonment, disease and enforced removal of their children (a process to be repeatedly applied to "aboriginal" people elsewhere, and most notably in Australia up to the late 1960s). As with indigenous lands in Southern Africa, New Caledonia and arid Australia, the lands of the Apache were given over to grazing by the livestock of the invader. With the final military defeat of the Plains Indians came their confinement in each case to reservations. The Indian population fell from about 400,000 in 1850 to about 250,000 in 1890.[51]

The defeat and dispossession of the Indians by the United States was paralleled by the more benign conquest of the western and northern wildernesses of Canada. A substantial body of Canadians were Scots and Irish forced from their homelands by English rapacity. The assimilatory ethnocide practised by the Americans also applied in Canada and such policies (notably those applying to children) extended vigorously into the 20th century in Canada and indeed in other parts of the English-speaking world, including Australia. Such policies have a continuing impact today in all of these countries.

Finally a brief comment must be made about the West Indies that was the first site of colonial exploitation in the New World. The islands of the Caribbean Sea were variously seized by the Spanish, Dutch, French, British and Danes and the sugar plantations were the earliest targets of the slave trade from Africa. Prior to Spanish conquest, parts of the West Indies had been conquered by Caribs from the mainland who enslaved the Arawak-speaking women and put to death the menfolk. European colonial rule disposed of both groups. The Caribbean islands saw the whole gamut of colonial excesses: the genocide of the original inhabitants; African slavery (from 1501 onwards); the violent suppression of revolts by slaves or former slaves (notably that in Jamaica in 1865 that was suppressed by Governor Eyre with controversial ferocity); successful slave revolt (in Haiti against the French in 1804); and the introduction of indentured labour from India after the abolition of slavery .[52]

The works of V.S. Naipaul and his brother S. Naipaul give a delightful insight into the latter experience as well as a more sombre view of the wash-up of British colonialism elsewhere in the world. While V.S. Naipaul's An Area of Darkness (1967) appears insufficiently responsive to the courage and dignity of the impoverished people of India, the realistic perceptions of this precise observer must be taken very seriously as the Third World approaches a catastrophic era. The writings of both V.S. Naipaul [53] and Shiva Naipaul [54] are splendid examples of the rich outflowings from the cultural fusions of the British Empire. [55] [My wife introduced me to V.S. Naipaul's glorious A House for Mr Biswas over 30 years ago, her grandparents having left India for the sugar cane plantations of Fiji as opposed to those of Natal, Mauritius or Naipaul's Trinidad]. [It is not surprising that British commercial and military activity in the West Indies as well as India should actually score mentions (albeit very brief) in particular Jane Austen novels given the interests of her connections in both places. The Reverend George Austen was the trustee for an estate in Antigua owned by James Langford Nibbs of St John's College (as well as being trustee for the fund set up for Eliza by Warren Hastings). Francis and Charles Austen had sailed the waters of both places in the British Navy; James Austen's father-in-law General Matthew had served as Governor of Granada and Charles Austen's father-in-law was John Palmer, the Attorney General of Bermuda; Cassandra's fiancé the Reverend Thomas Fowle had died at San Domingo in 1797 under the command of Lord Craven, in turn connected with Jane Austen's sisters-in-law Mary and Martha Lloyd.[56] In addition, Mrs Austen's sister-in-law Jane Leigh-Perrot (née Cholmeley) was heiress to an estate in Barbados and the Reverend George Austen's relatives William and George Walter worked on the Jamaica estates of Sir George Hampson, a relative of his mother Rebecca (née Hampson)]. [57]

13.8. Australia

The first settlement of Australia, the convict settlement that eventually became Sydney, was made by the "First Fleet" under Captain Phillip in 1788. Strategic naval considerations relating to the naval defence of British India against the French were important factors in this settlement (as well as the often-stated need for a place for convicts after the loss of America) [We have already seen in Chapter 2 how close Jane Austen's aunt Jane Leigh-Perrot came to transportation to "Botany Bay"]. Settlement in other parts of Australia followed over the next century, namely settlements that were destined to become the following State capital cities: Hobart (Tasmania, 1804), Brisbane (Queensland, 1824), Perth (Western Australia, 1829), Adelaide (South Australia., 1834) and Melbourne (Victoria, 1835). The Mainland Australian colonies were associated with relatively well-watered coastal regions and vast interior regions suitable for "wheat and wool" at best, for only livestock when more marginal and ultimately giving way to the interior desert. [58]

The aboriginal inhabitants ("aborigines") quickly came into conflict with the settlers and were rapidly dispossessed of their land and remorselessly exterminated through disease (including deliberately introduced disease), shooting, bludgeoning and the poisoning of water holes and flour. They did not give up their land without a fight but were ultimately defeated by disease, weight of numbers, a mounted enemy and guns. The aborigines, ethnically connected with the Dravidians of South India, had lived in Australia for some 50,000 years (some suggest 60,000 years). While they had a major impact on the environment through the use of fire, they did not practise cereal agriculture and maintained a population compatible with a hunter-gatherer culture. They had a sophisticated civilization involving a large number of distinct cultures and languages throughout the Continent. Their vulnerability is dramatically illustrated by the fact that one well-armed European with his family could occupy a water-hole at the cross-roads of a transcontinental aboriginal trade route, shoot or drive away the aborigines and destroy a sophisticated continental inter-tribal trading system that had been operating for millennia. [59]

The insidiousness of this genocidal evil can be seen from the accounts of the writer Dame Mary Gilmore. [60] She recalled seeing with her parents a murdered tribal group lying dead in the vicinity of a poisoned water-hole. [61] The last major massacre of Australian aborigines occurred in Western Australia in 1926 in which about 100

aborigines were gunned down, the survivors being led away in chains.
[62]

There were perhaps 300,000 aborigines in Australia in 1788 although other estimates go as high as several million. [63] By 1890 this had been reduced to about 85,000. Those now living a culturally more or less intact "tribal" existence are largely confined to the Northern Territory (the last region to be colonized). Today [2008] there are perhaps about 50,000 "full-blood" aborigines and some 450,000 part-aboriginals who nevertheless very strongly identify with their aboriginal heritage. An appalling large-scale policy of deliberate ethnocide applying for much of the 19th and 20th centuries involved simply taking aboriginal children from their parents. This policy stopped in West Australia as recently as 1967 and the after-effects continue to have a major impact on a substantial proportion of aborigines in Australia to this day. An extraordinary account of this process is given by Sally Morgan in her astonishingly light-hearted book My Place .[64] The conservative Australian Government refused to officially apologize for this crime against humanity.

Aborigines were finally officially regarded as Australians for the purpose of the National Census and Federal legislation in 1967. [65] However the process of dispossession and abuse continues today despite a political consensus dictating at the very least "politically correct" deference and public respect for aborigines in public life. Aboriginal mortality, morbidity and living conditions in many areas are appalling even by Third World standards. The rates of imprisonment of aborigines are extraordinarily high and the incidence of "aboriginal deaths in custody" proportionately exceeded that in Apartheid South Africa and remains an outrageous national blemish. While the celebrated "Mabo" case decision of the Australian High Court (1992) disputed the concept of terra nullius and established the possibility of "land rights" for some Torres Strait Islanders and thence by implication for other indigenous Australians, [66] a current conservative thrust is impelling continuation and final legitimation of the dispossession of aborigines that started over 2 centuries ago.

13.9. New Zealand

The Australian aborigines were almost completely exterminated in the rich coastal areas of South Eastern Australia through a combination of European weaponry, genocidal settler ferocity, disease and enforced ethnocidal assimilation through child removal. In addition the determined and courageous aboriginal resistance was made more difficult because they had a multiplicity of tribes that spoke different languages and were spread out over a vast continental expanse. In New Zealand the British encountered indigenous people, the Maoris, who were more concentrated geographically, extremely war-like, armed with modern weapons and who were able to unite and give the invaders a much more difficult task. There were about 100,000 Maoris in New Zealand in the early 19th century when whalers and sealers started to arrive and merchants from Sydney started trading firearms for flax and timber. The first Church of England Mission was founded in 1814 in the Bay of Islands by the Reverend Samuel Marsden who, as a magistrate in Sydney, would have men flogged to death. The acquisition of firearms allowed coastal Maori tribes to impose upon those in the interior, but when all tribes obtained guns a modus vivendi was established and the so-called Musket Wars came to an end. Disease had a major impact but it was not as devastating to the Maoris as for indigenous people in other parts of Oceania and in Australia.

The first British colonists arrived en masse in 1840 and in that year 500 Maori chiefs signed the Treaty of Waitangi which was to be repeatedly violated for the next 150 years by the European (pakeha) invaders. Such violations and indeed different interpretations based on English/Polynesian semantic and cultural differences led to the First Maori War (1843-1848). The settlers were defeated by the Maoris at Wairau and eventually the British Army was brought into the conflict.

The Maoris developed excellent strategies to deal with the enemy, a notable one being the "disposable" pa (or fortification). While a pa in a coastal location was readily susceptible to naval attack or to Army shelling, a much greater investment in time and resources was required to invest a pa in the interior. When the Maoris saw impending defeat they would simply slip away and the British would have expended lives and effort for little gain. A further advance on this type of strategy was the construction of defensive earthworks, trenches and bunkers to allow shelter from shelling and gunfire and to allow for very effective ambushing of advancing British troops. These techniques bedevilled the campaigns of the British under General Cameron and General Pratt during the subsequent Second Maori War (1860-1870) and led to vindictive butchery of women and children by the British, as at the Battle of Orakau (1864).

While they were not able to defeat the British, the Maoris achieved considerable success against great odds in terms of numbers and arms. They did so with great skill and innovation by avoiding suicidal confrontations and in the design of the "modern pa". The sophistication of these latter fortifications was not appreciated by their immediate protagonists (presumably due to myths of racial superiority that in the event proved to be very expensive). However a 20th century British general was to describe these constructions as "perfect examples of field-fortification". Nevertheless weight of numbers ultimately defeated the skill and courage of the Maoris. [Charles Wilson Austen, great-grandson of Reverend George Austen's uncle and benefactor Francis Austen (Chapter 3), died in action in New Zealand]. Treaties notwithstanding, the Maoris became, in effect, second class citizens in their own country, this situation still obtaining today. [67]

13.10. Oceania

The French, British, Americans and Germans variously became involved in territorial expansion in Melanesia and/or Polynesia in the

19th century. The Polynesians of Tonga, Tahiti and Hawaii were particularly war-like. Indeed Captain Cook, so attentive to "noble savages" in Cowper's poem quoted earlier, was slain in Hawaii. The Polynesian aristocracy of Fiji derive from war-like invaders from Tonga lying to the east. The Polynesians, including the Tongans, Samoans, Tahitians, Hawaiians and Maoris were particularly war-like and in particular circumstances practised cannibalism (both of these sociopathies being linked to overpopulation relative to the "carrying capacity" of their island homes.) [68] [An anecdote involving an implausible one-upmanship: a Tongan is boasting of their past prowess and cannibalism to a visiting Australian who refers to cannibalism of their prisoners by Fijian warriors last century. The Tongan replies "But we didn't cook ours."] Horrendous tales are told of cannibalism in this region, of prisoners used as human rollers to launch war canoes, of victims offered a first bite of themselves and of missionaries intervening to save young women from being eaten. The Reverend Baker was followed village to village through the hills of Viti Levu (the main Fijian island) by a highly-prized whale's tooth (tabua, pronounced tambua) offered to those who would kill him for past discourtesies. The prize was secured and the missionary killed and eaten after he eventually committed the double discourtesy of re-possessing his comb from the head of a ratu (chief) (in their culture of keri keri you simply give something to a person if it is desired and you do not touch the head of another, and especially not the head of a ratu). [69] Maoris on occasion welcomed Europeans sailors by chanting "Come ashore and be eaten" and practised great cannibalistic excesses on their enemies, the genocide of the Chatham Islands Morioris being a dreadful example. [70]

European imperialism was actively sought in one case at least. The Fijian chief Cakobau (pronounced Thakembau) of Ovalau, off the coast of the main island of Viti Levu, was being threatened by the American Navy for impossible claims for compensation and approached the English in relation to cession and protection. The

English were not particularly enthusiastic but eventually accepted cession of Fiji to Britain in 1874. [71]

The major consequence of European imperialism in the Pacific was massive population decline due to disease. It is estimated that the population of Fiji declined by one third in 1874 due to measles. Similar massive depredations due to disease occurred in the late 19th century in the Solomons and the New Hebrides, disease being introduced by missionaries and by "blackbirders", the last British adventurers to be engaged in slave-trading. Polynesia suffered enormously also and it has been asserted that a high proportion of the French Polynesian colony of Tahiti are European-Polynesian hybrids selected for survival through disease epidemics.[72]

The development of the sugar industry in Fiji and in Queensland led to a need for cheap labour which was met through "blackbirding" or kidnapping of labour from the Solomon Islands and the New Hebrides as well as the Santa Cruz, Ellice and Tokelau groups. Tens of thousands of "Kanakas" were brought to Australia in the late 19th century, half a century after the ostensible abolition of slavery in the British Empire. These people were treated with great brutality in all facets of the process. In Fiji another source of slaves was from the Fijians themselves, Ratu Cakobau having sold men of Lovoni in 1871 as plantation workers. The death rate of such Melanesian workers in Fiji in 1875 was estimated to be about 50% as compared to the death rate among Indian indentured labourers of about 2%. The British installed a Pacific Islanders Protection Act in 1871 and attempted to enforce it. [73]

The squeeze on "blackbirding" led to the need for labour from another source and as a consequence the indentured Indian labour system (girmit) was introduced in 1879. Indians would commit themselves to 5 years of effective slavery in Fiji in return for a remuneration ostensibly much greater than they already received for labour and the promise of a free trip home. In the event neither of these promises were satisfied and the indentured labourers had a very hard time. They worked 6 days a week, this involving heavy physical labour in a hot humid environment. They were flogged for not working hard enough and often those unable to cope went out to the jungle and killed themselves. The typically Australian overseers and Indian sirdars could be brutal and impose upon women, single or married. As in the South African system, there was a major disparity of men over women in the ratio of as high as about 3 to 1. This system ended in 1920. [74]

Finally the European colonial takeover of the major western parts of Melanesia - New Guinea and the adjoining islands of New Caledonia, Bougainville, the Solomon Islands and Vanuatu - requires a brief mention. Tropical disease (especially malaria) took a heavy toll of British soldiers in the West Indies, Cassandra Austen's fiancée being one of 80,000 dying in the campaign against the French in the Caribbean sector of the Napoleonic Wars. [75] There were also very high casualties from disease in Bengal at about the same time. [76] The Melanesians and the related people of the Torres Straits Islands and the north coast of Australia were in a sense protected from European settlement by the scourge of malaria, against which they had some degree of immunity.[77] However the Kanaks of New Caledonia had to suffer massive European settlement because of the discovery of nickel and land seizure for cattle ranching. Cattle and mining continue to conflict with indigenous interests in Northern Australia. Gold was discovered in New Guinea and the Melanesians there had the pleasure of European company. [78] Environmentally destructive mining and massive logging of tropical rainforests continues to have a massively destructive effect in Melanesia.

13.11. China and South East Asia

No account of British imperialism would be complete without brief mention of British interactions with China and South East Asia, the emigration of Chinese throughout the British Empire and their differential treatment in the various locations. The East India Company had a major trade involving export of opium from India to China to secure the bullion required for the purchase of tea. In addition to tea, Chinese porcelain and silk were important imports for Britain. These goods had an additional major impact through encouraging the scientific and technological advances required for European manufacture of replacement products. The opium trade was lucrative and a key component of the British exploitation of Bengal. [We have already seen the involvements of Francis Austen with the East India Company including a highly profitable trip to China involving opium, bullion and the death of a Chinese]. The end of the East India Company monopoly of the China trade lead to British negotiations with the Chinese who were unhappy about opium per se and losses of bullion from the trade. This led to the Opium War of 1840-1842 that in turn resulted in the cession of Hong Kong to Britain and the opening up of a number of Chinese ports to trade.

Britain and other European powers had their way with China throughout the 19th century and the middle of the century saw the Taiping rebellion that was inspired in part by western Christian notions and fuelled by the erosion of Imperial authority by the Europeans. This conflict disrupted China in the period 1850-1864 and associated famine and distress is estimated to have taken 20-100 million lives. Key events specifically associated with European incursion include the Treaty of Tientsin that opened up further trade (1858), the occupation of Beijing by British and French troops (1860), recognition of British occupation of Burma (1886) [we remember that Charles Austen died of cholera on the Irrawaddy in 1852 during a war with the Burmese] and intervention by Britain and other powers in the Boxer rebellion (1900-1901). The flavour of these interactions can be gauged from stories and illustrations in Chums' Own Annuals for British boys (in which there seemed to be a peculiar hatred for the Chinese) and the notorious park sign in European Shanghai "No dogs or Chinese allowed". Unfortunately for the Chinese, the 20th century saw the

Japanese militarists emulating European colonial conduct on a Chinese stage with unimaginable ferocity and carnage. [79]

The discovery of gold in Australia and in California produced a large migration of Chinese to these goldfields. In about 1855 20% of the male population in the State of Victoria in Australia was Chinese but their hard work excited envy and antagonism. Anti-Chinese riots on Victorian and other Australian goldfields, "Chinaman hunts", restrictions on entry to Australia and deportations ultimately reduced the Chinese population drastically. The Chinese goldminers by their simple presence contributed to the genesis of a deep anti-Asian strand in Australian consciousness that was close to the heart of the working class and the Labour movement who felt a threat to the employment and minimal social position of European workers. This found concrete expression in the White Australia policy constraining non-European immigration into Australia. [80]

Chinese emigrated throughout the British Empire, from Malaya to the West Indies. Some 64,000 Chinese indentured labourers were brought to South Africa to work in the goldmines of the Witwatersrand. They were in effect "3-year slaves" and were subject to maltreatment including flogging. Considerable concern in South Africa and Parliamentary debate in Britain led to their repatriation in 1907. [81] One of Churchill's most celebrated comments is that related to the effective slavery of indentured Chinese labourers in South Africa: "It cannot in the opinion of His Majesty's Government be classified as slavery in the extreme acceptance of the word without some risk of terminological inexactitude." [82]

The cruelties and human toll of European colonialism in East Asia and South East Asia - principally by the British in Burma, Malaya and China, by the French in Indo-China and the Dutch in the Dutch East Indies - was dwarfed by the carnage inflicted by Japanese imperialism in the 20th century. It has been estimated that war waged by Japan in China in the 1930s and 1940s consumed as many as 35 million lives, a carnage tragically approached postwar by the approximately 30 million lives lost due to the presumably well-intentioned but tragically misplaced Great Leap Forward (1959-1961). [83] We will see in Chapter 15 how bad advice to government contributed to the death of millions of people in the Bengal Famine of 1943-1945.

13.12. Celtic Britain and the Irish famine

The English conquest and final subjugation of the Gaelic-speaking areas of Britain had the inevitable consequences of changes in land tenure and progressive ethnocide. By the 19th century Welsh, Cornish and Irish and Scottish Gaelic were still being spoken but English had made major inroads in the respective areas of Britain. However there was explicit discouragement of the retention of these cultures as seen in the prohibition of talk in Welsh in Welsh schools and the clearing of the Scottish Highlands. [84]

The Corn Laws of England artificially maintained high prices for British grain through imposition of duties on imported grain and there was considerable agitation for their repeal coming from a variety of quarters in English society for various obvious reasons (the labourers and the poor for cheaper food, the manufacturers for lower subsistence wages and the farmers for free trade and a consequent lower cost of living). The Tory landowners - the people of Jane Austen novels - were opposed to repeal and were unmoved by the misfortunes of their own people.

The ruin of the Irish potato crop by Phytopthera infestans (potato blight fungus) took away the basic staple of the impoverished Irish and led to the Irish famine or An Gorta Mor (The Great Hunger) (1845-1852). This led to the death from starvation and attendant disease of 1 million Irish and 1.5 million emigrated to Australia or America. [85] The Tory Prime Minister Peel instituted a relief Commission in November 1845 and by the beginning of 1846 the man in charge was Charles Edward Trevelyan, Assistant Secretary of the Treasury. Trevelyan was a rigidly upright, evangelical who disapproved of the Irish and, while of Cornish background, regarded Celts such as himself as having been ameliorated and rendered "practical men" by "long habits of intercourse with the Anglo-Saxons". Trevelyan permitted export of food from Ireland and approved of exorbitant prices charged by grain dealers during the famine in the name of "free trade". [86] However one should appreciate the cruel logic involved for an Irish tenant farmer: in the absence of potatoes, sale of grain for rent to avoid eviction meant starvation. Peel repealed the Corn Laws in 1846 in the face of the mounting disaster but his government paid the political price of being overthrown by Disraeli and his supporters. [87]

The relief measures based on public works and workhouses were by definition grossly insufficient. Trevelyan regarded the event as a "local distress" and took the relief provided by the Government as a powerful argument for continued association between Ireland and England: "The poorest and most ignorant Irish peasant must, I think, by this time, have become sensible of the advantage of belonging to a powerful community like that of the United Kingdom, the establishments and pecuniary resources of which are at all times ready to be employed for his benefit." [88] Trevelyan had a cold-blooded attitude to the Irish population/food discrepancy that could be summed up as "let nature take its course". In his own obscene words: "This being altogether beyond the power of man, the cure has been applied by the direct stroke of an all-wise Providence in a manner as unexpected and as unthought of as it is likely to be effectual." [89]

This devoutly Christian bureaucrat, having done his job with the Irish, went out to preside over post-Mutiny famine and distress in India in 1858-1860 and thence in 1862-1865. C.E. Trevelyan married the sister of the great historian T.B. Macaulay, his son G.O. Trevelyan (1838-1928) becoming an historian, Chief Secretary for Ireland (1882-1884) and an opponent of Irish Home Rule. C.E. Trevelyan's grandson was the historian G.M. Trevelyan (1876-1962), Regius Professor of Modern History at Cambridge University, whose History of England (1952 revision) totally ignores both the Bengal Famine of 1769-1770 and that of 1943-1945, and indeed any Indian famine whatsoever including those occurring during his grandfather's sojourn in India.[90] This omission is the more surprising because of the passion with which his great-uncle had written about the Bengal famine of 1769-1770. [91] This is all that G.M. Trevelyan had to say in this work about the most appalling event in Irish history and indeed in the history of the British Isles:

"and partly because of the potato-blight in Ireland in 1845-6 left him [Peel] no other choice than either to suspend the Corn Laws or to allow the Irish to die by tens of thousands." [92]

The same blight that, together with the English, devastated Ireland in 1845-1850, affected much of Western Europe in the middle to late 1840s and precipitated a potato famine in the Scottish Highlands. In that sorry land the English had already been busily engaged for a hundred years replacing the Highland Scots with sheep just as the settlers were to do to the aborigines in Australia. "Free trade" ruled despite the relief works that were instituted and desperate men and women faced the red-coat bayonets in Inverness trying to stop grain ships leaving port. [93]

Of interest in the context of Austenizing history, Harriet Beecher Stowe, famous for her abolitionist novel Uncle Tom's Cabin, was visiting friends in the Highlands at the time of the famine and continuing clearances. However not a skerrick of these troubles disturbs the happiness of her Highland holiday record, Sunny Memories of Foreign Lands. [94]

13.13. The genocide of the Tasmanian aborigines

The extermination of the Tasmanian aborigines is one of the best documented accounts of genocide and has a special place in the sad litany of the crimes of British global expansion. [95] We have already seen in Chapter 3 how the English sheep farming gentlemen with the help of convict labour recreated the Home Counties in the Tasmanian midlands replete with Georgian mansions, stone churches and bridges, sheep, horses, cattle and rabbits. There were about 6,000 Tasmanian aborigines at the time of settlement and they divided into a number of tribes who waged war on each other in a gentlemanly way (like the Papuans, quitting after the first death in an encounter). They were relatively small people. This would have surprised the Dutch sailors of Abel Tasman in 1642 who were alarmed on seeing footholds 6 feet apart on the trunks of Tasmanian trees - they should have determined that the footholds actually spiralled around the trunks. These hunter-gatherers came into conflict with the European settlers in the 19th century.

Government propaganda "cartoons" attempted to convince the aborigines that they would be protected from abuse by whites and vice versa. In 1830 a celebrated "Black Line" of soldiers and settlers moved across the island in an attempt to capture all of the surviving aborigines but they secured only 2. George Augustus Robinson was commissioned to persuade the aborigines to "come in". He had some success (at the cost of spreading disease that was a major cause of their demise) and the aborigines were shipped to Flinders Island off the north east coast of Tasmania in 1832. The aborigines declined on Flinders Island and eventually in 1847 the 4 dozen survivors were relocated to Oyster Cove near Hobart in southern Tasmania where they finally all succumbed to disease. Robinson, "Protector of the Aborigines", returned home and died at 78 on the hill in Bath where Catherine Morland was to walk with her friends in Northanger Abbey.

The last male "full-blood" aboriginal "King Billy" Lanney lived in Hobart and died in 1869. The last full-blood female aborigine was Truganini ("seaweed"). Her mother had been murdered by a European and her sister was captured by sealers. Truganini had been captured and raped while her man was mutilated and drowned. Taken

to New South Wales with 2 male and 2 female Tasmanians by
Robinson in 1839, she was charged with them over the death of a
European. The aboriginal men were hanged and Truganini and the
other women were returned to Tasmania. Truganini died in 1876 at the
age of 73 and was buried in the grounds of the Cascades Female
Factory, located in South Hobart by the Cascades Creek at the outlet of
a gully in the foothills of Mount Wellington. [This eventually became
a timber yard where I used to play as a 6 year-old child]. Truganini's
body was disinterred and her standing skeleton was one of the key
exhibits in the Hobart Museum in my youth, together with the
panoramas of the long-lost aborigines, stuffed Tasmanian tigers and
the dreadful "dunking boxes" for the aquatic torture of British
seamen.]

The Tasmanian aborigines did not totally disappear due to
kidnapping and rape perpetrated by bushrangers, shepherds, sealers
and others. There are several thousand Tasmanians today who are
proud of their aboriginal heritage deriving from women violated after
being kidnapped from the Mainland or in Tasmania. I remember a very
poor, dark boy and his pretty, athletic sister in my primary school in
the foothills of Mount Wellington by the Lenah Valley Creek. The
Creek springs from the wind-blasted dolorite massifs of the Mountain
and makes its way down to the River Derwent through fern-tree and
sassafrass forest glades.[96] About half a century ago the boy showed us
how to "tickle" fish in the Creek and the exquisite native orchids on
the bush track leading up to the Mountain.

13.14. 2008 Postscript

An outstanding account of the evolution of European racist ideas and
their translation to colonialism and genocide is given in Sven
Lindqvist's "Exterminate All the Brutes" [97], this title and a key subject
of the book deriving from Joseph Conrad's novel "Heart of Darkness"
about Belgian colonialism in the Congo (later made into the movie
"Apocalypse Now" based in Indo-China). [98] There have been further

recent accounts of genocides and European colonial atrocities. [99] For detailed histories of European colonialism on all continents see "Body Count". [100] Horrendous post-invasion excess deaths are associated with the ongoing Palestinian Genocide (0.3 million), Iraqi Genocide (2 million) and Afghan Genocide (3-7 million). [101] Now in 2008 biofuel-, climate change- , oil price-, meat diversion-, globalization- and speculation-driven food prices are being translated into Third World famine, biofuel famine and climate genocide threatening billions. [102]

Chapter 14

The Bengal Famine of 1943-1944

"In the standard of life they have nothing to spare. The slightest fall from the present standard of life in India means slow starvation, and the actual squeezing out of life, not only of millions but of scores of millions of people, who have come into the world at your invitation and under the shield and protection of British power."

- Winston Churchill, speech to the House of Commons (1935) [1]

"It therefore seems that, given the necessary controls, the famine could have been averted by wheat imports. By a curious coincidence the amount of the deficit in the province (about 700,000 tons) was almost exactly the amount needed to feed Calcutta (a city of 4 millions consuming on average 1 lb per head per day) for a year."

- C.B.A. Behrens (1955) [2]

"Now he [Churchill] cut down sailings to the Indian Ocean from 100 a month to 40 in order to sustain his Mediterranean campaign. This decision had disastrous consequences. The harvest had failed in Bengal. Imports of food were urgently needed and did not come. A million and a half Indians died of starvation for the sake of a white man's quarrel in North Africa."

- A.J.P. Taylor (1965) [3]

"I hate Indians. They are a beastly people with a beastly religion."

- Winston Churchill to Leo Amery, Secretary of State for India (1942) [4]

"No great portion of the world population was so effectively protected from the horrors and perils of the World War as were the peoples of

Hindustan. They were carried through the struggle on the shoulders of our small Island."

- Winston Churchill (1954) [5]

14.1. Churchill's racist and deadly ignoring of the Bengali Holocaust

Churchill's assertion quoted above is an extraordinary perversion of reality since the total war-time, man-made death toll in India was about ten times greater than the total of such military and civilian deaths in the rest of the British Empire combined. The penultimate horror in our catalogue of British Imperial crimes is the man-made Bengal Famine that had maximal effect in 1943 and 1944 and which had finally largely run its course by 1946.

A variety of estimates of the human toll have been made of which the best documented and most carefully argued is that of Greenough (1982) which calculated 3.5 to 3.8 million as the famine-induced "excess mortality" in the period 1943-1946. [6] However this estimate assumes a constant pre-famine "normal" baseline mortality frequency in the Bengal population in this period independent of major medical advances (antibiotics, cholera and smallpox vaccination and preventative education). Assumption of a small consequent decline in "normal" baseline mortality frequency ameliorated by such medical health advances can yield an excess mortality figure of about 4 million. Depending upon the magnitude of such baseline assumptions, the estimates can go over 5 million. Another estimate of the impact of the famine comes from conservative demographic considerations by Uppall (1984) based on a comparison of population growth in Bengal in 1931-1941 (11 million) and in 1941-1951 (only 3 million as compared to a conservatively calculated expected 13.5 million increase). There is a "demographic deficit" here of over 10 million people. [8] We recall from Chapter 10 that after the 1770 Bengal Famine it took nearly 20 years before the population started to increase again.

This effect was attributed to differential famine mortality with children being particularly susceptible. As we will see, children represented the most famine-susceptible group in 1943-1944 as in 1769-1770.

We will now consider the genesis and course of the Bengal Famine of 1943-44. Notwithstanding the extraordinary "holocaust denial" of Churchill quoted above, we should bear in mind that the losses of human life in the Bengal Famine represented about 90% of the total military plus civilian losses of the British Empire during the Second World War. [9]

14.2. The context of the Second World War

The Bengal Famine occurred against the backdrop of total war being waged by the Allies against the unspeakable barbarism and inhumanity of German and Japanese militarism and imperialism. We will return at the end of this chapter to a more precise moral accountancy but for the moment it is appropriate to note the desperate struggle of Britain and her allies in mid-1942 against the Axis powers in North Africa, Europe, the Pacific, China and indeed on the borders of Bengal. The Second World War began on September 1 1939 with the German invasion of Poland. Britain and France declared war against Germany on September 3. The subsequent successive major events [10] are briefly outlined below interspersed (in square brackets) with some events of particular importance to our Indian disquisition.

14.3. German victories:

Hitler-Russian Pact dividing Poland (September 28 1939); German occupation of Denmark, Norway, Belgium, the Netherlands, Luxembourg and France (April-May 1940); Winston Churchill Prime Minister (May 10 1940); German-French Armistice (June 22 1940); Germany-Italy-Japan Three-Power Pact (September 27 1940); United States Lend Lease Act enabling supplies to strategically vital countries (March 11 1941); Soviet-Japan Neutrality Treaty (April 13 1941); Germany invaded the Soviet Union (June 22 1941); the Germans swept all before them to Leningrad, Moscow and Stalingrad (1941-1942); the Atlantic Charter between the USA and Britain declaring aims for a peaceful world (August 14 1941);

[Indian provinces were given autonomy over their food supplies (December 1 1941); Churchill fails to warn F.D. Roosevelt about Pearl Harbor or John Curtin and the Australian Government about the indefensibility of Singapore.]

14.4. Japanese victories:

The Japanese attacked the US Pacific Fleet at Pearl Harbor, Hawaii and attacked the Philippines, Guam, Midway Island, Hong Kong and Malaya (December 7 1941); US declared war on Japan (December 8 1941); Germany and Italy declared war on the US (December 11 1941); the Japanese successively captured Hong Kong, the Philippines, the Dutch East Indies islands of Celebes and Amboina, Rabaul and Pacific islands including New Ireland and the Solomons (December 1941-January 1942); the Japanese took Malaya and Singapore surrendered (February 15 1942);

[of 90,000 Allied soldiers captured at Singapore about 50,000 were Indians];

the Japanese secured the Dutch East Indies and Burma (February - March 1942);

[the Indian Nationalist leaders rejected the postwar autonomy offer of Sir Stafford Cripps, demanding immediate independence (April 11 1942); they were thence imprisoned; Nationalist violence in parts of India including Bengal was suppressed vigorously with several thousand killed, thousands injured, 60,000 detained and 14,000 imprisoned];

14.5. Allied victories:

The US Navy defeated the Japanese at the Battle of the Coral Sea, thereby preserving Australia (May 7 1942) and at the Battle of Midway, thereby opening up the "island hopping" rolling back of the Japanese (June 4-7 1942); US forces under Eisenhower landed in North Africa (November 8 1942); General Wavell's forces captured Tobruk and defeated the Italians in North Africa (January-February 1942); the Germans under Rommel counter-attacked but failed to capture Tobruk, were held at El Alamein and pushed back from Tripoli by the British Army under General Bernard Montgomery (April 1942-January 1943);

[Indian forces played a major role in British victories in the Middle East, notably in Syria and North Africa in 1942-1943; misplaced use of Allied planes for massive bombing of German cities in 1942-1943 affected the Battle of the Atlantic with bad consequences for shipping availability for India];

Soviet forces relieved Leningrad and pushed back the Germans (January 1943); the Germans surrendered at Stalingrad (February 2 1943); the Casablanca Conference between Roosevelt and Churchill resolved upon unconditional surrender of the Axis forces (January 14-24 1943);

[Churchill cut Indian Ocean shipping by about half with disastrous consequences for India];

Axis forces were finally defeated in North Africa by Allied forces (May 8-12 1943); US, British and Canadian forces invaded Italy (July 10 1943); the Red Army defeated the Germans in the Battle of Kursk (July-August 1943); Teheran Conference of Stalin, Roosevelt and Churchill (November 28 1943-January 12 1944); US forces enter Rome (June 4 1944); invasion of Normandy (June 4 1944);

[British and Indian forces won the battle for Imphal and Kohima in Assam and thus opened the way for the recapture of Burma (June 1944)];

14.6. Final defeat of the Germans:

The Red Army recaptured Pskov, the last important Russian city in German hands (July 24 1944); Paris was liberated (August 29 1944); the Warsaw revolt was crushed in the absence of Soviet assistance (October 2 1944); Athens was liberated by the Allies (October 13 1944); Belgrade was liberated by the Red Army and Yugoslav forces (October 20 1944); the end of the Greek civil war (January 11 1945); the Yalta conference between Stalin, Churchill and Roosevelt (February 7-12 1945); Mussolini killed (April 28 1945); Hitler suicided as the Red Army fought for Berlin (May 1 1945); German surrender and Victory in Europe (May 8 1945);

14.7. Final defeat of the Japanese:

After a succession of US "island hopping" victories throughout 1944, US General Douglas MacArthur "returned" to Leyte in the Philippines (October 19 1944), Iwo Jima fell (March 17 1945); British and Indian forces under General William Slim, US forces under General R. Stilwell (and thence Lt. General Sultan) and Chinese forces of Chiang Kai Shek defeated the Japanese and ultimately this opened the Burma Road to China (January 18 1945). Massive bombing destroyed Japanese industrial cities (May-August 1945); Hiroshima atomic bombed (August 6 1945); Nagasaki atomic bombed (August 9 1945); Japan offers surrender (August 10); formal Japanese surrender (September 2 1945).

14.8. Genesis of the Bengal Famine

At this point the reader is referred a number of detailed accounts of the Bengal Famine. [11] The Japanese had occupied Burma at the beginning of 1942, Rangoon falling on March 10 1942. This cut off additional rice supplies to Bengal that had come from Burma. While the autumn (August-September harvest) aus rice crop was down a little compared to previous years, the winter (November-December harvest) aman crop was down by about one sixth. A cyclone and tidal wave had affected the coastal western region of Midnapore badly and excessive rain elsewhere in Bengal had led to fungal infection of rice crops, both of these circumstances contributing to the significantly lower aman crop. While there was no catastrophic decline in the amount of rice or other grain available in Bengal, the price of rice edged up slightly during 1942 and by December 1942 the wholesale price of rice in Calcutta had increased to be double that in December 1941. By mid-1943 it had doubled again to be over 4 times greater than the price in December 1941.

A variety of factors contributed to the greatly increased market price of rice but the absolute amount of rice and other grain was not a critical determinant as has been argued from a superficial analysis of the situation. As described above, the loss of rice from Burma and decreased rice production because of cyclonic damage and fungal infestation decreased rice yields but Sen (1981a) has calculated that the 1943 rice supply was actually greater than that in the non-famine year of 1941. Further, the rice plus wheat supply was similarly greater in 1943 than in 1941 as was the per capita supply of food. The explanation for the disaster advanced by Sen (1981a) relates to changes in social "exchange entitlements" and specifically entitlement to rice: while the wages for agricultural labourers remained roughly the same in the 1942-1944 period, the price of rice quadrupled. The famine was a substantially rural phenomenon and if the landless rural poor could not afford to buy rice they simply starved unless they made it to the cities and begged for relief. We should accordingly consider the reasons for the dramatic rise in the price of rice.

Heavy-handed government intervention had caused uncertainty in the rice markets. Disturbances in West Bengal had met with rough responses from the British authorities especially in the Midnapore region that was already recovering from the effects of a cyclone. In April 1942 the government introduced a policy for several months that involved removal of surplus stocks of grain from particular coastal areas of Bengal, ostensibly in order to prevent such stocks falling into the hands of the Japanese if they indeed invaded Bengal from the sea. While this Rice Removal Policy was enforced for only a few months, it would have caused considerable nervousness on the part of grain supply holders and diminished confidence in the rice market.

A further measure that had a big impact on distribution of rice in a waterway-rich country was the Boat Denial Policy that required owners of boats capable of carrying more than 10 people to register them at police stations. Again the ostensible purpose of this edict was to deny a potentially useful resource from the Japanese if they invaded. This order was issued in April 1942 and some 25,000 boats were rapidly removed from use. This had a major impact on fishing (and hence on fish for rice for fishermen, of which more later) and also impeded the movement of sorely needed rice supplies throughout the country. This edict was reversed at the end of March 1944 and the Government agreed to immediately build 5,000 new boats to replace boats destroyed by the Denial Policy and to build 5,000 further boats later. However immense harm had been done to a huge number of people. The impact of this measure can be seen from the tripling of the price of fish in Calcutta by mid-1943 in comparison with the price in December 1941.

Sen (1981a) has described the Bengal famine as a "boom famine" caused by inflationary pressures in a war economy. [12] Calcutta was a major industrial city of the Empire and there was a major war-related economic expansion, an increasing military presence and major military-related construction. In a sense a rich city with money sucked rice out of an increasingly devastated countryside. The industrial workers and soldiers were able to buy rice (assisted in some cases by direct government subsidy). The rural labourer was increasingly excluded from the rice market by price rises. The relatively poor winter rice crop of 1942, panic, speculation and decreased confidence led to hoarding by producers that amplified the effect on market availability of the initial short-fall. Heavy-handed attempts by the Government to free up rice supplies simply had the opposite effect, causing a "freezing" of the rice market in the countryside due to further withholding by suppliers. This withholding would have been stimulated by the evidence of increasing famine distress, noting that many rice producers were not that far away from disaster themselves.

The provincial autonomy granted in late 1941 in relation to grain supplies prevented such supplies coming into Bengal from other provinces and hence bringing down the price of rice. The Government permitted free trade in rice in eastern India in mid-1943 but this then led to considerable price rises in the adjoining states and the policy was reversed. It has been asserted that this "divide and rule" policy of provincial autonomy in relation to food supplies was the crucial administrative mistake in the genesis of the famine. [13] [However after reading Chapter 15 and noting the timing of the administrative decision - the week before the attack on Pearl Harbor - the reader might reasonably hypothesize that this was not necessarily an administrative "mistake" but a deliberate act of policy that had the effect of isolating and crushing a restless and populous province]. The retention of rice supplies by producers added a further complicating factor to the situation. Less rice for market meant less money available for expenditure on services, whether these were for crafts, other manufactures or for labour. This then led to further groups of people being forced into the ranks of the destitute and starving in rural Bengal.

14.9. The course and nature of the famine

It should be appreciated that the typical poor Indian agricultural worker or peasant farmer at that time was living close to the edge anyway and a substantial decline in food availability would be quickly translated into physiological distress and thence into dangerous susceptibility to disease. In late 1942 scarcity became apparent in parts of Bengal that became translated into famine involving starvation from about March 1943 onwards. From late 1943 through 1944 starvation as such began to decline but epidemics devastated the starved and weakened population. The mortality was decreased in 1945 but was still very substantial and an excess mortality was still evident in 1946.

There were big differences between the impact of the famine in Calcutta and the countryside. The Government subsidized food for various Government workers (e.g. Port, railway and City workers) and food was also subsidized for industrial workers. Soldiers were of course well fed (this having been a sine qua non of 2 centuries of British occupation). Destitutes flooded into Calcutta and sought relief by begging "rice water" from the cooking of rice by householders. Relief of a kind was offered by charitable organizations and in August 1943 relief was offered by the Government. As discussed further below, the relief was inadequate, this inadequacy being compounded by malabsorption of food. By October 1943 there were about 100,000 destitutes in Calcutta and the Bengal Destitute Persons (Repatriation and Relief) Ordinance passed in that month directed the removal of destitutes from the city to "camps". When destitutes refused to go they were removed by force. The relief offered was an inadequate gruel that was provided simultaneously at various centres in the City each day to prevent destitutes from having more than one serve. Nevertheless it could be supplemented with scraps or "rice water" and one can understand why destitutes were reluctant to leave the City.

The removal of destitutes from Calcutta to the country fits exactly with the thrust of this disquisition - that the British ruling classes wanted the world to conform to their nice social sensibilities, orderly perception being preferred to the exigencies of reality. In the noblest form of this aberration, men went over the top to their deaths on the Somme or stood to attention as the Titanic went down in the icy Atlantic. In its most ignoble manifestation the starving Calcutta destitutes were removed from the city to die out of sight, out of mind.

In pre-famine years the average Bengali consumed about 140 kg of rice per year and a bare subsistence rural Bengali about 90 kg per year. It can be calculated that the relief gruel amounted to a diet of only about 30 kg per year. The inadequacy of the diet (complicated by unsatisfactory taste and malabsorption due to disease) was evidenced by the dead and dying littering the City. Survival was greatly enhanced by getting to Calcutta or another big city and females had additional survival options involving sexual exploitation. [14]

14.10. Sexual exploitation of famine victims

Gross demographic statistics indicate that children were the most vulnerable to this famine but among children and young people there are sex differences consistent with sexual exploitation of famine victims. A nearly two-fold increase in the percent mortality increase of males as compared to females in the age groups of 10-15 and 15-20 has indicated that females had a major additional survival option of sexual submission. Similarly, a greatly decreased ratio of females to males in the 10-15 year age group among destitutes in Calcutta has been interpreted in terms of female prostitution. Such sexual exploitation had to clearly be of very substantial incidence in order to have such a big effect on these demographic statistics and this appalling aspect of the catastrophe is recorded by a number of observers. [15]

Greenough (1982) has recorded the testimonies of female famine victims forced into sexual submission or prostitution by famine circumstances. There was a major military presence in Bengal at the time since military campaigns were being conducted against the Japanese in Assam, Burma and the coastal Arakan region south of Chittagong. Service through prostitution in the Military Labour Corps represented a major avenue of survival for single females or women desperate to keep their children alive. The world is now familiar with the massive system of enforced prostitution involving "comfort women" for the Japanese Army during the Second World War. In war-time Bengal such large-scale sexual submission was enforced by the exigencies of survival in a devastating famine. Greenough (1982) reproduces an account of a mother forced into prostitution with the Military Labour Corps in order to keep herself and her child alive. After withdrawing for obvious reasons, she returns to "service" but succumbs to disease. [16] So much for the "honour of the regiment".

Bhowani Sen (1945) describes the impact on families and women:

"The whole life of the people was disrupted. Parents were forced to throw their children and babies on the roadside in the hope that somebody might pick them up and feed them. Husbands were forced to leave their wives and the whole family at the mercy of events. Women were forced to sell themselves and enter brothels. Out of the 125,000 destitutes who came to Calcutta, it is estimated that quite about 30,000 young women joined brothels to be able to continue their breathing." [17]

Jog (1944) described the disaster as follows:

"an unprecedented famine in Bengal gathered about two million people to their forefathers, drove countless more to utter destitution, sent innumerable women to brothels and sapped the very life-force of the province for generations to come." [18]

The abuse of scores of thousands of enslaved "comfort women" by Japanese soldiers in the conquered lands of the Second World War has been recently well documented. [19] The similar abuse of Bengali women on a similar scale during that conflict is a well-kept secret in the English-speaking world. The contempt with which the Bengalis were regarded by some Allied soldiers is revealed by the account of an appalled American officer who had to stop his soldiers amusing themselves (in rail transit through starving Bengal to Assam) by using paddy field peasants ("wogs" in their parlance) and their livestock as target practice. [20]

14.11. The biological and social realities of mass starvation

The mortality in this famine was initially largely due to explicit starvation. Infants with no milk from starving mothers simply starved. Adult men had greater freedom to roam more widely for food. Infants and mothers were necessarily more constrained. Accordingly children represented the major group of victims in 1943/44 as in 1769/70. The death through starvation of 1943 gave way to death through disease in 1944 onwards as cholera and malaria had a devastating impact on a starving, weakened population.

The famine had big differential effects on social groups involved in different occupations. The worst affected by the famine were fishermen and transport workers. In order of decreasing suffering the occupations have been ranked thus by Greenough (1982): fishermen, transport workers, agricultural labourers, other agricultural workers, non-agricultural labourers, raft workers, tradespeople, professional and other service providers, non-cultivating owners, part peasant-part labourers and peasant farmers and share-croppers. The latter people, being directly involved in the production of rice, were the least affected by the famine but were certainly not immune from the disaster.

The enforced removal of boats through the Boat Denial Policy meant denial of food in the form of fish and of rice in exchange for fish or transport services. The famine had a catastrophic effect on people dependent on boats for subsistence. [My wife's paternal grandfather (dada) Kasim may have originally worked as a boatman on the Hooghly River in Bengal before he went as an indentured labourer to Fiji, where he worked on boats on the Rewa River. One presumes that those of his remaining clan dependent on boating and fishing for survival would have been very vulnerable in the Bengal Famine]. With the rural economy crippled, transport workers suffered from loss of business as did other people providing services in the countryside. One class of labourers, the Namasudras, numbered 3 million in Bengal and suffered 1 million dead. [21]

The great Bengali film-maker Satyajit Ray made an immensely moving film, Distant Thunder, that describes the Bengal Famine from the perspective of an educated man, a pandit, and his wife in a rural village environment. The husband provided medical, educational and religious services to the neighbourhood in return for money or food. Like other service providers such as labourers, hair-dressers and tradesmen, he was dependent on adequate return for service and critically affected by the price of rice and indeed the actual availability of rice. As the drama unfolds we see scarcity, disease, compassion of the husband and his wife for an old man and the husband's guilt at having been fed at a rich man's house far removed from his home and his hungry wife. We see the rising collective anger and violence of the hungry towards the rich hoarder, the woman driven to the shame of prostitution, the women driven to collecting weeds and snails and their increasing vulnerability in a society that is collapsing. The wife turns to husking paddy for survival. I am moved as I recall a tragic vignette: a dying girl finally expires with a little parcel of food at her finger tips in all the lushness and beauty of a tropical field and a waif creeps out to take the unneeded food. The film ends as the old man from many kilometers away now returns with a whole band of his destitute kinsfolk. The famished wife turns to her husband who says that they must now share what they have with 10 rather than 2 people - it is actually 11 with a baby coming. The film ends, against a backdrop of the silhouettes of hobbling, starving people, with the words: "Over 5 million died of starvation and epidemics in Bengal in what has come to be known as the man-made famine of 1943." [22]

The level of violence associated with this distress was to all account surprisingly low. Calcutta was well supplied with food and destitutes died in the streets in sight of bountiful markets. Theft of grain in the fields clearly occurred and seizure of harvested food by desperate men also happened. Greenough (1982) and Ghosh (1944) in particular have provided graphic records of the impact of the famine on individuals. The individual tragedies are innumerable: Hindu pandits forced to accept conditions inconsistent with the purity dictates of their Brahminic station; women and girls forced into prostitution; desperate men murder the rich man who shoots at them; a dying mother tells of her return to prostitution with the Military Labour Corps in a vain attempt to save her child; mothers murder their children to stop their suffering; parents give their children away; agonizing deaths, alone and unsupported by the roadsides, in the streets or in the lush fields of the Bengal countryside. The mass of dead and dying was a feast for vultures and dogs in 1943/44 as in 1769/70. Awful accounts tell of people too weak to resist being eaten alive. Bodies were left to rot by roadsides and in fields, there often not being enough able-bodied men to bury or otherwise sensibly dispose of the dead. Reporters graphically describe the sight of masses of dead bodies and the stench of rotting corpses. [23]

14.12. British administrators and the disaster

An extraordinary feature of the Bengal Famine was that a famine was not actually declared under the terms of the Famine Codes, apparently on the basis that invoking the famine codes would have meant being committed to the expenditure involved in doing something about it. Thus Sir T. Rutherford wrote to Viceroy Linlithgow explaining that he had not declared a famine to avoid the obligations set down in the regulations. [24] Amartya Sen, a leading scholar in the analysis of famines in general and of famines in Bengal in particular, concludes that this omission may well have been largely responsible for the immense loss of life in this famine. [25]

The net importation of grain into India in the 6 financial years up to and including the beginning of the famine is instructive (millions of tons in parentheses): 37/38 (+ 0.624), 38/39 (+ 1.044), 39/40 (+ 2.221), 40/41 (+ 0.993), 41/42 (+ 0.431) and 42/43 (- 0.361). A similar picture is seen for net imports of rice into India (millions of tons in parentheses): 37/38 (+ 1.165), 38/39 (+ 1.235), 39/40 (+ 2.139), 40/41 (+ 1.097), 41/42 (+ 0.723) and 42/43 (- 0.259). Thus in the financial year that saw the commencement of the worst famine in India in 2 centuries the British authorities oversaw a massive net export of grains and rice from an increasingly impoverished country. This situation no doubt contributed to the price of grain and rice in Bengal during the famine and the ability of other parts of India to make a contribution when the provincial autonomy in this respect was over-ridden in a restricted region for a limited time during the emergency.

It is important to consider the conditions underlying this famine. Before the outbreak of the Second World War, India (population about 400 million) could largely feed herself with a short-fall of about 1 million tons of grain (representing only about 2% of the total requirement) that was met by an excess of imports over grain exports. This level of existence involved chronic undernourishment of a large proportion of the population, which accordingly did not have the literal or metaphorical fat to surmount a major famine of the Bengal famine kind without major loss. The above figures demonstrate the sheer callousness of the administering authorities in permitting net imports to steadily decline from the minimal requirement to a substantial net export by mid-War. [26]

It is of interest to note that in major past famines in Bengal the same obscenity occurred. In the 1770 famine that killed 10 million people a ban was temporarily placed on exports of grain from Bengal but with the typical laissez-faire of the times the ban was ignored and the ban was indeed rescinded in mid-November of that year. It was asserted that "as much grain was exported from lower parts of Bengal as would have fed the number who perished for a whole year." In the famine of 1866 that killed over a million and devastated Orissa (750,000 dead), exports of rice continued during the famine period at only a modestly decreased level (30% down on the pre-famine 1864/65 level). In the famine of 1873-74, the Lieutenant Governor of Bengal, Sir George Campbell (a decent and good man), pleaded unsuccessfully for a cessation of exports which continued at near-maximal levels. A similar near-maximal export of rice from India occurred during the appalling famine decade from 1892 to 1901 that saw some of the worst general famine conditions in India in general. [27]

The opinion of the British Raj Foodgrains Policy Committee in 1943 is instructive in relation to the loss of imports - it considered that, the absolute deficit aside, it "seriously affects the sense of security generally". As we have seen it was the loss of that sense of security that lead to hoarding, consequent catastrophic price rises in Bengal and hence to the disaster in rural Bengal. [28]

That the disaster would be of a huge magnitude was eventually apparent to Viceroy Linlithgow who felt able to predict losses of the order of a million people in mid-1943. Nevertheless Linlithgow and the Governor of Bengal, Sir John Herbert, felt unable to respond effectively to the emergency. They were quite happy, however, to interfere with the provincial government of Bengal. Sir John Herbert was replaced by a stand-in Governor of Bengal, Sir T. Rutherford, who in October 1943 was still uncertain about the extent of shortages but offered a short-fall figure of 655,000 tons, a figure to be revised upwards by Linlithgow to 1 million tons. It was Sir T. Rutherford who wrote to the Viceroy explaining that a famine had not been declared to avoid the relief obligations set down by the Famine Codes. One may be presuming too much to assume that the unfolding disaster and the incompetence of the administration led to the replacement of Linlithgow in October 1943 by General Wavell of North Africa fame. The Australian R.G. Casey came from the same theatre in January to become Governor of Bengal. The view of Bhattacharya (1967) on the famine and the changeover is instructive:

[there was an] increase in the British India Army from 175,000 to more than 2 million ... But the war effort involving mounting expenditure and the pursuit of a policy of the scorched earth in Bengal culminated in the outbreak of a severe famine there in 1943 which the administration of Linlithgow failed to tackle and he was soon relieved by his successor, Lord Wavell, who brought his military experience and push to bear on the situation." [29]

Unlike his predecessor, Wavell immediately visited Bengal and took the immediate step to recovery of ensuring that Calcutta would be supplied by the rest of India and not by starving rural Bengal. The army was deployed for famine relief. In Bengal under Casey there was a major program of cholera innoculations and smallpox vaccination that involved millions of people. The Boat Denial Policy was reversed at the end of March 1944 enabling surviving fishermen and boatmen to resume their occupations. Nevertheless the juggernaut of starvation, social collapse and disease had been set in motion and the death toll would only slightly decline in 1944. There would still be a substantial excess mortality in 1945 and 1946, even if one assumes that the medical and preventative measures taken had no effect on the underlying "normal" pre-famine mortality rate. [30]

14.13. Wavell

Wavell was a decent, concerned and vigorous man and he pleaded continually (but unsuccessfully) with Churchill for 1 million tons of grain for 1944 to ensure that the price of food declined and to ward against further disasters in Bengal and elsewhere in India. Churchill was unmoved, his hatred for India and Indians combining with cold-blooded strategic considerations to hold him to a course that from early 1942 onwards had deprived India of minimal food requisites in the name of maximizing supplies to the North African campaign and thence for the Italian theatre and Normandy. Nevertheless Wavell's persistence paid off and he was able to squeeze commitments for 450,000 tons of grain out of the British Government in his first year in office, the Chiefs of Staff (if not Churchill) recognizing the importance of India as a base for military operations. Churchill began to regret Wavell's appointment before he even left England for India, Wavell having merely expressed some concern over food for India and the desirability of at least talking to the Congress leaders. While our concern here is with Wavell in relation to the Bengal famine, it is also important to note that he was involved in the time-tabling of Indian Independence and the decision for Partition (which he did not desire) was actually taken by the Indian leadership before he left India for England.

Wavell's diaries [31] give a fascinating insight into exchanges of the high and mighty in this awful time. He accepted the position of Viceroy of India in June 1943. His entries relating to India's British rulers before he had left England are very revealing. Wavell differed from Churchill in style and morality over India. Wavell was a conservative empire man like Churchill but was concerned to have sensible dialogue with the Indian politicians in order to assist the war effort and was also most concerned about the food problems. Churchill had hatred and contempt for India and Indians.

On July 3 1943 Wavell attended a Cabinet meeting on Palestine occasioned by increasing Arab-Jewish tension. Churchill was a confirmed Zionist. Wavell, struck by the complete absence of support for the Arab point of view, defended their rights pledged under the Balfour Agreement and argued that the Jews were likely to win any conflict and that the Arabs needed protection. Churchill countered that the Arabs had done nothing to help in the war. Wavell rejoined that Ibn Saud was friendly, that his country could have harmed Britain and that "the Jews, as a race, had not helped us" - an extraordinary assertion that leaves one nonplussed and in the circumstances raises the suspicion that Wavell might have felt to some extent about Jews as Churchill felt about Indians. We will return to the Jewish-Arab-Muslim-Indian connection in Chapter 15 of this book.

On July 17 1943 at a Cabinet meeting Churchill complained bitterly about the fact that Britain owed India 800 million pounds. Wavell asserts "He hates India and everything to do with it" and records that Secretary of State for India Amery pushed him a note saying that Churchill "knows as much of the Indian problem as George III did of the American colonists". Wavell records that "Winston drew harrowing picture of British workmen in rags struggling to pay rich mill-owners, and wanted to charge India the equivalent of our debt to her for saving her from Japanese invasion." Wavell's only contribution was to point out India's defence of Britain in the Middle East theatre (where Indian troops had figured prominently in the action).

On August 1 1943 Wavell has a walk and conversation with Amery and they discuss the failure of the British to mix with the Indians: "Amery thought that intermarriage might have been no bad thing, and that the ban we put on the Indian Princes marrying English women was wrong." Wavell thought that Hindu and Moslem customs rather than colour had been involved.

On September 14 1943 Wavell records the preparation of a paper for a Cabinet Sub-Committee in which they propose discussions to bring Indian leaders of the Centre into a government willing to support the war effort. On September 24 Wavell dines with the King and the Queen. "H.M. again referred to undue length of Viceroy's telegrams and told me to make them shorter." At a Cabinet meeting on food for India Churchill spoke scathingly of Indian inefficiency, the supply of 150,000 tons of grain from Iraq and the need for reserves in the Middle East for Greece and the Balkans. Wavell disapproves in his diary of the preference for Greeks and liberated countries as opposed to Indians. He commented on the major Indian war effort at the meeting.

On September 29 1943 the India Paper was restructured to a much vaguer proposition. On September 30 1943 Wavell discusses India with William Phillips (American representative in India 1942-1943) who said that the "P.M. had a blind spot about India, was most unreasonable and "riding for a fall" over it". Mountbatten supported Wavell's position. On October 6 there was a Government dinner for Wavell. Churchill was so annoyed with the India Paper that he almost refused to come. He told Wavell he could not possibly accept it but nevertheless praised Wavell in his speech and eulogised Britain's record in India. At the Cabinet meeting on October 7 the "bogey" of Gandhi was raised, Eden spoke as if Wavell was proposing to "enthrone Gandhi" and Churchill had a tirade about Congress and the potential for the politicizing of the Indian Army.

On October 15 1943 in Cairo on his way out to India, Wavell inspected Indian troops and spoke to Casey about food. Casey said Australia had had a bad wheat harvest, Canada could just supply U.S. and British deficiencies and that the Argentinians had burnt their surplus of 2 million tons as fuel on the railways in the absence of coal, of which there was a world shortage.

On March 24 1944 Wavell records a British Government (H.M.G.) offer of 250,000 tons of wheat for 1944 and a further 150,000 tons of wheat if India will export 150,000 tons of rice. The Secretary of State for India suggested that he announce the import of 400,000 tons of wheat and conceal the export of 150,000 tons of rice. Wavell writes in his journal: "I shall certainly do nothing so dishonest or stupid", notes the refusal of H.M.G. to approach the Americans for shipping and refers to his position that 1 million tons is the minimum needed.

On April 14/15 1944 Wavell is visited by Louis Mountbatten (M.B.), Commander in Chief for South East Asia, who is optimistic about clearing the Japanese out of Assam. An explosion and fire in the Bombay docks had destroyed shipping and 50,000 tons of food. He comments on the tough time that M.B. is having with the "Japs, the P.M. and the Americans" and that he "has lost that first fine, careless confidence that caused my predecessor to call him the Boy Champion." M.B. nevertheless tells a very funny story about the visit of the ultra-orthodox Maharajah of Benares to the Maharaja of Rampur. "Benares" believes that a cow should be the first object he sees each day but the guest rooms are on an upper floor. "Rampu" gets a crane from a local sugar factory and rigs up a platform to ensure that "a rather astonished cow was elevated every morning to His Highness' bedroom window."

On June 4 1944 Wavell refers to Roosevelt refusing a request by the P.M. for shipping. On June 24 1944 he refers to a wire to the S. of S. asking for a decision on food imports and comments on a conversation with George Giffard about American denigration of British efforts and how they mutually concluded that "we were a very great nation, greater than the Americans." On June 26 1944 Wavell is very chuffed to have got a promise from H.M.G. to ship a further 200,000 tons in the next 3 months, with more to be considered: "I have extracted 450,000 tons since the War Cabinet regretted that nothing could be done." Gandhi had been very ill and on July 5 1944 Wavell writes: "Winston sent me a peevish telegram to ask why Gandhi hadn't died yet. He has never answered my telegram about food."

On July 22 1944 Wavell is told about a secret conference in Cairo in May in which everyone, civil and military, had opposed the H.M.G. decision for Partition of Palestine. Wavell is peeved because India has 90 million Moslems with strong feelings about Palestine and H.M.G. has not informed him. On August 15 1944 Wavell alludes to his differences with Churchill and Cabinet that he had set out in a very frank letter to the Secretary of State dealing with his desire for a courteous reply to a letter from Gandhi, application of "Section 93" in Bengal (resumption of British administration) and his requests for food imports. In the event Cabinet ignores his plea and forces him to send a "rude" and "arrogant" reply to Gandhi. On August 22 Wavell says "Cabinet has destroyed at one blow my reputation for fairness and good temper in my correspondence with Gandhi" and speculates that it was indeed probably the P.M.'s intention to weaken his usefulness in dealing with the Congress.

On August 31 1944 Wavell consults with Casey about forgoing "Section 93" British interference with the Bengal Provincial Government and Congress worries about his interference - a cartoon in the Hindustan Times shows Wavell as an octopus with a governor's head at the end of each tentacle. However Congress paranoia about Wavell is more than matched by Churchill's paranoia about Congress. On September 7 1944 M.B. comes up to Simla and indicates that the "P.M. was as intractable as ever about India" and seemed to regard food for India as "appeasement" of Congress. Only the strategic sense of the Chiefs of Staff had ensured food for India as a stable operational base. Wavell suspected that there was more shipping available than claimed and comments on medical scarcities and its relief. An extraordinary insight into Churchill is given: "P.M. was quite furious about Gandhi's release and subsequent activities, and in fact quite impossible about India. Leo Amery [Secretary of State for India], who does stand up to him, had accused the P.M. of a "Hitler like attitude" to India, and had got a first class rocket."

In a communication to the P.M. summarizing his term (October 25 1944) Wavell frankly refers to the neglect of India by H.M.G. He agrees with the P.M. that encouragement of Indian independence 25 years before was "misplaced liberal sentimentality" that has nevertheless had permanent political consequences that cannot be ignored. Wavell is concerned with the neglect of India at a meeting of Dominion Premiers, the presence of only 40 members at the big India debate in the Commons and how, despite the lessons of the Bengal Famine, he has had to fight to secure food imports to prevent food prices soaring again as they had in 1943. Wavell was finally replaced as Viceroy of India by Lord Mountbatten in 1947. From his journal entries we can see his determination to prevent a repetition of the Bengal Famine in the face of hostility from Churchill. Wavell died in 1950 and was buried in the same city as Jane Austen - not in Winchester Cathedral where she lies, but in the chantry cloister of Winchester College, which he had attended as a boy.

14.14. The record of history

The Bengal Famine of 1943-1944, for all of its absence from general public perception, is a well-documented event and without being exhaustive I have briefly catalogued below some of the historical sources:

1. Contemporary newspapers and public records: The famine was described by the Bengali and Indian press at the time and indeed by the British press, notably by the Manchester Guardian and the Calcutta Statesman. [32] The normal bureaucratic processes of the Raj and the British Empire in general ensured a thorough record of all kinds of germane matters. The biographies, autobiographies, correspondence or other memoirs of relevant great men (such as Churchill, Mountbatten, Amery and Wavell) [33] or of lesser, albeit distinguished, men (such as Casey) [34] inevitably had to turn to one of the most extraordinary events of that time. The matter was debated in the House of Commons, albeit to a miniscule audience. [35] In the end there was an official Famine Commission that analyzed the event and enormously under-estimated the carnage. [36]

2. Diaries and memoirs: People connected with the famine in various capacities recorded their impressions. Viceroy Wavell's published diaries record his attempts to secure additional supplies of grain for India and Bengal in particular. [37] R.G. Casey (later Lord Casey) has recorded his perception of the famine, dismissing the assertion that it was "man-made" (it was a simple shortage of food in his opinion) and grossly under-estimating the carnage (in his opinion only 1 million may have died). [38] Jog (1944) records the outrage of Senator James M. Mead of New York who visited India in 1943. In the words of Jog:

"[Mead] was shocked that at the time when thousands of shivering people lay on the sidewalks of Calcutta, the authorities were still devoting precious space in freight cars to race horses en route for the

Calcutta Gold Cup! India made him angrier than anything else he saw during his 45,000-mile trip." [39]

The Calcutta Gold Cup in 1943 and the British war-time dilemma of resources for war or starving millions, respectively, recall the obscenity of the Great Durbar at Delhi in 1900 at a time of immense famine [40] and Viceroy Lord Curzon's resolution then that famine relief would not be permitted to cut into military expenditure. [41]

3. Specific contemporary histories: A major analysis of the famine involving the destitutes of Calcutta was conducted and prepared for publication by Das in 1944 and indeed the bulk of this material was submitted to the Famine Inquiry Commission in 1944. This extraordinary work could not be published until 1949. [41] Ghosh published an account of famines in Bengal (1770-1943) in 1944. [42] The succinct but potent book by Jog (1944), Churchill's Blind-spot:India, had to deal in part with the dreadful famine and British unresponsiveness. Jog was among the first to apply the term "holocaust" to an event of man-made mass death in World War 2 in applying this descriptive to the Bengal Famine. [43] The Report of the Famine Commission (1946) [44] and the account by Bhowani Sen (1945) [45] are further key documents. Other contemporary accounts and novels relate to this event, and the reader is referred to Villager (1945) and to Das (1949) for photographs of famine victims that recall images of the inmates of Nazi death camps. [46]

4. Further specific accounts of the Bengal Famine: Accounts of the Bengal Famine are included in a variety of works in addition to those of Ghosh (1944) and Das (1949) and the list of the most comprehensive treatises includes Bhatia (1991), Drèze & Sen (1989), Sen (1981a,b), Greenough (1982), Uppal (1984) and Villager (1945). [47] However a variety of other works mention or otherwise deal, albeit briefly, with the Bengal Famine from a number of different specific perspectives. [48]

5. Histories of India: It is difficult to imagine a history of India ignoring what was one of the most awful events in the history of India and indeed of mankind. Indeed a wide range of Indian histories dealing with modern times refer to the Bengal Famine. [49] However inevitably we find the malignant effects of the historiographical malaise anglaise and a number of histories dealing with India of this period this period somehow failed to notice this horrendous event, Britain's Auschwitz. [50]

6. Related histories: A number of historical accounts dealing with related events such as the war in Burma and elsewhere in South East Asia and the major players involved inevitably have to refer at least in passing to the famine. [51] Thus an account of the life of Subhas Chandra Bose, the leader of the Axis collaborationist Indian National Army, refers to his offer of 100,000 tons of rice for the Bengalis (an offer which was ignored by the British). [It is noteworthy that Bose's German "handler" participated in the plot against Hitler and a film of his strangulation by piano wire was made for the pleasure of the Fuehrer.] [52] Nevertheless it is disturbing to find related histories and other histories that for whatever reason overlook the sustained suffering and death of millions in the region. [53] [Again, the reader is cautioned that "experimental error" by the author may have inadvertently resulted in missing brief or non-indexed references to the disaster. Further, such absences in themselves may merely reflect the general value "First World" society as a whole places upon such "Third World" victims. As we will see in Chapter 17, a "moral responsiveness test" applied recently to the media and the intellectual and political leadership of Australia in relation to the Bengal Famine yielded minimal response.]

7. Histories of Britain and the British Empire: The Americans are an earnestly moralistic lot (thank goodness) and remain all too conscious of the nuclear destruction of Hiroshima and Nagasaki (even if many feel that these nuclear cataclysms were necessary evils). It is almost inconceivable that a history of the American people up to the post-war era would ignore these events. What is the perception in the

English-speaking world of the man-made Bengal Famine - an event that swept away an incomprehensible 25 times as many people? I dare say that British historiography can account an almost zero perception of these events as one of its greatest Austenizing triumphs. A large number of British histories - including classics of G.M. Trevelyan (1952) and H.G.Wells (1951) - completely ignore the Bengal Famine and even any mention of famine in Bengal at all. [54]

G.M. Trevelyan, like his inhumane grandfather Charles Trevelyan of Irish famine and Indian notoriety, is simply beyond the comprehension of ethical primitives such as myself. G.M. Trevelyan is the British Austenizer par excellence in relation to the glories of the 18th century, the Irish famine and 2 centuries of famine in India. His History of England (1952) virtually ignores the actuality of the Irish Famine and totally ignores any famine in India at all, whether in 1770, the 19th century or in 1943. [55] Humphrey Trevelyan, great-nephew of C.E. Trevelyan, served in India and in his account of his sojourn almost completely fails to notice the Bengal Famine of 1943. This holocaust simply appears in his account of his subsequent sojourn in Washington as a joke:

"As the end of the war came near, visitors from India flooded in ... [including] a mission to obtain aid for Bengal famine relief, led inappropriately by a globular politician who had clearly never missed a meal in his life." [56]

Humphrey Trevelyan went on to become the British Ambassador to Egypt and this somewhat unobservant fellow who had overlooked the demise of about 4 million Bengalis was amazed when he saw British warplanes overflying Cairo during the collusive Suez invasion of 1956.

Of H.G. Wells we have some evidence of human warmth in his enthusiastic sexual debauchery and one can only speculate about possibly not unconnected racial or psychosexual misperceptions on the part of the great man. Certainly, in retrospect, H.G. Wells had a certain ideological unevennness that could accommodate socialism and social justice on the one hand and ambivalence towards the working class on the other. [57] In his Outline of History (heavily biased towards an Anglocentric picture of the world), H.G. Wells ignores both the 1770 and 1943 Bengal Famines and yet devotes 3 dozen of 100 dozen pages of this work to a prejudiced diatribe against Islam, Islamic culture and the Prophet Mohammed. (It should be noted that while this was a Hindu plus Muslim Holocaust, most of the victims were Muslims and it can indeed be described as a "Muslim Holocaust"). Perhaps he had a problem with "the East", and since he also ignores the horrendous Ukrainian Famine of 1928-1933 one might further suppose that he also subscribed to the view that "Asia begins east of Vienna". However while ignoring the Bengal Famines and the Ukrainian Famine, H.G. Wells does wax strong about the ghastly post-revolutionary famine in Russia at the beginning of the twenties. [58]

One would like to credit those historians of Britain and the British Empire who grace their pages with a mention of "famine in Bengal" in at least a few words. However I have had great trouble discovering such historians. One hopes that a list of such Oskar Schindlers of British History could be generated by more dogged researchers. Apart from the 1961 edition of the generalist Encyclopaedia Britannica (but not the 1977 and 1979 editions) and Taylor (1965), English History 1914-1945 (that mentions the Bengal famine in the quotation given at the beginning of this chapter), I have found no works dealing specifically and comprehensively with the general history of Britain and the British Empire that mention the Bengal Famine of 1943-1944. [59] This apparent total absence of such reportage of such a major event in British history - as perceived from analysis of one of the best academic libraries "in the Southern Hemisphere" (as we say in the Antipodes) - is surely one of the most extraordinary examples of Austenizing that can be offered in this book.

British historiography stands condemned for the effective deletion from British history of one of the most immense disasters in

the British realm and indeed in human history. One can only speculate
on the socio-economic basis of this extraordinary aberration. While
Holocaust Denial is a criminal offence in Germany, [60] it is clear that
postwar Japan has yet to come to grips with the ghastly realities of its
20th century military imperialist phase. [61] As an Anglo-Celtic,
Australian anglophile I feel ashamed that our culture has chosen a path
of deliberately blotting out the reality of war-time Bengal. We have
chosen to "walk by on the other side", a position for a sophisticated
and liberal culture that bodes ill for the coming world of the 21st
century.

8. General histories of the World: One can glibly rationalize the
British coyness in relation to their dark past as stemming from national
pride and a perfectly natural desire to not wash dirty linen in public or
reveal such an enormous collection of literal skeletons in the cupboard.
In support of this we see that the Bengal Famine surfaces in general
histories. Nevertheless of a sample of 30 more general histories dealing
with Twentieth Century history, [62] only 9 mention the Bengal Famine,
namely Cook (1991), Embree (1988), Encyclopaedia Britannica
(1961), Grun (1975), Howat & Taylor (1973), Rosenberger & Tobin
(1945) [Keesing's Contemporary Archives (1943-1945)], Spear
(1968), Taylor (1965) and Trager (1979).

9. Histories of World War 2 and of Winston Churchill: The Bengal
Famine was a major event of World War 2 by any reasonable standard
and may well have consumed as many people as died in combat in that
conflict. It is reasonable to expect that it might merit some mention in
such histories including those specifically dealing with the life of
Winston Churchill in view of his intimate connection with the genesis
and duration of the Bengal Famine as clearly recorded by Wavell (and
others). Unfortunately we look largely in vain and there is an all too
long list of such histories of World War 2 or of Winston Churchill that
are silent on the death of millions of Bengalis. Of a selection of 38
histories dealing relatively specifically with World War II, only 9 even
briefly mention this major event, namely Behrens (1955), Calvocoressi

et al. (1972), Encyclopaedia Britannica (1961), Dear & Foot (1995), Kitchen (1990), Renouvin (1969), Romanus & Sunderland (1956), Taylor (1965) and Weinberg (1994). However, while not mentioning the Bengal Famine, Macmillan (1967) notes how he was mistakenly congratulated by Giraud in June 1943 for appointment as Viceroy of India and the importance of the Muslim world (as perceived by the actual appointee, Wavell): "No doubt the experience which I had been able to gain on "la question mussulmane" in North Africa during the last five months had served me well. I disclaimed this high honour was to come to me." It should be noted that nearly all of these works mention the Jewish Holocaust. [63]

Of a selection of 25 historical works specifically dealing with Winston Churchill [64] in only 2 is mention made of the Bengal Famine, namely in Jog (1944) and in the analysis of S. Gopal in the collection of essays edited by Blake and Louis (1994) (both of these works being hostile towards Churchill and written by Indians).

The most extraordinary example is Churchill (1954), the 6 volume History of the Second World War. This was published over the period 1948-1954, noting that Churchill was awarded the Nobel Prize for Literature in 1953. Despite the fact that Churchill was intimately involved in life and death decisions that ultimately meant death for millions of Bengalis, there is total silence on the matter. Nevertheless there is an intriguing, inexplicit letter from the Viceroy of India Linlithgow in Churchill's treatise that may be germane in the sense that it probably is referring to 1942 anti-British violence and we will consider this in Chapter 15. The following quotations from Churchill (1954) are potent "from the horse's mouth" assertions that impinge on the matter. However while the Bengal Famine is not revealed, these passages are very revealing about Churchill and his attitude towards his Indian victims:

"The President ... cautioned Stalin against bringing up the problem of India with Churchill and Stalin agreed that this was undoubtedly a sore subject. Roosevelt said that reform in India should begin from the bottom, and Stalin replied that reform from the bottom would mean revolution." (Volume V, p306).

"I feel that you cannot have looked into the extraordinary consequences of our coming out of this war owing India a bigger debt, after having defended her, than we owed the United States at the end of the last war. Your note does not seem at all to take into consideration these frightful consequences." (Volume V, p625).

"I was also glad to record that although the British Empire had now entered the sixth year of the war it was still keeping its position, with a total population, including the Dominions and Colonies, of only seventy million white people. Our effort in Europe, measured by divisions in the field, was about equal to that of the United States. This was as it should be, and I was proud that we could claim equal partnership with our great ally." (Volume VI, pp132-133). [65]

Churchill's silence on the Famine even during war-time provoked this comment from Jog (1944):

"Though he has scrupulously avoided referring to it, Churchill will nevertheless have to admit that the situation went slightly out of hand in the latter half of 1943, when an unprecedented famine in Bengal gathered about two million people to their forefathers, drove countless more to utter destitution, sent innumerable women to brothels and sapped the very life-force of the province for generations to come. The famine of 1943 has thrown into shade even its terrible predecessor of 1770, about which Macaulay [read by Churchill] wrote in such flesh-creeping phrases in his essay on Robert Clive. Churchill must surely be remembering the latter, even if he has had no time to attend to the former due to his numerous preoccupations." [66]

Of the few general histories of World War 2 that do refer to famine in India or more specifically to the Bengal famine, of particular interest to our account of the Bengal famine is a very detailed work by

C.A Behrens, Merchant Shipping and the Demands of War (1955) that
is referred to by Taylor (1965) in his English History 1914-1945
quoted above. Drastic reductions in the amount of shipping in the
Indian Ocean in 1943 enabled supply of Britain and forces in North
Africa at the expense of famine relief for India. In her opinion the
North African priority condemned any deficit area of India to
starvation. [67]

In Chapter 15 of this book we will explore the connections
between Bengal and the Holocaust in Europe, the role of Churchill in
the Bengal Famine and his secretiveness not only about Bengal but in
relation to other major events of World War 2 with which he was
intimately involved namely the attack on Pearl Harbour and the fall of
Singapore. This will lead us to consider the importance of correct
scientific advice to government and the major decisions facing world
governments in relation to population growth and global warming.

14.15. An Australian view of a Holocaust

This could be considered a form of "colonial cringe", but many
Australians would feel that they lack the sangfroid and ruthlessness of
those in the "metropolitan" Old World. Further, Australians regard
their country as the land of the "fair go" and that human decency and
responsiveness are more evident in the mores of a less stratified and
less class-ridden society such as that found in Australia. Be that as it
may, the response of an on-the-spot Australian diplomat to the Bengal
Famine is of interest in relation to our unquenched (if probably
seriously misplaced) hope for future social responsiveness to such
matters. The reader is referred to detailed accounts of Richard Casey's
experiences in war-time Bengal as a Governor of the famine-wracked
province [68], the most recent of these being the excellent biography of
Casey's wife Maie by Langmore (1997). However this work deals with
the indisputable Bengal Famine in 2 disputable sentences - 40 words
for 4 million victims - but has a running innuendo throughout the work
about the arguable and unknowable, namely the alleged homosexual

passion of Maie Casey and its possible physical consummation. [Reviews indicating the differential treatment given to horrendous reality as compared to surmised and unknowable minutiae were ignored by Anglo media - a testament to the continuing unresponsiveness of our dominant Anglo culture].

After stints in Washington and the Middle East, Richard Casey (later Lord Casey) was offered the job of Governor of Bengal by Churchill in November 1943. Casey was sworn in on January 22, 1944. Casey records his indifferent welcome and his initial impressions:

"I could not have had a worse Press before I arrived. They protested to high heaven against an Australian being sent to govern them, "Have we become a colony of Australia?" - "How are we to endure the humiliation of a Governor from a country that prohibits Indians from entering it?" [69]

"The province was grossly over-populated, with an out-of-date system of administration and a microscopically small and over-tired staff. It had just been through a very bad famine, and there was no reserve of food. The health of the people was very bad." [70]

Casey was justifiably proud of the massive preventative medical programs in Bengal in 1944-1945:

"In the course of 1944 and 1945 over 54,000,000 individuals were vaccinated against smallpox, and 27,000,000 inoculated against cholera, a total of over 81,000,000 treatments against one or other of these diseases out of a total population of 65,000,000. I doubt whether an effort in preventative medicine on this scale had ever been made before in any country." [71]

Nevertheless Casey had a self-recorded attitude to the Bengal Famine that minimizes the holocaust. Thus he declares:

"When I arrived in Bengal [January 1944] the famine of 1943 was only just over, and the November 1943 rice crop had been quite good, so that the outlook for 1944 was reasonably good, although, of course, there were no reserves of rice." [72]

In reality the death rate in 1944 was much the same as in 1943, albeit for different reasons (starvation-induced disease susceptibility as opposed to explicit starvation). [73] Casey's estimate of a death toll of "probably 1,000,000 over and above the normal mortality - about a 50% increase in the normal death-rate" [74] is at the lower end of estimates and about 14% of the likely actuality. [75]

Casey's final verdict is incorrect in substance and completely absolves the rulers for the devastation of the ruled:

"Many people have sought to make political capital out of the Bengal famine of 1943. It was said that the famine was man-made. This is untrue. Even had there been no hoarding and black-marketing, there would have been a grievous famine in 1943 simply because there was not nearly enough rice to go round. Hoarding and black-marketing merely intensified the shortage." [76]

Casey's written accounts of his Indian experiences minimize the Bengal Famine but he was clearly sufficiently moved by his experiences in Bengal to write bluntly to Wavell in 1945, expressing a judgement he was to later deliberately omit from his account of the exchange:

"the Empire has cause for shame in the fact that, in Bengal at least, after a century and a half of British rule, we can point to no achievement worth the name in any direction." [77]

The minimizing, softening, blunting and erasing - this Austenizing - of historical reality by even well-intentioned "decent chaps" such as Richard (later Lord) Casey has made the Bengal Famine the Forgotten Holocaust of the Twentieth Century. The world remains well aware of the Japanese use of prisoner of war and other slave labour on the Burma-Siam railway in the same region through the testament of survivors [78], films such as The Bridge on the River Kwai [79] and the commitment of the survivors and their compatriots to the memory of the fallen. The wartime Bengal Famine (and indeed the previous similar horrors of British-occupied Bengal) have disappeared from public perception and from our history books. Those members of the global village likely to have glimpsed the realities of wartime Bengal would be mostly specialist Indian and economic historians, those interested in the sociology and economics of famine, people who have read novels based on the disaster such as Amritlal Nagar's Hunger: A Novel [80] and those "serious film" lovers familiar with Satyajit Ray's moving film Distant Thunder. [81]

14.16. Never again

It is unacceptable that an event of such a magnitude as the war-time Bengal Famine could occur over such a prolonged period, meet with resolute unresponsiveness and then be essentially blotted out of public perception for ever. If we compare the Holocaust of the Jews of Europe with the "Forgotten Holocaust" of Bengal - events that occurred at about the same time - we see that both events occurred over a period of several years and the world resolutely failed to respond to either tragedy. However in the aftermath of the Jewish Holocaust there has been sustained public documentation and public trials of a small number of those responsible. A large number of war criminals involved in the Holocaust escaped justice through a well-organized process of escape from Europe and assisted emigration to the Americas and Australia involving elements of American intelligence. Aarons and Loftus (1997) have documented this outrageous process as well as the related smuggling of Nazi money and close American and British corporate links with Nazi Germany. [82] Nevertheless the trials and punishment of a few have had an educative effect in relation to social moral responsiveness. The world has got the message from the survivors and those who will never forget: "Never again." The

Forgotten Holocaust of Bengal was substantively ignored while it was happening, has been effectively erased from public perception and there has been no perceived accountability.

Arising out of the extraordinary lack of perception of the war-time Bengal Famine and of profound concern is the widespread and morally detached expectation that catastrophic famine will be the lot of the Bengalis and other people of the Third World in the coming century. How can we sit back and regard our fellow human beings in this way? Knowing that more than half the victims of such events are children, how can we walk by on the other side?

The words of "Villager" (ca 1945) are salutary:

"Public opinion must never be allowed to forget the tragedy that was enacted in Bengal in 1943 unless and until action has been taken to make a recurrence impossible. After the capitulation of Germany in May, 1945, considerable publicity was given through the press, the radio and the cinema to the conditions that existed in the German Concentration Camps. Expressions of horror that such conditions could exist in the twentieth century reverberated around the world. The conditions under which the respectable, inoffensive, decent, law-abiding citizens of Bengal died in 1943 were equally bad, if not worse. It was no uncommon thing to hear reports from widely separated parts of the province of bodies being attacked and devoured by vultures, dogs and jackals even before life was extinct." [83]

We will now see how Winston Churchill, ruler of the British Empire, was involved in the tragic fate of millions of his humblest subjects.

14.17. 2008 Postscript

According to Dr Sanjoy Bhattacharya, Wellcome Institute, University College London, the death toll in the Bengal Famine totalled 6-7 million in Bengal and the adjoining provinces of Bihar, Assam and

Orissa in 1943-1945. [84] Colin Mason and others have suggested that the Bengal Famine was as a result of a deliberate British scorched earth policy. [85] Further histories have referred, albeit briefly, to the WW2 Bengal Famine [86] but there are a number of further exceptions found [87] (e.g. leading UK historian Simon Schama recently wrote about the 18th century Great Bengal Famine and 19th century famines in British India but ignored the WW2 Bengal Famine in his 3-volume "A History of Britain"). Leading Australian historian Geoffrey Blainey failed to mention the WW2 Bengal Famine in his recent history of the 20th century [88] and failed to mention any Indian or Bengal famines or even Bengal at all in his recent "Short" and "Very Short" histories of the world except for identical references to Bangladesh "later Bangladesh became a third nation" and to the (largely fictional) Black Hole of Calcutta incident: "In June 1757 [sic], one of the blackest months in Britain's colonial history, more than 100 of its soldiers died while imprisoned in the Black Hole of Calcutta". [89]

Chapter 15

Pride and Prejudice - Churchill, Science, the Bengal Famine and the Jewish Holocaust

"The British Empire ... population in 1900 stood at 370 million. Since there were 37 million people in Britain herself in 1901, one can see that every Briton had 10 colonial slaves working for him overseas."

- V.G. Trukhanovsky in Winston Churchill (1978) [1]

"It cannot in the opinion of His Majesty's Government be classified as slavery in the extreme acceptance of the word without some risk of terminological inexactitude."

- W.S. Churchill to the House of Commons on Chinese indentured labourers in South Africa (1906) [2]

"Traditions! What traditions? Rum, sodomy and the lash!"

- W.S. Churchill on the British Navy (circa 1916) [3]

"We shall declare war on Japan."

- W.S. Churchill, jumping to his feet on being told by his butler of the radio announcement of the Pearl Harbor attack (1941) (he was dining at Chequers with the American Ambassador John Winant and Roosevelt's special envoy Averell Harriman) [4]

"I had, moreover, given it as my considered opinion in October 1941 that Japan's former desire to avoid war with the United States at almost any cost could no longer be counted upon as a factor in the situation should Japan feel herself to be finally driven into a corner ... there can be no doubt that the absence of any British moderating influence, whether at Washington or Tokyo, increased the chances of that breakdown which eventually occurred."

- Sir R. Craigie, British Ambassador to Japan in 1941, in his final report to Foreign Secretary Anthony Eden (1943) [5]

15.1. Churchill's hidden roles in the WW2 Bengal Famine and the WW2 Jewish Holocaust

The above quotations provide the essence of this Chapter and an indication of the British imperial attitudes that contributed to the genesis and remorseless carnage of two of the most appalling events of human history. The Jewish Holocaust in Europe and the Bengal Famine in Asia were events that overlapped in time and which were tragically connected through British Imperial policy. Winston Churchill, wartime Prime Minister of Great Britain, was critically involved in the Bengal Famine [6] and was also involved in the Allied policy preventing Jews escaping from Nazi Europe. [7] There is a huge literature specifically dealing with the life of Churchill of which the biography by Pelling (1974) is particularly comprehensive. However this huge literature overwhelmingly fails to address Churchill's connection with the demise of these 13 million innocent people during the Second World War. [8]

15.2. Churchill and Jane Austen

Winston Spencer Churchill (1874-1965) has appeared at various stages of this treatise. His forebear John Churchill, the Duke of Marlborough, was the patron of Jane Austen's forebear James Brydges, the Duke of Chandos, and we have already perceived that the two of them started a long tradition in English establishment life of personal enrichment in the "national interest" at the expense of humanity both at home and abroad. The wealth of Marlborough was exhibited at Blenheim Palace and that of Chandos was revealed at his palace Canons that, when it stood, rivalled the palaces of royalty in its magnificence. Winston Churchill was born in 1874 at Blenheim Palace, the son of Lord Randolph Churchill (MP for Woodstock, Oxfordshire and younger son of the 7th Duke of Marlborough) and his

American wife Jennie née Jerome (the daughter of a New York businessman and a descendant of Captain Smith and Pocahantas). The actual legal family name was actually Spencer because John Churchill had not had a son and his line was initiated through his daughter Anne who had married Charles Spencer, the Earl of Sunderland. Given the stratification of English society and the relatively small size of the upper class, it would be likely that Winston Spencer Churchill would be directly connected with Jane Austen in a familial sense and indeed this is so. Winston Churchill, Pitt the Elder, Pitt the Younger, Jane Austen and Lady Hester Stanhope (oriental traveller) all can be traced back to Sir Thomas and Dame Alice Leigh née Barker (the great-great-great-great grandparents of Jane Austen (see Chapter 2). The genetic flow is as follows: Sir Thomas Leigh X Alice Barker → Winifred Leigh X Sir George Bond → Dionisia Bond X Sir Henry Winston → Sarah Winston X John Churchill → Sir Winston Churchill X Elizabeth Drake → John Churchill, First Duke of Marlborough X Sarah Churchill → → → Lord Randolph Churchill X Jennie Jerome → Sir Winston Churchill. [9]

15.3. Churchill as a young man

Churchill was reported by various people to have had an unreasoning detestation of Indians. Since his actions led to the death of millions of Indians in World War 2 it is not unreasonable to make some minimal attempt to explore the possible basis of this hatred. Some sort of sexual and associated physical contributing factors might excite our attention through natural curiosity, voyeurism and the widely held perception that such matters can be very powerful behavioural determinants. Thus Freud initially connected childhood sexual abuse with later psychopathy but, according to Masson (1985), he later decided upon a more socially acceptable position that claims of such abuse were more likely to be fantasy. [10] Morris gives dramatic examples of physical sexual experiences and their effects on subsequent behaviour. [11] More germane to this sketch, Sartre (1946) and Baldwin (1963) have made the connection between the psychology of sex and anti-semitism and American white anti-black racism, respectively. [12] Perhaps the secret of Churchill's deep antipathy for Indians lies in his full-blooded life as a youth and as a young man.

During his childhood the Churchill family was in disfavour with the Prince of Wales and his set. In 1876 the Marquess of Blandford (brother of Lord Randolph) had contemplated elopement with Lady Aylesford whose husband was a close friend of the Prince and was indeed accompanying him on a trip to India. Lord Randolph wrote to the Prince urging him to dissuade Aylesford from instituting divorce proceedings and, in what was perceived as close to blackmail, had indicated that if unsatisfied in his request, he would publish the Prince's own correspondence with Lady Aylesford. It took a number of years and Lord Randolph's success as a politician to overcome the consequent social exclusion. Lord Randolph administered a relief fund for Ireland set up by his mother in 1879 as a result of food shortages that year. Lord Randolph became Secretary of State for India in 1885 and strengthened the Indian Army under Sir Frederick Roberts (due to worries about the Russians) and annexed Upper Burma (because of similar concerns about the French). After the General Election of 1886 the Conservative Prime Minister made Lord Randolph Chancellor of the Exchequer and Leader of the House of Commons. However he differed with Salisbury on policy matters, Lord Randolph favouring closer ties with Germany and Austria and a decrease in military expenditure. Attempting to force his views by offering his resignation, he was retired to the back benches. Suffering from syphilis, he took a world tour with his wife but died in 1895 at the age of only 46. Marital conjugal satisfaction being precluded, Lady Jennie Churchill found pleasure in the company of other men, including the Prince of Wales, and her most significant romance was with the Austrian Count Charles Kinsky.

Churchill and his brother Jack had a devoted nurse Mrs Elizabeth Everest ("Woom") who was with them before they moved to Ireland temporarily in 1876 and on whom they were very much dependent as children. Churchill went to Harrow (on a par with Eton as the top public school in England) where he was well known but lonely and he described these years as "the only barren and unhappy period of my life". One can only speculate on likely exposure to the sorts of sexual experiences for which the Great English Public Schools are famous. It is quite likely that he would have encountered Indians at this stage of his life, both from the pages of history (such as the Nawab Siraj-ud-daulah of notoriety in relation to the Black Hole of Calcutta) and in the flesh as Indian Princes sent to school in England. Churchill went to Sandhurst and while there learned of the fatal illness of his father. 1895 was a critical year for Churchill: it saw the deaths of his father, his maternal grandmother and of his devoted nurse, Mrs. Everest. He graduated from Sandhurst in that year and was posted to the 4th Hussars.

Generous regimental leave arrangements allowed Churchill to go to New York and thence as a war correspondent to Cuba, where he was decorated for his courage. He had great plans on his return for service in the Lancers in South Africa with an explicitly expressed ambition of military adventure, decoration and subsequent political advance expressed as an intention to "beat my sword into an iron despatch box". However his lobbying efforts were unsuccessful (despite the powerful connections of his mother) and he remained with the 4th Hussars. However at this time the father of a fellow officer brought accusations of homosexuality against Churchill who in turn brought a libel suit that was settled out of court for 400 pounds. Nevertheless the father persisted in his complaints about other subalterns after his son left the regiment and the matter was reported in the radical journal Truth by Henry Labouchere. Churchill was advised against leaving the regiment as this might have indicated a desire to avoid inquiries. He was therefore compelled to go out to India when the regiment was posted there in 1896. [13]

Churchill arrived in Bombay and, before he even stepped on Indian soil, on landing at Sassoon Dock he suffered a severe injury that would plague him for the rest of his life. The boat rose and fell 4 or 5 feet with the surges of the waves and when he grasped one of the iron rings provided for hand-holds, the boat swung away and his right shoulder was severely dislocated. The dislocation meant that in future he played polo with his right arm strapped to his side and used a revolver in combat. For the rest of his life his arm would dislocate at odd times such as taking a book from a shelf or making an expansive gesture. [14]

In India Churchill's regiment was based in Bangalore but on leave in London he gained accreditation as a correspondent with the Malakand Field Force making war on tribes on the North-west Frontier. He joined this force after obtaining extra leave from his regiment. He had an exciting and dangerous time and described his experiences (with suitable circumspection in relation to the use of Dum-Dum expanding bullets and the murder of wounded prisoners) in newspaper accounts and in The Story of the Malakand Field Force. [15] He was appointed to the 31st Punjab Infantry but after a few days was returned to the 4th Hussars. On his return to Bangalore he wrote a "rattling" novel Savrola and in the meantime lobbied for a transfer to Kitchener in Egypt. One result of this Indian period was his declaration of love for a particular lady. No doubt other liaisons and adventures contributed to a pot pourri of race, sex and imperialism at this stage of his maturation.

In the event he secured leave from the 4th Hussars, secured a place in the 21st Lancers and made arrangements to act as a correspondent for the Morning Post. He took part in the Battle of Obdurman in the Sudan, being involved in the heroic charge of the 21st Lancers that earned them 3 Victoria Crosses. In this battle the Anglo-Egyptian forces crushed a numerically vastly greater force of 40,000 Dervishes, the critical element of the success being artillery and disciplined rifle fire on the part of the British forces. This battle and the subsequent occupation of Khartoum avenged the death of General Gordon in 1885 when his forces were defeated by those of the Mahdi.

Churchill had to return to India to rejoin his regiment but left India in 1899 for the last time. He published his account of the Sudan War as The River War. [16]

Churchill resigned his commission in 1899, sailed for South Africa as a correspondent for the Morning Post to cover the Boer War and on his arrival obtained a commission in the Lancashire Hussars. When a train was derailed by the Boers, Churchill was captured. He escaped and made it to Laurenco Marques in Portuguese Mozambique. He resumed coverage of the war with the South Africa Light Horse and, after the capture of Pretoria, returned home in 1900. Apart from a stint as a battalion commander on the Western Front in 1915, this was Churchill's last "active" involvement as a soldier. It was also the last time he was "on the ground" in a blood, sweat and tears sense in the great British Empire: in the non-metropolitan colonial world of plantations, mines, indigenous non-European subjects, indentured Indian labour and the "white man's burden". [17]

15.4. Churchill's public life 1899-1945

It is useful at this point to briefly document Churchill's subsequent career in the fashion of a somewhat biased curriculum vitae so that we can place events relevant to the present disquisition in context (the points at which he dealt with Indian and related matters are indicated below within square brackets):

15.5. Pre-World War 1

Unsuccessful Conservative candidate for Oldham (a cotton textile working-class Lancashire constituency near Manchester (1899); successful conservative candidate for Oldham (1900); lecture tour of Britain and America (1900); lecture tour of Canada (1901); supported freedom of trade, opposed restrictive tariff reforms of the Conservatives that could have inhibited the Lancashire cotton trade and reverted to the Liberal Opposition side of the House (1904); successfully opposed Conservative immigration restriction bill to the

approbation of his Manchester Jewish constituents and Lord
Rothschild (an old friend of his father) (1904); black-balled by the
Hurlingham Club as a polo-playing member (1904); Liberal
government (1905); Colonial Under-secretary to the Secretary of State
for the Colonies, Lord Elgin (former Viceroy of India) (1905);
successful Liberal and Free Trade candidate for Manchester North-
West (1906); supported Boer rights but was cool towards the rights of
Chinese "slaves" in South Africa, their flogging and other abuses -
repatriation of the Chinese resolved the matter (1907); toured East
Africa, wrote articles and a book My African Journey and commented
on future negative consequences of Indian migrant labour (1907);
joined Asquith's Cabinet as President of the Board of Trade (1908);
defeated in Manchester North-West (1908); successful Liberal
candidate for Dundee (1908); married Clementine née Hozier and
honeymooned in Italy (1908); his Labour Exchanges Bill was passed
(1909); he argued against conflict with Germany and argued for taxes
on land to meet naval armament expenses (1909); after the Lords
rejected Lloyd George's budget, he performed well in the subsequent
election campaign and was re-elected as a Liberal for Dundee (1910);
as Home Secretary (1910-1911) he was responsible for reform
legislation in relation to shop hours and mine safety and was
responsible for public order especially in relation to the South Wales
miners' strike and disturbances in the Rhondda Valley, the "battle of
Sidney Street" (involving East European revolutionaries) and a
national railway strike; as First Lord of the Admiralty (1911- 1915) he
oversaw pre-war naval preparations including fleet re-organizations
and technological innovations such as oil-burning vessels and larger
guns.

15.6. World War 1

Churchill was one of the more bellicose members of cabinet prior to
the outbreak of war (August 4th 1914); the naval Battle of Heligoland
Bight was an initial victory, but was followed by the loss of 3 old
British cruisers off the Dutch coast; Churchill was critically involved

in the delaying defence of Antwerp and when the Belgians capitulated
the British fell back to join a firm and unbroken stand at Ypres that
saved Dunkirk and a possible general catastrophe; the defeat of the
South American squadron under Cradock by von Spee at Coronel off
Chile was avenged by subsequent defeat of the Germans off the
Falklands by Sturdee's squadron (1914); the Battle of the Dogger Bank
was another British victory (1915); the scheme for a naval and military
attack on Gallipoli and the Dardanelles was designed to relieve Turkish
pressure on the Russians and was put by Churchill to the War Council
(January 1915); the campaign commenced in earnest with the British
and French naval bombardment of the Dardanelles forts with attendant
losses (February-April 1915); the Australian and New Zealand Army
Corps (the Anzacs) landed at Gallipoli on April 25 1915 only to
encounter withering fire from the well-prepared Turks; the campaign,
supported by British and Indian troops, developed into a bloody trench
warfare deadlock involving immense casualties before the final
withdrawal (1915).

[The total military casualties of the Dardanelles Campaign were
several hundred thousand, with disease taking a particularly heavy toll.
[18] However the day before the Anzac landing saw the beginning of the
rounding up of Armenian community leaders by the threatened and
xenophobic Turks. This inexorably led to the Armenian Genocide, a
major genocide of the 20th Century. An estimated 1 to 1.5 million
Armenians were killed through executions and mass civilian removal
from Anatolia into the Syrian desert. [19]]

The unpopularity of the Dardanelles campaign led to the Conservative
Bonar Law and the Liberal Prime Minister Asquith insisting on his
departure; Churchill was appointed to the junior Cabinet post of
Chancellor of the Duchy of Lancaster (1915); Churchill quit Cabinet
and joined his regiment, the Oxfordshire Hussars (Territorial Army)
first as a major and thence as a battalion commander in France
(November 1915-May 1916); the naval Battle of Jutland saw massive
losses on either side and Churchill agreed to release a suitably

convincing story for the public (May 1916); Churchill prepared a Cabinet paper on the folly of the Somme carnage caused by General Haig (July 1916); he testified before the Dardanelles Commission (late 1916) whose report criticised both him and Asquith while nevertheless largely exonerating Churchill (January 1917); he advocated greater recruitment of Africans and Indians (1917); he returned to Cabinet as Minister for Munitions (July 1917); with American intervention the Germans were finished and the War ended on November 11 1918.

15.7. Between the Wars

At the post-war general election Churchill was returned by Dundee as a Coalition Liberal (December 1918); Secretary of State for War and the Air Ministry (January 1919); he assisted anti-Bolshevik forces in Russia (1919).

[At this time Churchill excluded General Dyer from further employment in the Army. Dyer had been responsible for the notorious Amritsar massacre (1919) in which unarmed Indian demonstrators were gunned down by British forces in this Punjab city (379 people were killed and 1200 were wounded). An Army inquiry found that Dyer had committed "an error of judgement" but Dyer was condemned by a committee of the House of Commons. Nevertheless Dyer had engendered a certain amount of popular and Conservative support. Churchill made a strong speech that condemned the Amritsar massacre and hence Dyer in no uncertain terms. This was a most unusual occasion on which Churchill argued passionately for friendship binding the British and the Indians (1920).]

The Royal Air Force was employed in a successful and economical intervention in Somaliland (1920) which was to serve as a model for Imperial defence in Mesopotamia (1921) [including the strafing of Kurdish villages in the 1920s]; Churchill brought in the "Black and Tans" to deal brutally with Sinn Fein in Ireland, creating a bitterness that extends to this day (but which hopefully may soon finally evaporate); Churchill was appointed Colonial Secretary while retaining the Air Ministry (1921); Churchill recruited T.E. Lawrence, visited the Middle East, reasserted the British Government's support for a Jewish National Home in Palestine and agreed to the establishment (on Abdullah's insistence) of Transjordan as a territory separate from Palestine in which there would be no Jewish settlement (1921).

[Churchill prohibited Indians from purchasing land in the Kenya Highlands to preserve the position of the White settlers and, while recognizing principles of equality, saw the need for restrictions on Indian immigration there and on Indian citizenship: "The democratic principles of Europe are by no means suited to the development of Asiatic and African people." Montague, the Secretary of State for India, was more liberal than Churchill, criticized his views in Cabinet and initiated subsequent concessions to the Indians which greatly affronted the Kenyan and South African white racists who were implacably opposed to full citizenship for Indian immigrants. It should be noted that in the post-war years there was increasing Indian political activity in South and East Africa and of course in India. The return of Indian soldiers from France saw the appalling spread of the Spanish influenza that killed an estimated 17 million Indians in the immediately post-war years. [20]]

As Colonial Secretary Churchill was involved negotiations with Sinn Fein about Irish independence (1922); the Turks under Kemal Ataturk attacked the Greeks in Asia Minor but backed off in the face of tough diplomacy from Churchill (1922); the Coalition collapsed and in the subsequent election Churchill lost his seat (1922); Ramsay MacDonald became the first Labour Prime Minister (1924); Churchill was invited to stand for the Epping constituency as a "Constitutionalist" by the local Conservatives and was elected (1924); when the Labour government fell Stanley Baldwin was dissuaded from offering Churchill India and instead asked him to serve as "Chancellor" - the born-again Conservative Churchill thought he meant "of the Duchy of Lancaster" but it was indeed "of the Exchequer" (1924); differences between mine owners and miners - the latter declaring "not a penny off the pay, not a minute on the day" - led ultimately to the General Strike in which Churchill was prepared for military intimidation of the strikers (1926);

[The Statutory Commission of MPs was sent out to India under Sir John Simon to prepare for provincial self-government and was boycotted by Gandhi and the Nehrus.]

Churchill was again in opposition when a Labour government under Ramsay MacDonald was elected (1929); Churchill had to fall in with Stanley Baldwin and the Conservatives and support Empire Preference and Tariff Reform including imposts on food (1931);

[Lord Irwin as Viceroy of India renewed the ultimate commitment made in 1917 by Lloyd George for Indian Dominion status and organized a London Round Table Conference to enable expression of Indian views on the Simon Commission. Churchill was dead opposed to any encouragement of Indian self-rule and provoked Irwin who was concerned to keep a lid on Indian politicians. Churchill addressed the reactionary Indian Empire Society, set up at the time of the Conference, and advocated the crushing of Gandhi-ism (1930). Churchill's anti-Indian position brought him into conflict with the Conservative leadership who favoured the Labor policy of dialogue with the Indian Congress. When Gandhi and the Nehrus were released from prison in 1931and negotiated with Irwin, Churchill made his notorious comment that it was "alarming and also nauseating to see Mr. Gandhi, a seditious Middle Temple lawyer, now posing as a fakir of a type well-known in the East, striding half-naked up the steps of the Viceregal Palace." Churchill became associated with the reactionary India Defence League and opposed the White paper proposing Federal Indian government subject to support from the Indian States. Churchill and his supporters were conscious of the potential losses to Lancashire of cotton exports to India through loss of control of Indian fiscal policy and the Congress boycott of British goods.]

Hitler came to power (1933); throughout the thirties Churchill warned about German re-armament, the threat to Europe from German militarism (including the specific threat to European Jews) and the need for British preparedness; as described later, Churchill was brought into the committee of the Air Minister Lord Swinton to oversee air defence arrangements (1935).

15.8. World War 2

Germany invaded Poland and Churchill was invited to join Chamberlain's War Cabinet (September 1 1939); with the outbreak of war between Britain and Germany, Churchill was appointed First Lord of the Admiralty (September 3 1939); Churchill was appointed Prime Minister (1940); Pearl Harbor was attacked (Sunday December 7 1941); Singapore surrendered (January 1942);

[rioting and sabotage in India, including Bengal, occurred in 1942 and was dealt with strongly - 940 killed, 1630 injured, 60,000 arrested, 14,000 detained.]

Casablanca Conference (January 1943);

[At the Casablanca Conference in January 1943 Churchill substantially cut shipping in the Indian Ocean, a decision that sentenced millions of Indians to death in the Bengal Famine of 1943-1944.]

D-Day (June 4 1944); on May 8 1945 Churchill announced all hostilities would terminate at 0001 on May 9; Churchill and the Conservatives were defeated in the first post-war elections (1945).

15.9. Churchill's Secret War - Singapore and Pearl Harbor

Churchill realised that victory against Germany depended upon the entry of the United States into the conflict as an ally of Britain and that this would occur if Japan could be induced to go to war. J. Rusbridger and E. Nave have published a very detailed account of their perception of how Churchill secured American participation in their book Betrayal at Pearl Harbor. How Churchill Lured Roosevelt into World War II. [22] Nave was a Japanese-speaking Australian naval intelligence officer who was on secondment to the British Navy from the end of World War 1 to the end of World War 2. He was intimately involved in decoding Japanese naval signals and further testament to his credentials and responsibility is given by his period of leadership in the Australian Security and Intelligence Organisation (ASIO).

According to the account of Rusbridger and Nave (1991), in November 1940 a German raider under Captain Rogge captured the merchant vessel the Automedon in the Indian Ocean and it was found that the ship's safe contained a Chiefs of Staff report approved by the British War Cabinet and destined for the Commander at Singapore. Recognizing the importance of the document, Rogge immediately sailed for Japan. After authorization from Hitler, the document was given to the Japanese who thus by the beginning of 1941 realized that the British recognized that Singapore was essentially indefensible (I know that you know that I know ...). Rogge was awarded a samurai sword of honor by the Emperor - this award having only been made to 2 other Germans, namely Erwin Rommel and Hermann Goering.

The successful torpedo attack on the Italian fleet at Taranto in November 1940 demonstrated the potential for what could be done at Pearl Harbor. The British report revealing the indefensibility of Singapore confirmed the feasibility of attacking the American Pacific fleet without concern for British naval forces at Singapore. Rusbridger and Nave concluded that "the incident remains one of the worst intelligence disasters in history". These researchers assert that the British knew of the loss of this material but that Churchill did not inform Singapore or the Australians. The Australian Prime Minister, John Curtin, was apprised of the general situation after Pearl Harbor and insisted on bringing Australian soldiers back to Australia from the Middle East. Churchill diverted British forces to Singapore and inevitable capture at the fall of Singapore (January 1942).

15.10. Churchill and Pearl Harbor

The Americans had been able to break the machine-based code ("Purple") that the Japanese used for top secret diplomatic purposes and provided 2 such de-crypting machines to the British early in the war. However the British did not respond in kind and kept mum about details of the Japanese naval code which was code book-based and which the Americans were to subsequently break for themselves. With increasing tension between America and Japan and progressive Japanese intervention in French Indochina, it became obvious that conflict was inevitable. The critical question was when and where the conflict would begin.

The first shots against Britain and her allies may possibly have been fired several weeks before Pearl Harbor off the Australian coast. On November 19 1941 the Australian cruiser HMAS Sydney sank the German raider Kormoran but was hit by a torpedo (possibly not from the Kormoran) and disappeared with all hands. While three quarters of the Germans survived, no Australians lived to tell the tale, and this singularity has led to persistent speculation of a comprehensive massacre perpetrated by the crew of a Japanese submarine. The jury is still out.

The Japanese fleet bound for Hawaii had gathered initially in the north of the Kuriles in early November 1941 but (according to the account of Rusbridger and Nave) British naval intelligence was in a position to detect, decode and interpret messages associated with this initial movement and with the movement of the fleet when it set sail towards Hawaii. Rusbridger and Nave make it clear that the British would have known 2 weeks before the event that a large Japanese force was in the north Pacific and that "one of the most likely targets was Pearl Harbor." Churchill did not alert the Americans and indeed, on the contrary, at a time when he evidently would have been aware of this likelihood, he sent a message to Roosevelt (November 26 1941) asserting in relation to Japan that "we certainly do not want an additional war". Even if one discounts the above expert judgement of Nave, who was intimately involved with British naval intelligence at the time, this statement of Churchill's is manifestly disingenuous in the light of further events and his reaction to them.

According to the British ambassador in Tokyo, Sir Robert Craigie, in his report to Anthony Eden in February 1943 on conclusion of his mission to Japan, peace was still achievable with the Japanese in December 1941. In Craigie's view the balance of the War, as perceived from Tokyo, had shifted significantly by late 1941: the British and the Russians were shifting to a more offensive rôle, the Americans were assisting with supplies and with an "undeclared" war against German submarines in the Atlantic. The Japanese had presented a pacifying proposal involving their withdrawal from Indo-China and Craigie had strongly urged British acceptance (with some modifications) of this modus vivendi but evidently without success for this proposal was not acceptable to the Americans (November 26 1941). It is likely that the decision to go to war was taken by the Japanese on November 27. [22]

Craigie was conscious of the theory that American participation in the War was so vital for victory that it had to be incurred at the cost of war with Japan. He held a contrary view and felt that American-Japanese conflict could curtail American trans-Atlantic aid. Accordingly Craigie had strongly favoured continuing Japanese neutrality. Churchill had a completely different view in hindsight (and one can also reasonably presume in foresight): he was highly critical of Craigie's report and asserted: "It was a blessing that Japan attacked the United States and thus brought America wholeheartedly into the war. Greater good fortune has rarely happened to the British empire than this event." Craigie reflects that the Tripartite Pact between Japan, Germany and Italy may have been regarded in both Washington and London as committing Japan irretrievably to the War as an ally of the Axis powers - a view that he did not personally accept. In relation to the final breakdown of Japanese-American negotiations Craigie makes the critical observation: "there can be no doubt that the absence of any

British moderating influence, whether at Washington or at Tokyo, increased the chances of that breakdown which eventually occurred."

Rusbridger and Nave (1991) refer to a communication of Churchill to Roosevelt on November 26 1941 that is so secret that it cannot be released for the best part of 70 years and one of the American Pearl Harbor inquiries refers to critical (but not revealed) evidence received on November 26 indicating impending Japanese attack against Britain and America. Hawaii was warned in a general, as opposed to a specific sense, of the danger of Japanese attack on the same day that the Americans rejected the final Japanese proposal. 2 weeks later British forces in Malaya were at battle stations when attacked by the Japanese at dawn on December 8 1941, having had prior warning of major Japanese naval movements across the Gulf of Siam several days before. The Americans in Hawaii had no warning of the attack to come, although precise information was available to both British and American naval intelligence people the day before the attack.

A coded message sent to the Japanese Consulate in Melbourne on November 19 was intercepted and decoded. It specified warning messages to be incorporated into Japanese broadcasts in the event of the impending commencement of hostilities. The message indicating an impending outbreak of Japanese-American hostilities was "east wind rain" inserted in the text of a weather report ("west wind clearing" was to mean a Japanese-British crisis). The point of this was to ensure timely destruction of documents in Japanese consulates and embassies. The "east wind rain" radio message - indicating an impending Japanese attack on the Americans - was indeed picked up in Melbourne by the Australian Special Intelligence Organisation officer on December 4 1941. That intelligence was immediately passed on to Nave (who had been seconded to SIO) and thence to higher authority - but not to the Americans. The same message was picked up, correctly interpreted and passed on to higher authority by naval intelligence in Maryland - but according to Rusbridger and Nave, this direct warning of an impending Japanese attack on American forces was not acted upon to ensure the preparedeness of American forces in the Pacific.

The attack on Pearl Harbor on the morning of December 7 1941 caused massive damage to the US Navy and Air Force - 5 battleships and 3 cruisers sunk or severely damaged, 177 aircraft destroyed, 2,343 American servicemen dead, 876 missing and 1,272 injured. At that time Churchill was dining with Roosevelt's special envoy, Averell Harriman, and the American ambassador, John Winant. The butler brought the news and Churchill phoned Roosevelt immediately to inform him that Britain would declare war on Japan. The conclusion of Rusbridger and Nave (1991) is that denial of British naval intelligence information from the Americans allowed the Pearl Harbor attack to happen, turned a potential Japanese disaster into an American one and was "no accident but the deliberate policy of Churchill himself to achieve his aim of dragging America into the war." While "revisionists" have sought to implicate Roosevelt in a process of forcing Japan into a corner and thence into war, an analysis of this by Goldstein and Dillon (1982) concluded: "But in a thorough search of more than thirty years, including all documents released up to May 1 1981, we have not discovered one document or one word of sworn testimony that substantiates the revisionist position on Roosevelt and Pearl Harbor." [23]

15.11. Churchill, Lindeman and the Air War in Europe

We are indebted to C.P Snow's classic analysis Science and Government (1961) for the next key element of our saga. We have seen that Lord Swinton, the Air Minister, invited Winston Churchill onto his air defence committee in 1935. This was a sensible move to bring Churchill, a very public critic of defective defences, into a committee concerned with defence. He had already in 1934 publicly challenged the Government underestimation of the German air force using accurate estimates provided by his friend and adviser Lindeman, Professor of Physics at Oxford University. Churchill insisted on

Lindeman joining the technical "Tizard Committee" chaired by H. Tizard and including the leading scientists Hill and Blackett. Although Tizard and Lindeman had worked together in Berlin many years before and had been friends for years, this relationship fell apart on the Committee. Tizard wanted first priority to be given to development of radar for air defence. Lindeman favoured infrared detection and the use of parachute mines and bombs to destroy attacking aircraft. The aggressive attitude of Lindeman led to Blackett and Hill resigning in 1936. The Committee was subsequently reconstituted with the radio expert E.V. Appleton replacing Lindeman. The radar research and development work overseen by the Tizard Committee, carried out in close cooperation with the Royal Air Force, led to a working radar system in place in time to play a crucial role in the Battle of Britain.

In May 1940 Germany launched its massive assault on France and Churchill became Prime Minister. On June 4 Tizard was summoned to see Lindeman at 10 Downing Street. Placed in an intractably difficult position, within 3 weeks Tizard had resigned from his position as official scientific adviser of the Air Ministry. He was later directed to go to America with J. Cockroft to share British radar advances, including the cavity magnetron, with the Americans and was later put on the Air Council. However, despite his excellent scientific administrative track record in relation to radar defences, Tizard was effectively excluded from key scientific decision making, which was now in the hands of Churchill's man Lindeman.

Tizard and Blackett were to have a significant argument with Lindeman in 1942 over strategic bombing. They should have won the argument at the time and were thoroughly vindicated in hindsight, but Lindeman was Churchill's man and won the day. Lindeman (now Lord Cherwell) had proposed a policy of strategic bombing of "working class" areas of German towns, the objective being to kill or render homeless as many Germans as possible. His calculations were based on data from German air raids on British cities and towns. However his analysis evidently did not allow for a significant proportion of bombs landing essentially on the same spot. Blackett and Tizard independently analyzed the data and concluded that Lindeman's estimates of housing destruction were 6 and 5 times too high, respectively. A survey of bombing after the war revealed that Lindeman's estimate had been 10 times too high. Lindeman, obsessed by the predicted efficacy of this course, had his way by virtue of his association with Churchill. The policy of massive strategic bombing of German cities was ultimately adopted at the Casablanca Conference in January 1943 as a joint US-British policy.

Lindeman's incorrect judgement in relation to strategic bombing was compounded by his conservative attitude to the introduction of "Window", a procedure whereby metallized paper strips were dropped from aircraft and interfered with accurate analysis of radar signals. It was estimated that interference with radar-controlled and radar-controlled anti-aircraft guns would have saved 35% of aircraft being shot down over Occupied Europe. Lindeman felt that "Windows" could interfere with British night fighter operations and was successful in delaying its introduction for about 1 year. It was estimated that use of "Window" in April to Mid-July 1943 would have saved 230 Allied bombers but only 16 German bombers would have been saved if the Germans had applied this device.

The cost of the Strategic Bombing campaign was analyzed after the war. 500,000 German civilians were killed at the cost of 160,000 dead Allied airmen. However the objective of the campaign, to demoralize the industrial work-force and thereby reduce war production, was certainly not achieved. German war production kept rising steadily until it reached a peak in August 1944 when Allied forces were well into France and Poland and it was clear that Germany itself would shortly face invasion from both the west and the east. C.P. Snow (1961) quotes Blackett's assertion that with a more intelligent use of air power for military targets in Germany, in other war zones and in the Battle of the Atlantic the war would have ended a half a year or a year earlier. In addition to the massive air losses, the Allies suffered major shipping losses for want of sufficient air protection.

In the middle of 1943 naval analysts determined that there was a deficiency of 800 aircraft for anti-submarine protection of merchant shipping convoys. Nevertheless the Air Ministry won out in the continuing massive commitment to bombing of Germany. The losses could be counted not only in men and ships but in the cargoes vital for the war effort. C.P. Snow (1961) quotes the judgement of the Naval historian that in 1943 the Allies came close to defeat in the Battle of the Atlantic through the major deficiency in aircraft for convoy protection, a view shared by others. [24] The losses of shipping had a major impact on the crisis that was developing in India.

15.12. The shipping crisis and famine in India

At the Casablanca Conference between Churchill and Roosevelt in January 1943, the decision was made in relation to the joint strategic bombing offensive against Germany with the continuing consequences outline above. Shipping losses and the shipping requirements for the North African campaign and the supply of Britain led Roosevelt to promise the transfer of some shipping from the Pacific. During 1942 the needs of the North African campaign and the armament and food needs of Britain had steadily eroded ship sailings in the Indian Ocean. In January 1943 Indian Ocean shipping was cut by about one half. This edict from Churchill cut sailings to the Indian Ocean in the first half of 1943 to 40 ships a month, about 40% of the level obtaining in the first half of 1942. This restriction had a compounding effect since it also reduced the intra-Indian Ocean "cross route" shipping. An eventual horrendous result of this situation, as perceived by Taylor (1965), was mass-starvation in India:

"A million and a half Indians died of starvation for the sake of a white man's quarrel in North Africa."

In the first half of 1943 major shortages of food became apparent in Ceylon (labourers were leaving rubber plantations to seek food), East Africa (where labour involved in naval support and agricultural production was in danger), Southern Rhodesia, Mauritius and the Seychelles. Severely compounding this problem had been the promise of 150,000 tons of grain to Turkey made at the Casablanca Conference. (Even though Turkey was a "neutral" country it occupied a very strategic position between the Nazis and Middle East oil). By the middle of 1943 there was severe famine in Bengal and there were also severe shortages in Rajasthan and South India. It is useful to consider estimates of the food needs and to what extent they were actually met.

The population of India at that time was about 400 million and total grain production was 50 to 70 million tons annually. The population was growing at a rate of about 5% per year and there was a requirement of net imports of about 1-2 million tons of grain per annum to make up for deficiencies. The loss of rice from Burma (occupied by the Japanese) and the decrease in shipping (for the reasons outlined above) resulted in a major decrease in net imports of grain into India at this time. The decrease in the Bengal rice crop in the winter of 1942/43 was estimated in hindsight by the post-war Famine Inquiry Commission to have been about 700,000 tons (the normal annual Bengal total being about 9 million tons in those years). In December 1942 the Secretary of State for India estimated the need for delivery of 600,000 tons of grain to India by April 1943. It is useful to reiterate the key points made earlier deriving from the incisive analyses of Sen (1989) and of Greenough (1982): while ultimately there is an absolute need for a particular amount of food over a given period, at any point in time people need to be able to obtain food at a socially feasible price. As we have seen in Chapter 14, a variety of factors (including modest decreases in crop yield, the massive decrease in net food imports and provincial food control autonomy) resulted in uncertainty and fatal food price rises in Bengal. According to the figures of Ghosh (1944), while the net import of all food grains into

India by sea in 1939-40 was 2.2 million tons, by the 1942/43 this had become a net export of 0.4 million tons. It should be noted that Ghosh (1944) and Behrens (1955) differ slightly in terms of the amount of grain imported into India in this period, the estimates being 0.02 or at least 0.06 million tons, respectively. These estimates are 2 orders of magnitude lower than the estimated annual import requirement of 1-2 million tons.

The analysis of Behrens (1955) of the role of war-time shipping shortages on the Bengal famine concludes that "the North African campaign doomed almost irrevocably to starvation any deficit area in India where the harvest failed", a view with which Taylor (1965) concurs. [25]

15.13. Churchill and the resumption of grain shipments to India

We have seen in Chapter 14 the urgency and persistence with which Wavell pleaded with the British Government for food for India after he took up his appointment as Viceroy of India in October 1943. Churchill repeatedly opposed food for India, his priorities being the North African campaign (legitimate up to a point), the promised Turks (not our allies but having to be kept neutral) and ultimately the famine-wracked Greeks when they were liberated (and fell to civil war, the Allies supporting the "right" against the unequivocally anti-Nazi "left"). Churchill opposed the Canadian offer to ship grain to India and specifically blocked the provision of 10,000 tons of grain offered by Prime Minister King of Canada. The offer of 100,000 tons of rice from Burma made by the collaborationist head of the Indian National Army, Subhas Chandra Bose, was totally ignored. [26] We will recall R.G. Casey's intelligence at this time of the Argentinians using 2 million tons of surplus wheat in their railway system in lieu of coal. [27]

While Churchill rejected Wavell's urgent and repeated pleading for 1 million tons of grain for India, he did accede to pressure from Wavell to write to Roosevelt at the end of April 1944 requesting

American assistance in the actual shipment of the wheat from Australia. However in making this request Churchill qualified it in the most extraordinary terms: "I am no longer justified in not asking for your help." Jane Austen could hardly have put it better. Not unsurprisingly Churchill's request, couched in such less than enthusiastic terms, failed to move Roosevelt to a concrete response. Since this is the only substantial written comment made by Churchill that I have found that actually refers to the Bengal famine - Churchill's genocide - it deserves to be reproduced in full here:

"London, April 29 1944. Prime Minister to President Roosevelt Personal and Top Secret.

1. I am seriously concerned about the food situation in India and its possible reactions on our joint operations. Last year we had a grievous famine in Bengal through which at least 700,000 people died. This year there is a good crop of rice, but we are faced with an acute shortage of wheat, aggravated by unprecedented storms which have inflicted serious damage on the Indian spring crops. India's shortage cannot be overcome by any possible surplus of rice even if such a surplus could be extracted from the peasants. Our recent losses in the Bombay explosion have accentuated the problem.

2. Wavell is exceedingly anxious about our position and has given me the gravest warnings. His present estimate is that he will require imports of about one million tons this year if he is to hold the situation, and so meet the needs of the United States and British and Indian troops and of the civil population especially in the great cities. I have just heard from Mountbatten that he considers the situation so serious that, unless arrangements are made promptly to import wheat requirements, he will be compelled to release military cargo space of SEAC in favour of wheat and formally advise Stilwell that it will also be necessary for him to arrange to curtail American military demands for this purpose.

3. By cutting down military shipments and other means, I have been able to arrange for 350,000 tons of wheat to be shipped to India from Australia during the first nine months of 1944. This is the shortest haul. I cannot see how to do more.

4. I have had much hesitation in asking you to add to the great assistance you are giving us with shipping but a satisfactory situation in India is of such vital importance to the success of our joint plans against the Japanese that I am impelled to ask you to consider a special allocation of ships to carry wheat from Australia without reducing the assistance you are now providing for us, who are at a positive minimum if war efficiency is to be maintained. We have the wheat in Australia but we lack the ships. I have resisted for some time the Viceroy's request that I should ask you for your help, but I believe that, with this recent misfortune with the wheat harvest and in the light of Mountbatten's representations, I am no longer justified in not asking for your help. Wavell is doing all he can by special measures in India. If however he should find it possible to revise his estimates of his needs, I would let you know immediately." [28]

Lord Louis Mountbatten, Commander in Chief of South East Asia Command, attempted assistance by using shipping under his control to get grain to India. Churchill intervened, blocked this avenue and promptly reduced Mountbatten's available shipping by 10%. Mountbatten continued in his resolve and used 10% of what remained of his shipping resources to convey grain to India. [29]

Figures documented by Behrens (1955) of grain shipments to India in 1942-1945 give an idea of the amounts involved and the human implications of the shipments in a biological and social sense. To sharpen the implications of this data, imagine that we are not simply adherents to "all men are created equal" who are considering food for living, feeling, thinking fellow human beings (and, more specifically, for children, the major victims of famine and scarcity). Let us attempt to distance ourselves emotionally to some extent and consider the following figures as applying to an agricultural or industrial "livestock" resource seen from the perspective of an inspector from the Royal Society for the Protection of Cruelty to Animals (RSPCA). One supposes that economists would be happy with this approach since historically the Indians were essentially "farmed" by the British colonialists and indeed "farming" was the technical term used to describe the taxing of Bengali farmers under the East India Company.

Behrens' figures for grain shipments (in tons) for India in 1942-1945 are as follows: 1942 (30,000), 1943 (303,000), 1944 (639,000) and 1945 (871,000). The 1942 shipment involved 2 lots from Australia contracted for at the rate of 15,000 tons per month to supply the Indian Army (the balance of the demand was not shipped that year). 2.4 million men served in the Indian Army during World War 2. This estimate can be "reduced" since not all of these were in the Army at the same time, scores of thousands were in the Mediterranean theatre (250,000 served there), had been captured by the Japanese or had died. Taking the gross Indian annual grain production estimates of about 60 million tons for 400 million people, we see that the average consumption was 0.15 tons per person per year (obviously more for adults and less for children). The annual requirement for about 2 million men in the "reduced" Indian Army was therefore 0.3 million tons. We can arrive at a figure having a similar order of magnitude from the 1942 contracted requirement of 15,000 tons per month i.e. 0.18 million tons for a whole year. If we assume that an Indian Army soldier required 50% more food than the average Indian we would estimate that the annual grain requirement for a 2 million strong Indian Army would be about 0.45 million tons. The average yearly importation in 1942-1945 was 0.46 million tons and thus we can see that the grain actually imported was merely enough to feed the Indian Army. It is interesting to note that Churchill's letter to Roosevelt quoted earlier indeed specifies US, British and Indian soldiers as well as civilians in the big cities (and therefore directly involved in the war-effort) as the people for whom the urgent food supplies were needed. [30]

One can perform all kinds of similar numerical exercises, but the fact remains that the grain actually imported into India each year in these dreadful years was sufficient to feed less than 1% of the Indian population at a bare subsistence level. Such was Britain's reward for India's major contribution to the war effort that involved 2.4 million serving soldiers and almost complete and comprehensive civil peace. However this "gratitude" on the part of Churchill and his colleagues was to continue after the war. The average market "price" of the 4 million victims can be estimated in various ways but consideration of the annual per capita income of rural Bengalis today provides an estimate of about US$100 per head in today's money.

15.14. Bengal and the Burma Campaign

Bengal and Assam share borders with Burma, the furthest extent of the Japanese advance. The armed insurrection against the British in West Bengal in 1942 was put down with great ferocity. The Indian National Army led by Bose in collaboration with the Japanese was on the frontier with India. Forcing the Japanese back from Burma was crucial for defence of India and for supplying China via the Burma Road to Kunming in Yunnan. Willmott (1989) writes of the critical situation facing the British:

"In April 1942, at a time when two divisions were sent by sea to Rangoon and carrier forces raided Ceylon, a Japanese landing in Bengal could not have been repulsed by the British forces in north-east India, and a British defeat around Calcutta, coming on top of those in Malaya and Burma, would have destroyed the British position throughout the subcontinent." [31]

This situation was complicated by British sensitivities over requisite American involvement in this British Empire theatre. The Americans in turn were conscious of British ambivalence and distasteful colonial impositions. Thus Kitchen (1990) writes:

"American attitudes toward India vividly illustrate this problem [of Allied tensions]. With Gandhi in prison and apparently intent on starving himself to death, and with the appalling famine in Bengal, American anti-colonialists had ample material for their accusations against British imperialism." [32]

The following opinions of the American commander in this theatre, General Stilwell, reflect these tensions:

On British-Chinese interactions: the British couldn't work with Chinese "because they looked down on them".

Disgust at swagger sticks: the English officer "is a mess. At least here in Hong Kong. Untidy, grouchy, sloppy, fooling around with canes, a bad example for the men."

Admiration for English drill sergeants : "[who] for commands, appearance and results beat our average officer 500%."

On the English commanders: "The more I see of the Limeys, the worse I hate them"; "The bastardly hypocrites do their best to cut our throats on all occasions. The pig fuckers." [33]

On the 43 year-old Lord Louis Mountbatten, Supreme Commander of South East Asia Command : "a fatuous ass", "childish Louis, publicity crazy", "piss pot"; "The Glamour Boy is just that. He doesn't wear well and I begin to wonder if he knows his stuff. Enormous staff, endless walla-walla but damned little fighting." [34]

On the other hand, President Roosevelt felt that "Stilwell obviously hated the Chinese." The Americans had contempt for the Indians who they referred to as "wogs" and, with other Allied servicemen, enjoyed the pleasures of rest and recuperation in the cities of starving Bengal. This included the violation of destitution- and starvation-driven young girls and mothers surviving on the open market or associated with the Military Labour Corps. The following incident reveals something of such attitudes:

"on the way to Ledo by train some of the men were discovered by a horrified officer to be shooting out the windows at the "wogs" and their cows in the field." [36]

The British evidently shared these attitudes towards the Indians and clearly mistrusted the will of the Indian Army in India to fight for the British Empire. Churchill was keen to dismantle much of the huge Indian Army in India that amounted to about 2 million men:

"There ought to be a continuous reduction in the vast mass of low-grade troops now maintained under arms in India. Nearly two million men are on our pay-lists and ration strength, apart from the British troops in the country and on the frontier." [37]

In the event, Allied forces, notably British and Indians, under the brilliant General Slim, defeated the Japanese in Assam and thence drove them out of Burma, relieving the threat to India and enabling supply of the Chinese campaigns against the Japanese invader.

15.15. Famine as a successful strategic weapon

The British decision-making that produced and sustained the man-made Bengal Famine took place over a substantial part of the war years and was deliberate, considered and informed. The magnitude, nature and duration of the Bengal Famine, the resolute and sustained unresponsiveness of the British authorities, the manifold strategic benefits arising from this course and the contempt for Indians from the top to the bottom among the Allies, compel one to the conclusion that the disaster arose from deliberate, considered and informed policy. The reality is that the Bengal Famine happened and that about 4 million people died awful, slow agonizing deaths. A restless, densely populated province bordering the limit of Japanese expansion was contained by the horrendous grip of general starvation. Valuable resources of food, medical supplies and shipping were freed for the primary task of the global defeat of the Axis forces. Provincial autonomy ensured that the strategic problem was contained for a substantial part of the emergency and that the other Indian provinces were suitably pacified under the unspoken threat that there, but for the grace of God and Churchill, might be their fate as well.

Famine, or the threat of famine, has been an effective weapon of pacification and was certainly used by the Germans during World War 2 and by Stalin in the crushing of the Ukraine in 1928-33. [38] In the instance of war-time Bengal - and indeed of India as a whole - huge populations were kept on the edge of survival through deliberate policy extending over 6 years and the outcome was minimal civil disturbance.

There is a further strategic dimension to the British supervision of the Bengal Famine that has direct implications in relation to that other, contemporary Holocaust, the deliberate destruction of the Jews of Europe by the Germans. There was a substantial Muslim majority in Bengal and especially in the eastern half of the province, the region that was closest to the enemy and which suffered the worst privations of the disaster. The British were extraordinarily sensitive to the problem of containing the huge Muslim populations under their control in India and the Middle East. As is described below, a major reason for the refusal of the Allies to allow the Jews of Europe to escape stemmed from an extremely realistic fear of renewed Arab revolt in the Middle East if massive Jewish immigration to Palestine occurred. Seen in that light, any situation involving the need for unrestrained exercise of military force in densely populated, restless and heavily Muslim Bengal would have been extraordinarily dangerous.

India was held through defence of the frontier against the Japanese, the presence of a 2 million strong army, the confinement of political leaders, the arrest of 60,000 other activists and the detention of 14,000 of them, ruthless suppression of disturbances and strategic parsimony in relation to food supplies. War-time Bengal can be seen to have been secured through the quiet, cowardly and utterly evil stratagem of deprivation and consequent mass starvation, just as nearly 2 centuries earlier man-made, devastating famine delivered the crushed Bengali and Bihari survivors into servitude.

15.16. Muslim containment and the Jewish Holocaust

Churchill, our bête noire in this account, was nevertheless one of the first major figures to warn of the danger to the Jews of Eastern Europe in a speech made in 1935 in which he predicted that the "odious" treatment of Jews current in Germany would be extended to a general pogrom in the East after conquest by the Germans. [39] While having considerable sympathy with the anti-communist, anti-socialist and economic orientation of the Nazis, Churchill found anti-semitism a sticking point. This position was at variance with that of many of his British Establishment peers and indeed of many others in British society. "Good mannered" anti-semitism surfaces in the literature of the period from the pens of authors such as Agatha Christie, Somerset Maugham and H.G. Wells, of which the following extract from H.G. Wells' Postscript to an Experiment in Autobiography (1936) is a good example:

"And on another occasion about that time we [Wells and his current lover Odette Keun] met the Mathiases and they took us over to lunch with Sir Alfred Mond and Lady Mond at Monte Carlo. Odette was put near Sir Alfred. Two gems of conversation flashed down the table to me. One was Odette saying "When you say "Ve", Sir Alfred, do you mean "Ve English" or "Ve Jews" ?" Then I lost the thread for a time. Then I heard Sir Alfred, excessively wrath, saying: "In Judaea we would have stoned you - and serve you right!" She had raised that little matter of the Well of Loneliness again [a suppressed novel of female homosexuality by Radclyffe Hall]. It is impossible to dislike a woman who can create such a situation altogether." [40]

Churchill's sympathy for the Jews may have stemmed in part in a personal sense from his Manchester constituency and friendship with the Rothschilds. Nevertheless the Nazis evidently wanted to do to Eastern Europeans what the British were doing in India. Surely one of the biggest "ifs" in History relates to what would have happened if Churchill and Hitler had struck a deal to carve up the world peacefully before the "phony war" had degenerated into global carnage.

The Jehovah's Witnesses were among the first people to publicly oppose Nazism (in 1929) and were among the first to expose the existence of concentration camps (in 1933). These good people suffered catastrophically under the Nazis and continued to inform the world to the bitter end. An appalling aspect of the extermination of Jews and Gypsies by the Nazis was the failure of the world to accept what was going on. The Jehovah's Witnesses bore explicit witness every year of the Third Reich, 10,000 of their total of 25,000 adherents in Germany having been incarcerated for at least some time and 2,000 having been sent to concentration camps. [41] They were not listened to and indeed the formerly pro-Fascist conservative government of Australia made them an illegal organization in 1941 (a determination that was struck out by the Australian High Court in 1943). [42] Finally on December 17 1942 Foreign Secretary Sir Anthony Eden, in the name of 11 Allied governments, informed a shocked House of Commons of their receipt of:

"numerous reports from Europe that the German authorities, not content with denying to persons of Jewish race in all the territories over which their barbarous rule has been extended the elementary rights, are now carrying into effect Hitler's oft-repeated intention to exterminate the Jewish people of Europe. The number of victims of these bloody cruelties is reckoned in many hundreds of thousands of entirely innocent men, women and children." [43]

The Balfour Declaration of November 2 1917 announced that the British Government supported "the establishment in Palestine of a national home for the Jewish people ... it being clearly understood that nothing shall be done which may prejudice the civil and religious rights of existing non-Jewish communities in Palestine". The impact of this short statement, released in the form of a letter to Lord Walter Rothschild, has been so profound that it is reproduced below in full:

"Foreign Office. November 2nd 1917.

Dear Lord Rothschild,

I have much pleasure in conveying to you on behalf of His Majesty's Government, the following declaration of sympathy with Zionist aspirations which have been submitted to, and approved by, the Cabinet.

"His Majesty's Government view with favour the establishment in Palestine of a national home for the Jewish people, and will use their best endeavours to facilitate the achievement of this object, it being clearly understood that nothing should be done which may prejudice the civil and religious rights of existing non-Jewish communities in Palestine, or the rights and political status enjoyed by Jews in any other country."

I should be grateful if you would bring this declaration to the knowledge of the Zionist Federation. Yours, Balfour." [44]

Massive Jewish immigration to Palestine and massive alienation of Arab lands had finally led to the communal violence of the Arab revolt in the mid-1930s. This in turn led to the formation of the Jewish Haganah and the Jewish Special Night Squads backed by General Wavell and led by the remarkable British military officer Orde Wingate in the period 1936-1939. [Wingate (1903-1944) later led the "Gideon Force" in the liberation of Ethiopia, the daring Chindit expeditions behind Japanese lines in Burma and died in an air crash in Burma in 1944. His unorthodox but highly successful operations are themselves a matter of surprising historiographic differences as to their

effectiveness.] [45] The British finally contained the situation by the issue
of a White Paper on May 17 1939 that severely constrained land
transfer and limited Jewish immigration to 75,000 over the next 5
years, with final cessation unless the Arabs agreed to continuance. A
major factor in the issuance of the Chamberlain White Paper was
concern over the danger of unrest in the Middle East and among
Muslims in India if Jewish immigration was to continue unabated, a
danger heightened by the imminence of war. According to the Colonial
Secretary Malcolm MacDonald, the British Government had received
"unanimous advice" of this kind from military advisers and from its
representatives in India and the Middle East. According to Kedourie
(1968):

"It is clear that Great Britain embarked on this policy because she
considered the cost of supporting the Zionists against the Arabs too
high. By 1939 the Arabs were being increasingly wooed and
encouraged by the Axis powers, and, as they occupied lands of
strategic importance, it was considered that they had to be conciliated;
hence the abandonment of partition, to which the Arabs objected, and
hence, too, the White Paper."

A major part of that "strategic importance" stemmed from the
discovery of oil in Bahrain in 1932 and thence in Saudi Arabia in 1933,
leading to intense German and American interest in what had
previously been a British patch. This "strategic importance" bolstered
American and British Establishment anti-Semitism, massive and
critical American and British investment in Nazi Germany, genocidal
German anti-Semitism and ultimately sealed the fate of 6 million Jews,
martyred innocents in "the wrong place at the wrong time". [46]

It is notable that one of the leading Jewish figures of the
Empire was a supporter of the Chamberlain White Paper. Sir Isaac
Isaacs, a distinguished jurist, was the Governor-General of Australia
(1931-1936) and wrote a series of letters to the press in Australia in the
war years in which he opposed further substantial Jewish immigration

and the notion of Palestine as a National Home for Jews as contrary to principles of international justice. His position created great controversy in the Jewish community in Australia, the more so because of the realization of what was happening to the Jews of Europe. [47]

The Second World War began on September 1 1939 with the German invasion of Poland and the declaration of war by Britain. It seems likely that the first shots of that conflict by the British were fired on September 2 1939 in Palestine, killing 2 illegal Jewish immigrants attempting to land from a ship off Tel Aviv beach. [48] Enforcement of the White Paper, made more urgent by the need to placate the Arabs and Indian Muslims during the war, was to kill many more ship-borne Jewish refugees and helped seal the fate of millions of Jews in Nazi-occupied Europe. While the Germans were happy to see Jews leave Europe during the first few years of the war, the British and the Americans were not happy to receive them. Thus in the event 23,000 Jews entered Palestine in 1943-1944 and only 4,700 entered the U.S.A. in 1943. The total number of Jewish refugees making it to Britain, the United States and the British Dominions during the war can be estimated at about 40,000, 70,000 and 4,000, respectively. [49] [My father, John (Janos) Bela Polya, and his brother Michael (Mihaly) had the opportunity and good sense to leave Hungary before the war and thence went to Australia in 1939. Their sister Susie (Zsuzsanna) left for America before the war].

By late 1941 the Germans had already murdered 1,400,000 Jews in Eastern Europe, this process involving Einsatzgruppen murder squads and mass shootings. In 1941 use of mobile gas chambers accelerated the process and from 1942 extermination camps equipped with permanent gas chambers were set up at Belzec, Sobibor, Treblincka, Maidanek and at the Birkenau section of Auschwitz. By the end of the war 6 million (possibly 7 million) Jews and 0.5 million (possibly 1 million) Gypsies had been murdered by the Germans.[50]

While Churchill was pro-Jewish and anti-Arab, most of his
Cabinet colleagues were pro-Arab and anti-Jewish. Anthony Eden was
firmly in the latter camp (and indeed many years later had managed to
excite great anger in Israel through his pro-Arab position a year before
the collusive invasion of Egypt in 1956.) [51] Thus while Churchill
argued for arming and training the Jews in Palestine, this was
resolutely opposed by the dominant lobby concerned to keep the Arabs
and the Indian Muslims on-side. Thus when Chaim Weizmann wrote to
Churchill in 1940 offering him 50,000 Jewish soldiers, Churchill
declined for fear of an Islamic backlash and General Wavell estimated
that he would need a further division to hold down Palestine alone if
the Arabs became disaffected. [52]

The major lobbyists for saving Jewish refugees in the latter half
of the war were Palestine and U.S. Jews. However practical assistance
to the Jews of Europe was not forthcoming. Attempts to save the last
surviving Jewish community in Europe, that of Hungary, failed. In
1944 Joel Brand negotiated with the Nazis and the Allies for the lives
of surviving Hungarian Jews and any surviving regional remnants. The
survivors were to go anywhere other than Palestine after release
through Turkey. The value placed on 1 million people was 10,000
lorries (for the eastern front only), 2 million bars of soap, 8000 tons of
coffee, 200 tons of cocoa and 800 tons of tea (in money terms about 10
pounds per head). [What price then for each of those saved by my
martyred grandfather who performed some 50,000 surgical
interventions in his abbreviated lifetime? Confident in humanity, he
declined offers to remain in America in 1939, returned to his hospital
duties in Budapest and was eventually killed in 1944/45. His last words
in Polya (1941) The Story of Medical Science: "This is the end of the
narrative but not of the story. It will never end as long as humane
people inhabit the Earth. The struggle for the life and health of man
will only cease with the last man."] Soviet fears about separate German
deals with the Western Allies helped scotch the deal. Churchill rejected
the proposal, and after the story leaked, the British Press endorsed his

decision. 200,000 out of 700,000 of the Jews of Hungary perished in the Holocaust.[53]

The Bengal Famine and the Jewish Holocaust occurred at about the same time but at different ends of the earth and involved different perpetrators and victims. They are tragically linked by the strategic imperatives of the British Empire and have common causes in greed, racism, militarism and the denial and unresponsiveness of the world.

15.17. Food supplies and the UNRRA

The United Nations Relief and Rehabilitation Administration (UNRRA) was set up by an international agreement signed by 44 nations at the White House in Washington on November 9 1943. The first contribution of funds came from the Government of Iceland. The aims of the UNRRA were to:

"Plan, coordinate, administer or arrange for the administration of measures for the relief of victims of war in any area under the control of any of the United Nations through the provision of food, fuel, clothing, shelter and other basic necessities, medical and other essential services."

The United States made immense contributions to the UNRRA that totalled $5.4 billion in the period 1944-1946. This continuing act of immense humanity and generosity is in stark contrast to the callous indifference of Churchill to the sufferings of his 0.4 billion Indian subjects. India was initially not a recipient of benefits although it was clearly in desperate need in the latter half of the War and indeed in the immediately postwar years. Indians and others engaged in considerable lobbying in the US (notably to Eleanor Roosevelt) with the result that in March 1944 a so-called "India clause" was inserted into US legislation that (while not naming India explicitly) permitted India to receive support in the following fashion:

"in so far as funds and facilities permit, any area (except within enemy territory and while occupied by the enemy) important to the military operation of the United Nations which is stricken by famine or disease may be included in the benefits to be made available through the United Nations Relief and Rehabilitation Administration."

Unfortunately the British did not request such assistance and Churchill rejected Wavell's suggestion that it should. India received no support from the UNRRA. Indeed the British ensured that India became the 6th largest contributor to the UNRRA funds, providing the equivalent of over $24 million. When India was asked to increase this contribution at the Third Council Meeting in 1947, its representative declined because it was only averting wholesale famine by massive food imports. [54]

India was similarly treated differentially after the war in relation to compensation for war-associated damage and the cost of the war to the Indian people. India was a subject dominion of 400 million people which had contributed 2.4 million men to the Army, 250,000 men to the Mediterranean theatre, 100,000 men to the defence of Malaya and Singapore and a similar number to the defence of Assam and the liberation of Burma. India had suffered some bombing damage, scores of thousands of military casualties, scores of thousands of men captured by the enemy and millions of civilian famine deaths (mostly in Bengal and adjoining provinces but also in South India and Rajasthan). Yet India received less in compensation than Canada and only about twice the amount given to New Zealand plus Australia. [55]

Food shortages continued after the War. Thus a letter from Churchill's successor, the Labor Prime Minister Attlee, to Ben Chifley, Prime Minister of Australia, detailed grave concerns about food shortages in India, the need for food supplies from Australia and the dangers of famine-induced disorders in India:

".... India must thus have an import of at least two million tons of rice, wheat or millet, during 1946, if famine of a dimension and intensity greater than the Bengal famine of 1943 (is) to be avoided. This is an increase of 500,000 tons on their earlier request and I should not be surprised if in point of fact they do not need more. In the circumstances of political crisis which are approaching, a famine in India would be bound to lead to disorders and would be likely to remove the last hope of an orderly solution of the Indian problem ... As regards the use of wheat for feed, I am very grateful for the action you have taken to withhold it from dairy stock. As regards poultry and pigs, while in the new circumstances we shall be more than ever dependent on Australia for our supplies of bacon and eggs, and while we should very much regret any reduction in them, we feel that so long as human beings are exposed to famine and starvation as a result of the present wheat shortage, human needs must have a priority." [56] [We will see from Chapter 16 that humanity in general will not be eating meat by the end of the 21st Century.]

15.18. Churchill's final legacy to India

Churchill had a steadfast position over several decades of opposing constitutional reform in India, spoke with contempt of Gandhi and the other Indian leaders, opposed their release from prison and only permitted token Indian participation in the essential war-time government of India. The Stafford Cripps mission to involve the Indian leadership in the war effort in return for constitutional reforms was stymied by Churchill who expressed concern about any deals a Congress-based national government of India might concoct with the Japanese. The Cripps mission failed but ultimately postwar Britain had to leave India and Churchill's resolute imperialism was brought to nought. [57] However one aspect of Churchill's policies towards India did survive to cause immense post-war carnage and suffering and indeed exists to this very day with the added threat of nuclear devastation. Churchill was dead opposed to wartime suggestions of increasing amity between the Muslims and Hindus, maintaining that the Muslim-Hindu antipathy was crucial to maintaining British rule in India. That ugly antipathy, the converse of the humane course advocated by wise and good men such as Rabindranath Tagore and Gandhi, led to Partition and its attendant horrors, the India-Pakistan stand-off that continues to this day and the barely suppressed fanatical communalism (in utter contradiction of the humane wisdom of Gandhi and Rabindranath Tagore) that is a growing menace in India. [58]

15.19. The re-writing of history

It is now useful to pick up the historiographical thread of our disquisition and pose the question: to what extent has Churchill's involvement in the Bengal Famine of 1943-1944 been Austenized by historians? We can apply the same sort of analysis that we have applied to the other matters raised in this book. As in the matters of Jane Austen's connections, the Bengal Famine of 1769-1770 and the Bengal Famine of 1943-1944, our survey is made much easier by the paucity of data. The sources to be considered are of various kinds including writings of Churchill himself, biographies of Churchill, histories of the Second World War and specific books dealing with the Bengal Famine that we considered in Chapter 14.

15.20. Churchill's writing and the Bengal Famine

It is utterly extraordinary that someone can dispose of 4 million people in relatively recent times without just about anybody noticing including the perpetrator himself. As Henry Tilney says in Northanger Abbey: "Does our education prepare ourselves for such atrocities? [NO] Do our laws connive at them? [YES] Could they be perpetrated in a country like this, where social and literary discourse is on such a footing, where every man is surrounded by a neighbourhood of voluntary spies, and where roads and newspapers lay everything open? [YES]. [59]

Churchill's 6-volume History of the Second World War is a great tour de force by the "man on the spot" which resulted in the award of the Nobel Prize for Literature to Churchill in 1953. Astonishingly there is not a word about the Bengal Famine in this mammoth work. The closest we get to a reference to a major disaster in India is a rather inexplicit letter from Viceroy Linlithgow to Churchill (dated August 20 1942) referring to some major problem in India that will hopefully be overcome:

"I am much encouraged by your kind message. We are confronted by an awkward situation, and I am by no means confident that we have yet seen the worst. But I have good hope that we may clear up position before either Jap or German is well placed to put direct pressure on us." We can reasonably infer that the reference is to the civil disturbances that were firmly put down in August 1942. [60]

In this context it is appropriate to recall the extraordinary assertion of Churchill (1952) in relation to the war effort:

"No great portion of the world population was so effectively protected from the horrors and perils of the World War as were the people of Hindustan. They were carried through the struggle on the shoulders of our small Island." [61]

Churchill certainly knew about the Bengal Famine as we have seen from his detailed account given to Roosevelt that contains his "700,000" estimate of the casualties. His omission of this immense event from The History of the Second World War demands some explanation beyond his contempt and hatred for Indians expressed in his notorious assertion: "I hate Indians. They are a beastly people with a beastly religion." [62] The absence of the Bengal Famine from Churchill's immense body of "public" writings surely represents a powerful statement of guilt.

Notwithstanding Churchill's dismissal of India's contribution and sacrifice, the factual record has it that 2.4 million Indians served in the war-time army, about 15,000 died in combat and scores of thousands perished as prisoners of the Japanese. [63] The reward of India was deliberately imposed, massive civilian privation of which the death of some 4 million Bengalis was the most appalling result. Of the total civilian plus military war-caused deaths in the British Empire in World War 2, over 90% were famine victims in Bengal.

It is notable in this context that about 1.4 million Jews saw active service in the Allied forces during World War 2 with deaths in combat of at least 170,000. The breakdown by country (with deaths in combat in parentheses) is as follows: USA 555,000 (11,000), Palestine 26,000 (500), Canada 16,550 (386), South Africa 10,000 (283), Australia plus New Zealand 4,222 (150), USSR 500,000 (120,000), Poland 150,000 (33,000), UK 60,000 (1,150), France 80,000, Yugoslavia 5,000, Greece 5,000 and Belgium 500. [64] Their reward was the almost total failure of the world to respond to the systematic murder of 6 million European Jews.

15.21. The record of the historians

Churchill historians: Of a sample of 25 historical works specifically dealing with Winston Churchill in only 2 is mention made of the Bengal Famine, namely in Jog (1944) and in the analysis of S. Gopal in the collection of essays edited by Blake and Louis (1994). The remaining 23 works manage to totally ignore this horrendous disaster for which Churchill must bear a substantial responsibility. [65] Given this immense capacity for Austenizing, one can understand how the war-time treason of Edward Duke of Windsor has been kept out of public perception until very recently. [66]

The record of the World War II historians: Historians of World War II or of the Twentieth Century in general do a little better than the Churchill historians when it comes to mentioning the Bengal Famine. Of a selection of 38 histories dealing specifically with World War II, only 9 mention this major event, namely Behrens (1955), Calvocoressi et al. (1972), Encyclopaedia Britannica (1961), Dear & Foot (1995), Kitchen (1990), Renouvin (1969), Romanus & Sunderland (1956), Taylor (1965) and Weinberg (1994). [67]

Histories dealing with the 20th century: Of a sample of 30 more general histories dealing with Twentieth Century history, only 8 mention the Bengal Famine, namely Cook (1991), Embree (1988), Encyclopaedia Brittanica (1961), Grun (1975), Howat & Taylor (1973), Rosenberger & Tobin (1945) [Keesing's Contemporary Archives (1943-1945)], Spear (1968), Taylor (1965) and Trager (1979)[68].

While denial of the Jewish Holocaust is an offence in both France and Germany (attracting a maximum sentence of 5 years in prison in the latter country),[69] denial (or to be more exact, non-reportage) of the World War 2 Bengal Famine is evidently de rigeur for historians in the English- speaking world. Further, the closer one gets to the heart of the matter, namely to the conduct of the Second World War and thence the conduct of Churchill, the amnesia becomes progressively more severe. Remembering that famine had not actually been declared in the Bengal Famine of 1943-1944 (ostensibly for financial and bureaucratic reasons),[70] the commentary of Edwardes (1967) is an astonishing testament to the Austenizing of this part of British history:

"Although famines continued - the last under British rule was that of Bengal in 1943 - the Famine Code remains the earliest and, despite all qualifications, one of the greatest examples of the acceptance by the state of responsibility for the welfare of those it rules."[71]

In Chapters 10 and 14 we have already seen the deficiencies of The Cambridge History of India in relation to reporting the Bengal Famines of both 1769-1770 and of 1943-1944, this deficiency being reversed in the various volumes of The New Cambridge History of India.[72] We find a similar remarkable divergence between the first and second editions of The New Cambridge Modern History Volume XII. In the first edition, The Era of Violence, Lewis (1964), in dealing with the Middle East, ignores the 1939 White Paper that slammed the door on millions of European Jews who would subsequently die in the

Holocaust. In the second edition, The Shifting Balance of World Forces 1898-1945, Kedourie (1968) pin-points the basis for this crucial change in policy. In the first edition, Phillips (1964), in dealing with India, fails to notice the Bengal Famine of 1943-44, whereas in the second edition, Spear (1968) does deal with this major event of the War and indeed of human history. [73]

From this sad catalogue of deficient historiography we will turn to the "business end" of our disquisition: the scientific prediction of environmental change and the prospect of major changes in the food/population balance of the world. The ultimate problem perceived by Malthus (1798) [74] of population outrunning food supply is likely to become a reality in the next half century as described in Chapter 16. The steadfast failure of a remorselessly Austenizing world to accept the realities of the past does not auger well for a timely and humane global response to the coming crisis that is set to consume hundreds of millions of men, women and children.

15.22. 2008 Postscript

A number of additional sources identified variously report the Bengal Famine [75] or fail to report this horrendous, man-made, British war-time atrocity. [76]

Chapter 16

Global warming and the unthinkable world of 2050

16.1. Global warming and planetary homeostasis

There has been mounting speculation in the last century - and particularly in recent decades - about global warming due to increasing atmospheric carbon dioxide and other "greenhouse" gases due to a combination of industrial activity, fuel burning by internal combustion engines, deforestation and livestock agriculture. The Swedish physical chemist S. Arrhenius (of thermodynamic Arrhenius Plot fame) suggested one hundred years ago that a doubling of atmospheric carbon dioxide (CO_2) would lead to an increase of average global temperature of about 5^0 C (degrees Celsius). [1] The current consensus appears to be that a doubling of atmospheric CO_2 in the absence of other mitigating factors will cause an increase of about 3^0 C in mean global temperature. It is now recognized that other gases contribute to atmospheric warming through absorption of solar radiation, including methane (CH_4) (produced by rotting living matter and through the digestion of vegetable matter by cattle and termites), nitrous oxide (N_2O) (contributed to significantly by agricultural application of man-made nitrogenous fertilizers) and chlorofluorocarbons (CFCs) (refrigerant and spray-can gases made notorious through their contribution to the depletion of the stratospheric, UV-absorbing ozone layer). [2]

The wholesale destruction of the world's forests (most notably those of Africa, the Amazon basin and of South East Asia) contributes to atmospheric CO_2 through the burning of timber and through the loss of photosynthetic capacity. [3] Photosynthesis by trees involves the reductive immobilizing of CO_2 (as cellulose and related polysaccharides that constitute the bulk of timber). This process involves trapping solar radiation (solar energy) for the "photolysis" of water (H_2O) to produce O_2 (oxygen) and the "hydrogenating" or "reducing" power required for "fixing" of CO_2 into the monosaccharide monomers (mainly glucose) that eventually polymerize into polysaccharides such as starch and cellulose. The process of combustion of trees involves the "oxidative" reverse of this process - O_2 reacts with cellulose to generate CO_2 and H_2O and energy in the form of heat and light. [4]

It should be noted that there are negative feedbacks applying to this situation. Thus increased atmospheric CO_2, atmospheric temperature (within limits) and water availability (through increased precipitation in particular regions) will result in increased rates of photosynthesis and hence CO_2 removal.[5] The oceans represent a CO_2-dissolving reservoir that also represent a major locus for algal photosynthesis. [6] Desertification and clearing for agriculture increase the amount of atmospheric dust and aerosols that are involved in global cooling through the reflection of solar radiation. The SO_2 (sulphur dioxide) produced through the burning of the fossil fuels (coal and oil, the products of past photosynthesis) is oxidized further to sulphuric acid (H_2SO_4) and this in turn forms light-scattering aerosols of "non-sea salt sulphate" (n.s.s. SO_4^{2-}). Indeed it has been estimated that man-made (anthropogenic) sulphate aerosols make a major contribution to global cooling. In addition to "anthropogenic" atmospheric components contributing to atmospheric temperature balances, we must include the contribution of volcanoes (dust and sulphur dioxide-derived aerosols that reflect solar radiation) [7] and dust generated by wind and through the bombardment of the earth by extraterrestrial material. About 10,000 tons of comet and meteoritic material is captured by the earth per annum and it has been concluded that variations in the amount of this extraterrestrial "rain" of dust-generating material may have driven glaciation cycles through effects on global cooling. [8] Finally the albedo (light reflecting capacity) of the earth's surface and of clouds is of importance. A forest will absorb solar radiation but clouds and snow-fields will substantially reflect solar radiation. [9]

In all of this we can see the warming and cooling effects of different environmental components and the elements of negative feedback. Thus we can see that burning of forests and of fossil fuels will generate CO_2 which will warm the atmosphere, cause more water evaporation (and hence cooling cloud cover) and increase rates of photosynthesis, which will tend to decrease atmospheric CO_2. It is such notions of negative feedback that are explicit in Lovelock's Gaia model of the world - a world in which such homeostatic (or "stasis"-maintaining) mechanisms are so effective and inter-locked that the whole "system" begins to have the superficial attributes of an "organism". The nicest example of such a homeostatic system involves a "Daiseyworld" planet covered by flowering plants with flowers that could be white, gray or black. If, for example, the flowers were all white, the resultant high albedo would cause a substantial reflection of solar radiation and a cooling of the planet. Mutant black-flowered plants are able to absorb more solar radiation, have a "selective advantage" over the white-flowered plants and accordingly multiply at their expense. Accordingly the blackening planet warms up. However there are limits to the efficacy of such biological or indeed non-biological homeostatic mechanisms. [10]

Our solar system provides us with examples of non-homeostatic progressions. Mars, being more distant from the Sun than the Earth and without (as far as we know) having had an ameliorating, homeostatic, biological component, descended into a deep freeze. Venus, closer to the Sun, became the victim of a run-away "greenhouse" effect. [11] The Earth, like the baby bear's soup, was neither too hot nor too cold but became "just right" through a combination of biological and non-biological homeostatic processes. The real concern we have is that the planet is becoming more and more drastically "simplified" in the service of an impossibly expanding human population and homeostatic mechanisms vital for our survival are being over-ridden through the consequences of our massive interventions. [12]

Of course we can surely all grasp the obvious point that nearly everyone is apparently missing - that there is a limit to how much energy can be released at the earth's surface in the course of our activities without rendering life on earth impossible for all but thermophilic micro-organisms. The dreams of "inexhaustible energy" for terrestrial mankind from nuclear fission or nuclear fusion are hollow dreams indeed - except for those who would go out into the universe, "to go where no man has ever gone before". For the purposes of argument, in relation to biodiversity, quality of life and global energy output we have essentially reached the limits of growth. The vast majority of mankind, who by their actions could be taken to think otherwise, are remorselessly pushing towards the ultimate blasphemy of terracide. [13]

16.2. Global warming - is it happening?

Naive inspection of a plot of global temperature change as a function of time from 1880 to the present reveals 3 apparent phases: a steady rise of about 0.4^0 C over the period 1880 to 1930, a plateau from 1930 to 1970 and a resumption of a steady but sharper steady rise of about 0.5^0 C over the period 1970 to 1990. [14] However the temperature change fluctuations are such that alternative interpretations can be put on the data. Thus, rather than concluding that global temperature is now increasing at a rate of about 0.25^0 C per decade, we could infer from the data that there is merely an underlying trend (described by a "line of best fit" through the data) of only 0.5^0 C per 100 years (i.e. 0.25^0 C per 5 decades). This example of 2 quite different interpretations of the same data illustrates well the type of considerations that have made scientists very cautious in interpreting apparent trends in this area. However the "warming" trend has continued through the 1990s and as outlined below there is now a strong scientific consensus that global warming is a reality. [15] This consensus has now been reflected in the recent global political decision at Kyoto to make a start at constraining global warming through initial constraints on CO_2 emission.

The Working Group 1 of the Intergovernmental Panel on Climate Change (IPCC) concluded in a report issued in late 1995 that "the balance of evidence suggests that there is a discernible human influence on global climate". This was reported in the top scientific (and accordingly necessarily conservative) journal Science under the headline "It's official: first glimmer of greenhouse warming seen" in the News section. [16] The equally reputable British scientific journal Nature reported this in its News section under the banner "Climate panel confirms human role in warming, fights off oil states". [17]A key element of this synthesis of available data was the recognition that aerosols were making a major negative contribution to global warming. These aerosol contributions were coming from volcanic activity (notably from the Philippino Mount Pinatubo eruption of June 1991), dust and smoke from agricultural practices and SO_2-derived sulphuric acid aerosols from industrial activity. Consideration of a combination of aerosol cooling contributions and greenhouse gas warming contributions yielded more accurate models. [18]

The IPCC Report concluded that the last few years had been the warmest since the mid-nineteenth century, that global mean temperature had increased by between 0.3 and 0.6^0 C and that sea levels had risen by 10 - 25 cm (centimeters) in the last century. The IPCC predicted a further increase in global temperature by about 1^0 C over the next century with a parallel increase in sea level of about 15 cm accompanying an increase of atmospheric CO_2 from the current 330 ppm (parts per million) to about 500 ppm. [19]

Evidence of global warming of a more arguable but nevertheless more dramatic kind has come from the disappearing glacial remnants in the highlands of New Guinea. These tropical glaciers have declined dramatically in size over recent decades [20], and similar phenomena have been observed in Antarctica in relation to ice-shelf shrinkage. Atmospheric warming has occurred in Antarctica as determined from inspection of long-term meteorological records kept over half a century. This warming has been associated with the retreat of some ice-shelves that fringe the coast of Antarctica but some ice-shelves have not been so clearly affected. This has been interpreted as indicating that there are sharp temperature limits to the viability of ice-shelves and that global warming in conjunction with other factors has led to a southerly movement of the zone of instability and the consequent very dramatic declines of some of these geographical structures. Thus representations of the Wordie Ice Shelf from 1936 to 1992 show that this huge floating ice geographic structure diminished by about half in 50 years and then diminished by half again in the subsequent 5 years. Nevertheless the authors of this detailed study were properly cautious in their attribution of the causes of this phenomenon. [21]

Evidence of changes that may be linked to global warming has also come from damage to life in Canadian lakes that is reflected in a decreased amount of "dissolved organic carbon". Climate warming, lake acidification (from industrial SO_2) and increasing exposure of lake organisms to "UV B" (ultraviolet B) radiation correlate with a decline of dissolved organic carbon content in the Canadian lakes studied. The researchers concluded that warming and acidification could be more effective in enhancing aquatic life exposure to UV radiation than depletion of the protective stratospheric "ozone layer". [22]

Evidence of a more anecdotal kind comes from the meteorologist Harold Bernard who in his dramatic book Global Warming Unchecked gives one a feel for a pattern of drought, flood and hurricane in the United States this century. He perceives a pattern of a drought every 22 years that correlates with a cycle of increased sun-spot activity every 11 years, severe drought occurring immediately after a prior succession of 2 peaks of enhanced sun-spot activity. He believes that this climatic cycle will simply be superimposed upon a background of increasing temperature and with consequently magnified effects. Thus if the effects of global warming are normally relatively imperceptible (or even blanketed by the global cooling effects of volcanic eruptions such as those of Mount St Helens or

Pinatubo), the effects will be most apparent to people (as well as to monitoring machines) in drought years. These effects will be complicated by possible changes to the Northern atmospheric jet-stream component of the Westerlies that heavily determines patterns of cooler/wetter or warmer/drier climate in particular parts of North America, Europe and North and Central Asia. Thus he suggests that the1930s experience of elevated temperature and superdrought in the Mid-West and horrendous hurricanes (such as the Florida Labor Day Hurricane of 1935 and the New England "Long Island Express" Hurricane of 1938) will provide a good model for what he expects to happen in the mid-1990s. [23]

1995 saw an extremely hot summer in the United States that actually killed people at risk (notably poor and old people) in big American cities such as Chicago and New York. However the assertion that "1995 was the warmest year" on record has been criticized because the global mean temperature in 1995 was a statistically insignificant mere 0.04^0 C above that in 1990. [24] Nevertheless in 1996 drought and forest fires affected the United States and the high incidence of hurricanes was reported to have created a problem for those charged with naming them on an alphabetically-ordered Christian name basis.

While there is a scientific consensus about the reality of global warming there is a mixed political response. Thus the recent Berlin Climate Change Conference failed to agree on any agreed national or global targets for greenhouse gas emission. The Conference concluded by adopting a generalized agreement to continuing to assess the situation. [25] However major dangers from this passivity are that entrenched interests may become even better entrenched and that future collective action may be vetoed by countries with economies that are heavily dependent on activities associated with greenhouse gas emission. Thus Australia, while having among the world's best per capita prospects for solar energy conservation, is per capita one of the world's major greenhouse gas emitters through coal production and utilization. Not surprisingly there is a low-key, bipartisan consensus in Australia from both the ostensibly "labour"- and "business"-oriented sides of politics against doing anything substantial at present in relation to global warming. Saudi Arabia and Kuwait are major oil producers and are very much opposed in practice to adoption of concrete steps to limit greenhouse gas emission, as is Australia, a major coal exporter and consumer. [26] It has been argued that imposition of tough and rigid timetables and targets may not be the way to go initially and that it would be better to have an informed, sensibly negotiated process taking special circumstances into account. One now senses a growing movement towards effective action by both the EEC (EU) and the US [27], and indeed the 1997 Kyoto world conference has finally decided on some limits to CO_2 emission (with a surprising and exceptional status granted to energy-exporting Australia).

One prospect that one hopes should spur urgent international action on the matter is that climate change may on occasion occur in a precipitate fashion as opposed to developing in a gradual fashion that would allow plenty of time for social and industrial response. Recent discoveries have raised serious concerns in this respect. Thus temperature records from Greenland ice cores show marked changes in sea surface temperature occurring over a decade rather than over centuries or millennia. The general possibility of such short-term changes has awful implications for an increasingly crowded world. In this specific instance these dramatic and relatively rapid temperature changes were likely to have been brought about by changes to the amount of fresh water entering the North Atlantic Ocean, a process likely to be affected by global warming. [28]

16.3. The coming holocaust

Accepting the conservative assessment of the IPCC Report, what are the possible consequences of global warming for the world and, more specifically, for third world regions such as West Bengal and Bangladesh? The major effects fall into 4 inter-connected categories relating to climate change and hurricanes, sea level rises, agricultural productivity changes and health. Of course the nature and magnitude of the consequences to be considered will depend upon the size of the actual global warming achieved by international profligacy. We will briefly consider these areas in turn.

Climate changes will involve a global background of elevated temperature that will be much greater in particular regions and at particular times of year. Changes to the disposition of prevailing winds will cool certain regions and greatly elevate the average temperature of others. The scenario advanced by Bernard (1993) predicts super-hurricanes for tropical regions such as the Bay of Bengal and the Gulf of Mexico. These coming events will have a much more energy-rich environment to feed upon and their victims will now regularly experience extraordinarily destructive events that they would previously have expected to encounter only once in their life-times. Thus Bangladesh experienced a major cyclonic disaster in 1970 that killed about 300,000 people in coastal regions. In 1991 a similar event claimed 140,000 lives in Bangladesh. The hurricanes of a much hotter world will be much more likely to be extraordinarily destructive super-hurricanes of this kind and the destructiveness of these events will be seriously compounded by increases in population density and by the effects of sea-level rises brought about through global warming.[29]

All kinds of estimates have been made about the sorts of sea-level rises to be expected next century. However even modest estimates become very significant in relation to storm-surges that are associated with hurricanes. The hurricane essentially forces up a broad hump of water that translates into a tidal wave tens of feet high that is typically responsible for most of the deaths associated with hurricanes in coastal regions. The relatively shallow northern reaches of the Bay of Bengal are very susceptible to this problem. About 15 million people live on coastal chars, islands built up from the silt brought down from their catchments by the Ganges and the Brahmaputra. After the 1970 hurricane disaster concrete refuges were constructed but the 1991 disaster showed the limited utility of those installed. Even modest sea-level rises will seriously compound the storm-surge potential of the super-hurricanes of a century hence. [30]

The UN IPCC Working Group 1 developed a series of pathways for achieving stabilization of atmospheric CO_2 at various levels over the next few centuries. These pathways involve anthropogenic CO_2 emission peaking next century at various times. Thus for a pathway resulting in an approximate doubling of atmospheric CO_2 the emission maximum occurs in the middle to late 21st Century (depending upon the particular model employed). While the average global temperature increase stabilizes in these conditions at about 2° C by the early 22nd Century, the sea-level continues to steadily creep up century after century, up about 40 cm by 2100, about 80 cm by 2200 and 90 cm by 2300. We could regard these estimates as conservative given the typical tardiness of international responsiveness. Nevertheless these sorts of sea level rises become highly significant in terms of inundation of low-lying delta lands and salination of river-derived fresh water supplies in high-tide and storm-surge conditions. [31] What happens to delta communities in situations in which the world is insufficiently resolute or timely in its response? Indeed, as discussed later, it is quite likely that the considerable benefits that global warming (or its genesis) will have for some societies will in an all too familiar fashion act as a compelling brake upon requisite drastic international action.

In the case of low-lying island countries such as the Maldives (in the Indian Ocean) and the Marshall Islands (in the Pacific Ocean), a 1 metre sea-level rise would see these countries repeatedly devastated by hurricane-driven storm-surges. With a 2 metre sea-level rise these island communities would simply disappear. In the case of Bangladesh a 2 metre rise would inundate the rich coastal 20% of the country that supports 10% of the population. By the middle of the 21st century this would mean the displacement of some 20 million people. In the case of Egypt this scenario would similarly flood the most highly productive agricultural land. This would be the lot of other delta and coastal communities throughout the world including the US Gulf states, Holland, Indonesia and the river delta regions of Africa, South America, Thailand, Vietnam and China. While Australia is behaving in a troglodytic fashion in relation to greenhouse gas emission control, it is actually under some threat because most of the population is confined to major coastal cities. [32]

Temperature rise and CO_2 concentration rise will have different effects in different regions of the world. In short there will be winners and losers and the nature of the winners (primarily affluent and powerful "First World" countries) leads to a cynical conclusion that humane and equitable international responses to the potential threat of the events outlined above will be severely delayed and circumscribed. Already people are arguing for a global "market forces" approach to this new "problem". According to this analysis the severely affected poor countries will be unable to "pay" for the economic losses to rich countries occasioned by requisite mitigation of global warming. [33]

It is hard for people in liberal democracies to accept that quintessential Nazism was not extirpated in the Battle for Berlin in 1945 but lives on alive and well in the board rooms of our corporations and the faculty common-rooms of our universities. "Truth" and reason exercised in relation to economic productivity and profit will prevail over "emotional" sentiment for the losers in an ostensibly efficient "market forces" world. Of course all of this begs the indisputable reality from the perspective of a biological scientist such as myself: that the Bengali peasant subsisting on a coastal char is easily one of the most efficient human users of the resources of the biosphere.

Cereal grain production projections have been made by Rosenzweig and Parry (1996) based upon a 2060 scenario in which CO_2 levels have approximately doubled to about 600 ppm, average global temperature has increased by about 4^0 C and average precipitation has increased by about 11% as predicted independently and in reasonable agreement by 3 different groups namely the NASA Goddard Institute for Space Studies (GISS), the Geophysical Fluid Dynamics Laboratory (GFDL) and the United Kingdom Meteorological Office (UKMO). Rosenzweig (from Columbia University, New York) and Parry (from the Environmental Change Unit, Oxford University) employed crop growth models in a very extensive international collaboration to predict crop yields in various countries and geographic regions with different versions of the above climate change scenario. Climate scenarios were predicted from 3 "general circulation models" (GCMs) for a doubling of atmospheric CO_2 as developed by the 3 groups listed above. The crop yield modelling took advantage of other such modelling studies and was based on the predicted temperature and precipitation effects from the 3 climate modelling groups. Global pictures of potential change in grain yield were developed employing each of the 3 climate change models and with 4 further sets of assumptions: (a) with the physiological effect of only the current CO_2 level of 330 ppm on crop photosynthesis and water retention through leaf "stomata" opening incorporated; (b) as for (a) but with the physiological effect of 550 ppm CO_2 incorporated; (c) as for (b) together with minimal adaptations of farmers to the changing circumstances; and (d) as for (b) but with national adaptations included such as major investment in irrigation works. We receive "the good news and the bad news".

The bad news is that global warming together with the positive effects of elevated CO_2 on crop yields is predicted to cause a decline in grain yields in tropical and sub-tropical regions of South America, Africa and Asia. These are precisely the regions that are currently struggling to maintain minimal human subsistence in the face of high population growth rates and barely sufficient food production. The ratio of available food/population will be drastically reduced in the "2 times CO_2" world of the 2060s. On the other hand for Chinese, Japanese and Europeans the news is good - and this in itself may make things much worse for the "Third World" through a predicted disinclination of beneficiaries of the "developed" world to do anything timely and substantial about global warming. The predicted picture is particularly good for Canada and China in the Northern Hemisphere and Australia in the Southern Hemisphere in all 3 climate models and with direct CO_2 effects and sensible human adaptations incorporated. If we look at the "best" scenario (GISS climate model with all extras) temperate South America, the United States, Europe and the CIS also have an increased grain yield. However the tropical and sub-tropical regions of South America, Africa and Asia suffer a decrease in grain yield in all situations examined. [34]

Ultimately whether the world acts in an adequate and timely fashion about global warming will be the outcome of a complex function of economic power and self-interest. The current indications are that global warming will greatly increase disparities in agricultural production between the developing world and the developed world. The Kyoto "first steps" aside, a worry persists that the developed world countries will be doubly disinclined initially to do anything too drastic about it. They have complex, high energy-utilization economies strictly dependent on the very industrial activity that is producing global warming and are also set to benefit enormously in an absolute (and certainly in a relative sense) in relation to global warming-induced increases in agricultural production.

16.4. Global warming and human health

Global warming-induced health problems are currently being discussed in terms of the spread of tropical diseases such as malaria, dengue fever and cholera to temperate zones through the increasing effective geographic range of organisms that harbour these diseases or which otherwise act as vectors. Thus global warming has created concerns about mosquito-borne malaria extending northwards in North America, Europe, China and the CIS. This is a particular concern in Australia which has a substantial if relatively unpopulated northern tropical region. The malarial problem is complicated through the development of resistance in malarial populations against major anti-malarials such as chloroquine, a process that was very likely to have been spurred on by use of such anti-malarials during the massive, long-term American involvement in Vietnam. However a major benefit for tropical third world countries in relation to malaria is the increasing likelihood of anti-malarial vaccines and new chemotherapeutic agents. The latter have little to commend themselves at present to major drug companies as prospects for major research investment since there would be little profit to be made from this source from the impoverished, malaria-infested Third World. However global warming and the predicted spread of malaria to the rich "white folks" of formerly temperate zones will make anti-malarial chemotherapeutics increasingly attractive to pharmaceutical industry. That in turn may produce one of the rare benefits of global warming for the tropical Third World.

Global warming dangers for the temperate zones are illustrated by health effects of the El Nino/Southern Oscillation (ENSO) phenomenon that affects the central and southern Pacific rim countries. In one phase of the ENSO phenomenon warm water moves from the western Pacific to the central and eastern Pacific. This influx of warm water brings plankton blooms that can harbour cholera bacteria (Vibrio cholerae) and this indeed has been connected with the major cholera epidemic in Central and South America in 1990-1991. The increasing temperatures and precipitation on the west coast of the Americas in this cycle of the ENSO phenomenon has the potential to promote disease vectors such as ticks, mosquitoes and rodents. The boost in the population of the deer-mouse due to such climatic changes led to enhanced probabilities of human contact and the consequent outbreak of mouse-borne Hantavirus pulmonary syndrome in South-Western United States in 1993. [35]

The major medical problems associated with global warming will occur in the impoverished Third World and will directly relate to susceptibility to disease of people weakened by starvation. This susceptibility will be dramatically intensified in regions currently suffering epidemics of HIV infection (Africa and Thailand) and regions about to experience an escalation of HIV infection (India). We have already seen that while explicit starvation was the major killer in the Bengal Famine in 1943, in 1944 the major famine-induced mortality was due to cholera and malaria.

16.5. The impact of the population explosion

The mathematical inevitability perceived by Malthus over 2 centuries ago [36] is now seen to be a major threat to the world as we know it. [37] Past events such as the Irish Famine have been taken as early warnings of requisite food/population inequalities and we have seen the obscene opinion of Charles Trevelyan that the only solution is starvation-induced population correction. [38] We have seen in Chapters 10, 13, 14 and 15 that some famine events in the past have been deleted from "history" and rationalized as "acts of God" whereas the reality has been that enslaved people forced to the edge of survival and deprived of adequate exchange means to obtain food in emergency have simply been sentenced to death by their rulers. [39] These singularities of the past that have been swept aside from general perception must be restored to global consciousness to the same extent as the "deliberate" mass murder of Cambodians by the Khmer Rouge or of the Jews and Gypsies by the Nazis. The "passive" starvation of millions of helpless subjects is surely per se a far worse way of killing people than the "active", quick , "industrial" shooting or gassing of victims but is paradoxically regarded somehow as "acceptable", as being an "act of God" rather than down to economic hegemony.

The world is facing a prospect of a massive gap between available food and population demands in the coming century. Even with a radical change in global attitude to the economic realities (and specifically, the inequalities) of famine, there will be a crisis of moral responsiveness in the face of a situation well beyond normal human experience and conception. We have seen that agricultural projections for the tropical Third World are bleak, this problem being compounded by desertification, storm inundation, salination, deforestation, loss of sustainable fish stocks and continuing soil degradation. While population growth in the prosperous parts of the world has declined markedly, population growth in the tropical Third World of Latin America, Africa and Asia remains out of control in relation to biological sustainability. This has serious consequences for the environment, biological diversity, sustainable agriculture and socio-economic decency. [40]

The current world population is about 6 billion (6.6 billion in 2008) and there are various projections of where we are going. [41] Thus Porrit (1991) estimated a population of 7.5 billion by 2100 if the "replacement" 2-child average family were achieved by 2010 and 11 billion or 14.2 billion if this was attained by 2035 or 2065, respectively. [42] We can already see the impact of circa 6 billion people on the planet in terms of diminution of marine and forest resources, biodiversity and water quality, ozone layer depletion and global warming. We are actually already approaching one kind of limit - at a global population of about 6 billion people we are already consuming about 40% of land-based photosynthetic production. [43] There is a large literature dealing with the current departure from the homeostasis of a sustainable global biological system and suggestions of how this can be addressed. [44] However whatever solutions that are found for a given global population at a particular average standard of living will be eroded by increases in population and per capita consumption and departures from a sustainable equilibrium through environmental degradation. Thus China has instituted the "one child policy" and the birth rate is further constrained by economic advance and improved education, health and life expectancy. However economic advance in China is dangerously and irreversibly consuming what Bochuan (1991) has called "environmental capital". [45] A converse situation occurs in Bangladesh where the population is still increasing catastrophically but per capita consumption is highly constrained. [46] An intermediate situation occurs in the Indian State of Kerala where there is a much higher female literacy than in the rest of India coupled with better economic independence and security, a lower infant mortality and a better expectation of child survival - all of these factors contributing to a lowered birth-rate, albeit in a very poor part of the country. [47]

The solutions to the global crisis will have to be put in place in the next decade or so to prevent catastrophe. In the words of Gordon & Suzuki (1990):

"There has never been a bigger crisis than the one we now face. And we are the last generation that can pull us out of it. We must act because this is the only home we have. It is a matter of survival" [48]

We are all in this together in the sense of a common atmosphere, ocean and global economy. It is clear that the First World countries consume vastly more per capita than the Third World countries and are having an increasingly negative impact on the impoverished nations through crushing debt impositions, economic control, environmental degradation and resource depletion. Industrial growth and resultant global warming is a reflection of this inequitable occupancy and exploitation of the planet and will differentially impact upon the impoverished tropical Third World countries.

More general education and a modest increase in economic security would have a very substantial ameliorating effect on the global impact of Third World countries. [49] However unless there is a profound change in global ethos, it is likely that the greed of the First World resource consumers will deny them such relief and indeed compound their problems by imposing the damaging consequences of global warming upon the Third World. [50] Ben Elton (1990) has provided a powerful metaphor for this tightening situation in his play Gasping in which the Third World huddle black and blue having been forced to sell the very oxygen they breathe to the Corporation. However the anti-hero eventually becomes a victim of the circumstances he has created and of his incorrect perceptions. [51]

Our final Chapter considers the moral problem of effective response to increasing environmental degradation, loss of biodiversity, declining food production [52] and burgeoning human population. [53] We have already seen how conquered Bengal was rapidly transformed from a rich, prosperous, sophisticated and sustainable society into an impoverished, enslaved "human farm". That state, punctuated by the most appalling famines, persisted for 2 centuries, ignored by the world. We have seen how the massive Bengal holocausts of 1769-1770 and of 1943-1945 have been effectively deleted from history. It is apparent that Bengal, and indeed the tropical Third World in general, is facing a major catastrophe in the next century. It has been the purpose of this book to inform, so that a world apprised of past "forgotten" holocausts may be more likely to effectively respond to the looming holocaust of the 21st century. The last Chapter adopts an empirical approach to assessing this likelihood. We will consider the 2 centuries of genocide, ecocide and environmental degradation since the initial British invasion of Australia and assess the responsiveness of this presently prosperous, educated and liberal society to social decency imperatives and the crisis of biological sustainability.

16.6. 2008 Postscript

My dire 1998 predictions have been exceeded by 2008 realities. In 2007 the IPCC published its Fourth Assessment Report based on an international consensus of thousands of climate scientists but with a literature cut-off date of about 2005. [54] The dire findings of the latest IPCC Report in relation to threats to agricultural productivity, natural resources and sustainability have been rapidly supplanted by findings that ice is melting much faster than predicted in the Arctic, the Antarctic, Greenland and the Siberian and North American tundra. The atmospheric carbon dioxide (CO_2) concentration is now 385 parts per million (ppm) by volume and increasing at about 2.5 ppm per year but "positive feedback" can increase this rate (e.g. the solar radiation-reflecting white ice to radiation-absorbing black water "albedo flip"; release of the greenhouse gases methane and CO_2 from melting tundra;

melt water lubrication of glacier movement to the sea; and loss of CO_2 sequestration by phytoplankton, forests and storm-stirred oceans). [55] Above about 450 ppm CO_2 (in 26 years' time at current rates) the world's coral reefs – including Australia's Great Barrier Reef – will start dying because of ocean acidification and ocean warming. [56] At about 500 ppm (in about 115 years' time at current rates) there is huge damage to the ocean phytoplankton system (crucial for ocean food chains and for global temperature homeostasis (balance) by sequestering CO_2 and for light-reflecting cloud formation through production of cloud-seeding dimethylsulphide) and the Greenland ice sheet melts with huge attendant circa 7 meter sea level rise. [57] At the current 385 ppm atmospheric CO_2 concentration we have already passed a "tipping point" for the complete loss of Arctic summer sea ice that may be completely gone within a decade with huge implications for polar warming, Greenland and West Antarctic ice sheet melting, tundra melting and sea level rise. [58] At current levels of human impact (e.g. 0.8^0C above pre-industrial, current 385 ppm CO_2) we already have species extinction rates that are 100-1,000 times greater than that of the fossil record. [59] Atmospheric CO_2 pollution is increasing rapidly at an annual rate of 3.2% increase per annum (2000-2005) as compared to 0.8% (1990-1999), corresponding to the very worst of the various scenarios envisaged by the IPCC i.e. the scenario of unaddressed carbon pollution. [60] Top US climate scientist Dr James Hansen (Head, NASA Goddard Institute for Space Studies, GISS) says we've gone too far: "The evidence indicates we've aimed too high -- that the safe upper limit for atmospheric CO_2 is no more than 350 ppm"; he wants a "negative CO_2 emissions" policy of cessation of CO_2 pollution and reducing atmospheric CO_2 pollution (e.g. by use of renewable and geothermal energy, re-afforestation, and returning biochar carbon to soils). [61] However the world is already facing a global food price crisis [62] driven by global warming effects (drought), globalized markets (with big demand from India and China), oil price rises, grain use for meat production and legislatively-mandated US, UK and EU food to biofuel diversion (notwithstanding the reality that crop-based biofuel is highly CO_2 polluting). [63] The global food price crisis threatens "billions" (UK Chief Scientist Professor John Beddington FRS) [64] and unaddressed climate change will kill over 6 billion people this century (Professor James Lovelock FRS). [65] As predicted in 1998 the US and Australia are still top CO_2 polluters and continue to sabotage global action against greenhouse gas pollution and man-made global warming. [66]

Chapter 17

Antipodean epilogue - the moral dimension of the Lucky Country and the world

"I am afraid," replied Elinor, "that the pleasantness of an employment does not always evince its propriety." [Elinor]

"On the contrary, nothing can be stronger proof of it, Elinor; for if there had been any real impropriety in what I did, I should have been sensible of it at the time, for we always know when we are acting wrong, and with such a conviction I could have had no pleasure." [Marianne]

- Elinor and Marianne discussing the Marianne's indiscreet outing with Mr. Willoughby in Sense and Sensibility (1811)[1]

"Elinor agreed to it all, for she did not think he deserved the compliment of rational opposition."

- Elinor putting up with Robert Ferrars' conversation in Sense and Sensibility (1811) [2]

"We have learned nothing and we have conserved nothing compared to what we might have had. Unhindered we let the most ignorant settler, and the most brutal stockman, shoot, starve, burn, poison, break and destroy the most living record of an ancient world that the later centuries have known ... We killed the tellers, and the genealogies died with them."

- Dame Mary Gilmore on the destruction of Australian aboriginal society and culture [3]

"Man has lost the capacity to foresee and to forestall. He will end by destroying the earth."

- Dr. Albert Schweitzer, quoted by Rachel Carson (1962) [4]

17.1. Will Australia and the World respond sufficiently to the existential climate crisis?

The great Dr. Albert Schweitzer's pessimistic view quoted above is the central arguable proposition of this final chapter. How can we approach the likelihood of this outcome? How can we put all of humanity on the psychiatrist's couch? We have already seen how historians can resolutely ignore the most massive human disasters and how humanity in general has an immense capacity for moral and intellectual unresponsiveness. In this final chapter I will approach the problem empirically by adducing the example of my own country, Australia.

Australia has been called the Lucky Country [5] because of a variety of historical, geographic, resource, strategic, institutional and social blessings. In short, the Lucky Country is a well-endowed democracy with a well-educated, prosperous and liberal population cognizant of the dark shadows of its past and the problems of the future. If such an "ideal" First World, high technology society is presently unable or unwilling to come to grips with its substantial contribution to global degradation and with the appalling human disaster that is the continuing lot of its own very small residual aboriginal population, will such a society be able to respond adequately to the approach of the global Bergen-Belsen that may be a mere half century away? And if such a resource-rich society is unable to respond in a proper and timely fashion, how then will the world respond? Let us now briefly explore the origins and social evolution of the Lucky Country. In doing so we must consider past attitudes of "White Australia" to non-Europeans, and to "black" people in particular, from the Jane Austen era of settlement to the present. The degree of retention of racist attitudes will determine the extent to which "lifeboat" Australia and other prosperous countries contribute to humane solutions for the potential catastrophe that is set to devastate the Third World. We have seen that 2 centuries of the British colonial holocaust has been largely deleted from generally accessible history and there is a need for a major change in perception if the world is to withdraw from the edge of the abyss.

17.2. Pre-invasion Australia

The first aboriginal people came to Australia some 60,000 years ago. Waves of expansion by different human cultures are inferred from the discovery and dating of artefacts and skeletal remains throughout the continent. The aboriginal people had a major effect on the biogeography of the continent through the use of fire to regenerate rangelands. Dramatic consequences of this impact were extensive rangelands and an extensive fire-compatible flora. [6] Further consequences of aboriginal activity included the disappearance of certain impressive megafauna such as the diprotodon, the giant cow-sized version of the contemporary herbivorous wombat, and giant versions of the present-day flightless bird, the emu.

While the aboriginal tribes were scattered over a whole continent of 8 million square kilometers and were also separated linguistically by the existence of some hundreds of different languages, there was an extensive, continental communication involving trade that could ultimately reach between tribes located respectively on the Gulf of Carpentaria in the North and those on the shores of the Great Southern Ocean and indeed between northern Australian tribes and islands to the north. [7] The linguistic differences between neighbouring tribes could be overcome by exchanges of particular children who became "interpreters". [8] An extreme case of isolation was that of the Tasmanian aborigines who were cut off from the Mainland by the rising of the sea occasioned by the end of the last major Ice Age about 15,000 years ago. [9]

The aboriginal societies did not have large scale agriculture (because of the absence of suitable indigenous plants) but evolved very sophisticated population/food resource management policies that enabled sustainable use and replenishment of natural resources. In this sense the Australian aborigines had found an exquisite solution to the major continuing problem of sustainable longterm human existence thousands of years ago. Men hunted game such as kangaroos, wallabies, possums, emus, flying birds, fish, snakes and goannas. Various weapons were developed to assist this process such as specialized spears, throwing sticks and, of course, the celebrated boomerang that was aerodynamically perfected by particular tribes. Women gathered grubs, and plant material such as fruit, leaves, tubers and seeds. [10]

An extraordinary aspect of this continental culture was the sophistication with which the aborigines assured sustainability of natural resources. Extensive fish traps were set up on rivers to ensure retention of fish breeding stock. Reserves were set aside as sanctuaries for animal resources to permit replenishment of the countryside with breeding stock after drought or to permit food for periodic large tribal gatherings. Seeds were planted during food gathering and consumption as a matter of course to ensure replenishment of plant resources. [11] Gilmore (1934, 1935) describes her own experiences with aborigines as a child in the late 19th century in inland South Eastern Australia and her wonder at the fish traps (fish-balks), the planting of fire-damaged seeds, the seeding of new areas after drought with possums and sophisticated medicine including the use of medicinal plants. [12]

The aborigines had a rich and sophisticated oral culture, art, spiritual life and systems of belief and social ritual. Their oral traditions connected them with the deep past of their origins (the Dreamtime), rituals provided "rites of passage" through birth, puberty, marriage and death, corroborees or tribal ceremonial gatherings bound the members of their society and male- and female-specific mysteries and rituals were supervised by the elders, the transmitters of ancient traditions. The stylistically varied rock painting, rock and wood carving and bark painting of these people attest to rich artistic insights and cultural traditions. [13]

Dame Mary Gilmore (1934, 1935) (of Highland Scottish origins) has provided remarkable accounts of aboriginal culture seen from the perspective of a young settler girl - their ability to count objects (notably large numbers of animals or stars) with great accuracy and speed employing a five-based number system (thus stockmen would ask aborigines and indeed young Mary Gilmore precisely how many animals they had in a mob of hundreds); the handling of complex multivariable patterns (as in tracking, an infant being trained to find a discarded twig or in scores of different "cat's cradle" hand-worked string games); the remarkable astronomical observations that enabled them to know the precise time of year and to be able to predict dawn and sunset accurately; and their skill in relation to herbal medicine and the importance of aboriginal women for the medical problems of settler women, especially in relation to wounds and child-birth. [Puerperal fever was unknown to aboriginal women of Mary Gilmore's acquaintance in the 19th century. They would be taken by other women for childbirth well away from the infection sources of their encampment to a specially prepared hut having a floor of carefully-placed leaves elaborating antiseptic oils. My grandfather (a Semmelweiss Medal awardee in 1917) recounts the acute distress of Ignaz Semmelweiss at the postpartum death of women in the best hospitals of Vienna and his eventual discovery that the best hospitals had the best surgeons and hence the greatest chance for infection of such women and their consequent death from puerperal fever. Aborigines used particular plants that burned with a hot blue flame for the successful cauterising of wounds. At a time when major wounds and childbirth were fraught with danger in the best hospitals of Europe, "naked" aborigines were achieving remarkable success.] [14]

17.3. Invasion and genocide

While the date of European invasion is usually set at January 26 1788, the date of the arrival of the First Fleet under Captain Phillip, the aborigines had been beset by Europeans for over a century before this, especially on the western coast of Australia. Aborigines soon became aware of the vile ways of European sailors and the violence, rape, murder and disease (the "Dampier Disease") brought by the European ships. After the first settlement the initial process of unorganized, reflex murdering of aborigines (e.g. in response to attacks on livestock) slowly degenerated into systematic extermination conducted with appalling savagery and brutality. [15]

Dame Mary Gilmore recalls appalling stories of bestial treatment of aborigines from her own family's experience in the mid-19th century. Her grandparents provide refuge for 2 aboriginal survivors of the genocide but general community hostility forces them to enable the escape of these survivors to the hills. A young aboriginal girl rushes in and clings to the skirts of Mary Gilmore's grandmother but to no avail: settlers invade the house and club the girl to death in the doorway. Mary Gilmore's grandparents are forced out of the district for being "abolitionists" who oppose the genocide. Mary Gilmore recalls hearing an uncle recounting to his fellow stockmen how he has acquired a whip. Riding through the bush he finds the dead body of a 12 year old aboriginal girl tied to a tree by means of the stock whip, her rapist and murderer having forgotten where he left her during the massacre of her tribe. [16] Mary Gilmore recollects an aboriginal woman Flora who was noted for her drawing and singing and then concludes "I never saw Flora again, for soon after the secret unofficial leave for "extermination" came from Sydney. From that time on, the blacks were fugitives." [17] Mary Gilmore's eye-witness account of this holocaust is chilling:

"And death was always near; but though always in the mind no one thought very much about it. I least of all. I had seen too much of death:

too many acres of dead blacks, slain as a part of life's necessity, to think that death mattered. At least among men... It was then that men said in fear: "If once the blacks procure arms..." So the poor black had to die." [18]

There are many graphic accounts of the genocide applied to aboriginal people throughout Australia, a process that continued up to the late 1920s. [19] There may well be people still alive today whose fathers participated in the last massacres of large numbers of aborigines in the north of Western Australia in 1926. [20] Lines (1991) and others catalogue the ghastly abuses that decorated this holocaust: the beating of children to death; kicking in the heads of largely-buried infants; the chaining of aboriginal women for repeated gratification; a woman raped and hung by the heels and left to die; a woman in a tree stuffs leaves in to the wounds as she is repeatedly shot until she falls dead to the ground; men caught and then freed to run away bleeding to death, their testicles having been severed. [21]

The genocide was not simply left to stockmen and the settlers who had seized aboriginal land (the "squatters"). Formal government programs accelerated the process. Thus "Native Police" forces set up in Victoria and Queensland provided for efficient killing that contributed to the decimation of the aboriginal populations in these states, the numbers falling by over 90% in the latter half of the 19th century. In Victoria the Native Police was set up by the Port Phillip administrator Charles La Trobe in 1841. These were involved, in collaboration with settlers, in the systematic murder of aboriginals in Victoria, a process involving poisoning, starving, burning, clubbing and shooting and accompanied by torture and rape. [22] Nevertheless La Trobe raised the ire of the settlers for being insufficiently effectual and subordinate to the governor in Sydney, being sarcastically referred to as "The Second Fiddle". La Trobe's life is well-documented and his name has been generously applied to the geography of Victoria and Tasmania. [23] It is sad to admit that my own university, arguably Australia's top "non-medical" university, is named after this administrator who painted

watercolours of the depopulated countryside. [One recalls however that
Hitler and Churchill both painted landscapes. Frederick the Great was a
patron of the arts, a flautist and a composer, for which effeteness he
was deeply resented by his father Frederick I, who extracted
"protection" money from Jews, had Gypsies in Prussia scourged,
branded and expelled and finally had all Gypsies over 18 hanged.
Warfare aside, Frederick the Great hated inflicting pain and abolished
torture of civilians but nevertheless still demanded the expulsion of
poor and unemployed Jews from West Prussia.] [24] La Trobe's Native
Police provided the hard edge to genocide in Victoria. La Trobe
University, like other good universities in Australia, is currently
threatened by "economic rationalist" social and governmental
philistinism that may yet create its obverse, an ebortal institution in
which the cutting edge for scholarly discovery is blunted or ripped out.

17.4. Body count

It is generally asserted that there were about 300,000 aborigines
in Australia before the European invasion [25] but others give much
higher estimates of as many of 1.5 million. [26] Dame Mary Gilmore
estimates several millions. [27] By the turn of the century, through
disease and active genocide, the aboriginal population had shrunk
catastrophically in the eastern and the southern parts of Australia. The
Queensland population had fallen from 200,000 to less than 15,000, the
Victorian population from about 20,000 to less than 1,000 and the full-
blood Tasmanian population from 6,000-8,000 to zero. By 1938 the
population was about 50,000 "full-bloods" and 25,000 "half-castes" in
the parlance of the day. [28] The current Australian aboriginal population
is about 300,000 [500,000 in 2008] of which perhaps only about
50,000 are "full-blood" aborigines, these latter being largely confined
to the remote central desert and northern tropical areas of Australia. [29]

17.5. Black labour, white labour and "White Australia"

Australia was founded on slave labour of white convicts who endured appalling savagery at places such as Norfolk Island, Botany Bay (New South Wales), Macquarie Habour and Port Arthur (Tasmania), Morton Bay (Queensland) and the Swan River (Western Australia). Transported for offences that were relatively trivial in many cases, the convicts were readily abused, flogged and hanged. Parcelled out to free settlers, convict slave labour provided the raw muscle of the new colonies that had a penal basis. [30] Labour shortages led to limited introduction of Indian labour into New South Wales in the 1840s but already the notion of Australia for white people had crept into public consciousness. [31] With the discovery of gold in New South Wales and Victoria in the mid-19th century came greatly expanded immigration, including a major influx of Chinese from coastal regions of Southern China. This in turn led to anti-Chinese sentiment, riots, entry restrictions, deportations, massacres and "Chinaman hunts" that provided a variation on the hunting down of aborigines associated with the aboriginal genocide. The Chinese influx into goldmining areas was so substantial that Chinese could represent a significant proportion of the male population. [32]

While there was a massive process of extermination of aborigines in some regions, for example along major riverways and in coastal areas, aboriginal remnants could survive and supplement their needs through limited employment. [33] The need for tropical workers in the Queensland sugar cane fields led to massive importation of Melanesian slaves ("Kanakas") from the Western Pacific Islands in the late 19th century. The slaves were badly treated but the greatest impact of the so-called "black-birding" was the transmission of European diseases to Pacific Island communities resulting in an appalling loss of life. [34] Growing hostility to black labour among white workers and their representatives led to cessation of the trade and substantial repatriation. [35] The need for cheap quasi-slave labour for the sugar cane industry in Fiji was met by indentured labourers (5-year slaves) from

India who were compelled to slave under the régimes of brutal Australian overseers. [36]

Despite the near-extermination of the aborigines, the very presence of other non-Europeans, such as Chinese and Kanakas, exacerbated European racial antagonism that sprang from psycho-sexual fears as well as from the more practical employment and income concerns of white workers. This found expression in all kinds of State, trade union and other organizational restrictions directed against non-Europeans. The industrial concerns of white workers became acute in the 1890s associated with economic recession and saw a final expression in the "unofficial" but very real restrictions on non-European immigration known as the "White Australia Policy". The rather inexplicit legislative basis for this was passed by the Australian Federal Parliament in 1901. [37]

At this point it is useful to have a glimpse of the seething psychoses of the more articulate exponents of racism in young Australia. It is also important to note that this is not a disease of the past. Since the Whitlam Labor Government's removal of the White Australia Policy (1974) and introduction of laws banning racial discrimination (1975), Australia had 20 years of getting used to the idea that "all men are created equal". However Australia is now in the hands of "revisionists" and the racial discrimination laws and minimal land rights of indigenous people are under threat in the name of "economic efficiency" and "equal rights for all Australians". On the global stage, Australian opposition to effective international greenhouse gas controls is set to contribute to the coming holocaust in Bengal and indeed throughout the Third World.

17.6. Racism - in their own words

Re Aborigines

"They are the most degraded of the human race, and never seem to wish to change their habits and manner of life."

- Reverend Samuel Marsden (1819), the notorious clergyman and merciless flogging magistrate, commenting on Sydney aborigines. [38]

"The Native soon saw that in yielding to his natural aggressive impulses he would be opposed to those who were not only his equals in savage cunning and endowment, but his superiors by alliance with the Europeans."

- Port Phillip Administrator Charles La Trobe (1840s) commenting on the efficacy of the Australian Native Police that he set up in colonial Victoria (1841). [39]

"I have the honour to state that there are no aboriginals in my District."

- The Reverend James Walker, MA, Minister of the Church of England, North Parramatta (1846). [40]

"Of the Australian black man we may certainly say that he has to go. That he should perish without unnecessary suffering should be the aim of all who are concerned in the matter."

- Anthony Trollope (1873). [41]

"Whether the Blacks deserve any mercy at the hands of the pioneering squatters is an open question, but that they get none is certain. They are a doomed race, and before many years they will be completely wiped out of the land."

- Harold Finch-Hatton (1885). [42]

"... white kids in Cowra running after us yelling "Nigger, nigger, pull the trigger,"

- Mum Shirl (Colleen Shirley Perry), aboriginal community leader, recalling outback racism while waiting to receive her MBE (Member of the British Empire award) from the Governor of New South Wales (circa 1975). [43]

The poetry of "the outback" or "the bush" gives an insight into attitudes to aborigines. Thus in 'Tis True not Many Years Ago by J.E. Liddle tells a story of times when "The niggers there were all bad then" and ends with the ultimate retribution in which "Many wild nigs were hunted down". Lex Talionis by Francis Myers tells a tale of murderous retribution by a white boy orphaned by blacks:

"'Twas to kill and to kill, and in killing pay

His debt to the devils the proper way.

He is dead, God rest him, and all his tracks

Are marked with the bones of the cursed blacks."

Powell's Revenge by F.C. Urquart tells a similar story of merciless extermination. However Moneenee (Anonymous) tells a story of self-sacrifice by an aboriginal boy working for a white man tracking other aborigines - the boy dies fetching a doctor for his master's wife. In The Grave of a Nigger (Anonymous) an aborigine dies saving a white woman and her child from a madly galloping horse. Other more light-hearted poems relate the condition of other "assimilated" aborigines. Thus in Mac's Half-Caste by E.S. Emerson ("Milky White"), Mac's half-caste wife is sold to the amorous Englishman Fancy Fred for 40 pounds. However she eventually goes "bush", he returns home to England and the half-caste returns to her lawful husband (but for how long?) In On the Arrow Track J.H.G. recounts meeting a "nigger family, tramping on the way, The meanest, poorest wretches I had seen in W.A.". One of the children starts singing what initially appears to be an unusual aboriginal song but which is eventually recognized as "Ta-ra-ra Boom-dee-ay!" (a Music Hall song). [44]

Re Chinese

"He ... saw no more injustice in preventing the landing of this degraded race, who would not only lower and demoralize, but also endanger the safety of the country, than he saw in stopping the "running " of a cargo of contraband opium or brandy."
- Daniel Henry Deniehy, speech to Parliament on restriction of Chinese immigration (1858). [45]

"I asked a cove for shearin' once along the Marthaguy:
"We shear non-union here" says he. "I call it scab," says I.
I looked along the shearin' floor before I turned to go -
There was eight or ten dashed Chinamen a-shearin' in a row ...
It was shift, boys, shift, for there wasn't the slightest doubt.
It was time to make a shift with the leprosy about.
So I saddled up my horses and I whistled to my dog,
And I left his scabby station at the old jig-jog."

- A.B. "Banjo" Patterson, A Bushman's Song (1891). ["Banjo" Patterson is a national hero and had a place on one whole side of the A$10 note.] [46]

"There was strife about the Chinamen, who came in days of old
Like a swarm of thieves and loafers when the diggers found the gold ...
What's the good of holding meetings when you only talk and swear?
Get a move upon the Pig-tails when you've got an hour to spare.

It was nine o'clock next morning when the Chows began to swarm

But they weren't so long in going, for the white men's blood was warm."

- Henry Lawson poem Cambaroora Star, written to commemorate the closure of the Boomerang, a Labor journal edited by racist Laborite William Lane (who was to found the Australian socialist Paraguay colony with most definitely non-racist Mary Gilmore and others.)

[Henry Lawson is also a national treasure and also had a place on one whole side of the A$10 note.] [47]

"The doctrine of the equality of man was never intended to apply to the equality of an Englishman and the Chinaman."

- Australia's first Prime Minister Edmund Barton debating the Commonwealth Immigration Restriction Bill (1901). [48]

"Beware of the East, O Christian, for the sake of your fairest and best;

It is written, and written, remembered, that the tide of invasion goes west."

- Henry Lawson poem The Old, Old Story (1913). [49]

Re browns and other hues

[He would prefer his daughter] "dead in her coffin than kissing one of them on the mouth or nursing a little coffee-coloured brat that she was mother to. If this is a wicked thing to say, then I am one of the wicked ones, and don't want to be good either; and I'd pray daily to be kept wicked if I thought there was any chance of my ever getting to think that colour didn't matter."

- William Lane, racist labour leader (1892). [50]

"Total exclusion of coloured and other undesirable races."

- Federal Australian Labor Party platform (1900). [51]

"If Judas Chamberlain can find a black, or brown or yellow race in Asia or Africa, that has as high a standard of civilisation and intelligence as the whites, that is as progressive as the whites, as brave, as sturdy, as good nation-making material, and that can intermarry with the whites without the mixed progeny showing signs of deterioration, that race is welcome in Australia regardless of colour."

- An attack by the racist Bulletin on Joseph Chamberlain, British Secretary of State for the Colonies over his rejection of racist Queensland legislation (1901). [52]

"We are here upon a continent set apart by the Creator for a Southern empire - for a Southern nation - and it is our duty to preserve this island continent for all eternity to the white race, irrespective of where they may come from."

- King O'Malley, Federal Parliamentary speech (1901). [53]

"Yea, will we steel us to the death to fight -
In such poor means alone avail - whome'er,
Or Asian throng, or island brown, or white
Blood-brother e'en, would cloud our prospect fair,
To guard the future from exotic blight!"

- Bernard O'Dowd (circa 1900). [54]

"I see the colour line so drawn
(I see it plain and speak I must),
That our brown masters of the dawn
Might, aye, have fair girls for their lusts."

- Henry Lawson poem To Be Amused (ca 1910) [55]

"For the "money" and "sporting" madness - and here in a land that was white!
You mated a black-man and white-man to stand up before you and fight
And many - God knows how many! - sons of a white man's son
"Backed the nigger to beat him" - and flocked to see it done ...

You paid and you cheered and you hooted, and this is your need of disgrace;
It was not Burns that was beaten - for a nigger has smacked your face.
Take heed - I am tired of writing - but O my people take heed,
For the time may be near for the mating of the Black and the White to breed."

- Henry Lawson poem The Great Fight concerning the fight in which white boxer Tommy Burns was beaten by American black boxer Jack Johnson in Sydney, Boxing Day, 1908. [56] [The racists finally got him, but Jack Johnson had the last laugh in addition to his numerous victories. Aware of the sexual element of racism, he was supposedly wont to stuff socks into his boxing shorts to make his largely white male audience think that he had prodigious genitals].

Re Jews

The Bulletin, Australia's leading magazine for the educated, had a long tradition of racism. Its motto at one period was "Australia for the White Man" and it had a long tradition of racist cartoonists and racist writers. Thus the following in the tradition of the genocidal anti-Semitic canard about Jews drinking the blood of poor little Hugh of Lincoln:

"The Jackal of the world can choose
Disdainfully his prey.
He slinks about your trade, your wars;
His mouth is ripe to drain
The red wine of the conquerors -
The red blood of the slain."

- A.H. Adams, a writer and editor for the Bulletin from the early 20th century. [57]

There was a major media campaign against allowing Jewish refugees from Nazism to enter Australia, as detailed by Cyril Pearl in his account of the Jewish and other refugees sent as "enemy alien" prisoners to Australia from Britain on the Dunera in 1940. Sir Frank Clarke, a Melbourne dignitary, charmingly referred to Jewish refugees as "shrinking, rat-faced men" and another Victorian dignitary and member of the War Cabinet declared "One of the best jobs Adolph Hitler ever did for Germany was when he drove some of these out of his country." [A leading men's club and a leading golf club in Melbourne supposedly black-balled Jews and there is certainly a determined, residual anti-Semitic streak in Victorian society that regularly manifests itself, like a wolf from the forest.] Bulletin writers and cartoonists excelled themselves during the thirties in applying Nazi-style stereotypes to Jewish refugees from Nazism. [58]

Such attitudes were not just from the Fascist era. Thus at one point in the 19th century Tasmania was excited over a "Hebrew invasion" that in the event turned out to be only a couple of Jewish families coming out from England. The capital, Hobart, has the oldest synagogue in Australia. [59]

We will return to Australian racism later to see how things are in this regard as we approach the new millennium and the pressing need for uncluttered, humane and rational responses to humanity's most extraordinary challenge.

17.7. White Australia, Empire and Japan

The latter half of the nineteenth century saw the consolidation of the British conquest of Australia. In addition to the initially convict-based settlements of New South Wales, Van Dieman's Land and Queensland came the burgeoning of the "free settler" colonies of Victoria and South Australia. An additional penal colony was established on the Swan River in Western Australia. The resolute genocide of the original inhabitants was largely concluded in the southern and eastern states by the end of the century and had been vigorously extended to the Kimberley region of the north of Western Australia and to the Northern Territory. The wealth from western agriculture (and in particular from wool, wheat and meat) and from gold and other mining created a very prosperous society. This prosperity was reflected in magnificent Victorian public buildings, the creation of universities and the expansion of manufacturing industry to meet a plethora of sophisticated hardware needs. [60] McQueen (1971) cites the import of 700,000 pianos into Australia during the nineteenth century at the end of which it had a population of only several millions. [61]

Nevertheless with wealth came anxiety. Just as greed for land and fear of properly armed aborigines led to the near total destruction of the indigenous societies, so burgeoning wealth led to possessiveness and xenophobic fear. Chinese were excluded and persecuted to the extent that Victoria had a very substantial Chinese population in the mid-nineteenth century but a negligible Chinese population by 1900. The "black-birding" of Melanesian "Kanaka" slaves was eventually halted and substantial repatriation effected. Racial fears and the economic fears of the Australian Worker (especially after the economic recession of the 1890s) led to State and ultimately Federal racially-oriented legislation. Fear of the Russians led to the construction of key coastal fortifications in south eastern Australia. The dependence on the British Navy (after all, a major reason for the foundation of Australia in the first place) led to enthusiastic flesh and blood support for British military adventures in New Zealand (the Maori Wars), India (during the Indian Mutiny), the Sudan (with Kitchener), China (during the Boxer Rebellion) and in South Africa (the Boer War). [62] The latter conflict was immortalized in a film about the volunteer Australian horseman "Breaker" Morant ("Edwin Henry Murrant" and thence "Harry Harbord Morant"), a great horse-breaker (and possible "remittance man" of noble birth, exiled by his British family) who married outback station governess Daisy Bates (later famous for her aboriginal researches). Morant was executed by the British for war crimes against the (white, Christian) Boers. [63]

The fear of Russian expansion was ameliorated by the rise of Japan as a major military and economic power and the victories of Japan in the Russo-Japanese War at the turn of the century created a well-justified fear of the Japanese in Australia. The psychotic hatred and contempt for Asians and aborigines that expressed itself in riots, Chinaman hunts or casual murder of aborigines was quickly converted into urgent fear with the prospect of such people being armed. The Maori Wars showed what original Antipodeans could do in the possession of equalizers and the naval victories of the Japanese over the Russians produced well-justified fears of Japanese imperial expansion. The rise of the Japanese and their alliance with Britain in the early 20th century had a big impact on the legislative outcomes of Australian racial fears. Thus the inexplicit nature of the legislative basis of the "White Australia Policy" arose from British objections to explicit offence being given to the 90% of the British Empire that was not European and from Japanese objections to being discriminated against or indeed being lumped with "lesser races" from elsewhere in Asia. The alliance with Japan in World War I and the Imperial deployment of huge numbers of Indian soldiers crystallized these fears for Australians. [64]

World War I involved massive sacrifice of Australian manhood in the name of the British Empire. Thus as much as 10% of the adult male population of the State of Victoria was killed or wounded in that conflict. The Australian and New Zealand Army Corps (the Anzacs) distinguished themselves in the futile Gallipoli campaign that has become the key component of national remembrance. [65] [While April 25 1915 marks the beginning of the violent end of one of the oldest civilizations in the world (that of the Anatolian Armenians), in Australia it is remembered as the date of the invasion of the Dardanelles that led to the carnage of Gallipoli. Indeed Anzac Day is our day of national remembrance for those who fell in war. That the invasion contributed to the Armenian Genocide has been a well-kept secret in Australia that is beginning to falter since Australian Armenians have taken to public demonstrations over the matter on Anzac Day in recent years. The extent of the Big Lie can be seen in the award of the Order of Australia to the Genocide-denying "trampler of human rights" Turkish President Turgut Ozal on the occasion of the 75th Anzac Day. The continuing persecution of the very substantial Kurdish population of Turkey today is a further instance of the danger of Austenizing history. Thus with lack of effective global recognition of the Armenian Genocide and the Greek and Kurd Massacres, present Turkish rulers feel that it is "business as usual" in their treatment of the Kurds.] [66]

Australians fought in Turkey, Palestine, Flanders and France [67] and then, like their Indian comrades, brought the Spanish influenza back home. This disease caused more global deaths than those occasioned by the worst war the world had yet seen. [68] [It is likely that my maternal grandmother and grandfather met as nurse and doctor, respectively, in the context of caring for victims of the influenza epidemic in Melbourne in 1919. My paternal grandfather, the great surgeon Jeno Polya, was awarded a Semmelweiss Medal in 1917 for his immense surgical work during World War I while his brother, the great mathematician George Polya, had to teach in a Swiss gymnasium as a "punishment" for conscientious objection to military service. Their brother Laszlo Polya disappeared on the Eastern Front as an officer in the Austro-Hungarian Army but who knows what he would have become if he had survived. [69] The great Australian physicist Lawrence Bragg survived service on the Western Front and was awarded the Nobel Prize for Physics in 1915 with his father William Bragg for the development of X-ray crystallography, a technology enabling the determination of the structure of molecules, including very complex molecules such as proteins. [70] 80 years later in Melbourne this technology has been the basis for the molecular design of a potent anti-influenza drug that fits precisely into a highly conserved, relatively invariant part of a key influenza virus enzyme. [71]]

World War I scarred the Australian consciousness in various ways. While Federation in 1900 provided self-government under the British Crown, the issue of conscription during the War to End All Wars had brought the Irish/English dichotomy of Australian culture to the fore. While the later Cardinal Gilroy of Sydney had served in the Australian Navy, the later Catholic Archbishop Mannix of Melbourne had been arrested by the British as a pro-Irish activist. [72] The post-war independence of Ireland and the orchestration of right-wing Australian-cum-British nationalism would ameliorate these passions. The greatest Australian political novel, Power Without Glory by Frank Hardy, describes the gaining of Establishment, pro-Fascist respectability and mainstream political power by an Irish Catholic entrepreneur-cum-gambling crook in Melbourne. [73] The death and mangling of the War had a huge impact on the families of the dead and of the "Returned Soldiers". While the War and subsequent economic depression consolidated the Australian "mateship" ethos implicit in Australian democratic socialism it also gave rise to an Australian equivalent of German or Italian veteran fascism. Expressions of the latter came in political violence against socialists [74] that has been transmuted in various works including D.H. Lawrence's Kangaroo and Peter Carey's Illywhacker. [75] The most celebrated expression of this thuggery was the disruption of the opening of the Sydney Harbor Bridge (the "Coat-hanger") in 1932 by sabre-wielding Captain De Groot of the fascist New Guard mounted on a white charger. [76]

The cataclysm of World War I is commonly taken as the defining moment of acquisition of Australian nationhood, a message that is repeated annually at thousands of shrines and cenotaphs around the country on Anzac Day. Dame Mary Gilmore, one of the greatest Australians, had a horror of the War and published a book of poems The Passionate Heart conveying this. [77] [She donated the royalties to blind soldiers, recording that "I would have felt like eating blood had I kept them."] [78] Dame Mary Gilmore wrote thus of the "new" Australia in 1936:

"When all that stuff used to be written during & after the war about Australia's virgin page I used to stand in wonder. Not two hundred years old & our first hundred years saw the Convict System, the destruction of at least half a million blacks, and in the '80's the thousands of dead black-birded kanaka "slaves". - and after that the war. A virgin page! The "cat" alone marked it." [79]

The Depression Years in Australia saw up to 25% of the population unemployed and while there was not starvation there was certainly privation and hunger for the poor. The thirties represented the first decade since 1788 in which there was no large-scale killing of aborigines although the appalling process of large-scale forcible removal of aboriginal children from their mothers was to continue apace for a further 3 decades.

The thirties and World War 2 saw a further distancing of Australia from Britain. The dismissal of the Jack Lang Labor Government by the governor of New South Wales at the apparent behest of British bankers underscored our "neo-colonial" position. Labor leaders indulged in domestic and colonial entrepreneurial adventures, a notable example being that of "Red Ted" Theodore, one time Federal Treasurer, former Premier of Queensland and Royal Commission survivor, who founded the Emperor Goldmine in Fiji in cahoots with his media business associate newspaper tycoon Frank Packer and Melbourne businessman and powerbroker John Wren (the John West of Frank Hardy's Power Without Glory). [80] The conservative side of politics had evident respect for the Nazis in Germany and the Italian Fascists and a celebrated case that says it all was the forced deportation of Czech socialist intellectual Egon Kisch. Having been refused entry to Australia, Kisch broke his leg jumping from the ship taking him away from Melbourne (where he was to address an anti-fascist peace conference). A highly educated and multilingual man, he was unable to pass the "White Australia Policy" "dictation test" given in Gaelic in Sydney. Although the High Court of Australia found that Scottish Gaelic was not a European language under the terms of the Immigration Act "entrance test", Kisch was eventually deported back to Europe. [81]

The War years represented a great divide for Australian-British relations. Conservative Prime Minister Robert Menzies was an admirer of fascism, sold scrap iron to the Japanese and to Nazi Germany (earning himself the sobriquet "Pig Iron Bob") and argued for peace with the Nazis and common cause against Communism. Thus hostile Lockwood (1987) records a Menzies' 1938 speech made on returning from a trip including a sojourn in Nazi Germany, several months after the invasion of Austria. In his speech he attacked anti-Fascist Australians who "proclaim their disdain for the governments of Italy or Germany where enthusiasm for service to the State, although it perhaps went too far, could well be emulated in Australia." Sympathetic Perkins (1968) records pre-war Attorney General Menzies' attempts to give an optimistic view of Germany but notes that "In some quarters the Attorney General's statements on Germany were interpreted to mean that he was an admirer of Hitler." Menzies (1967) in his memoirs makes his support for appeasement quite clear but notably starts his account of his adult life in politics in 1939 (excluding his recent visit to Nazi Germany and his failing to enlist in World War 1 while arguing for conscription of others). [82] As we will have perceived from the treatment of famine in India by British historians, it is what they leave out that is most revealing.

When Japan entered the war, Labor under Curtin took over the government and insisted on bringing Australian troops home from the Middle East to defend Australia. [83] The fall of Singapore, the rapid collapse of the Western colonial empires in Asia, the bombing of Darwin and the inability of Great Britain to defend Australia had a big impact on Australia. Australia irrevocably threw in its lot with the USA and remains firmly - indeed desperately - linked to that Power. The Battle of the Coral Sea (in which the US Navy defeated the Japanese) and the desperate courage of Australian soldiers in New Guinea saved Australia. The Battle of Midway confirmed the

inevitability of the victory that immediately followed the nuclear
bombing of Japan. For all the cultural impact of the US servicemen in
wartime Australia (notably that of black GIs and the feelings reflected
in the saying about the "Yanks" as "Overpaid, oversexed and over
here"), there was an immense gratitude for the American salvation. [84]

17.8. Postwar attitudes in Australia - the tale of Arthur Calwell

After the Second World War and the realization of the enormity
of the Jewish Holocaust, the entrenched racism in Australian society
abated substantially. Nevertheless there was a learning process and
some entrenched fears were resistant to change. Substantial
unreasoning hatred of Asians has persisted in a significant minority.
The recent massive support for blatantly racist anti-Asian sentiment in
Australia has been contained and ameliorated in part by fears of
economic damage in the areas of Asian tourism to Australia and
Australian trade in Asia.

The postwar journey of one Arthur Calwell (1896-1973), a
leading Labor Party politician, is instructive. Australia embarked on a
major immigration postwar program that literally brought in millions
of migrants to feed the labour needs of a burgeoning economy. Until
the middle of the 1960s this "populate or perish" immigration was
necessarily confined to Europeans because of the "unofficial" dictates
of the White Australia Policy. Calwell was the Minister of Immigration
in the postwar Labor Government (1945-1949) and his officers scoured
the Displaced Persons camps of Europe for suitable migrants.
Anecdotal accounts have it that "blond and blue eyed" people were
regarded as particularly suitable.migrants in these years immediately
following the liberation of the concentration camps. [We have already
noted the emigration of a large body of Nazi war criminals to Australia
at this time with the assistance of American intelligence.]

Calwell made some appalling assertions in the late 1940s in
commenting on the deportation of particular Asians he found

undesirable. In relation to the deportation of a Chinese refugee Wong in 1947 Calwell made the following notorious declaration of racial inequality in Federal Parliament:

"There are many Wongs in the Chinese community, but I have to say - and I am sure that the honourable member for Balaclava [T.W. White, Liberal] will not mind me for doing so - that "two Wongs do not make a White." [85]

Defending his attempt to deport an Indonesian woman Mrs Annie O'Keefe and her eight children in 1949, Calwell declared to Parliament:

"We can have a white Australia, we can have a black Australia, but a mongrel Australia is impossible, and I shall not take the first steps to establish the precedents which will allow the floodgates to be opened." [86]

Mrs O'Keefe, the Ambonese widow of a war-time Dutch refugee from the Dutch East Indies and who had married a retired Australian, John O'Keefe, was eventually able to stay after protracted legal action. Not to be outdone, Calwell generated special legislation to enable removal of war-time evacuees such as Mrs O'Keefe and the Filipino American serviceman Lawrence Gamboa, who had married an Australian. Mrs O'Keefe attributed her eventual success in remaining in Australia to the defeat of the Labor Government in 1949.

Major difficulties were placed in the way of Japanese "war brides" of Australian Occupation Forces soldiers being united with their husbands. Attributed to Calwell is the virulent assertion that "We will not let the yellow hordes contaminate our golden shores."

Calwell defended his assertion as being directed not at Asians in general but to Japanese in particular:

"I said the Japanese women should not be allowed to pollute our shores... I spoke of the Japanese and nobody else... I was expressing the opinion that the Australian people have formed owing to the brutalities of the Japanese army and the attitude of the Japanese people in World War II." [87]

As the British Empire slowly disintegrated under the "winds of change", attitudes warmed to our newly "equal" citizens of the world. Robert Menzies (1894-1978), the conservative Prime Minister of Australia for 17 years and resolute Empire loyalist, finally actually had to shake hands with a non-European Commonwealth leader. Increasing interactions occurred between Australians and Asians (especially through university students and in particular Asian students brought to Australia under the Colombo Plan tertiary training scheme). The White Australia policy began to be softened in the middle sixties and in 1967 a national referendum determined that aboriginal Australians were now to be counted in the Census. In 1967 the State of Western Australia ceased the ethnocidal forcible removal of aboriginal children from their mothers [Stolen Generations]. [88] Massive demonstrations were held in Australia against the carnage of the Vietnam War and the vicious racism of South Africa.

Nevertheless the White Australia Policy was to persist until the Whitlam Labor government was elected in 1972. Anecdotal account has it that in the late sixties the Australian diplomatic representatives in the U.S. still demanded colour photographs of intending migrants. [When I had to go down to the Australian Government Immigration Offices in 1966 to obtain a visa for my non-European fiancé to come to Australia they asked me whether she was a prostitute. I wanted the visa stamped so I adopted the pragmatic course of replying politely in the negative rather than satisfying honour.]

Late 1972 saw the election of the Whitlam Labour Government and the end of 22 years of conservative rule. The new government oversaw the cessation of Australian involvement in the mass killing in

South East Asia and the start of a new era in European-aboriginal relations in Australia. The Labor Government Minister for Immigration, Al Grassby (of Irish and Italian origin), oversaw the final removal of racial discrimination as applied to immigration i.e. the formal end of the White Australia Policy. Grassby paid the price of vicious anonymous hatred and ultimately political oblivion for his role in this piece of moral spring-cleaning - he lost his seat in the 1974 election after an unprecedented campaign of vilification against him. However as a Government consultant Grassby helped design the 1975 law that outlawed racial discrimination in Australia. In a panegyric for Grassby, Whitlam commented on this achievement: "For the first time the Nation solemnly affirmed it opposition to all forms of racial discrimination and established machinery to deal with it." [89] [There is currently intense concern that the current conservative government's "Wik legislation" will over-ride this law in order to rob many aborigines of even minimal rights in relation to their traditional lands.]

Nevertheless, Calwell remained true to his "traditional" position, declaring only a few months before this change of national direction:

"No red-blooded Australian wants to see a chocolate-coloured Australia in the 1980s." [90]

Since it is likely that much racism is linked intimately with matters sexual, it is always so satisfying when sex comes to the aid of the forces of light. Thus it was highly amusing when a prominent supporter of international sporting tours of Apartheid South Africa was arrested in a toilet. In David Williamson's biting play The Department (1975) some academics are discussing Arthur Calwell's less than photogenic visage and one tells a (fictional) story of Calwell door-to-door campaigning in Toorak (the richest and "poshest" suburb of Melbourne) :

"...and there was a lad of 15 or so. "You're Arthur Calwell!" he said. "I've got a picture of you hanging in my bedroom." Arthur was overcome. A Labor supporter in the heart of Toorak. "You're one of us, "he said. "Not rahly," said the lad. "Mother put it there to show me what I look like when I masturbate." [91]

Calwell did not live to see the non-Parliamentary ousting of the first Labor government in 22 years by the Queen of England's representative on November 11 1975 in a process widely believed to have had impetus from America. However the sorts of racial positions Calwell espoused played a significant part in that demise and its subsequent democratic ratification in the election held in December 1975. Key items of evidence for the "unsoundness" of the Whitlam Government in the minds of "traditional" Australians were government dealings with an Asian businessman, Tirath Khemlani, and the fact that a beautiful Eurasian woman, Juni Morosi, had been the private secretary of Dr Jim Cairns, a leading Labor politician who had been compelled to resign his post as Deputy Prime Minister some months before the election. [92]

For all this, Calwell was a humanitarian and a committed Christian who had devoted his life to social justice for ordinary people. He attacked the disgraceful treatment of aborigines but could still declaim against a "chocolate coloured Australia". He supported the entry of Jewish refugees into Australia against ugly opposition and his admiration for the Chinese had led him to learn Mandarin. Calwell's great contribution to Australia was his initiation and supervision of the massive postwar immigration that has so beneficially transformed "melting-pot Australia". [93] The paradox of Calwell is indeed that of many Australians today - the coexistence of explicit or subliminal racist attitudes with determined egalitarianism and non-elitism in everything except competitive sport.

17.9. The apogee of Australian decency

Australia has had an outstanding record of innovative social decency. It is one of very few countries in the world with a record of continuous democratic administration over the last one and a half centuries (other such countries - allowing for military occupation by invaders in some cases - include the U.K., the Netherlands, Belgium, Luxembourg, Denmark, Sweden, Norway, Switzerland, New Zealand, Canada and the USA). In addition to basic democratic institutions and the rule of law, Australia has had free trade unions, women's suffrage and free and compulsory education for over a century. Even under postwar conservative governments there was a basic social safety net involving good hospital services, charitable institutions, old-age pensions, disabled pensions and unemployment relief. The notion of a "basic wage" was legislatively determined, the right to strike was an empirical reality and an Arbitration Commission determined industrial "awards" for workers. A real sense of freedom was provided by free speech, a multiplicity of media, access to tertiary education and the social security provided by a relatively benign police and the rule of law.

The country has produced a plethora of outstanding creative people from which we can somewhat arbitrarily single out Charles Conder, Frederick McCubbin, Arthur Streeton and Tom Roberts ("Heidelberg School" impressionist landscape painters) [as I write this I am looking out over the Yarra Valley from one of their vantages on the Heidelberg Heights of Melbourne], William Farrer (wheat breeding), Lawrence Hargraves (first manned flight, 1894), John Flynn and Fred Hollows (outback medicine), Norman Lindsay, William Dobell, Arthur Boyd, Sidney Nolan, Albert Namatjira and Brett Whiteley (painters), Christopher Koch, Peter Carey, Frank Moorehouse, Frank Hardy, Xavier Herbert, Patrick White, Tim Winton, Elizabeth Jolley, Judith Wright and David Williamson (literature), Percy Grainger and Peter Sculthorpe (composers), Nellie Melba and Joan ("our Joan") Sutherland (singers) and a large body of musicians and experimental scientists. A less arbitrary list of Nobel Prize winners includes William and Lawrence Bragg (X-ray crystallography), Howard Florey (penicillin), John Cornforth (isoprenoid biochemistry) [deaf as George Austen probably was; who knows what forgotten George might have attained in a more sympathetic age?], MacFarlane Burnett (immunology), John Eccles (neurobiology), Patrick White (literature) and Peter Doherty (immunology).[94]

The brief interlude of the Whitlam Labor Government (1972-1975) was a major period of reform that removed racial discrimination in immigration and other areas, dramatically widened access to tertiary education through abolition of fees, expanded access to legal services and health services (through the Medicare free public health system) and generally widened social access in areas of cultural expression. However behind this bold and fair facade was the ugly reality of the poverty, disease, dispossession and victimization of the aboriginal inhabitants of Australia. Aborigines had been finally recognized as "countable" citizens of their own land by referendum in the late sixties and that period also saw the ending of the outrageous system involving large-scale, forcible removal of aboriginal children from their mothers [for which the 1996-2007 government refused to offer a formal apology]. Aborigines were still dispossessed of their land, subject to wage discrimination and abused by arbitrary authority. Aboriginal housing and health in a prosperous country remained a scandal. The brief Whitlam administration at least publicly recognized the problems and took faltering steps toward their amelioration.

The "New Jerusalem" ushered in by the Whitlam Government had foundations of clay that paradoxically derived from the very strengths of Australian society that relate to egalitarianism, pragmatism, social compromise and consensus. Labor had lost power in 1950 and had remained out of power until 1972 because of a three-way split between the doctrinaire Left that cooperated with Communists at the industrial level, a fiercely anti-Communist Catholic Right (that held the balance of electoral power and in consequence kept the conservatives in power for over 20 years) and a pragmatic Centre-

Right. In the end electoral victory in 1972 depended upon a dominant pragmatic Centre-Right, neutralization of the idealistic Left and massive vote-buying through generous social policies.

The contradictions of the Whitlam Government are very relevant to our general "global morality" disquisition. The Labor Government moved against racism and thereby abolished the "unofficial" White Australia policy in a backdoor fashion - a referendum on the matter would have been soundly defeated then as it probably would be now. The right noises about aboriginal rights and welfare were about as effectual as comparable noises at the same time about the nuclear threat, neo-colonialism and the obscenity of Apartheid in South Africa. While Labor stopped our involvement in the concluding carnage in Vietnam it pragmatically indirectly contributed to and accepted the Indonesian invasion of Portuguese East Timor that would lead to the death of as many as 200,000 people out of a total population of 600,000. Despite firm commitment to our participation in the nuclear standoff of the Cold War (principally through key telecommunications and monitoring bases), romantically leftish Labor rhetoric convinced the Americans otherwise. Financial looseness and massive vote-buying finally even made the recipients nervous. The democratically-elected Whitlam Government was finally dismissed by the Queen's Representative (the Governor-General, Sir John Kerr) on Remembrance Day, 11 November 1975, after a lengthy standoff between the 2 Houses of Federal Parliament (the Senate and the House of Representatives) over the Budget. It is widely speculated that the Americans were involved directly or indirectly in the Dismissal. The conservative electorate democratically endorsed Whitlam's undemocratic removal a month later. [95]

The looseness and indulgence of the reformist Whitlam government was mirrored in the subsequent conservative administration of Malcolm Fraser. Strong on rhetoric and weak on action (albeit in an obverse direction to that of his predecessors), this conservative administration also failed to put the house in order and was thrown out in 1983 in favour of the ultimate Labor pragmatist Bob Hawke. Hawke was a national trade union leader who could gain support from the anti-American Left while simultaneously being one of America's best friends in Australia. With a huge proportion of the country now recipients of Federal largesse, Hawke Labor felt compelled to continue the spendthrift policies of the previous conservative and Labor administrations as long as money could be raised by taxes, borrowing or "selling the farm". The increasing gap between perception and reality was papered over by "Lib-Lab", consensus rhetoric.[96] Hawke could weep publicly over the tribulations of his family but failed in the area of the continuing aboriginal health disaster. Hawke wept publicly and responded humanely over the Tianenman Square Massacre but departed from dominant global opinion in recognizing the conquest of East Timor.

Despite the ambivalence and contradictions of Bob Hawke Labor, one is tempted to place the apogee of Australian decency somewhere towards the middle of the eighties when incompetent, racist conservatism had just been electorally rejected together with knee-jerk industrial confrontation; the free public health Medicare system survived to continue providing excellent general access to top medical services; widespread, sensible liberal sentiment had not yet degenerated into shrill political correctness; the universities were having an Indian summer before their intrinsic weakening by Dawkins later in the decade; national debt had not yet blown out to dangerous proportions; environmental activism was blossoming in defence of Australia and the planet; and when Uluru (Ayer's Rock) in Central Australia was returned to its traditional aboriginal owners (11 November 1983). [97] From this point on (with some sparkles of light) it is all downhill.

17.10. Decline and fall

The latter half of the eighties degenerated into a destructive spending spree: billions were poured into Canberra and notably into a massive new Parliament House, both enterprises being more appropriate for a country with ten times the population; the binary tertiary education sector was critically damaged by the fusion of Colleges of Advanced Education (essentially teaching-only and vocationally-oriented institutions) with the traditional high-quality research and teaching Universities; massive commercial as well as State and Federal borrowing blew out the national debt, this being compounded by the market collapse of 1987; massive long-term unemployment, and especially youth unemployment, became an entrenched reality of Australian society; massive drought, soil degradation and salination, lowered world commodity prices and high interest rates impacted upon agricultural communities of the "bush"; Australian society restructured radically with an increasingly "American" spectrum from the fabulously rich to bottom line Third World degradation and radical social discrepancies in income, health, education and welfare in urban environments [e.g. Hawke's unsustainable promise that has entered the national lexicon: "No Australian child will live in poverty by the year 1990"]; environmental damage in relation to forests, rivers, marine preserves and biodiversity has continued apace while decorated with a veneer of rhetorical concern; corporate and governmental implication or involvement in human rights and environmental abuse in our region has expanded - a classic example being Australian environmental violation of Bougainville followed by government support for Papua and New Guinea military intervention in the consequent rebellion that has taken thousands of lives, principally through disease and lack of medical services and supplies.

The Hawke Labor administrations finally degenerated into the last gasp Paul Keating Labor government that was elected by default because the conservatives had been too honest in their bitter economic prescriptions. Led by Keating, an astute, young Labor politician who had left school at 14 (and is now a Visiting Professor at the University of New South Wales), this mob evidently believed their own confident rhetoric to their ultimate cost. One of Keating's great contributions to public life was his ripping Parliamentary language e.g. re John Hewson (conservative Opposition Leader) "This little flower, this delicate little beauty, this little cream puff, is supposed to be beyond personal criticism ... he was simply like a shiver, looking for a spine to run up"; re Andrew Peacock (sun-lamp tanned, well-groomed, conservative Opposition Leader) "They were not for the show-pony. He wanted to get back in the 747 to hightail it to Washington to check into the cocktail party circuits - that is when he was not standing at the mirror running a little dye through his hair"; re a second political attempt by Andrew Peacock "Does a soufflé rise twice?"; re John Howard, conservative Leader of the Opposition: "He is the greatest job and investment destroyer since the bubonic plague". As for himself, he was the "world's greatest treasurer" who could handle "the big picture." [98]

The conservatives learned their lesson well and stormed back in 1996 under John Howard on the basis of an inexplicit "nudge-nudge, wink-wink" platform involving financial reform and a return to the good old politically incorrect days of calling a spade a spade. Australia has now resolutely turned the clock back by about half a century. While not yet having the courage to institute badly needed taxation reforms, the Howard government has commenced a slashing and burning program that is set to cripple the universities, cut ordinary people off from realistic access to the law and to progressively restore the social inequities of 50 years ago in relation to access to health services and good secondary and tertiary education. This mounting inequity will impact differentially on the 40% of the community who have a non-Anglo-Celtic origin and who are proportionally represented by vastly fewer representatives in Australia's 9 parliaments than were non-Europeans in South Africa before the collapse of Apartheid.

Most importantly, Howard has failed to properly address ugly, resurgent racism in Australia that may have already cost Australia hundreds of millions this year and threatens multi-billion dollar tourism and tertiary export education industries directed at Asian clients. A fish-and-chip shop owner from Ipswich, Pauline Hanson, was disendorsed as the Liberal candidate for the safe Labor seat of Oxley for making disparaging remarks about aboriginal matters. She was returned to Federal Parliament as an independent with a huge majority as were several other similarly opined politicians. Her maiden speech oncerned itself with Asian migrants, aborigines and the desirability of a return to White Australia and provided immense offence both here and in Asia. A key part of her address is as follows:

"I believe we are in danger of being swamped by Asians. Between 1984 and 1995, 40 per cent of all migrants into this country were of Asian origin. They have their own culture and religion, form ghettos and do not assimilate. Of course, I will be labelled a racist but, if I can invite who I want into my home, then I should have the right to have a say in who comes into my country. A truly multicultural country can never be strong or united. The world is full of failed and tragic examples, ranging from Ireland to Bosnia to Africa and, coming closer to home, Papua New Guinea, America and Great Britain are paying the price. Arthur Calwell was a great Australian and Labor leader, and it is a pity that there are not men of his stature sitting on the Opposition benches today. Arthur Calwell said and I quote: "Japan, India, Burma, Ceylon and every new African nation are fiercely anti-white and anti-one another. Do we want or need any of these people here?" I am one red-blooded Australian who says no and who speaks for 90 per cent of Australians." [99]

With the media stirring the pot for all it was worth, Ms Hanson generated great popular support that only began to wane when the economic implications of giving offence to Asian customers began to strike home. The wittiest responses to Ms Hanson's offending views were the suggestions that she should not take the national anthem Advance Australia Fair literally and if she wanted to find out what xenophobia means she shouldn't look under Z.

Of course there is nothing very new in this but Australians had got used to referring to their fellow human beings in a courteous fashion in the dozen years since the "Australian decency apogee" of circa 1985. Indeed in the middle 1980s distinguished historian Geoffrey Blainey had caused great public and academic controversy in relation to his articulate advocacy of less Asian migration and his thoughts on the economic transformation of Australia by European settlement. [100] The bottom line in these arguments is of course that Australia is a "multicultural" immigrant country like Canada and the USA and that the original aboriginal societies maintained quite substantial populations in a homeostatic, biologically sustainable fashion..

For all that Australians have a self-image as tolerant people who believe in an equitable deal (a "fair go"), the reality is that a substantial body of Australians are intrinsically racially prejudiced as revealed by polling and other public responses to Ms Hanson. Whatever the courtesies of "politically correct" public utterance, I suspect that retention of "White Australia" would win hands down in a referendum. We have come a long way since we laid down our guns and had a "smoke-oh" after complementing introduced disease and murdering nearly all of the indigenous inhabitants of Southern and Eastern Australia last century. But it is quite apparent that there is still a substantial undercurrent of racism that had merely been driven into the recesses of the national consciousness by the "political correctness" (and indeed prohibitive legislation) of the "small l" liberal 1980s. How will this prosperous society on "lifeboat Australia" respond to global disaster? Since this final part of our disquisition is concerned with the likelihood of effective moral and intellectual responsiveness to the coming food/population disaster, let us digress to briefly reconsider responsiveness to the World War 2 Jewish Holocaust and the contemporaneous man-made Bengal Famine.

17.11. Moral responsiveness to the Jewish Holocaust and the Forgotten Holocaust of Bengal

The failure of the world to recognize the extermination of the Jews and Gypsies as it was happening, to permit the persecuted to escape from Nazi-occupied Europe and to take substantive steps to bring the Holocaust to a halt is an awful indictment of the Allies and of global humanity at the time. This appalling failure of humanity is well documented but remains substantially forgotten even though the actuality of the Jewish Holocaust is burnt into global sensibility. The survivors have quite understandably not qualified their appreciation of their liberation and the destruction of Nazism. Indeed Aarons and Loftus (1997) document the pragmatic use of blackmail by Zionists against a corrupted American intelligence system (involved in Nazi collaboration and postwar "rescue" of Nazi money and Nazi war criminals) in order to secure the smuggling of Jews out of postwar Europe and US and Latin American support for the UN vote on the establishment of the State of Israel. [101]

Nevertheless the impact of the Holocaust has been quite variable. For those who were present at the liberation of the camps a strange desensitization was manifest as even battle-toughened soldiers subliminally protected themselves from unimaginable horror. Richard Crossman (1945) recorded the consequent relative inaction of the shocked liberators of Dachau:

"How else can one explain that ten days after the liberation no one thinks it strange that there are no trucks to carry the dying to hospital and no proper diet in the hospital? If a town of 32,000 people had been struck by a cyclone, an immense rescue apparatus would be organised. But these 32,000 outcasts are so remote from civilization as we know it that we are content to leave them as they are, improving slightly their living standards." [102]

James Baldwin (1963) provides a chillingly honest view of the Holocaust from the perspective of a black American subject to a remorselessly racist society:

"White people were, and are, astounded by the holocaust in Germany. They did not know that they could act in that way. But I very much doubt whether black people were astounded - at least, in the same way. For my part, the fate of the Jews, and the world's indifference to it, frightened me very much. I could not but feel, in those sorrowful years, that this human indifference, concerning which I knew so much already, would be my portion on the day that the United States decided to murder its Negroes systematically instead of little by little and catch-as-catch-can." [103]

James Baldwin's fears were well justified and his testimony provides powerful support for the thesis of this book, namely that unimaginable horror on a gigantic scale will be the inevitable consequence of human indifference to the fate of remote, different and unseen people. It is more than likely that James Baldwin, like the overwhelming majority of people in the world at the time and since, was completely unaware of the man-made famine of Bengal that destroyed as many as 5 million innocent Bengalis (mostly Muslims and children) at the same time as 6 million Jews and half a million Gypsies (Roma) were being just as remorselessly destroyed by their rulers. Those in positions of authority who were aware steadfastly refused to act, notable exceptions being Lord Louis Mountbatten, Lord Wavell and Prime Minister King of Canada. The rest was silence. [104]

How will the post-globalisation world respond to comparable events in the future? How will the well-fed of the world respond to the Bergen-Belsen Third World of 2050? Some idea can be gained from the absence of world response to the horrendous famine in China occasioned by the Great Leap Forward in 1959-1962 and which killed as many as about 30 million people - the "global village" was almost completely unaware of what was happening. [105] In contrast, domestic public pressure over a decade in the USA eventually brought the carnage of Vietnam to a halt just as the same rational and humanitarian perceptions contributed to French withdrawal from Indochina and from the bloodbath of Algeria.

With an increasingly global economy and astonishingly quick and pervasive communications, the world is ostensibly more responsive now. The obscenity of war in Bosnia-Herzegovina was permitted to run for several years and take several hundred thousand lives but eventually the moral leadership of the USA won out over the moral cowardice of Western Europe and the guns of the murderers were silenced. However South African Apartheid - like the monstrous Soviet tyranny - evidently succumbed to global economic realities rather than to a global moral unanimity. Nevertheless the imminence and likelihood of the genocide in Rwanda was no doubt quite obvious to a small number of Western experts and yet the world was unable to act decisively. Mass starvation in Sudan and North Korea in recent years has similarly met with inadequate global responses.

Clearly there has to be some enhanced appreciation of humanity, some depth of perception that can overcome an immense "activation energy" barrier to compel requisite effective action. Clearly racism and racial and cultural prejudices can severely blunt such humanitarian thrusts. In addition we know that we respond most deeply to individual horrors but cannot properly comprehend massive disaster. Who knows but that the tragic public murder of the young Sarajevo lovers - one Serbian, one Bosnian Muslim - had a vastly greater impact on the President of the United States or his advisers than the massive statistics on ethnic cleansing?

We will now briefly return to the Antipodes to see how a prosperous, educated, racially diverse, resource-rich country such as Australia can deal with problems that are trivial compared to the coming global food/population problem.

17.12. Genocide, ethnocide, ecocide and terracide in Australia

We have already seen how Europeans in Australia destroyed a sophisticated set of aboriginal cultures, wiping out something of the order of a million people and destroying for ever all but about a dozen of several hundred distinct languages. The process was accompanied by racial vilification that continues to this day. It is notable in comparison that even the firm intentions, efficiency and technical sophistication of the Nazis was unable to totally destroy any particular culture or people (although one can argue that Yiddish-speaking Jewish groups were in effect deleted from particular Eastern European national cultures). This process of murder, violence, forced child-removal, dispossession and marginalisation has had a huge effect on the cultural continuity of the survivors in addition to language loss. This process of ethnocide is still continuing. A major aspect of aboriginal survival in Australia today involves differential aboriginal morbidity and mortality. The current statistics are appalling as the following examples will serve to illustrate:

1. Aboriginal infant mortality in Australia is about 24 per 1000 live births as opposed to 8 per 1000 for Australia as a whole and 22 (Canadian Indians), 18 (New Zealand Maoris), 10 (US Indians) and 5 per 1000 in Japan. Contributing factors include poor living conditions, lack of medical services and antenatal care, poor education, alcohol and tobacco abuse, a high incidence of teenage mothers and low infant birth weights. In about 1990 the 0-24 death rate among aborigines was 2 times the national average but among the 15-24 year olds the death rate for both male and female aboriginals was about 4 times the national average. The death rate among 25-54 year old aborigines is about 7 times the national average. The life expectancy for aboriginal males is about 59 years (as opposed to a national male average of about 75 years); the corresponding female figures are 63 for aboriginals as compared to a national average of 81 years. [106]

2. Aboriginal women of childbearing age have about 3 children as compared to the national average of about 2. While maternal death in childbirth has fallen nationally since 1970, the incidence for aboriginal women has increased. In 1988 aboriginal maternal death during childbirth represented 30% of all such deaths although aboriginal women represented only 2% of women giving birth each year. [107]

3. The incidence of a variety of preventable diseases among aboriginals is appallingly high and this in turn relates to poor living conditions, education and access to medical services. Major health problems relate to poor diet, obesity, diabetes, alcoholism and cardiovascular and other problems associated with smoking and alcohol abuse. Glaucoma and diabetes are major problems with HIV infection a major threat. Only about 30% of aborigines live in cities and 20% live in particularly remote areas. Of the 265,000 aborigines counted in 1991, 40% were under 15 (as opposed to 22% nationally). [108]

4. A major problem is differential imprisonment of aboriginals and aboriginal deaths in custody. Aborigines represent 1.6 % of the total population but contribute 12% of the prison population. Despite a Royal Commission into the appalling incidence of aboriginal deaths in custody, the solutions are still being ignored and this utterly avoidable tragedy continues. [109]

5. Differential access to educational services results in the following discontinuities: about half the aboriginal population have left school under 15, fewer than 1% have tertiary qualifications and about 5% have never gone to school. [110]

6. In social conditions there are immense differences as shown by the 38% unemployment rate of aboriginal males (as opposed to a 9% national average), 65 % of aborigines rent (as opposed to a 26% national incidence) and while aboriginal home ownership is about half the national average, the number of person per dwelling (such as it is) is about double the national average. [111]

Many "outback" aborigines are still living in conditions that are among the worst in the world and this in a country that is one of the richest in the world. These obscene, continuing differentials clearly contribute to the appalling differences in morbity and mortality of aborigines. The awful Australian aboriginal living conditions that reduced the great black American singer Paul Robeson to tears nearly 50 years ago remain today. In a very real sense the undeclared War of Occupation is continuing and one wonders when Australia will be brought to the International Court of Justice or indeed to a War Crimes Tribunal in The Hague.

There is currently a thoroughly justified national and international horror of evil, psychotic paedophiles (stimulated by the recent Belgian horrors and the continuing European, Asian and Australian "sex tours" of Asia). However there is no recognition of a dominant global culture of greedy, cold-blooded paedophobes - powerful people having a relaxed attitude to the past, present and future suffering and death of millions of children throughout the world as victims of national and corporate economic interests. Whether it is in the man-made famines of Bengal or the man-made continuing abuse of Australian aborigines, a substantial proportion of the suffering is borne by children and one cannot go much further than the New Testament plea of Jesus (Matthew chapter 18, verse 6): "But whoso shall offend one of these little ones which believe in me, it were better that a millstone were hanged about his neck, and that he were drowned in the depth of the sea."

The celebrated Australian High Court "Mabo" decision of June 1992 overturned the terra nullius proposition of the first 2 centuries of European invasion by establishing (6 to 1) that the Torres Straits Meriam people had rights to the possession of the Murray Islands on which they had lived from time immemorial. Subsequent Federal legislation has addressed the consequences of this landmark decision to reverse the colonial fiction of terra nullius but current conservative reaction in Australia is set to put the clock back. In particular the Wik people of northern Queensland recently won a High Court case over their fight to regain at least qualified "cultural" access to lands occupied by their forbears for thousands of years. However there has been an immense political reaction to the "Wik decision" and calls for "total extinguishment" of aboriginal residual rights relating to land use of an immense area of Australia leased to miners and pastoralists. This has now been translated into essentially race-specific legislation that curbs and threatens the legitimate land rights of indigenous Australians. It is with forboding that we see that the current Australian Government has recently refused to sign a "human rights" article associated with trade arrangements with the European Union. Residual rights in relation to the lands that they have occupied for millennia is crucial for the cultural survival of the remaining aboriginal societies and the intended continuing dispossession will amount to continuing deliberate ethnocide by White Australia. [112]

Successive recent Australian governments have pointed to massive funding of Aboriginal organizations and services as evidence of good intentions. This begs the question of why such unfavourable outcomes obtain. The critical argument that has been applied to British rule in India over several centuries, and indeed of Bengal in 1943-1946, can be equally well applied to continuing European rule of aboriginal Australians - the administering authority is inescapably responsible for the welfare of its subjects. Comparing the appalling state of aboriginal Australia with the ostensibly massive financial expenditure for their benefit is a classic example of inappropriate use of numbers to which our Gadarene economists remain enthusiastically committed. This is simply a matter of comparing "goats with sheep" and the same idiocy dictates that the crucial, "unpaid" labor of several billion people (mostly women) in subsistence economies cannot contribute to official "dollar-based" estimates of social productivity. [113]

Not unconnected with the genocide and ethnocide of aborigines is the massive diminution of biological diversity in Australia since the invasion. One third of our remarkable fauna are facing extinction. Of an estimated 22,000 native plants, 10% are facing extinction. There has been a massive invasion of Australia by introduced flora and fauna. Many marsupials have become extinct since European settlement, the most obvious and dramatic (likely) extinction being that of the Tasmanian Tiger (Thylacinus cynocephalus). The largest mammal currently facing extinction in Australia is the dugong of tropical waters but the current Australian government has recently given the "go-ahead" for commercial development of a highly sensitive area of the Queensland coast that is a major refuge for these rare creatures. Of Australia's indigenous mammals 10 are extinct, 20 are endangered and 135 are potentially threatened with extinction (including species not sighted for over 50 years). In the words of William Lines (1991) in The Taming of the Great South Land:

"Nowhere else on earth have so few people pauperised such a large proportion of the world's surface in such a brief period of time. In under 200 years, a natural world millions of years in the making, and an Aboriginal culture of 60,000 years duration, vanished before the voracious, insatiable demands of a foreign invasion." [114]

Massive environmental degradation of the continent of Australia has occurred over the last 200 years. Major outback rivers of the Murray-Darling System are contaminated with the toxic blue-green algae Anabaena (that produces the neurotoxic anatoxin) and Microcystus (that elaborates the hepatotoxic and secondary tumour promoting microcystins). Massive irrigation in the New South Wales Riverina and in Victoria has contributed to this problem and irrigation and tree removal in the same region has led to massive salination. Overstocking has led to areas of vegetation removal on rectilinearly-defined properties that can be discerned from Landsat images from space. [30 years ago I made several trips to the University of Adelaide Botany Department Kurnamore reserve in the arid centre of South Australia. The several square kilometers that had been fenced off from sheep for about 40 years had a richness, lushness and complexity comparable with well-watered coastal areas and was in stark contrast to the salt-bush desert outside the fence having 6 feet of red sand between each salt-bush clump.] The criminal destruction of forests and the associated complex habitats has excoriated the most complex ecosystems of Australia from the tropical rainforests of Queensland to the temperate rainforests of Tasmania. Even the ostensibly ecologically simpler plains have been devastated by the hard hooves of cattle and sheep. Feral creatures such as rabbits, buffalo, dogs, cats, horses and pigs have contributed to animal extinctions and massive environmental damage. [115]

Mining has devastated particular regions of which the most dramatic examples are the dead rivers and vegetation-free hills near Queenstown on the west coast of Tasmania that are set in the midst of lush, dense rainforests watered with 180 inches of rainfall per year. As previously mentioned, this destructiveness has been extended to mud and heavy metal pollution of major river systems in New Guinea and ugly coastal degradation on Bougainville that has driven the indigenous Melanesian people to a continuing rebellion that has cost thousands of lives. [116]

Given this appalling litany of genocide, ethnocide and ecocide one would have thought that some sensible constraint would be exercised now. The reality is that appalling aboriginal health and welfare differentials are being sustained by government irresponsibility and a major new assault is underway on hard won, minimal aboriginal land rights. Renewed attack on the Australian environment is afoot in a more pragmatic and selfish society. The release of calicivirus-infected rabbits may lead to benign reversal of 2 centuries of damage from the rabbit plague but there are concerns over diminution of effectiveness. For all the vastness of the continent, much of Australia is desert and large areas of the best agricultural land are being degraded through salination, erosion, loss of soil and urbanization. [117] Per capita, Australia is one of the major greenhouse gas producers in the world through massive exports of black coal, use of huge black and brown coal resources for production of electricity, use of oil and gas reserves

and massive deforestation. It is remarkable that on his recent visit to
Australia, President Clinton was moved to comment unfavourably on
Australia's tardiness in relation to greenhouse gas emission controls.
[118]

From this quick sketch we can see that Australia, a resource-
rich, highly-educated, liberal, democratic and orderly nation with an
extraordinarily high standard of living, declines to act in a fashion
consistent with global environmental responsibility in relation to
greenhouse gas emissions. In addition, it is continuing the 200 year
process of environmental degradation and biodiversity destruction. If
that were not enough, it is continuing the process of destruction of its
indigenous cultures and is a passive witness to massive environmental
damage and human rights abuse in a swathe of tropical countries to our
north.

17.13. An experimental test of the moral responsiveness of White Australia

1995 marked the 50th anniversary of the end of World War 2
and Australian public figures and media repeatedly acknowledged this
through an "Australia Remembers" program throughout the year. Since
the Bengal Famine represented one of the largest single catastrophes of
the War (contributing about 10% of the victims of that conflict and
about 90% of total British Empire casualties) and since it had been
essentially forgotten, I thought it timely to inform Australia of this in
1995. However a detailed account of that catastrophe [119] sent to
politicians, media and others fell largely on deaf ears. It was utterly
ignored by mainstream media but was the subject of a speech and
tabled in the Senate by Green Senator Chamarette [120]. A version was
published by the Sydney-based Centre for Comparative Genocide
Studies. [121]

While Holocaust denial is a criminal offence in Germany, [122]
Australia's mainstream media were unanimous in steadfastly ignoring

the Bengal Famine in the year Australia remembered the 50th anniversary of the end of World War 2. Nevertheless in the same year the Australian literary establishment awarded, rewarded and lionized a "Holocaust" novel by a supposedly first generation Ukrainian-Irish Australian woman. Ukrainian participation in the Holocaust was causally linked in this fictional work to alleged Jewish participation in the Ukrainian Famine of the early 1930s. The authoress, "Helen Demidenko", repeated this as historical fact in an article in The Age (a leading Australian newspaper, published in Melbourne and having a liberal stance). She went further and indeed specified that "Jewish Russian Communists" had murdered members of her family in the Ukraine in the 30s. [123] After "Helen Demidenko" was revealed to be Helen Darville, the daughter of English migrants, The Age steadfastly refused to retract and apologize for her false assertions published opposite their editorial page. They were upheld in their resolution by the Australian Press Council after formal hearing of my complaint. In the year marking the 50th anniversary of the liberation of the concentration camps the same newspaper steadfastly declined to remember the Forgotten Holocaust of Bengal. However it did publish a "Holocaust" cartoon in very poor taste: Melbourne has a major new casino industry and the cartoon showed subdued civilians guarded by police entering a facsimile of Auschwitz with the gateway sign reading "Gambling Makes Freedom" (rather than "Arbeit Macht Frei") and with the caption "The Victorian Solution" as a "joke" about the "Final Solution". [124] Several years later the same newspaper (which has a supportive, Voltairean attitude to the entry of presently-excluded, Holocaust revisionist historian David Irving into Australia), offered the following historical revision of the Bengal Holocaust in its Entertainment section in relation to the screening of Satyajit Ray's film Distant Thunder: "The Japanese demands for rice during 1943 caused a famine in India, resulting in five million deaths and a hard struggle for survival for millions of others." [125].

In addition to its historical involvement in the near-complete genocide of Tasmanian and Mainland Australian aborigines and slavery in the Pacific, White Australia has been intimately (if indirectly) connected in various ways with the 200 year holocaust that was British India, the Armenian Genocide, the Bengal Famine, the massacre of Chinese Indonesians, the Cambodian Genocide, the Timorese Genocide and, most recently, the genocide applied to Kurds in Iraq. Like a postnatal psychotic mother who has murdered her child, Australia just does not want to know. As thorough genocidists in our own right, we have a long history as running dogs of the Big Boys and well-founded national insecurity will keep us on track. Our present conservative Prime Minister John Howard indeed has denied that we should feel any guilt about our past: "I sympathize fundamentally with Australians who are insulted when they are told that we have a racist, bigoted past ... but to tell children ... that we're all part of a a sort of racist, bigoted history is something that Australians reject." [126] However it is not so much the past as the present and the future we are ultimately concerned about in this disquisition. Will Australia over-ride anti-racist legislation and global sentiment to enable a massive extinguishment of native title over a substantial part of Australia? Will Australia continue to play "dog in the manger" in relation to the commerce-driven ecocide and global warming that threatens the Third World?

For all the mythology of the outspoken egalitarianism of "rough diamond" Australians, the reverse can appear to be the case. It is argued that the poor diction of Australians derives from the same source as the Great Australian Salute i.e. Australians talk with their mouths nearly closed to avoid inadvertently eating flies just as they are forever brushing them away. A more likely hypothesis is that it derives from the Australian horror of expressing moral or intellectual commitment. This spiritual disease is in epidemic proportions in our universities wherein one can now perceive an insidious evolution from the "Those who can, do. Those who can't, teach" of Williamson's The Department [127] to "Those who can, mislead. Those who can't, blather." As our universities evolve from "research and teaching institutions" into "ethically fluid deregulated businesses", so we see the departure from the elegant games of Cornford's Microcosmographica Academica or a host of delightful academic novels [128] to power debates in which some assert and diminish with abandon (or more exactly, crudely mislead with remorseless regularity) and others are reduced to frozen silence. We have already seen the remarkable lying by omission of British historians over several centuries. However the new style of academia is bringing Australian universities out of a "Truth only zone" into the real world of salesmen, competition, moral ambivalence and deceit as analyzed in Lying by Bok (1978). [129]

Alison Lurie has wickedly put her finger on the uncomfortable blather of the English in avoiding the unpleasant, in this instance as upstate New York academic Fred Turner enquires after his estranged love Lady Rosemary Radley in Foreign Affairs:

"His questions about Rosemary are passed over as if unheard, or met with what he is beginning to recognize as the classic waffling manner of the British upper classes when confronted with the insignificant unpleasant." [130]

The Australians, lacking the verbal agility of the English, tend to keep mum in ignoring the undesirable. To be fair to them, one should realize that there can be severe financial penalties for free speech in Australia and there is a long tradition of intellectual suppression and constraint on free speech going back to First Settlement. [131] Thus in Sydney in 1789 John Callaghan was sentenced to 600 lashes and 6 months' labor in irons for uttering a simple truth that was held by Judge Advocate David Collins to be "an untruth and scandalous falsehood". [132]

If a highly-resourced, highly-educated liberal democracy such as Australia is unable to even minimally constrain its greed and irresponsibility, what hope is there for the rest of the world that in general is overpopulated, under-educated, under-resourced and lacking longstanding democratic traditions and institutions? If fabulously rich Australia cannot deal with relatively minor problems such as preserving biological sustainability, rare ecosystems and the limited biodiversity of an arid continent or providing decent health services and living conditions for a mere three hundred thousand [currently 500,000] indigenous inhabitants, what hope is there for a world crowded with 6 billion mostly impoverished people?

17.14. How we can prevent the Apocalypse

The world is facing a catastrophe involving massive continuing loss of biodiversity, [133] irreversible environmental change through global warming, deforestation, desertification, soil degradation and pollution [134] and a looming gap between population needs and available resources of food and water. [135] Clearly in the short term there are steps that can be urgently effected to ameliorate the situation. Thus the world has acted collectively on specific biodiversity issues (such as saving romantically-perceived large creatures such as the whale and the elephant), has banned chlorofluorohydrocarbons (CFCs) (implicated in destruction of the UV-absorbing ozone layer), has largely quarantined Antarctica from human destructiveness (but not from the effects of the ozone hole), exercised some control over nuclear waste and nuclear proliferation and is now (from Kyoto) evidently beginning to get serious about greenhouse gas emission (despite dissent from "greenhouse gas" nations such as Australia). Action, such as it is, has been informed by a large, concerned literature. [136]

Clearly there needs to be a radical change in the current global ethos which is still, in effect, that which sent off the European fleets to scour the world for treasure and slaves centuries ago to support Jane Austen's class. There are major matters crying out for global collective action. Thus the continuing massive assault on the remaining forests of the world and the consequent huge loss in biodiversity should be halted - no more species and ecosystems should be lost. While the developed world consumes a very high proportion of the world's resources we are facing the transformation of Asian nations with high growth economies into First World countries. However given the evidence of massive environmental damage to date, this development cannot be sustained. The current world evidently cannot support Western Europe, North America, Australasia and Japan without massive environmental damage. Can it seriously contemplate China and India with an American middle class lifestyle? [137]

From this it follows that there is a need for some global consensus on acceptable and sustainable environmental load (an immediately useful suggestion would simply be the abolition of the private car). The people of Bengal provide an example of unparallelled economic efficiency that is one possible boundary condition for high density human survival, with Long Island providing another extreme. Between the 2 there is a huge amount of room for sensible global consensus on where we are going. Given evidence for global warming, there must be effective action to limit emissions and provide a new form of enforceable "environmental accounting" or "renewable resource rental" that encompasses the real cost and impact of human activity. The same type of "environmental accounting" or "commercial decency" [138] should apply to industrial pollution, desertification, ecosystem destruction and displacement of high-efficiency subsistence agriculture with low efficiency monoculture cash crops. There must be recognition that "smallholder" agriculture in the Third World is highly efficient and sustainable but, unlike large-scale cash-crop farming, is largely excluded from the "dollar economy". [139] This has been cogently argued by Marilyn Waring (1988) in relation to "women's work", whether in the affluent West or in the economic subsistence that is the highly efficient and tightly focussed process occupying half the people of the world. [140]

There is a need for a rational, sustainability-directed economics that rewards efficiency and minimal use of resources and penalizes the reverse. In the parlance of biochemistry and electronics, there has to be "positive feedback" to encourage desirable outcomes and "negative feedback" to constrain undesirable courses. Despite the "New Order" of the United Nations and the post-Cold War Pax Americana, there is still in place a positive feedback mechanism that rewards and encourages wasteful and destructive activity (deforestation, desertification, industrial pollution, irreversible "mining" of biological and other resources, greenhouse gas emission and militarism). There is a complementary negative feedback mechanism that effectively punishes the most efficient and most minimal resource users, the people of the Third World, through largely externally imposed environmental degradation, crushing debt and unaffordable militarism. This utterly misplaced feedback arrangement has to be reversed emphatically. In a very real sense we are victims of our own social evolutionary success. The arrogant urban "winners", who are increasingly detached from basic biological sustainability realities, are irreversibly destroying whole swathes of the biosphere. The world is manifestly best left in the hands of the humble, low-impact "losers" who have a deep, intimate attachment to the richness of the world. We can draw the same message from St. Matthew, Chapter 5, Verse 5: "Blessed are the meek, for they shall inherit the earth."

It is already apparent that the world is beginning to appreciate the urgency of our situation and is becoming more responsive. The global action taken over CFCs may now be extended in at least some limited fashion to greenhouse gases. However a key corollary of sensible and comprehensive global action is the need for international accountability and free information flow. The revolution in information technology is rapidly achieving the latter. Some key experimental tests of whether the world has the collective will to enable humanity to get through the next century without catastrophic disaster would be global action (resolutely backed by onerous collective sanctions) on some "smaller", immediately soluble problems that would meet with general global approbation: e.g. restoration of Aung San Suu Kyi as the democratically elected ruler of Myanmar and indeed similar global insistence on basic human rights throughout the world; effective conventions and mechanisms for the rapid cessation of all military conflict on the planet; international protection of residual "aboriginal" people in countries such as Australia and Brazil; a just, sustainable and quintessentially normal life for Palestinians and other displaced people in their own lands; drastic reduction of Third World debt and an increase in women's rights, security and education to ameliorate disastrous population increases; resolute support for the highly efficient, sustainable, low cost, multi-faceted, "smallholder" or "village" integrated agriculture and industry that keeps half the world alive; weighted, global financial penalties for murder, genocide, unacceptable "enhanced mortality" gaps, population irresponsibility, ecosystem destruction, extinctions and other damage to the biosphere; a readily addressable computer-based register of all humanity, from those hiding in the jungles to those incarcerated in prison or "refugee camps", so that no more Ann Franks, Jeno Polyas or Raoul Wallenbergs can simply be "disappeared" from the face of the earth without remorseless international inquiry and penalty that may save them from oblivion. [141]

While environmentalists call for world government and global action, [142] it must be appreciated that there is a very real downside to globalisation and surrender of uninhibited national "rights" to pollute and otherwise violate the world. There is the notion of "managing" the biosphere, for example, [143] whereas there is an ideal we could aspire to of a world with a much lower population that enables normal global biosphere homeostatic mechanisms to operate. [144] While "global" decision-making is required, there is a very real danger that "global" management will fall into the perverting and malignant hands of major élites, corporations and powerful industrial societies. [145] In the interim, before we arrive at the New Jerusalem, the world should collectively employ the accountancy of Babylon to our noble ends, and apply the "user pays" principle. The humble subsistence villagers that cherish the earth will be rewarded, the Gadarene blasphemers will pay for their derelict stewardship. Unfortunately the forces of darkness are presently firmly in control. However there is at least some hope that a healthy start can be made by ensuring that at least vulnerable "middle ranking" environment-destroying nations (notably those in the Southern

Hemisphere such as Brazil and Australia) can be brought to heel by international inspection and the threat of sanctions.

17.15. The population nightmare

The fundamental problem the world is facing is catastrophic population increase. [146] The shortfall of food in the food/population equation can be met by cessation of meat eating and and other even more profound lifestyle adjustments that will maximize available resources for food production. However even when such radical adjustments are made their effects will be overcome by further increases in population. It is clear that all kinds of steps have to be taken urgently on both the food and industrial production side and the human consumption side in order to achieve a sustainable solution for the world. No doubt there is a world-wide move in the right direction but the current constraint on population growth is woefully insufficient in many areas and in an overall global sense.

China has acted with great responsibility in this area through the government-proscribed "one child" policy. In contrast, the laissez-faire of India will lead to humanitarian disaster as will religious proscription of birth control. While there is a general observation (most dramatically seen in Scandinavia and also in Kerala) that birth rates are inversely related to female education, [147] this can only make a partial contribution to the urgent need for effective action. It is also clear that childbirth is dangerous in the Third World. Thus in Sierra Leone the pregnancy-related death rate is 1800 per 100,000 births - contributing one seventh of women's deaths - as opposed to 27 per 100,000 in industrialized countries. A small increase in economic and personal security would decrease the birth rate in poor countries as women (and their partners) perceive a greater likelihood of their children making it to adulthood. [148]

It will take a long time before the Juggernaut is slowed to a stop and indeed can be moved in the opposite direction so that the world can return to a more sustainable population of several billion people. Apart from specific conception-related processes to be discussed below, major advances would involve education and a deliberate choice by the rich nations of the world to loosen the economic screws and admit the possibility of increased economic security for the highly efficient, low resource users of the Third World.

17.16. Selective contraception

While effective government proscription (albeit draconian) can have a major impact on population growth (as in the excellent example of China), other possible anti-fertility mechanisms can be suggested that are more compatible with the "Western" or "American" ethos involving the overriding importance of "rights of the individual". However in doing so we should keep in mind the ways in which global or local environmental strategies can burden particular groups. Thus Seager (1993) has analyzed how environmental activism in a variety of areas impinges selectively upon women. In relation to biodiversity and animal rights she cites the anti-fur propaganda showing a fur clad female model and the caption "It takes up to 40 dumb animals to make a fur coat. But only one to wear it"; and the fur-clad model ("rich bitch") and the animal caught in a leg-hold trap ("poor bitch"). In the population control area, the "blame" is typically also applied to women, whereas female literacy, female empowerment and economic security for women are sensible avenues for improvement. [149]

Only females bear children and accordingly an effective and conceivably socially solution to contain and reverse population growth would be application of fertility technologies and procedures that change the sex ratio at birth to maximize the proportion of males. This is already occurring in effect in India (where females are an expensive burden in terms of dowry provision) and in China (where the one-baby policy translates for many as a one male baby policy). Of course the methods involved (amniocentesis and female abortion in middle class India and female infanticide in peasant or working class India and

China) are gruesome, expensive and ultimately simply murder when postnatal or something that comes conceptually uncomfortably close to murder if circa mid-term. In about 1800 in certain parts of India, an unwanted (typically female) child could be deprived of sustenance, suckled on a nipple painted with poison (usually opium) or put in a sack and thrown into a river. In Bengal, if a formerly childless woman gave birth to children, one could be cast into the Ganges as an offering. [150] Infanticide was practised in Australian aboriginal societies. [151] Thus a new-born child who would clearly not survive the rigours of nomadic existence might be placed just far enough away from the fire in the desert night cold to ensure an endless sleep.

A variety of mechanical and chemical contraceptive devices or procedures are available for both males and females, as is effective chemical abortion. [152] However where childbirth is desired, cheap and reliable, peri-conception sex selection would be a useful technological advance to avoid the awfulness of mid-term abortion and the evil of infanticide and to provide choice for women in the Third World for whom each child birth carries a substantial risk. [153] Thus, for example, Falloux and Talbot (1993) cite the following United Nations assertion: "if all the women who say they do not want more babies could cease to conceive, the number of births would diminish by 27% in Africa ... And the maternal mortality would diminish by half." [154] Humane, choice-providing, in vitro possibilities can be contemplated such as in vitro fertilization involving biochemically isolated Y-chromosome-carrying spermatozoa or in vitro implantation of XY (male) embryos. However such procedures, while readily perfectable in a research and development sense and a Western context, would be very expensive for the Third World. Achievable low-cost technologies can be readily contemplated e.g. fertilization procedures favouring Y-sperm success and hence a male outcome if that is desired. While potentially much more ethically arguable and difficult to achieve, XX (female)-specific, "morning-after" chemical abortion could be a very cheap option for women wishing to "invest" in a male child.

One has great confidence that such protocols can be readily developed to deal with the human emergency in a fashion that is more acceptable, empowering and effective than at present. Such protocols have the major advantage that they would be applied through individual choice and may well not require government proscription or social pressure to achieve the desired result. However the social consequences of a markedly altered sex ratio are problematical. Botswana has a high female/male ratio (due to men going to South Africa to find work) and as a consequence is apparently a very happy society with minimal social violence or other crimes. One might suppose that the reverse would be true in a society with even a temporary high male/female ratio and that this might yield a violent, pressure-cooker society with a higher predisposition to human rights abuse in all kinds of ways. However this would not be necessarily so and there would be a long lead time before such potential psychopathies and sociopathies might emerge. Thus precisely this type of social engineering in Fiji a century ago resulted in a remarkably peaceful society. My wife's dadi (paternal grandmother) crossed the kala pani (the Black Water) to Fiji as an indentured labourer (5-year slave) and recalled that there were about 3 men to 1 woman. The British and Australian agents considered this a suitable ratio that maximized economic return with a concession for social and biological realities. The famous Australian journalist John Norton (1858-1916) commented on this from his perspective in 1916:

"The importation of black labor into this country [Australia] having been stopped, it was perhaps only to have been expected that the Colonial Sugar Refining Co. should have gone elsewhere, where it was still open them to purchase human bone and muscle in the cheapest possible market. They consequently established a black colony on one of the Pacific Islands [Fiji], and numbers of Indian coolies were imported to it. The most horrible code of morality was also imported to this ghastly settlement, where the prevailing conditions can only be described as hellish. It is not possible for a black to live there morally in marriage, but one woman is imported for a fixed number of men.

Not more women than are physically necessary are brought, but just as few as can be made to do." [155]

Human beings are very adaptable and the Indian slaves made the best of it, although some who could not take the hard labour and beating would go into the jungle and hang themselves. A similar indentured labourer sex ratio was applied in the South African context and a very high male suicide rate was attributed to this factor. [156] Mutual support and collective strength fostered survival in adversity. Hilarious stories are told of groups of women tricking and ambushing an insistent Indian foreman (sirdar) or an importuning Australian overseer and beating or urinating upon their persecutors. Nevertheless Indian women were forced by economic circumstances and social pressure to deal sexually with a multiplicity of men and with Europeans at the gora barak (European men's barracks). Most importantly this inauspicious social arrangement led to a remarkably peaceful and law-abiding society of great humanity and racial and religious tolerance. Sharing one's sexual partner with others surely involves a considerable exercise in tolerance and pragmatism as does acceptance of relations with multiple partners. That humane and tolerant ethos persists to this day in Fiji despite radical racial, religious, linguistic and cultural differences in that society that are vastly greater than differences between, for example, Northern Irish Catholics and Protestants. [157]

One can envisage a Brave New World in which the sex ratio is temporarily, markedly altered through a combination of intense global pressure for 1 child families, increases in economic security and literacy for Third World people (especially women), a strong temporary bias of both citizenry and governments for male children and the relatively simple and cheap, non-invasive technology to match the predilection. Of course women might feel endangered by being substantially outnumbered (albeit for a relatively brief period). One could argue to outraged women that this solution would be temporary and that a necessary corollary would be global consensus on exquisite observance of the rights of women. In this scheme of things women would necessarily be extraordinarily well protected, empowered and socially elevated as a matter of general global convention. No doubt other schemes can be suggested that would have a similar capacity to contain and reverse population growth. However it is likely that effective solutions will involve global governmental constraints on childbirth with effective sanctions or rewards to encourage compliance. The suggestion of a sex ratio change has the merits that it is effective, non-invasive, would comply with governmental and overall individual biases, is "pro-choice" for women and would lessen the need for draconian pressure for absolute compliance. Thus having 2 male children might be very indulgent and anti-social but would not have the potential environmental impact of having 1 female child.

17.17. The Jane Austen option

An ameliorating accompaniment to such schemes of humane, global consensus social engineering would be popularization and active encouragement of the "Jane Austen option" in which individual women make the decision to eschew or strictly limit child-bearing and find intellectual, artistic, industrial, social or spiritual avenues for creative fulfilment. Jane Austen, we will recall, changed her mind over Harris Bigg-Wither's proposal and finally decided in the morning to retract her acceptance and hence a conventional married life with a wealthy husband and no doubt numerous children. Both Jane Austen and her sister Cassandra lost the men with whom they were in love and remained unmarried. Their good friend Martha Lloyd, who lived with them for many years in Southampton and in Chawton, was also childless and was past childbearing age when she married the widowed Francis Austen in 1828. [158]

The "Jane Austen option" has much to commend it and we all have friends who have followed this path by accident or design. Jane Austen had the satisfaction of being an Aunt to a large swag of nieces and nephews and escaped the miseries and dangers of child bearing and the responsibilities of child rearing. The last 2 decades of her adult life were spent in the congenial company of her mother, her sister and their dear friend Martha Lloyd. Jane Austen's exquisite literary work was written (as is this) with absorption but also in the midst of the daily bustle of domestic life. The truth, reason and beauty of her work has made her easily the most popular serious English woman writer and has secured for her an affectionate place in the hearts of millions over 2 centuries.

The "Jane Austen option" is a net for a wider human catch. Generalized, it applies to all of humanity and instructs that modest absorption with truth and beauty is an alternative to the aggression, aggrandisement and obsessive material acquisition that is threatening the very survival of humanity. The Nobel Prize-winning Australian writer Patrick White, in a speech in Melbourne to a packed audience shortly before his death, was caustic in his condemnation of the mindlessly peripatetic. After castigating Australian "kiddults" (rather typical Australian adults who use self-effacing, diminutive "kid's talk"), he lashed out at the pointlessness of "City to Surf" and "Surf to City" races and "flogging poor camels across the stony desert" (a recent trans-continental competitive event). Why don't these people stay home, he argued, make themselves a nice meal and curl up with a good book? Patrick White adopted a version of the "Jane Austen option", living a civilized, highly creative life in the company of his male partner. Indeed in the Braver New World, in which humanity actively seeks to realistically address the crisis of biological sustainability, there will be many versions of the "Jane Austen option" that should be encouraged, ranging from homosexual relations to monastic celibacy. In this light we can see that the psychopathy of homophobia is not merely a threat to homosexual men and women and to a decent society but is also a constraint on sensible, humane, sympathetic approaches to the crisis of sustainability.

17.18. Conclusion

The world is facing a catastrophe from the impact of economic
activity attendant on continuing population growth. [159] China has
responded to the emergency with draconian constraints but its
population will continue to increase from the present 1 billion before
hopefully plateauing at 1.5 billion in the 21st century. Further, the
environmental impact of the currently greatly increased economic
activity in countries such as China and India is already immense and
there is a huge social pressure for continued economic advance. [160] The
warning of Paul Ehrlich (1968) in The Population Bomb is even more
urgent 30 years on: "Remember, above all, that more than half the
world is in misery now. That alone should be enough to galvanize us
into action, regardless of the exact dimensions of the future disaster
now staring Homo sapiens in the face." [161] Suzuki (1990) has cogently
stated the problem and the general nature of the solution: "The rapid
increase in human numbers at the very time that technological muscle
has also leapt ahead has generated the environmental crisis of today.
Scientists like Harvard's Edward Wilson and Stanford's Paul Ehrlich
point out the need for a profound shift in attitude towards the natural
world. The change must be a "quasi-religious"' shift in the spiritual
value that we place on other organisms." [162]

The exquisitely sustainable, Arcadian world of the Australian
and Amazonian aborigines has largely disappeared. The extraordinarily
efficient and potentially sustainable solution of Bengal survives as a
continuing, dignified lesson for humanity but faces the external threat
of man-made global environmental change and the internal threat due
to female disempowerment and utterly irresponsible, unchecked
population growth. [163] We have now seen the immense man-made
human disasters of the British Imperial era and how they have been
almost completely removed from general perception by a sustained and
continuing tradition of utterly distorted historiography. We must peer
outside our hygienic and beautiful Jane Austen worlds and appreciate
the seriousness of the crisis facing the world as a whole. Global

salvation demands that we now look honestly at the past and resolve with the survivors of the Holocaust: "Never Again". Practical translation of that resolution half a century from the Apocalypse will require urgent action guided by commitment to truth, reason, open communication and love of humanity.

Our world faces destruction as the Juggernaut lurches towards catastrophe. There is still time for acceptance of the homeostatic wisdom of the Australian aborigines that biological sustainability and the preservation of biodiversity and the richness of the world is our only path. But more than simple rational acceptance is required for our survival - we must love Truth, Reason and Beauty and accept that such appreciation is an end in itself. In the words of the Bengali poet Rabindranath Tagore: "We have come into this world to accept it, not merely to know it. We may become powerful by knowledge, but we attain fullness by sympathy." [164] Profound sympathy for the richness of the world will be the salvation of humanity.

17.19. 2008 Postscript - Epilogue

Ten years on after publication of "Jane Austen and the Black Hole of British History" in 1998, the greed, racism and lying persist and the world is now on the verge of disaster from an immediate global food price crisis that currently threatens billions [165] and a global climate emergency and sustainability emergency that may kill over 6 billion people by the end of this century. [166]

It is useful to repeat here the message on the back cover of the 1998 edition:

"Repetition of immense crimes against humanity such as the WW2 Holocaust is made less likely when the responsible society acknowledges the crime, apologizes, makes amends and accepts the injunction "Never again".

This book is concerned in part with the 2 century holocaust in British India that commenced with the Great Bengal Famine of 1769-1770 (10 million victims), concluded with the WW2 Bengal Famine (4 million victims) and took tens of millions of lives in between.

However these events have been almost completely written out of history and removed from general perception, there has been no apology nor amends made and indeed it is generally accepted that, in the absence of effective global action, these horrors will be repeated on an unimaginably larger scale in the coming century.

This carefully documented "J'accuse" addresses what the author terms the "Austenizing" of history or the deletion of awful realities from historical writing.

While it was legitimate for Jane Austen, the artist, to render her exquisite novels free of the contemporary awfulness in which her connections participated, the Austenizing of British history is a holocaust-denying outrage that threatens humanity."

Unfortunately the lying continues. In recent years global warming-exacerbated storms have devastated India, Bangladesh, Burma and other mega-delta regions (notably Louisiana). [167] In 2008 legislatively-mandated Biofuel Famine, Biofuel Genocide and climate criminal-imposed Climate Genocide are exacerbating the hunger of billions and the horrendous Global Avoidable Mortality Holocaust (16 million annual excess deaths). [168]

Since 1998 pollution of the planet with greenhouse gases has remorselessly continued and indeed accelerated (increasing annually by 3.2% in 2000-2005 as compared to 0.8% in 1990-1999). [169] The most recent international Climate Change Conference, that in Bali in December 2007, was sabotaged by the major Anglo-American polluters, the US, Australia and Canada, who opposed any explicit pollution reduction targets. [170] However the latest scientific discoveries point to a situation that is much graver than even the dire predictions of the 2007 IPCC Fourth Assessment Report. [171]

Thus top US climate scientist Dr Hansen and his colleagues say that the world has already reached a "tipping point" in relation to the melting of Arctic sea ice which has declined dramatically in recent years – indeed it may completely disappear in the coming decade. Dr Hansen argues that the current atmospheric CO_2 concentration of 385 ppm is too high and that we must return to a safe and sustainable concentration of 300-350 ppm in order to avoid massive damage to the biosphere through Arctic, Antarctic, Greenland and tundra ice melting, huge sea level rises, devastating global warming to temperatures several degrees Centigrade above pre-industrial, ocean acidification, massive loss of ocean and land photosynthetic capacity, huge agricultural productivity decline and massive depopulation. [172] Indeed top UK climate scientist Professor James Lovelock says that over 6 billion people will die this century if climate change is not addressed urgently. [173]

However the world is still dominated by a climate criminal, "climate sceptic" US Administration which still refuses to even sign the Kyoto protocol, let alone curb its world-leading greenhouse gas pollution. 2004 data from the US Energy Information Administration reveal that the "annual per capita fossil fuel-derived CO_2 pollution" in tonnes per head per year was 19.2 tonnes for Australia (40.3 if we include Australia's world-leading coal exports) as compared to 20 (the US), 20 (Canada), 4.2 (the World), 3.7 (China), 1.0 (India), 0.7 (Pakistan) and 0.25 (Bangladesh). [174]

Australia has a new Labor Government which is strong on nice-sounding rhetoric (e.g. the farcical 2008 Australia 2002 Summit) but which does not stand up to close scrutiny in a "politically correct racist" (PC racist) country committed to genocidal Bush-ite war policies and in which Coal is King. As recounted in Chapter 17, 50 years ago Australian Immigration Minister Arthur Calwell stated "two

Wongs do not make a White" and yet the above data indicate Australia's annual per capita CO_2 pollution is over 10 times that of China's i.e. "Ten Wongs do not make a White" (more embarrassing still, if it were actually reported by racist, lying Australian mainstream media, because the current Australian Federal Climate Change Minister is Senator Penny Wong). [175]

2008 has seen the emergence of the horror of Biofuel Famine and Biofuel Genocide that is threatening 4 billion malnourished people on Spaceship Earth. Global food prices have soared due to the CO_2-polluting biofuel perversion (legislatively mandated by the US, the UK and the EU), oil price rises (due to war and its immense cost), global warming (drought in Australia and the CIS), increasing agricultural cost, "market forces" in a globalized market for food (including meat from grain-fed livestock) and unilateralist, export-ban actions by major rice-exporting countries. [176]

We are seeing a re-run of the WW2 Bengal Famine but on possibly a 100-fold greater scale. Rice has doubled in price in just a few months in 2008; major rice-exporting countries have imposed export bans; and the West has legislatively mandated the use of food for transport, just as the Argentinians burned wheat to run their railways during WW2 (Chapters 14 and 15). [177]

The post-Holocaust protocol adopted by the Germans after 1945 can be summarized by the acronym C4A (CAAAA) – Cessation of the killing, Acknowledgment of the crime, Apology, Amends and Assertion "never again to anyone". Unfortunately, the killing continues and extraordinary media censorship in the Western Murdochracies ensures that there is essentially no Acknowledgment of the ongoing genocides on Spaceship Earth. Post-invasion excess deaths in the ongoing Palestinian, Iraqi and Afghan Genocides now total 0.3 million, 2 million and 3-7 million, respectively; Biofuel Genocide is increasing the 16 million annual avoidable deaths due to deprivation; and Climate

Genocide, already impacting the World, may kill over 6 billion people by the end of the century. [178]

What can decent people do? In short, we are obliged to (a) inform others about man-made atrocities; (b) act ethically in all our dealings with countries, corporations and individuals complicit in such atrocities (e.g. by Sanctions and Boycotts); and (c) act positively to create a safer world. [179]

Fundamental to rational risk management from the personal level (e.g. healthy life-style choices) to the global level (e.g. dealing with First World-imposed Biofuel Genocide and Climate Genocide) is a basic protocol successively involving (a) accurate data, (b) scientific analysis and (c) systemic change to minimize risk. [180] Thus in 2007 I published a huge book entitled "Body Count. Global avoidable mortality since 1950" detailing the horrendous 1950-2005 Global Avoidable Mortality Holocaust involving an estimated 1.3 billion excess deaths, a figure consonant with an independent estimate of 0.9 billion 1950-2005 under-5 infant deaths.

The causes of this catastrophe have fundamentally been violence, occupation- or hegemony-related deprivation, deprivation-exacerbated disease and lying. [181] While people are appalled by the egregious violence of man-made atrocities such as the Rwanda Tutsi Genocide, the Balkans War, the Cambodian Genocide and the Darfur Genocide, they have difficulty appreciating the awfulness of the vastly greater non-violent avoidable deaths through deprivation and deprivation-exacerbated disease.

In "Body Count" as in Chapter 17 above, I offered a variety of simple, cheap solutions based on wonderful examples of some very poor countries such as Cuba which have achieved remarkable success in addressing the fundamental human right of "right to life" through high female literacy, good governance, focussed investment and good primary health care. The same intelligent and humane approaches can effectively deal with the problems of excessive population and demands that have pushed the biosphere to a point of Climate Emergency and Sustainability Emergency. [182] Indeed 10,000 times more solar energy hits the earth each day than man currently uses and we already have highly efficient renewable energy technologies for cheaply and safely harvesting this resource. [183]

Fundamental to any rational risk management – as urgently needed today for Spaceship Earth - is accurate data and general reportage. Further, just as we take the advice of top medical specialists very seriously in relation to life-threatening conditions, so sensible risk management demands that we take very seriously the advice of top scientists at the cutting edge of research and the advice of top scientific bodies. Thus the Melbourne-based Yarra Valley Climate Action Group and the Australian climate action group umbrella organization, the Climate Emergency Network, have provided detailed and documented summations of such information from top scientists and top scientific organizations in relation to the Climate Emergency and Sustainability Emergency facing the World. [184] The continuing, entrenched lying in mainstream cultures acutely threatens humanity. History ignored yields history repeated. Peace is the only way but silence kills and silence is complicity. Please inform everyone you can.

Chapter 18.

2022: neoliberal ignoring of reality now existentially threatens Humanity and the Biosphere

18.1. British-imposed Indian Holocaust 1757-1947

British mythology has it that Britain brought wonderful things to India such as railways, canals, civil service, judiciary, Pax Britannica and cricket. The horrible reality is that the hugely outnumbered British with the help of well-fed Indian soldiers (sepoys) were able to control several hundred million Indians for over 2 centuries by keeping them in a state of bare survival. Under the British India suffered massive man-made famines over 2 centuries, from the 1769-1770 Great Bengal Famine (10 million deaths) to the 1942-1945 WW2 Bengal Famine (6-7 million deaths), with regular massive famines in between. [1]

India contributed an army of 2.4 million men to assist the British war effort in World War 2. However India was rewarded by a British-imposed Bengal Famine (WW2 Bengali Holocaust, WW2 Indian Holocaust) that killed 6-7 million Indians in Bengal, Assam, Bihar and Odisha (Orissa) in the period 1942-1945. Australia was a major producer of wheat but in WW2 only exported 9 million tonnes out of 24 million produced. Australia deliberately by-passed starving India, this boosting British food stocks and what was evidently a starvation-based military strategy to prevent Japanese advance into Bengal. [2]

In over 2 centuries of genocidal British rule avoidable deaths in India from British-imposed deprivation in the period 1757-1947 totaled 1.8 billion, an Indian Holocaust and an Indian Genocide as defined by Article 2 of the UN Genocide Convention. Using census and other estimates of Indian population in these periods, post-invasion excess deaths totaled 0.6 billion, 1757-1837; 0.5 billion, 1837-1901 under Queen Victoria; and 0.4 billion in 1901-1947; this being 1.5 billion in total and 1.8 billion victims if the carnage in the various royalty-ruled Indian British Protectorate States are included. [3]

Winston Churchill was well aware of the consequences of imposed deprivation on Britain's Indian subjects. Thus Churchill back in 1935 in a speech to the UK House of Commons made the following astonishing confession: "In the standard of life they have nothing to spare. The slightest fall from the present standard of life in India means slow starvation, and the actual squeezing out of life, not only of millions but of scores of millions of people, who have come into the world at your invitation and under the shield and protection of British power" [4]

From the quantitative perspective of avoidable deaths the 2 century British-imposed Indian Holocaust involving 1.8 billion avoidable deaths from deprivation has been the worst holocaust in human history. From a qualitative perspective the 1788 onwards Australian Aboriginal Genocide and Ethnocide was the worst in human history – of about 750 distinct Indigenous languages and dialects before the British invasion only about 120 survive today with all but 20 endangered. [5] The horrendous, British-imposed Indian Holocaust has been largely white-washed from public perception, and the Australian Aboriginal Ethnocide continues.

18.2. The "forgotten" 2-century Indian Holocaust in the context of a catalogue of mostly European-imposed genocides and holocausts

To the end of humane bearing witness it is useful to catalogue over 60 holocausts and genocides, mostly of recent centuries and European-imposed. [6]

Estimates of deaths in holocausts, genocides and famines and deriving from actual violence and from imposed deprivation are given in brackets as follows for the following alphabetically listed atrocities:

1978-1997 Afghan Genocide and Afghan Holocaust (6 million),

2001 onwards Afghan Genocide and Afghan Holocaust (7 million),

15th – 19th century African Holocaust (slave trade; 6 million),

16th century onwards Amerindian Genocide, American Holocaust (90 million),

19th century Argentinian Indian Genocide (1 million),

1915-1923 Armenian Genocide (1.5 million),

1950 onwards Asian Holocaust due to Australia-complicit US Asian Wars (40 million),

1914-1924 Assyrian Genocide (Syriac Genocide; 0.2-0.3 million),

1788 onwards Australian Aboriginal Genocide and Aboriginal Ethnocide (2 million),

1769-1770, Bengal Famine (10 million),

1942-1945 WW2 Bengali Holocaust, WW2 Bengal Famine and WW2 Indian Holocaust (6-7 million),

1971-1972 Bengali Holocaust and gendercide (3.0 million),

1967-1970, Biafran Genocide (2 million),

1990s Bosnian Genocide (circa 0.1 million),

20th century Brazilian Indigenous Genocide (1 million),

1969-1998 Cambodian Genocide (6.0 million),

19th century Chinese Holocaust (Opium slavs trade and Tai Ping rebellion; 20-100 million),

1937-1945 WW2 Chinese Holocaust (35-40 million),

1958-1961 Chinese Holocaust of the Great Leap Forward (20-30 million),

19th -20th century Congo Genocide (Belgian Congo) (10 million),

1960 onwards Congolese Genocide and Congolese Holocaust (20 million),

1984-1985 Ethiopian famine (1 million),

13th century, Mongol-imposed Eurasian Holocaust (40-60 million),

1939-1945 WW2 European Holocaust (30 million Slavs, Jews and Roma killed),

1941-1950 German Genocide and German Holocaust (9 million),

Post-1950 Global Avoidable Mortality Holocaust (1,500 million since 1950),

1960-1996, Guatemala Mayan Indian Genocide (1.9 million),

1890s and 1990s, Hazara Genocide (Afghanistan) (circa 0.1 million),

1757-1947 Indian Holocaust from famine and deprivation (1,800 million),

1947 Indian Holocaust due to Partition (1.0 million),

1918-1920 Influenza epidemic in India (17 million),

1918-1920 Influenza Epidemic (50 million deaths out of 500 million cases),

1917-1919 Iranian Famine (2 million),

1978 onwards Iranian Holocaust and Iranian Genocide (3 million),

2003-2011 21st century Iraqi Genocide and Iraqi Holocaust (2.7 million),

1990-2011 Iraqi Genocide and Iraqi Holocaust (4.6 million),

1914-2011 Iraqi Genocide and Iraqi Holocaust (9 million),

1939-1945 WW2 Jewish Holocaust, Shoa (5-6 million),

1950-1953 Korean Genocide and Korean Holocaust (5.2 million),

1840s Irish Famine (2 million),

1955-1975 Laotian Genocide (1.2 million),

2011 Libyan Genocide (0.2 million),

19th century Maori Genocide in New Zealand (0.2 million),

2000 onwards 21st century Muslim Genocide and Muslim Holocaust (32 million),

1900s Namibian Genocide (0.1 million),

17th – 19th century North American Indian Genocide (up to 18 million),

1916 onwards Palestinian Genocide and Palestinian Holocaust (2.2 million),

1865-1870 Paraguay Genocide (1 million),

14th century Plague, Black Death (75-200 million in Eurasia and North Africa),

1939-1945 WW2 Polish Genocide and Polish Holocaust (6 million),

21st century Rohingya Genocide (circa 0.1 million),

1921-1922 Russian famine, Povolzhye famine (5 million),

1930-1953 Russian Holocaust under Stalin (3 million),

1994 Rwandan Genocide (0.9 million),

2019 onwards, SARS-CoV-2 coronavirus (Covid-19) Pandemic (possibly 18 million as of May 2022)

18th-19th century, Scottish Highland Clearances (circa 0.1 million),

1992 onwards Somali Genocide and Somali Holocaust (2.2 million),

19th century South Pacific Genocide via disease (0.1 million),

1930-1953 Soviet Holocaust of purges under Stalin (10 million),

1941-1945 WW2 Nazi Germany-imposed Soviet Holocaust (25 million),

1955-2018 Sudan Genocide and Sudan Holocaust (13 million),

2011 onwards Syrian Genocide (1.0 million),

1990-2018 Tamil Genocide in Sri Lanka (0.2 million),

1975-1999 East Timorese Genocide (0.3 million),

1930s Ukrainian Famine, Holodomor (7 million),

1950- US Asian Wars (40 million),

2001- US War on Terror aka the US War on Muslims (32 million),

1945-1975 Vietnamese Genocide and Vietnamese Holocaust (15.3 million),

1914-1918 World War 1 (20 million),

1939-1945 World War 2 (100 million),

2015 onwards Yemeni Genocide (circa 0.1 million)

(my sincere apologies for any absences or underestimates).

As of early May 2022 there were 6.3 million deaths out of 514 million infection cases in the Covid-19 Pandemic due to the SARS-Cov-2 coronavirus, but there may be a 3-fold under-reportage in Developing Countries. Covid-19 deaths per million of population were 3,052 (US, population 334.5 million), 2,552 (UK, population 68.5 million), 278 (Australia, population 26.0 million) and 4 (China, population 1,439.3 million). Taking the China result as a baseline for what could and should have been achieved, avoidable Covid-19 deaths (January 2020 to May 2022) total 1,020,000 (US), 175,000 (UK) and 7,100 (Australia). [7] Should President Donald Trump (US), PM Boris Johnson (UK) and PM Scott Morrison (Australia) be held responsible for their failures?

Almost totally ignored in its totality, about 1.7 million Americans die preventably each year from "life-style choice" and "political choice" reasons, and accordingly about 35 million Amercians have died thus in an Amercian Holocaust since 9/11 in 2001. However successive US governments have committed to a long-term accrual cost of $6 trillion for the War on Terror. Further, it was estimated in 2015 that 32 million Muslims had died from violence, 5 million, and imposed deprivation, 27 million, in 20 countries invaded by the US Alliance since the US Government's 9/11 false flag atrocity that killed about 3,000 innocent people. Thus successive US goverments have committed $6 trillion to killing over 30 million Muslims abroad for oil and hegemony rather than trying to save the lives of over 30 million Americans at home. [8]

Climate change has generated about 20 million climate refugees in the last decade, and about 1 million people die avoidably from climate change-imposed deprivation each year. It has been estimated that 9 million people die from air pollution each year, this including 75,000 people dying from the long-term effects of pollutants from burning Australian exported coal and 10,000 Australians dying from air pollution. [9] It is estimated that in the absence of requisite action 10 billion people will die this century in a worsening Climate Genocide en route to a sustainable human population of only 1 billion in 2100. [10]

The greater the actual or prospective carnage the more assiduously do the Mainstream journalist, editor, politician, academic and commentariat presstitutes suppress the Awful Truth in the interests of the One Percenters and remorseless neoliberalism. Thus the Uighur population of China's Xinjiang province is subject to harsh treatment (1 million confined for "re-education") but there is essentially no state killing and Uighur health outcomes are excellent, comparable to those in China as a whole, and vastly better than in US Alliance-occupied Afghanistan. Yet the US Alliance refers to a "Uighur Genocide" despite essentially no violent Uighur deaths. However a Google Search for "Uighur Genocide" (essentially no killing) yields 55,000 results, whereas a Google Search for "Bengali Holocaust" (6-7 million Indians deliberately starved to death in 1942-1945 for strategic reasons by the British with Australian complicity) yields 3,000 results, and a Google Search for "Afghan Holocaust" (7 million Afghan deaths from violence and war-imposed deprivation, 2001-2021) yields 5,000 results. [11] The reader is invited to do their own comparative Google Searches in relation to the genocide and holocaust atrocities summarized above. For the US genocide has only been committed in recent decades by non-European countries the US doesn't like and by Serbs and Russians.

18.3. Fake news through Mainstream presstitutes lying by omission

"Fake news" is a term popularized by former US President Donald Trump who achieved the remarkable feat of telling an astonishing 30,000 lies and falsehoods in his 4 year administration. [12]

"Fake news" or "lying" comes in 2 varieties – lying by omission and lying by commission. Lying by omission is far, far worse than lying by commission because the latter at least admits public refutation and public debate. [13] The example above at the end of section 18.2 illustrates both perversions. The wide dissemination of the falsehood of a "Uighur Genocide" (despite zero deaths) illustrates lying by commission, whereas the minimal mention of the horrendous "Bengali Holocaust" (6-7 million deaths) and the "Afghan Holocaust" (7 million deaths) illustrates lying by omission.

Similarly, the war criminal Russian invasion of Ukraine in February 2022 (already thousands of Ukrainian deaths) is deservedly massively reported but the West almost totally ignores the 1916 onwards and ongoing Palestinian Genocide (2.2 million deaths from violence, 0.1 million, and imposed deprivation, 2.1 million) [14]. Similarly, almost totally ignored in the appalling Ukraine War context are US invasion of 52 countries since WW2 [15], post-1950 US Asian Wars (40 million Asian deaths) [16], the post-9/11 US War on Terror (32 million deaths from violence and imposed deprivation) [17], the Iraqi Holocaust and Iraqi Genocide (5 million deaths, 1990 onwards), and the continuing Afghan Holocaust (7 million deaths, 2001 onwards) [18]. In vain one protests that black lives, brown lives and non-European lives matter.

Professors Edward Herman and Noam Chomsky have cogently exposed American Mainstream media (MSM) as endlessly mendacious propaganda agents of US government. [19] This corporate subversion of American democracy is compounded by the massive Zionist subversion of the US and US Alliance countries after Apartheid Israel acquired nuclear weapons by 1967. The horrible reality is that Zionism is genocidal racism and Nazism without gas chambers but with 90 nuclear weapons. Anti-racist Jewish American scholar Professor Bertell Ollman: "An all out struggle against Zionism by Jews, therefore, is also the most effective way to fight against real anti-Semitism. Furthermore, if Zionism is indeed a particularly virulent form of nationalism and, increasingly, of racism and if Israel is acting toward its captive minority in ways that resemble more and more how the Nazis treated their Jews, then we must also say so. For obvious reasons, the Zionists are very sensitive about being compared to the Nazis (not so sensitive that it has restrained them in their actions but enough to bellow "unfair" and to charge "anti-Semitism" when it happens). Yet, the facts on the ground, when not obscured by one or another Zionist rationalization, show that the Zionists are the worst anti-Semites in the world today, oppressing a Semitic people as no nation has done since the Nazis.". [20]

Google is owned by Alphabet which is the world's number 1 media organization and has a Zionist-dominated Board. However Google grossly violates journalistic standards by blatantly censoring the views of numerous anti-racist Jewish humanitarians as recorded in a series of public interest websites. Thus 5 websites recording criticism by anti-racist Jews of genocidally racist Zionism, Apartheid Israel, Israeli state terrorism, the Gaza Concentration Camp and the Palestinian Genocide are well hidden on Google Searches whereas Bing Searches reveal these sites as number 1 to 10 on page 1. This constitutes extraordinary censorship by Google of anti-racist Jewish opinion. [21] While numerous anti-racist Jewish intellectuals are resolutely critical of the ongoing Palestinian Genocide, Western Mainstream Media variously censor or white-wash the nuclear terrorist, genocidally racist, and grossly human rights-abusing conduct of Apartheid Israel. A part explanation for this huge moral discrepancy is that the American 60% of the world's 30 biggest media companies have a disproportionately high Jewish Board membership. Jews and females represent 2% and 51%, respectively, of the US population but average 33% and 19%, respectively, of Board members of the top 18 US media companies. [22]

The US became increasingly Zionist subverted after Apartheid Israel gained nuclear weapons by 1967. Support for Apartheid Israel (and hence of apartheid) is now a pillar of US politics, with anti-racist critics of Israeli apartheid ferociously attacked, side-lined, and falsely defamed as anti-Semitic. However Zionist control and hubris are now blatant: 32 percent or about one third of President Joe Biden's Cabinet are Jewish Zionists and the remainder are moderate Christian Zionists (as opposed to the fervently fundamentalist Pentecostal Evangelical Christian Zionists who support Trump). [23] Slavishly US-backed Apartheid Israel subjects Israeli Palestinians to 65 Nazi-style, race-based discriminatory laws but the fanatical and mendacious Zionists falsely condemn any Nazi comparisons as "anti-Semitism". In horrible reality one can make a shocking list of 52 Zionist- and Apartheid Israeli-Nazi Germany comparisons. [24] Massive Zionist subversion of America and the American Establishment has made ordinary Americans subject to egregious lying by commission, lying by omission, and fake news through lying by omission . [25]

18.4. War is the penultimate in racism, genocide the ultimate in racism – revealing genocidally racist Churchill and Zionist quotes re brutally colonized Palestine

For all that the wonderful Palestinian humanitarian Jesus left us the profoundly humane memes of "Do unto others as you would have them do unto you" and "Love thy neighbor as thyself", Humanity has regularly violated these injunctions, and most appallingly so in the holocausts and genocides summarized above in section 18.2. War is the penultimate in racism, and genocide the ultimate in racism.

The Anglosphere democracies (the US, UK, Canada, Australia and New Zealand) are internally peaceful, are cognizant of human rights, have the rule of law, and these days fervently eschew explicit racism.

However as members of the US Alliance they have variously been involved in horrendous invasions, occupations and genocidal devastations of non-European countries across the world in the post-WW2 era. This Anglosphere moral disease involving peace, rule of law, and non-racism at home but repeated genocidal violence abroad since WW2 means that their position must be described as politically correct racism (PC racism).

All the overseas countries of the Anglosphere derive from British colonizarion and decimation of Indigenous peoples. The Anglosphere countries profess regret for this genocidal record but the regret is hollow because they all (with the possible exception of modern New Zealanders) fervently support the ongoing Zionist colonization and ethnic cleansing of Palestine. Under the Coalition led by Christian Zionist PM Scott Morrison racist White Australia is second only to the US as a supporter of Apartheid Israel. [26]

In 1880 the 0.5 million population of Palestine was about 90% Muslim and 10% Christian, with about 25,000 Jews, half of them immigrants. By 1947 the population of Palestine was 1,970,000 comprising 630,000 Jews (32.0%), 143,000 Christians (7.3%) and 1,181,000 Muslims (59.9%) i.e. two thirds were Indigenous Palestinians. 1n 1948 the non-Semitic European Zionist colonizers rejected calls by Palestinians, anti-racist Jews, the UN, the Arab World and civilized humanity for a secular, democratic and multicultural state, and seized nearly 80% of Palestine, emptied over 500 villages, killed 10,000 Palestinians, forcibly expelled 800,000 Palestinians (about 60% of the Indigenous Palestinian population) in the Nakba (or Catastrophe), and proclaimed the race-based settler state and democracy-by-genocide pariah state of "Israel" (but better described as "Apartheid Israel"). In the 1967 Naksa (Setback) a genocidal Apartheid Israel invaded all of its neighbours, seized all of Palestine plus territory of all its neighbours, and expelled a further 400,000 Arabs.

A Zionist-subverted West ignores the present reality that Apartheid Israel rules all of a 90% ethnically cleansed Palestine (plus ethnically cleansed parts of Syria and Lebanon) and of its 14.4 million Subjects 6.8 million (47.0%) are Jewish Israelis, 0.4 million (2.8%) are non-Jews and non-Arabs, 2.0 million (13.9%) are Palestinian Israelis, and 5.2 million (36.1%) are Occupied Palestinians with zero human rights. Despite a century of a Palestinian Genocide involving killing, deprivation and repeated mass expulsions, Indigenous Palestinians today still represent 50% of the Subjects of Apartheid Israel in Palestine. Further, 72% of the 7.2 million Indigenous Palestinian Subjects of Apartheid Israel are excluded from voting for the government ruling them i.e. they are subject to egregious Apartheid as perceived by leading human rights groups and anti-racist Jewish and non-Jewish humanitarians around the world (including heroes in the fight against South Afrcian apartheid, notably Nobel laureates Nelson Mandela and Desmond Tutu). [27]

Winston Churchill (a fervent Zionist. responsible for secretly deciding post-war partition of Palestine in 1944, and also a supporter of the disastrous Partition of India) had a great hatred of Indians ("I hate Indians. They are a beastly people with a beastly religion"). Churchill's racism extended to Indigenous Palestinian, Indigenous Americans and Indigenous Australians: "I do not apologize for the takeover of the region by the Jews from the Palestinians in the same way I don't apologize for the takeover of America by the whites from the Red Indians or the takeover of Australia from the blacks [i.e. Australian aborigines]. It is natural for a superior race to dominate an inferior one". Zionist leaders from the founder of Zionism (racist psychopath Theodor Herzl) to the recent PM of Apartheid Israel, Benjamin Netanyahu, were frank in espousing genocide of the Indigenous inhabitants. Thus, for example, Herzl ("We shall try to spirit the penniless population across the border by procuring employment for it in the transit countries, while denying it employment in our country. The property owners will come over to our side. Both the process of expropriation and the removal of the poor must be carried out discretely and circumspectly") and Netanyahu ("Israel should have exploited the repression of the demonstrations in China, when world attention focused on that country, to carry out mass expulsions among the Arabs of the territories"). [28]

18.5. A new and dangerous anti-science culture of blatant Trumpist lying

We expect authoritarian governments to lie, and anti-racist Jewish American writer I .F. Stone famously generalized that "Governments lie". However the Australian Coalition Government under PM Scott Morrison has adopted blatant, in-your-face lying and falsehood to an extraordinary, Orwellian and Trumpist degree as revealed by Bernard Keane in his scathing book "Lies and Falsehoods. The Morrison Government and the new culture of deceit". Keane has perceived a distinct shift to a culture of blatant lying in the US Alliance democracies. This change is dramatically and quantitatively exampled by the case of John Profumo, a leading UK Conservative Minister who resigned from parliament in 1963 because the press revealed that he had lied to the House of Commons over his affair with Christine Keeler. Similarly, back in 1998 US President Bill Clinton was impeached because he had lied over his affair with Monica Lewinski: "I did not have sexual relations with that woman". From these dire consequences from what many would see as "white lies" about personal matters, we jump to unpunished war criminal US President George W. Bush (whose Administration told 935 lies about Iraq between 9/11 and the illegal and massively deadly invasion of Iraq that killed 2.7 million Iraqis), and thence to US President Donald Trump (who astonishingly made over 30,000 false or misleading assertions during his 4-year Administration). [29]

There was always massive Mainstream lying by omission (as described in this book in relation to the WW2 Bengali Holocaust), but the "quality" Mainstream media and good-mannered politicians tried to avoid blatant lying by commission. However now there is massive lying by commission and as well as lying by omission, notably by the Trumpists and the anti-science climate change deniers.

In science there is zero tolerance for lying because it simply short-circuits the scientific process. Science-based rational risk management that is crucial for societal safety, successively involves (a) accurate data, (b) scientific analysis, this involving the critical testing of potentially falsifiable hypotheses, and (c) informed systemic change to minimize risk.

Unfortunately, this rational risk management protocol is typically perverted at the individual, family or local level, or at the level of the family of nations by (a) lying, self-deception, spin, obfuscation, intimidation and censorship, (b) anti-science spin, this involving the selective use of asserted facts to support a partisan position, and (c) blame and shame that is counterproductive because it blocks reportage crucial for rational risk management and in the worst cases leads to war. [30]

 Accordingly, my view in 2022 is that ignoring of reality through an entrenched culture of lying by omission and lying by commission now existentially threatens Humanity and the Biosphere.

18.5. Selective Western indignation re Russia's criminal Ukraine War but not regarding Apartheid Israel's Palestinian Genocide and genocidal US wars for oil and hegemony

The war criminal Russian invasion of Ukraine that has presently killed thousands of innocent Ukrainians is rightly condemned by the West which has applied massive sanctions on Russia in response. However there is deafening silence over the war criminal Apartheid Israeli invasion and occupation of Palestine and the ongoing, century-long British- and Zionist-imposed Palestinian Genocide (2.2 million Palestinian deaths from violence, 0.1 million, and imposed deprivation, 2.1 million, since the British invasion of the Middle East in 2014 for oil and imperial hegemony). Indeed presently each year Israel violently kills an average of about 550 Occupied Palestinians and passively murders a further 4,000 through imposed egregious deprivation. Indeed some Western media have falsely claimed images of bombing-devastated Gaza as coming from war-ravaged Ukraine, and in a celebrated instance claimed the image of a fair Occupied Palestinian child remonstrating with an Israeli solider as that of a Ukrainian child castigating a Russian soldier. Likewise mendacious and racist Western Mainstream journalist, editor, politician, academic and commentariat presstitutes utterly ignore the US invasion of 52 countries since WW2 and in particular the post-1990 US Alliance-imposed Iraqi Holocaust (5 million Iraqis actively and passively killed) and the post-9/11 Afghan Holocaust (7 million Afghans actively and passively killed). [31] While the West has rightly applied massive economic sanctions to Russia over its war criminal invasion of Ukraine, the application of peaceful Boycotts, Divestment and Sanctions (BDS) against Apartheid Israel over its genocidal war crimes is falsely condemned by the Zionist-subverted West as "anti-Semitism". Boycotts, Divestment and Sanctions were successfully applied against Apartheid South Africa but the Zionist-subverted West indignantly denies what human rights groups and anti-racist humanitarians identify as Israeli apartheid. [32]

18.6. Anti-Arab anti-Semitism, anti-Jewish anti-Semitism, holocaust-ignoring, nuclear terrorism, and colonial atrocities of US- and Zionist-subverted IHRA countries

The International Holocaust Remembrance Alliance (IHRA) has 34 European members and has a false Zionist definition of "anti-Semitism" that has been used to smear anti-racist critics of genocidal Zionism, Apartheid Israel and Apartheid Israel's ongoing Palestinian Genocide. Indeed the IHRA definition was used to falsely defame and politically cripple UK Labour's most outstanding anti-racist leader, Jeremy Corbyn. In short, the IHRA is anti-Arab anti-Semitic (by falsely defaming anti-racist Palestinian, Arab and Muslim critics of Apartheid Israel), anti-Jewish anti-Semitic (by falsely defaming anti-racist Jewish critics of Apartheid Israel), and holocaust-denying (ignoring all WW2 holocausts other than the WW2 Jewish Holocaust (5-6 million killed by violence and deprivation), namely (deaths from violence and imposed deprivation in brackets) the WW2 European Holocaust (30 million Slavs, Jews and Gypsies killed), the WW2 Bengali Holocaust (6-7 million Indians deliberately starved to death for strategic reasons by the British with Australian complicity in 1942-1945), the WW2 Chinese Holocaust (35-40 million Chinese killed under the Japanese, 1937-1945), and indeed ignoring and hence denying about 60 other horrendous genocides and holocausts). Of the 34 IHRA countries:

(1) all 34 are European;

(2) the 5 outside of Europe (Argentina, Australia, Canada, Apartheid Israel, and the USA) are societies based on horrendous genocide of the Indigenous inhabitants;

(3) 4 are nuclear terrorist states (Apartheid Israel, France, the UK, and the US) who have adopted the unspeakably evil military strategy of mass incineration of billions of human beings;

(4) of the 29 members in Europe, all but 6 (Austria, Finland , Ireland, Serbia, Sweden and Switzerland), i.e. 23, belong to nuclear-armed NATO (together with Canada and the US), and thus support nuclear mass murder of women, children and men as a military strategy;

(5) of the 29 members in Europe, 7 were notably complicit in the WW2 Jewish Holocaust and the WW2 European Holocaust (Croatia, France, Germany, Hungary, Italy, Latvia, and Romania);

(6) of the 34 members, 14 were notably involved in the brutal conquest and genocide of Indigenous non-European people (Argentina, Australia, Belgium, Canada, Denmark, France, Germany, Apartheid Israel, Italy, Netherlands, Portugal, Spain, the UK and the USA);

(7) of the 34 members, 25 are among the 30 members of nuclear-armed NATO, namely (non-IHRA NATO members in bold): (**Albania**, Belgium, Bulgaria, Canada, Croatia, Czech Republic, Denmark, Estonia, France, Germany, Greece, Hungary, **Iceland**, Italy, Latvia, Lithuania, Luxembourg, **Montenegro**, Netherlands, **North Macedonia**, Norway, Poland, Portugal, Romania, Slovakia, Slovenia, Spain, **Turkey**, the United Kingdom, and the   United States);

(8) of the 34 members, only 2 (Austria and Ireland) have had the moral decency to sign and ratify the Treaty on the Prohibition of Nuclear Weapons (TPNW) that was the great accomplishment of the Melbourne-founded and 2017 Nobel Prize-winning International Campaign to Abolish Nuclear Weapons (ICAN). [33]

Over 40 anti-racist Jewish organizations have condemned the IHRA Definition of anti-Semitism. [34] The almost exclusively US Alliance and Western adoption of the anti-Arab anti-Semitic, anti-Jewish anti-Semitic and holocaust-denying IHRA definition of anti-Semitism is an extraordinary example of massive and indeed Orwellian lying by omission and lying by commission in the Zionist-subverted West.

18.7. World hero Julian Assange imprisoned for revealing a huge body of secret US documents

The world's most famous journalist, world hero and Australian hero, Julian Assange, has been imprisoned for 10 years for truth-telling and is facing life imprisonment in a US prison. Not content with massive lying by omission and lying by commission, the US Alliance and Western Mainstream presstitutes are committed to the destruction of truth-telling Julian Assange. The Julian Assange-released video showing the massacre of unarmed Iraqi civilians (including journalists and children) by a US Apache helicopter crew is unforgettable. The huge body of US documents released by Julian Assange (with the collaboration of some Mainstream journalists who have not been persecuted) does not actually reveal how many people the Americans killed in Iraq and Afghanistan – because as stated by US General Tommy Franks: "We don't do body counts".

Julian Assange has been horribly maltreated for invading the sanctum of US secrets. In contrast, as a science-informed scholar I have been writing for nearly 30 years in 8 huge books and in hundreds of carefully researched articles about the scientifically-assessed body count from Anglosphere atrocities from the "forgotten" WW2 Bengali Holocaust (6-7 million Indian deliberately starved to death) to the

Mainstream-ignored carnage of the 1990 onwards Iraqi Holocaust (5 million killed by violence and imposed deprivation) and the 2001 onwards Afghan Holocaust (7 million killed by violence and imposed deprivation). [35] However while Julian Assange faces endless abusive imprisonment and eventual death in custody for violating the secrecy of the genocidal American war criminals, I have merely been ignored and rendered "invisible" in my own country, Australia, in the last decade by the gate-keepers (surmised to be Australian intelligence, traitorous Zionist and Mainstream media gate-keepers).

However I was very pleased to note that John Shipton (the father and indefatigable supporter of Julian Assange) has variously acknowledged my efforts to quantitate the ever-increasing carnage in American wars. Thus John Shipton as reported by the UK Independent (2021): "Shipton points to the work of Australian academic Dr Gideon Polya and others, who have estimated the US-led invasion of Iraq and Afghanistan led to millions of deaths. He also says millions of people were turned into migrants or refugees as a result of the conflicts", and by Sydney Criminal Lawyers (2021): "Melbourne academic Dr Gideon Polya has calculated 6 to 7 million excess deaths in the Middle East due to western intervention over the last two decades, Shipton told the rally in Sydney's CBD, adding that these are the crimes his son has exposed." [36]

18.8. Nuclear weapons and climate change existentially threaten Humanity and the Biosphere

The world is acutely threatened by nuclear weapons, poverty and man-made climate change. A comprehensive Nuclear Weapons Ban is needed to avoid an accidental or deliberate full-scale nuclear catastrophe and a consequent Nuclear Winter that will wipe out most of Humanity and the Biosphere through cessation of life-sustaining photosynthesis. As of 2020 poverty was killing about about 7.4 million people each year in an ongoing Global Avoidable Mortality Holocaust in which about 1,500 million people, mostly children, have died thus since 1950. With a species extinction rate 1,000 times greater than normal, crucial tipping points being exceeded or approached, atmospheric carbon dioxide (CO_2) and methane (CH_4) steadily increasing at record rates, and oil and gas use increasing at record and increasing rates (coal use has flattened out at a record rate), it appears effectively too late to avoid a catastrophic plus 2 degrees Centigrade temperature rise. Nevertheless, we are all obliged to do everything we can to make the future "less bad" for future generations. As amplified below, to avoid horrendous human mass mortality and destruction of most of the remaining Biosphere there must be a total ban on nuclear weapons, an end to deadly poverty in the global South, and reversal of man-made global warming. [37] It bears endless repetition that one of Humanity's greatest minds, Stephen Hawking, has declared: "We see great peril if governments and societies do not act NOW [my emphasis] to render nuclear weapons obsolete and stop further climate change" [38].

18.9. Treaty on the Prohibition of Nuclear Weapons (TPNW)

The Treaty on the Prohibition of Nuclear Weapons (TPNW) opened for signature at the United Nations in New York on 20 September 2017 and entered into force on 22 January 2021. There are currently only 86 signatories and 60 states parties. The Article 1 prohibitions are salutary: "Each State Party undertakes never under any circumstances to:
(a) Develop, test, produce, manufacture, otherwise acquire, possess or stockpile nuclear weapons or other nuclear explosive devices;
(b) Transfer to any recipient whatsoever nuclear weapons or other nuclear explosive devices or control over such weapons or explosive devices directly or indirectly;
(c) Receive the transfer of or control over nuclear weapons or other nuclear explosive devices directly or indirectly;
(d) Use or threaten to use nuclear weapons or other nuclear explosive devices;
(e) Assist, encourage or induce, in any way, anyone to engage in any

activity prohibited to a State Party under this Treaty;
(f) Seek or receive any assistance, in any way, from anyone to engage
in any activity prohibited to a State Party under this Treaty;
(g) Allow any stationing, installation or deployment of any nuclear
weapons or other nuclear explosive devices in its territory or at any
place under its jurisdiction or control." [39]

There are presently 9 states that possess nuclear weapons. [40] According
to the Nobel Prize-winning International Campaign Against
NuclearWeapons (ICAN) the numbers of nuclear weapons held are as
follows: Russia (6,255), US (5,550), China (350), France (290), UK
(225), Pakistan (165), India (156), Apartheid Israel (90), and North
Korea (40-50). [41]

There are presently crippling sanctions applied to North Korea for
possession of 40-50 nuclear weapons. Crippling sanctions are also
applied against Iran (that does not possess nuclear weapons) on the
basis that the mendacious, serial war criminal and nuclear terrorist
states of the US and Apartheid Israel claim that Iran is seeking to
obtain nuclear weapons (a claim denied by Iran). On this basis it would
seem reasonable to apply crippling sanctions against all 9 nuclear
weapons-possessing states, and that until this regime of sanctions is
emplaced all sanctions against Iran should be lifted. The US is the only
state so far to have used nuclear weapons against cities (Hiroshima and
Nagasaki in 1945). However one notes that Itzhak Yaakov was the
Apartheid Israeli engineer and brigadier general in charge of
development of an Israeli nuclear bomb to be detonated in the Egyptian
Sinai Peninsular as a demonstration if the 1967 War did not go as
planned; he was later punished when he revealed this secret. [42]
One can only declare utter repugnance for states that have a military
strategy involving nuclear mass murder of hundreds of millions and
possibly billions of human beings. In particular one notes that nuclear
terrorist, racist Zionist-run, genocidally racist, serial war criminal,
grossly human rights-abusing, international law-violating, child-
abusing, mother-abusing, women-abusing and democracy-by-genocide

Apartheid Israel is ruled by a 47% minority population of 6.8 million mostly non-Semitic Ashkenazi Jewish Israelis and possesses 90 nuclear weapons. On the basis of racial equality in nuclear terrorism this indicates that 15 million Indigenous Palestinians (5.2 million Occupied Palestinians, 2.0 million Israeli Palestinians and 8 million Exiled Palestinians) would have about 200 nuclear weapons and the whole world would have 105,000. Already much of the world applies Boycotts, Divestment and Sanctions (BDS) against Apartheid Israel for its manifold crimes against Humanity, and the whole world should certainly immediately apply crippling sanctions against genocidally racist and serial war criminal Apartheid Israel for possession of 90 nuclear weapons and missile delivery systems.

18.10. A catastrophic plus 2 degrees Centigrade of heating is now effectively unavoidable

The national commitments to the Paris Climate Change Conference amount to a plus 3.2 degrees Centigrade of warming by 2100, whereas the Paris "target" was ideally less than 1.5C and certainly no more than a catastrophic plus 2C. The average temperature rise is presently about 1.2C and 1.5C will be reached within this decade. Gas and oil use steadily increases at record rates but annual coal use has flattened, albeit at a record level. Key tipping points are being exceeded or approached, and atmospheric carbon dioxide (CO_2) and methane (CH_4) are steadly increasing at record levels and record rates. The pre-Industrial Revolution atmospheric CO_2 was no higher than 280 ppm CO_2 for about a million years but is now about 420 ppm CO_2. Coral started dying at 320 ppm CO_2 and sustainable retention of the Arctic summer sea ice requires abour 320 ppm CO_2. Without the global dimming and masking effect of atmospheric sulphate aerosols deriving from the burning of sulphur-containing coal the average temperature rise would already be about plus 2 degrees Centigrade. [43] According to the Intergovernmental Panel on Climate Change (IPCC) coral reefs would decline by 70-90 percent with global warming of 1.5°C, whereas virtually all (> 99 percent) would be lost with 2°C. [44]

18.11. Worsening Climate Genocide en route to only 1 billion people left by 2100

Some leading climate scientists have warned of possible catastrophic depopulation this century due to man-made global heating. In the absence of requisite action on climate change it is estimated that 10 billion people could die this century in a worsening Climate Genocide en route to a sustainable human population of only about 1 billion in 2100. [45] This would mean an average of 100 million people dying annually this century from this cause, noting that presently 7.4 million people die annually from deprivation, and in 2004 16.0 million people died thus. [46]

18.12. Catastrophic biodiversity loss in the Anthropocene Era

About 2 decades ago the species extinction rate was estimated to be 100-1,000 times greater than normal. In 2022 it is estimated that the species extinction rate is 10,000 times greater than normal, 28% of species are under critical threat of extinction, and that 50% of all species will be facing extinction by 2100. [47] For this reason the present era has been called the Anthropocene to reflect the huge negative impact of Humanity on Biodiversity [48]. It has been estimated that for everyone to have an American lifestyle would require 7 planets and that 3 planets would be needed for a European lifestyle. Presently we are exploiting the planet on a 2 planet basis, and it is this over-exploitation and burgeoning population compounded with an ever-worsening climate crisis that are responsible for the continuing catastrophic loss of Biodiversity.

18.13. Negative carbon emissions back to 300 ppm CO_2 needed plus halving population and halving economic activity

Numerous climate scientists and science-informed climate activists have urged a return of the atmospheric CO_2 to the pre-Industrial Revolution level of circa 300 ppm CO_2 for a safe and sustainable planet for all peoples and all species. The excellent 350.org organization demands a return to at most 350 ppm CO_2 from the present atmospheric level of 420 ppm CO_2 and which is increasing at a record rate. Professor James Hansen has stated that 320 ppm CO_2 is needed for sustainable summer sea ice in the Arctic, and the Royal Society reported that world coral started dying at an atmospheric level of 320 ppm CO_2. [49] Indeed coral reefs can be used as a "canary in the mine" to determine where we should be for safety. Thus the atmospheric CO_2 was 320 ppm CO_2 in 1962 when the human population was about 3.5 billion. From this we can estimate that the human population needs to roughly halve from the present 7.8 billion, with a corresponding halving of economic activity (noting that the economic de-growth burden must be mainly borne by rich European societies to permit the Global South to advance to a modest level of existence). [50]

18.14. Deadly poverty, famine from war and climate change, entitlement, the global South, and terracidal neoliberalism versus sustainable social humanism (socialism)

Presently 7.4 million people die each year from deprivation on Spaceship Earth with the endlessly greedy neoliberal One Percenters in charge of the flight deck. However the refusal of the world to take requisite action on man-made climate change will mean an average of 100 million avoidable deaths annually en route to a sustainable human population in 2100 of only 1 billion people. [51] Indeed the First Edition of "Jane Austen and the Black Hole of British History" (1998) was written to expose horrendous Indian famines due to merciless colonial rapacity, and to warn that climate change was set to wreak even greater carnage on India and the world.

As cogently argued by Nobel Laureate economist Amartya Sen, food is a relatively cheap commodity, and that famines occur when populations are deprived of their "entitlement" to food for survival when the price of food exceeds the capacity of people to pay. Thus in the WW2 Bengali Holocaust (the WW2 Indian Holocaust, the man-made Bengal Famine in British-ruled India) the price of the staple rice rose up to 4-fold for a variety of reasons, and the 6-7 million people who could not pay simply starved to death or died from famine-associated diseases. Calcutta was a major industrial city of the war-time British Empire and simply sucked food out of a starving but food-producing countryside. A real strategic reason for this disaster inflicted on India by the British with Australian complicity was evidently to present potential Japanese invaders with a food-less north-east India. [52]

Today in 2022 a similar scenario is being played out associated with the war criminal Russian invasion of Ukraine that was provoked by anti-Russian US machinations (notably involving Ukrainian neo-Nazis) and the NATO eastward expansion in the decades after the break-up of the Soviet Union in 1991. Indeed one can speculate that a resolutely anti-Russia and anti-China US may have had a secret policy of implicitly encouraging this war criminal Russian action with the prospect of massive harm to Russia and China via global sanctions, just as the US "greenlighted" the Iraqi invasion of Kuwait with resultant devastation of Iraq. Russia and the Ukraine are major producers of wheat and vegetable oil, and Russia is a major supplier of wheat to the world and of gas and oil to Europe. Russia's war criminal Ukraine War and the well-justified application of sanctions against Russia has resulted in huge and variously inter-connected global price rises for wheat, vegetable oil, gas, oil, fertilizer, and transport. For the circa 1 billion people in the global South who suffer serious food insufficiency this is already a growing disaster. Populous Egypt has already capped the price of bread. While thousands of innocent Ukrainians have been killed in this appalling war, it seems likely that millions of people will die in the Global South as a consequence of increases in the price of food. Unfortunately future estimates of the consequent global excess mortality associated with the Ukraine War (and using the pre-Covid-19 2020 statistical base-line established in the Second Edition of my book "Body Count. Global avoidable mortality since 1950" [53]) will be complicated by tens of millions of Covid-19-related deaths in the global South.

At the heart of these disasters is Enlightenment libertarianism that while enabling huge intellectual, scientific and technological progress had the massive downsides of increasingly deadly high technology wars and freedom of capitalists to mercilessly exploit the world for private profit. The presently globally dominant neoliberal ideology demands maximal freedom for the smart and advantaged to exploit the natural and human resources of the world for private profit with a hypothetical "trickle down" benefit for the poor. This ruthless ideology has led us to decimation of the Biosphere and to the edge of the Climate Genocide precipice.

In 2020 the richest 1% (the One Percenters) owned 46% of the world's wealth whereas the poorest 55% owned a mere 1.3%. Inequality.org on the worsening wealth inequality: "In 2009 the combined wealth of the world's richest 380 people equaled the wealth of the bottom half. By 2018, just 26 billionaires had as much as the bottom half" [54] . Capital begets capital and Oxfam reports: "The world's small elite of 2,755 billionaires has seen its fortunes grow more during Covid-19 than they have in the whole of the last fourteen years combined. The wealth of the 10 richest men has doubled, while the incomes of 99% of humanity are worse off, because of COVID-19… Inequality is deadly. We estimate that it contributes to the deaths of at least 21,300 people each day—or one person every four seconds [7.8 million people per year; my exhaustive estimate is 7.4 million in 2020 [55]]… Twenty of the richest billionaires are estimated, on average, to be emitting as much as 8,000 times more carbon than the billion poorest people" [56] This latter statistic suggestes a novel partial solution to the Climate Crisis and the Wealth Inequality Gap. Thus monogamy is generally accepted for everyone, even for billionaires, although great Kings and Sultans in the past had large harems. However an even more compelling constraint would be that each human being (including billionaires) could have no greater carbon footprint than that of, say, an average American. Billionaires would accordingly be compelled to give away their wealth or to expend it only on "green" projects such as re-afforestation and renewable energy schemes.

French economist Thomas Piketty has cogently argued that wealth inequity is bad for economics (the poor cannot afford to buy the goods and services they produce) and bad for democracy (Big Money buys votes). Piketty has suggested an annual wealth tax of up to circa 1%, noting that until recently France had such a tax and for 1,400 years the Muslim World has had an annual wealth tax of 2.5% (zakkat). [57] Indeed in 2014 I estimated that a 4% Annual Global Wealth Tax could stop the Global Avoidable Mortality Holocaust of (then) 17 million poverty-related deaths annually by bringing the annual per capita GDP of all poor countries up to that of China and Cuba, countries for which annual avoidable mortality from deprivation was zero. [58]

In his recent book "Time for Socialism", Thomas Piketty (a relatively conservative socialist) further explores the wealth inequity gap, capital begetting more capital, intergenerational inequity, patriarchy, the colonial legacy and the worsening climate crisis. As a way of addressing the poverty trap of the young without rich parents, he suggests a minimum inheritance for all at the age of 25 of $180,000. [59] Of course this phenomenon of capital begetting capital was identified 2,000 years ago by the wonderful Palestinian humanitarian Jesus in observing in the Gospel of Matthew "For unto every one that hath shall be given, and he shall have abundance: but from him that hath not shall be taken away even that which he hath". This has been subsequently descibed as "the Matthew effect" (e.g. "the Matthew effect in science" involves those with research grants getting even more research grants). However in the same chapter in Matthew Jesus demands care for the poor, this no doubt prompting Mikhail Gorbachev to describe Jesus as the first socialist. [60]

While neoliberalism demands morally and environmentally unsustainable maximal freedom for the smart and advantaged to exploit natural and human resources for private profit, social humanism (socialism, ecosocialism, democratic socialism, human rights-cognizant communism, Universal Basic Income (UBI) and the welfare state) seeks to sustainably maximize the happiness, opportunity and dignity of everybody through culturally sensitive and evolving intra-national and international social contracts.[61] The bottom line is that there is no Planet B and with major climate science-informed constraints on sustainable resource utilization, there must be much greater sharing and social equity, not just intra-nationally but between the Global North and the Global South.

18.15. Rich, neoliberal and racist Australia's ongoing commitment to US wars, genocide, nuclear terrorism, and climate criminality

Chapter 17 of the previous editions of "Jane Austen and the Black Hole of British History" posed an existential dilemma: will the world meet the climate crisis challenge if a rich, peaceful, prosperous, highly educated and progressive democracy like Australia won't? Sadly the answer in 2022 is no as coal-rich Australia and our similarly greed-driven neoliberal world as a whole continues to rush headlong towards a catastrophic plus 2C and worse. [62]

Australia was among the first countries in world history to have free trade unions, the 8 hour working day, the living wage, free, secular and compulsory education, university education for the smart, free university education (albeit only for 1974-1989), female suffrage, an independent judiciary, a free press, and the great institution of compulsory and preferential voting in elections. However there is another serial war criminal and genocidally racist side to Australia, and these great social advances did not apply to the sorely oppressed Indigenous Australians (aka Aborigines, Aboriginals, Black Australians) until they were finally "counted" as citizens after a Referendum in 1967.

Indigenous Australians and those sympathetic to their lot quite properly regard 26 January (Australia Day) as Invasion Day that marks the British invasion of Australia on 26 January 1788 and commencement of the ongoing Aboriginal Genocide in which some 2 million Indigenous Australians have died untimely deaths due to violence (0.1 million) or due to dispossession, deprivation, and disease (the remainder). The Indigenous population dropped from about 1 million to 0.1 million in the first century after the invasion in 1788, mainly through violence, dispossession, deprivation and introduced disease. The last massacres of Aborigines occurred in the late 1920s in Central Australia. Throughout much of the 20th century there was a policy of forcibly removing Aboriginal children (especially mixed race children) from their mothers, a systematic genocidal policy involving the removal of perhaps 0.1 million children (the Stolen Generations). This practice ended in the 1970s, and in 2008 Labor Prime Minister Kevin Rudd offered a formal apology, but removal of Aboriginal children from their mothers continues (albeit for ostensibly different reasons) at a record rate, this leading Kevin Rudd to warn of a "second stolen generation".

Before the British invasion in 1788 there were 350-750 different Indigenous Australian (Aboriginal) tribes and a similar number of languages and dialects, of which only 150 survive today and of these all but about 20 are endangered in a process of continuing Australian Aboriginal Ethnocide and Cultural Genocide of remaining Indigenous Australian societies. Removal of Aboriginal children from their mothers and communities, removal of Federal and State government support for remote Aboriginal communities, and substantial removal of instruction of Aboriginal children in their own language are all ultra-conservative measures that threaten destruction of most of the surviving Aboriginal languages and dialects (Australian Aboriginal Ethnocide). [63]
White Australians did not confne their greed-driven genocidal racism to extermination of Indigenous Australians. Variously as UK or US lackeys Australians have invaded 85 countries with 30 of these invasions being genocidal. [64] After Pearl Harbor (7 December 1941) Australia shifted its allegiance to the US and has been a slavish US lackey ever since. Australia joined the Australia, New Zealand and US (ANZUS) alliance in 1951 as a protection against a perceived "Yellow Peril" from Asia that had prompted the racist White Australia Policy

(1901-1973) that excluded non-Europeans (a huge, yellow-painted modern sculpture in Melbourne was immediately dubbed "The Yellow Peril"). ANZUS excluded New Zealand in 1987 after the New Zealand Government objected to nuclear warships in the South Pacific.

Australia has been involved in all post-1950 US Asian wars (atrocities associated with 40 million Asian deaths from violence and war-imposed deprivation). Australia was an enthusiastic partner in the US War on Terror that has been associated with 32 million Muslim deaths from violence (5 million) and imposed deprivation (27 million) in 20 countries invaded by the US Alliance since the US Government's 9/11 false flag atrocity that killed 3,000 innocent people, mostly Americans. There is slavish bipartisan agreement over the US Alliance between the extreme right-wing to far right Liberal Party-National Party Coalition and the right-dominated Labor Party. This means that Australia (under fervently pro-Zionist Coalition rule for the last decade) is second only to the US as a fervent supporter of nucear terrorist, racist Zionist-run, genocidally racist, serial war criminsal, international law-violating, grossly human rights-violating, child-abusing, mother-abusing, women-abusing, democracy-by-genocide Apartheid Israel. [65]

With exclusion of decent New Zealand from ANZUS, Australia has recently formed the anti-China AUKUS (Australia, UK and US) and Quad (Australia, India, US and Japan) Alliances to contain a supposedly aggressive China. In reality a US lackey, nuclear terrorist, climate criminal, serial invader and subversive Australia has actually violated all circa 80 Indo-Pacific countries in the last 80 years (i.e. within living memory). The joint US-Australian telecommunications and spying base at Pine Gap in Central Australia targets continuing war criminal US drone strikes on 7 Muslim countries from Africa to South Asia. As UK and thence US lackeys Australia has been involved militarily against many Indo-Pacific countries in the last 80 years. As US lackeys Australians have been involved with the US in covert subversion of many Indo-Pacific countries, and were successful in achieving regime change in 8 instances, namely Laos (1960), Indonesia

(1965), Cambodia (1970), Chile (1973), Australia (1975), Fiji (1987), Fiji (2000), and Australia (2010) (the latter 3 also involving Apartheid Israel). All Indo-Pacific countries are existentially threatened by man-made climate change. Tropical Island Nations and tropical mega-delta countries like Bangladesh are the most direly threatened. Climate criminal Australia is among world leaders in 16 areas of climate criminality, is a world leader in coal and gas exports, ranks worst for climate policy out of 64 major GHG-polluting countries, and Australia's annual greenhouse gas (GHG) pollution (Domestic plus Exported) is about 5% of the world's total GHG pollution despite the Australian population being only 0.3% of the world's total. [66] Look-the-other-way Australia ignores these extraordinary realities. War is the penultimate in racism and genocide the ultimate, but serial war criminal and pro-Apartheid Israel Australia endlessly declares that it rejects racism in an ongoing process of extraordinary politically correct racism (PC racism). Australia professes to be shocked by allegations of dozens of war crimes committed by Australian soldiers in Afghanistan but totally ignores the horrendous war criminality of the politicians who sent Australian soldiers to Afghanistan and to Iraq in the first place. Thus avoidable deaths from violence and imposed deprivation in Iraq and Afghanistan have totalled 5 million (1990 onwards) and 7 million (2001 onwards), respectively. This horrendous carnage is evidence of gross violation iof the Fourth Geneva Convention by the US Alliance, including Australia. Thus Articles 55 and 56 of the Fourth Geneva Convention (the Geneva Convention relative to the Protection of Civilian Persons in Time of War) unequivocally state that the Occupier is obliged to provide its conquered Subjects with life-sustaining food and medical requisites "to the fullest extent of the means available to it". My personal view is that meritorious prosecutions of war crimes allegedly committed by Australian soldiers against dozens of Indigenous people should not proceed until Australian politicians are prosecuted for vastly greater war crimes involving the avoidable deaths of millions. Indeed John Valder (former Federal president of the conservative Liberal Party that has supported all 1950 onwards US Asian wars) has called for the prosecution of John Howard (the Liberal PM of Australia who illegally invaded Iraq): "Bush, Blair, and Howard, as leaders of the three members of the coalition of the willing, inflicted enormous suffering on the people of Iraq. And, as such, they are criminals. I believe the only deterrent to a repetition of the Iraq situation is punishment in some form as war criminals." [67]

Nearly 30 years ago 30 years of global Boycotts, Divestment and Sanctions (BDS) against US-, UK- and Apartheid Israel-backed Apartheid South Africa finally succeeded in abolishing apartheid in South Africa. However the US, UK, Canada and Australia fervently support Apartheid Israel and hence the crime of apartheid that is condemned as a crime against Humanity by the UN International Convention on the Suppression and Punishment of the Crime of Apartheid, and implicitly so by the International Covenant on Civil and Political Rights, the Universal Declaration of Human Rights, and the International Convention on the Elimination of All Forms of Racial Discrimination. Nearly 100% of Australian Coalition MPs and most Labor MPs fervently support Apartheid Israel and hence apartheid, but look-the-other-way Australia evidently does not realize that by the global anti-apartheid standards from the 1960 Sharpeville Massacre to the fall of South African apartheid in 1993 anyone supporting apartheid was persona non grata. Australian politicians supporting Apartheid Israel and hence apartheid are unfit for public life in a one-person-one-vote democracy like Australia. [68]

Yet in 2022 Australia's top university, the University of Melbourne, declared that a motion of the University of Melbourne Students Union (UMSU) supporting Boycotts, Divestment and Sanctions (BDS) against institutions and corporations complicit in Israeli apartheid was "anti-Semitic". My indignant response sent to the leading Melbourne newspaper (but not published) was as follows: "Melbourne University's condemnation as "anti-Semitic" of its students' support for boycotting Israeli institutions and corporations complicit in Israeli apartheid (The Age, 4/5) is utterly false (this trashing the university's reputation because there is zero tolerance for lying by all genuine

scholars and institutions of learning), anti-Arab anti-Semitic (by falsely
defaming anti-racist Palestinians, Arabs and Muslims critical of
Apartheid Israel), anti-Jewish anti-Semitic (by falsely defaming anti-
racist Jews such as myself who are critical of Apartheid Israel), and
indeed falsely defamatory of all decent people around the world critical
of Israeli apartheid. Israeli apartheid has been condemned by leading
human rights groups (Amnesty International, Human Rights Watch,
Israeli B'Tselem and Israeli Yesh Din) and by anti-racist humanitarians
around the world (notably by Jewish and non-Jewish heroes in the fight
against South African apartheid, notably Ronnie Kasrils and Nobel
Laureates Nelson Mandela and Desmond Tutu). Indeed the architect of
South African apartheid, Dr Hendrik Verwoerd, famously declared that
"Israel is an apartheid state". I and my non-European wife managed to
overcome the White Australia Policy in the 1960s but had to strictly
avoid egregious apartheid in South Africa, the US Deep South and
Apartheid Israel."

Australia violates other international conventions and decencies. Thus
for 2 decades Australia has been violating the Refugee Convention and
other human rights conventions by indefinitely and highly abusively
imprisoning boat-borne refugees to Australia - men, women and
children - in remote and off-shore concentraton camps without charge
or trial. When World Number 1 tennis player Novak Djokovic was
imprioned for a few days in a Melbourne CBD detention centre when
the corrupt, racist and mendacious Australian Coalition Government
cancelled his visa, the world discovered that some of his fellow
inmates were refugees who had been imprisoned as children and
detained without charge or trial for 9 years. What sort of moral
degenerates do such things to refugees and to children in particular?
The answer: political correct racist Australian politicians supported by
90% of the voting population.

The fundamental problems with prosperous Australia are its
commitment to neoliberal greed, toleration of massive corruption,
servile support for a serial war criminal US, gross human rights abuse,

and above all to egregious lying by omission. Australia that once led the world for democracy (albeit only for White Australians) has now become a kleptocracy, plutocracy, Murdochracy, lobbyocracy, corporatocracy and dollarocracy in which Big Money purchases people, parties, policies, public perception of reality, votes and hence more political power and more private profit. A former Coalition PM and a former Labor PM have joined forces with half a million other petitioners in demanding a judicial investigation into the mendacious US Murdoch media empire that has captured 70% of Australia's daily newspaper readership. Australia has become a look-the-other-way and corrupt fake democracy in which several billionaires can play kingmaker at election time. [69]

18.16. Polya's 3 Laws of Economics, user pays, carbon price, carbon tax, and intergenerational equity

Fundamental to the physical sciences and the explosion of the Industrial Revolution in the 19th century are the 3 Laws of Thermodynamics that can be simply stated as follows. The First Law of Thermodynamics states that the energy of a closed system is constant. The Second Law of Thermodynamics states that the entropy (disorder) of the world strives to a maximum i.e. the world inexorably tends to randomness, chaos, disorder and minimum information content. The Third Law of Thermodynamics states that the entropy (disorder) of a pure crystal of a pure chemical at the absolute zero temperature of zero (0) degrees Kelvin (minus 273.15 degrees Centigrade) is zero i.e. in a universe full of motion and increasing disorder there is a boundary state of zero disorder. Polya's 3 Laws of Economics mirror the 3 Laws of Therrnodynamics and are (1) Price minus COP (Cost of Production) equals profit; (2) Deception about COP strives to a maximum; and (3) No work, price or profit on a dead planet. [70]

These fundamental laws help to expose the failure of neoliberal capitalism in relation to wealth inequality, massive tax evasion by multinational corporations, disastrous failure to apply a carbon pollution price to establish and pay for the true Cost of Production in economic activity, and horrendous avoidable deaths from poverty and pollution culminating in eventual general ecocide, speciescide, climate genocide, omnicide and terracide. Thus science-trained Pope Francis has stated that the environmental and social cost of pollution should be "fully borne" by the polluters. [71] Eminent economist Lord Nicholas Stern has stated that "Climate change is a result of the greatest market failure that the world has seen" because the price of energy does not reflect the "externality" of the climate change-related costs of producing it. [72]

Climate economist Dr Chris Hope (Cambridge) has estimated a damage-related carbon price of about $200 per tonne CO_2 [73] and a similar estimate derives from estimates by eminent climate scientist Professor James Hansen (Columbia) of the cost of reducing atmospheric CO_2 . [74] Applying this value of $200 per tonne CO_2 one can estimate that the World has an unpaid Carbon Debt of $270 trillion that is increasing at $10 trillion per year, and that climate criminal Australia has an unpaid Carbon Debt of about $6 trillion that is increasing at about $600 billion per year, and is increasing at about $70,000 per head per year for under-30 year old Australians (these estimates including Exported as well as Domestic GHG pollution). [75]

Of course unlike conventional debt that is inexorably recovered by "the rule of law" and can be evaded by measures such as defaulting, printing money, declaring bankruptcy, or running away, Carbon Debt is inescapable. Thus, for example, unless sea walls are built at immense cost, low-lying cities, towns and arable land will be inundated. When young Australians and young people in general recognize the horrendous magnitude of their remorselessly increasing and inescapable per capita Carbon Debt there will be Climate Revolution (non-violent one hopes). [76] Fortunately for the climate criminals the young are presently unaware of the precise magnitude in dollar terms of this ever-increasing per capita Carbon Debt, although they are aware in a general fashion that the older generations are bequeathing them a devastated and dying planet. This ignorance is maintained by mendacious Mainstream journalist, editor, politician, academic and commentariat presstitutes who slavishly serve the endlessly rapacious One Percenters.

A recent International Monetary Fund (IMF) report on climate change mitigation advocates a Carbon Tax of \$75 per ton of CO_2 by 2030 that, if progressively implemented in the G20 countries alone, would prevent an estimated 4 million air pollution deaths by 2030. However the effective climate change denialist Coalition Government of Australia, a G20 country that is among world leaders in 16 areas of climate criminality, has flatly rejected a global Carbon Tax. If all G20 countries followed Australia's rejection of a global Carbon Tax then they would be complicit in an unconscionable Climate Genocide and Climate Holocaust killing 4 million people over the next decade. The IMF estimated that the average applied Carbon Price in the World was merely \$2 as compared to the desired \$200 per tonne CO_2. [77] I explained this discrepancy thus to my grandchildren at a Chinese restaurant: the owner gives us bill for \$200 but we say that we will only pay him \$2.

Non-inclusion of the Carbon Price in the Cost of Production (COP) is utter mendacity, grand larceny, massive theft and a glaring example of Polya's Second Law of Economics, to whit "Deception about COP strives to a maximum". In corrupt, dishonest, neoliberal and climate criminal Australia there is bipartisan agreement that prohibits endorsement of a Carbon Tax to address the huge and ever-increasing Carbon Debt. Indeed any proposal that might have some Carbon Tax implication is roundly condemned in pro-coal, pro-gas, climate criminal Australia in which "Carbon Tax" is "that which must not be spoken".

18.17. Covid-19-related avoidable deaths, Gerocide, holding rulers responsible, and the 2020 pre-Covid-19 mortality baseline

As of early May 2022 "Covid-19 deaths per million of population" were 3,052 (US, population 334.5 million), 2,552 (UK, population 68.5 million), 278 (Australia, population 26.0 million), and 4 (China, population 1,439.3 million). Taking China as a best-case standard, "avoidable Covid-19 deaths per million of population" are 3,048 (US), 2,548 (UK) and 274 (Australia), and "avoidable Covid-19 deaths" have totaled 1,020,000 (the US), 175,000 (the UK), and 7,100 (Australia). About 95% of Covid-19 deaths have been of people aged 60 years or older and hence this huge mass mortality in the US, UK, Australia (and elsewhere) can be described as Gerocide. The ruler is responsible for the ruled, and accordingly US President Donald Trump, UK PM Boris Johnson, Australian PM Scott Morrison (and many other leaders) must be held responsible at the ballot box and before the International Criminal Court.

The extensively revised and updated 2022 Second Edition of my book "Body Count. Global avoidable mortality since 1950" includes 12 Tables that list under-5 infant mortality and avoidable mortality for every country in the world as estimated by the UN Population Division for 2020 before the Covid-19 Pandemic. This data provides an invaluable resource for estimating changes in under-5 infant mortality and avoidable mortality in subsequent years and thus associated with both direct and indirect effects of the Covid-19 Pandemic (e.g. deaths from Covid-19 per se and deaths associated with collateral impacts of the Covid-19 pandemic such as economic impacts).

18.18. All human rights for all including the sorely oppressed Palestinians

Decent people who believe that "all people are created equal" demand all human rights for all, of which the "right to life" is the most fundamental. Yet in the religion-perverted and serial war criminal US most of the population support horrendously deadly US wars and internal inequities that have killed millions of people but are fervent in their belief in the "right to life" of week-old human embryos regardless of the reproductive rights of the women concerned.

 This absurd and deadly moral dichotomy is presently best illustrated by Western reactions to the war criminal Russian invasion of Ukraine that is rightly condemned and sanctioned over the thousands of deaths whereas the US and the US lackey West ignore the horrendous deaths of tens of millions of people in 52 post-WW2 US invasions, most notably the 1990 onwards Iraqi Holocaust and Iraqi Genocide (5 million deaths from violence and imposed deprivation) and the 2001 onwards Afghan Holocaust and Afghan Genocide (7 million deaths from violence and imposed deprivation). [78]

The most determined Western ignoring of human rights violations is reserved for the sorely oppressed Palestinians. Of 15 million mostly impoverished Indigenous Palestinians in the world, 8 million are Exiled Palestinians, 5.2 million are Occupied Palestinians and 2.0 million are Israeli Palestinians The 8 million Exiled Palestinians represent about 10% of the World's refugees, are mostly confined without civil rights to dire poverty in refugee camps, and are prevented on pain of death from returning to the land continuously inhabited by their forebears for over 4,000 years.

The 5.2 million Occupied Palestinians are highly abusively confined without human rights to ever-dwindling West Bank ghettoes or the blockaded and bombed Gaza Concentration Camp – the per capita GDP is $3,400 for Occupied Palestine as compared to $46,400 for Apartheid Israel, and careful analysis shows that Occupied Palestinians are excluded from all the human rights set out in the 30 articles of the Universal Declaration of Human Rights .[79] Despite a century of ethnic cleansing, colonizarion and Palestinian Genocide (8 million Exiled Palestinians and 2.2 million Palestinian deaths from violence, 0.1 million, and imposed deprivation, 2.1 million), today Indigenous

Palestinians represent 50% of the Subjects of Apartheid Israel but only the 2.0 million Israeli Palestinians can vote for the government ruling them, albeit as Third Class citizens subject to 65 Nazi-style, race-based discriminatory laws. [80]

Rania Muhareb (2018): "Yet, neither the Universal Declaration nor the UN Charter have succeeded in preventing the resurgence of armed conflicts and rights abuses, which, continued to ravage the world since 1948, notably in Palestine. Indeed, the Universal Declaration also came in the aftermath of the Palestinian Nakba, or 'catastrophe', during which Zionist forces destroyed 531 Palestinian villages, killed over 10,000 of Palestine's native population, and forcibly displaced some 800,000 Palestinians from their homes and property. Denied return by Israel ever since, Palestinians have suffered an 'ongoing Nakba', forced to live as refugees in neighbouring countries or within the former territory of Mandate Palestine. The drafters of the Universal Declaration were not oblivious to the war that had ravaged Palestine nor to the fate of Palestinian refugees scattered across the region. Indeed, the plight of the refugees was discussed in the drafting of the provisions on the right to freedom of movement and on the right to asylum." [81] A further 400,000 Arabs were expelled from Palestine and the Syrian Golan Heights in 1967. [82]

Occupied Palestinians and indeed all Palestinians are effectively invisible to the deeply racist and Zionist-subverted West. There nevertheless is some hope for Western decency over this matter. One is reminded of the 1899 poem "Antigonish" by William Hughes Mearns: "As I was going up the stair / I met a man who wasn't there! / He wasn't there again today!/ I wish, I wish he'd go away!" [83]

It would still be very unfair, but one could envisage a fairy tale in which the Occupied Palestinians were granted all human rights today but with the caveat that, for whatever unexplained reasons, in return they would remain occupied – but occupied by a nice, peaceful, human rights-respecting country like Fiji, Costa Rica, Ireland or Switzerland, so that this would at least bring to an end the appalling, highly abusive, deadly, and 55 year occupation by nuclear terrorist, racist Zionist-run, genocidally racist, anti-Arab anti-Semitic, serial war criminal, grossly humnan rights–abusing, child-abusing, mother-abusing, women-abusing, democracy-by-genocide, neo-Nazi Apartheid Israel.

The "two-state solution" has been a convenient fig-leaf for pro-Apartheid Western dishonesty and inaction over Palestine. The ethnic cleansing of 90% of Palestine has rendered the "two-state solution" dead but the continuing obscenity of a grossly human rights-abusing Apartheid Israel is intolerable to decent people around the world. However the racist Jewish Nation-State Law makes it abundantly clear that the racist Zionists running Apartheid Israel are resolutely committed to a neo-Nazi Apartheid State and endless, deadly subjugation of the Indigenous Palestinians with the ever-present threat of 100% ethnic cleansing of Palestine i.e. the forcible removal of all Indigenous Palestinians from Palestine. The world must act firmly and decisively over Apartheid Israel as it did over Apartheid South Africa. A clear, humane solution to the continuing human rights catastrophe in Palestine is a secular and democratic unitary state (a "one state solution") as in post-Apartheid South Africa that would involve return of all refugees, zero tolerance for racism, equal rights for all, all human rights for all, one-person-one-vote, justice, economic justice, truth-telling, goodwill, reconciliation, airport-level security, nuclear weapons removal, internationally-guaranteed national security initially based on the present armed forces, and untrammelled access for all citizens to all of Palestine. It can and should happen tomorrow. [84]

18.19. One-person-one-vote World Parliament for economics, human rights, entitlement and sustainability

The world is badly running out of time to deal with the worsening Climate Crisis and it is already clear that the Global South will suffer disproportionately in a worsening Climate Genocide. [85] A useful suggestion would be that in addition to a one-nation-one-vote UN General Assembly and the world power-dominated UN Security

Council (5 world powers, not including India, having a veto power) there is an urgent need for a third new World Government element, specifically a World Parliament that is elected on a one-person-one-vote basis, and is devoted to human rights, equitable economics, and environmental sustainability. Since half the world's population are female, it is males who are involved in forcibly maintaining the world order, and the world is still subject to the patriarchy that came about with the Agrarian Revolution 10,000 years ago, it would be useful if the World Parliament had gender equality. Further, since even in informed democracies wealth inequality subverts democracy (Big Money buys votes) there would have to be an electoral process that minimizes the anti-democratic impact of wealth inequality (e.g. by UN supervised elections, solely UN-funded candidate electioneering, and guaranteed sanctity of all MPs). [86]

18.20. Speak out!

History ignored yields history repeated. Genocide ignored yields genocide repeated. Holocaust ignored yields holocaust repeated. Peace is the only way but silence kills and silence is complicity. Zero tolerance for lying by commission and lying by omission. We cannot walk by on the other side. All people are created equal. Love thy neighbor as thyself. Do unto others as you would have them do unto you. All human rights for all. All species and ecosystems are priceless. We are responsible for what we do and for what we do not do. We are running out of time. There is no Planet B. Bear witness. Tell everyone you can. Make noise! Speak out! Speak out! Make Kindness and Truth prevail!

NOTES

Preamble

1. Austen (1818b), Northanger Abbey, Chapter 14, p108.

2. Santayana (1953), p397.

3. Aarons and Loftus (1997), The Secret War Against the Jews, p12.

4. Rachel Carson (1964), Silent Spring, p257.

5. Koestler (1974), The Heel of Achilles, p11.

6. Rabindranath Tagore quoted in Henry Miller (1992), Moloch or, this Gentile World., p257.

2008 Preface

7. Ray (1973).

8. Polya (2003b) in Elias & Elias (2003), pp 201-202.

9. Grun (1975).

10. Polya (1995).

11. Chamarette, C. (1995).

12. Austen (1818b), Northanger Abbey, Chapter 24, pp210-202.

13. Polya (1998a).

14. Polya (1999d).

15. see Polya (1995) to Polya (2008).

16. Polya (1999b).

17. Polya (2003a).

18. Reason (2000).

19. Polya (2008a, b, c).

20. Polya (2008d, e, f, g, h); Spratt, D. and Sutton, P. (2008a, b).

21. Hansen (2008); Whitesides (2007).

22. Hansen et al. (2008)

23. Lovelock (2006); Goodell (2007); see also Lovelock (1979, 1988, 1991, 2007).

24. Polya (2008a, b, c).

25. Smith & Elliott (2008) re Professor John Beddington.

26. Fargione et al. (2008); see also Searchinger (2008).

27. Polya (1998a).

28. Polya (2007a).

29. Singer (2000).

30. Kuhse & Singer (1985).

31. Polya. (2007b).

32. UNICEF (2008); UN (2008); Polya (2006c,d).

33. WHO (2008).

34. Geneva Convention Relative to the Protection of Civilian Persons in Time of War (1950).

35. News.com (2008).

36. Scholars for 9/11 Truth (2008); Gore (2007).

37. Polya (2007c).

38. Polya (2008k,l).

39. UN Genocide Convention (1950).

40. Polya (2005l, m); Polya (2008i,j).

2022 Preface

41. Polya (1998a).

42. Polya (2020a).

43. Polya (2007a).

44. Polya (2008q).

45. Polya (2021).

46. Polya (2020b).

47. Hawking (2018), chapter 7.

48. Keane (2021); Polya (2022).

Chapter 1. Introduction - truth, reason, science and history

1. Austen (1791), The History of England, p71.

2. George Santayana (1953): "Progress, far from consisting in change, depends upon retentiveness. Those who cannot remember the past are condemned to repeat it." Quoted by Daintish et al., (1991), p176; Davidoff (1955), p267; Mc Cormick (1987), p173, in his biography of George Santayana in a section dealing with the latters's discourse on history in Santayana (1953), The Life of Reason; "He who forgets His history is condemned to relive it", attributed to Santayana by Young (1966), p422. Of course there are numerous versions of this, of which the following are from McKenzie (1980), p237: "Seems like every time history repeats itself the price doubles; why is it nobody listens when history repeats itself? ; history repeats itself - and that's one of the things wrong with history; a lot of history isn't fit to repeat itself; the reason history repeats itself is that people weren't listening the first time; we sincerely hope that history will repeat itself at longer intervals." Other variations include: "History does not repeat itself. Historians repeat each other" , attributed to Arthur Balfour by Daintish et al. (1991), p175; "Alas! Hegel was right when he said that we learn from history that we never learn anything from history", G.B. Shaw in the preface to Heartbreak House, quoted by Evans (1968), p316.

3. Chatterjee (1944); Ghosh (1944); Greenough (1982); Hunter (1871); Kachhawaha (1992).

4. Enbree (1962); Ghosh (1944); Hunter (1871; Khan (1969).

5. Bansil (1958); Bhatia (1991); Chatterjee (1944); Chopra (1988); Das (1949); Greenough (1982); Uppal (1984); Ghosh (1944); Dreze & Sen (1989); Sen (1981).

6. Bernard (1993); Eastwood (1991);. Edgerton (1991); Kennedy (1993); Leggett (1990); Rosenzweig & Parry (1996).

7. Barrio (1990); Bennett & George (1987); Bernard (1993); Chaliand & Rageau (1985); Kennedy (1993); Kidron & Segal (1987); McKibben (1990).

8. Austen (1817), Sanditon, Chapter 11, p206.

9. Ali (1979); Gravelle (1983).

10. Robertson & Tamanisau (1988); Sutherland (1992).

11. Gedye (1994), reporting that "Denying that that Nazi Holocaust occurred became a criminal offence in Germany yesterday, punishable by up to 5 years in jail", The Telegraph-Mirror (Sydney), 23 September 1994, p33.

12. Jog (1944).

13. The Manchester Guardian (1944).

14. Brust (1929); Polya (1986); Taylor & Taylor (1993).

15. Smith (1776).

16. Edwards & Bouchier (1991), pp435-436; Edwards et al. (1995), pp430-431; Friel (1985), pp 927, 1026; Leonardo (1950); Polya (1941); American College of Surgeons & Physicians (1941); Polya (1986); Taylor & Taylor (1993).

17. Alexanderson (1987); Boas (1974a,b); Polya (1945), How to Solve It; Taylor & Taylor (1993)

18. Polya (1986, 1996); Taylor & Taylor (1993).

19. Davis (1985); Eddy (1961); Martin et al.(1986); Polya (1955); Polya (1962a,b); Polya (1964); Polya (1965); Polya (1986); Polya & Solomon (1996); Pybus (1995); Smith (1992, 1993); Solomon (1994).

20. Bone (1957); see also Ignotus (1964); Koestler (1968); Levi (1979); Laffin (1968); Solzhenitsyn (1963, 1968, 1974); Timmerman (1982); Tyler (1977).

21. Aarons and Loftus (1997); Blumberg (1975); Gilbert (1969, 1982); Laqueur (1982); Parkes (1964); Wasserstein (1988); Weissberg (1958).

22. Churchill (1952); Churchill (1965).

23. Ceram (1955).

24. Shakespeare (1623), The Tragedy of King Richard the Third.

25. Drewett & Redhead (1984); Tey (1951).

26. Hicks (1992).

27. Einbinder (1972); Little (1913); Macfarlane (1975).

28. Honan (1987); Lane (1986, 1996).

29. Honan (1987); Weldon (1984).

30. Honan (1987); Hodge (1972); Johnson (1984).

31. Reynolds (1966); Wilson (1979).

32. Rothenstein (1966); Wilton (19750; Wilson (1979); Lloyd (1996).

33. Trevelyan (1952).

34. Levi (1979).

35. Greenough (1982).

36. Austen (1818b), Northanger Abbey, Chapter 24, pp210-202.

37. Magee (1975); Popper (1976).

38. Kuhn (1965).

39. Koestler (1964).

40. Soros (1987); Soros (1990); Soros (1991); Soros et al. (1995); Slater (1996).

41. Sharpe (1971).

42. Calvin (1969); Lehninger (1975), Chapter 37.

43. Cohen (1996); Denton (1985).

44. Trevelyan (1952).

45. Rosenzweig & Parry (1994).

46. Kennedy (1993); United Nations Population Division (1992).

47. Birch (1980); Bochuan (1991); Ehrlich (1968); Ehrlich et al. (1973); Falk & Brownlow (1989); Falloux & Talbot (1993); Goldsmith et al. (1990); Gordon & Suzuki (1990); Lovelock (1979, 1988, 1991); McKibben (1990); Porritt (1991); Saunders et al. (1993); Suzuki (1990); Washington (1991).

48. Santayana in Lucifer, A Theological Tragedy, p31; quoted in Cardiff (1964), p1.

49. Cartoons of George Booth reproduced in Heller (1981), pp26-33.

2008 Postscript

50. American Association for the Advancement of Science (AAAS) (2007).

51. Wikipedia (2008) re US National Academy of Sciences and other national Academies of Science re climate change threats.

52. Royal Society (UK) (2007).

53. Wikipedia (2008) re US National Academy of Sciences and other national Academies of Science re climate change threats.

54. Intergovernmental Panel on Climate Change (IPCC) (2007); Polya, G. (2007d).

55. Whitesides (2007); Hansen (2008).

56. Goodell (2007); Lovelock (2006); see also Lovelock (1979, 1988, 1991, 2007).

57. Polya (2008a, b, c); Smith, L. and Elliott, F. (2008) re Professor John Beddington.

58. Polya, G. (2005-2008); Polya (2008d,e,h); Spratt, D. and Sutton, P. (2008).

Chapter 2. The editing of Jane Austen's maternal connections - the Leighs and Brydges

1. Austen (1813) Pride and Prejudice, Volume 1, Chapter 1, p1.

2. Austen (1818a) Persuasion, Chapter 16, p162.

3. Jane Austen letter to Cassandra from Castle Square, Southampton (20 November 1808), reproduced in: Chapman (1964), p231; Le Faye (1995), p153.

4. Austen-Leigh (1870); Austen-Leigh & Austen-Leigh (1913); Austen-Leigh (1920); Bailey (1931); Bradbrook (1966); Bush (1975); Cecil (1978); Chapman (1949); Fergus (1978); Grey (1986); Halperin (1984); Hodge (1972); Honan (1987); Howard (1995); Johnson (1926); Johnson (1927); Lane (1984); Lane (1986); Lane (1996); Lascelles (1939); Llewellyn (1977); McDonagh (1991); Lauber (1993); Nicolson (1991); Rees (1976); Sherry (1966); Smith (1890); Smithers (1981); Tucker (1983); Watkins (1990); Weldon (1984); Wilks (1978).

5. Honan (1987).

6. Austen-Leigh (1870).

7. Austen-Leigh (1920).

8. Austen-Leigh (1870); Austen-Leigh & Austen-Leigh (1913); Austen-Leigh (1920); Bush (1975); Cecil (1978); Chapman (1949); Fergus (1978); Halperin (1984); Hodge (1972); Honan (1987); Howard (1995); Jenkins (1973); Johnson (1926); Johnson (1927); Lane (1984); Lane (1986); Lane (1996); Lascelles (1939); Llewellyn (1977); McDonagh (1991); Nicolson (1991); Pinion (1975); Rees (1976); Sherry (1966); Smith (1890); Thomson (1929); Tucker (1983); Watkins (1990); Weldon (1984); Wilks (1978).

9. Hodge (1972); Halperin (1984); Honan (1987); Lane (1984, 1986, 1996); Smithers (1981); Tucker (1983).

10. Austen-Leigh (1870); Austen-Leigh & Austen-Leigh (1913); Austen-Leigh (1920); Bush (1975); Cecil (1978); Chapman (1949); Fergus (1978); Howard (1995); Johnson (1926); Johnson (1927); Lascelles (1939); Llewellyn (1977); McDonagh (1991); Nicolson (1991); Rees (1976); Sherry (1966); Smith (1890); Watkins (1990); Weldon (1984); Wilks (1978).

11. Beckett (1984); Churchill (1947); Halperin (1984); Holmes (); Honan (1987); Johnson (1984).

12. Encyclopaedia Brittanica (1977), Macropaedia, vol. 5, pp31-32; Hudson (1992); Shepher (1983); Twitchell (1987).

13. Bell (1993); Brain (1979); Edwards (1987).

14. Bernstein (1991); Dukas & Hoffmann (1979); Encyclopaedia Brittanica (1977), Macropaedia, vol. 6, pp510-514; Forsee (1963).

15. Hudson (1992); The Old Testament, Leviticus, Chapters 18 & 20; for a detailed analysis of consanguinity in Jane Austen's novels see Hudson (1992), Sibling Love and Incest in Jane Austen's Fiction.

16. Beckett (1984); Churchill (1947); Holmes (1984); Johnson (1984);

17. Carter & Mears (1962); Plumb (1963); Trevelyan (1952); Wells (1951).

18. Jane Austen letter to Cassandra from Steventon (25 November 1798); reproduced in Chapman (1964), p32; Le Faye (1995), p20.

19. Bradbrook (1966); Cecil (1978).

20. Beckett (1984); Halperin (1984); Honan (1987); Johnson (1984).

21. Austen-Leigh (1870).

22. Embree (1962); Feiling (1966); Gardner (1971); Malleson (1894); Reid (1947); Wilbur (1945).

23. Feiling (1966).

24. Jane Austen letter to Charles Austen from Chawton (6 April 1817); reproduced in: Chapman (1964), p491; Le Faye (1995), p338.

25. Austen-Leigh (1870).

26. Embree (1962); Feiling (1966); Gardner (1971); Malleson (1894); Reid (1947); Wilbur (1945).

27. Feiling (1966).

28. Jane Austen letters to Cassandra from the Paragon, Bath (12-13 May & 1801); reproduced in: Chapman (1964), pp 126-129; Le Faye (1995), pp84-86.

29. Jane Austen letter to Cassandra from the Paragon, Bath (26-27 May, 1801); reproduced in : Chapman (1964), pp134-138; Le Faye (1995), pp89-92.

30. Spear (1971).

31. Embree (1962); Gopal (1963); Grieve (1974); Grant (18xx); Hastings (1772) [and other eye-witnesses of the event and its aftermath quoted by Hunter (1871)]; Khan (1969); Roberts (1953, 1958); Robinson (1984)); Sinha (1967); Smith (1776); Spear (1979); Teignmouth (1843).

2008 Postscript

32. Nokes (1997); Polya (1998a); Fullerton & Harbers (2001).

33. Fullerton, S. (2002).

34. Spence (2008).

Chapter 3. The editing of the Austens and the consequences of rustic amusement

1. Jane Austen letter to Cassandra from Steventon (1-2 December 1798); reproduced in: Chapman (1964), pp33-37; Johnson (1926), p51-56; Le Faye (1995), pp23-25.

2. Austen (1791) The History of England in Austen (1791), p71.

3. Austen (1811) Sense and Sensibility, Chapter 42, pp295-296

4. Austen-Leigh (1870); Austen-Leigh & Austen-Leigh (1913); Austen-Leigh (1920); Bush (1975); Cecil (1978); Chapman (1949); Fergus (1978); Halperin (1984); Hodge (1972); Honan (1987); Howard (1995); Jenkins (1973); Johnson (1926); Johnson (1927); Lane (1984); Lane (1986); Lascelles (1939); Llewellyn (1977); McDonagh (1991); Nicolson (1991); Pinion (1975); Rees (1976); Sherry (1966); Smith (1890); Thomson (1929); Tucker (1983); Watkins (1990); Weldon (1984); Wilks (1978).

5. Halperin (1984); Hodge (1972); Honan (1987); Lane (1984).

6. Williamson (1975), The Department, p23.

7. Davies (1935); Feiling (1966); Gleig (1841); Lawson (1905); Lyall (1907); Moon (1947); Malleson (1894); Trotter (1890); Stephen & Lee (1964); Turnbull (1975)..

8. Feiling (1966); Malleson (1894); Spear (1971), especially pp100-104.

9. Letter of Philadelphia Hancock to Warren Hastings (3 March 1780) quoted in Lane (1994), p71.

10. Letter from Lord Robert Clive to Lady Clive (1765) quoted in Bence-Jones (1974); Lane (1984), p44; Honan (1987), p423.

11. Austen (1792), Catherine or The Bower ; also see Halperin (1982) reproduced in: Chapman (1965), pp195-240; Grey (1989) (editor), pp23-44.

12. Letter of Jane Austen to Cassandra Austen from Henrietta Street, London (15-16 September 1813) in Chapman (1964), p318-325; Le Faye (1995), pp217-222.

13. Honan (1987); Lane (1984, 1986; 1996); Tucker (1983); [Hodge (1972) (p23) suspects something funny. In relation to the 10,000 pound bequest she says "It does make one wonder, just a little, about the relationship between them, but Hastings was known for his generosity." Ruoff (1992) speculates about Hastings' paternity of Eliza.]

14. Flannery (1994); Lines (1991).

15. Flannery (1994); Lines (1991); Morris, J. (1972) The Final Solution, Down Under reproduced in Chalk & Jonassohn (1990), pp204-222; Reynolds (1990); see also Strahan (1984) for details of the marsupials.

16. Flannery (1994); Strahan (1984), pp81-83.

17. Clark (1969, 1971, 1986); Clarke (1885), For the Term of his Natural Life; Conrad (1988); Hughes (1987); Koch (1987); Lines (1991).

18. Collings & Durrant (1977); Norris (1990).

19. Angus (1975): a collection of the superb wilderness photographs of Olegas Trehanas; Australian Parliament Inquiry into the Proposal to Drain and Restore Lake Pedder (1995) & the extraordinarily moving Lake Pedder slide collection set to music of Frederic Delius and performed at the University of Melbourne, 1995 as part of an as yet unsuccessful campaign to restore this vandalized treasure; Aulich

(1992); Bennett (1991); Brown (1986); Burt (1980); Collings & Durrant (1977); Conrad (1988); Davies (1965); Dombrovskis et al. (1996); Gilpin (1980); Koch (1986); Lines (1991); Pullan (1986); Rankin (1989); Tassell & Wood (1981); of particular note are the paintings by Elspeth Vaughan of the South West Wilderness of Tasmania.

20. This law against homosexuals was an extraordinary blemish on Tasmania and indeed Australia.

21. Prebble (1963).

22. Flannery (1994); Lines (1991); Morris, J. (1972) The Final Solution, Down Under reproduced in Chalk & Jonassohn (1990), pp204-222; Robinson & York (1977).

23. Broomhall (1991); Cooke (1993); Fenner & Ratcliffe (1965); Matthams (1921); Williams et al. (1995).

24. Fenner & Ratcliffe (1965).

25. Tyndale-Biscoe (1993); Cooke (1993); Williams et al. (1995); Goss (1995).

26. Cooke (1993); Lenghaus (1993); Williams et al. (1995).

27.Anderson (1995a,b); Goss (1995).

28. Dickson (1996).

29. Abbott (1996).

30. Bernard (1993); Brown (1995); Carson (1962); Eastwood (1993); Edgerton (1991); Kennedy (1993); Leakey & Lewin (1996); Leggett (1990); Mitchell (1991); Myers (1990); Rosenzweig & Parry (1994).

31. Mann (1924), The Magic Mountain (Der Zauberberg).

32. Bullfinch's Mythology (1984 edition); Larousse Encyclopaedia of Mythology (1959).

33. Anderson (1995c), Australia the brave?; Anderson (1995d), Australia's green dissenters gagged; Martin et al. (1986); Masood (1996b), Climate report "subject to scientific cleansing".

34. Austen-Leigh (1870); Austen-Leigh & Austen-Leigh (1913); Austen-Leigh (1920); Bush (1975); Cecil (1978); Chapman (1949); Fergus (1978); Halperin (1984); Hodge (1972); Honan (1987); Howard (1995); Jenkins (1973); Johnson (1926); Johnson (1927); Lane (1984); Lane (1986); Lane (1996); Lascelles (1939); Llewellyn (1977); McDonagh (1991); Nicolson (1991); Pinion (1975); Rees (1976); Sherry (1966); Smith (1890); Thomson (1929); Tucker (1983); Watkins (1990); Weldon (1984); Wilks (1978).

35. Hodge (1972); Ruoff (1992).

2008 Postscript

36. Nokes (1997); Polya (1998a); Fullerton & Harbers (2001).

37. Flanagan (2001).

Chapter 4. Jane Austen's siblings and their descendants

1. Jane Austen letter to Cassandra from Godmersham (17-18 November 1798); reproduced in: Chapman (1964), pp27-30; Le Faye (1995), pp19-21.

2. Jane Austen letter to Cassandra from Queen's Square, London (2 June 1799); reproduced in: Chapman (1964), pp62-65; Johnson (1926), p57-60; Le Faye (1995), pp41-43.

3. Austen (1818b) Northanger Abbey, Chapter 14, p110.

4. Halperin (1984); Hodge (1972); Honan (1987); Lane (1984, 1986, 1996).

5. Austen, C (18xx), My Aunt Jane Austen, a Memoir; Austen-Leigh, J. (1983) The Austen-Leighs and Jane Austen or "I have always maintained the value of Aunts" in Todd (1983), pp11-28; Austen-Leigh, J.E. (1870), A Memoir of Jane Austen; Austen-Leigh, M.A. (1920), Personal Aspects of Jane Austen; Austen-Leigh, W. and Austen-Leigh, R.A. (1913), Jane Austen Her Life and Letters. A Family Record. Hubback, J.H. and Hubback, E.C. (1906), Jane Austen's Sailor Brothers; Hugesson, H.M. (1960) Kentish Family; Knatchbull-Hugesson, E.H. (1884) (editor), Letters of Jane Austen.

6. Austen-Leigh (1870); Austen-Leigh & Austen-Leigh (1913); Austen-Leigh (1920); Bush (1975); Cecil (1978); Chapman (1949); Fergus (1978); Halperin (1984); Hodge (1972); Honan (1987); Howard (1995); Jenkins (1973); Johnson (1926); Johnson (1927); Lane (1984); Lane (1986); Lane (1996); Lascelles (1939); Llewellyn (1977); McDonagh (1991); Nicolson (1991); Pinion (1975); Rees (1976); Sherry (1966); Smith (1890); Thomson (1929); Tucker (1983); Watkins (1990); Weldon (1984); Wilks (1978).

7. Jenkins (1973).

8. Honan (1987).

9. Lodge (1986), Changing Places.

2008 Postscript

10. Nokes (1997); Polya (1998a); Fullerton & Harbers (2001).

Chapter 5. The editing of Jane Austen's life and connections

1. Jane Austen letter to Cassandra from Steventon (20-21 November 1800); reproduced in : Chapman (1964), pp90-95; Johnson (1926), pp60-66; Le Faye (1995), pp60-63.

2. Austen (1813) Pride and Prejudice, Volume 3, Chapter 15, p323.

3. Halperin (1984); Hodge (1972); Honan (1987); Lane (1984, 1986, 1996).

4. Howard (1995); Lane (1984, 1986, 1996).

5. For the Juvenilia see Austen (1790, 1791, 1792).

6. For a picture of Eliza see Lane (1996), p59.

7. Austen (1792, 1811; 1814; 1818b).

8. Mary Russell Mitford letter to Sir William Elford (April 1815), reproduced in Wilks (1978), p35; for a rebuttal of the "butterfly" assertion see Austen-Leigh (1870), p305.

9. Jane Austen letter to Cassandra from Steventon (9-10 January 1796); reproduced in Chapman (1964), pp1-4; Le Faye (1995), pp1-3.

10. Jane Austen letter to Cassandra from Steventon (14-15 January 1796); reproduced in Chapman (1964), pp4-6; Le Faye (1995), pp3-4.

11. Jane Austen letter to Cassandra from Steventon (17-18 November 1798); reproduced in Chapman (1964), pp27-30; Le Faye (1995), pp19-21.

12. Austen (1794, 1811, 1813, 1818b).

13. Jane Austen letters to Cassandra from the Paragon, Bath (12-13 May & 1801), reproduced in: Chapman (1964), pp 126-129; Le Faye (1995), pp84-86.; Jane Austen letter to Cassandra from the Paragon, Bath (26-27 May, 1801), reproduced in : Chapman (1964), pp134-138; Le Faye (1995), pp89-92.

14. Austen (1811, 1813).

15. Austen (1795, 1804, 1818b); Austen & Another (1977).

16. Austen (1804, 1816); Austen & Another (1977).

17. Jane Austen letter to Francis Austen from Bath (22 January 1805); reproduced in Chapman (1964), pp145-147.

18. Jane Austen letter to Cassandra from Godmersham re George Moore (20-22 June 1808); reproduced in Chapman (1964), pp192-198; Le Faye (1995), pp128-132.

19. Austen (1811, 1816).

20. Honan (1987), p270; for portraits of Jane Austen: see Lane (1996), pp20-21; Austen (1818a).

21. Austen (1813, 1814, 1816, 1818a,b).

22. Austen (1816).

23. Mary Russell Mitford letter to Sir William Elford (April 1815), reproduced in Wilks (1978), p35.

24. A delightful letter from Jane Austen to her favourite "neice" Fanny Knight from Chawton (20 February 1817); reproduced in : Chapman (1964), pp478-482; Le Faye (1995), pp328-331.

25. Jane Austen letter to Charles Austen from Chawton (6 April 1817); reproduced in: Chapman (1964), p491; Le Faye (1995), p338.

26. Jane Austen letter to her nephew James Edward Austen (27 May 1817) re doctors; reproduced in Chapman (1964), pp496-497; Le Faye (1995), p342.

27. Jane Austen's last words recorded in a letter from Cassandra Austen at Winchester to her niece Fanny Knight (20 July 1817); reproduced in: Chapman (1964), pp513-516; Le Faye (1995), pp343-346.

28. Austen-Leigh (1876); Honan (1987).

29. Mary Russell Mitford letter to Sir William Elford (April 1815), reproduced in Wilks (1978), p35; see also Austen-Leigh (1870), p305.

30. Austen-Leigh (1870); Austen-Leigh & Austen-Leigh (1913); Austen-Leigh (1920); Bush (1975); Cecil (1978); Chapman (1949); Fergus (1978); Halperin (1984); Hodge (1972); Honan (1987); Howard (1995); Jenkins (1973); Johnson (1926); Johnson (1927); Lane (1984); Lane (1986); Lane (1996); Lascelles (1939); Llewellyn (1977); McDonagh (1991); Nicolson (1991); Pinion (1975); Rees (1976); Sherry (1966); Smith (1890); Thomson (1929); Tucker (1983); Watkins (1990); Weldon (1984); Wilks (1978).

2008 Postscript

31. Nokes (1997); Polya (1998a); Fullerton & Harbers (2001).

Chapter 6. The rare intrusions of social reality into Jane Austen's novels

1. Austen (1794) Lady Susan, Lettter 21, p74.

2. Austen (1804) The Watsons, p110.

3. Austen (1814) Mansfield Park, Chapter 1, p41.

4. Austen (1814) Mansfield Park, Chapter 22, p226.

5. Jane Austen letter to Fanny Knight from Chawton (13 March 1817); reproduced in : Chapman (1964), p482-486; Johnson (1926), pp158-162; Le Faye (1995), pp331-334.

6. Carter & Mears (1962); Howard (1995); Lane (1986, 1996); Trevelyan (1952).

7. Carter & Mears (1962); Honan (1987); Trevelyan (1952).

8. Weldon (1984); Polya (1941); Cartwright (1977).

9. Honan (1987); Lane (1996).

10. Clark (1969, 1971, 1986); Clarke (1885), For the Term of His Natural Life; Hughes (1987); Shaw (1971).

11. Clarke (1885); Pullan (1984); Hughes (1987);

12. Honan (1987); Hughes (1987); Lane (1996).

13. Cameron & Spies (1992); Gopal (1963a,b); Prebble (1963); Porter (1984).

14. Chalk & Jonassohn (1990); Freund (1984); Lane (1996).

15. Gopal (1963a,b); Hunter (1871); Khan (1969); Cunningham (1996); Edwards & Williams (1957); Litton (1994); Woodham-Smith (1962).

16. Chalk & Jonassohn (1990); Lines (1991); Flannery (1994); Reynolds (1990); Robinson & York (1977).

17. Edwardes (1967); Embree (1962); Feiling (1966); Gardner (1971); Gopal (1963); Hunter (1871); Kaye (1853); Khan (1969); Lyall (1916); Majumdar (1976); Malleson (1894); Marshall (1993); Misra (1959); Reid (1947); Roberts (1958); Sinha (1967); Smith (1776); Spear (1965, 1971); Wilbur (1945).

18. Austen (1794), Lady Susan.

19. Austen (1818b), Northanger Abbey.

20. Austen (1818b), Northanger Abbey, Chapter 24, pp201-202.

21. Austen (1804), The Watsons.

22. Austen (1804), The Watsons, p110.

23. Austen (1811), Sense and Sensibility.

24. Austen (1811), Sense and Sensibility, Chapter 10, p49.

25. Anonymous (1842); Gardner (1971); Feiling (1966); Khan (1969); Malleson (1894); re the Chawton Middletons see Honan (1987).

26. Gardner (1971); Wilbur (1945).

27. Johnson (1984).

28. Spear (1971).

29. Anonymous (1842); Gardner (1971); Feiling (1966); Khan (1969); Malleson (1894); re the Chawton Middletons see Honan (1987).

30. Halperin (1984); Honan (1987); Lane (1984, 1996).

31. Gardner (1971); Reid (1947).

32. Gardner (1971); Feiling (1966); Malleson (1894).

33. Letter from Jane Austen to Cassandra from Henrietta Street (15 September 1813); reproduced in Chapman (1964), pp318-325; Le Faye (1995), pp217-222.

34. Austen (1813), Pride and Prejudice.

35. Austen (1814), Mansfield Park.

36. Honan (1987); Lane (1996); Lane (1996).

37. Austen (1814), Mansfield Park, p91.

38. Austen (1816), Emma.

39. Jane Austen comment in Austen-Leigh (1870) (1926 edition, p157); quoted in Chapman (1964), p xx2.

40. Jane Austen letter to Cassandra from Castle Square, Southampton (1-2 October 1808); reproduced in : Chapman (1964), pp209-219; Le Faye (1995), pp139-142.

41. Austen (1816), Emma, Volume 1, Chapter 7, pp47-48.

42. Austen (1816), Emma, Volume 3, Chapter 19, p438.

43. Austen (1816), Emma, Volume 3, Chapter 19, pp438-439.

44. Austen (1816), Emma, Volume 3, Chapter 19, p440.

45. Austen (1818a), Persuasion.

46. Austen (1817), Sanditon.

47. Austen (1817), Sanditon, Chapter 6, p181.

48. Honan (1987).

49. Cartwright (1977); Cochrane (1972); Polya (1941).

50. Malthus (1798), An Essay on the Principle of Population as it Affects the Future Improvement of Society.

51. Cartwright (1977).

52. Gopal (1963a,b); Hunter (1871); Sinha (1967).

53. Blankert et al. (1988); Dupart & Powell (1996); Jacob & Bianconi (1967); Levey (1962); Read (1965); Wheelock (1988) [of particular relevance to Jane Austen's life are the following masterpieces: Girl reading a letter (circa 1657); Woman in blue reading a letter (circa 1662-1664); The girl with a pearl earring (circa 1665); A lady writing (circa 1665-1666); Lady writing a letter with her maid (circa 1670).]

54. Wallace (1983) has provided a technically precise comparison of the work of Jane Austen and Mozart.

2008 Postscript

55. Polya (1999b, c; 2001a, b; 2005a).

56. Polya (2008p).

Chapter 7. The sensibilities of Jane Austen's literary contemporaries

1. Austen (1811) Sense and Sensibility, Chapter 3, p16.

2. Austen (1811) Sense and Sensibility, Chapter 10, p45.

3. Cowper (1785), The Task in Milford (1963), pp129-219.

4. Jane Austen letter to Cassandra from Henrietta Street, London (15-16 September 1813); reproduced in Chapman (1964), pp; Le Faye (1995), pp217-222.

5. Jane Austen letter to Cassandra from Godmersham Park (21 October 1813); reproduced in Chapman (1964), pp335-358; Le Fay (1995), pp241-243.

6. Jane Austen letter to Cassandra from Godmersham Park (6-7 November 1813); reproduced in Chapman (1964), pp369-375; Le Faye (1995), pp251-254.

7. Crabbe poem, Letter XX, The Poor of the Borough: Peter Grimes from The Borough (1810), quoted in Sherry (1966), p77..

8. Crabbe poem, The Village; quoted in Sherry (1966), p77.

9. Crabbe Letter XXII, The Poor of the Boroug : Peter Grimes from The Borough in Eastman et al. (1970), pp518-524.(1810)

10. Anonymous contemporary poem quoted in Howard (1995), p12.

11. Goldsmith (1770) The Deserted Village in Eastman et al. (1970), pp500-507.

12. Wright (1892); Milford (1963); Eastman et al. (1970).

13. Wright (1892); Honan (1987).

14. Cowper (1803) To Warren Hastings, Esq. by an Old School-Fellow of his at Westminster in Milford (1963), p416.

15. Cowper (1782) Expostulation in Milford (1963), pp43-59.

16. Fanning (1970); Maclean (1972); Gould (1978); Clark (1986).

17. Cowper (1782) Charity in Milford (1963), pp76-89.

18. Flannery (1994); Lines (1991); Morris, J. (1972) The Final Solution, Down Under reproduced in Chalk & Jonassohn (1990), pp204-222; Reynolds (1990).

19. Cowper (1785) The Task; Cowper (1785) The Task, Book II, The Time-Piece in Milford (1963), pp146-163.

20. Cowper (1793) The Negro's Complaint in Milford (1963), pp371-372.

21. Cowper (1788) The Morning Dream in Milford (1963), pp373-374.

22. Cowper (1836) Sweet Meat has Sour Sauce in Milford (1963), pp374-375.

23. Cowper (1800) Pity the poor African in Milford (1963), pp375-376.

24. Burns (1769) The Ploughman in Barke et al. (1966), pp146-147.

25. Burns(1786) The Author's Earnest Cry and Prayer to the Scotch Representatives in the House of Commons in McFurlan (1994), pp79-84.

26. McFurlan (1994), pp i-x.

27. Burns The Creed of Poverty in Cunningham (18xx), p125.

28. Prebble (1963).

29. Cunningham (18xx), Life of Robert Burns in Cunningham (18xx), pp i-xlvii.

30. Burns (1787), Dedication to Poems Chiefly in the Scottish Dialect.

31. Burns Written in a Lady's Pocket-Book in Cunningham (18xx), p125.

32. Burns The Slave's Lament in McFurlan (1994), p485.

33. John Shore, 1st Baron Teignmouth (circa 1810), poem on the 1769-1770 Bengal famine quoted by Shore (1843) & Woodruff (1965), p138.

34. Macaulay (1841), p584; Feiling (1966); Woodruff (1965).

35. Johnson (1778) in Postgate (1949), p193.

36. Johnson (1778) in Postgate (1949), p238.

37. Johnson (1783) in Postgate (1949). p286.

38. Anonymous (1842); Rhodes (1962); Durant (1975); Ayling (1985); Morwood (1985).

39. Anonymous (1842), an editing of the speeches of Sheridan by a "constitutional friend".

40. Sheridan (1799) Pizarro, A Tragedy in Five Acts in Rhodes (1962).

41. More (1905).

42. Lord Byron poem, reproduced in Anonymous (1842), The Speeches of the Right Honorable Richard Brinsley Sheridan, p viii.

43. More (1905).

44. Carter & Mears (1962); Honan (1987); Lane (1996); Trevelyan (1952).

45. Austen (1816), Emma, Volume 2, Chapter 18, p280.

46. Jane Austen letter to Cassandra from Chawton (6 June 1811); reproduced in: Chapman (1964), pp288-291; Le Faye (1995), pp192-194.

47. Austen (1816), Emma, Volume 2, Chapter 17, pp270-271.

48. Emily Bronte (1847), Wuthering Heights; Charlotte Bronte (1847), Jane Eyre.

Chapter 8. The judgement of Jane Austen's peers and successors

1. Jane Austen letter to Cassandra from Steventon (27-28 October 1798); reproduced in: Chapman (1964), pp22-26; Johnson (1926), pp37-42; Le Faye (1995), pp15-18.

2. Jane Austen letter to Cassandra from Steventon (24-26 December 1798); reproduced in: Chapman (1964), pp41-46; Johnson (1926), pp51-56; Le Faye (1995), pp28-31.

3. Jane Austen letter to Cassandra from Queen's Square, Bath (17 May 1799); reproduced in: Chapman (1964), pp59-62; Le Faye (1995), pp39-41.

4. Jane Austen letter to Cassandra from Godmersham Park (14-15 October 1813); reproduced in: Chapman (1964), pp; Johnson (1926), pp89-99; Le Faye (1995), pp236-241.

5. Jane Austen letter to James Edward Austen from Chawton (16-17 December 1816); reproduced in: Chapman (1964), pp467-470; Johnson (1926), pp467-470; Le Faye (1995), pp322-324.

6. Austen-Leigh (1870), p348.

7. Letter of Jane Austen to Cassandra from Henrietta Street, London (15-16 September 1813) in Chapman (1964), p318-325; Le Faye (1995), pp217-222.

8. Austen (1816), Emma, dedication to His Royal Highness the Prince Regent.

9. Austen letter re Emma to the Reverend J.S.Clarke, 11 December 1815, reproduced in Heath (1961).

10. Austen letter to the Reverend J.S.Clarke re a suggested "House of Saxe Coburg" novel (1 April 1816), reproduced in Heath (1961).

11. Anonymous review (1818), British Critic, new series,vol. IX (March 1818) pp293-301, reproduced in Southam (1976a), pp41-47.

12. Sir Walter Scott (Journal 14 March 1826), quoted by Howard (1995), p6 & by Southam (1976b), p155.

13. Sir Walter Scott in the Quarterly Review vol. XIV (October 1815), reproduced in Southam (1976b), pp36-39. & in Heath (1961); see also Halperin (1975).

14. Sir Walter Scott, Journal (18 September 1827), reproduced in Southam (1976b), p53.

15. Halperin (1975); Heath (1961); Southam (1975a,b).

16. Macaulay essay, Edinburgh Review (January 1843), reproduced in Southam (1976b).

17. Jane Austen letter to Cassandra from Henrietta Street, London (15-16 September 1813); reproduced in Chapman (1964), pp; Le Faye (1995), pp217-222.

18. Austen-Leigh (1870), p282.

19. Austen-Leigh (1870), p373.

20. Whately (anonymous) review (1881) in the Quarterly Review vol. 24, pp352-376; reproduced in Heath (1961).

21. Lewes (1852) in the Westminster Review vol. 58, pp 134-135; reproduced in Southam (1976b).

22. Brontë letter to G.H. Lewes (12 January 1848), quoted in Southam (1976b, pp55-56; reproduced in Heath (1961).

23. Brontë letter to G.H. Lewes (18 January 1848) quoted in Southam (1976b), p56; reproduced in Heath (1961).

24. Brontë letter to W.S. Williams (12 April 1850) quoted in Southam (1976b), pp56-57; reproduced in Heath (1961).

25. G.H. Lewes essay (1859), quoted by Monaghan (1981), p89.

26. Kavanagh (1862) in English Women of Letters (1862) quoted in Southam (1976b), p60.

27. Simpson in 1870, quoted by Monaghan (1981), pp89-90.

28. Simpson in 1870, quoted in Southam (1976b), p63.

29. Smith (1890), p185.

30. Southam (1987).

31. Joseph Conrad in 1913 in a lettter to H.G. Wells, quoted in Lauber (1993), p133.

32. Samuel Clemens (Mark Twain) in 1896, quoted in Southam (1987), p232.

33. Samuel Clemens (Mark Twain) in 1898, quoted in Southam (1987), p232.

34. Samuel Clemens (Mark Twain) in 1909, quoted in Southam (1987), p232.

35. Samuel Clemens (Mark Twain) in 1909, quoted in Southam (1987), pp232-233.

36. Henry James in 1906, quoted in Southam (1987), pp229-230.

37. Henry James in 1914, quoted in Southam (1987), p234.

38. Wilson (1945), A long talk about Jane Austen, reproduced in Watt (1963), pp35-40.

39. Villard (1924), p67.

40. Villard (1924), p71.

41. Jane Austen letter to James Edward Austen from Chawton(16 December 1816) as quoted in Villard (1924), p129; for precise transcription see Chapman (1964), pp467-470; Johnson (1926), pp467-470; Le Faye (1995), pp322-324.

42 Villard (1924), pp129-130.

43. Villard (1924), p248.

44. Bailey (1931); Bradbrook (1966); Bush (1975); Cecil (1935); Chapman (1949); Craik (1965); De Rose (1980); Gooneratne (1970); Halperin (1975); Hardy (1984); Hardy (1979); Harris (1989); Heath (1961); Johnson (1924); Lascelles (1939); Lauber (1993); Litz (1965); McMaster (1976); Morris (1987); Moler (1978); Mudrick (1968); Scott (1982); Sherry (1966); Southam (1964, 1976a, 1976b, 1987); Thompson (1951); Villard (1924); Watt (1963); Weldon (1984); Wiesenfarth (1967); Wiltshire (1976).

45. Halperin (1975); Southam (1987); Watt (1963).

46. Virginia Woolf in 1923, quoted by Southam (1987), p301.

47. Virginia Woolf (1924); reproduced in Heath (1961); quoted in Southam (1987), p281.

48. Johnson (1924), p4.

49. Johnson (1924), p19.

50. Arnold Bennett in 1922-1928 in the Evening Standard, quoted in Southam (1987), pp287-288.

51. Bailey (1931), p23.

52. Johnson (1924), p53.

53. Johnson (1927), pp163-164.

54. Auden poem, Letter to Lord Byron in Auden (1937), Letters from Iceland; quoted in Southam (1987), p299; Watt (1963), pp11-12.

55. Wells (1938), The Brothers, p15; quoted in Southam (1987), p301.

56. Amis (1957), What became of Jane Austen? (a critique of Mansfield Park); reproduced in Watt (1963), pp141-144.

57. C.S.Lewis (1954), A note on Jane Austen, reproduced in Watt (1963), pp25-34.

58. Southam, B.C. (1977), Encyclopaedia Brittanica (1977), Macropaedia, Volume 2, pp377-378.

59. Lane (1986, 1996); Weldon (1984).

60. Weldon (1984).

61. Lord Halifax's Advice to His Daughter quoted in Monaghan (1981), Jane Austen and the position of women, chapter 7 in Monaghan (1981), pp105-121.

62. Alexander Pope poem Of the Characters of Women, reproduced in Hayward (1978), pp208-212.

63. Austen (1813), Pride and Prejudice; Austen (1814), Mansfield Park.

64. Sulloway (1989).

65. **Jane Austen's life:** Austen-Leigh (1870); Austen-Leigh (1920); Austen-Leigh & Austen-Leigh (1913); Fergus (1991); Halperin (1984); Hodge (1972); Honan (1987); Hubback & Hubback (1906); Hugesson (1960); Jenkins (1973); Lane (1984, 1986, 1996); MacDonagh; Pinion (1975); Smith (1890); Smithers (1981); Thomson (1929); Tucker (1983); Wilks (1978).

66. **Literary criticism:** Bailey (1931); Bloom (1986); Bradbrook (1966); Brown (1973); Bush (1975); Butler (1975); Cecil (1935); Chapman (1949); Craik (1965); De Rose (1980); Dussinger (1990); Dwyer (1989); Gard (1992); Gay (1990); Gooneratne (1970); Halperin (1975); Handler & Segal (1990); Hardy (1984); Hardy (1979); Harris (1989); Heath (1961); Johnson (1924); Lascelles (1939); Lauber (1993); Liddell (1966); Litz (1965); Lodge (1991); Maker (1989); Mansell (1978); McMaster (1976); Morris (1987); Moler (1978); Monaghan (1980); Mooneyham (1988); Morgan (1980); Mudrick (1968); Nardin (1973); Nordhjem (1987); Oldmark (1981); O'Neill (1971); Paris (1978); Powell (1993); Rubinstein (1969); Ruoff (1992); Scott (1982); Sherry (1966); Southam (1964, 1968, 1976a, 1976b, 1987); Tanner (1986); Thompson (1951); Villard (1924); Warner (1964); Watt (1963); Weldon (1984); Wiesenfarth (1967); Wilkes (1991); Williams (1986); Wiltshire (1976); Wiltshire (1992); Wood (1993); Wright (1957).

67. **Word use & language:** Burrows (1987); Page (1970); Phillips (1970); Stokes (1991).

68. **Sociology, history & philosophy:** Brown (1979); Devlin (1975); Fergus (1983); Grey (1989); Hudson (1992); Johnson (1988); Kent (1989); Koppel (1988); Lane (1984, 1986, 1996); Monaghan (1981); Myer (1980); Roberts (1979); Weldon (1984).

69. **Music:** Wallace (1983); Piggott (1979) [while Handel appears, his patron and important Jane Austen family connection, James Brydges, does not rate a mention]; Wallace (1983).

70. **Youthful works:** Austen (1791); Austen (1800); Austen & Another (1975); Austen & Another (1977); Chapman (1932, 1954); Grey (1989); Johnson (1926); Kaplan (1992); Knatchbull-Hugesson (1884).

71. **Female & feminist perspective:** Brown (1979); Horwitz (1991); Johnson (1988); Kaye-Smith & Stern (1943); Kirkham (1983); Muckherjee (1991); Smith (1983); Sulloway (1989); Todd (1983); Weldon (1984).

72. **Life, health and lifestyle:** Howard (1995); Lane (1986, 1996); Nicolson (1991); Watkins (1990); Weldon (1984); Wiltshire (1992).

73. Hudson (1992).

74. Wallace (1983).

75. Burrows (1987).

76. Disraeli read Pride and & Prejudice 17 times according to the Encyclopaedia Brittanica (1961), Volume 2, p699; Trevelyan (1952).

77. Fraser (1980).

78. Cunningham (1996); Edwards & Williams (1957); Litton (1994); Woodham-Smith (1962).

79. Churchill (1952), vol. 5, p377.

2008 Postscript

80. Polya (2008i-m).

81. Dawkins (2006), pp254-259 – describing a very disturbing survey by Israeli psychologist George Tamarin of Jewish childrens' attitudes to Joshua's extermination of the Palestinians.

82. Fullerton & Harbers (2001).

Chapter 9. The East India Company, the Black Hole and the conquest of Bengal

1. Jane Austen letter to Cassandra (15-16 September 1796); reproduced in: Chapman (1964), pp13-15; Faye (1995), pp9-11; Johnson (1926), p5.

2. J.Z.Holwell quoted by Forbes, Oriental Memoirs, II, p457 & Spear (1971), p195.

3. Famous Robert Clive assertion during the Parliamentary inquiry, 1973; quoted by: Cohen & Cohen (1961), p112; Palmer (1981), p73; Churchill (1965), p225.

4. Capper (1853; Carey (1882); Chaudhuri (1975); Churchill (1965); Datta (1977, 1978); Davies (1935, 1939); Dodwell (1963, 1967); Dunbar (1936, 1943, 1951); Edwardes (1961, 1967, 1977); Embree (1962); Feiling (1966); Gardner (1971); Garnett (1976); Ghosh (1944); Gleig (1841); Gopal (1963a,b); Greenough (1982); Grieve (1974) [T.B. Macaulay's essays on Lord Clive & Warren Hastings]; Gupta (1977); Hastings (1787); Hunter (1871); Islam (1982); Kaye (1853); Khan (1969); Kopf (1969); Lawford (1976); Lawson (1905); Lyall (1907, 1916, 1989); Majumdar (1960, 1969, 1976, 1977); Malleson (1885, 1894); Marshall (1965,1976, 1993); Masani (1960); Mason (1916); Misra (1961); Moon (1947, 1989); Muckherjee (1958); Muir ((1917, 1929); Nolan (18xx); Philips (1961); Reid (1947); Richmond (1984); Roberts (1958); Sinha (1967); Smith (1776); Spear (1971, 1975, 1979); Srivastava (1981); Teignmouth (1843); Thompson & Garratt (1934); Traeger (1979); Trotter (1890); Turnbull (1975); Wheeler (1860); Wilbur (1945); Woodruffe (1953).

5. Embree (1962); Ghosh (1944); Gopal (1963a); Grieve (1974); Grant (18xx); Greenough (1982); Hastings (1772); Hunter (1871); Khan (1969); Roberts (1953, 1958); Robinson (1984); Sinha (1967); Smith (1776); Spear (1979); Teignmouth (1843).

6. Barber (1966); Capper (1853); Carey (1882); Chaudhuri (1975); Datta (1977); Davies (1935, 1939); Dodwell (1963, 1967); Dunbar (1936, 1943, 1951); Edwardes (1977); Feiling (1966); Gardner (1971); Garrett (1976); Gleig (1841) [he assumed the reader was familiar with the story]; Grieve (1963) [including Macaulay's account in his essay Lord Clive]; Holwell (1778) - his own account, reproduced in Macfarlane (1975); Lawford (1976); Lyall (1907); Macaulay (1840); Malleson (1885); Moon (1947, 1989); Nolan (18xx); Spear (1975, 1979) [more critical views ; maybe 64 into the Black Hole and 21 surviving]; Trotter (1890); Turnbull (1975); Wheeler (18600; Woodruff (1953) [p96; "Everyone knows what happened that evening of a Calcutta June"]

7. Datta (1977) in Majumdar & Dighe (1977); Einbinder (1972), pp184-187; Little (1915); Majumdar & Dighe (1977).

8. Gopal (1963b); Macfarlane (1975), pp229-230; Mukherjee (1958), p261

9. Gopal (1963a,b); Hunter (1871); Sinha (1967).

10. Datta (1971); Gopal (1963b); Macfarlane (1975).

11. Churchill (1965); Edwardes (1967); Embree (1962); Feiling (1966); Gardner (1971); Ghosh (1944); Gopal (1963a); Hunter (1871); Islam (1982); Kaye (1853); Khan (1969); Lyall ,1916, 1989); Majumdar (1960); Majumdar (1976); Malleson (1894; 1985); Marshall (1976); Marshall (1993); Mason (1916); Misra (1961); Moon (1947, 1988); Muir ((1917, 1929); Reid (1947); Roberts (1958); Sinha (1967); Smith (1776); Spear (1971); Spear (1979); Srivastava (1981); Teignmouth (1843); Thompson & Garratt (1934); Traeger (1979); Trotter (1890); Turnbull (1975); Wilbur (1945); Woodruff (1953).

12. Bhatia (1991); Chatterjee (1944); Chopra (1988); Das (1949); Ghosh (1944); Greenough (1982); Sen (1981); Uppal (1984).

13. Kennedy (1993); Rosenzweig & Parry (1994); United Nations Population Division (1992).

14. Capper (1853); Carey (1882); Datta (1977, 1978); Dodwell (1963, 1967); Dunbar (1943); Gardner (1971); Hunter (1890, 1912); Majumdar & Dighe (1977); Moon (1989); Mukherjee (1958); Nolan (18xx); Reid (1947); Spear (1979); Wheeler (1860); Wilbur (1945); Wooruff (1953).

15. Smith (1776), pp600-601.

16. Smith (1776), p601.

17. Gardner (1971), p38.

18. Johnson (1984), chapter 3, pp53-89.

19. Smithers (1981), p124; Honan (1987), p409.

20. Trevelyan (1938), p240.

21. Sinha (1967).

22. Datta (1971); Gopal (1963b); Macfarlane (1975); Sinha (1967).

23. Barber (1966); Reid (1947); Wilbur (1945).

24. Holwell (1758) A Genuine Narrative of the Deplorable Deaths of the English Gentlemen and Others who were Suffocated in the Blasck Hole in Fort William, at Calcutta; reproduced in Macfarlane (1975).

25. Stanhope (1784); partly reproduced in Nair (1984).

26. Jog (1944).

27. Little (1915-1916) in Bengal Past and Present; July 1915 &
January 1916, quoted by Einbinder (1972), pp184-187 & Dodwell
(1963a), p156.

28. Einbinder (1972), pp184-187.

29. Gopal (1963b), Appendix, Note on the Black Hole, pp351-357.

30. Macfarlane (1975).

31. Barber (1966).

32. Clayton (1931); Cohn (1967); Farmer (1985); Koestler (1971),
Anatomy of a Canard (a review of Edgar Morin (1970), Rumour in
Orleans), reproduced in Koestler (1974), pp89-91; Sartre (1946);
Woolley (1927), pp115-116.

33. Datta (1977), p112.

34. Spears (1979), p156.

35. Edwardes (1977), pp89-91.

36. Nolan (18xx), pp245-247.

37. Samuel Johnson in Boswell's Life , 7 April, 1775; quoted by Evans
(1968).

38. Bickerton & Pearson (1991); Darwish & Alexander (1991); Hiro
(1992).

39. Wells (1951).

40. Rusbridger & Nave (1991).

41. Churchill (1952).

42. Kimball (1984).

43. Macfarlane (1975), Chapter 9, p207.

44. Hunter (1890), p381.

45. Curzon (1925).

46. For Lord Curzon's parsimony see Edwardes (1967), pp230-231.

47. Ranindranath Tagore, quoted in Macfarlane (1975), Chapter 9, p207.

48. Keesing's Contemporary Archives, 12-19 October 1940, p4279B.

49. Bhatia (1991); Das (1949); Drèze & Sen (1989); Ghosh (1944); Greenough (1982); Sen (1981).Uppal (1984).

50. Carey (1882); Garrett (1976); Macauley (1840), p506; Nair (1975); Stanhope (1778).

51. Dunbar (1951); Lawford (1976); Macaulay (1840); Moon (1947, 1969); Mukherjee (1958).

52. Dodwell (1967).

53. Dodwell (1967); Moon (1989).

54. Feiling (1966).

55. Chaudhuri (1975); Davies (1939).

56. Dodwell (1963).

57. Lyall ((1916), pp143-144.

58. Davies (1939); Edwardes (1977); Garrett (1976); Malleson (1885).

59. Davies (1939); Dunbar (1936).

60. Gardner (1971); Lyall (1916); Reid (1947); Wilbur (1945); Woodruffe (1953).

61. A remarkable set of examples includes those that dismiss the major event of the period, the Great Bengal Famine of 1769-1770, in a few words: Ballhatchett (1965); Churchill (1965); Edwardes (1967); Gardner (1971): Kaye (1853): Lyall (1916) and Wilbur (1945); and those that fail to mention this disaster at all [according to my reading of their work] : Ayling (1991); Barber (1986); Baxter (1988); Barraclough (1982); Black (1992); Carter & Mears (1960); Chaudhuri (1988); Dodwell (1963b); Derry (1962); Edwardes (1967); Ehrman (1969); Encyclopaedia Brittanica (1961 edition); Grun (1975); Hunt (1905); Halliday (1986); Langer (1953); Mabbett (1988); Plumb (1950); Porter (1986); Reilly (1978); Roberts (1963a,b); Rose (1925); Rosebery (1902); Stanhope (1861); Trevelyan (1960); Vadgama (1984); Wells (1956); Williams (1966).

62. Bolts (1772); Embree (1986); Gopal (1963a); Grant (18xx); Grieve (1974) [Macaulay's account]; Hunter (1871); Khan (1969); Malleson (1885); Roberts (1958); Robinson (1984); Smith (1776); Spear (1979); Teignmouth (1843).

63. Smith (1776).

64. Gopal (1963a,b); Macfarlane (1975); Sinha (1967).

65. Dodwell (1963b), p156.

66. Dodwell (1963a,b).

Chapter 10. The Great Bengal Famine of 1769-1770

1. Austen (1814) Mansfield Park, Chapter 48, p446.

2. Austen (1818b) Northanger Abbey, Chapter 24, p201.

3. Churchill (1965), Book 8, Chapter 15, p225.

4. Weldon (1984), Letters to Alice on First Reading Jane Austen, p93.

5. Ballhatchet (1965); Bayly (1988); Bolts (1772); Bose (1993); Carey (1882); Churchill (1965); Datta (1961, 1978); Davies (1935, 1939); Dunbar (1943; Edwardes (1961, 1967); Embree (1962); Feiling (1966); Fortescue (1967); Gardner (1971); Ghosh (1944); Gleig (1841); Gopal (1963); Greenough (1982); Grieve (1974) [T.B. Macaulay's essay on Clive]; Hastings (1787); Hunter (1871, 1890); Islam (1982); Kaye (1853); Khan (1969); Kopf (1969); Lovett (1963a,b); Lyall (1907, 1916, 1989); Macaulay (1840); Majumdar (1969, 1976, 1977); Malleson (1894; 1985); Marshall (1976, 1987, 1993); Mason (1916); Mason (1985); Misra (1961); Moon (1947, 1989); Muir ((1917, 1929); Mukherjee (1958); Reid (1947); Richmond (1984); Roberts (1909a,b,1958); Sinha (1967); Smith (1776); Spear (1971); Spear (1979); Srivastava (1981); Teignmouth (1843); Thompson & Garratt (1934); Traeger (1979); Trotter (1890); Turnbull (1975); Wheeler (1860); Wilbur (1945); Woodruff (1953 , 1965).

6. Austen (1811), Sense and Sensibility, Chapter 10, p49.

7. Greenough (1982)

8. Bissio (1990); Chaliand & Rageau (1985); Greenough (198); Kidron & Segal (1987).

9. Edwardes (1967); Embree (1962); Feiling (1966); Gardner (1971); Gopal (1963); Hunter (1871); Kaye (1853); Khan (1969); Lyall (1916); Majumdar (1976); Malleson (1894); Marshall (1993); Misra (1959);

Reid (1947); Roberts (1958); Sinha (1967); Smith (1776); Spear (1965, 1971); Wilbur (1945).

10. Marshall (1993), The Company and the coolies, in Marshall (1993) (editor), pp23-38.

11. The 1765 exchange rate can be calculated to be 1 Rupee = 0.1125 pound according to Dunbar (1951), p91; the 1782 figure was about 1 Rupee = 0.105 pound according to Hunter (1871), p83.

12. Greenough (1982).

13. Ghosh (1944); Greenough (1982).

14. Edwardes (1967); Embree (1962); Feiling (1966); Gardner (1971); Gopal (1963); Hunter (1871); Kaye (1853); Khan (1969); Lyall (1916); Majumdar (1976); Malleson (1894); Misra (1959); Reid (1947); Roberts (1958); Sinha (1967); Spear (1965); Wilbur (1945).

15. Austen (1811), Sense and Sensibility.

16. Marshall (1993), The Company and the coolies, in Marshall (1993) (editor), pp23-38.

17. Hunter (1871), The Annals of Rural Bengal.

18. Embree (1962); Gopal (1963); Grieve (1974); Grant (18xx); Hastings (1772) [and other eye-witnesses of the event and its aftermath quoted by Hunter (1871)]; Khan (1969); Roberts (1953, 1958); Robinson (1984)); Sinha (1967); Smith (1776); Spear (1979); Teignmouth (1843).

19. Ghosh (1944); Greenough (1982);

20. Crossman (1946); Crossman's observations (1945), quoted in Wasserstein (1988), pp356-357.

21. Letter from the President and Council at Fort William to the Court of Directors, 11 September 1770, quoted in Hunter (1871), p30.

22. John Shore (Lord Teignmouth) poem quoted in: Hunter (1871), p26; Teignmouth (1843), vol. 1, pp25-26; Woodruff (1965), p138.

23. Charles Grant, Observations of the State of Asia, quoted at length in Embree (1963).

24. Warren Hastings report to the " Hon'ble the Court of Directors for Affairs of the Hon'ble the United Company of Merchants of England trading to the East Indies", 3 November 1772; reproduced in Hunter (1871), appendix A.

25. Hunter (1871).

26. Stanhope (1784; 1909 edition), reproduced in Nair (1984), 166-179.

27. Nair (1984), chapter 10, pp166-179.

28. Hunter (1871).

29. Uppall (198).

30. Hunter (1871).

31. De Grandpre (1801), reproduced in Nair (1984), chapter 14.; Stanhope (1784), reproduced in Nair (1984); Nair (1984); Spear (1971).

32. Hunter (1871).

33. Ghosh (1944); Greenough (1982); Kachhawaha (1992).

34. Hunter (1871).

35. Ballhatchet (1965), p220, quoting a Despatch from Bengal, 3 November 1771, India Office Records, Letters from Bengal, vol.XI, p84.; Bose (1993), pp17-18;Embree (1962); Hastings (1772); Hunter (1871); Khan (1969); Roberts (1909b), p566; Sinha (1967); Smith (1876).

36. Hunter (1871).

37. Drèze & Sen (1989); Sen (1981).

38. Gardner (1971); Hastings (1772); Hunter (1871).

39. Bolts (1772); Embree (1962); Grant (18xx); Hastings (1772) [he quotes eye-witness accounts and Company reports]; Hunter (1871); Nair (1984); Stanhope (1774); Teignmouth (1843).

40. Warren Hastings report to the Company Directors, 3 November 1772; reproduced in Hunter (1871), appendix A.

41. Hunter (1871).

42. Bolts (1772); Bose (1993); Embree (1986); Gopal (1963a); Grant (18xx); Grieve (1974) [Macaulay's account]; Hunter (1871); Khan (1969); Malleson (1885); Roberts (1958); Robinson (1984); Smith (1776); Spear (1979); Teignmouth (1843).

43. Hunter (1871).

44. Smith (1776).

45. Ballhatchet (1965); Bayly (1988); Bhatia (1991); Bhattacharya (1967); Black (1971); Churchill (1965); Davies (1935, 1939); Embree (1988); Encyclopaedia Brittanica (1977, 1779); Feiling (1966); Fortescue (1967); Greenough (1982); Hunt (1905); Jog (1944); Kopf (1969); Mehra (1985); Macfarlane (1975); Majumdar (1976); Malleson (1894); Maloo (1987); Marshall (1976, 1987); Mason (1985); Mehra

(1985); Misra (1959); Muir (1929); Raychaudhuri (1988) in Embree (1988); Reid (1947); Roberts (1909); Sen (1981); Spear (1965, 1971); Watson (1960).

46. Carey (1882); Churchill (1965); Dunbar (1951); Edwardes (1961, 1967); Feiling (1966); Hunter (1871, 1890); Gardner (1971); Gleig (1841); Kaye (1853); Lovett (1963a,b); Lyall (1907, 1916); Wilbur (1945).

47. Kaye (1853), p168.

48. Lyall (1916), chapters 8-10, pp138-183.

49. Lyall (1907), p35.

50. Wilbur (1945), chapters 18 & 19, pp254-288.

51. Churchill (1965), A History of the English-Speaking Peoples. The Age of Revolution, pp225-226.

52. Edwardes (1961), pp211-212; Edwardes (1967), pp228-231.

53. Gardner (1971), pp103-105.

54. Carey (1882), p54.

55. Dunbar (1951), p91.

56. Feiling (1966), p85.

57. Hunter (1871).

58. Hunter (1890), pp387-388.

59. Gleig (1841), Volume 1, p150.

60. Ayling (1991); Barber (1986); Baxter (1988); Barraclough (1982); Black (1992); Capper (1853); Carter & Mears (1960); Chaudhuri (1988); Derry (1962); Dodwell (1963a,b); Edwardes (1967); Ehrman (1969); Encyclopaedia Brittanica (1961 edition); Grun (1975); Hunt (1905); Halliday (1986); Langer (1953); Lawson (1905); Mabbett (1988); Masani (1960); Plumb (1950); Porter (1986); Reilly (1978); Roberts (1963a,b); Rose (1925); Rosebery (1902); Stanhope (1861); Trevelyan (1960); Vadgama (1984); Ward (1965); Wells (1956); Williams (1966) [my apologies if I have missed a footnote or a "10 words for 10 million victims" entry].

61. Porter (1986), p88.

62. Bayly (1988); Bose (1993); Marshall (1987); Dodwell (1963a,b); Lovett (1963a,b) in Dodwell (1963a).

63. Langer (1952); Grun (1975).

64. Darlington (1969).

65. Freund (1984); Martin (1929) in Rose et al. (1929).

66. Wells (1956), The Outline of History.

67. Trevelyan (1952), History of England.

68. Edwards & Williams (1957); Encyclopaedia Brittanica (1977), Slavery, serfdom and forced labour, Volume 16, pp853-866; Woodham-Smith (1962).

69. Einbinder (1972), pp184-187.

70. Holwell (1778), reproduced in Macfarlane (1975);

71. Gopal (1963b); Little (1913); Macfarlane (1975), pp229-230.

72. Barber (1966); Carter & Mears (1960); Encyclopaedia Brittanica (1961 edition); Grun (1975); Halliday (1986); Langer (1953); Porter (1986).

73. Joseph Stalin aphorism, quoted in Marsden (1988), p23.

74. Elton (1996), Popcorn, p267.

75. Macfarlane (1975), p230.

76. Encyclopaedia Brittanica (1977, 1979), Macropaedia, vol. 9, p405.

77. Gopal (1969a), p32.

78. Feiling (1966), p75.

79. Muir (1929), p437.

80. Grant (1792), p8; quoted in Embree (1962), p38.

81. Woodruff (1965), p138.

82. Trager (1979), p314.

83. Malleson (1985), pp199-200.

84. Misra (1959), p113.

85. Hunter (1871), p63.

86. Majumbar (1976), p157.

87. Gopal (1963a), p17.

88. Horace Walpole quoted in: Kopf (1969), pp13-14; see also Dodwell (1963a) (editor), The Cambridge History of India, Volume V,

p187 [Walpole quoted but with the part mentioning of the Bengal Famine of 1770 deleted.].

89. Moon (1989), p146.

90. Mukherjee (1958), pp351-352.

91. Trotter (1890), p53.

92. Wheeler (1860), pp55-56.

93. Majumdar & Dighe (1977), p357.

94. T.B. Macaulay (1840) essay on Lord Clive, reproduced in Grieve (1974), pp 479-549.

95. Trevelyan (1952).

96. Churchill (1965), pp225-226.

97. Das (1949); Drèze & Sen (1989); Greenough (1982); Sen (1981); Uppal (1984).

2008 Postscript

98. Schama (2002).

99. Polya, G.M. (2003), pp 204, 530.

100. Blainey (2000, 2004); Garratty & Gay (1972); McNeil (1979); Ponting (2000).

101. Polya, G. (2008m).

Chapter 11. Warren Hastings and the conquest of India

1. Austen (1811) Sense and Sensibility, Chapter 10, p49.

2. Hastings letter to the East India Company Secret Committee, 1772; reproduced in Fortescue (1967) (editor), pp 385-392.

3. Hastings letter to the East India Company Directors, 5 May 1781; reproduced in Islam (1982), p5.

4. Jane Austen letter to Cassandra from Ibthrop (Ibethorp), 30 November - 1 December 1800; reproduced in Le Faye (1995), pp63-64; for details of the "faithful" Maria Payne see Le Faye (1995), pp373, 534 & 561; Smithers (1981), pp116-117.

5. Jane Austen letter to Cassandra from Godmersham, 30 June - I July, 1802; reproduced in Le Faye (1995), p138; see also Le Faye (1995), p390 re the William Hodges painting at Daylesford of Mrs Hastings' heroic Ganges journey to nurse Warren Hastings, Mrs Hastings at the Rocks of Colgong.

6. Davies (1935); Feiling (1966); Gleig (1841); Grieve (1961), T.B. Macaulay essay, Warrren Hastings; Macaulay (1841); Hastingss (1787); Kopf (1969); Lawson (1905); Lyall (1907); Marshall (1965); Malleson (1894); Mehra (1985); Moon (1947); Trotter (1890); Turnbull (1975); Woodruff (1965), Warren Hastings, Chapter 4.

7. Capper (1853; Carey (1882); Chaudhuri (1975); Churchill (1965); Datta (1977, 1978); Davies (1935, 1939); Dodwell (1963, 1967); Dunbar (1936, 1943, 1951); Edwardes (1961, 1967, 1977); Embree (1962); Feiling (1966); Gardner (1971); Garnett (1976); Ghosh (1944); Gleig (1841); Gopal (1963a,b); Greenough (1982); Grieve (1961, 1974) [T.B. Macaulay's essays on Lord Clive & Warren Hastingd]; Gupta (1977); Hastings (1787); Hunter (1871); Islam (1982); Kaye (1853); Khan (1969); Kopf (1969); Lawford (1976); Lawson (1905); Lyall (1907, 1916, 1989); Majumdar (1960, 1969, 1976, 1977);

Malleson (1885, 1894); Marshall (1965,1976, 1993); Masani (1960); Mason (1916); Misra (1959); Moon (1947, 1989); Muckherjee (1958); Muir ((1917, 1929); Nair (1984); Nolan (18xx); Philips (1961); Reid (1947); Richmond (1984); Roberts (1958); Sinha (1967); Smith (1776); Spear (1971, 1975, 1979); Srivastava (1981); Teignmouth (1843); Thompson & Garratt (1934); Traeger (1979); Trotter (1890); Turnbull (1975); Wheeler (1860); Wilbur (1945); Woodruffe (1953).

8. Hastings (1772); reproduced in Hunter (1871).

9. Honan (1987), p411.

10. Stanhope (1784).

11. Marshall (1965), p133.

12. Capper (1853); Dodwell (1967); Khan (1969); Majumdar & Dighe (1977).

13. Majumdar & Dighe (1977), p374.

14. Anstey (1962, 1966); Forbath (1978); Martelli (1962).

15. Macaulay (1841), p584.

16. Feiling (1966); Woodruff (1965).

17. Macaulay (1841); quoted by Moon (1947), p160.

2008 Postscript

18. Chomsky (2007).

19. Polya (2008k, l, m).

20. UN Genocide Convention (1948), Article 2: "In the present Convention, genocide means any of the following acts committed with

intent to destroy, in whole or in part, a national, ethnic, racial or religious group, as such: a) Killing members of the group; b) Causing serious bodily or mental harm to members of the group; c) Deliberately inflicting on the group conditions of life calculated to bring about its physical destruction in whole or in part; d) Imposing measures intended to prevent births within the group; e) Forcibly transferring children of the group to another group".

Chapter 12. The impeachment of Warren Hastings and the judgement of history

1. Jane Austen letter to Cassandra from Henrietta Street, London, 15-16 September 1813; reproduced in: Chapman (1964), pp318-325 ; Le Faye (1995), pp217-222. For further analysis see Le Faye (1995), pp 419, 486-487, 534.

2. Austen (1818b) Northanger Abbey, Chapter 14, p111.

3. Robert Clive letter (30 December 1758); quoted in: Forrest, Life of Clive, Volume 2, p120; Spear (1971), p195.

4. Edmund Burke (circa 1790) quoted by: Bose (1960), pp2-3; Islam (1982), p5.

5. Warren Hastings speech to Parliament; quoted by Malleson (1894), p439.

6. Davies (1935); Feiling (1966); Lyall (1989); Malleson (1894); Mason (1985); Moon (1947); Moon (1988); Trotter (1890); Turnbull (1975); Woodruff (1953).

7. Grieve (1974), T.B. Macaulay essay on Warren Hastings, pp550-649.

8. Embree (1962, 1988); Fortescue (1967); Gardner (1971); Ghosh (1944); Gopal (1963a); Greenough (1982); Grieve (1974); Hunter (1871); Kaye (1853); Khan (1969); Kopf (1969); Lyall (1916); Malleson (1985); Marshall (1976, 1993); Misra (1959); Nair (1984); Reid (1947); Roberts (1958); Sinha (1967); Spear (1971, 1979); Srivastava (1981); Stanhope (1784); Teignmouth (1843); Thomson & Garratt (1934); Wilbur (1945)

9. Carter & Mears (1962); Muir (1917); Trevelyan (1952); Wells (1984).

10. Anonymous (1842); Ayling (1985); Durant (1975); Morwood (1985); Rhodes (1962).

11. Anonymous (1842), The Speeches of the Right Honourable Richard Brinsley Sheridan.

12. D'Alpuget (1982); McClelland (1991); Morosi (1975); Whitlam (1979).

13. Feiling (1966); Gardner (1971); Marshall (1965), p47; see also Turnbull (1975), p206.

14. Edmund Burke speech to Parliament (1790?), quoted in: Gardner (1971), p132; Reid (1947), pp132-133.

15. Edmund Burke assertions, quoted by Feiling (1966), pp354-355.

16. Gardner (1971), p132.

17. Austen (1818b), Northanger Abbey, Chapter 24, pp201-202.

18. Morwood (1985), p124.

19. Feiling (1966), pp394-395.

20. Woodruffe (1965), p132.

21. Grieve (1974), Macaulay

22. Malleson (1894), p547.

23. Kaye (1853), p88.

24. Greenough (1982); Ghosh (1944).

25. Lyall (1916), p297.

26. Reid (1947), pp133-136.

27. Gardner (1971), pp130-131.

28. Woodruffe (1965), p132.

29. Wilbur (1945), chapters 19 & 20, pp274 -303.

30. Wells (1959), p1050.

31. Muir (1929), p443.

32. Encyclopaedia Brittanica (1977), Warren Hastings, Macropaedia, vol. 8, 665-666.

33. Trevelyan (1952), p594.

34. Carter & Mears (1962), p742.

35. Speech by Sir George Cornewall Lewis, House of Commons Debates, February 12, 1858; quoted by Gopal (1963a), p9.

36. Nair (1984).

37. Mackintosh (nom de plume) (1782), A day as it is commonly spent by an Englishman in Bengal, Letter 55 to J.M. Esq., Calcutta December 23, 1779, reproduced in Nair (1984), pp184-186; (This work was revised, printed and possibly even written by Philip Francis, presumed author of Letters of Junius).

38. Corbett (1966); De Grandpre ((1801); Mitchell (ca 1775); Nair (1984); Spear (1971); Stanhope (1784); Stavorinus (1798).

39. Fane (ca 1840), p33.

40. Corbett (1966); De Grandpre ((1801); Mitchell (ca 1775); Nair (1984); Stanhope (1784); Stavorinus (1798).

41. Allen & Mason (1975); Allen & Diwedi (1984), p263.

42. Broad (1951, 1963); Churchill (1952); Gilbert (1988); Rose (1995).

2008 Postscript

43. Polya (2008i, j, k, l, m).

44. Pinter (2005).

45. Brussells Tribunal (2008).

46. Polya (2005l, m, 2008i, j).

Chapter 13. Colonial famine, genocide and ethnocide

1. Lord Hastings (1813), Private Journal I, p30 quoted by Spear (1971), p198 and by Plumb (1963), p178.

2. C.E. Trevelyan (1835), British Treasury bureaucrat, Report on the Inland Customs and Town Duties of the Bengal Presidency; quoted by Sinha (1967), pp116-117.

3. C.E. Trevelyan (1840), evidence on textile trade and tariffs given to a British Parliamentary Enquiry Committee; quoted in Gopal (1963a).

4. Letter of C.E. Trevelyan to Lord Monteagle (1846), quoted in Edwards & Williams (1957), p257.

5. Famine Commission Report (1880); quoted in Kachhawaha (1985), p32..

6. Lord Curzon (January 1900) quoted in Edwardes (1967), pp230-231.

7. Reverend James Walker, M.A., Church of England Minister, North Parramatta, Sydney, New South Wales, Australia (1846); quoted by Buggy & Cates (1982), p8.

8. Abbate (1972); Bussagli & Sivaramamurti (1978).

9. Abbate (1972); Blurton (1992); Bussagli & Sivaramamurti (1978); De Smedt (1983); Guirand (1959), Mythology of India, pp339-392; Harle (1986); Havell (1974); Lawrence (1963); Pal (1988).

10. Hunter (1871); Sinha (1967).

11. Drèze & Sen (1989); Sen (1981a,b).

12. Gopal (1963a); Muckherjee (1958), p304; Sinha (1967).

13. Bhatia (1991); Gopal (1963a); Greenough (1982); Ghosh (1944); Hunter (1871); Sinha (1967).

14. Drèze & Sen (1989); Gangrade & Dhadda (1973); Loveday (1914); Merewether (1985); Singh (1991).

15. Bhatia (1991); Drèze & Sen (1989).

16. Ghosh (1944); Greenough (1982); Kachhawaha (1985).

17. Kachhawaha (1985), p310.

18. Greenough (1982).

19. Cook & Stevenson (1991), Ghosh (1944), Greenough (1982), Kachhawaha (1992), Langer (1952), Maloo (1987), Roberts (1958), Sen (1981) and Spear (1965).

20. Drèze & Sen (1989); Sen (1981).

21. C.E. Trevelyan (1835), British Treasury burcaucrat, Report on the Inland Customs and Town Duties of the Bengal Presidency; quoted by Sinha (1967), pp116-117; see also Gopal (1963a); Lanyi & McWilliams (1966); Marx (1853); Roberts (1958); Sinha (1967); Spear (1965)..

22. Kachhawaha (1992); Maloo (1987).

23. Ghosh (1944); Greenough (1982); Hunter (1871); Kachhawaha (1992); Maloo (1987).

24. Ghosh (1944).

25. Ghosh (1944); Greenough (1982).

26. Bolts (1772), p194; quoted in Gopal (1963a), p7; Mukherjee (1958), p304.

27. Marx (1853); reproduced in Lanyi & McWilliams (1966), pp112-116.

28. Embree (1962); Hunter (1871).

29. Smith (1776).

30. Sinha (1967), pp116-121.

31. Edwards & Williams (1957).

32. Report of Justice H.B.L. Braund on the Bengal Famine (1943), quoted by Voight (1987), pp154, 337.

33. Drèze & Sen (1989); Edwardes (1967); Kachhawahara (1992); Maloo (1987);

34. Drèze & Sen (1989), p212.

35. Freund (1984).

36. Cameron & Spies (1992); Chalk & Jonassohn (1990); Freund (1984); Langer (1952).

37. Cameron & Spies (1992); Walter (1969) pp137-142, reproduced in Chalk & Jonassohn (1990), pp223-229.

38. Cameron & Spies (1992); Langer (1952); Porter (1984).

39. Langer (1952); Pelling (1974); Porter (1984).

40. Cameron & Spies (1992); Langer (1992).

41. Anstey (1962, 1966); Forbath (1978); Martelli (1962); Morel (1907).

42. Martelli (1962).

43. Drechsler, H. (1980), Let Us Die Fighting: The Struggle of the Herero and the Nama against German Imperialism (1884-1915) (transl. B.Zollner) (Zed Books, New York), reproduced in part in Chalk & Jonassohn (1990), pp230-248.

44. Bhana & Pachai (1984); Cameron & Spies (1992); Freund (1984); Mehta (1976).

45. Ross (1993), p719.

46. Chalk & Jonassohn (1990), Indians of the Americas, 1492 to 1789, pp173-194..

47. Langer (1952).

48. Chalk & Jonassohn (1990), Indians of the Americas, 1492 to 1789, pp173-194..

49. Honan (1987).

50. Chalk & Jonassohn (1990), Indians of the Americas, 1492 to 1789, pp173-194..

51. Chalk & Jonassohn (1990), Indians of the United States in the Nineteenth Century, pp195-203; Langer (1952); Washburn (1988), History of Indian-White Relations, Volume 4 in Sturtevant (1988), Handbook of North American Indians.

52. Chalk & Jonassohn (1990), pp195-203; Langer (1952).

53. V.S. Naipaul, (1957), The Mystic Masseur; (1958), The Suffrage of Elvira; (1959), Miguel Street; (1961), House for Mr Biswas; (1962), The Middle Passage; (1963), Mr Stone and the Knights Companion; (1964), An Area of Darkness; (1967), The Mimic Men; (1967), A Flag on the Island; (1969), The Loss of El Dorado; (1971), In a Free State; (1972), The Overcrowded Barracoon; (1975), Guerillas; (1977), A Wounded Civilization; (1991), India. A Million Mutinies Now.

54. Shiva Naipaul (1970), Fireflies; (1970), The Chip-Chip Gatherers; (1983), A Hot Country; (1985), Beyond the Dragon's Mouth; (1986), An Unfinished Journey.

55. Other examples of excellent "British colonial" literature include: Boldrewood (1889), Robbery Under Arms; Clarke (1885), For the Term of his Natural Life; Conrad (1898), Tales of Unrest; Conrad (1905), Typhoon; Forster (1924), A Passage to India; Forster (1965), The Hill of Devi; Fraser (1979), Flashman's First Omnibus: Flash; Royal Flash; Flash for Freeedom; Gordimer (1992), Jump and Other Stories; Herbert (1983), Poor Fellow My Country; Herbert (1938), Capricornia; Kipling (1891), Life's Handicap; (1901), Kim; Kipling (1924), The Jungle Book; Kipling (1926), Just So Stories for Children; Kipling (1960), Soldiers Three; The Story of the Gadsbys; In Black And White; Kipling (1960), Plain Tales From the Hills; Lawrence (1950), Kangaroo; Lessing (1983), Martha Quest; Manning (1983), The Rain Forest; Maugham (1951), The Complete Short Stories; and, of course, Anonymous (1934), Letters From An Indian Judge.

56. Honan (1987).

57. Honan (1987); Lane (1996), pp78-79.

58. Clark (1969, 1971, 1986); McQueen (1971);.Shaw (1960, 1971).

59. Buggy & Cates (1985); Chalk & Jonassohn (1990); Flannery (1994); Lines (1991); Robinson & York (1977); Ross (1993).

60. Gilmore (1934, 1935).

61. Dame Mary Gilmore testament on film, "The 7.30 Report", Australian Broadcasting Commission (ABC) Television, broadcast 16 January 1997.

62. Bradfield (1996).

63. Bradfield (1996); Gilmore (1934); Lines (1991); Shaw (1960).

64. Morgan (1987), My Place.

65. Ross (1993), p667.

66. Ross (1993), p732.

67. Belich (1989).

68. Belich (1989); Flannery (1994); Gravelle (1980).

69. Gravelle (1980).

70. Flannery (1994).

71. Gravelle (1980).

72. Belich (1989); Darlington (); Gravelle (1980).

73. Buggy & Cates (1985); Gravelle (1980); McQueen (1970).

74. Ali (1979); Cannon (1981); Gravelle (1980); for the South African indentured labour system see Bhana & Pachai (1984); Cameron & Spies (1992).

75. Lane (1996), p79.

76. Spear (1971).

77. Flannery (1994).

78. Nelson (1976).

79. Bochuan (1991); Langer (1952).

80. Buggy & Cates (1985); Cannon (1981); McQueen (1971).

81. Cameron & Spies (1992).

82. Churchill speech to the House of Commons, 22 February 1906; quoted in: Palmer (1981), p71; R.S.Churchill (1967), Winston S. Churchill, volume 2, p167.

83. Bachman (1988), Great Leap Forward, in Embree (1988a), pp520-523; Chang (), Wild Swans; Dreze & Sen (1989); Embree (1988a); Greenough (1988), Famine, in Embree (1988a), pp457-459; Newman (1990).

84. Prebble (1963).

85. Cunningham (1996); Edwards & Williams (1957); Litton (1994); Woodham-Smith (1962).

86. Woodham-Smith (1962).

87. Langer (1952); Trevelyan (1952);

88. C.E. Trevelyan letter (1846) quoted in Edwards & Williams (1957), p255.

89. C.E. Trevelyan letter to Lord Moneagle (1846), quoted in Edwards & Williams (1957), p257.

90. Trevelyan (1952).

91. Grieve (1974), Macaulay essay on Lord Robert Clive and the Great Bengal Famine.

92. Trevelyan (1952), pp644-645.

93. Prebble (1963).

94. Stowe (1857); quoted in Prebble (1963).

95. Chalk & Jonassohn (1990); Flannery (1994); Lines (1991); Morris (1972), Final solution Downunder, Horizon vol. 14, pp60-71, reproduced in Chalk & Jonassohn (1972), pp204-222.

96. Dombrovskis, Flanagan & Kirkpatrick (1996).

2008 Postscript

97. Lindqvist (1992).

98. Conrad (1899); Coppola (1979).

99. Blum (2006); Chomsky (2007a, b); Davis (2001); Diamond (1997, 2005); Elkins (2005); Flannery (1994); Gilbert (1969, 1982); Mason (2000); Polya (2007a).

100. Polya (2007a).

101. Polya (2008i, j, k, l, m).

102. Polya (2008a, b, c, m).

Chapter 14. The Bengal Famine of 1943-1944

1. Hansard of the House of Commons, Winston Churchill speech, Hansard Vol. 302, cols. 1920-21, 1935; quoted by Jog (1944), p195.

2. Behrens (1955), p348.

3. Taylor (1965), p563.

4. Diary of Amery (Secretary for India), September 9, 1942; quoted by Ziegler (1988), pp 351-352.

5. Churchill (1954), vol. 4, p181.

6. Greenough (1982).

7. Uppal (1984).

8. Das (1949); Drèze & Sen (1989); Ghosh (1944); Greenough (1982, 1988); Uppal (1984); Satyajit Ray film, Distant Thunder; Sen (1989); Villager (ca 1945).

9. World War 2 losses included 303,000 British Armed forces personnel killed, 109,000 Empire losses, 60,000 civilians killed in air raids and 30,000 merchant seamen killed according to Taylor (1965); if we take a figure of 4 million Bengalis having perished in the famine then the famine victims represented about 90% of total British Empire losses.

10. Langer (1952).

11. Drèze & Sen (1989); Ghosh (1944); Greenough (1982, 1988); Uppal (1984); Satyajit Ray film, Distant Thunder; Sen (1989).

12. Sen (1981).

13. Report of Justice H.B.L. Braund on the Bengal Famine (1943), quoted by Voight (1987), pp154, 337.

14. Das (1944); Ghosh (1944); Greenough (1982).

15. Das (1949); Greenough (1982); Jog (1944); Sen (1945).

16. Greenough (1982); Jog (1944).

17. Bhowani Sen (1945), Rural Bengal in ruins; quoted in Gopal (1963a), pp55-56.

18. Jog (1944), p192.

19. Hicks (1995).

20. Tuchman (1970), p433.

21. Ghosh (1944); Das (1949); Greenough (1982).

22. Satyajit Ray film, Distant Thunder.

23. Ghosh (1944); Greenough (1982).

24. Sir T. Rutherford letter to the Viceroy of India, qiuoted by Dreze & Sen (1989), p212.

25. Sen (1981).

26. Behrens (1955); Dreze & Sen (1989); Ghosh (1944); Greenough (1982); Uppal (1984); Sen (1981).

27. Ghosh (1944); Hunter (1871); Kachhawaha (1985).

28. Famine Commission (1946); Greenough (1982).

29. Bhattacharya (1967), p550.

30. Casey(1962); Greenough (1982); Hudson (1986); Moon (1973); Uppal (1984).

31. Moon (1973).

32. Manchester Guardian, 1943; Calcutta Statesman supplement, Maladministration in Bengal, October 1943, quoted by Greenough (1982).

33. Barnes & Nicholson (1988); Moon (1973); Kimball (1984), p117; Lewin (1980).

34. Casey (1947, 1962); Hudson (1986); Ziegler (1985).

35. Ghosh (1944).

36. Famine Commission Report, India (1945), Report on Bengal.

37. Moon (1973).

38. Casey (1962).

39. Jog (1944), p193.

40. Kachhawahara (1985), pp37-38.

41. Ross (1992).

42. Ghosh (1944).

43. Jog (1944).

44. Famine Commission Report, India (1945), Report on Bengal.

45. Narayan (1944), quoted in Greenough (1982), p145; Bhohowani Sen , Rural Bengal In Ruins (translated by Chakravarty),1945 (Calcutta); quoted in Greenough (1982); Gopal (1965a);

46. Johnson (1947); Nagar (1990).

47. Bhatia (1991); Das (1949); Dreze & Sen (1989); Ghosh (1944); Greenough (1982); Sen (1981); Uppal (1984).

48. Aykroyd (1974); Bhattacharya (1967); Behrens (1955); Brown & Eckholm (1974); Chatterjee (1984); Grun (1975); Encyclopaedia Britannica (the 1961 edition but not the 1977 or 1979 editions); Kimball (1984); Kitchen (1990); Lewin (1980); Maloo (1987); Mehra (1985); Robinson (1984); Romanus & Sunderland (1956); Taylor (1965); Spear (1965, 1968); Stephens (1966); Voight (1987).

49. Bhattacharya (1967); Chatterjee (1984); Mehra (1985); Robinson (1984); Spear (1965); Voight (1987).

50. Dodwell (1963a); Porter (1984); Thomson (1965); Sethi (1963); Vadgama (1984).

51. Gordon (1990); Taylor (1965).

52. Gordon (1990).

53. Churchill (1950); Kinvig (1992); Moore (1979).

54. Carter & Mears (1960); Encyclopaedia Brittanica (1977, 1979); Halliday (1986); Langer (1952); Morgan (1984); Peacock (1980); Porter (1984); Roberts & Roberts (1980); Thomson (1965); Trevelyan (1952); Wells (1951).

55. Trevelyan, G. (1952).

56. Trevelyan, H. (1972).

57. Wells (1936); Wells (1984)

58. Wells (1951).

59. Encyclopaedia Brittanica (1961).

60. Gedye, R. (1994), Holocaust denial banned.

61. Hicks (1995).

62. Brownstone & Franck (1990); Carter & Mears (1960); Cook & Stevenson (1991); Dunan (1968); Embree (1988); Encyclopaedia Brittanica (1961, 1977, 1979); Grun (1975); Howat & Taylor (1973); Langer (1952); Lenman & Boyd (1993); Morgan (1984); Mowat (1968); Natkiel et al. (1982); Palmer (1973); Palmer (1992); Pascoe (1991); Phillips (1964); Rosenberger & Tobin (1945) [Keesing's Contemporary Archives (1943-1945]; Ross (1990); Shafritz et al. (1993); Spear (1968); Taylor (1965); Teed (1992); Thackrah (1993); Thomson (1965); Trevelyan (1960); Trager (1979); Trevelyan (1960); Wells (1951); Williams (1966).

63. Behrens (1955); Bosworth (1993); Calvocoressi et al. (1972); Campbell (1985); Churchill (1954); Davies (1984); Dear & Foot (1995); Encyclopaedia Brittanica (1961, 1977, 1979); Esposito (1964); Gilbert (1988, 1989); Hoyt (1988); Keegan (1989); Kitchen (1990); Leckie (1987); Lee (1989); Liddell Hart (1970); Lyons (1989); Macmillan (1967); Messenger (1989); Michell (1975); Miller (1945); O'Neill & Krauskopf (1976); Parker (1987); Polowetzky (1989); Renouvin (1969); Romanus & Sunderland (1956); Snyder (1960); , 1975); Taylor (1965); Vyas (1982); Warner (1988); Weinberg (1994); Willmott (1989); Wright (1968); Young (1966).

64. Albjerg (1973); Ben-Moshe (1992); Broad (1951, 1963);; Charmley (1993); Churchill (1954); Encyclopaedia Brittanica (1961, 1977, 1979); Gilbert (1988); Gilbert (1991); S. Gopal in Blake & Louis (1994), Chapter 26; Irving (1987); Jablonsky (1991); Jog (1944); Kimball (1984); Lambakis (1993); Longford (1974); Manchester (1983); Martin (1991); Moore (1979); Pearson (1991); Pelling (1974); Rose (1995); Trukhanovsky (1978).

65. Churchill (1954), The Second World War.

66. Jog (1944), p192.

67. Behrens (1955).

68. Casey (1947, 1962); Hudson (1986); Langmore (1997).

69. Casey (1962), p178.

70. Casey (1962), p179.

71. Casey (1962), p188.

72. Casey (1962), p192.

73. Greenough (1982).

74. Casey (1962), p190.

75. Das (1949); Drèze & Sen (1989); Greenough (1982); Sen (1981); Uppal (1984).

76. Casey (1962), p193.

77. Casey letter to Wavell (March 1, 1945), quoted in Hudson (1986), p169; this letter is reproduced but with this key part omitted in Casey (1962), A Letter to a Viceroy, Chapter 9, pp209-215.

78. Kinvig (1992).

79. Feature film, The Bridge on the River Kwai.

80. Nagar (1990), Hunger: A Novel.

81. Satyajit Ray feature film Distant Thunder.

82. Aarons and Loftus (1997).

83. Villager (ca 1945), Famine or Plenty, p4.

2008 Postscript

84. BBC (British Broadcasting Corporation) (2008).

85. BBC (British Broadcasting Corporation) (2008); Mason (2000).

86. Bayly & Harper (2004); Brown & Finsterbusch (1972); Bulliet (1998); BBC (British Broadcasting Corporation) (2008); Embree (1999); Gilbert (1999); Mason (2000); Polya (1998a, 2003a, 2007a); Ponting (2000); Stanton (1999).

87. Braudel (1993); Duiker & Spielvogel (2006); Garratty & Gay (1972); McNeil (1979); Schama (2002); Stokesbury (1980).

88. Blainey (2005).

89. Blainey (2000, 2004).

Chapter 15. Pride and Prejudice - Churchill, science, the Bengal Famine and the Jewish Holocaust

1. Trukhanovsky (1978), p30.

2. Churchill (1906), House of Commons, 22 February 1906 , quoted in Palmer (1981), p71.

3. Churchill (1915) quoted in Pearson (1991), p138.

4. Churchill (1941) quoted by Rusbridger & Nave (1991), p28.

5. Report of Sir R. Craigie (former British Ambassador to Japan) to Mr. Eden (British Foreign Secretary) in 1943, reproduced in Rusbridger & Nave (1991), Appendix I.

6. Jog (1944); Uppall (1984); Moon (1988).

7. Weissberg (1958); Laqueur (1982); Wasserstein (1988).

8. Albjcrg (1973); Ben-Moshe (1992); Blake & Louis (1994); Charmley (1993); Churchill (1938); Churchill (1952); Gilbert (1991); Irving (1987); Jablonsky (1991); Jog (1944); Kimball (1984); Lambakis (1993); Longford (1974); Manchester (1983); Martin (1991); Moore (1979); Pearson (1991); Pelling (1974); Rusbridger & Nave (1991); Snow (1961); Trukhanovsky (1978); Ziegler (1988).

9. Halperin (1984); Hodge (1972); Honan (1987); Tucker (1983), pp57-58..

10. Masson (1985).

11. Morris (1967, 1984).

12. Sartre, J-P. (1946); Baldwin (1963).

13. Pelling (1974).

14. Jog (1944); Pelling (1974).

15. Churchill (1898).

16. Churchill (1899).

17. Cameron & Spies (1986).

18. Tyquin (1993).

19. El-Ghusein (1917); Gurun (1988); Walker (1990).

20. Robinson (1989), pp48-52.

21. Rusbridger & Nave (1991).

22. Craigie (1943) letter to Anthony Eden, reproduced in Rusbridger & Nave (1991), Appendix.

23. Goldstein & Dillon (1982), Revisionists revisited in Prange (1982), Appendix, pp839-852 and Forward, ppix-xiii; Martin (1991); Prange (1992); Rusbridger & Nave (1991);

24. Snow (1961).

25. Behrens (1955); Churchill (1952), volume IV, p823; Taylor (1965).

26. Moon (1973); Polya (1995); Uppall (1984); Ziegler (1988).

27. Moon (1973).

28. Churchill (1944) letter to Roosevelt, reproduced in Kimball (1984), p117.

29. Gopal (1994) in Blake and Louis (1994), chapter 26, pp465-466; Behrens (1955); Uppall (1984); Ziegler (1988)

30. Behrens (1955); Das (1949); Greenough (1982); Kimball (1984).

31. Willmott (1989), p326.

32. Kitchen (1990), pp160-161.

33. Tuchman (1970), p38.

34. Ziegler (1985), p247.

35. Tuchman (1970), p383.

36. Tuchman (1970), p433.

37. Churchill (1952), volume V, p600.

38. Chalk & Jonassohn (1990); Anatoli (Kuznetsov) (1966).

39. Gilbert (1991), p516.

40. H.G. Wells (1936) Postscript to an Experiment in Autobiography in G.P. Wells (1984), pp133-134.

41. Awake, August 22, 1995.

42. Kiernan (1976).

43. Laqueur (1980), appendix 4, pp223-228; Wasserstein (1983), pp172-182.

44. Langer (1953), p1100-1102.

45. Mosley (1955); Slim (1956); Sykes (1959); Mead (1987).

46. Aarons and Loftus (1997); Kedourie (1968), esp. p295; Moon (1973); Wasserstein (1983).

47. Gordon (1963), especially pp196-203.

48. Wasserstein (1983), p40.

49. Wasserstein (1983).

50. Aarons and Loftus (1997); Bermant (1979); Blumberg (1975); Clarke (1960); Gilbert (1969); Gilbert (1982); Lacqueur (1980); Parkes (1964); Russell, Lord (1956); Van den Haag (1969); Wasserstein (1983); Weissberg (1958).

51. Dayan (1967).

52. Moon (1973); Albjerg (1973), p211.

53. Weissberg (1958); Lacqueur (1980); Wasserstein (1983).

54. Woodbridge (1950); Uppall (1984).

55. Report by E.R.Walker to H.V. Evatt (January 7, 1946) in Hudson et al. (1991), pp22-27.

56. Letter from C.Attlee to B. Chifley (February 4, 1946) in Hudson et al. (1991), pp105-107.

57. Jog (1944); Mehta (1976); Ziegler (1988).

58. Allen & Mason (1975), pp209-211; Lewin (1980); Mehta (1976).

59. Austen (1817) Northanger Abbey, Chapter 24, pp201-202.

60. Letter of Lord Linlithgow, Viceroy of India, to Winston Churchill (August 20, 1942), quoted in Churchill (1952), volume IV, p456.

61. Churchill (1952), volume IV, p181.

62. S. Gopal (1994) in Blake and Louis (1994) (editors), Chapter 24, p464..

63. Jog (1944); Gilbert (1988).

64. Gilbert (1969), p91.

65. Albjerg (1973); Ben-Moshe (1992); Broad (1951, 1963); Charmley (1993); Churchill (1954); Encyclopaedia Brittanica (1961, 1977, 1979); Gilbert (1988); Gilbert (1991); S. Gopal in Blake & Louis (1994), Chapter 26; Irving (1987); Jablonsky (1991); Jog (1944); Kimball (1984); Lambakis (1993); Longford (1974); Manchester (1983); Martin (1991); Moore (1979); Pearson (1991); Pelling (1974); Rose (1995); Trukhanovsky (1978).

66. Bloch (1982); Bill Blauber , Baltimore Sun, Papers show Duke of Windsor's Nazi leanings, report in The Age 5 December 1996, p10.

67. Behrens (1955); Bosworth (1993); Calvocoressi et al. (1972); Campbell (1985); Churchill (1954); Davies (1984); Dear & Foot (1995); Encyclopaedia Brittanica (1961, 1977, 1979); Esposito (1964); Gilbert (1988, 1989); Hoyt (1988); Keegan (1989); Kitchen (1990); Leckie (1987); Lee (1989); Liddell Hart (1970); Lyons (1989); Macmillan (1967); Messenger (1989); Michell (1975); Miller (1945); O'Neill & Krauskopf (1976); Parker (1987); Polowetzky (1989); Renouvin (1969); Romanus & Sunderland (1956); Snyder (1960); , 1975); Taylor (1965); Vyas (1982); Warner (1988); Weinberg (1994); Willmott (1989); Wright (1968); Young (1966).

68. Bullock (1967); Brownstone & Franck (1990); Carter & Mears (1960); Cook & Stevenson (1991); Dunan (1968); Embree (1988); Encyclopaedia Brittanica (1961, 1977, 1979); Grun (1975); Howat & Taylor (1973); Langer (1952); Lenman & Boyd (1993); Morgan (1984); Natkiel et al. (1982); Palmer (1973); Palmer (1992); Pascoe

(1991); Phillips (1964); Rosenberger & Tobin (1945) [Keesing's Contemporary Archives (1943-1945]; Ross (1990); Spear (1968); Shafritz et al. (1993); Taylor (1965); Teed (1992); Thackrah (1993); Thomson (1965); Trevelyan (1952); Trager (1979); Trevelyan (1960); Wells (1951); Williams (1966).

69. Gedye (1994), Holocaust denial banned.

70. Dreze & Sen (1989); Greeenough (1982).

71. Edwardes (1967), p231.

72. Bayly (1988); Bose (1993); Marshall (1987); Dodwell (1963a,b); Sethi (1963).

73. Kedourie (1968); Lewis (1964); Mowat (1968); Phillips (1964); Spear (1968); Thomson (1964).

74. Malthus (1798), An Essay on the Principle of Population as it Affects the Future Improvement of Society.

2008 Postscript

75. Bayly & Harper (2004); Brown & Finsterbusch (1972); Bulliet (1998); BBC (British Broadcasting Corporation) (2008); Embree (1999); Gilbert (1999); Mason (2000); Polya (1998a, 2003a, 2007a); Ponting (2000); Stanton (1999).

76. Blainey (2000, 2004, 2005); Braudel (1993); Duiker & Spielvogel (2006); Garratty & Gay (1972); McEvedy (1984); McNeil (1979); Schama (2002); Stokesbury (1980).

Chapter 16. Global warming and the unthinkable world of 2050

1. Svante Arrhenius (circa 1900) quoted by Bernard (1993), p5.

2. Bach (1984); Bernard (1993); Falk & Brownlow (1989); Goldsmith et al. (1990); Lovelock (1979, 1988, 1991); MacKenzie (1995b); McKibben (1990); Pickering & Owen (1994); Prather et al. (1996); Washington (1991).

3. McKibben (1990).

4. Lehninger (1975), Chapter 22; Rawn (1989), Chapter 18; Darnell et al. (1990), Chapter 16; Alberts et al. (1994), Chapter 14; Garrett & Grisham (1995), Chapter 22; Lodish et al. (1995), Chapter 18; .Stryer (1995), Chapter 26; Mathews & Van Holde (1996), Chapter 17.

5. Reilly (1994); Rosenzweig & Parry (1994).

6. Weier et al. (1974).

7. Kerr (1994); Simkin (1994); Andreae (1996); Li et al. (1996).

8. Brownlee, D.E. (1995); Farley & Patterson (1995).

9. Cess & Zhang (1996).

10. Lovelock (1979, 1988, 1991); Kump (1996).

11. Lovelock (1988); Newsom (1996).

12. Lovelock (1991); Mc Kibben (1990).

13. Bernard (1993); Birch (1980); Bochuan (1991); Ehrlich (1968); Ehrlich et al. (1973); Falk & Brownlow (1989); Goldsmith et al. (1990); Gordon & Suzuki (1990); Lovelock (1979, 1988, 1991); McKibben (1990); Mestel (1995); Porritt (1991); Saunders et al.

(1993); Schneider (1989); Silver & De Fries (1990); Suzuki (1990); Washington (1991).

14. Bernard (1993).

15. Kerr (1996a,b); Masood (1996); Rosenzweig & Parry (1996); Thomson (1995); Walker (1995).

16. Kerr (1996a,b).

17. Masood (1996).

18. Wigley et al. (1996).

19. IPCC Report (1995).

20. The Age June 6 1995.

21. MacKenzie (1995a); Vaughan & Doake (1996).

22. Schindler et al. ((1996); Gorham (1996).

23. Bernard (1993).

24. Kerr (1996b).

25. Victor & Salt (1995); Anderson (1995); Pearce (1995b).

26. Masood (1995).

27. Victor & Salt (1995).

28. Manabe & Stouffer (1995).

29. Bernard (1993).

30. Leggett (1990); Edgerton (1991); Eastwood (1991); Bernard (1993).

31. Wigley et al. (1996).

32. Bernard (1993); Eastwood (1991); Edgerton (1991); Leggett (1990).

33. Pearce (1995a); Pearce (1995c).

34. Rosenzweig & Parry (1996).

35. Sprigg (1966).

36. Malthus (1798).

37. Birch (1980); Bochuan (1991); Ehrlich (1968); Ehrlich et al. (1973); Falk & Brownlow (1989); Falloux & Talbot (1993); Goldsmith et al. (1990); Gordon & Suzuki (1990); Lovelock (1979, 1988, 1991); McKibben (1990); Porritt (1991); Saunders et al. (1993); Suzuki (1990); Washington (1991).

38. Letter of C.E. Trevelyan to Lord Monteagle (1846), quoted in Edwards & William (1957), p257.

39. Chalk & Jonassohn (1990); Hunter (1871); Jog (1944); Uppal (1984).

40. Bissio (1990).

41. Bochuan (1991); Falloux & Talbot (1993); Porrit (1991); Washington (1991).

42. Porrit (1991).

43. Falloux & Talbot (1993).

44. Birch (1980); Bochuan (1991); Ehrlich (1968); Ehrlich et al. (1973); Falk & Brownlow (1989); Falloux & Talbot (1993); Goldsmith et al. (1990); Gordon & Suzuki (1990); Lovelock (1979, 1988, 1991); McKibben (1990); Porritt (1991); Saunders et al. (1993); Suzuki (1990); Washington (1991).

45. Bochuan (1991).

46. Bissio (1990); Chaliand & Rageau (1985); Kidron & Segal (1987).

47. Bissio (1990).

48. Gordon & Suzuki (1990), p238.

49. Bissio (1990); Falloux & Talbot (1993).

50. Bernard (1993); Kennedy (1993).

51. Elton (1990), Gasping, a play.

52. Mestel (1995); Rosenzweig & Parry (1994).

53. Bissio (1990); Bochuan (1991); Falloux & Talbot (1993).

2008 Postscript

54. Intergovernmental Panel on Climate Change (IPCC) (2007); Polya (2007d); Science Daily (2007).

55. Intergovernmental Panel on Climate Change (IPCC) (2007); Lovelock (2006, 2007); Polya (2007d, 2008e, d); Spratt & Sutton (2008); Whitesides (2007).

56. Hoegh-Guldberg et al (2007); Science Show (2007); Veron (2008).

57. Lovelock (2006, 2007).

58. Hansen et al. (2007a, b); Hansen (2008); NASA Goddard Institute for Space Studies (GISS) (2007); Polya (2008h); Spratt & Sutton (2008).

59. Science Daily (2002); Whitty (2007).

60. Brahic (2006).

61. McKibben (2007); Whitesides (2007).

62. Brown (2008); Polya (2008a, b, c, d, m. n).

63. Fargione et al. (2008); Searchinger et al. (2008).

64. Smith & Elliott (2008).

65. Gainor (2007).

66. Polya (2007e).

Chapter 17. Antipodean epilogue - the moral dimension of the Lucky Country and the w orld

1. Austen (1811), Sense and Sensibility, chapter 13, p66.

2. Austen (1811), Sense and Sensibility, chapter 36, p246.

3. Gilmore (1934), chapter 24, The ungathered script, p175.

4. Dr. Albert Schweitzer, quoted by Rachel Carson (1962) in dedicating Silent Spring to him.

5. Horne, D. (1968), The Lucky Country.

6. Flannery (1994); Lines (1991); Parv (1984); Rolls (1994); Ross (1993).

7. Hardjono (1994); Ross (1993).

8. Gilmore (1934), Chapter 22, They had their culture, pp160-166.

9. Flannery (1994); Lines (1991); Ross (1993).

10. Flannery (1994); Gilmore (1934); Gilmore (1935); Ross (1993).

11. Gilmore (1934); Gilmore (1935); White (1992).

12. Gilmore (1934); Gilmore (1935).

13. Bates (1985); Brain (1979); Caruna (1993); Collings & Durrant (1977), p39; Davidson (1984); Edwards (1975); Hardy (1968); Lockwood (1962); Massolo (1971); Norton (1975); Ryan & Akerman (circa 1980); Ross (1993); Stubbs (1974); Wertheim (1995); White (1992).

14. Gilmore (1934); Gilmore (1935); Polya (1941), Chapter 13, The saviour of mothers, pp96-102.

15. Chalk & Jonassohn (1990); Gilmore (1934); Gilmore (1935); Lines (1991).

16. Gilmore (1935).

17. Gilmore (1935), p218.

18. Gilmore (1935), pp101-104.

19. Bradfield (1996); Chalk & Jonassohn (1990); Flannery (1994); Gilmore (1934); Gilmore (1935); Hassell (1966); Lines (1991); Morris (1972); Pollard (1988).

20. Bradfield (1996); Ryan & Akerman (1980).

21. Gilmore (1934, 1935); Lines (1991).

22. Blainey (1987); Lines (1991); Reynolds (1990); Robinson & York (1977).

23. Garden (1984); Garran (1986); Lines (1991); Murray-Smith (1984); Pratt (1934); Turner (1973).

24. Duffy (1988); Ergang (1941); Hindley (1987), p230; Hubatsch (1975); Jenks (1960); Longford (1974), p202: "Asked why he preferred to paint landscapres, Churchill replied: "Because a tree doesn't complain that I haven't done it justice." ; Mitford (1970); Payne (1973).

25. Lines (1991); Shaw (1960).

26. Bradfield (1996).

27. Gilmore (1934), p104.

28. Lines (1991); Shaw (1960).

29. Bradfield (1996); Lines (1991).

30. Blainey (1982); Clarke (1885), For the Term of His Natural Life; Hughes (1987); Shaw (1971).

31. Dunn (1984).

32. Buggy & Cates (1985); Lines (1991); McQueen (1971).

33. Lines (1991).

34. Cannon (1981); Buggy & Cates (1985); Gravelle (1980); McQueen (1971).

35. Buggy & Cates (1985); Lines (1991); McQueen (1971).

36. Ali (1979); Cannon (1981); Gravelle (1980); Norton (1914), reproduced in Cannon (1981), pp99-101.

37. Buggy & Cates (1985); McQueen (1971).

38. Reverend Samuel Marsden (1819) quoted in Lines (1991), p43.

39. Charles La Trobe (1840s) quoted in Lines (1991), p108.

40. Reverend James Walker, Church of England Minister, North Parramatta (1846), quoted in Buggy & Cates (1985), p8.

41. Trollope (1873), p76.

42. Finch-Hatton (1975) quoted in Lines (1991), p109.

43. Perry (circa 1975) quoted in Murray-Smith (1984), p237.

44. Stewart & Keesing (1962), collected poems about "blacks" , Australian Bush Ballads pp99-122.

45. Deniehy (1858), parliamentary speech quoted in Murray-Smith (1984), p64.

46. A.B."Banjo" Paterson, A Bushman's Song quoted in Murray-Smith (1984), p214.; Stewart & Keesing (1962), pp391-392. [A. B. "Banjo" Paterson, author of Australia's national song Waltzing Matilda and The Man From Snowy River, is pictured on the current Australian $10 note. We of course learned all three poems at school in Australia in the 1950s.]

47. Henry Lawson, poem quoted by: Hardy (1968), pp246-247; McQueen (1971), p51. [Henry Lawson was up to several years ago pictured on the Australian $10 note]; see also Wilde & Inglis (1980) pp xxi-xxvii, for the Lawson, Lane and Gilmore friendships.

48. Barton (1901) speech to Federal Parliament concerning the Commonwealth Immigration Restriction Act 1901, quoted in Buggy and Cates (1985), p145.

49. Lawson (1913), poem The Old, Old Story quoted in Mc Queen (1971), p 113.

50. William Lane (1892) in the Wagga Hummer, April 1892; quoted in McQueen (1971), p48.

51. McQueen (1971); Murray-Smith (1984). p9.

52. The Bulletin (1901) attacking Joseph Chamberlain, British Secretary of State for the Colonies, quoted in Murray-Smith (1984), p31.

53. O'Malley (1901), Commonwealth Parliamentary Debates, House of Representatives, 6 September 1901, vol.4, p4639; quoted in Murray-Smith (1984), pp206-207..

54. Bernard O'Dowd (circa 1900), poem Our Land, quoted in McQueen (1971), p102.

55. Henry Lawson (circa 1910), poem To Be Amused, quoted in McQueen (1971), p112.

56. Henry Lawson (1908), poem The Great Fight, quoted in McQueen (1971), pp111-112.

57. Adams (circa 1906), poem The Jew, quoted in McQueen (1971), p103.

58. Coleman & Tanner (1978); King (1983); Pearl (1983).

59. Polya & Solomon (1996), p181.

60. Clark (1969, 1971, 1986); Crawford (1963); Dunn (1984); Hardjono (1994); McQueen (1971); Mulvaney & White (1987); Ross (1993); Shaw (1960); White (1992);

61. McQueen (1971), chapter 9, Pianists, pp117-119.

62. Buggy & Cates (1982); Coleman & Tanner (1978); McQueen (1971); Ross (1993).

63. "Breaker Morant", a feature film starring Edward Woodward as "Breaker" Morant; Blackburn (1994).

64. Cannon (1981); McQueen (1971); Ross (1993).

65. Adam-Smith (1978); Facey (1981); Ross (1993); Tyquin (1993).

66. El Ghusein (1917); Gurun (1985); McClelland (1991), p6; Walker (1990).

67. Adam-Smith (1978); Ross (1993).

68. Ross (1993).

69. Polya (1986).

70. Caroe (1978); Jenkin (1986);

71. Von Itzstein et al. (1993); Von Itzstein & Smalec (1994).

72. Brady (1934); Kiernan (1984); Murphy (1972); Santamaria (1984).

73. Hardy (1962), Power Without Glory. [Frank Hardy, great writer, raconteur, humanist and champion of aboriginal rights, was unsuccessfully charged with criminal defamation over the love affair of the anti-hero's wife Mrs West with a tradesman, Mrs West having being identified as the wife of the actual Catholic businessman and powerbroker John Wren.]

74. Ross (1993).

75. Lawrence (1950), Kangaroo; Carey (1985), Illywhacker.

76. Ross (1993).

77. Gilmore (1918), The Passionate Heart.

78. Wilde & Moore (1980), pxxv.

79. Gilmore (1936), letter to Hugh McCrae in Wilde & Moore (1980), pp119-121. The "cat" is the "cat o' nine tails" used for flogging convicts.

80. Hardy (1962); Whitington (1971), p125; Young (1971).

81. Kisch (1969); Smith (1936).

82. Menzies' speech to Old Scotch Collegians, 16 October 1938 shortly after his return from Nazi Germany, Lockwood (1987), p151;

Menzies (1967), especially 23 August 1939 appeasement speech, p14; Perkins (1968), notably another appeasement speech of mid-September 1938 and commentary, pp61-62.

83. Rusbridger & Nave (1991).

84. Moore (1981); Ross (1993); Shaw (1960).

85. Calwell speech to Parliament (1948), Commonwealth Parliamentary Debates, 2 December 1947, vol. 194, p2948; quoted in Murray-Smith (1984), p36; quoted and discussed in Kiernan (1978), chapter 5, pp114-135.

86. Calwell speech to Parliament (1949), Commonwealth Parliamentary Debates, 9 February 1949, vol. 201, p64; quoted by Murray-Smith (1984), p36; quoted and discussed in Kiernan (1978), chapter 6, pp136-153.

87. Calwell (circa 1950) quoted by Kiernan (1978), p134.

88. Morgan (1987), My Place, a superb account of the impact of aboriginal children being removed from their mothers.

89. Grassby (1979); E.G. Whitlam, Forward to Grassby (1979), pxv.

90. Calwell assertion (1972), Observer 7 May 1972; quoted in Murray-Smith (1984), p36; quoted and discussed in Kiernan (1978), p133.

91. Williamson (1975), The Department, p13.

92. Morosi, J. (1975); D'Alpuget (1985), p276.

93. Kiernan (1978).

94. Shaw (1960); Ross (1993).

95. D'Alpuget (1982); Frost (1974); McClelland (1991); Morosi (1975); Whitlam (1979).

96. D'Alpuget (1985);

97. Ross (1993); Singleton (1977).

98. Bookman Press (1992).

99. Tingle (1996), a critique of Pauline Hanson's maiden speech.

100. Blainey (1982, 1994).

101. Aarons and Loftus (1997); Lacqueur (1978); Wasserstein (1988); Weissberg (1958).

102. Crossman, R.H.S. (1946), p21, quoted in Wasserstein (1988), p356-357.

103. Baldwin (1964), pp50 -51.

104. Greenough (1982); Moon (1973); Uppall (1984).

105. Chang (1991); Chalk & Jonassohn (1990).

106. Tingle (1996); Australian Government Report concerning the Convention on the Rights of the Child (CROC) (1995); Australian Health Ministers' Conference : the Health of Young Australians (1995).

107. Australian Government CROC Report (1995).

108. Australian Government CROC Report (1995).

109. Tingle (1996); McClelland (1991), pp4-6.

110. Tingle (1996).

111. Tingle (1996).

112. Ross (1993); reported in the Weekend Australian 8-9 February 1997: "The Deputy Prime Minister and leader of the National Party, Mr. Fischer, yesterday called for legislation to overturn the High Court's Wik decision by extinguishing native title on pastoral leases."

113. Netting (1993); Pollard (1988); Waring (1988).

114. Dovers (1994); Flannery & Kendall (1990); Flannery (1994); Morton (1994), Chapter 8 in Dovers (1994), pp141-166; Washington (1991).

115. Gilpin (1980); Flannery & Kendall (1990); Flannery (1994); Anderson Ehrlich.

116. Collings & Durrant (1977), pp116-133; Tassell & Wood (1981), esp. pp98-131;

117. Anderson, I. (1995a), Bad science breeds contempt [concerning the calicivirus release.]; Da Silva (1996).

118. Reported in the Weekend Australian 23-24 December 1996: Clinton fires salvo at PM on Greenhouse: "The United States President , Mr Clinton, yesterday rebuffed the Howard government's refusal to accept legally binding limits to greenhouse gas emissions."; ibid 8-9 January 1997: "It is understood that the [Australian] Federal Government is prepared to step outside the Climate Change Convention process, risking possible trade sanctions, if a differentiated appoach is not adopted at the Kyoto [climate change] meeting in December."

119. Polya (1995a), The Forgotten Holocaust - The 1943 Bengal Famine.

120. Chamarette (1995), Australian Senate Speech on the Bengal Famine, Hansard, No.14, September 1995, p1158.

121. Polya (1995b), The Famine of History: Bengal 1943.

122. Geyde (1994), Holocaust denial banned.

123. Demidenko (1995) The Hand That Signed the Paper; Demidenko (1995), Stories and stereotypes: critics miss the mark, The Age, 27 June 1995; I am truly sorry. Demidenko comes clean, Weekend Australian, 26-27 August 1995.

124. Michael Leunig cartoon, The Age, 28 September 1995.

125. Editorial, The Age, 9 November 1996; movie summary, The Age entertainment "Green Guide", 17-23 January 1997, p37..

126. John Howard speech, reported in The Age, 12 December 1996. For an argument sympathetic to John Howard's "no guilt" position see J.King (first settler descendant), The other side of history, The Age 14 November 1996.

127. Williamson (1975), The Department (a play).

128. Amis (1953); Bradbury (1979); Cornford (1908); Lodge (1980, 1981, 1984, 1986, 1988, 1992); Jacobson (1984); Sharpe (1974).

129. Bok (1978).

130. Lurie (1985), Foreign Affairs.

131. Martin et al. (1986); Pullan (1984).

132. Pullan (1984), chapter 2, Concealing the truth, pp36-51.

133. Flannery & Kendall (1990); Flannery (1994).

134. Bernard (1993); Kennedy (1993).

135. Barrio (1990); Chaliand & Rageau (1985); Kidron & Segal (1987); McKibben (1990).

136. Birch (1980); Bochuan (1991); Ehrlich (1968); Ehrlich et al. (1973); Falk & Brownlow (1989); Falloux & Talbot (1993); Goldsmith et al. (1990); Gordon & Suzuki (1990); Lovelock (1979, 1988, 1991); McKibben (1990); Porritt (1991); Saunders et al. (1993); Suzuki (1990); Washington (1991).

137. Bochuan (1991).

138. Hawken (1993).

139. Agarwal & Narain (1993) in Sachs (1993); Netting (1993).

140. Waring (1988).

141. Frank (1944), The Diary of Ann Frank; Leonardo (1950); Polya (1986); Taylor & Taylor (1993); Wasserstein (1988).

142. Bernard (1993); Birch (1980); Bochuan (1991); Ehrlich (1968); Ehrlich et al. (1973); Falk & Brownlow (1989); Falloux & Talbot (1993); Goldsmith et al. (1990); Gordon & Suzuki (1990); Harun ur Rashid (1993); Kennedy (1993); Lovelock (1979, 1988, 1991); McKibben (1990); Polunin & Burnett (1993); Porritt (1991); Redclift (1987); Sachs (1993); Saunders et al. (1993); Schneider (1989); Shiva (1993); Silver & De Fries (1990); Suzuki (1990); Washington (1991).

143. Clark & Munn (1986).

144. Lovelock (1979, 1988, 1991); Washington (1991).

145. Redclift (1987); Sachs (1993); Shiva (1993), Chapter 10 in Sachs (1993).

146. Bennett & George (1987); Bissio (1990); Bochuan (1991); Chaliand & Rageau (1985); Falloux & Talbot (1993); Kennedy (1993), esp. p111; Kidron & Segal (1987); Porritt (1991).

147. Bissio (1990).

148. Bissio (1990); Coghlan (1996); Seager (1993).

149. Greer (1984); Seager (1993).

150. Majumdar (1976), pp74-75.

151. Bates (1985).

152. Vines (1994).

153. Coghlan (1996).

154. Dr. Nafis Sadik, UNFPA, cited by Falloux & Talbot (1993), p175.

155. Norton article (1914), Sugar Swindle. What the C.S.R. Co. is after in Cannon (1981), pp99-101.

156. Bhana & Pachai (1984).

157. Ali (1979); Gravelle (1980).

158. Honan (1987).

159. Bennett & George (1987); Bissio (1990); Bochuan (1991); Chaliand & Rageau (1985); Falloux & Talbot (1993); Kennedy (1993), esp. p111; Kidron & Segal (1987); Porritt (1991).

160. Bochuan (1991).

161. Ehrlich (1968), p198.

162. Suzuki (1990), p229.

163. Bissio (1990); Harun ur Rashid (1993).

164. Rabindranath Tagore quoted in Miller (1992), Moloch or, this Gentile World, p257.

2008 Postscript - Epilogue

165. Brown (2008); Polya (2008a, b, c, d, m. n).

166. Intergovernmental Panel on Climate Change (IPCC) (2007); Lovelock (2006, 2007); Polya (2007d, 2008e, d); Spratt & Sutton (2008); Whitesides (2007).

167. Polya (2005d).

168. Brown (2008); Polya (2007a, 2008a, b, c, d, m. n).

169. Brahic (2006).

170. Polya (2007e).

171. Intergovernmental Panel on Climate Change (IPCC) (2007); Lovelock (2006, 2007); Polya (2007d, 2008e, d); Spratt & Sutton (2008); Whitesides (2007).

172. Hansen et al. (2007a, b); Hansen (2008); NASA Goddard Institute for Space Studies (GISS) (2007); Polya (2008h); Spratt & Sutton (2008).

173. Gainor (2007).

174. Polya (2007f).

175 Polya (2008d, f, g, i, j).

176. Brown (2008); Polya (2008a, b, c, d, m. n).

177. Polya (2008m, n).

178. Polya (2008m),

179. Polya (2008o).

180. Reason, J. (2000).

181. Polya (2007a).

182. Climate Emergency Network (2008); Polya (1998a, 2007a); Sachs (2005); Spratt & Sutton (2008a, b); Yarra Valley Climate Action Group (2008).

183. Polya (2007g).

184. See the Climate Emergency Fact Sheets of the Yarra Valley Climate Action Group (2008); Climate Emergency Network (2008); Spratt & Sutton (2008a, b).

Chapter 18. 2022: ignoring of reality now existentially threatens Humanity and the Biosphere

1. Polya (1995a, b, 1998a).

2. Polya (2011a).

3. Polya (2011b).
4. Churchill (1935), Polya (2017c, 2018b).

5. Aboriginal Genocide.

6. Polya (2020a); Report Genocide.

7. Worldometer (2022).

8. Experts: US did 9/11; Polya (2015); Polya (2020a) chapters 8 & 20;

9. Stop Air Pollution Deaths.

10. Climate Genocide; Polya (2020b).

11. Afghan Holocaust Afghan Genocide; Polya (2018a, c); Polya (2021c)

12. Keane (2021); Polya (2022c).

13. Lying By Omission; Mainstream Media Censorship; Mainstream Media Lying;

14. Palestinian Genocide; Polya (2022b).

15. Stop State Terrorism; Polya (2013).

16. Polya (2021a).

17. Polya (2015).

18. Afghan Holocaust Afghan Genocide; Iraqi Holocaust Iraqi Genocide; Muslim Holocaust Muslim Genocide; Polya (2020a, 2021a).

19. Herman and Chomsky (2002)

20. Jews Against Racist Zionism.

21. Polya (2018d).

22. Polya (2018b, 2018d).

23. Polya (2022a).

24. Polya (2021c)

25. Lying By Omission; Polya (2017a).

26. Polya (2021a).

27. Polya (2021b).

28. Zionist quotes re racism and Palestinian Genocide.

29. Keane (2021); Polya (2022e).

30. Gideon Polya.

31. Polya (2022d).

32. Polya (2009, 2014b, 2022a, c).

33. Polya, G. (2021e).

34. Jewish Voices for Peace (2018).

35. Polya (1995a, b; 1998a, b; 2003a; 2007a; 2008q; 2011a, b; 2020a, b; 2021a).

36. Buncombe (2021); Gregoire (2021).

37. Nuclear Weapons Ban, End Poverty & Reverse Climate Change; Polya (2020a, b; Polya 2021a).

38. Hawking (2018).

39. ICAN (2022).

40. Nuclear Weapons Ban, End Poverty & Reverse Climate Change.

41. ICAN (2022).

42. Zionist quotes re racism and Palestinian Genocide.

43. Glikson (2019); Polya (2020b).

44. IPCC (2019); Polya (2020b).

45. Climate Genocide; Polya (2020b).

46. Polya (2007a, 2021a).

47. Polya (2021a); The World Counts (2022).

48. Kolbert (2014); Lewis and Maslin (2018); Polya (2021a).

49. 300.org – Return Atmosphere CO_2 to 300 ppm CO_2.

50. Polya (2021a).

51. Climate Genocide; Polya (2020b).

52. Polya (1998a, 2008q).

53. Polya (2021a).

54. Inequality.org.

55. Polya (2007a, 2021a).

56. Oxfam (2021).

57. Pickety (2014).

58. Polya (2014a).

59. Piketty (2021).

60. Jesus, Matthew, The Holy Bible, King James Version, Chapter 25, verse 29.

61. Ellis, B. (2012); Polya (2012).

62. Polya (1998a, 2008q).

63. Aboriginal Genocide.

64. Stop State Terrorism.

65. Experts: US did 9/11; Polya (2015a, 2020a, 2021 a, b).

66. Polya (2021f, g).

67. Iraqi Holocaust, Iraqi Genocide.

68. Boycott Apartheid Israel.

69. Boycott Murdoch Media.

70. Polya (2015b).

71. Pope Francis (2015).

72. The Climate Group (2013).

73. Hope (2011).

74. Hansen (2018).

75. Carbon Debt, Carbon Credit.

76. Climate Revolution Now.

77. International Monetary Fund (IMF) (2019); Polya (2020b).

78. Afghan Holocaust, Afghan Genocide; Iraqi Holocaust, Iraqi Genocide; Muslim Holocaust Muslim Genocide; Polya (2020a).

79. Muhareb (2018); Polya (2009).

80. Abulhawa (2018); Discriminatory laws in Israel.

81. Muhareb (2018).

82. Polya (2021b).

83. Mearns (1899).

84. One-state solution, unitary state, bi-national state for a democratic, equal rights, post-apartheid Palestine.

85. Polya (2020b).

86. Polya (2021a).

BIBLIOGRAPHY

300.org – Return Atmosphere CO_2 to 300 ppm CO_2:
https://sites.google.com/site/300orgsite/300-org---return-atmosphere-co2-to-300-ppm

Aarons, M. and Loftus, J. (1997), The Secret War Against the Jews. How Western Espionage Betrayed the Jewish People (Mandarin, Melbourne).

Abbate, F. (1972) (editor), Indian Art and the Art of Ceylon, Central and South-East Asia (Octopus Books, London).

Abulhawa, S (2018), Israel's "nation-state law" parallels the Nazi Nuremburg Laws, Al Jazeera, 27 July 2018:
https://www.aljazeera.com/indepth/opinion/israel-nation-state-law-parallels-nazi-nuremberg-laws-180725084739536.html .

Aboriginal Genocide: https://sites.google.com/site/aboriginalgenocide/

Adam-Smith, P. (1978), The Anzacs (Thomas Nelson, Melbourne). Afghan Holocaust, Afghan Genocide:
https://sites.google.com/site/afghanholocaustafghangenocide/ .

Agarwal, A. and Narain, S. (1993), Towards green villages in Sachs (1993), Chapter 17.

Alberts, B., Bray, D., Lewis, J., Raff, M., Roberts, K. and Watson, J.D. (1994), Molecular Biology of the Cell (3rd edition) (Garland, New York).

Albjerg, V.L. (1973), Winston Churchill (Twayne, New York).

Alexanderson, G.L. (1987) (editor) The Polya Picture Album. Encounters of a Mathematician (Birkhauser, Boston & Basle).

Ali, A. (1979), Girmit, the indenture experience in Fiji, Bulletin of the Fiji Museum No.5, 1979.

Allen, C. and Diwedi, S. (1984), Lives of the Indian Princes (Century Publishing, London).

Allen, C. and Mason, M. (1975) (editors), Plain Tales from the Raj: Images of British India in the Twentieth Century (Andre Deutsch & BBC, London).

American Association for the Advancement of Science (AAAS) (2007), AAAS President John P. Holdren Urges Swift Action to Build a Sustainable Future, AAAS news release: http://www.aaas.org/news/releases/2007/0216am_holdren_address.shtm .

Amis, K. (1953), Lucky Jim (Penguin, London).Amis, K. (1957), What became of Jane Austen? The Spectator, 4 October, No. 6745, pp339-340.

Anatoli (Kuznetsov), A. (1966), Babi Yar: A Document in the Form of a Novel (translated by D. Floyd, 1970) (Jonathan Cape, London).

Anderson, A. (1995), Sweating it out together, New Scientist April 15, 3.

Anderson, I. (1995a), Bad science breeds contempt New Scientist 18 October, p3 (editorial).

Anderson, I. (1995b), Killer rabbit virus on the loose, New Scientist, 21 October, p4.

Anderson, I. (1995c), Australia the brave? New Scientist 18 November, p3 (editorial).

Anderson, I. (1995d), Australia's green dissenters gagged, New Scientist, 18 November, p4.

Andreae, M.O. (1996), Raising dust in the greenhouse, Nature vol. 380, 389-390.

Angus, M. (1975), The World of Olegas Truchanas (Olegas Truchanas Publication Committee, Hobart).

Anonymous (1842) (editor), The Speeches of the Right Honourable Richard Brinsley Sheridan with a Sketch of his Life, Edited by a Constitutional Friend, Volumes I-III (Henry G. Bohn, London).

Anonymous (1934), Letters of an Indian Judge to an English Gentlewoman (Peter Davies, London, 1939).

Anstey, R. (1962), Britain and the Congo in the Nineteenth Century (Clarendon Press, Oxford).

Anstey, R. (1966), King Leopold's Legacy. The Congo Under Belgian Rule 1908-1960 (Oxford University Press, London).

Agarwal, A. and Narain, S. (1993), Towards Green Villages in Sachs (1993), Chapter 17, pp242-256.

Aulich, T. (1992), The River's End (Kerr, Sydney).

Austen, C. (18xx), My Aunt Jane Austen, a Memoir (Jane Austen Society, London, 1952).

Austen, J. (1790), Love and Freindship - a Novel in Letters in: Jane Austen. Love, Freindship and Other Works (The Women's Press, London, 1978); Chapman (1954), The Works of Jane Austen vol. 6, Minor Works.

Austen, J. (1791), The History of England in: Jane Austen. Love, Freindship and Other Works (The Women's Press, London, 1978); Chapman (1954).

Austen , J. (1792), Catharine or The Bower in Chapman (1954).

Austen, J. (1794), Lady Susan (Penguin, London, 1974).

Austen, J. (1800), Sir Charles Grandison or The Happy Man. A Comedy in Five Acts (Oxford University Press, London, 1980.

Austen, J. (1804), The Watsons (Penguin, London, 1974).

Austen, J. (1811), Sense and Sensibility (Penguin, London, 1995).

Austen, J. (1813), Pride and Prejudice (Oxford University Press, Oxford, 1988).

Austen, J. (1814), Mansfield Park (Penguin, London, 1979).

Austen, J. (1816), Emma (Oxford University Press, Oxford, 1980).

Austen, J. (1817), Sanditon (Penguin, London, 1974).

Austen, J. (1818a), Persuasion (Penguin, London, 1975).

Austen, J. (1818b), Northanger Abbey (Thomas Nelson, London, circa 1960).

Austen, J. and Another (1975), Sanditon (Houghton & Mifflin, USA).

Austen, J. and Another (1977), The Watsons (Peter Davies, London).

Austen-Leigh, J. (1983), The Austen-Leighs and Jane Austen or "I have always maintained the value of Aunts" in Todd (1983), pp11-28.

Austen-Leigh, J.E. (1870), A Memoir of Jane Austen (Penguin, London, 1972).

Austen-Leigh, W. and Austen-Leigh, R.A. (1913), Jane Austen Her Life and Letters. A Family Record (2nd edition, Russell & Russell, New York, 1965).

Austen-Leigh, M.A. (1920), Personal Aspects of Jane Austen (John Murray, London).

Australian Council of National Trusts (1979), Historic Places of Australia, vol. 2 (Cassell, Sydney).

Awake (1995), The Holocaust. Who Spoke Out? 50th Anniversary of Liberating the Camps, Awake, August 22, pp1-15.

Aykroyd, W.R. (1974), The Conquest of Famine (Chatto & Windus, London).

Ayling, S. (1985), A Portrait of Sheridan (Constable, London).

Ayling, S. (1991), Fox. The Life of Charles James Fox (John Murray, London).

Aziz, S. (1975), Hunger, Politics and Markets: The Real Issues in the Food Crisis (University Press, New York).

Bach, W. (1984), Our Threatened Climate. Ways of Averting the CO_2 Problem Through Rational Energy Use (translated by J. Jäger) (Reidel, Boston).

Bachman, D. (1988), Great Leap Forward in Embree, A.T. (1988a) (editor), Encyclopaedia of Asian History (Collier Macmillan, London).

Bahtia, B.M. (1991), Famines in India. A Study in Some Aspects of the Economic History of India with Special Reference to the Food Problem 1860-1990 (Koonark Publishers, Delhi, 3rd edition).

Bailey, J. (1931), Introduction to Jane Austen (Oxford University Press, London).

Baldwin, J (1963), The Fire Next Time (Penguin, London).

Ballhatchet, K.A. (1965), European relations with Asia and Africa 1. Relations with Asia in Goodwin (1965), Chapter, pp218-236.

Bansil, P.C. (1958), India's Food Resources & Population (A Historical and Analytical Study) (Vora & Co., Bombay).

Barber, N. (1966), The Black Hole of Calcutta. A Reconstruction (Houghton Mifflin, Boston).

Barke, J., Smith, S.G. and Ferguson, J.D. (1965), The Merry Muses of Caledonia. A Collection of Bawdy Folksongs (Panther, London).

Barnes, J. & Nicholson, D. (1988), The Empire at Bay. The Leo Amery Diaries 1929-1945 (Hutchinson, London).

Barnett, C. (1974), Marlborough (Eyre Methuen, London).

Bates, D. (1985), The Native Tribes of Western Australia (I. White, editor) (National Library of Australia, Canberra).

Bayly, C.A. (1988), Indian Society and the Making of the British Empire, Volume II.1 of The New Cambridge History of India (Cambridge University Press, Cambridge).

Bayly, C. & Harper, T. (2004), Forgotten Armies. The Fall of British Asia 1941-1945 (Allen Lane, London).

BBC (British Broadcasting Corporation) (2008), Bengal Famine, The Things We Forgot to Remember (radio broadcast including Dr Gideon Polya, Dr Sanjoy Bhattacharya, Professor Amartya Sen and other scholars, January 2008): http://www.open2.net/thingsweforgot/bengalfamine_programme.html .

Beckett, J.V. (1994), The Rise and Fall of the Grenvilles: Dukes of Buckingham and Chandos, 1710 to 1921 (Manchester University Press, Manchester).

Behrens, C.B.A. (1955), Merchant Shipping and the Demands of War (Longman's, Green, London, 1955).

Belich, J. (1989), The Victorian Interpretation of Racial Conflict. The Maori, the British, and the New Zealand Wars (McGill-Queen's University Press, Montreal).

Bell, D. (1993), Daughter of the Dreaming (Allen & Unwin, Sydney).

Bence-Jones, M. (1984), Clive of India (Constable, London).

Ben-Moshe, T. (1992), Churchill. Strategy and History (Harvester Wheatsheaf, London).

Bennett, J. and George, S. (1987), The Hunger Machine. The Politics of Food (Polity Press, Oxford).

Bennett, T. (1991), South West Tasmania (Bennett, Hobart).

Bermant, C. (1979), The Jews (Sphere Books, London).

Bernard, H.W. (1993), Global Warming Unchecked (Indiana University Press,

Bloomington & Indianopolis).

Berstein, J. (1991), Einstein (Fontana, London).

Bhana, S. and Pachai, B. (1984), A Documentary History of Indian South Africans (David Philip, Cape Town).

Bhatia, B.M. (1991), Famines in India. A Study in Some Aspects of the Economic History of India with Special Reference to Food Problem 1860-1990 (Konark Publishers, Delhi).

Bhattacharya, S. (1967), A Dictionary of Indian History (University of Calcutta, Calcutta).

Bickerton, I. and Pearson, M. (1991), 43 Days. The Gulf War (The Text Publishing Company, Melbourne).

Bindoff, S.T. (1950), Tudor England (Pelican, 1961).

Birch, C. (1980), Confronting the future. Australia and the World: the Next Hundred Years (Penguin Books, Sydney).

Bissio, R.R. (1990), Third World Guide 91/92 (Instituto del Tercer Mundo, Montevideo).

Black, J. (1992), Pitt the Elder (Cambridge University Press).

Blackburn, J. (1994), Daisy Bates in the Desert (Secker & Warburg, London).

Blainey, G. (1982), The Tyranny of Distance: How Distance Shaped Australia's History (Sun, Melbourne).

Blainey, G. (1982), The Blainey View (Macmillan, Sydney).

Blainey, G. (1987), A Land Half Won (Sun Books, Melbourne).

Blainey, G. (1994), A Shorter History of Australia (Heinemann, Melbourne).

Blainey, G. (2000), A Short History of the World (Viking, Melbourne).

Blainey, G. (2004), A Very Short History of the World (Viking, Melbourne).

Blainey, G. (2005), A Short History of the 20th Century (Penguin, Melbourne).

Blake, R. and Louis, W.R. (1994) (editors), Churchill (Oxford University Press, London).

Blankert, A., Montias, J.M. and Aillaud, G. (1988), Vermeer (Rizzoli, New York).

Bloch, M. (1982), The Duke of Windsor's War (Weidenfeld & Nicolson, London).

Bloom, H. (1986) (editor), Modern Critical Views. Jane Austen (Chelsea House Publishers, New York).

Blum, W. (2006), Rogue State, A guide to the world's only superpower (Zed Books, London).

Blumberg, H.M. (1975), Weizmann. His Life and Times (St. Martin's Press, New York).

Blurton, T.R. (1992), Hindu Art (British Museum Press, London).

Boas, R.P. (1974a) (editor), George Polya Collected Papers Volume I Singularities of Analytic Functions (The MIT Press, Cambridge Massachusetts & London).

Boas, R.P. (1974b) (editor), George Polya Collected Papers Volume II Location of

Zeroes (The MIT Press, Cambridge Massachusetts & London).

Bochuan, H. (1991), China on the Edge. The Crisis of Ecology and Development (China Books & Periodicals, San Francisco).

Bok, S. (1979), Lying. Moral Choice in Public and Private Life (Vintage Books, New York).

Boldrewood, R. (1889), Robbery Under Arms (Macmillan, Sydney, 1968).

Bolts, W. (1772), Considerations on Indian Affairs (London).

Bone, E. (1957), Seven Years' Solitary (Hamish Hamilton, London).

Bookman Press (1992), Paul Keating's Book of Insults (Bookman Press, Melbourne).

Bose, N.S. (1960), The Indian Awakening and Bengal (Firma K. L. Mukhopadhay, Calcutta).

Bose, S. (1993), Peasant Labour and Colonial Capital: Rural Bengal Since 1770, Volume III.2 in The New Cambridge History of India (Cambridge University Press, Cambridge).

Bosworth, R.J.B. (1993), Explaining Auschwitz and Hiroshima. History Writing and the Second World War 1945-1990 (Routledge, London).

Boycott Apartheid Israel.

Boycott Murdoch Media.

Braeburne, Lord (1884) (editor), Letters by Jane Austen (Bentley & Son, London).

Bradbrook, F.W. (1966), Jane Austen and Her Predecessors (Cambridge University Press, London).

Bradbury, M. (1979), The History Man (Secker & Warburg, London).

Bradfield, S. (1996), Australia's Genocide, Centre for Comparative Genocide Studies Newsletter vol.2 (4), 7-10.

Brady, E.J. (1934), Doctor Mannix Archbishop of Melbourne (Library of National Biography, Melbourne).

Brahic, C. (2006), Carbon emissions rising faster than ever, New Scientist, 10 November 2005:
http://www.newscientist.com/article/dn10507-carbon-emissions-rising-faster-than-ever.html .

Brain, R. (1979), Rites, Black and White (Penguin, Melbourne).

Braudel, F. (1993), A History of Civilizations (Penguin, New York).

Bridgewater, P. and Potter, C. (1993), Endangered species: the rabbit's role in Cooke (1993), pp26-34.

British Broadcasting Corporation (BBC) (2008), Bengal Famine, The Things We Forgot to Remember (radio broadcast including Dr Gideon Polya, Dr Sanjoy Bhattacharya, Professor Amartya Sen and other scholars, January 2008):
http://www.open2.net/thingsweforgot/bengalfamine_programme.html .

Broad, L. (1951), Winston Churchill 1874-1951 (Hutchinson, London).

Broad, L. (1963), Winston Churchill. The Years of Achievement (Hawthorn Books, New York).

Brontë, E. (1847), Wuthering Heights (Penguin, London, 1965)

Brontë, C. (1847), Jane Eyre (Penguin, London, 1966).

Broomhall, F.H. (1991), The Longest Fence in the World. A History of the No.1 Rabbit Proof Fence From its Beginning Until Recent Time (Hesperian Press, Perth).

Brown, B. (1986), Lake Pedder (The Wilderness Society, Hobart).

Brown, J.P. (1979), Jane Austen's Novels. Social Change and Literary Form (Harvard University Press, Cambridge).

Brown, L.P. (1973), Bit of Ivory. Narrative Techniques in Jane Austen's Fiction (Louisiana State University Press, Baton Rouge).

Brown, L.R & Finsterbusch, G.W. (1972), Man and his Environment: Food (Harper & Row, New York)

Brown, L.R. (1995), Who will feed China? (Norton, Earthscan).

Brown, L.R. (2008), Why ethanol production will drive world food prices even higher in 2008, Earth Policy Institute, 24 January 2008: http://www.earth-policy.org/Updates/2008/Update69.htm .

Brown, W.R. and Anderson, N.R. (1976), Historical Catastrophes: Famines (Addison-Wellesley, Reading, Massachusetts).

Brown, W.R. and Eckholm, E.P. (1974), By Bread Alone (Pergamon Press, Oxford).

Brownlee, D.E. (1995), A driver of glaciation cycles? Nature vol. 378, 558.

Brownstone, D.M. and Franck, I.M. (1990), Dictionary of 20th Century History (Prentice Hall, London).

Brussells Tribunal (2008), Messages to the People, commemorating five years of war against Iraq:
http://www.brusselstribunal.org/Messages190308.htm .

Brust, D. (1929), Family memoir (unpublished manuscript, Budapest).

Bryant, A. (1957), The Turn of the Tide 1939-1943: A Study based on the Diaries and Auto-biographical Notes of the Viscount Alanbrooke (London).

Buggy, T. and Cates, J. (1985), Race Relations in Colonial Australia (Nelson, Melbourne).

Bullfinch, T. (circa 1860), Bullfinch's Mythology (Spring Books, London).

Bulliet, R.W. (1998) (editor), The Columbia History of the 20th Century (Columbia University Press, New York).

Bullock, A. (1967) The Life and Times of Ernest Bevin. Volume 2. Minister of Labour 1940-1945 (Heinemann, London).

Buncombe, A. (2021), Julian Assange's father says "greatest fear is they will take him to the US and break him for revenge", Independent, 1 January 2021:
https://www.independent.co.uk/news/world/americas/julian-assange-father-wikileaks-court-b1781104.html .

Burns, R. (1776-) in McFurlan, D. (1994) (editor), The Works of Robert Burns (Wordsworth Poetry Library, London).

Burns, R. (1787), Poems Chiefly in the Scottish Dialect (William Creech, Edinburgh).

Burrows, J.F. (1987), Computuation into Criticism. A Study of Jane Austen's Novels and an Experiment in Method (Clarendon Press, Oxford).

Burt, J. (1980), Australia's Beautiful Places (Rigby, Sydney).

Bush, D. (1975), Jane Austen (Macmillan, London).

Bussagli, M. and Sivaramamurti, C. (1978), 5000 Years of the Art of India (Harry Abrams, New York).

Butler, M. (1975), Jane Austen and the War of Ideas (Oxford University Press, Oxford).

Calvin, M. (1969), Chemical Evolution. Molecular Evolution Towards the Origin of Living Systems on the Earth and Elsewhere (Clarendon Press, Oxford).

Calvocoressi, P., Wint, G. and Pritchard, J. (1972), Total War. The Causes and Courses of the Second World War. Volume I. The Western Hemisphere; Volume II. The Greater East Asia and Pacific Conflict (Penguin, London).

Cameron, T. and Spies, S.B. (1992), A New Illustrated History of South Africa (Human & Rousseau, Cape Town).

Campbell, C. (1985), The World War II Fact Book (Macdonald, London),

Cannon, M. (1981), That Damned Democrat. John Norton, an Australian Populist, 1858-1916 (Melbourne University Press, Melbourne).

Capper, J. (1853), The Three Presidencies of India: A History of the Rise and Progress of the British Indian Possessions from the Earliest Records to the Present Time (Ingram Cooke, London).

Cardiff, I. (1964) (editor), The Wisdom of George Santayana (Atoms of Thought) (Peter Owen, London).

Carey, P. (1985), Illywhacker (University of Queensland Press).

Carey, W.H. (1882), The Good Old Days of Honorable John Company, Being Curious Reminiscences During the Rule of the East India Company from 1600 to 1858 (Quins Book Company, Calcutta, 1964).

Caroe, G.M. (1978), W.H. Bragg (1862-1942): Man and Scientist (Cambridge University Press, Cambridge).

Caruna, W. (1993), Aboriginal Art (Thames & Hudson, Singapore).

Carson, R. (1962), Silent Spring (Penguin, London).

Carter, E.H. and Mears, R.A.F. (1962), A History of Britain (Clarendon Press, Oxford).

Cartwright, F.F. (1977), A Social History of Medicine (Longman, London).

Casey, R. (1947), An Australian in India (London).

Casey, R. (1962), Personal Experience 1939-1946 (Constable, London).

Cecil, D. (1935), Jane Austen. The Leslie Stephen Lecture, University of Cambridge (Cambridge University Press, London).

Cecil, D. (1978), A Portrait of Jane Austen (Constable, London).

Cess, R.D. and Zhang, M.H. (1996), How much solar radiation do clouds absorb? Science vol. 271, 1131-1136.

Chaliand, G. and Rageau, J-P. (1985), Strategic Atlas. World Geopolitics (Penguin, London).

Chalk, F. and Jonassohn, K. (1990), The History and Sociology of Genocide. Analyses and Case Studies (Yale University Press, New Haven & London).

Chamarette, C. (1995), Speech to the Australian Senate on the Bengal Famine, 20 September, Australian Senate Weekly Hansard, No. 14, September, p1158:
http://parlinfoweb.aph.gov.au/piweb/view_document.aspx?ID=385062&TABLE=HANSARDS .

Chang, (1991), Wild Swans. Three Daughters of China (Harper Collins, London).
Chapman, R.W. (1932) (editor), Jane Austen's Letters to Her Sister Cassandra and Others (Oxford University Press, London, 1964).

Chapman, R.W. (1949), Jane Austen. Facts and Problems (Clarendon Press, Oxford).

Chapman, R.W. (1954) (editor), The Works of Jane Austen, vol. 6, Minor Works (Oxford University Press, London, 1965).

Charmley, J. (1993), Churchill: the End of Glory (Harcourt Brace, New York).

Chatterjee, S.K. (1944), The Starving Millions (Asoka Library, Calcutta).

Chatterjee, P. (1984), Bengal 1920-1947. Volume 1. The Land Question (K.P. Bagchi, Calcutta).

Chaudhuri, N.C. (1975), Clive of India. A Political and Psychological Essay (Barrie & Jenkins, London).

Chomsky, N. (2003), Imminent crises: threats and opportunities, Monthly Review, 59 (2), June 2007: http://www.monthlyreview.org/0607nc.htm .

Chomsky, N. (2007a), Interventions (Penguin, London).

Chomsky, N. (2007b), What We Say Goes. Conversations on US power in a changing world (Allen & Unwin, Sydney).

Chopra, R.N. (1988), Food Policy in India. A Survey (Intellectual Publishing House, New Delhi).

Churchill, R.S. and Gilbert, M. (1966-1990), Winston S. Churchill, Volumes I-VIII (Heinemnann, London).

Churchill, W.S. (1898), The Story of the Malakand Field Force: An Episode of Frontier War (Norton, London, 1989).

Churchill, W.S. (1899), The River War (London, 1973).
Churchill, W.S. (1935), Speech to the House of Commons about Indians (1935); 1. Hansard of the House of Commons, Winston Churchill speech, Hansard Vol. 302, cols. 1920-21, 1935.

Churchill, W.S. (1938), While England Slept. A Survey of World Affairs 1932-1938 (Books for Libraries Press, New York, 1971).

Churchill, W.S. (1947), Marlborough. His Life and Times. Books I & II (George Harrap, London).

Churchill, W.S. (1954), The Second World War. Volumes I-VI (Cassell, London).

Churchill, W.S. (1965), A History of the English-Speaking Peoples. The Age of Revolution (Dodd, Mead & Co., New York).

Clark, G. (1961), The Later Stuarts 1660-1714 (Oxford University Press, London, 2nd edition, 1972).

Clark, G. (1971), English History. A Survey (Oxford University Press, London).

Clark, M. (1969), A Short History of Australia (Mentor, London, revised 6th edn.).

Clark, C.M.H.(1971), A History of Australia (Melbourne University Press, Melbourne).

Clark, M. (1986), A Short History of Australia (Penguin, Sydney, revised & illustrated).

Clark, W.C. & Munn, R.E. (1986), Sustainable Development of the Biosphere (Cambridge University Press, Cambridge).

Clarke, C. (1960), The Savage Truth (World Distributors, Manchester).

Clarke, M.A.H. (1885), For the Term of His Natural Life (Richard Bentley, London).

Clayton, J. (1931), St Hugh of Lincoln. A Biography (Burns, Oats & Washburne, Publishers to the Holy See, London).

Climate Emergency Network (2008): http://www.climateemergencynetwork.org/ .

Climate Genocide: https://sites.google.com/site/climategenocide/ .

Clive, J. and Pinney, T. (1972) (editors), Thomas Babington Macaulay. Selected Writings (University of Chicago Press).

Coates, K. (2006), editor, Haditha Ethics. From Iraq to Iran? (Spokesman, Bertrand Russel Peace Foundation, Nottingham, UK).

Cochrane. A.L. (1972), Effectiveness and Efficiency: Random Reflections on Health Services (Nuffield Provincial Hospitals Trust, London).

Coghlan, A. (1996), Poorest women die "needlessly" in childbirth, New Scientist 17 February 1996, p5.

Cohen, J.M. and Cohen, M.J. (1961), The Penguin Dictionary of Quotations (Penguin, London).

Cohen, P. (1996), Let there be life, New Scientist 6 July, pp22-27.

Cohn, N.F.C. (1967), Warrant for Genocide. The Myth of the Jewish World-Conspiracy and the Protocols of the Elders of Zion (Eyre & Spottiswoode, London).

Coleman, P. and Tanner, L. (1978), Cartoons of Australian History (Nelson, Melbourne).

Collings, L. and Durrant, L.L. (1977), Tasmania (Murray, Sydney).

Colvin, I.D. (1917), The Unseen Hand In British History (The National Review Office, London).

Conrad, J. (1898), Tales of Unrest (Thomas Nelson, London, circa 1960).

Conrad, J. (1899), Heart of Darkness (Penguin, London, 1983).

Conrad, J. (1903), Typhoon (Thomas Nelson, London, circa 1960).

Conrad, P, (1988), Down Home, Revisiting Tasmania (Chatto & Windus, London).

Cook, C. and Stevenson, J. (1991), The Longman Handbook of World History Since 1914 (Longman, London & New York).

Cooke, B.D. (1993) (editor), Australian Rabbit Control Conference, 2-3 April (Anti-rabbit Research Foundation of Australia, Adelaide, South Australia.

Coppola, F.F. (1979), Apocalypse Now (Movie, Omni Zoetrope, San Francisco).

Corbett, J. (1966), Man-Eaters of Kumaon (Oxford University Press, London).

Cornford, F.M. (1908), Acta Microcosmographica Academica. Being a Guide For the Young Academic Politician (Bowes & Bowes, London, 1966 edition).

Craigie, R. (1943), Final Report to Mr. Eden on Conclusion of his Mission to Japan, published in Rushbridger, J. and Nave, E. (1991), Betrayal at Pearl Harbor. How Churchill Lured Roosevelt into World War II (Summit, New York).

Craik, W.A. (1965), Jane Austen. The Six Novels (Methuen, London).

Crawford, R.M. (1963), Australia (Hutchinson University Library, London).

Crossman, R.L.H. (1946), Palestine Mission (London).

Cunningham, A. (18xx) (editor), The Complete Works of Robert Burns: Containing the Poems, Songs and Correspondence (George Virtue, London).

Cunningham, A. (1996), An Gorta Mor (The Great Famine), Centre for Comparative Genocide Studies Newsletter 2, 8-10.

Curzon, K.G. (1925), British Government in India. The Story of the Viceroys and Government Houses. Volumes 1 & 2 (Cassell, London).

Daintish, J., Fergusson, R., Stibbs, A. & Wright, E. (1991) (editors), Bloomsbury Thematic Dictionary of Quotations (Bloomsbury, London).

Darlington, C.D. (1969), The Evolution of Man and Society (George Allen & Unwin, London).

Darnell, J., Lodish, H. and Baltimore, D. (1990), Molecular Cell Biology (2nd edition) (Scientifc American Books, New York).

Darwish, A. and Alexander, G. (1991), Unholy Babylon. The Secret History of Saddam's War (Victor Gollancz, London).

Das, T. (1949), Bengal Famine (1943) as Revealed in a Survey of Destitutes of Calcutta (University of Calcutta, Calcutta).

Da Silva, W. (1996), Long Dry Spells, Outlook Gloomy, New Scientist, 12 December, p9.

Datta, K. (1971), Siraj-ud-daulah (Orient Longman, Bombay).

Datta, K.K. (1977), Disruption of the Mughul Empire (a) Bengal Subah in Majumdar (1977), pp104-112.

Datta, K. (1978), Survey of India's Life and Economic Conditions in the Eighteenth Century 1707-1813 (Munshiram Manoharlal, New Delhi).

Davidoff, H. (1955), The Pocket Book of Quotations (Pocket Books, New York).

Davidson, R. (1984), Tracks (Granada, Sydney).

Davies, A. (1984), Where did the Forties Go? A Popular History. The Rise and Fall of the Hopes of a Decade (Pluto Press, London).

Davies, A.M. (1935), Strange Destiny. A Biography of Warren Hastings (G.P. Putnma's Sons, New York).

Davies, A.M. (1939), Clive of Plassey. A Biography (Nicholson & Watson).

Davies, J.L. (1965) (editor), Atlas of Tasmania (Tasmanian Government, Hobart).

Davis, M. (2001), Late Victorian Holocausts: El Nino Famines and the Making of the Third World (Verso, London).

Davis, R. (1985), Free academics or council servants? Tasmanian University staff before the Murray Report, Vestes No. 2, pp28-34.

Dawkins, R. (2006), The God Delusion (Bantam Press, London).

Dayan, M. (1967), Diary of the Sinai Campaign 1956 (Sphere Books, London).

Dear, I.C.B. and Foot, M.R.D. (1995) (editors), The Oxford Companion to the Second World War (Oxford University Press, Oxford).

De Grandpre, L. (1801), Voyage dans l'Inde et au Bengale, Fait dans les Années 1789 et 1790; English version: Voyage in the Indian Ocean and to Bengal (1803); reproduced in part in Nair (1984), pp210-274.

Demidenko, H. (1995), The Hand That Signed the Paper (Allen & Unwin, Sydney).

Denton, M. (1985), Evolution: A Theory in Crisis (Burnett Books, London).

De Rose, P.L. (1980), Jane Austen and Samuel Johnson (University Press of America, Washington).

Derry, J.W. (1962), William Pitt (B.T. Batsford, London).

De Smedt, M. (1983), The Kama-Sutra. Erotic Figures in Indian Art (Liber, Fribourg-Geneve).

Devlin, D.D. (1975), Jane Austen and Education (Macmillan, London).

Diamond, J. (1997), Guns, Germs and Steel. The Fates of Human Societies (Jonathan Cape, London).

Diamond, J. (2005), Collapse. How societies choose to fail or survive (Penguin, London).

Dickinson, W.C. (1990), Sidney Godolphin, Lord Treasurer 1702-1710 (Edwin Mellen Press, New York).

Dickson, D. (1996), Britain may set up genetics advisory body as ethics report clears xenografts, Nature Volume 380, 6.

Discriminatory laws in Israel, Adalah, https://www.adalah.org/en/law/index?page=4 .

Dodwell, H.H. (1929) (editor), The Cambridge History of the British Empire, Volume IV (= Volume V of the Cambridge History of India) (Cambridge University Press, Cambridge).

Dodwell, H.H. (1963a) (editor), The Cambridge History of India, Volumes I-VI (Chand, Delhi).

Dodwell, H. H.(1963b), Bengal 1760-1772 in Dodwell (1963a), Volume V, Chapter IX, pp166-180.

Dodwell, H. (1967), Dupleix and Clive. The Beginning of Empire (Frank Cass, London).

Dogra, B. (1987), Empty Stomachs and Packed Godowns (Aspects of the Food System in India).

Dombrovskis, P., Flanagan, R. and Kirkpatrick, J. (1996), On the Mountain (West Wind Press, Hobart).

Dovers, S. (1994) (editor), Australian Environmental History. Essays and Cases (Oxford University Press, Oxford).

Drechsler, H. (1980), Let Us Die Fighting: The Struggle of the Herero and the Nama against German Imperialism (1884-1915) (translated by B.Zollner) (Zed Books, New York).

Drewett, R. and Redhead, M. (1984), The Trial of Richard III (Alan Sutton, London).

Dreze, J. and Sen, A. (1989), Hunger and Public Action (Clarendon, Oxford).

Duffy, C. (1988), Frederick the Great. A Military Life (Routledge & Kegan Paul, London).

Duiker, W.J. and Spielvogel, J.J. (2006), World History (Thomson, Belmont, CA).

Dukas, H. and Hoffmann, B. (1979) (editors), Albert Einstein. The Human Side (Princeton University Press, Princeton).

Dunan, M. (1968) (editor), Larousse Encyclopaedia of Modern History from 1500 to the Present Day (Paul Hamlyn, London, 4th edition).

Dunbar, G. (1936), Clive (Duckworth, London).

Dunbar, G. (1943), A History of India from the Earliest Times to the Present Day, Volumes 1-2 (Nicholson & Watson).

Dunbar, G. (1951), India and the Passing of Empire (Nicholson & Watson, London).

Dunn, M. (1984), Australia and the Empire: From 1788 to the Present (Fontana / Collins, London).

Dupart, F.J. and Powell, E.A. (editors), Johannes Vermeer (Nationall Gallery of Art Washington, Yale University Press, New Haven).

Durant, J.D. (1975), Richard Brinsley Sheridan (Tayne, Boston).

Dussinger, J.A. (1990), In the Pride of the Moment. Encounters in Jane Austen's World (Ohio State University, Columbus).

Dutta, K.K. (1971), Siraj-ud-daulah (Calcutta).

Dwyer, J. (1989), Jane Austen (Continuum, New York).

Eastman, A.M., Allison, A.W., Barrows, H., Blake, C.R., Carr, A.J. and English, H.M. (1970) (editors), The Norton Anthology of Poetry (W.W. Norton, New York).

Eastwood, P. (1991), Responding to Global Warming. An Examination of the Prospects for Effective Action (Berg, New York).

Eddy, J.J. and Nethercote, J.R. (1987) (editors), From Colony to Coloniser. Studies in Australian Administrative History (Hale & Iremonger, Sydney).

Eddy, W.H.C. (1961), Orr (Jacaranda, Brisbane).

Edgerton, L.T. (1991), The Rising Tide. Global Warming and World Sea Levels (Island Press, Washington).

Edwardes, M. (1961), A History of India from the Earliest Times to the Present Day (Thomas & Hudson, London).

Edwardes, M. (1967), British India 1772-1947 (Sidgwick & Jackson, London).

Edwardes, M. (1977), Clive. The Heaven-Born General (Harte-Davis, MacGibbon, London).

Edwards, C. (1980), Man-Made Wonders (Cathay Books, Hong Kong).

Edwards, C.R.W. and Bouchier, I.A.D. (1981) (editors), Davidson's Principles & Practice of Medicine (16th edition) (Churchill Livingstone, London).

Edwards, C.R.W., Bouchier, I.A.D., Haslett, C. and Chilvers, E.R. (1995) (editors), Davidson's Principles & Practice of Medicine (17th edition) (Churchill Livingstone, London).

Edwards, R. (1975) (editor), The Preservation of Australia's Aboriginal Heritage. Australian Aboriginal Studies No. 54 (Australian Institute of Aboriginal Studies, Canberra).

Edwards, R.D. and Williams, T.D. (1957) (editors), The Great Famine. Studies in Irish History 1845-52 (New York University Press, New York).

Edwards, W.H. (1987) (editor), Traditional Aboriginal Society. A Reader (Macmillan Education Australia, Melbourne).

Ehrlich, P.R. (1968), The Population Bomb (Ballantine Books, New York).

Ehrlich, P.R., Ehrlich, A.H. and Holden, J.P. (1973), Human Ecology. Problems and Solutions (W.H. Freeman, San Francisco).

Ehrlich, P.R., Ehrlich, A.H. and Daily, G.C. (1995), The Stork and the Plow (Grosset, Putnam).

Ehrman, J. (1969), The Younger Pitt. The Years of Acclaim (Constable , London).

Einbinder,H. (1972), The Myth of the Britannica (Johnson Reprint Corporation, New York).

El-Ghusein, F. (1917), Martyred Armenia (C. Arthur Pearson, London).

Elias, P. and Elias, A. (2003) (editors), A Few From Afar. Jewish Lives in Tasmania from 1804 (Hobart Jewish Congregation, Hobart, Tasmania).

Elkins, C. (2005), Britain's Gulag. The Brutal End of Empire in Kenya (Pimlico, London).

Ellis, B. (2012), Social Humanism. A New Metaphysics, Routledge , UK , 2012.

Elton, B. (1990), Gasping (Sphere Books, London).

Elton, B. (1996), Popcorn (Simon & Schuster, London).

Embree, A.T. (1962), Charles Grant and British Rule in India (Columbia University Press, New York).

Embree, A.T. (1988a) (editor), Encyclopaedia of Asian History (Collier Macmillan, London).

Embree, A.T. (1988b), India in Embree, A.T. (1988a) (editor), Encyclopaedia of Asian History (Collier Macmillan, London) pp111-126.

Embree, A.T. (1988c), Rajasthan in Embree, A.T. (1988a) (editor), Encyclopaedia of Asian History (Collier Macmillan, London) pp321-322.

Embree, A.(1999) Imperialism and decolonization, Chapter 7 in Bulliet, R.W. (1999) (1998) (editor), The Columbia History of the 20th Century (Columbia University Press, New York), pp147-171.

Encyclopaedia Britannica (1977), The New Encyclopaedia Britannica (Benton, Chicago).

Ergang, R. (1941), The Potsdam Führer. Frederick William I, Father of Prussian Militarism (Columbia University Press, New York).

Esposito, V.J. (1964) (editor), A Concise History of World War II (Pall Mall Press, London).

Etienne, G. (1977), Bangladesh: Development in Perspective (Graduate Institute of International Studies, Geneva).

Evans, B. (1968), Dictionary of Quotations (Delacorte Press, New York).

Experts: US did 9/11: https://sites.google.com/site/expertsusdid911/ .

Facey, A.B.(1981), A Fortunate Life (Penguin, Melbourne).

Falk, J. and Brownlow, A. (1989), The Greenhouse Challenge. What's to be Done? (Penguin, Melbourne).

Falloux, F. and Talbot, L.M. (1993), Crisis and Opportunity. Environment and Development in Africa (Earthscan, London).

Famine Inquiry Commission, India (1945), Report on Bengal (Government of India).

Fane H.E.H.(ca 1840), Five Years in India (Department of Languages, Punjab, !970).

Fanning, P. (1970), James Cook: His Early Life and the Endeaavour Voyage (National Library of Australia, Canberra).

Fargione, J., Hill, J., Tilman, D., Polasky, S. and Hawthorne, P. (2008), Land Clearing and the Biofuel Carbon Debt, Science 29 February 2008, Vol. 319. no. 5867, pp. 1235 – 1238: http://www.sciencemag.org/cgi/content/abstract/1152747 .

Farmer, D.H. (1985), Saint Hugh of Lincoln (Darton, Longman & Todd, London).

Feiling, K. (1966), Warren Hastings (Macmillan, London).

Fenner, F. and Ratcliffe, F.N. (1965), Myxomatosis (Cambridge University Press, London).

Fergus, J. (1983), Jane Austen and the Didactic Novel. Northanger Abbey, Sense and Sensibility and Pride and Prejudice (Macmillan, London).

Fergus, J. (1991), Jane Austen. A Literary Life (Macmillan, London).

Firth, C. (1964), A Commentary on Macaulay's History of England (Frank Cass, London).

Flanagan, R. (2001), Gould's Book of Fish. A Novel in Twelve Fish (Picador, Sydney).

Flannery, T and Kendall, P. (1990), Australia's Vanishing Mammals: Extinct and Native Species (RD Press, Sydney).)

Flannery, T.F. (1994), The Future Eaters. An Ecological History of the Australasian Lands and People (Reed Books, Melbourne).

Foot, M. (1995), HG: The History of Mr Wells (Doubleday, London).

Forsee, A. (1963), Albert Einstein: Theoretical Physicist (Macmillan, New York).

Forster, E.M. (1924), A Passage to India (Penguin, London, 1965).

Forster, E.M. (1965), The Hill of Devi (Penguin, London).

Fortbath, P. (1978), The River Congo. The Discovery, Exploration and Exploitation of the World's Most Dramatic River (Secker & Warburg, London).

Fortescue, J. (1967) (editor), The Correspondence of King George the Third from 1760 to December 1783 (Frank Cass, London).

Frank, A. (1944), The Diary of Ann Frank (Penguin, London).

Fraser, G.M. (1979), Flashman's First Omnibus: Flash; Royal Flash; Flash for Freedom (Barrie & Jenkins, London).

Fraser, T.G. (1980) (editor), The Middle East 1914-1979 (Edward Arnold, London).

Freund, B. (1984), The Making of Contemporary Africa (Indiana University Press, Bloomington).

Friel, J.P. (1985) (editor), Dorland's Illustrated Medical Dictionary (26th edition) (Saunders, London)

Frost, D. (1974) (editor), Whitlam and Frost (Sundial, London).

Fullerton, S. & Harbers, A. (2001), Jane Austen Antipodean Views (Wellington Lane, Sydney).

Fullerton, S. (2002), Jane Austen and Adultery in Persuasions: The Jane Austen Journal (January 1, 2002): http://www.encyclopedia.com/doc/1G1-135180163.html .

Gainor, D, (2007), Lovelock: warming will kill 6 billion, Business & Media Institute, 19 October 2007: http://www.businessandmedia.org/printer/2007/20071022221333.aspx .

Gangrade,K.D. and Dhadda, S. (1973), Challenge and Response. A Study of Famines in India (Rachaua Publications, Delhi).

Gard, R. (1992), Jane Austen's Novels. The Art of Clarity (Yale University Press, New Haven).

Garden, D. (1984), Victoria - A History (Nelson, Melbourne).

Gardner, B. (1971), The East India Company (Dorset Press, New York).

Garnett, R. (1976), Robert Clive (Arthur Baker, London).

Garran, A. (1886) (editor), Historical Sketch of Victoria (Lansdowne Press, Sydney; 1974).

Garratty, J.A. and Gay, P. (1972), The Columbia History of the World (Harper & Row, New York).

Garrett, R.H. and Grisham, C.M. (1995), Biochemistry (Saunders College Publishing, New York).

Gay, P. (1990), Jane Austen's Pride and Prejudice (Sydney University Press, Sydney).

Gedye, R. (1994), Holocaust denial banned Telegraph-Mirror (Sydney), 23 September, p33.

Geneva Convention Relative to the Protection of Civilian Persons in Time of War (1950): http://www.unhchr.ch/html/menu3/b/92.htm .

Ghosh, K.C. (1944), Famines in Bengal 1770-1943 (National Council of Education, Calcutta, 2nd edition 1987).

Gideon Polya: https://sites.google.com/site/drgideonpolya/home .

Gilbert, M. (1969) (with Banks, A., cartographer), Jewish History Atlas (Weidenfeld & Nicolson, London).

Gilbert, M. (1982), Atlas of the Holocaust (Michael Joseph, London).

Gilbert, M. (1988), Road to Victory. Winston Churchill 1941-1945, Volume VII of Churchill & Gilbert (1966-1990) (Heinemann, London).

Gilbert, M. (1989), Second World War (Weidenfeld & Nicolson, London).

Gilbert, M. (1991), Churchill. A Life (Heinemann, London).

Gilbert, M. (1999), A History of the Twentieth Century (W. Morrow, New York).

Gilmore, M. (1918), The Passionate Heart (Angus & Robertson, 1918).

Gilmore, M. (1934), Old Days: Old Ways. A Book of Recollections (Angus & Robertson, Sydney).

Gilmore, M. (1935), More Recollections (Angus & Robertson, Sydney).

Gilpin, A. (1980), The Australian Environment. 12 Controversial Issues (Sun Books, Melbourne).

Gleig, G.R. (1841), Memories of the Life of the Right Hon. Warren Hastings, First Governor-General of Bengal Volumes I-III (Richard Bentley, London).

Glikson, A. (2019), Inferno: from climate denial to planetary arson, Countercurrents, 8 September 2019: https://countercurrents.org/2019/09/inferno-from-climate-denial-to-planetary-arson/ .

Goldsmith, E., Hildyard, N., McCully , P. and Bunyard, P. (1990), Imperiled Planet. Restoring our Endangered Ecosystems (MIT Press, Cambridge).

Goldstein, D.M. and Dillon, K.V. (1982), Revisionists revisited in Prange (1982), pp839-852; Forward in Prange (1982), ppix-xiii.

Goodell, J. (2007), The Prophet of Climate Change, James Lovelock: (see: http://www.rollingstone.com/politics/story/16956300/the_prophet_of_climate_change_james_lovelock .

Goodwin, A. (1965) (editor), The New Cambridge Modern History, Volume VIII, The American and French revolutions 1763-93 (Cambridge University Press, Cambridge).

Gopal, R. (1963), How the British Occupied Bengal. A Corrected Account of the 1756-1765 Events (Asia Publishing House, New York).

Gopal, R. (1963), British Rule In India. An Assessment (Asia Publishing House, Bombay).

Gopal, S. (1994), Churchill and India in Blake, R. and Louis, W.R. (1994) (editors), Churchill (Oxford University Press, London).

Gooneratne, Y. (1970), Jane Austen (Cambridge University Press, Cambridge).

Gordimer, N. (1992), Jump and Other Stories (Penguin, London).

Gordon, A. and Suzuki, D. (1990), It's a Matter of Survival (Allen & Unwin, Toronto).

Gordon, L.A. (1990), Brothers Against the Raj (Columbia University Press, New York).

Gordon, M. (1963), Sir Isaac Isaacs. A Life of Service (Heinemann, London).

Gore, A. (2007), The Assault on Reason (Bloomsbury, London)

Gorham, E. (1996), Lakes under a three-prolonged attack, Nature vol. 381, 109.

Goss, H. (1995), While contraceptive virus is pitched at the rabbit plague, New Scientist 7 October, p8.

Gould, R.T. (1978), Captain Cook (Duckworth, London).

Grant, C. (18xx), Observations on the State of Asia (London).

Grassby, A. (1979), The Morning After (Judicator, Canberra).

Gravelle, K. (1980), Fiji's Times. A History of Fiji (Fiji Times, Suva).

Greenough, P.R. (1982), Prosperity and Misery in Modern Bengal: the Famine of 1943-1944 (Oxford University Press, Oxford & New York).

Greenough, P.R. (1988), Famine in Embree, A.T. (1985a) (editor), Encyclopaedia of Asian History (Collier Macmillan, London) pp457-459.

Greer, G. (1984), Sex and Destiny. The Politics of Human Fertility (Picador,London).

Gregg, E. (1980), Queen Anne (Routledge & Keegan Paul, London).

Gregoire, P. (2021), "Until we win": Assange's father John Shipton on the home run tour for Julian, Sydney Criminal Lawyers, 15 March 2021: https://www.sydneycriminallawyers.com.au/blog/until-we-win-assanges-father-john-shipton-on-the-home-run-tour-for-julian/ .

Grey, J.D. (1986) The Jane Austen Handbook with a Dictionary of Jane Austen's Life and Works (The Athlone Press, London).

Grey, J.D. (1989) (editor), Jane Austen's Beginnings. The Juvenilia and Lady Susan (UMI Research Press, Ann Arbor).

Grieve, A.J. (1961) (editor), Thomas Babington Macaulay. Critical and Historical Essays. Volumes I & II (Everyman's Library, London).

Grun, B. (1975), The Timetables of History. A Chronology of World Events Based on Werner Stein's Kulturfahrplan (Thames & Hudson, London).

Guirand, F. (1959) (editor), Larousse Encyclopaedia of Mythology (translated by R. Aldington & D. Ames) (Batchworth Press, London).

Gupta, A.K.D. (1977), Consolidation of British Power in Bengal in Majumdar (1977), pp339-387.

Gupta, B.K. (1962), Siraj-ud-daulah and the East India Company (Calcutta).

Gurun, K. (1985), The Armenian File. The Myth of Innocence Exposed (Weidenfeld & Nicolson, London).

Halliday, F.E. (1980), A Concise History of England (Thames & Hudson, London).

Halperin, J. (1982), Unengaged laughter: Jane Austen's Juvenilia South Atlantic Quarterly, vol. 81, 3, Summer 1982.

Halperin, J. (1984), The Life of Jane Austen (Johns Hopkins University Press, Baltimore).

Halperin, J (1975) (editor), Jane Austen Bicentenary Essays (Cambridge University Press, London).

Handler , R. and Segal , D. (1990), Jane Austen and the Fiction of Culture (University of Arizona Press, Tucson).

Hansen, J. et al. (2007a), Dangerous human-made interference with climate: A GISS modelE study, Atmos.Chem. Phys., vol. 7, 2287-2312: http://pubs.giss.nasa.gov/abstracts/2007/Hansen_etal_1.html .

Hansen, J., Sato, M., Kharecha, P., Russell, G., Lea, D.W., & M. Siddall, M. (2007b), Climate change and trace gases. Phil. Trans. Royal. Soc. A, vol. 365, 1925-1954: http://pubs.giss.nasa.gov/abstracts/2007/Hansen_etal_2.html .

Hansen, J. (2008), The need for an International moratorium on coal power, Bulletin of the Atomic Scientists On-line: http://www.thebulletin.org/columns/james-hansen/20080124.html .

Hansen, J. et al (2008), "Target atmospheric CO_2: where should humanity aim?": http://arxiv.org/abs/0804.1126 .

Hansen, J. (2018), Climate change in a nutshell: the gathering storm, Columbia University, 18 December 2018: http://www.columbia.edu/~jeh1/mailings/2018/20181206_Nutshell.pdf .

Haque, W., Mehta, N., Rahman, A. and Wignaraja, P. (1975), Towards a Theory of Rural Development (UN Asian Development Institute, Bangkok).

Hardjono, R. (1994) White Tribe of Asia. An Indonesian View of Australia (Hyland House, Melbourne).

Hardy, B. (1979), A Reading Of Jane Austen (The Athlone Press, London).

Hardy, F. (1962), Power Without Glory (Sphere Books, London, 1970).

Hardy, F. (1968), The Unlucky Australians (Nelson, Melbourne).

Hardy, J. (1984), Jane Austen's Heroines. Intimacy in Human Relationships (Routledge & Kegan Paul, London).

Harle, J.C. (1986), The Art and Architecture of the Indian Subcontinent (Yale University Press, New Haven).

Harris, J. (1989), Jane Austen's Art of Memory (Cambridge University Press, Cambridge).

Harvell, E.b. (1974), A Handbook of Indian Art (Reprints & Trans Publications, Delhi).

Harun ur Rashid, H.E. (1993), The environmental situation in Bangladesh in Polunin, N. & Burnett, J. (1993), pp29-30.

Hassell, K. (1966), The Relations Between the Settlers and Aborigines in South Australia, 1836-1860 (Libraries Board of South Australia, Adelaide).

Hastings, W. (1772), Letter to the Secret Committee of the Honorable Court of Directors for the Affairs of the Honorable United East India Company (Cossimbuzar, 1st September 1772) in Fortescue, J. (1967) (editor), The Correspondence of King George the Third from 1760 to December 1783 (Frank Cass, London), pp385-392.

Hastings, W. (1787), Memoirs Relative to the State of India (Murray, London).

Hawken, P. (1993), The Ecology of Commerce. A Declaration of Sustainability (Phoenix, New York).

Hawking, S. (2018), Brief Answers to the Big Questions (John Murray, UK).

Hayward, J. (1978) (editor), The Penguin Book of English Verse (Allen Lane, London).

Heath, W. (1961) (editor), Discussions of Jane Austen (Heath, Boston).

Heller, S. (1981), Man Bites Man. Two Decades of Satiric Art (Hutchinson, London).

Herbert, X. (1983), Poor Fellow My Country (Fontana, Sydney).

Herbert, X. (1938), Capricornia: A Novel. (Lloyd O'Neil, Melbourne, 1971).
Herman, E.S. and Chomsky, N. (2002), Manufacturing Consent. The political economy of the mass media, Pantheon, 2002.

Hicks, G. (1995), The Comfort Women: Sex Slaves of the Japanese Imperial Forces (Allen & Unwin, Sydney).

Hicks, M. (1992), Richard III. The Man Behind the Myth (Collins & Brown, London).

Hindley, G. (1987) (editor), The Larousse Encyclopaedia of Music (Hamlyn, London).

Hiro, D. (1992), Desert Shield to Desert Storm. The Second Gulf War (Paladin, London).

Hodge, J.A. (1972), The Double Life of Jane Austen (Hodder & Stoughton, London).

Hoegh-Guldberg, O. et al (2007), Coral reefs under rapid climate change and ocean acidification, Science, vol. 318 (5857), 1737-1742.

Holmes, G. (1984), Britain After the Glorious Revolution 1689-1714 (Macmillan, London).

Honan, P. (1987), Jane Austen. Her Life (Weidenfeld & Nicolson, London).

Hope, C. (2011), How high should climate change taxes be?, Working Paper Series, Judge Business School, University of Cambridge, 9.2011:
http://www.jbs.cam.ac.uk/fileadmin/user_upload/research/workingpapers/wp1109.pdf .

Hopkins, E.J. (1967) (editor), Ambrose Bierce. The Enlarged Devil's Dictionary (Penguin, London).

Horne, D. (1965), The Lucky Country. Australia Today (Penguin, Sydney).

Horwitz, B.J. (1991), Jane Austen and the Question of Women's Education (Peter Lang, London).

Howard, T. (1995), Austen Country (Grange Books, London).

Howat, G.M.D. and Taylor, A.J.P. (1973) (editors), Dictionary of World History (Nelson, London).

Hoyt, E.P. (1988), Hitler's War (McGraw-Hill, New York).

Hubatsch, W. (1975), Frederick the Great of Prussia. Absolutism and Administration (translated by P. Doran) (Thames & Hudson, London).

Hubback, J.H. and Hubback, E.C. (1906), Jane Austen's Sailor Brothers.

Hudson, G.A. (1992) Sibling Love and Incest in Jane Austen's Fiction (Macmillan, London).

Hudson, W.J. (1986), Casey (Oxford University Press, Melbourne).

Hudson, W.J. and Way, W. (1991) (editors), Documents on Australian Foreign Policy 1937-49. Volume IX: January-June 1946 (Australian Government, Canberra).

Hugesson, H.M. (1960) Kentish Family (Methuen, London).

Hughes, R. (1987), The Fatal Shore. A History of the Transportation of Convicts to Asutralia, 1787-1868 (Collins-Harvill, London).

Hunt, M.A. (1905), The History of England From the Accession of George III to the Close of Pitt's First Administration (1760-1801) (Longman's, London).

Hunter, W.W. (1871), Annals of Rural Bengal (Smith, Elder & Co., London).

Hunter, W.W. (1890), The Indian Empire: Its People, History and Products (Kegan Paul, Trench & Trubner, London)

Hunter, W.W. (1912), A History of British India (Longman, Green & Co., London).

ICAN (International Campaign to Abolish Nuclear Weapons) (2022): https://www.icanw.org/ .

Ignotus, P. (1964), Political Prisoner (Collier, New York).

Inequality.org: https://inequality.org/facts/global-inequality/ .

International Monetary Fund (IMF), "Fiscal Monitor: how to mitigate climate change". Executive Summary", September 2019: file:///C:/Users/Gideon/AppData/Local/Temp/execsum-6.pdf .

IPCC (Intergovernmental Panel on Climate Change) (2007), Fourth Assessment Report: http://www.ipcc.ch/ .

IPCC (2019), Global Warming of 1.5°C: https://www.ipcc.ch/site/assets/uploads/sites/2/2019/06/SR15_Full_Report_High_Res.pdf .

Iraqi Holocaust, Iraqi Genocide: https://sites.google.com/site/iraqiholocaustiraqigenocide/ .

Irving, D. (1987), Churchill's War (Veritas, Melbourne).

Islam, M. (1982), A History of Folktale Collections in India, Bangladesh and Pakistan (Punchali Prakasan, Calcutta).

Jablonsky, D. (1991), Churchill, the Great Game and Total War (Frank Cass, London).

Jacobson, H. (1984), Coming From Behind (Black Swan, London).

Jacob, J. and Bianconi, P. (1967) (editors), The Complete Paintings of Vermeer (Weidenfeld & Nicolson, London).

Jenkin, J. (1986), The Bragg Family in Adelaide: A Pictorial Celebration (Melbourne).

Jenkins, E. (1973), Jane Austen. A Biography (Victor Gollancz, London).

Jenks, W.A. (1960), Vienna and the Young Hitler (Columbia University Press, New York).

Jesus in Matthew, The Holy Bible, King James Version, Chapter 25, verse 29.

Jewish Voices for Peace, "First ever: 40+ Jewish groups worldwide oppose equating antisemitism with criticism of Israel", 17 July 2018: https://jewishvoiceforpeace.org/first-ever-40-jewish-groups-worldwide-oppose-equating-antisemitism-with-criticism-of-israel/#english .

Jews Against Racist Zionism: https://sites.google.com/site/jewsagainstracistzionism/ .

Jog, N.G. (1944), Churchill's Blind-Spot: India (New Book Company, Bombay).

Johnson, A. (1947)., Another's Harvest (Bookman, Calcutta).

Johnson, C.L. (1988), Jane Austen. Women, Politics and the Novel (University of Chicago Press, Chicago).

Johnson, J. (1984), Princely Chandos. James Brydges 1674-1744 (Alan Sutton, London).

Johnson, R.B. (1924), A New Study of Jane Austen (George Routledge, London).

Johnson, R.B. (1926) (editor), The Letters of Jane Austen (Dial Press, London).

Johnson, R.B. (1927), Jane Austen (Haskell House, London, !974).

Kachhawaha, O.P. (1985), Famines in Rajasthan (1900 A.D. - 1947 A.D.) (Hindi Sahitya Mandir, Jodhpur).

Kachhawaha, O.P. (1992), History of Famines in Rajasthan (Research Publications, Jodhpur).

Kaplan, D. (1992), Jane Austen Among Women (Johns Hopkins University Press, Baltimore).

Kaye, J.W. (1853), The Adminsitration of the East India Company. A History of Indian Progress (Kitab Mahal, Allahabad, 1966).

Kaye-Smith, S. and Stern, G.B. (1943), Talking of Jane Austen (Cassell, London).

Keane, B. (2021), Lies and Falsehoods. The Morrison Government and the new culture of deceit, (Hardie Grant Books, Melbourne).

Kedourie, E. (1968), The Middle East 1900-1945 in Mowat (1968), Volume XII, Chapter X, pp269-296.

Keegan, J. (1989), The Second World War (Hutchinson, London).

Kendall, P.M. (1955), Richard the Third (London).

Kennedy, P. (1993), Preparing for the Twenty-First Century (Harper Collins, London).

Kent, C. (1981), "Real solemn history" and social history in Monaghan, D. (1981) (editor), Jane Austen in a Social Context (Macmillan, London).

Kent, C. (1988), Learning history with, and from, Jane Austen in Grey, J.D. (1988) (editor) Jane Austen's Beginnings. The Juvenilia and Lady Susan (UMI Research Press, New York).

Kerr, G.J.A. and Donnelly, T.A. (1982), Fiji in the Pacific. A History and Geography of Fiji (Jacaranda, Brisbane).

Kerr, R.A. (1994), Did Pinatubo send climate-warming gases into a dither? Science vol. 263, 1562.

Kerr, R.A. (1996a), It's official : first glimmer of greenhouse warming seen, Science vol. 270, 1585-1587.

Kerr, R.A. (1996b), 1995 the warmest year? Yes and no, Science vol. 171, 137-138.

Khan, A.M. (1969), The Transition in Bengal, 1756-1775. A Study of Saiyid Muhammad Reza Khan (Cambridge University Press, Cambridge).

Kidron, M. and Segal, R. (1987), The New Revised State of the World Atlas (Pan, London).

Kiernan, C. (1978), Calwell. A Personal and Political Biography (Nelson, Melbourne).

Kiernan, C. (1984), Daniel Mannix and Ireland (Alella, Morwell, Victoria).

Kimball, W.F. (1984) (editor), Churchill & Roosevelt. The Complete Correspondence Volume I. Alliance Emerging October 1933 - November 1942 (Princeton University Press, Princeton).

King, J.(1983), A Cartoon History of Australia. A Social History of Australia in Cartoons (Savvas Publishing, Adelaide).

Kinvig, C. (1992), River Kwai Railway. The Story of the Burma-Siam Railway (Brassey's, London).

Kipling, R. (1891), Life's Handicap (Oxford University Press, 1987).

Kipling, R. (1901), Kim (Macmillan, London, 1966).

Kipling, R. (1924), The Jungle Book (Macmillan, London).

Kipling, R. (1926), Just So Stories for Children (Macmillan, London).

Kipling, R. (1960), Soldiers Three; The Story of the Gadsbys; In Black and White (Macmillan, London).

Kipling, R. (1960), Plain Tales From the Hills (Macmillan, London).

Kirkham, M. (1983), Jane Austen, Feminism amd Fiction (Harvester Press, Sussex).

Kisch, E. (1969), Australian Landfall (translated by J. Fischer, I. Fitzgerald and K. Fitzgerald) (Macmillan, Melbourne).

Kitchen, M. (1990), A World In Flames. A Short History of the Second World War in Europe and Asia, 1939-1945 (Longman, London).

Knathcbull-Hugesson, E.H. (1884) (editor), Letters of Jane Austen.

Koch, C. (1986), The Doubleman (Triad Grafton, London).

Koch, C. (1987), Crossing the Gap. A Novelist's Essays (Hogarth Press, London).

Koestler, A. (1964), The Sleepwalkers (Penguin, London).

Koestler, A. (1968), Arrival and Departure (Bantam, New York).

Koestler, A. (1971), Anatomy of a canard, Sunday Times 4 July; reproduced in Koestler (1974), pp89-91.

Koestler, A. (1974), The Heel of Achilles (Picador, London).

Kolbert, K. (2014), The Sixth Extinction. An unnatural history, Bloomsbury, 2014.

Kopf, D. (1969), British Orientalism and the Bengal Renaissance. The Dynamics of Indian Modernization 1773-1835 (University of California Press, Los Angeles).

Koppel, G. (1988), The Religious Dimension of Jane Austen's Novels (UMI Research Press, Ann Arbor , London).

Kuhn, T.S. (1970), The Structure of Scientific Revolutions (University of Chicago Press, Chicago).

Kuhse, H. & Singer, P. (1985), Should the Baby Live? The Problem of Handicapped Infants (Oxford University Press, Oxford).

Kump, L.R. (1996), The physiology of the planet, Nature vol. 381, 111-112.

Kuznetsov, A. (Anatoli, A.) (1966), Babi Yar: A Document in the Form of a Novel (translated by D. Floyd, 1970) (Jonathan Cape, London).

Laffin, J. (1968), The Anatomy of Captivity (Abelard-Schuman, London).

Lambakis, S.J. (1993), Winston Churchill, Architect of Peace. A Study of Statesmanship and the Cold War (Greenwood Press, London).

Lane, M. (1984), Jane Austen's Family. Through Five Generations (Robert Hale, London).

Lane, M. (1986), Jane Austen's England (Robert Hale, London).

Lane, M. (1996), Jane Austen's World (The Book Company, Sydney).

Langer, W.L. (1952), An Encyclopaedia of World History (3rd edition) (G.G.Harrap, London).

Langmore, D. (1997), Glittering Surfaces. A Life of Maie Casey (Allen & Unwin, Sydney).

Lanyi, G.A. and McWilliams, W.C. (1966) (editors), Crisis and Continuity in World Politics. Readings in International Relations (Random House, New York).

Laqueur, W. (1982), The Terrible Secret. Suppression of the Truth About Hitler's "Final Solution" (Penguin, London).

Lascelles, M. (1939), Jane Austen and her Art (Oxford University Press, London).

Lauber, J. (1993), Jane Austen (Twayne Publishers, New York).

Lawford, J.P. (1976), Clive. Proconsul of India. A Biography (George Allen & Unwin, London).

Lawrence, D.H. (1950), Kangaroo (Penguin, London),

Lawrence, G. (1963), Indian Art. Paintings of the Himalayan States (Methuen, London).

Lawson, C. (1905), The Private Life of Warren Hastings. First Governor-General of India (Macmillan, New York).

Leadam, I.S. (1909), The History of England. From the Accession of Anne to the Death of George II (1702-1760) (London).

Leakey, R. and Lewin, R. (1996), The Sixth Extinction: Biodiversity and its Survival (Weidenfeld & Nicolson).

Leckie, R. (1987), Delivered from Evil. The Saga of World War II (Harper & Row, New York).

Lee, L.L. (1989), The War Years. A Global History of the Second World War (Unwin Hyman, Boston).

Le Faye, D. (1995), Jane Austen's Letters (Oxford University Press, Oxford, 3rd edition).

Leggett, J. (1990), Global Warming. The Greenpeace Report (Oxford University Press, Oxford).

Lehninger, A.L. (1975), Biochemistry. The Molecular Basis of Cell Structure and Function (Worth, New York, 2nd edition).

Lenghaus, C. (1993), Rabbit haemorrhagic disease: assessing the potential of a new virus to control wild rabbits in Australia in Cooke (1993), pp18-22.

Lenman, B.P. and Boyd, K. (1993) (editors), Chambers Dictionary of World History (Chambers, Edinburgh).

Leonardo, R.A. (1950), Lives of Master Surgeons (Froben Press, New York).

Lessing, D. (1983), Martha Quest (Granada, London).

Levey, M. (1962), A Concise History of Painting from Giotto to Cezanne (Thames & Hudson, London).

Levi, P. (1979), If This is a Man and The Truce (both translated by S. Woolf) (Penguin).

Lewin, R. (1980), The Chief. Field Marshall Lord Wavell Commander-in-Chief and Viceroy 1939-1947 (Hutchinson, London).

Lewis, B. (1964), The Western question in Asia and North Africa 1. The Near and Middle East 1900-45 in Thomson (1964), Chapter IX, pp207-209.

Lewis, S.L. and Maslin, M.A. (2018), The Human Planet. How we created the Anthropocene, Pelican, 2018.

Li, X., Maring, H., Savoie, D., Voss, K. and Prospero, J.M. (1996), Dominance of mineral dust in aerosol light-scattering in the North Atlantic trade winds, Nature vol. 380, 416-422.

Liang, C-T. (1972), General Stilwell in China 1942-1944: The Full Story (St. John's University Press).

Liddell, R. (1966), The Novels of Jane Austen (Longmans, London).

Liddell Hart, B.H. (1970), History of the Second World War (Cassell, London).

Lindqvist, S. (1992), Exterminate All the Brutes (Granta Books, London, 2002).

Lines, W.J. (1991), Taming the Great South Land. A History of the Conquest of Nature in Australia (Allen & Unwin, Sydney).

Little, J. H. (1915-1916), in Bengal Past and Present, July 1915 & January 1916; quoted by Einbinder (1972), pp184-187 & Dodwell (1963a), p156.

Litton, H. (1994), The Irish Famine, An Illustrated History (Wolfhound Press, Dublin).

Litz, A.W. (1965), A Study of her Artistic Development (Chatto & Windus, London).

Litton, H. (1994), The Irish Famine - An Illustrated History (Wolfhound Press).

Llewelyn, M. (1977), Jane Austen. A Character Study (William Kimber, London).

Lloyd, M. (1996) (editor), Turner (National Gallery of Australia, Melbourne).

Lockwood, D. (1962), I, the Aboriginal (Rigby, Sydney).

Lockwood, D. (1987), War on the Waterfront. Menzies, Japan and the Pig-ron Dispute (Hale & Iremonger, Melbourne).

Lodge, D. (1980), How Far Can You Go? (Penguin, London).

Lodge, D. (1981), The British Museum is Falling Down (Penguin, London).

Lodge, D. (1984), Small World (Penguin, London).

Lodge, D. (1986), Changing Places (Penguin, London).

Lodge, D (1988), Nice Work (Penguin, London).

Lodge, D. (1991) (editor), Jane Austen. Emma. A Casebook (Macmillan, London).

Lodge, D. (1992), Paradise News (Penguin, London).

Lodish, H., Baltimore, D., Berk, A., Zipursky, S.L., Matsudara, P. and Darnell, J. (1995), Molecular Cell Biology (3rd edition) (Scientific American Books, New York).

Longford, E. (1974), Winston Churchill (Sidgwick & Jackson, London).

Loveday, A. (1914), The History and Economics of Indian Famines (G. Bell & Sons, London)

Lovelock, J.E. (1979), Gaia, A New Look at Life on Earth (Oxford University Press, London).

Lovelock, J.E. (1988), The Ages of Gaia: A Biography of our Living Earth (Norton, New York).

Lovelock, J.E. (1991), Gaia, the Practical Science of Planetary Medicine (Gaia Books, London).

Lovelock, J.E. (2006), The Revenge of Gaia: Why the Earth is Fighting Back – and How We Can Still Save Humanity (Allen Lane, London).

Lovelock, J.E. (2007), Humans at War with Earth on Climate Change says James Lovelock, Royal Society Science News: http://royalsociety.org/news.asp?id=7226%20 .

Lovett, H.V. (1963a), District Administration in Bengal 1818-1858 in Dodwell (1963a), Volume VI, Chapter II.

Lovett, H.V.(1963b), The Development of Famine Policy in Dodwell (1963a), Volume VI, Chapter XVII, pp294-313.

Lukas, R.C. (1988), The Forgotten Holocaust. The Poles under German Occupation 1939-1944 (The University of Kentucky Press, Lexington).

Lurie, A. (1985), Foreign Affairs (Abacus, London).

Lyall, A. (1894), The Rise and Expansion of British Dominion in India (John Murray, London, 4th edition, 1910).

Lyall, A.C. (1907), Warren Hastings (Macmillan , London).

Lying By Omission: https://sites.google.com/site/mainstreammedialying/lying-by-omission .

Lyons, M.J. (1989), World War II. A Short History (Prentice Hall, New York).

Macaulay, T.B. (18xx) The History of England From the Accession of James II. Volumes I-VI (C.H. Firth, editor, Macmillan, London).

Macaulay, T.B. (1840), Lord Clive in Grieve (1974) (editor), Thomas Babington Macaulay. Critical and Historical Essays in 2 Volumes, Volume 1, pp479-549 (Dent, London).

Macaulay, T.B. (1841), Warren Hastings in Grieve (1974) (editor), Thomas Babington Macaulay. Critical and Historical Essays in 2 Volumes, Volume 1, pp550-649 (Dent, London).

MacDonagh, O. (1991), Jane Austen. Real and Imagined Worlds (Yale University Press, New Haven & London).

Macfarlane, I. (1975), The Black Hole or The Making of a Legend (George Allen & Unwin, London).

MacKenzie, D. (1995a), Polar meltdown fulfils worst prediction, New Scientist, 12 August, p4.

MacKenzie, D. (1995b), Ozone's future is up in the air, New Scientist, 16 December, p14.

Mackintosh, W. (1782) (nom de plume; Philip Francis printed, revised and may indeed have authored this as well the Letters of Junius), Travels in Europe, Asia and Africa (J. Murray, London); reproduced in part in Nair (1984), pp184-186.

Maclean, A. (1972), Captain Cook (Collins, London).

Macmillan, H. (1967), The Blast of War (Macmillan, London).

Magee, B. (1975), Popper (Fontana / Collins, London).

Mahapatra, J. (1988), Orissa in Embree, A.T. (1985a) (editor), Encyclopaedia of Asian History (Collier Macmillan, London) pp 157-158.
Mainstream Media Censorship:
https://sites.google.com/site/mainstreammediacensorship/home .

Mainstream Media Lying:
https://sites.google.com/site/mainstreammedialying/home .

Majumdar, R.C. (1969), The History and Culture of the Indian People. Struggle for Freedom (Bharatiya Vidya Bhavan, Bombay).

Majumdar, R.C. (1976), Renascent India. Frst Phase (G. Bharadwaj, Calcutta).

Majumdar, R.C. and Dighe, V.G. (1977) (editors), The History and Culture of the Indian People. The Maratha Supremacy (Bharatiya Vidya Bhavan, Bombay).

Maker, K.L. (1989), Pride and Prejudice. A Study in Artistic Economy (Twayne Publishers, Boston).

Malleson, G.B. (1885), Lord Clive and the Establishment of the English in India (Kaushal Prakashan, Delhi, 1985).

Malleson, G.B. (1894), Life of Warren Hastings First Governor-Gencral of India (Chapman & Hall, London).

Maloo, K. (1987), The History of Famines in Rajputana (1858-1900 A.D.) (Himanshu, New Delhi).

Malthus, T.R. (1798), An Essay on the Principle of Population as it Affects the Future Improvement of Society (anon.) (London).

Manabe, S. and Stouffer, R.J. (1995), Stimulation of abrupt climate change induced by freshwater input to the North Atlantic, Nature vol. 378, 165-167.

Manchester, W. (1983), The Last Lion: Winston Spencer Churchill. Visions of Glory: 1874-1932 (Michael Joseph, London).

Mann, T. (1924), The Magic Mountain (Der Zauberberg) (translated by H.T. Lowe-Porter) (Penguin, London, 1964).

Manning, O. (1983), The Rain Forest (Penguin, London).

Mansell, D. (1978), The Novels of Jane Austen. An Interpretation (Macmillan, London).

Marchand, L.A. (1971), Byron. A Portrait (Futura, London).

Marsani, R.P. (1960), Britain In India. An Account of British Rule in the Inhdian Subcontinent (Oxford University Press).

Marsden, C.R.S. (1988), The Dictionary of Outrageous Quotations (Xanadu, London).

Marshall, P.J. (1965), The Impeachment of Warren Hastings (Oxford University Press, London).

Marshall, P.J. (1976), East Indian Fortunes. The British in Bengal in the Eighteenth Century (Oxford University Press, London).

Marshall, P.J. (1987), Bengal: The British Bridgehead Eastern India 1740-1828 (Cambridge University Press, Cambridge).

Marshall, P.J. (1993) (editor), Trade and Conquest. Studies on the Rise of British Dominance in India (Variorum, London).

Martelli, G. (1962), Leopold to Lumumba. A History of the Belgian Congo 1877-1960 (Chapman & Hall, London).

Martin, B., Baker, C.M.A., Manwell, C. and Pugh, C. (1986) (editors), Intellectual Suppression. Australian Case Histories, Analysis and Responses (Angus & Robertson, Sydney & London).

Martin, E.C. (1929), The English Slave Trade and the African Settlement in Rose et al. (1929), The Cambridge History of the British Empire, Volume I, pp437-459.

Martin, J. (1991), Downing Street. The War Years (Bloomsbury, London).

Marx, K. (1853), The British Rule In India, New York Tribune, June 25 reproduced in Lanyi & McWilliams (1966), pp112-116.

Masani, R.P. (1960), Britain in India. An Account of British Rule in the Indian Subcontinent (Oxford University Press, London).

Masefield, G.B. (1963), Famine: Its Prevention and Relief (Oxford University Press, Oxford).

Mason, C. (2000), A Short History of Asia. Stone Age to 2000AD (Macmillan, London).

Mason, P. (1985), The Men Who Ruled India (Johnathan Cape, London).

Masood, E. (1996a) Climate panel confirms human role in warming, fights off oil states, Nature vol. 378, p424.

Masood, E. (1996b), Climate report subject to "scientific cleansing", Nature, vol. 381, p546.

Massolo, A. (1971), The Aborigines of South-Eastern Australia As They Were (Heinemann, Melbourne).

Mathews, C.K. and Van Holde, K.E. (1996), Biochemistry (2nd edition) (Benjamin / Cummings, New York).

Matthams, J. (1921), The Rabbit Pest in Australia (The Specialty Press, Melbourne).

Maugham, W.S. (1951), The Complete Short Stories (Heinemann, London).

McClelland, J. (1990), Conversations in Cabs (Penguin, Melbourne).

McCormick, J. (1987), George Santayana, a Biography (Alfred Knopf, New York).

McEvedy, C. (1984), The Century World History Factfinder (Century, London).

McFurlan, D. (1994) (editor), The Works of Robert Burns (Wordsworth Poetry Library).

McHenry, D.F. and Bird, K. (1977), Food Bungle in Bangladesh, Foreign Policy No. 27, Summer.

McInnes, A. (1969), The revolution and the people in Holmes, G. (1984) (editor), Britain After the Glorious Revolution (Macmillan, London), Chapter 3, pp30-94.

McKenzie, E.C. (1980), 14,000 Quips & Quotes (Wings Books, New York).

McKibben, W. (2007), Remember this: 350 parts per million, Washington Post, 28 December 2007: http://www.washingtonpost.com/wp-dyn/content/article/2007/12/27/AR2007122701942.html .

McMaster, J. (1976), Jane Austen's Achievement. Papers Delivered at the Jane Austen Bicentennial Conference at the University of Alberta (Macmillan, London).

McNeil, W.H. (1979), A World History (3rd edition, Oxford University Press, Oxford).

McQueen, H. (1971), A New Britannia (Penguin, Melbourne).

Mead, P. (1987), Orde Wingate and the Historians (Merlin Books, Braunton, Devon).

Mearns, H. (1899), Antigonish; see: https://missprint.wordpress.com/2017/04/21/poetically-speaking-about-antigonish-i-met-a-man-who-wasnt-there-by-hughes-mearns/ .

Mehra, P. (1985), A Dictionary of Modern Indian History 1707-1947 (Oxford University Press, Delhi).

Mehta, V. (1976), Mahatma Gandhi and His Apostles (Penguin, London).

Menzies, R.G. (1967), Afternoon Light. Some Memoirs of Men and Events (Penguin, Adelaide).

Merewether, F.H.S. (1985), A Tour Through the Famine Districts of India (Usha, Delhi).

Messenger, C. (1989), World War Two. Chronological Atlas. Who, Where, How and Why (Bloombury, London).

Mestel, R. (1995), "Doomsters" take on global bet, New Scientist 2 June, p5.

Michel, H. (1975), The Second World War (translated by D. Parmée) (Andre Deutsch, London).

Milford, H.S. (1963) (editor), The Poetical Works of William Cowper (Oxford University Press, London).

Miller, F.T. (1945), History of World War II (John Winston, Philadelphia).

Miller, H. (1992), Moloch or, This Gentile World (Grove Press, New York, published posthumously).

Misra, B.B. (1959), Central Administration of the East India Company 1773-1834 (Manchester University Press, Manchester).

Mitchell, G.J. (1991), World on Fire. Saving an Endangered Earth (Charles Scribner's Sons, New York).

Mitchell, J. (ca 1775), Journal of a Voyage to the East Indies in His Majesty's Ship Harwich of 50 Guns and 350 Men (transcribed by A. Cassells), Bengal Past & Present, Volume XLV, part II, pp79-119; reproduced in Nair (1984), pp93-102.

Mitchell, L. (1997) (editor), Distant Thunder summary, The Age Greenguide, 17-23 January, p37.

Mitford, N. (1970), Frederick the Great (Hamish Hamilton, London, 1988)

Moler, K.L. (1978), Jane Austen's Art of Allusion (University of Nebraska Press. Lincoln & London).

Monaghan, D. (1980), Jane Austen. Structure and Social Vision (Macmillan, London).

Monaghan, D. (1981) (editor), Jane Austen in a Social Context (Macmillan, London).

Monaghan, D. (1981), Jane Austen and the position of women in Monaghan, D. (1981) (editor), Jane Austen in a Social Context (Macmillan, London).

Moon, P. (1947), Warren Hastings and British India (Hodder & Staughton, London).

Moon, P. (1973) (editor), Wavell. The Viceroy's Journal (Oxford University Press, London).

Moon, P. (1989), The British Conquest and Dominion of India (Duckworth, London).

Mooneyham, L.G. (1988), Romance, Language and Education in Jane Austen's Novels (Macmillan, London).

Moore, J.H. (1981), Over-Sexed, Over-paid, Over-Here: Americans in Australia 1941-1945 (University of Queensland Press, Brisbane).

Moore, R.J. (1979), Churchill, Cripps and India 1939-1945 (Clarendon Press, London).

Moore, T.G. (1995), Why global warming would be good for you, The Public Interest vol. 118, 83-99.

More, P.E. (1905) (editor), The Complete Poetical Works of Byron (Riverside Press, Cambridge).

Morel, E.D. (1907), Red Rubber. The Story of the Rubber Slave Trade Flourishing on the Congo in the Year of Grace 1907 (T.Fisher Unwin, London).

Morgan, K.O. (1984), The Oxford Illustrated History of Britain (Oxford University Press, Oxford).

Morgan, S. (1980), In the Meantime. Character and Perception in Jane Austen's Fiction (University of Chicago Press, Chicago).

Morgan, S. (1987), My Place (Freemantle Arts Centre Press, Freemantle).

Morosi, J. (1975), Sex, Prejudice and Politics (Widescape, Melbourne).

Morris, D. (1967), The Naked Ape (Corgi, New York, 1972).

Morris, D. (1984), The Human Zoo (Triad / Panther, London).

Morris, I. (1987), Mr Collins Considered. Approaches to Jane Austen (Routledge & Kegan Paul).

Morris, J. (1972), The Final Solution Down Under Horizon vol . 14 (1), 60-71, reproduced in Chalk & Jonassohn (1990), pp204-222.

Morton, S.R. (1994), European Settlement and the Mammals of Arid Australia, chapter 8, pp 141-166 in Dovers (1994) (editor), Australian Environmental History: Essays and Cases (Oxford University Press, Melbourne).

Morwood, J. (1985), The Life and Works of Richard Brinsley Sheridan (Scottish Academic Press, Edinburgh).

Mosely, L. (1955), Gideon Goes to War (Charles Scribner's Sons, New York).

Mowat, C.L. (1968) (editor), The New Cambridge Modern History, Volume XII, The Shifting Balance of World Forces 1898-1945 [A second edition of Thomson (1964) (editor), the previous Volume XII, The Era of Violence.]

Muckherjee, M. (1991), Women Writers. Jane Austen (Macmillan, London).

Muckherjee, R. (1958), The Rise and Fall of the East India Company. A Sociological Appraisal (Veb Deutscher Verlag der Wissenschaften, Berlin).

Mudrick, M. (1968), Jane Austen. Irony as Defence and Discovery (University of California Press, Berkeley & Los Angeles).

Muhareb, R. (2018), The Universal Declaration of Human Rights and the ongoing Nakba: 70 years of exile, rights abuses and Israeli impunity. Al-Haq, 10 December 2018: https://www.alhaq.org/advocacy/6124.html .

Muir, R. (1929), British History. A Survey of the History of All the British Peoples (George Philip & Son, London).

Mulvaney, D.J. and White, J.P. (1987) (editors), Australians - A Historical Library (Fairfax, Syme & Weldon, Melbourne).

Murphy, F. (1972), Daniel Mannix. Archbishop of Melbourne 1917-1963 (The Poldinf Press, Melbourne).

Murray-Smith, S. (1984) (editor), The Dicitionary of Australian Quotations (Heinemann, Melbourne).

Muslim Holocaust Muslim Genocide: https://www.sites.google.com/site/muslimholocaustmuslimgenocide/home.

Myers, N. (1990), The Gaia Atlas of Future Worlds. Challenge and Opportunity in an Age of Change (Penguin Books, London).

Myer, V.G. (1980), Authors in Their Age. Jane Austen (Blackie, London).

Nagar, A. (1990), Hunger: A Novel (translated from Hindi by Sarala Jag Mohan) (Abhinov Publications, New Delhi).

Naipaul, S. (1970), Fireflies (Hamish Hamilton, London).

Naipaul, S. (1970), The Chip-Chip Gatherers (Hamish Hamilton, London).

Naipaul, S. (1983), A Hot Country (Hamish Hamilton, London).

Naipaul, S. (1985), Beyond the Dragon's Mouth (Abacus, London).

Naipaul, S. (1986), An Unfinished Journey (Abacus, London).

Naipaul, V.S. (1957), The Mystic Masseur (Pelican, London).

Naipaul, V.S. (1958), The Suffrage of Elvira (Pelican, London).

Naipaul, V.S. (1959), Miguel Street (Pelican, London).

Naipaul, V.S. (1961), House for Mr Biswas (Pelican, London).

Naipaul, V.S. (1962), The Middle Passage (Pelican, London).

Naipaul, V.S. (1963), Mr Stone and the Knights Companion (Pelican, London).

Naipaul, V.S. (1964), An Area of Darkness (Pelican, London).

Naipaul, V.S. (1967), The Mimic Men (Pelican, London).

Naipaul, V.S. (1967), A Flag on the Island (Pelican, London).

Naipaul, V.S. (1969), The Loss of El Dorado (Pelican, London)

Naipaul, V.S. (1971), In a Free State (Pelican, London).

Naipaul, V.S. (1972), The Overcrowded Barracoon (Pelican, London).

Naipaul, V.S. (1975), Guerrillas (Pelican, London).

Naipaul, V.S. (1977), A Wounded Civilization (Pelican, London).

Naipaul, V.S. (1991), India. A Million Mutinies Now (Heinemann, London).

Nair, P.T. (1984), Calcutta in the 18th Century. Impressions of Travellers (Firma Klm, Calcutta).

Narayan, T.G. (1944), Famine Over Bengal (The Book Company, Calcutta).

Nardin, J. (1973), Those Elegant Decorums. The Concept of Propriety in Jane Austen's Novels (State University of New York Press, Albany).

NASA Goddard Institute for Space Studies (GISS) (2007), Research finds that Earth's climate is approaching "dangerous" point, 30 May 2007: http://www.giss.nasa.gov/research/news/20070530/ .

Natkiel, R., Sommerville, D. and Westwood, J.N. (1982), Atlas of 20th Century History (Hamlyn-Bison, London).

Nelson, H. (1976), Black White & Gold. Goldmining in Papua New Guinea 1878-1950 (Australian National University Press, Canberra).

Netting, R.McC. (1993), Smallholders, Householders. Farm Families and the Ecology of Intensive, Sustainable Agriculture (Stanford University Press, Stanford).

Newman, L.F. (1990) (editor), Hunger in History. Food Shortages, Poverty and Deprivation (Basil Blackwell, London).

News.com (2008), George Bush, White House told 935 lies after September 11, News.com, January : http://www.news.com.au/story/0,23599,23098129-401,00.html

Newsom, H.E. (1996), Martians in a deep freeze, Nature vol. 379, 205-206.

Nicolson, N. (1991), The World of Jane Austen (Weidenfeld & Nicolson, London).

Nokes, D. (1997), Jane Austen (Fourth Estate, London).

Nolan, E.H. (18xx), The Illustrated History of the British Empire in India and the East from the Earliest Times to the Suppression of the Sepoy Mutiny in 1859 (James Virtue, London).

Nordhjem, B. (1987), What Fiction Means. An Inquiry into the Nature of Fiction With a Study of Three Comic Novels (Publication of the Department of English, University

Normile, D. (1996), Polar regions give cold shoulder to theories, Science vol. 270, 1566.

Norton, F. (1975), Aboriginal Art (The Western Australian Art Gallery, Perth).

Norris, K. (1990), Australia's Heritage Sketchbook (PR Books, Sydney).

Nuclear Weapons Ban, End Poverty & Reverse Climate Change, 300.org: https://sites.google.com/site/300orgsite/nuclear-weapons-ban .

Oldmark, J. (1981), An Understanding of Jane Austen's Novels. Character, Value and Ironic Perspective (Basil Blackwell, Oxford).

O'Neill, J. (1971), Critics on Jane Austen. Readings in Literary Criticism (George Allen & Unwin, London).

O'Neill, J.E. and Krauskopf, R.W. (1976) (editors), World War II.. An Account of its Documents (Harvard University Press, Washington).

One-state solution, unitary state, bi-national state for a democratic, equal rights, post-apartheid Palestine
: https://sites.google.com/site/boycottapartheidisrael/one-state-solution
.

Oxfam (2021), A deadly virus: 5 shocking facts about global extreme inequality, https://www.oxfam.org/en/5-shocking-facts-about-extreme-global-inequality-and-how-even-it .

Page, N. (1970), The Language of Jane Austen (Basil Blackwell, Oxford).

Pal, P. (1988), A Pot-Pourri of Indian Art (Marg Publications, Calcutta).
Palestinian Genocide:
https://sites.google.com/site/palestiniangenocide/ .

Palmer, A.W. (1973), A Dictionary of Modern History 1789-1945 (Penguin, London).

Palmer, A. (1992), The Penguin Dictionary of Twentieth Century History 1900-1991

(4th edition) (Penguin, London).

Palmer, B.J. (1981) (editor), The Concise Oxford Dictionary of Quotations (2nd edition) (Oxford University Press, Oxford).

Paris, B.J. (1978), Character and Conflict in Jane Austen's Novels. A Psychological Approach (The Harvester Press, Brighton).

Parker, R.A.C. (1987), Struggle for Survival. The History of the Second World War (Oxford University Press, Oxford).

Parkes, J. (1964), A History of the Jewish People (Penguin, London).

Parliament of the Commonwealth of Australia (1995), Inquiry into the Proposal to Drain and Restore Lake Pedder (Australian Government, Canberra).

Parv, V. (1984), The Changing Face of Australia. The Impact of 200 Years of Change on Our Environment (Bay Books, Sydney).

Pascoe, L.C. (1991) (editor), Encyclopaedia of Dates and Events (3rd edition) (Hodder & Staughton, London).

Payne, R. (1973), The Life and Death of Adolph Hitler (Johnathan Cape, London).

Pearce, F. (1995a), Greenhouse warming goes to market, New Scientist January 21, 4.

Pearce, F. (1995b), Don't stop talking about tomorrow, New Scientist April 15, 4.

Pearce, F. (1995c), The Costa del Carbon Dioxide, New Scientist May 6, 14-15.

Pearl, C. (1983), The Dunera Scandal (Angus & Robertson, Sydney).

Pearson, J. (1991), The Private Lives Of Winston Churchill (Simon & Schuster, New York).

Pelling, H. (1972), Britain and the Second World War (Collins, London).

Pelling, H. (1974), Winston Churchill (Macmillan, London).

Perkins, K. (1968), Menzies. Last of the Queen's Men (Rigby, Adelaide).

Philips, C.H. (1961), The East India Company 1784-1834 (Indian Branch Oxford University Press, London).

Phillips, C.H. (1964), The Western question in Asia and the North Africa, 1900-45 2. India in Thomson (1964), Chapter IX, pp212-218.

Phillips, K.C. (1970), Jane Austen's English (Andre Deutsch, London).

Pickering, K.T. & Owen, L.A. (1994), An Introduction to Global Environmental Issues (Routledge, London).

Piggott, P. (1979), The Innocent Diversion. A Study of Music in the Life and Writings of Jane Austen (Clover Hill, London).

Piketty, T. (2014), Capital in the Twenty-First Century, Harvard University Press, 2014.

Piketty, T. (2021), Time for Socialism, Yale University Press, 2021.

Pinion, F.B. (1975), A Jane Austen Companion. A Critical Survey and Reference Book (Macmillan, London).

Pinter, H. (2005), Art, Truth and Politics, Countercurrents: http://www.countercurrents.org/arts-pinter081205.htm .

Plumb, J.H. (1950), England in the Eighteenth Century (Penguin, London, 1957).

Plumb, J.H. (1963), England in the Eighteenth Century (Penguin Books, London).

Pollard, A.F. (1912), The History of England: A Study in Political Evolution, 55 B.C. - A.D. 1911 (Oxford University Press, London).

Pollard, D. (1988), Give & Take. The Losing Partnership in Aboriginal Poverty (Hale & Iremonger, Sydney).

Polowetzky, N. (1989) (editor), World War II. A 50th Anniversary History by the Writers and Photographers of the Associated Press (Robert Hale, London).

Polya, G. (1945), How to Solve It (Princeton University Press, Princeton; Doubleday Anchor, New York, Second edition, 1957).

Polya, G.M. (1995a), The Forgotten Holocaust - The 1943 Bengal Famine (version tabled in the Australian Senate by Senator Christobel Chamarette).

Polya, G.M. (1995b), The Famine of History: Bengal 1943, International Network on Holocaust and Genocide vol.10, 10-15.

Polya, G.M. (1998a), Jane Austen and the Black Hole of British History. Colonial rapacity, holocaust denial and the crisis in biological sustainability (First edition, Polya, Melbourne).

Polya, G.M. (1998b), Holocaust denial in an open society and the crisis in biological sustainability. Australian Humanist, Spring 1998, pp6-7.

Polya, G.M. (1999a), Austenizing British Atrocities in India, Sulekha web magazine, 5 May [see: http://www.sulekha.com/blogs/blogdisplay.aspx?cid=748 and

http://gideon.sulekha.com/blog/post/1999/05/austenizing-of-british-atrocities-in-india.htm].

Polya, G.M. (1999b), ABC Ockham's razor broadcast, 21 February, Bengali famine [see: http://www.abc.net.au/rn/science/ockham/stories/s19040.htm].

Polya, G.M. (1999c), Bengali famine. Austenizing history, holocaust denial and the crisis in biological sustainability. Tirra Lirra, Vol. 9 (3), pp37-41.

Polya, G.M. (2001a). Dr Gideon Maxwell Polya, Australia, in Jane Austen Antipodean Views (eds, S. Fullerton and A. Harbers), pp81-85 (Wellington Lane, Sydney).

Polya, G.M. (2001b). Jane Austen, Sense and Sensibility and truth in an open society. Observations, vol.1 (4), 75-83.

Polya, G.M. (2003a), Biochemical Targets of Plant Bioactive Compounds. A Pharmacological Guide to Sites of Action and Biological Effects (Taylor & Francis, London).

Polya, G.M. (2003b), John Bela Polya (1914-1992), organic chemist and academic in Elias & Elias (2003), pp 201-202.

Polya, G. (2004), US Profits from jihadist terrorism, Countercurrents, 19 November [see: http://countercurrents.org/us-polya191104.htm].

Polya, G.M. (2005a), Jane Austen and Blog [see: http://janeaustenand.blogspot.com/].

Polya, G.M. (2005b), Global Avoidable Mortality Blog [see: http://globalavoidablemortality.blogspot.com/].

Polya, G (2005c), Gideon Polya Website [see:

http://members.optusnet.com.au/~gpolya/links.html].

Polya, G.M. (2005d), New Orleans tragedy exposes US racism & passive mass murder, MWC News, 5 September 2005: http://mwcnews.net/content/view/1256/26/ .

Polya, G.M. (2005e), Search for Gideon Polya on Rumor Mill News [see: http://rumormillnews.com].

Polya, G.M. (2005f), Search the Web and websites for Gideon Polya on Al-Jazeerah, Bellaciao, Coalitionforfreethoughtinmedia, Countercurrents, Media Monitors, MWC News, News Central Asia, NASPIR, Crosswire and Newsvine.

Polya, G.M. (2005g), Submission to Australian Senate Committee Inquiry on proposed Anti-Terror Laws [see submission #112: http://www.aph.gov.au/senate/committee/index.htm].

Polya (2005h), Slies, lies and media breakthrough over 9/11, MWC News [see: http://www.mwcnews.net/index.php].

Polya, G.M. (2005i), The Forgotten Holocaust – the 1943/1944 Bengal famine, Global Avoidable Mortality Blog [see: http://globalavoidablemortality.blogspot.com/2005/07/forgotten-holocaust-194344-bengal.html].

Polya, G. (2005j), Australian complicity in Iraq mass mortality, ABC Radio National, Ockham's Razor, 28 August 2005 [see: http://www.abc.net.au/rn/science/ockham/stories/s1445960.htm].

Polya, G. (2005k), Afghan opium and 50,000 US deaths, Countercurrents, 28 October [see: http://www.countercurrents.org/us-polya281005.htm].

Polya, G. (2005l), MWC political editor files formal complaint. Formal complaint to ICC over Coalition war crimes: http://mwcnews.net/content/view/3087/247/ .

Polya, G. (2005m), Indict the Coalition Governments: http://www.countercurrents.org/us-polya211205.htm .

Polya, G.M. (2006a), Soviet rule, Cold War, radiation and excess deaths of Hungarians, Austrians, Germans, Czechs, Bulgarians, Estonians, Latvians and Ukrainians, Global Avoidable Mortality Blog [see: http://globalavoidablemortality.blogspot.com/2006/01/soviet-rule-cold-war-radiation-excess.html].

Polya, G. (2006b), Cricket & Iraq – exposing politically correct Australian racism [see: http://www.countercurrents.org/au-polya060106.htmhttp://www.countercurrents.org/au-polya060106.htm].

Polya, G. (2006c), Layperson's Guide to Counting Iraq Deaths, MWC News, April: http://mwcnews.net/content/view/5872/26/ .

Polya, G. (2006d), Iraq and Afghanistan: how many dying? In Coates, K. (2006), editor, Haditha Ethics. From Iraq to Iran? (Spokesman, Bertrand Russel Peace Foundation, Nottingham, UK), pp 78-80.

Polya, G. (2007a), Body Count. Global avoidable mortality since 1950 (First edition, GM Polya, Melbourne).

Polya, G. (2007b), US Terror & Occupation. War crimes & huge infant deaths, MWC News, January: http://mwcnews.net/content/view/11968/42/ .

Polya, G. (2007c), Were US and Israel behind the 9/11? MWC News, December: http://mwcnews.net/content/view/18569/26/ .

Polya, G. (2007d), Summary of the Summary of the 2007 IPCC AR4 Synthesis Report, Green Blog: http://green-blog.org/2007/11/21/summary-of-the-summary-of-the-2007-ipcc-ar4-synthesis-report/ .

Polya, G. (2007e), Climate criminal, Bali-wrecker Rudd Australia faces World sanctions, Green Blog, 14 December 2007: http://green-blog.org/2007/12/14/climate-criminal-bali-wrecker-rudd-australia-faces-world-sanctions/ .

Polya, G. (2007f), Climate criminals & climate genocide. Anglo-Celtia threatens final Bengali Holocaust, MWC News, 30 March 2007: http://mwcnews.net/content/view/13576/26/ .

Polya, G. (2007g), Solar energy & the end of war. US balloon technology to slash solar energy cost 90% by 2010, MWC News, 10 December 2007: http://mwcnews.net/content/view/18667/42/ .

Polya, G. (1999-2008) – articles in Sulekha: http://gideon.sulekha.com/blog/posts.htm .

Polya, G. (2005-2008) – articles in MWC News: http://mwcnews.net/content/view/1375/247/ .

Polya, G. (2008a) World food price crisis and global famine from biofuel perversion, climate change and globalization, Green-Blog, April: http://green-blog.org/2008/04/04/world-food-price-crisis-and-global-famine-from-biofuel-perversion-climate-change-and-globalization/ .

Polya, G. (2008b), Global food crisis. US Biofuel & CO2 threaten billions, MWC News, March: http://mwcnews.net/content/view/21277/42/ .

Polya, G. (2008c), World Food Price Crisis -Genocidal UK, EU, US Biofuel Perversion Threatens Billions, Countercurrents, March: http://www.countercurrents.org/polya310308.htm .

Polya, G. (2008d), Climate Emergency, Sustainability Emergency: http://climateemergency.blogspot.com/ .

Polya, G. (2008e), Risk Management, Science & Denial:

http://rationalriskmanagement.blogspot.com/ .

Polya, G. (2008f), Rudd Australia report Card: http://ruddaustraliareportcard.blogspot.com/ .

Polya, G. (2008g), Australia 2020 Ideas: http://australia2020ideas.blogspot.com/ .

Polya, G. (2008h), Book Review: Climate Code Red – the Case for a Sustainability Emergency, Green-Blog: http://green-blog.org/2008/03/07/book-review-climate-code-red-the-case-for-a-sustainability-emergency/ .

Polya, G.(2008i), Formal Complaint to the International Criminal Court (ICC) over Australia and Aboriginal, Iraqi, Afghan and Climate Genocides:

http://climateemergency.blogspot.com/2008/02/formal-complaint-to-international.html .

Polya, G. (2008j), ICC complaint over Australia and Aboriginal, Iraqi, Afghan and Climate Genocides, Countercurrents: http://www.countercurrents.org/polya030308.htm .

Polya, G. (2008k), Iraqi Genocide, Brussells Tribunal: http://www.brusselstribunal.org/Messages190308.htm#polya .

Polya, G. (2008l), Top US lawyer and UNICEF reveal Afghan Genocide, Countercurrents:

http://www.countercurrents.org/polya080208.htm .

Polya, G. (2008m), Palestinian, Iraqi, Afghan, Biofuel and Climate Genocide – silence kills and silence is complicity, Liberalati: http://www.liberalati.com/?q=node/261 .

Polya, G. (2008n), Biofuel famine, biofuel genocide and the global food price crisis: http://climateemergency.blogspot.com/2008/04/biofuel-famine-biofuel-genocide-and.html .

Polya, G. (2008o), What we could do to save the planet. New Year's resolutions, MWC News 1 January 2008: http://mwcnews.net/content/view/19121/42/ .

Polya, G. (2008p), The Sounds of Silence, 2008 Olympic Hype. Holocaust and Genocide Denial, MWC News, 12 August 2008: http://mwcnews.net/content/view/24575/42/ .

Polya, G. (2008q), Jane Austen and the Black Hole of British History. Colonial rapacity, holocaust denial and the crisis in biological sustainability (Second edition, Polya, Melbourne).

Polya, G. (2009), Universal Declaration of Human Rights & Palestinians. Apartheid Israel violates ALL Palestinian Human Rights", Palestine Genocide Essays, 24 January 2009: https://sites.google.com/site/palestinegenocideessays/universal-declaration-of-human-rights-palestinians .

Polya, G.M. (2011a), Australia and Britain killed 6-7 Million Indians in WW2 Bengal Famine, Countercurrents, 29 September 2011: http://www.countercurrents.org/polya290911.htm .

Polya, G.M. (2011b), Economist Mahima Khanna, Cambridge Stevenson Prize And Dire Indian Poverty, Countercurrents, 20 November 2011: https://countercurrents.org/polya201111.htm .

Polya, G. (2012), Book Review: "Social Humanism. A New Metaphysics" By Brian Ellis, Countercurrents, 19 August 2012: https://countercurrents.org/polya190812.htm .

Polya, G. (2013), The US Has Invaded 70 Nations Since 1776 – Make 4 July Independence From America Day, Countercurrents, 5 July: http://www.countercurrents.org/polya050713.htm .

Polya, M. (2014a), 4 % Annual Global Wealth Tax to stop the 17 million deaths annually, Countercurrents, 27 June 2014: https://www.countercurrents.org/polya270614.htm .

Polya, G. (2014b), Refutation of Mainstream-accepted racist Zionist lies behind Israel's Gaza Massacres and Palestinian Genocide,

Countercurrents, 26 July, 2014:
https://www.countercurrents.org/polya260714.htm .

Polya, G. (2015a), Paris atrocity context: 27 million Muslim avoidable
deaths from imposed deprivation in 20 countries violated by the US
Alliance since 9-11, Countercurrents, 22 November 2015:
https://countercurrents.org/polya221115.htm .

Polya, G. (2015b), Polya's 3 Laws Of Economics Expose Deadly,
Dishonest And Terminal Neoliberal Capitalism, Countercurrents, 17
October 2015: https://countercurrents.org/polya171015.htm .

Polya, G. (2017a), Mainstream media: fake news through lying by
omission, MWC News, 1 April 2017:
https://sites.google.com/site/mainstreammedialying/2017-04-01 .

Polya, G. (2017b), Dual Israeli citizenship & Zionist perversion of
America, Australia, India & Humanity, Countercurrents, 30 July 2017:
https://countercurrents.org/2017/07/dual-israeli-citizenship-zionist-
perversion-of-america-australia-india-humanity/ .
Polya, G.M. (2017c), Review: "Inglorious Empire. What the British
did to India" by Shashi Tharoor, Countercurrents, 8 September 2017:
http://www.countercurrents.org/2017/09/08/review-inglorious-empire-
what-the-british-did-to-india-by-shashi-tharoor/ .
Polya, G. (2018a), China's Tibet health success versus passive mass
murder of Afghan women and children by US Alliance', Global
Research, 7 January 2018: https://www.globalresearch.ca/chinas-tibet-
health-success-versus-passive-mass-murder-of-afghan-women-and-
children-by-us-alliance/5625169 .

Polya, G. (2018b), Zionist subversion, Mainstream media censorship,
Countercurrents, 9 March 2018:
https://countercurrents.org/2018/03/zionist-subversion-mainstream-
media-censorship/ .
Polya, G.M. (2018c), Richard Attenborough's UK "Gandhi" movie
ignored UK's WW2 Bengali Holocaust, Countercurrents, 15 March

2018: https://countercurrents.org/2018/03/richard-attenboroughs-uk-gandhi-movie-ignored-uks-ww2-bengali-holocaust/ .

Polya, G. (2018d), Google censors anti-racist Jews opposing Apartheid Israeli state terrorism & Palestinina Genocide, Countercurrents, 14 December: https://countercurrents.org/2018/12/google-censors-anti-racist-jews-opposing-apartheid-israeli-state-terrorism-palestinian-genocide/ .

Polya, G.M. (2020a), US-imposed Post-9/11 Muslim Holocaust and Muslim Genocide, Korsgaard Publishing, Germany).

Polya, G.M. (2020b), Climate Crisis, Climate Genocide & Solutions (Korsgaard Publishing, Germany).

Polya, G.M. (2021a), Body Count. Global Avoidable Mortality Since 1950 (Second edition, Korsgaard Publishing, Germany).

Polya,G (2021b), Australia must stop Zionist subversion and join the World in comprehensive Boycotts, Divestment and Sanctions (BDS) against Apartheid Israel and all its supporters, Subversion of Australia, 15 April 2021: https://sites.google.com/site/subversionofaustralia/2021-04-15 .

Polya, G. (2021c), A shocking list of 52 Zionist- & Apartheid Israeli-Nazi Germany comparisons, Countercurrents, 7 August 2021: https://countercurrents.org/2021/08/a-shocking-list-of-52-zionist-apartheid-israeli-nazi-germany-comparisons/ .

Polya, G. (2021d), Afghan Holocaust – the Awful Truth versus US Alliance lies, Countercurrents, 22 August 2021: https://countercurrents.org/2021/08/afghan-holocaust-the-awful-truth-versus-us-alliance-lies/ .

Polya, G. (2021e), Letter to Australian Labor MPs exposes Australian crimes & IHRA anti-Semitism, Countercurrents, 9 October 2021:

https://countercurrents.org/2021/10/letter-to-australian-labor-mps-exposes-australian-crimes-ihra-anti-semitism/ .

Gideon Polya, G. (2021f), Australia violates all Indo-Pacific countries, Stop state terrorism, 9 December 2021: https://sites.google.com/site/stopstateterrorism/2021-12-09-australia-violates-all-indo-pacific-countries .

Polya, G. (2021g), AUKUS & Quad in context: Australia violates all Indo-Pacific countries, Countercurrents, 9 December 2021: https://countercurrents.org/2021/12/aukus-quad-in-context-australia-violates-all-indo-pacific-countries/ .

Polya, G. (2022a), Zionist-subverted West ignores Desmond Tutu's opposition to Israeli Apartheid", Countercurrents, 2 January 2022: https://countercurrents.org/2022/01/zionist-subverted-west-ignores-desmond-tutus-opposition-to-israeli-apartheid/ .

Polya, G. (2022b), Zionist-subverted America: Jewish Zionists are One Third of the Biden Cabinet, Countercurrents, 27 January 2022: https://countercurrents.org/2022/01/zionist-subverted-america-jewish-zionists-are-one-third-of-the-biden-cabinet/ .

Polya, G (2022c), Amnesty's Israeli apartheid report versus Zionist, IHRA & US lies, Countercurrents, 6 February 2022: https://countercurrents.org/2022/02/amnestys-israeli-apartheid-report-versus-zionist-ihra-us-lies/ .

Polya, G. (2022d), West Rightly Supports Ukraine But Ignores Brutally Occupied Palestine, Countercurrents, 1 March 2022: https://countercurrents.org/2022/03/west-rightly-supports-ukraine-but-ignores-brutally-occupied-palestine/ .

Polya, G.M. (2022e), Review: "Lies and falsehoods" by Philip Keane: Australian Coalition Government lies, Countercurrents, 10 March 2022: https://countercurrents.org/2022/03/review-lies-and-falsehoods-by-bernard-keane-australian-coalition-government-lies/ .

Polya, J. (1941), The Story of Medical Science (translated from Hungarian by M. Polya, Canberra, 1996).

Polya, J.B. (1955), The State and the University, Australian Journal of Science vol. 18, pp1-8.

Polya, J.B. (1962a), The academic turmoil in Tasmania, Australian Quarterly vol. 34, pp27-35.

Polya, J.B. (1962b), The University of Tasmania. Scandal or Tragedy? Vestes vol. 5, 23-28.

Polya, J.B. (1964), Are we safe? (Cheshire, Melbourne).

Polya. J.B. (1986), Autobiography (unpublished manuscript, Melbourne).

Polya, J.B. and Solomon, R.J. (1996), Dreyfus in Australia (Fast Books, Sydney).

Ponting, C. (2000), World History. A new perspective (Chatto & Windus, London).

Pope Francis Encyclical Letter "Laudato si", 2015: http://w2.vatican.va/content/francesco/en/encyclicals/documents/papa-francesco_20150524_enciclica-laudato-si.html .

Popper, K. (1976), Unended Quest. An Intellectual Biography (Fontana Collins, Glasgow).

Porritt, J. (1991) (editor), Save the Earth (Angus, Sydney).

Porter, B. (1984), The Lion's Share (Longman, London).

Postgate, R. (1949) (editor), The Conversations of Dr. Johnson, Extracted From the Life by James Boswell (John Lehmann, London).

Potts, E.D. and Potts, A. (1985), Yanks Down Under 1941-45 (Oxford University Press, London).

Powell, V. (1993), A Jane Austen Compendium. The Six Major Novels (Heinemann, London).

Prange, G.W. (1982), At Dawn We Slept. The Untold Story of Pearl Harbor (Michael Joseph, London).

Prather, M., Midgley, P,, Rowland, F.S. and Skolarski, R. (1996), The ozone layer: the road not taken, Nature, Volume 381, 551-554.

Pratt, A. (1934), The Centenary History of Victoria (Robertson & Mullens, Melbourne).

Prebble, J. (1963), The Highland Clearances (Secker & Warburg, London).

Prior, R. and Wilson, T. (1994), The Churchill Industry, Quadrant, November, pp38-42.

Pullan, R. (1984), Guilty Secrets. Free Speech In Australia (Methuen, Sydney).

Pullan, R. (1986), Readers Digest to the Coast of Victoria, Tasmania and South Australia (Readers Digest, Sydney).

Pybus, C. (1993), Gross Moral Turpitude. The Orr Case Reconsidered (Heinemann, Melbourne)

Rankin, R. (1990), Classic Wild Walks of Australia (Rankin Publishers, Brisbane).

Rawn, J.D. (1989), Biochemistry (Neil Patterson, Burlington).

Ray, Satyajit (1973), director, Distant Thunder, a movie.

Rayner, R.M. (1948), A Concise History of England (Longmans, Green & Co, London).

Read, H. (1965), Vermeer, Volume 2 in The Masters (J. Rothenstein, editor) (Purnell & Sons, Bristol).

Reason, J. (2000), Human error: models and management, British Medical Journal, vol. 320, pp768-770.

Redclift, M. (1987), Sustainable Development. Exploring the Contradictions (Methuen, London).

Rees, J. (1976), Jane Austen . Woman and Writer (Robert Hale, London; St Martin's Press, New York).

Reid, C.L (1947), Commerce and Conquest. The Story of the Honourable East India Company (C & J Temple, London).

Reilly, J. (1994), Crops and climate change, Nature vol. 367, 118-119.

Reilly, R. (1978), Pitt the Younger 1759-1806 (Cassell, London).

Renouvin, P. (1969), World War II and its Origins. International Relations, 1929-1945 (translated by R. I. Hall) (Harper & Row, New York).

Report Genocide: https://sites.google.com/site/reportgenocide/ .

Reynolds, G. (1965), John Constable 1776-1837, The Masters Vol. 61 (Purnell & Sons, Bristol).

Reynolds, H. (1990), The Other Side of the Frontier. Aboriginal Resistance to the European Invasion of Australia (Penguin, Melbourne).

Rhodes, R.C. (1962) (editor), The Plays and Poems of Richard Brinsley Sheridan (Russell & Russell, New York).

Richmond, H. (1931), The Navy in India 1763-1783 (Ernest Benn, London).

Richmond, H. (1946), Statesman and Sea Power (Oxford University Press, London).

Roberts, C. and Roberts, D. (1980), A History of England (London).

Roberts, P.E. (1909a), The English and French in India in Ward et al. (1909), Chapter XV, part 2, pp529-550.

Roberts, P.E. (1909b), Clive and Warren Hastings in Ward et al. (1909), Chapter XV, part 3, pp551-585.

Roberts, P.E. (1958), History of British India Under the Company and Under the Crown (Oxford University Press, Oxford, 3rd edition).

Roberts, P.E. (1963a), The East India Company and the State 1772-1786 in Dodwell (1963a), Volume V, Chapter X, pp181-204.

Roberts, P.E. (1963b), The Early Reforms of Warren Hastings in Bengal in Dodwell (1963a), Volume V, Chapter XI, pp205-214.

Roberts, W. (1979), Jane Austen and the Revolution (Macmillan, London).

Robertson, R.T. and Tamanisau, A. (1988) Fiji. Shattered Coups (Pluto Press, Sydney).

Robinson, F. (1989), The Cambridge Encyclopaedia of India, Pakistan, Bangladesh, Sri Lanka, Nepal, Bhutan and the Maldives (Cambridge University Press, Cambridge).

Robinson, F. and York, B. (1977), The Black Resistance. An Introduction to the History of the Aboriginal Struggle Against British Colonialism (Widescope, Melbourne).

Rolls, E. (1994), More a New Planet than a New Continent in Dovers, S. (1994) (editor), Australian Environmental History. Essays and Cases (Oxford University Press, Oxford), chapter 2, pp22-36.

Romanus, C.F. and Sutherland, R. (1956), United States Army in World War II. China-Burma-India Theater. Stilwell's Command Problems (Department of the Army, Washington).

Rose, J.H. (1925), A Short Life of William Pitt (G.Bell, London).

Rose, J.H., Newton, A.P. and Benians, E.A. (1929), The Cambridge History of the British Empire, Volume 1 (Cambridge University Press, Cambridge).

Rose, N. (1995), Churchill. An Unruly Life (Simon & Schuster, London).

Rosebery, Lord (1902), Pitt (Macmillan, London).

Rosenberger, W. and Tobin, H.C. (1943) (editors), Keesing's Contemporary Archives, Vol. 4 (1940-1943) (Keesing's Publications, London).

Rosenberger, W. and Tobin, H.C. (1945) (editors), Keesing's Contemporary Archives, Vol. 5 (1943-1945) (Keesing's Publications, London).

Rosenberger, W. and Tobin, H.C. (1948) (editors), Keesing's Contemporary Archives, Vol. 6 (1945-1948) (Keesing's Publications, London).

Rosenzweig, C. and Parry, M.L. (1994), Potential impact of climate change on world food supply, Nature vol. 367, 133-138.

Ross, J. (1990) (editor), Chronicle of the 20th Century (Chronicle, Melbourne).

Ross, J. (1993) (editor), Chronicle of Australia (Chronicle, Melbourne).

Rothenstein, J. (1965), Joseph Turner 1775-1851, The Masters Vol. 12 (Purnell & Sons, Bristol).

Royal Society (UK) (2007a), Climate change controversies: a simple guide: http://royalsociety.org/page.asp?id=6229 .

Royal Society (2007b), Humans at war with earth on climate change, says James Lovelock, 29 October, 2007: http://royalsociety.org/news.asp?id=7226 .

Rubinstein, E. (1969) (editor), Twentieth Century Interpretations of Pride and Prejudice. A Collection of Critical Essays (Prentice-Hall, Englewood Cliffs).

Ruoff, G.W. (1992), Jane Austen's Sense and Sensibility (Harvester Wheatsheaf, New York).

Rusbridger, J. and Nave, E. (1991), Betrayal at Pearl Harbor. How Churchill Lured Roosevelt into World War II (Summit, New York).

Russell, Lord (1956), The Scourge of the Swastika. A Short History of Nazi War Crimes (Transworld, London).

Ryan, J. and Akerman, K. (198x), Images of Power. Aboriginal Art of the Kimberley (National Gallery of Victoria).

Sachs, J. (2005), The End of Poverty. How we can make it happen in our lifetime (Penguin, London).

Sachs, W. (1993) (editor), Global Ecology. A New Arena of Political Conflict (Zed Books, London).

Santamaria, B.A. (1984), Daniel Mannix. The Quality of Leadership (Melbourne University Press, Melbourne).

Sanatayana, G. (ca 1950), Lucifer, A Theological Tragedy (New York).

Santayana, G. (1953), The Life of Reason or The Phases of Human Progress (Charles Scribner's Sons, New York).

Sartre, J-P. (1946), Anti-semite and Jew (Reflexions sur la Question Juive) (trenslated by G.J. Becker) (Schocken Books, New York).

Saunders, D.A., Hobbs, R.J. and Ehrlich, P.R. (1993), Repairing a Damaged World: An Outline for Ecological Restoration (New York).

Schama, S. (2002), A History of Britain (BBC, London).

Schindler, D.W., Curtis, P.J., Parker, B.R. and Stainton, M.P. (1996), Consequences of climate warming and lake acidification for UV-B penetration in North American lakes, Nature vol. 379, 705-708.

Schneider, S.H. (1989), Global Warming. Are We Entering the Greenhouse Century? (Lutterworth Press, Cambridge).

Scholars for 9/11 truth (2008): http://www.scholarsfor911truth.org/ .

Science Daily (2002), Extinction rate across the globe reaches historical proportions, 10 January 2002: http://www.sciencedaily.com/releases/2002/01/020109074801.htm .

Science Daily (2007), IPCC Synthesis Report: risks and rewards of combating climate change, November 20, 2007: http://www.sciencedaily.com/releases/2007/11/071119122043.htm .

Science Show (2007), Corals and crustaceans in distress, 15 December 2007: http://www.abc.net.au/rn/scienceshow/stories/2007/2115399.htm .

Scott, P.J.M. (1982), Jane Austen: a Reassessment (Vision & Barnes & Noble, New Jersey).

Seager, J. (1993), Earth Follies. Feminism, Politics and the Environment (Earthscan, London).

Searchinger, T., Ralph Heimlich, R., Houghton, R.A., Dong, F., Elobeid, A., Fabiosa, J., Tokgoz, S., Hayes, D., & Yu, T-H (2008), Use of U.S. croplands for biofuels increases greenhouse gases through emissions from land-use change, Science 29 February 2008, Vol. 319. no. 5867, pp. 1238 – 1240: http://www.sciencemag.org/cgi/content/abstract/1151861 .

Sen (1945), Rural Bengal in Ruins (translated by Chakravarty; cited by Greenough, 1982).

Sen, A. (1981a), Poverty and Famines. An Essay on Entitlement and Deprivation (Clarendon Press, Oxford).

Sen, A. (1981b), Famine Mortality: A Study of the Bengal Famine of 1943 in Hobshawn, E. (1981) (editor), Peasants In History. Essays in Honour of David Thorner (Oxford University Press, New Delhi).

Sethi, R.R. (1963), The last phase 1919-1947 in Dodwell (1963a), The Cambridge History of India, Volume VI.

Shafritz, J.M., Williams, P. and Calinger, R.S. (1993), The Dictionary of 20th Century Politics (Henry Holt, New York).

Shakespeare, W. (1623), The Tragedy of King Richard the Third (Abbey Library, London, circa 1965).

Sharpe,T. (1971), Riotous Assembly (Secker & Warburg, London).

Sharpe, T. (1974), Porterhouse Blue (Prentice-Hall, Englewood Cliffs, New Jersey).

Shaw, A.G.L. (1960), The Story of Australia (Faber, London).

Shaw, A.G.l. (1971), Convicts and the Colonies. A Study of Personal Transportation from Great Britain and Ireland to Australia and Other Parts of the British Empire (Faber & Faber, London).

Shepher, J. (1983), Incest. A Biosocial View (Academic Press, New York).

Sheridan, R.B. (1780-1790), Speeches, Volumes 1-3 (Henry G. Bohn, London, 1842).

Sheridan, R.B. (1799) Pizarro, A Tragedy in Five Acts in Rhodes, R.C. (1962) (editor), The Plays and Poems of Richard Brinsley Sheridan (Russell & Russell, New York).

Sherry, N. (1966), Jane Austen (Evans Brothers, London).

Shiva, V. (1993), The greening of the global reach in Sachs (1993) (editor), Chapter 10, pp149-169.

Shore, C.J. (1843) (2nd Baron Lord Teignmouth), Memoirs of the Life and Correspondence of John Lord Teignmouth (John Shore, First Baron of Teignmouth) (London).

Silver, C.S. and De Fries, R.S. (1990), One Earth, One Future. Our Changing Global Environment (National Academy Press, Washington).

Simkins, T. (1994), Distant effects of volcanism - how big and how often? Science, vol. 264, 913-914.

Simons, H. (1994), The Other News On D-Day, Living Marxism, volume 68, June 1994.

Singer, P. (2000), Writings on an Ethical Life (Ecco Press, New York).

Singh, S.P. (1991), Poverty, Food, and Nutrition in India. Implications, Problems and Prospects (Chugh Publications, Allahabad).

Singleton, J. and Howard, B. (1977), Rip Van Australia (Cassell, Sydney).

Sinha, N.K. (1967), The History of Bengal 1757-1905 (University of Calcutta, Calcutta).

Sinha, P. (1988) Siraj ud-daulah in Embree, A.T. (1985a) (editor), Encyclopaedia of Asian History (Collier Macmillan, London) p479.

Slater, R. (1996), Soros. The Life, Times and Trading Secrets of the World's Greatest Investor (Irwin, New York).

Slim, W. (1956), Defeat into Victory (Cassell, London).

Smellie, K.B. (1962), Great Britain Since 1688 (University of Michigan Press, Ann Arbor).

Smith, A. (1776) An Inquiry Into the Nature and Causes of the Wealth of Nations (The Modern Library, New York, 1937).

Smith, G. (1890), Life of Jane Austen (Kennikat Press, London).

Smith, J. (1936), On the Pacific Front. The Adventure of Egon Kisch in Australia (Australian Book Company, Sydney).

Smith, L.W. (1983), Jane Austen and the Drama of Woman (Macmillan, London).

Smith, L. and Elliott, F. (2008), Biofuels threaten "billions of lives", The Australian, March 8: (see: http://www.theaustralian.news.com.au/story/0,25197,23336840-11949,00.html .

Smithers, D.W. (1981), Jane Austen in Kent (Hurtwood, London).

Smith, J. (1936), On the Pacific Front: the Adventures of Egon Kisch in Australia (Australian Book Services, Sydney).

Smith, P. (1992), Obituary: John Polya, UniTas, No. 29, March 3, p11.

Smith, P. (1993), Obituary. John Bela Polya (FRACI), Chemistry in Australia, April, p131.

Smollett, T.G. (1822), The History of England : From the Revolution in 1688 to the Death of George II (London).

Snow, C.P. (1961), Science and Government (The New English Library, London).

Snyder, L.L. (1960), The War. A Concise History 1939-1945 (Julian Messner, New York).

Solomon, R. (1994), The Orr Case, Quadrant July-August pp47-49.

Solzhenitsyn, A. (1963), One Day in the Life of Ivan Denisovich (Penguin, London).

Solzhenitsyn, A. (1968), The First Circle (Fontana , London).

Solzhenitsyn, A. (1974), The Gulag Archipelago (Fontana, Melbourne).

Soros, G. (1987), The Alchemy of Finance (Simon & Schuster).

Soros, G (1990), Opening the Soviet System (Weidenfeld & Nicolson, London).

Soros, G. (1991), Underwriting Democracy (The Free Press, New York).

Soros, G., Wien, B. and Koenen, K. (1995), Soros on Soros. Staying Ahead of the Curve (Wiley, New York).

Southam, B.C. (1964), Jane Austen's Literary Manuscripts. A Study of the Novelist's Development Through the Surviving Papers (Oxford University Press, London).

Southam, B.C. (1968) (editor), Critical Essays on Jane Austen (Routledge & Kegan Paul, London).

Southam, B.C. (1976a), Jane Austen, Northanger Abbey and Persuasion. A Casebook (Macmillan, London).

Southam, B.C. (1976b), Jane Austen, Sense and Sensibility, Prode and Prejudice and Mansfield Park. A Casebook (Macmillan, London).

Southam, B.C. (1977), Jane Austen, Encyclopaedia Brittanica, Macropaedia, Volume 2, pp377-380.

Southam, B.C. (1987) (editor), Jane Austen. The Critical Heritage 1870-1940. Volume 2 (Routledge & Kegan Paul).

Spear, P. (1965), The Oxford History of Modern India 1740-1975 (Oxford University Press, Delhi, 1978).

Spear, P. (1968), India and South East Asia 1. India in Mowat (1968), Chapter XI, pp297-328.

Spear, P. (1971) The Nabobs. A Study of the Social Life of the English in Eighteenth Century India (Peter Smith, Gloucester, Massachusetts).

Spear, P. (1975), Master of Bengal. Clive and His India (Thames and Hudson, London).

Spear, P (1979), The Oxford History of Modern India 1740-1975 (Oxford University Press, Delhi).

Spence, J. (2008), The Leighs. The Revelations of Stoneleigh, Jane Austen Society of Australia (JASA): http://www.jasa.net.au/l&t/stoneleigh.htm .

Spratt, D. and Sutton, P. (2008a), Climate Code Red – the Case for a Sustainability Emergency (Friends of the Earth, Melbourne).

Spratt, D. and Sutton, P. (2008b), Climate Code Red – the Case for Emergency Action (Scribe, Melbourne): http://www.climatecodered.net/ .

Sprigg, W.A. (1996), Doctors watch the forecasts, Nature vol. 379, 582-583.

Srivastava, B.B. (1981), Sir John Shore's Policy Towards the Indian States (Chugh, Allahabad).

Stanhope, Earl (1861), Life of the Right Honourable William Pitt (John Murray, London).

Stanhope, P.D. (1784) (under "Asiaticus" nom de plume), Genuine Memoirs of Asiaticus (London); reproduced in part in Nair (1984), pp167-179.

Stanton, B.F. 1999) Agriculture: crops, livestock and farmers, Chapter 15 in Bulliet, R.W. (1999) (1998) (editor), The Columbia History of the 20th Century (Columbia University Press, New York), pp345-380.

Statesman (1943), Supplement, Maladministration in Bengal, October 1943 (Statesman, Calcutta).

Stavorinus, J.S. (1798), Voyages to the East Indies (translated by S.H. Wilcocke) (G.G. & J. Robinson, London), reproduced in part in Nair (1984), pp153-166.

Stephen, L. and Lee, S. (1964) (editors), The Dictionary of National Biography (Oxford University Press, London).

Stephens, I. (1966), Monsoon Morning (Benn, London).

Stewart, D. and Keesing, N. (1962), Australian Bush Ballads (Angus & Robertson, Sydney).

Stokes, M. (1991) The Language of Jane Austen. A Study of Some Aspects of her Vocabulary (Macmillan, London).

Stokesbury, J. (1980), A Short History of World War II (William Morrow, New York).

Stop Air Pollution Deaths:
https://sites.google.com/site/300orgsite/stop-air-pollution-deaths .

Stop State Terrorism: https://sites.google.com/site/stopstateterrorism/ .

Stowe, H.B. (1852), Uncle Tom's Cabin; or Life Among the Lowly (W.W. Norton, New York, 1994).

Stowe, H.B. (1857), Sunny Memories of Foreign Lands (New York).

Strahan, R. (1983) (editor), The Australian Museum Complete Book of Australian Mammals (Angus & Robertson, Sydney).

Stryer, L. (1995), Biochemistry (4th edition) (Freeman, New York).

Stubbs, D. (1974), Prehistoric Art of Australia (Macmillan, Melbourne).

Sturtevant, W.C. (1988) (editor), Handbook of North American Indians (Smithsonian Institution, Washington).

Sulloway, A.G. (1989), Jane Austen and the Province of Womanhood (University of Pennsylvania Press, Philadelphia).

Sutherland, W. (1992), Beyond the Politics of Race. An Alternative History of Fiji (Research School of Pacific Studies, Australian National University, Canberra).

Suzuki, D. (1990), Inventing the future (Allen & Unwin, Sydney).

Swift, D. (1711), The Conduct of the Allies (London).

Swift, D. (1735), Gulliver's Travels (Oxford University Press, London)..

Sykes, C. (1959), Orde Wingate (Collins, London).

Tanner, T. (1986), Jane Austen (Macmillan, London).

Tassell, M. and Wood, D. (1981), Tasmanian Photographer. From the John Watt Beattie Collection (Macmillan, Melbourne).

Tatz, C. (2003), With Intent to Destroy. Reflecting on Genocide (Verso, London).

Taylor, A.J.P (1965), English History 1914-1945 (Oxford University Press, London).

Taylor, A.J.P. (1975), The Second World War. An Illustrated History (Hamish Hamilton, London).

Taylor, H. and Taylor, L. (1993), George Polya Master of Discovery ((Dale Seymour Publications, Palo Alto).

Teed, P. (1992), A Dictionary of Twentieth Century History 1914-1990 (Oxford University Press, Oxford).

Thackrah, J.R. (1993) (revised by R.F.Stapley), Twentieth Century History Basic Facts (Harper-Collins, Glasgow).

The Age June 6 1995, Global warming puts the threat on glaciers.

The Climate Group (2013), Carbon Pricing, May 2013: https://www.theclimategroup.org/sites/default/files/archive/files/May-Insight-Briefing—Carbon-Pricing.pdf .

The World Counts (2022), Life on Earth is under pressure: https://www.theworldcounts.com/challenges/planet-earth/forests-and-deserts/species-extinction-rate/story.

Thompson, J. (1951), Between Self and World. The Novels of Jane Austen (Pennsylvania State University Press, Philadelphia).

Thomson, C.L. (1929), Jane Austen. A Survey (Horace Marshall & Son, London).

Thomson, D. (1964) (editor), The New Cambridge Modern History, Volume XII, The Era of Violence 1898-1945 (Cambridge University Press, Cambridge)[The precursor of the second edition, Mowat (1968).]

Thomson, D. (1965), England in the Twentieth Century (1914-63) (Penguin Books, London).

Thomson, D. (1981) (new chapters by G. Warner), England in the Twentieth Century (1914-1979) (Penguin, 1981).

Thomson, D.J. (1995), The seasons, global precession and temperature Science, vol. 268, pp57-68.

Timmerman, J. (1981), Prisoner Without a Name, Cell Without a Number (Vintage Books, New York).

Tingle, L. (1996), Behind the lines. The speech that split a nation. The Age, 15 November, 1996, pA15.

Todd, J. (1983) (editor), Jane Austen. New Perspectives. Women and Literature New Series Volume 3 (Holmes & Meier, New York).

Trager, J. (1979) (editor), The People's Chronology. A Year-by-Year Record of Human Events from Prehistory to the Present (Holt, Rinehart & Winston, New York).

Trevelyan, G. (1886), Cawnpore (Macmillan, London).

Trevelyan, G.M. (1934), England Under Queen Anne. Volumes 1-3 (Longman's, Green , London).

Trevelyan, G.M. (1938), The English Revolution 1688-1689 (Thornton Butterworth, London).

Trevelyan, G.M. (1952), History of England (Longmans, London, 1960).

Trevelyan, H. (1972), The India We Left: Charles Trevelyan 1826-65, Humphrey Trevelyan 1929-47 (Macmillan, 1972).

Trollope, A. (1873), Australia and New Zealand (London).

Trotter, L.J. (1890), Rulers of India. Warren Hastings (Clarendon Press, Oxford).

Trukhanovsky, V.G. (1978), Winston Churchill (translated by K. Russell, A. Miller & C. English) (Progress Publishers, Moscow).

Tuchman, B.W. (1970), Stilwell and the American Experience in China 1911-45 (Macmillan, New York).

Tucker, G.H. (1983), A Goodly Heritage. A History of Jane Austen's Family (Carcanet New Press, Manchester).

Turnbull, P. (1975), Warren Hastings (New English Library, London).

Turner, H.G. (1973), A History of the Colony of Victoria from its Discovery to its Absorption into the Commonwealth of Australia, Volumes 1 & 2 (Heritage Publications, Melbourne).

Twitchell, J.B. (1987), Forbidden Partners. The Incest Taboo in Modern Culture (Columbia University Press, New York).

Tyler, M. (1977), My Years in an Indian Prison (Penguin, London).

Tyndale-Biscoe, II. (1993), Reducing rabbit numbers by controlling reproduction in Cooke (1993), pp11-17.

Tyquin, M.B. (1993), Gallipoli: The Medical War. The Australian Army Medical Services in the Dardanelles Campaign of 1915 (New South Wales University Press, Sydney).

UN Genocide Convention (1948): http://www.edwebproject.org/sideshow/genocide/convention.html .

UN (2008), Department of Economic & Social Affairs, Population Division, World Population Prospects: The 2006 Revision Population Database: http://esa.un.org/unpp/ .

UNICEF (2008), UNICEF report, 2008 : http://www.unicef.org/.

United Nations Population Division (UNPD) (1992), Long-Range World Population Projections: Two Centuries of Population Growth, 1950-2150 (UNPD, New York).

Uppal, J.N. (1984), Bengal Famine of 1943: A Man-Made Tragedy (Atma Ram & Sons, New Delhi).

Vadgama, K. (1984), Indians in Britain. The Indian Contribution to the British Way of Life (Robert Royce, London).

Van den Haag, E. (1969), The Jewish Mystique (Dell, New York).

Vaughan, D.G. and Doake, C.S.M. (1996), Recent atmospheric warming and retreat of ice shelves on the Antarctic peninsular Nature vol. 379, 328-331.

Veron, J.E.N. (2008), The plea of the Great Barrier Reef, ABC Radio National Ockham''s Razor, 5 April 2008: http://www.abc.net.au/rn/ockhamsrazor/stories/2008/2207734.htm .

Victor, D.G. and Salt, J.E. (1995), Keeping the climate treaty relevant, Nature vol. 373, 280-282.

Villager (ca 1945), Famine or Plenty (Sahityika, Calcutta).

Villard, L. (1924), Jane Austen . A French Appreciation (Translated by V.Lucas from Jane Austen: sa vie et son oevre) (George Routledge, London).

Vines, G. (1994), Time to throw away your old contraceptives? New Scientist, 30 April , pp36-40.

Voigt, J.H. (1987), India in the Second World War (Arnold Heinemann, Delhi).

Von Itzstein, M., Wu, W-Y., Kok, G.B., Pegg, M.S., Dyason, J.C., Jin, B., Phan, T.V., Smythe, M.L., White, H.F., Oliver, S.W., Colman, P.M., Varghese, J.N., Ryan, D.M., Woods, J.M., Bethell, R.C., Hotham, V.J., Cameron, J.M. and Penn, C.R. (1993), Rational design of potent sialidase-based inhibitors of influenza virus replication Nature vol. 363, 418-423.

Whitty, J. (2007), Animal extinction – the greatest threat to mankind, The Independent, 30 April 2007:
http://www.independent.co.uk/environment/animal-extinction--the-greatest-threat-to-mankind-397939.html .

Von Itzstein, M. and Smalec, B. (1994), Carbohydrates: drugs of the future Today's Life Science, April 1994, 22-24.

Vyas, M.R. (1982), Passage Through a Turbulent Era. Historical Reminiscences of the Fateful Years 1937-47 (Indo-Foreign Publications, Bombay).

Walker, C.J. (1990), Armenia. The Survival of a Nation (Routledge, London).

Walker, G. (1995), Fresh blow for greenhouse sceptics, New Scientist, 22 April, p5.

Wallace, R.K. (1983), Jane Austen and Mozart. Classical Equilibrium in Fiction and Music (University of Georgia Press, Athens).

Walter, E.V. (1969), Terror and Resistance: A Study of Political Violence (Oxford University Press, Oxford).

Ward, A.W., Prothero, G.W. and Leathes, S. (1909) (editors), The Cambridge Modern History, Volume VI The Eighteenth Century (Cambridge University Press, Cambridge).

Ward, W.R. (1965), The beginnings of reform in Great Britain: Imperial problems: politics and administration, economic growth in Goodwin (1965), Chapter XIX, pp537-564.

Waring, M. (1988), If Women Counted. A New Feminist Economics (Harper & Row, San Francisco).

Warner, G.T., Marten, C.H.K. and Muir, D.E. (1947), The New Groundwork of British History (Blackie & Son, London).

Warner, P. (1988), World War II. Untold Story (The Bodley Head, London).

Warner, S.T. (1964), Jane Austen (Longmans, London).

Warren, R. (1979), Jane Austen and the French Revolution (Macmillan, London).

Washburn, W.E. (1988) (editor), History of Indian-White Relations, Volume 4 in Sturtevant, W.C. (1988) (editor), Handbook of North American Indians (Smithsonian Institution, Washington).

Washington, I.H. (1991), Environmental Solutions for the World and for Australia (Boobook Publications, Sydney).

Wasserstein, B. (1988), Britain and the Jews of Europe 1939-1945 (Oxford University Press, Oxford).

Watkins, S. (1990), Jane Austen's Town and Country Style (Rizzoli, New York).

Watson, J.S. (1960), The Reign of George III 1760-1815 (Oxford University Press, London).

Watt, I. (1963), Jane Austen. A Collection of Critical Essays (Prentice-Hall, New Jersey).

Webb, R.K. (1970), Modern England. From the 18th Century to the Present (Dodd, Mead & Co., New York).

Weinberg, G.H. (1994), A World At Arms. A Global History of World War II (Cambridge University Press, London).

Weissberg, A. (1958), Advocate for the Dead (Andre Deutsch, London).

Weldon, F. (1984), Letters to Alice on First Reading Jane Austen (Coronet Books, Hodder & Stoughton, London).

Wells, G.P. (1984) (editor), H.G.Wells in Love. Postscript to an Experiment in Autobiography (Faber & Faber, London).

Wells, H.G. (1936), Postscript to an Experiment in Autobiography in Wells, G.P. (1984) (editor), H.G.Wells in Love. Postscript to an Experiment in Autobiography (Faber & Faber, London).

Wells, H.G. (1951) (revised by R. Postgate), The Outline of History (Cassell, London, 1956).

Wertheim, M. (1995), The way of logic, New Scientist, 2 December, pp38-41.

Wheeler, J.T. (1860), India Under British Rule (Discovery Publishing House, Delhi, 1986).

Wheelock, A.K. (1988), Jan Vermeer (Harry Abrams, New York).

White, C. (1992), Mastering Risk. Environment, Markets & Politics in Australian Economic History (Oxford University Press, Oxford).

Whitesides, L. (2007), NASA's James Hansen says Atmospheric CO2 is Already Beyond Safe Limit, Wired Science:
http://blog.wired.com/wiredscience/2007/12/nasas-james-han.html .

WHO (2008) : http://www.who.int/en/ .

Whitington, R.S. (1971), Sir Frank. The Frank Packer Story (Cassell, Melbourne).

Wiesenfarth, J. (1967), The Errand of Form. An Essay of Jane Austen's Art (Fordham University Press, New York).

Wigley,T.M.L., Richels, R. and Edmonds, J.A. (1996), Economic and environmental choices in the stabilization of atmospheric CO_2 concentrations, Nature vol. 379, 240-243.

Wikipedia (2008), United States (US) National Academy of Sciences: http://en.wikipedia.org/wiki/United_States_National_Academy_of_Sciences .

Wilbur, M.E. (1945), The East India Company and the British Empire in the Far East (Richard R. Smith, New York).

Wilde, W.H. and Moore, T.I. (1980) (editors), Letters of Mary Gilmore (Melbourne University Press).

Wilkes, J. (1991), Jane Austen's Persuasion (Sydney University Press, Sydney).

Wilks, B. (1978), Jane Austen (Hamlyn, London).

Williams, B. (1966), The Life of William Pitt, Earl of Chatham. Volume 2 (Frank Cass, London).

Williams, K., Parer, I., Coman, B., Burley, J. and Braysher, M. (1995), Managing Vertebrate Pests: Rabbits (Australian Government Publishing Service, Canberra).

Williams, M. (1986), Jane Austen: Six Novels and their Methods (Macmillan, London).

Williams, M.D. (1956), Out of the Mist (Oldham, Beddome and Meredith, Hobart, 5th edition).

Williams, N. (1966), Chronology of the Modern World 1763 to the Present Time (Barrier & Rockliff, London).

Williamson, D. (1975), The Department (Currency Press, Sydney).

Willmott, H.P. (1989), The Great Crusade (A New Complete History of the Second World War) (Michael Joseph, London).

Wilson, E. (1945), A long talk about Jane Austen, The New Yorker, October 13; reproduced in Watt (1963), pp35-40.

Wilson, S. (1979), British Art from Holbein to the Present Day (Tate Gallery & Bodley Head, London).

Wilton, A. (1975), Turner in the British Museum. Drawings and Watercolours (British Museum Publications, London).

Wiltshire, J. (1976), Jane Austen and Samuel Johnson: a Study in Intellectual Tradition and Literary Influence (PhD thesis, La Trobe University, Melbourne).

Wiltshire, J. (1992), Jane Austen and the Body (Cambridge University Press, Cambridge).

Wood, N. (1993) (editor), Mansfield Park (Open University Press, Buckingham).

Woodbridge, G. (1950), UNRRA. The History of the United Nations Relief and Rehabilitation Administration. Volumes I-III (Columbia University Press, New York).

Woodham-Smith, C. (1962), The Great Hunger. Ireland 1845-9 (Hamish Hamilton, London).

Woodruff, P. (1953), The Men Who Ruled India I. The Founders (Johnathan Cape, London, 1965).

Woodward, E.L. (1962), History of England (London).

Woolley, R.M. (1927), St. Hugh of Lincoln (Macmillan, New York).

World Health Organization (WHO) (2008) : http://www.who.int/en/ .

Worldometer (2022), Covid-19 coronavirus pandemic: https://www.worldometers.info/coronavirus/ .

Wright, A.H. (1957), Jane Austen's Novels. A Study in Structure (Chatto & Windus, London).

Wright, G. (1968), The Ordeal of Total War 1939-1945 (Harper & Row, New York).

Wright, T. (1892), The Life of William Cowper (T. Fisher Unwin, London).

Yarra Valley Climate Action Group (2008): http://sites.google.com/site/yarravalleyclimateactiongroup/Home .

Young, I. (1971), Theodore. His Life and Times (Alpha Books, Sydney).

Young, P. (1966), World War 1939-45. A Short History (Arthur Barker, London).

Ziegler, P. (1988), Mountbatten. The Official Biography (Collins, London).

Zionist quotes re racism and Palestinian Genocide, Palestinian Genocide : https://sites.google.com/site/palestiniangenocide/zionist-quotes .

Zubay, G.L., Parson, W.W. and Vance, D.E. (1995), Principles of Biochemistry , W.C. Brown, 1995.